Statement Type	Examples	Section
ON-GOTO	420 ON (FIX(N/10)+1) GOTO 500, 600, 700	7.3
GOSUB	280 GOSUB 3000	3.4, 5.5
ON-GOSUB	150 ON INSTR(1, "ABC", L$)+1 & GOSUB 1000, 2000, 3000, 4000	7.3, 9.5
RETURN	1150 RETURN	3.4, 5.5
READ DATA	200 READ NAMES$, SALARY, KIDS% 210 DATA "BILLY BUDD", 125.50, 2	1.3, 1.5, 4.3
INPUT	300 INPUT "YOUR NAME"; NAMES$ 450 INPUT #1, X, Y, STORE$	1.5, 4.3 11.3
INPUT LINE	120 INPUT LINE TITLE$ 250 INPUT LINE #2, INVEN.RECORD$	4.3 11.4
PRINT	200 PRINT 210 PRINT "X ="; X, "Y ="; Y 500 PRINT "X", "Y" \ PRINT X, Y 600 PRINT #1, X; ","; Y	1.3 1.5 3.1 11.3
PRINT USING	300 PRINT USING "###.##", X 500 PRINT USING HEAD$, COL1$, COL2$	11.1 11.1
OPEN	100 OPEN "TRANS.DAT" FOR INPUT AS FILE #1 110 OPEN "BAL.DAT" FOR OUTPUT AS FILE #2	11.2 11.2
CLOSE	3000 CLOSE #1, #2	11.2
ON ERROR GOTO	100 ON ERROR GOTO 9000 9040 ON ERROR GOTO 0 !DISABLE ERROR HANDLING	11.3 11.3
RESUME	9020 IF ERR = 11 THEN RESUME 290	11.3
CHAIN	2010 CHAIN "PROG3"	11.7
DIM	100 DIM A(20), B$(5,10), C%(1000) 120 DIM #1, X(1000) 130 OPEN "X.VIR" AS FILE #1	6.1, 10.1 11.5 11.5
MAT READ	150 DIM A(20), B$(32), C%(15,10) 210 MAT READ A, B$(25), C%	6.1, 10.1 10.3
MAT PRINT	120 DIM A(20), B(15,30) 250 MAT PRINT B, !5 VALUES/LINE 270 MAT PRINT #1, B !1 VALUE/LINE 290 MAT PRINT B(10,25); !10-BY-25 ARRAY	6.1, 10.1 10.3 11.4 10.3
MAT INPUT	100 DIM NAMES$(20) 220 MAT INPUT #3, NAMES$	6.1 11.4
MAT initialize	100 DIM B(10,10), A(10), C(5) 110 MAT C = CON !ALL ONES 120 MAT B = IDN !IDENTITY MATRIX 130 MAT A = ZER !ALL ZEROS	10.1 10.4 10.4 10.4
MAT operations	100 DIM A(15), B(15), C(15), D(15) 210 MAT C = A + B 220 MAT D = A - B 230 MAT B = (2) * A	6.1 10.4 10.4 10.4
RANDOMIZE	400 RANDOMIZE 410 LET X(I) = RND FOR I = 1 TO 10	4.2 4.2, 5.4

Problem Solving in Structured BASIC-PLUS and VAX-11 BASIC

ELLIOT B. KOFFMAN
FRANK L. FRIEDMAN

Temple University

 Addison-Wesley Publishing Company
Reading, Massachusetts • Menlo Park, California
London • Amsterdam • Don Mills, Ontario • Sydney

This book is in the
Addison-Wesley Series in Computer Science

Sponsoring Editor: James DeWolf
Production Editor: Fran Palmer Fulton
Project Supervisor: Cheryl Wurzbacher
Cover Designer: Marshall Henrichs
Text Designer: Volney Croswell
Manufacturing Supervisor: Hugh Crawford

The text of this book was composed in Videofont Melior by International
Computaprint Corporation (ICC). With the exception of Chapter 1, all artwork in
this book was electronically generated by ICC's IDACS System, wholly designed
and developed by ICC personnel.

Library of Congress Cataloging in Publication Data

Koffman, Elliot B.
    Problem solving in structured BASIC-PLUS and
in VAX-11 BASIC.

    (Computer science series ; 151A16)
    Includes index.
    1. Basic (Computer program language)
2. Structured programming. 3. Problem solving—
Data processing. I. Friedman, Frank L.
II. Title. III. Series.
QA76.73.B3K64   1984   001.64'24   83-2566
ISBN 0-201-10344-3

ISBN: 0-201-10344-3
BCDEFGHIJ-DO-8987654

To our wives:
   Caryn Koffman and Martha Friedman,
and our children:
   Richard, Debbie, and Robin Koffman
   Shelley and Dara Friedman

Preface

Preface for Students

The title of this book contains the terms *problem solving* and *structured BASIC-PLUS*. These terms describe the particular emphasis and direction that we have taken in teaching programming. Our primary goals are to help you develop your problem solving skills and to teach you how to practice structured programming in the BASIC-PLUS (or VAX-11 BASIC) programming language.

It is important to realize that a computer cannot solve problems. It can, however, carry out a limited set of instructions very quickly and without error. The instructions that you give the computer must specify the steps to be followed. This text will teach you how to develop and formulate these steps so that you can use the computer as a problem solving tool.

Structured programming is an approach to programming that has been widely adopted by professional programmers. Structured programming is a careful, disciplined approach to designing programs that are easy to read and understand. We feel that it is extremely important to adopt this technique right from the beginning. We will discuss features of structured programming and program style throughout the text and illustrate this approach in the solution of numerous problems. Careful study of the sample programs and style suggestions should enable you to adopt structured programming as your own programming approach.

Preface for Instructors

When our textbook *Problem Solving and Structured Programming in BASIC* was first published in 1979, we were a little concerned about whether or not there would be a significant demand for a textbook that emphasized structured programming in BASIC. The wide acceptance of that textbook affirmed our belief that it is important to teach the concepts of structured programming in a first programming course, regardless of the language used.

As we stated in the preface to that textbook, BASIC has evolved over the years from a language intended mainly for student use to a relatively sophisticated language that is often used for large-scale software development projects. The widespread availability of BASIC interpreters and compilers for personal computers should further stimulate the growth of BASIC as an important language for developing applications software in a variety of areas.

In addition, the low cost of microcomputers has made it economically feasible for many secondary schools to purchase their own computers and offer programming courses. Students will no longer learn just BASIC, but will move on to study other languages such as Pascal, FORTRAN, COBOL, and Ada in high school or college.

For these reasons, we feel it is important to teach BASIC in the same way that other high-level programming languages are taught. If BASIC is to be used as a serious tool for software development, then the principles of structured programming must be applied in order to design effective, reliable software that is readily maintained. If BASIC is to be a stepping stone to further study in computer science, then a firm foundation in the fundamentals of problem solving and programming is essential. It is unreasonable to expect students to discard unstructured programming techniques and practices that worked in BASIC just because a richer programming environment is available in a second programming language.

Consequently, we have stressed the development of good problem solving and programming habits throughout the textbook. We feel that these concepts should be introduced at the initial stages of development of a student's programming skills and that they are best instilled by examples, by frequent practice, and through instructor-student interaction. Therefore, we have concentrated on demonstrating problem solving and programming techniques through the presentation of many solved problems and example programs taken from a variety of applications areas. A minimal mathematical background is assumed.

Discipline and planning in both problem solving and programming are illustrated in the text from the beginning. We have attempted to integrate a number of relatively new pedagogic ideas into a unique, well-structured format that is uniformly repeated for each problem discussed. Three basic phases of problem solving are emphasized: the analysis of the problem; the step-wise specification of the algorithm (using flow diagrams); and, finally, the language implementation of the program.

Our goal is to bridge the gap between textbooks that stress problem solving approaches divorced from implementation considerations and programming manuals that provide the opposite emphasis. Language-independent problem analysis and algorithms are described in the same text as the language features required to implement the problem solution on the computer. For each new problem introduced in the text, the problem analysis and algorithm description are presented, along with the complete syntactic and semantic definitions of the new language features convenient for the implementation of the algorithm.

The top down or step-wise approach to problem solving is illustrated in the solution of each of the problems studied. The use of subroutines and functions is emphasized in the completed programs. Three pedagogic tools —a data definition table, a flow diagram, and a program system chart— are used to provide a framework through which students may practice the definition and documentation of program variables together with the step-wise development of algorithms.

The data definition tables provide a description of the attributes (initial values, sizes, etc.), and the use of each variable appearing in the problem solution. The flow diagram patterns that are used to represent decision and looping structures are similar to the D-chart of Dijkstra. Each algorithm is represented as a short sequence of individual flow diagram patterns corresponding to the algorithm subtasks; refinements of the subtasks are diagrammed separately. Program variables are added to the data table as they arise during algorithm development. The program system chart illustrates the system structure and the data flow between system modules.

We have also placed considerable emphasis on programming style. Program Style displays appear throughout the text to explain aspects of program style that we believe lead to the production of code that is more readable, easier to maintain and less prone to error.

BASIC-PLUS, BASIC-PLUS-2, and VAX-11 BASIC

All program examples in the text can be run in either BASIC-PLUS, BASIC-PLUS-2, or VAX-11 BASIC. In the main body of the text we have used only features that are supported in all three dialects. Thus, for example, we have used only subroutines and user-defined functions to implement separate program modules in the main body of the text.

Had we written the book solely for BASIC-PLUS-2 and VAX-11 users, we would have utilized subprograms as well as user-defined functions to implement separate program modules. To compensate for this, we have provided a complete discussion of the subprogram feature in Appendix I, along with a discussion of the VAX-11 BASIC DECLARE statement. Programs in Chapters 8–11 that would be improved by the use of the subprogram feature are redone in Appendix J for the benefit of BASIC-PLUS-2 and VAX-11 BASIC users. Appendix J also contains a text program (from Chapter 4) that is rewritten using the DECLARE statement (VAX-11 BA-

SIC) and the more general form of the IF-THEN-ELSE statement supported in BASIC-PLUS-2 and VAX-11 BASIC. Major differences among these three BASIC dialects are discussed in Appendix H.

Special Features of the Text

There is more than enough material for a one semester course in programming. The first eight chapters represent the core of the textbook and should be studied by all students. The last three chapters contain advanced material on string processing, matrixes, formatted output, and files (both ASCII files and virtual arrays). Each of these chapters can be studied independently of the others; consequently, the instructor should choose one or more of these chapters depending on student interest and time available.

Each chapter contains a description of common programming errors that may occur as well as hints for debugging. An extensive set of homework programming problems is provided at the end of each chapter, and exercises are inserted in the body of each chapter. Solutions to selected exercises are provided at the end of the text.

All chapters end with a summary and a table describing the BASIC-PLUS statements introduced in the chapter. A glossary of all BASIC-PLUS statements is provided in the end papers for quick reference and review.

The text is organized so that students may begin working with the computer as soon as possible. Chapter 1 provides a brief introduction to assignment statements and input and output in BASIC-PLUS as well as a description of how to use the BASIC-PLUS system.

As mentioned earlier, structured programming concepts are illustrated throughout the text. Long variable names are introduced in Chapter 1 and program documentation is discussed in Chapter 2. Chapter 2 also introduces the problem solving methodology practiced throughout the text and illustrates the step-wise refinement of algorithms.

A number of structured control statements are used in the text. The IF–THEN, IF–THEN–ELSE, and FOR loop control statements are introduced in Chapter 2 and described more completely in Chapter 3. The conditional loop forms (FOR–WHILE, FOR–UNTIL, WHILE, and UNTIL) are introduced in Chapter 5.

Modular programming is emphasized through the early introduction of subroutines. Subroutines are first used in Chapter 3 to implement true and false tasks in IF–THEN–ELSE statements. BASIC-PLUS library functions are described in Chapter 4. In Chapter 5, the subroutine is revisited as a tool for implementing program modules that reflect the step-wise refinement of algorithms. User-defined functions (single and multiple-line) are introduced in Chapter 8 and are used throughout the remainder of the text to implement separate program modules.

We have postponed discussion of the GOTO statement until Chapter 7. It is used relatively infrequently to implement loop exit (from within a nest of loops) and to transfer to a function FNEND statement (for function exit).

The ON–GOSUB, ON–GOTO, and other multiple-alternative decision forms are also introduced in Chapter 7.

One feature of this textbook that is hard to overlook is the use of color in flow diagrams and programs. We have used color to assist students in tracing the refinement of an algorithm step through to its final program implementation. The use of color is described in detail on page 49.

Finally, several appendixes are provided that should be a valuable aid to students using the BASIC-PLUS system. The appendixes list error messages and summarize various features of the BASIC-PLUS system.

Acknowledgments

Registered trademarks of Digital Equipment Corporation mentioned in this book are: VAX-11, PDP-11, BASIC-PLUS, BASIC-PLUS-2, VAX-11 BASIC, RSTS and Rainbow 100.

Many people have made substantial contributions to this text. We are grateful to Stephen Garland of Dartmouth College, who carefully reviewed the original BASIC text. We would also like to thank Randall S. Flint of California State University at Fullerton, Brad Wilson of Western Kentucky University, and Randy M. Kaplan of Smith, Kline and French Research Laboratories (Philadelphia), for their many detailed and valuable suggestions.

We would also like to thank Temple University students Stephen Stebulis, Linda Reichold, and Amelia Lignelli, who entered and tested the programs in the manuscript. We are also indebted to Helen Holzbaur of the Media Learning Center at Temple University for her cooperation in making this computer facility available to us and for providing her system expertise and program editing assistance.

Lastly, we would like to thank all of those involved in the production phases of the manuscript. In particular, we are, once again, extremely grateful to Fran Palmer Fulton, who served as production manager for the text. We are also grateful to Judith O'Shea Stebulis, who meticulously proofread numerous versions of the manuscript and provided solutions to the exercises. Thanks, too, to Marshall Henrichs of Addison-Wesley for his innovative design and effective use of color, and to Cheryl Wurzbacher also of Addison-Wesley, and Eileen Colahan of International Computaprint Corporation for their contributions to the production of this text. We also thank Marge Garcia and Mary McCutcheon for their excellent typing of manuscript drafts.

We are very much indebted to all of these people for their efforts in behalf of the text. Their graciousness and patience, as well as hard work, were a key factor in its successful and timely production. As always, the support and encouragement provided by Jim DeWolf, Computer Science Editor at Addison-Wesley, is very much appreciated.

Philadelphia, Pennsylvania   E.B.K.
September 1983   F.L.F.

Contents

6   Arrays and Subscripts   219

7   Nested Structures and Multiple-Alternative Decisions   267

8   User-Defined Functions and Program Systems   313

Appendixes

Answers to Selected Exercises

Indexes

Introduction to Computers and Programming

In this chapter we describe the general organization of computers and discuss the languages used for communicating with computers (programming languages). We shall see that all computers consist of four basic components: memory, central processor, input devices, and output devices. Also, we will learn how information is represented in the memory of a computer and how it is manipulated.

An introduction to the BASIC-PLUS programming language is also provided. Some simple computer operations are described and some short programs that perform these operations are presented. We also discuss how to create and test BASIC-PLUS programs on a computer.

1.1   Computer Organization

A computer is a tool for representing and manipulating information. There are many different kinds of computers, ranging in size from hand-held calculators to large and complex computing systems filling several rooms or entire buildings. In the recent past, computers were so expensive that they could be used only for business or scientific computations; now there are personal computers available for use in the home or office (see Fig. 1.1).

The size and cost of a computer is generally dependent upon the amount of work it can turn out in a given time unit. Larger, more expensive computers have the capability of carrying out many operations simultaneously, thus increasing their work capacity. They also have more devices attached to them for performing special functions, all of which increase their capability and cost.

Despite the large variety in the cost, size, and capabilities of modern computers, they are remarkably similar in a number of ways. Basically, a *computer* consists of the five components shown in Fig. 1.2. (The lines connecting the various units represent possible paths of information flow. The arrows show the direction of information flow.)

All information that is to be processed by the computer must first be entered into the computer *memory* via an *input device*. The information in memory is manipulated by the *central processor* and the results of this

Fig. 1.1 Rainbow 100 Personal Computer. (© Digital Equipment Corp. All rights reserved. Reprinted with permission.)

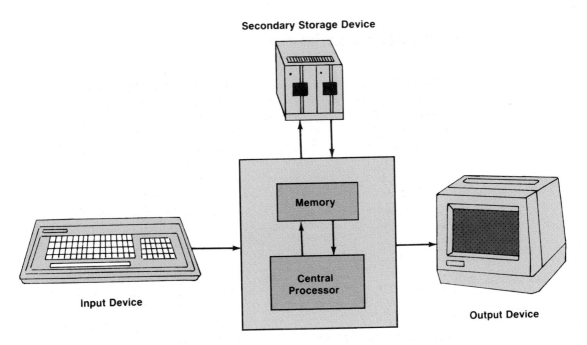

Secondary Storage Device

Memory

Central Processor

Input Device

Output Device

Fig. 1.2 Components of a computer.

manipulation are also stored in the memory of the computer. Information in memory can be displayed through the use of appropriate *output devices*. A *secondary storage device* is often used for storing large quantities of information in a semipermanent form. These components and their interaction are described in more detail in the following sections.

The Computer Memory

The memory of a computer may be pictured as an ordered sequence of storage locations called *memory cells*. Each cell has associated with it a distinct *address*, which indicates its relative position in the sequence. Figure 1.3 depicts a computer memory consisting of 1000 cells numbered consecutively from 0 to 999. Some large-scale computers have memories consisting of millions of cells.

The memory cells of a computer are used to store information. All types of information—numbers, names, lists, and even pictures—may be represented in the memory of a computer. The information that is contained in a memory cell is called the *contents* of the memory cell. Every memory cell contains some information—no cell is ever empty. Whenever new information is placed in a memory cell, any information already there is destroyed, and cannot be retrieved. In Fig. 1.3, the contents of memory cell 3 is the number −26, and the contents of memory cell 4 is the number 12.5.

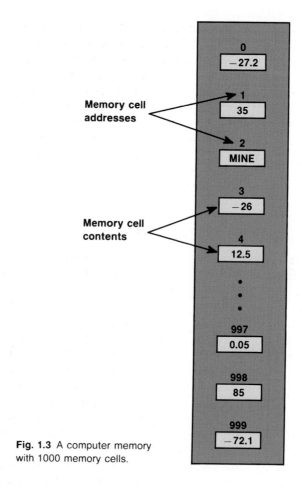

Memory cell addresses

Memory cell contents

Fig. 1.3 A computer memory with 1000 memory cells.

Exercise 1.1: What are the contents of memory cells 0, 2, and 997 in Fig. 1.3?

The Central Processor Unit

Modern computers can manipulate information stored in memory at phenomenal speeds. Most computers can perform more than one million operations in a second. This *manipulative* capability of the computer enables us to study problems that would otherwise be impossible because of their computational requirements. With appropriate directions, computers can generate large quantities of new information from old, solving many otherwise impossible problems, and providing useful insights into others; and they can do so in exceptionally short periods of time.

The heart of the manipulative capability of the computer is the *central processor unit* (CPU). The CPU can retrieve information from the memory unit. (This information may be either data or instructions for manipulating data.) It can also store the results of manipulations back into the memory unit for later reference.

The CPU coordinates all activities of the various components of the computer. It determines which operations should be carried out and in what order. The transmission of coordinating control signals and commands is the function of the *control unit* within the central processor.

Also found within the central processor is the *arithmetic-logic unit*. The *arithmetic* portion consists of electronic circuitry that performs a variety of arithmetic operations, including addition, subtraction, multiplication, and division. The speed with which it can perform these operations is on the order of a millionth of a second. The *logic* unit consists of electronic circuitry to compare information and to make decisions based upon the results of the comparison.

Input and Output Devices

The manipulative capability of the computer would be of little use to us if we were unable to communicate with the computer. Specifically, we must be able to enter information into the computer memory and display information (usually the results of a manipulation) stored in the computer memory. The *input devices* are used to enter data into the computer memory; the *output devices* are used to display results in a readable form.

Most of you will be using a computer terminal as both an input and an output device. Terminals usually consist of a typewriter-like keyboard on which information required by the computer is typed (see Fig. 1.4a). The results of a computation may be printed on a roll of paper fed through the terminal carriage or displayed on a video screen. Some terminals are equipped with *graphics capability* (see Fig. 1.4b) which enables the output to be displayed as a two-dimensional graph or picture, and not just as rows of letters and numbers. With some graphics devices, the user can communicate with the computer by moving an electronic pointer using a joystick or a game paddle.

Computer terminals are widely used in many facets of everyday life. They are used for confirming reservations and printing tickets. They are also used at checkout counters in department stores and supermarkets to assist in keeping track of customer purchases and for inventory control.

Secondary Storage Devices

There is another category of device, called a secondary storage device, that is found on most computer systems. These devices are used to provide additional data storage capability. Examples of secondary storage devices are magnetic tape and disk drives with their associated magnetic tapes or disks (see Fig. 1.5).

The memory described in the Computer Memory section is often called *main memory* to distinguish it from *secondary memory*, i.e., magnetic tape or disk. Main memory is relatively expensive and most computers can have only a limited amount of main memory. Consequently, it is often necessary to add one or more secondary memory devices in order to expand

Fig. 1.4a Printing terminal. (© Digital
Equipment Corp. All rights reserved.
Used with permission.)

Fig. 1.4b Computer with graphics
capability.

the computer system's capability for data storage in a practical fashion.
Results generated by the computer may be saved as *data files* on a magnetic tape or disk. These data files may be copied into main memory at a
later time for further processing.

A typical computer system, including memory, a central processor unit,
magnetic tape and disk drives, and terminals is pictured in Fig. 1.6. In the

Fig. 1.5 Inserting a floppy disk in a disk drive. (© Digital Equipment Corp. All rights reserved. Used with permission.)

Fig. 1.6 VAX-11/780 computer system. (© Digital Equipment Corp. All rights reserved. Used with permission.)

remainder of this text, we will learn how to use this *computer hardware* by writing appropriate *software* (computer programs) for specifying data manipulation.

Exercise 1.2: Describe the purpose of the control unit, the arithmetic, logic unit, main memory and secondary memory.

1.2 Programs and Programming Languages

Executing a Program

The computer is quite a powerful tool. Information (*input data*) may be stored in its memory and manipulated at exceptionally high speed to produce a result (*program output*). We can describe a data manipulation task by presenting the computer with a list of instructions (called a *program*) to be processed. Once this list has been stored in memory, the computer can then carry out (*execute*) these instructions.

In order to execute a program, the computer control unit examines each program instruction in memory, starting with the first, and sends out the command signals appropriate for carrying out the instruction. Normally, the instructions are executed in sequence; however, as we shall see later, it is possible to have the control unit skip over some instructions or execute some instructions more than once.

During execution, data may be entered into the memory of the computer, and the results of the manipulations performed on this data may be displayed. Of course, these things will happen only if the program contains instructions telling the computer to enter or display the appropriate information.

Figure 1.7 shows the relationship between a program for computing a payroll and its input and output, and indicates the *flow of information* through the computer during execution of the program. The data to be manipulated by the program (employee time cards) must first be entered into the computer memory (Step 1 in Fig. 1.7). As directed by the program instructions, the central processor unit manipulates the data in memory, and places the results of these computations back into memory (Steps 2–4). When the computation process is complete, the results can be displayed (Step 5) in the desired forms (as employee checks and payroll reports).

The BASIC Programming Language

The act of making up a list of instructions (writing a program) is called *programming*. Writing a computer program is very similar to describing the rules of a game to people who have never played the game. In both cases, a language of description understood by all parties involved in the communication is required. For example, the rules of the game must be de-

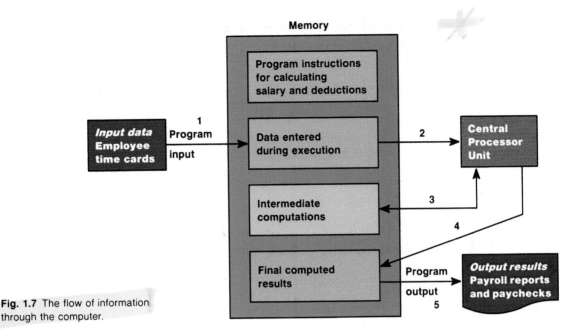

Fig. 1.7 The flow of information through the computer.

scribed in some language, and then read and carried out. Both the inventor of the game and those who wish to play must be familiar with the language of description used.

Languages used for communication between man and the computer are called *programming languages.* All instructions presented to a computer must be represented and combined (to form a program) according to the *syntactic rules* (grammar) of the programming language. There is, however, one significant difference between a programming language and a language such as French, English, or Russian. The rules of a programming language are very precise and have no "exceptions" or "ambiguities". The reason for this is that a computer cannot think! It can only follow instructions exactly as given. It cannot interpret these instructions to figure out what the program writer (*programmer*) meant it to do. An error in writing a single instruction may either prevent the program from executing at all, or, worse still, change the meaning of the program, and cause the computer to perform the wrong action.

In this book we shall concentrate on the BASIC (Beginner's All-purpose Symbolic Instruction Code) programming language that was originally developed at Dartmouth College. BASIC was designed for use by students and others who require a relatively simple language to learn programming. Many of the programming and problem-solving concepts you learn will be applicable to other programming languages as well as BASIC.

We shall emphasize the version of BASIC called BASIC-PLUS, which was developed by Digital Equipment Corporation for their PDP-11 computers. We shall use the special features of BASIC-PLUS that facilitate the development of *structured programs*—programs that are relatively easy to read, understand, and maintain (keep in good working order).

There are two other popular dialects of BASIC developed by Digital Equipment Corporation, BASIC-PLUS-2 (also for PDP-11 computers) and VAX-11 BASIC for the newer VAX-11 computer system. Almost everything that can be done in BASIC-PLUS can be done in these other dialects. However, BASIC-PLUS-2 and VAX-11 BASIC contain additional features that are not part of BASIC-PLUS. Special features of VAX-11 BASIC are described in Appendixes A, C, H, I, and J.

We should mention that the BASIC-PLUS language is not understood directly by PDP-11 computers. Each statement in a BASIC-PLUS program must be translated in order to be understood by the computer. This translation is performed by a large program called, appropriately enough, a *translator*. If the translator cannot translate a BASIC-PLUS statement, it will tell you so by typing a message such as

```
?Unrecognizable statement
```

We will discuss this later.

1.3 Introduction to BASIC-PLUS

Some Computer Operations and Their BASIC-PLUS Descriptions

There are a large number of computers available today and each has a unique set of operations that it can perform. These operations generally fall into three categories:

• Input and output operations
• Data manipulation and comparison
• Control operations

Despite the large variety of operations in these categories, there are a few operations in each that are common to most computers. These operations are summarized in Table 1.1. In the remainder of this chapter, we will describe some of these operations by showing how they are written in BASIC-PLUS.

Table 1.1 Common Computer Operations

Input/Output Operations	Data Manipulation and Comparison				Control Operations
Read Input	Add	Subtract	Multiply	Divide	Transfer
Print	Negate	Assign	Compare		Conditional execution
					Stop

Before beginning our study of BASIC-PLUS, we will examine two short programs. Don't worry about understanding the details of these programs yet; it will all come together later.

Example 1.1 Figure 1.8 contains a BASIC-PLUS program (top half) and a sample run or execution of that program (bottom half). Each program line begins with a number (100–140). The *system command* RUNNH initiates the execution of the program; the program output follows the word RUNNH.

```
100 PRINT "WHAT IS YOUR NAME";
110 INPUT N$
120 PRINT "HELLO "; N$
130 PRINT "WE HOPE YOU ENJOY STUDYING BASIC"
140 END

RUNNH
WHAT IS YOUR NAME? Bobo Derelict
HELLO Bobo Derelict
WE HOPE YOU ENJOY STUDYING BASIC
```

Fig. 1.8 Printing a welcoming message.

Each program statement starting with the word PRINT causes a line of output to be displayed during program execution. Each output line has the same color background as the PRINT statement that generates it.

The statement

```
110 INPUT N$
```

causes the characters "Bobo Derelict" typed in by the program user to be stored in a memory cell called N$. The next statement

```
120 PRINT "HELLO "; N$
```

causes these characters to be displayed after the message "HELLO".

Example 1.2 The program in Fig. 1.9 converts inches to centimeters. The number of inches (30) to be converted is specified as input data to the program in the line that begins with the word DATA (line 110). The equivalent number of

```
90 EXTEND
100 READ INCH
110 DATA 30
120 LET CENT = 2.54 * INCH
130 PRINT INCH; "INCHES EQUALS"; CENT; "CENTIMETERS"
140 END

RUNNH
30 INCHES EQUALS 76.2 CENTIMETERS
```

Fig. 1.9 Converting inches to centimeters.

centimeters (2.54 times 30) is printed as output (line 130). The actual program output is shown on the line following RUNNH. The system command EXTEND (line 90) allows us to use memory cell names that have more than one letter (e.g., INCH) as will be explained later in this chapter.

One of the nicest features of BASIC-PLUS is that it enables us to write program statements that resemble English. Even at this point, we can read and understand the example programs, although we have no idea how to write our own programs. In the next section we will examine another program and provide a detailed explanation of the BASIC-PLUS statements seen so far.

A BASIC-PLUS Payroll Program

Figure 1.10 shows a program that solves the following problem.

Problem 1A   Compute the gross salary and net pay for an employee of a company, given the employee's hourly rate, the number of hours worked, and a fixed tax deduction amount of $25.

Each statement in Fig. 1.10 is preceded by a unique _line number_ that indicates its relative position in the program. Any integer from 1 to 32767 may be used as a line number. It is generally a good idea to use increments of 10 between line numbers as this leaves room for inserting, at a later time, additional statements that may be needed. Each statement will be placed where it belongs in the program (according to line number sequence) regardless of when it is actually typed in.

Lines 100–120 in Fig. 1.10 are used to read and print the input data, 30 and 4.5, that are stored in HOURS and RATE. Then the gross salary (GROSS) and net pay (NET) are computed as functions of the input data, and, finally, these results are printed as the program output. The END statement at line 160 terminates the execution of the program and also marks the end of the list of BASIC-PLUS statements.

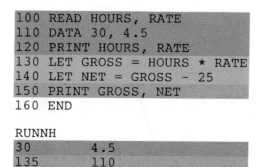

```
100  READ HOURS, RATE
110  DATA 30, 4.5
120  PRINT HOURS, RATE
130  LET GROSS = HOURS * RATE
140  LET NET = GROSS - 25
150  PRINT GROSS, NET
160  END

RUNNH
30          4.5
135         110
```

Fig. 1.10 The BASIC-PLUS program for Problem 1A.

Use of Symbolic Names in BASIC-PLUS

One of the most important features of BASIC-PLUS is that it permits us to reference data that are stored in memory through the use of symbolic names (called *variable names* or, simply, *variables*). BASIC-PLUS *allocates* (assigns) one memory cell for each variable name used in our program.

For the payroll problem, we used the variable HOURS (for hours worked), RATE (for hourly rate), GROSS (for gross salary) and NET (for net pay). These are pictured in Fig. 1.11. The question mark in each box indicates that we have no idea of the current values of these variables (although variables always have values).

Fig. 1.11 Using variable names to designate memory cells.

The rules below must be followed in forming variable names.

Variable names (EXTEND mode of BASIC-PLUS)

- Must always begin with a letter.
- May consist of up to 30 characters chosen from the letters, digits, and the symbol ".".
- May end with the symbol "$" or "%".
- Must not match any of the reserved keywords of BASIC-PLUS.

As we shall see later, variables that are used for storing *string data* (non-numeric data) must always end with the symbol "$" (e.g., N$ in Fig. 1.8). Variables that are used for storing only *integer data* (whole numbers) may end with the symbol "%".

The rules stated above apply to the EXTEND mode of BASIC-PLUS. The NOEXTEND mode is more restrictive and permits only variable names consisting of a single letter or a letter followed by a digit. From now on, we shall assume the EXTEND mode is being used. If it is not being used on your computer, the system command

    EXTEND

will place your system in EXTEND mode. This command should be typed before the first program statement.

As mentioned in the previous display, some words have special meaning in BASIC-PLUS. These BASIC-PLUS *reserved keywords* are listed in

Appendix C. They may not be used as variable names (with or without a "$" or "%"). The error message

```
?Syntax error
```

will be printed whenever a statement that attempts to use a reserved word as a variable is typed in. This error message means that the statement was not accepted by BASIC-PLUS as it violates the syntax rules. The statement in error should be corrected and retyped.

Program Style

Using meaningful variable names

Throughout this text we will use boxes such as this to discuss certain points that contribute to good program style. You may think that it is more important to get a program working correctly without being concerned with its style. However, computer scientists have found that programs that are written initially to conform to widely accepted style conventions are much easier to read and understand. They are also less likely to contain errors; moreover, any errors that might exist are easier to locate and correct.

As an example of good programming style, it is very important to choose variable names that can be readily associated with the information stored in the variable. Well chosen names can make programs considerably easier to read and understand. Avoid the temptation to use single letter variable names, such as R and H, instead of more meaningful names such as RATE and HOURS.

Exercise 1.3: Which of the following "strings" of characters can be used as legal variable names in EXTEND mode? Indicate the errors in the strings that are illegal. Which are legal in NOEXTEND mode?

```
ARK  MICHAEL  ZIP12  12ZIP  P$  ITCH  P$3  GROSS
X123459  I1  NINE-T  NEW.SAL  GROSS.PAY  END  DATA$
```

Simple Data Manipulation—Assignment Statements

As shown earlier, we will assume that the variables HOURS and RATE represent the number of hours worked and the hourly wage rate, respectively. GROSS and NET will be used to represent the computed gross salary and net pay, respectively. Our problem is to perform the two computations:

• Compute gross salary as the product of hours worked and hourly wage rate.
• Find net pay by deducting the tax amount from the gross salary.

We need to write BASIC-PLUS instructions to tell the computer to perform these computations. This is done in Fig. 1.10 using the *assignment statements*

```
130 LET GROSS = HOURS * RATE
140 LET NET = GROSS - 25
```

These data manipulation statements are called assignment statements because they specify the assignment of a value to a given variable. Fig. 1.12 illustrates the effect of these statements.

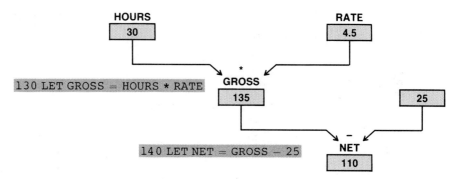

Fig. 1.12 Effect of assignment statements.

The first statement causes the value of the variable GROSS to be replaced by the *product* (indicated by *) of the values of the variables HOURS and RATE, or 135. The second statement causes the value of the variable NET to be replaced by the *difference* (indicated by −) between the values of the variable GROSS and the tax amount, 25. (We are assuming, of course, that meaningful data items are already present in the variables HOURS and RATE and that the value of 25 is also present in a memory cell.) Only the contents of GROSS and NET are changed by this sequence of *arithmetic operations*; the variables HOURS and RATE retain their original values.

The general form of the assignment statement is shown in the following display.

Assignment Statement

LET *result* = *expression*

Interpretation: The variable specified by *result* is assigned the value of the *expression*. The *expression* can be a single variable or value, or a computation involving variables and values and the arithmetic operators listed in Table 1.2. The previous value of *result* is destroyed when the expression value is stored.

Note: The word LET is optional and may be omitted; although we shall not do so.

Table 1.2 Some BASIC-PLUS Arithmetic Operators

Arithmetic operator	Meaning
+	Addition
–	Subtraction
*	Multiplication
/	Division

As we shall see, any arithmetic formula can be specified as an expression. For the time being, we will focus on simple expressions as illustrated in the following examples.

Example 1.3   It is perfectly permissible to write assignment statements of the form

```
200 LET SUM = SUM + ITEM
```

where the variable SUM is used on both sides of the equal sign. This is obviously not a mathematical equation, but it illustrates something that is often done in BASIC-PLUS. As shown next, this statement instructs the computer to add the current value of the variable SUM to the value of the variable ITEM and assign the result as the new value of the variable SUM. The previous value of SUM is destroyed in the process.

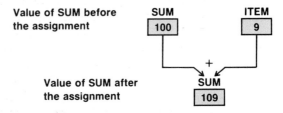

The above statement is discussed further in Chapter 2, where it is used to *accumulate* the sum of a large number of data items.

Example 1.4   A single variable or value can be used as an expression in an assignment statement. The statement

```
300 LET X.NEW = X.OLD
```

instructs the computer to *copy* the value of the variable X.OLD into X.NEW. The statement

```
400 LET X = 25.2
```

instructs the computer to store the number 25.2 in X.

Example 1.5   Although we shall wait until Chapter 4 to formally discuss the rules that are used in evaluating expressions with more than one operator, you should know that BASIC-PLUS follows the normal rules of algebra. This means that multiplication and division are done before addition and subtraction; parentheses may be used to group an operator with its operands. The meaning of some simple multiple-operator expressions are shown in Table 1.3.

Table 1.3 Simple BASIC-PLUS Expressions

BASIC-PLUS Expression	Meaning
X + Y + Z	The sum of variables X, Y, Z is computed.
X + Y * Z	The product Y * Z is added to X.
(X + Y) * Z	The sum of X and Y is multiplied by Z.
X - Y / Z	The quotient Y / Z is subtracted from X.

Storing Constants in Memory

Information cannot be manipulated by the computer unless it is first stored in memory. In this section and the next, we discuss two ways of initially placing information to be manipulated into computer memory: by writing constant values directly in an assignment statement, or by reading data into memory during the execution of the program. Normally, the first approach is taken for information with a value that is predetermined, or *constant*. Such values are usually given ahead of time, often in the statement of the problem to be solved. The second approach is taken for data that are likely to vary each time the program is used.

For example, in the payroll problem, the withholding tax amount is given as $25 regardless of which employee's net pay is to be computed. Since this value is given ahead of time as a constant, we may write it directly in the assignment statement

```
140 LET NET = GROSS - 25
```

When a constant is written *in-line* in this manner, the translator must make sure that the constant is placed in some memory cell prior to the execution of the program.

The READ and DATA Statements

Unlike the tax amount, which is given as part of the problem statement, the number of hours worked per week and the employee hourly rate may vary with each employee. Hence, these values should be read into memory during program execution. This operation must be performed prior to carrying out any calculations involving these values.

In the program of Fig. 1.10, the statement

```
100 READ HOURS, RATE
```

causes the computer to enter a data item into each of the variables listed (HOURS and RATE in this case). All of the data items (values) to be entered by the READ statement must be listed in a corresponding DATA statement. The effect of the READ and DATA statements

```
100 READ HOURS, RATE
110 DATA 30, 4.5
```

is indicated in Fig. 1.13. The previous values of the variables HOURS and RATE are destroyed by the data entry process.

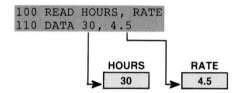

Fig. 1.13 Effect of READ and DATA statements.

READ Statement ✳

READ *variable list*

Interpretation: Data are entered into the variables specified in the *variable list*. Commas are used to separate the variable names in the list. The data values are provided in DATA statements.

DATA Statement ✳

DATA *data list*

Interpretation: Each value in the *data list* is entered into memory through the execution of a READ statement. Commas are used to separate the values in the *data list*.

The DATA statement may be placed anywhere in the program; however, we recommend placing it just after the READ statement which enters the data items in the list into memory. The order of the data items in the DATA statement must correspond to the order of the variable names in the associated READ statement. If the order of the data items were somehow interchanged during preparation of the program, the values read into HOURS and RATE would not be the ones desired.

To minimize the chance of this or other similar input errors going undetected, it is advisable to display or *echo print* the value of each variable used for storage of input data. Such a printout also provides a record of the data manipulated by the program. This record is often quite helpful to the programmer and to those who must read and interpret the program output. The statement used to display or print out the value of a variable is described in the next section.

The PRINT Statement

See pages 29-30, also

Thus far we have discussed the BASIC-PLUS statements required for the entry of employee hours and wage rate, and the computation of gross salary and net pay. The computational results have been stored in the variables GROSS and NET, respectively. Yet all of this work done by the computer is of little use to us since we cannot physically look into a memory cell to see what is there. We must, therefore, have a way to instruct the computer to display or print the value of a variable.

The statement

```
150 PRINT GROSS, NET
```

causes the values of the variables GROSS and NET to be printed on a line of program output (Fig. 1.14). The values of GROSS and NET are not altered by this operation.

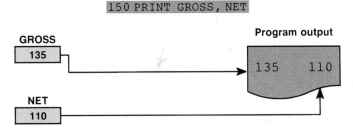

Fig. 1.14 Effect of PRINT statement.

The PRINT statement is described in the next display.

PRINT Statement

PRINT *output list*

Interpretation: The value of each item in the *output list* is printed in sequence across an output line. Commas or semicolons may be used to separate items in the *output list*. These items may be constants, variables or expressions. The *output list* is optional. If it is omitted, a blank output line results.

There are two PRINT statements in Fig. 1.10.

```
120 PRINT HOURS,  RATE
150 PRINT GROSS,  NET
```

The first PRINT statement follows the READ statement and echo prints the data values for HOURS (30) and RATE (4.5). The second PRINT statement displays the computed results, GROSS (135) and NET (110).

The output for a sample run of this program is shown below.

From the first line we see that the employee worked 30 hours (value of HOURS), and earned $4.50 per hour (value of RATE). The gross salary is $135 and the net pay is $110.

Stopping Computer Execution

Once all desired calculations have been performed and the results displayed, the computer must be instructed to terminate execution of the program. The instruction that does this (END) is described in the next display.

END Statement ✶

```
END
```

Interpretation: The END statement must always appear as the last line of a BASIC-PLUS program and nowhere else in the program. It causes program execution to be terminated and marks the physical end of the program.

The Complete Payroll Program

We will now arrange all of the instructions that have been discussed as a complete BASIC-PLUS program for Problem 1A. This program is shown in Fig. 1.15, along with a sample run.

The program in Fig. 1.15 prints the gross salary and net pay (second output line) for an employee whose hours worked and hourly rate are shown in the first output line. If we wished to rerun the program for a different

```
100 READ HOURS, RATE
110 DATA 30, 4.5
120 PRINT HOURS, RATE
130 LET GROSS = HOURS * RATE
140 LET NET = GROSS - 25
150 PRINT GROSS, NET
160 END

RUNNH
30          4.5
135         110
```

Fig. 1.15 Program and sample run for Problem 1A.

employee who worked 35 hours and was paid $3.18 per hour, we could simply modify the DATA statement as shown below.

```
110 DATA 35, 3.18
```

Program Style

Use of blank space

Program style is a very important consideration in programming. A program that "looks good" is easier to read and understand than a sloppy program. Most programs, at some time or another, will be examined or studied by someone else. It is certainly to everyone's advantage if a program is neat and its meaning is clear.

The consistent and careful use of blanks can significantly enhance the style of a program. Extra blanks in BASIC-PLUS programs are ignored and may be inserted as desired to improve the style and appearance of a program. As shown in Fig. 1.15, we shall always leave a blank space after a comma and before and after operators such as *, −, and =. Blanks should be used before and after BASIC-PLUS reserved keywords (e.g., LET, READ, DATA, PRINT) and variable names.

Exercise 1.4: Can the order of any of the statements in the program in Fig. 1.15 be changed in any way without altering the results of the program? Which statements can be moved? Which cannot be moved? Why?

Exercise 1.5: What values will be printed by the payroll program for the alternative DATA statement

```
110 DATA 35, 3.8
```

Exercise 1.6: Let HOURS, RATE, and TAX be the symbolic names of memory cells containing the information shown below:

HOURS	RATE	TAX
40	16.25	0.18

What values will be printed during the execution of the following sequence of instructions?

```
110 LET GROSS = HOURS * RATE
120 LET TAX = GROSS * TAX
130 LET NET = GROSS - TAX
140 PRINT HOURS, RATE, GROSS, TAX, NET
150 END
```

1.4 BASIC-PLUS with the RSTS/E Operating System

Many of you will be using BASIC-PLUS with Digital Equipment's *RSTS/E operating system*. An operating system is a supervisory program which schedules the resources of the computer and controls the order in which user programs are processed. The RSTS/E (Resource Sharing Timesharing System) enables several users to share the resources of the computer simultaneously. Normally each user will be unaware that others are using the computer.

In order to use BASIC-PLUS, you must become familiar with a set of system commands (e.g., RUN or RUNNH) that will enable you to communicate with the operating system. You will also have to learn how to *log in* (gain access to the computer).

The specific details of logging in are different at each computer installation; however, before beginning, you must make sure that your terminal is switched on. If your terminal is connected by telephone to the computer, it may be necessary to switch on the *acoustic coupler* beside the telephone and dial up the computer before proceeding further. If your terminal is directly wired (no coupler) then you may have to type HELLO before beginning.

Logging In

When your terminal is connected to the computer, a greeting message will be printed followed by the prompt symbol " # ". You should then type in your user identification number and a carriage return. (Each line should be terminated by a carriage return.) After you have entered your user number (146/5 below) the computer will prompt you for your password. This sequence is shown next.

```
RSTS    Version 7.0    11-Jan-84    10:50 AM
#146/5
Password:
```

Your password should be known only to you and typing it in at this point confirms your identity. Although your password will not be echoed on the screen, the letters you type will be entered into the computer. If the password is correct, you can begin using the computer; if either your user number or password is incorrect, the computer will print

```
Invalid entry - try again
```

and wait for you to re-enter your user number and password. (VAX-11 BASIC users should enter the BASIC command described in Appendix A once logged in.)

Old Files and New Files

Once you are identified as a valid user, a temporary *work area* in memory will be assigned to you and the computer will print a welcoming message followed by the prompt

```
Ready
```

The computer always types this prompt when it is waiting for your next system command. At this point you should specify whether you wish to create a new program (system command NEW) or transfer an existing program from disk storage to your work area (system command OLD). We will choose the first option and type the name PAYROL after the prompt "New file name—" as shown below

```
NEW
New file name—PAYROL
```

The two lines above can be combined by typing

```
NEW PAYROL
```

Each program that we create is treated as a *file* by the RSTS/E operating system. A file is a collection of related information with a unique name. A file name must always start with a letter and consists of one to six alphanumeric (letter or digit) characters. If no file name is typed in after the prompt, the system will use NONAME as the file name.

Deleting Characters and Lines

After the next prompt ("Ready") we can begin typing in the BASIC-PLUS program. We will enter the program shown in Fig. 1.15.

Ready

```
100 READ HOUR, RATE
110 DATA 35, 4.5
120 PRINT HOURS, RATE
            .
            .
            .
160 END
100 READ HOURS, RATE
```

Each line of the program should be terminated with a carriage return.

As shown above, it is permissible to retype a line (e.g., line 100 is typed twice) if it contains a mistake (HOUR instead of HOURS). The latest version of any line is the one retained in the work area. Line 160 is still the last line of the program.

If a mistake is noticed before the line is completed, you can erase one or more consecutive characters by pressing the DELETE (or RUBOUT) key. On a video screen, the *cursor* will back up and a character will disappear each time you press DELETE; on a printing terminal, the symbol "\" is printed (when DELETE is first pressed), then the deleted characters are printed, followed by another symbol "\" (after the last DELETE). When the erroneous characters are deleted, you can continue typing the line. In the line printed below, the DELETE key was pressed twice (deleting "R" and "I"); the word actually entered is PRINT.

```
100 PIR\RI\RINT "HI"
```

 To delete a line that was entered earlier, simply type the line number followed immediately by a carriage return. To delete lines 200 through 250, use the command

```
DELETE 200-250
```

 Be careful as the command

```
DELETE
```

will delete your entire work area.

Running a Program

Once the program is entered, you can use the command RUN or RUNNH (RUN with No Heading) to cause it to be executed.

```
RUN
PAYROL     10:59 AM     11-Jan-84
30     4.5
135     110
```

Ready

If RUNNH is used, the heading line shown under RUN will not be printed.

Listing a Program

If you desire to see the program in your temporary work area, use the command

LIST

or

LISTNH

where LISTNH lists with No Heading. The command

LIST 100-150

will display lines 100 through 150 of the program in your temporary work area.

Saving a Program

Unless you take steps to save the program in your temporary work area, it will be lost when the computer session is terminated or when the command NEW or OLD is used again. The command

SAVE

saves the contents of your work area as a *permanent file* in the disk storage area allocated to your account. The permanent file will have the same name as the file in the temporary work area.

After modifying the file in the temporary work area, you may try to save it again.

SAVE
File exists - RENAME/REPLACE

The diagnostic message above indicates that a permanent file with the same name as the file in the work area already exists so the SAVE operation was not performed. The command

REPLACE

replaces the original permanent file with the file currently in the work area, thereby destroying the original file. If you wish to save both the original and modified versions, the command

SAVE NEWNAM

saves the file currently in the work area as a new permanent file named NEWNAM without destroying the original file. Be wary about doing this as you can waste valuable disk space by saving several similar versions of a program.

It is generally a good idea to use the REPLACE command after every 10 lines of a lengthy program are entered. Then if the system should crash or you should somehow get disconnected from the computer, you will have to re-enter at most 10 lines of the program.

very good point

Changing a File Name

The command

    RENAME NEWPAY

changes the name of the file in the temporary work area to NEWPAY. The command

    NAME "PAYROL.BAS" AS "OLDPAY.BAS"

changes the name of the permanent file PAYROL.BAS to OLDPAY.BAS. Note that both the old and new names must be enclosed in quotes. The *extension* .BAS is automatically added to a permanent file name by RSTS/E to indicate that it contains a BASIC program. The extension must be used with the NAME command.

Deleting Files and Printing the Directory

The command

    UNSAVE OLDPAY

removes the permanent file OLDPAY (or OLDPAY.BAS) from the disk storage area. You should remove any extraneous files regularly in order to free up disk space.

The CAT command will provide you with a listing of the *file directory* for your account. For example:

```
CAT
OLDPAY.BAS  1  60  01-APR-84  05-JAN-84  11:55  AM
NEWNAM.BAS  1  60  01-APR-84  01-APR-84  10:20  AM
```

shows the name of both permanent files saved for our account, the number (1) of disk blocks used by each file, the protection code (60), the date each file was last used (01-APR-84), and the date and time each file was created. A *protection code of 60* means that each file can be accessed only by this account.

Logging Out

To terminate a computer session, type the command

BYE

The system will print the prompt

Confirm:

and wait for one of the following responses:

Y - Yes. The system continues the log out sequence.
N - No. The system terminates the log out sequence and types Ready.
I - The system lists each permanent file name followed by a ?. Typing a K (Kill) deletes the file from the disk. Typing any other character or RETURN retains the file.

The command

BYE Y

provides the response ("Y") without waiting for the prompt.

The Control Key

The control key (CTRL) can be used with other keys to perform special operations. For example, the command

CTRL/C

stops a running program. (The control key must be held down while the "C" is pressed.) The command

CTRL/S

can be used to temporarily halt a video terminal display so that you can read it. The command

CTRL/Q

resumes the display. These operations can also be performed by using the NO SCROLL key.

1.5 Additional Input and Output Features

Annotated Output

The printout for our payroll program consists of four numbers only, with no indication of what these numbers mean. In this section, we shall learn how output values may be annotated using *quoted strings* (or *strings*) to make it easier for us to identify the variable values they represent. We will learn more about the use of strings in Chapter 4, but for now it will be useful to know how to use them to clarify program output.

A *string* is a sequence of symbols enclosed in quotes. We can insert strings directly into BASIC-PLUS PRINT statements in order to provide descriptive messages in the program output. The string will be displayed exactly as it is typed (with the quotes removed).

For example, the statements

```
120 PRINT "HOURS ="; HOURS,  "RATE ="; RATE
150 PRINT "GROSS ="; GROSS,  "NET ="; NET
```

contain four strings and generate the two output lines:

```
HOURS = 30          RATE = 4.5
GROSS = 135         NET = 110
```

An additional example of the use of strings to annotate output is provided in Fig. 1.16, which computes the average trip time and cost using the formulas below:

1. time = distance / speed
2. gallons used = distance / miles per gallon
3. cost of trip = gallons used x cost per gallon

There are four data items for this program; trip distance (DISTANCE), average speed (SPEED), number of miles traveled on a gallon of gas (MPG) and cost of a gallon (GAL.COST). The program computes the estimated time of the trip (TRIP.TIME) and the total cost of gasoline (TRIP.COST).

The computations performed in this program are quite simple. Line 140 computes the time of a trip using formula 1 above; line 210 computes the number of gallons of gasoline (GALLONS) using formula 2; line 220 computes the cost of the trip using formula 3.

The remaining statements are used for data entry and display. Each output line has the same color background as the program statement that generates it.

A close examination of the program output for Fig. 1.16 reveals several important points concerning PRINT statements, which are summarized in the next display.

```
100  READ DISTANCE, SPEED
110  DATA 320, 50
120  PRINT "DISTANCE ="; DISTANCE; "MILES",
130  PRINT "AVERAGE SPEED ="; SPEED; "MPH"
140  LET TRIP.TIME = DISTANCE / SPEED
150  PRINT "TIME OF TRIP ="; TRIP.TIME; "HOURS"
160  PRINT
170  READ MPG, GAL.COST
180  DATA 19.5, 1.25
190  PRINT "MILEAGE RATE ="; MPG; "MILES PER GALLON"
200  PRINT "COST PER GALLON ="; GAL.COST; "DOLLARS"
210  LET GALLONS = DISTANCE / MPG
220  LET TRIP.COST = GALLONS * GAL.COST
230  PRINT "TRIP COST ="; TRIP.COST; "DOLLARS"
240  END

RUNNH
DISTANCE = 320 MILES
AVERAGE SPEED = 50 MPH
TIME OF TRIP = 6.4 HOURS

MILEAGE RATE = 19.5 MILES PER GALLON
COST PER GALLON = 1.25 DOLLARS
TRIP COST = 20.5128 DOLLARS
```

Fig. 1.16 Trip time and cost program and sample output.

Facts About PRINT Statements

- Either a comma or a semicolon may be used to separate items in an output list.
- Each PRINT statement initiates output on a new line, unless the previous PRINT statement ended with a comma or a semicolon. (The output from the PRINT statements at lines 120 and 130 appeared on the same line because the first PRINT—at line 120—was terminated with a comma.)
- The word PRINT by itself (line 160) generates a blank line.
- The blank character is printed after each number. The first character printed for a positive number is also a blank.
- Each string used as a message must be enclosed in either double quotes ("*message*") or single quotes ('*message*'). A PRINT statement may be used to print a message only or messages interspersed with variable values (lines 120, 130, 150, 190, 200, 230).
- BASIC-PLUS divides an output line into five *print zones* of 14 characters each. An output item following a comma separator is printed starting in the first print position (position 1, 15, 29, 43 or 57) of the next zone. A long string (more than 14 characters) will be printed in

two or more zones. An item will be printed on the next line if all zones of the current line are used.

- An output item following a semicolon separator is printed starting in the "next" print position of the current zone.

Example 1.6   Let the variables DEPOSIT and BAL contain the values 257.5 and −195.75, respectively. Then the statement

```
110 PRINT "DEPOSIT = "; DEPOSIT; "BALANCE = "; BAL
```

would produce the output

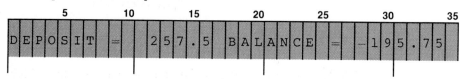

There is a blank space after each "=" sign in the strings in line 110; a second blank is printed before the positive number 257.5 as discussed in the display.

The statement

```
110 PRINT "THE CURRENT BALANCE IS", BAL
```

would produce the output

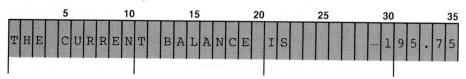

The statements

```
110 PRINT "DEPOSIT = "; DEPOSIT
120 PRINT "BALANCE = ", BAL
```

would produce the annotated output

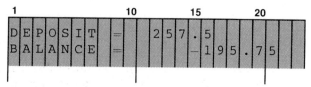

This output would also be produced by the statements

```
110 PRINT "DEPOSIT = ";
120 PRINT DEPOSIT
130 PRINT "BALANCE = ",
140 PRINT BAL
```

(Lines 120 and 140 do not initiate a new output line since lines 110 and 130 end with a semicolon and comma, respectively).

Exercise 1.7: Write the PRINT statements needed to print the TIC-TAC-TOE board configuration shown below.

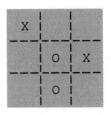

More on READ and DATA Statements

The DATA statement is a nonexecutable statement. This means it is not translated and executed; instead, the translator copies all items in each data list into a special area of memory as the program is translated. During execution, whenever a READ statement is encountered, the next group of data items is copied from this special area of memory into the variables specified in the READ statement.

Example 1.7   As an example, consider these two sets of READ and DATA statements:

```
100 READ A, B
110 DATA 30, 4.5
120 READ X, Y
130 DATA 6.8, 1.5
```

```
100 READ A, B
110 READ X, Y
120 DATA 30, 4.5, 6.8, 1.5
```

Both sequences of statements would cause the same values to be stored in memory

A	B	X	Y
30	4.5	6.8	1.5

We recommend the sequence on the left, even though it is longer, as each pair of data items appears directly below the READ statement that processes it.

Interactive Data Entry—The INPUT Statement

The program shown in Fig. 1.17 illustrates a second way in which data can be provided to a program: through the use of an INPUT statement. By using the INPUT statement, we can *interact* with a program while it is executing. It is not necessary to supply all of the problem data in advance; instead, we can supply data to the program as it is requested, during the running of the program.

If an *interactive program* is written properly, it will inform the user of important computational results, and *prompt* the user when it requires additional data. As shown in Fig. 1.17, the PRINT statement can be used to print both results and prompting messages. A prompting message (lines 100, 130-150) is printed each time additional information is needed by the program. The INPUT statement is then used to enter data items (25, 3, 2) that are typed at the terminal.

```
100 PRINT "HOW OLD ARE YOU";
110 INPUT AGE
120 PRINT AGE; "IS A GOOD AGE."
130 PRINT "HOW MANY BROTHERS AND SISTERS DO YOU"
140 PRINT "HAVE ENTER NUMBER OF BROTHERS, A COMMA,"
150 PRINT "NUMBER OF SISTERS"
160 INPUT BROTHER, SISTER
170 LET SIBLING = BROTHER + SISTER
180 PRINT "THAT MEANS YOU HAVE"; SIBLING; "SIBLINGS."
190 END

RUNNH
HOW OLD ARE YOU? 25
 25 IS A GOOD AGE.
HOW MANY BROTHERS AND SISTERS DO YOU
HAVE? ENTER NUMBER OF BROTHERS, A COMMA,
AND NUMBER OF SISTERS
? 3, 2
THAT MEANS YOU HAVE 5 SIBLINGS.
```

Fig. 1.17 Interactive data entry.

The INPUT statement is used exactly as a READ statement, except that data to be entered are typed at the terminal during program execution, rather than provided beforehand in a DATA statement as the program is initially typed. When an INPUT statement is executed by the computer, the running program is interrupted, a question mark is printed at the user's terminal, and the computer then waits for the user to supply the necessary data. As shown in Fig. 1.17, if the prompting message ends with a semicolon or comma (line 100), the question mark is printed on the same line as the prompt; otherwise, it is printed on the next output line (line 150). Once the data entry has been completed (usually indicated when the user presses the RETURN key), execution continues with the next statement in the program. The INPUT statement is described in the next display.

INPUT Statement

INPUT *variable list*
or INPUT *prompt*; *variable list*

Interpretation: A question mark is printed and program execution is interrupted. As many data items should be typed in (separated by commas) as there are variables in the *variable list*. If too few items are typed, the prompt "?" will be repeated; if too many items are typed, any extra data will be ignored. After data entry is complete, the RETURN key should be pressed to resume program execution. If a *prompt* (enclosed in quotes) is provided, it will be printed before the symbol "?".

A prompting message should always be printed before the program pauses for data entry. The prompt may also be included as part of the INPUT statement. Lines 100 and 110 in Fig. 1.17 could be combined as

```
110 INPUT "HOW OLD ARE YOU"; AGE
```

This would cause the prompting message

```
HOW OLD ARE YOU?
```

to be printed and the program would pause for data entry. Similarly, lines 130–160 could be rewritten as

```
130 INPUT "HOW MANY BROTHERS DO YOU HAVE"; BROTHER
140 INPUT "HOW MANY SISTERS"; SISTER
```

Remember, the INPUT statement processes data that are entered during the execution of the program. The READ statement processes data that are typed in DATA statements before program execution begins.

Exercise 1.8: Rewrite the programs in Figs. 1.15 and 1.16 as interactive programs.

1.6 Common Programming Errors

One of the first things you will discover in writing programs is that a program very rarely runs correctly the first time it is submitted. Murphy's Law, "If something can go wrong, it will," seems to be written with the computer programmer or programming student in mind. In most cases, an error message will be printed indicating that you have made a mistake and the number of the line in error. A listing of error messages is provided in Appendix G. We will discuss some common errors next.

Incorrect or Invalid Terminal Commands

Remember, the RSTS/E operating system controls your access to BASIC-PLUS and enables you to save and retrieve program files. If you use a system command that does not exist, the RSTS/E operating system will simply print the message

```
?What?
```

and wait for your next command. If you use a file name that is not legal in a system command, RSTS/E will print the message

```
?Illegal file name
```

and do nothing. If you try to SAVE (instead of REPLACE) a modified version of an existing file, RSTS/E will print

```
?File exists-RENAME/REPLACE
```

and do nothing.

It is also possible to get RSTS/E to perform an action that was not intended. For example, if you have a program file in the work area and issue the command OLD or NEW before saving that file, RSTS/E will erase the work area, thereby destroying your file. When you use the system command REPLACE, RSTS/E will delete the version of a file currently saved on disk regardless of whether you intended this to happen. These errors can be extremely frustrating because you may have to re-enter a large program that was inadvertently lost.

BASIC-PLUS Syntax Errors

A syntax error message is printed when the statement entered does not follow the precise *syntax rules* for forming BASIC-PLUS statements. In some cases (e.g., reserved keyword used as a variable name), an error message such as

```
?Syntax error at line 100
```

will be printed immediately after the statement (line 100) that contained the error. Whenever possible, BASIC-PLUS will provide a more descriptive diagnostic message.

```
120 PRINS X
?Illegal verb at line 120
```

If the syntax error is not corrected, line 120 will be preceded by the symbol "?" when it is listed. If the program is run, the message

```
?Illegal statement at line 120
```

will be printed when line 120 is reached and program execution will terminate.

If a line number is omitted from a statement, BASIC-PLUS tries to execute it immediately (*immediate mode*). Certain statements (e.g., READ, DATA) cannot be executed in immediate mode; hence, the error message

```
?Illegal in immediate mode
```

will be printed.

The use of immediate mode for *debugging programs* (correcting errors) will be discussed later (Chapters 3 and 4). For the time being, it is useful to know that the value of any variable can be printed by typing a PRINT statement (without a line number) immediately after program execution. This will enable you to see whether data or intermediate results were stored as expected if your program runs, but does not print the correct results.

Other Errors

The "nice" thing about syntax errors is that they are brought to the programmer's attention for immediate correction. There are other kinds of errors that do not violate BASIC-PLUS syntax rules and, consequently, will not be detected when the statement is typed.

An example is inconsistent spelling of variable names. If the same variable is spelled differently on two program lines, then BASIC-PLUS will assume that two distinct variables are used and will allocate a different memory cell for each. In line 110 of the program segment below

```
100 LET COUNT.N = 5
110 LET AVE = 20 / COUNT.M
```

COUNT.M is typed instead of COUNT.N. This would cause the message

```
%Division by zero at line 110
```

to be printed during program execution as COUNT.M has not been assigned a value. (All numeric variables are given an initial value of zero.) An error message beginning with the symbol "%" is a *warning message* and does not normally cause program execution to terminate. More often than not, an error message will not be printed when a variable name is misspelled, but an incorrect value will be computed.

BASIC-PLUS does not distinguish between upper-case and lower-case letters in variable names or reserved words. This means that the statements

```
100 LET COUNT.N = 5
110 LET AVE = 20 / count.n
```

would store the value 4 in the variable AVE since COUNT.N and count.n are treated as the same variable.

When the statement

```
120 INPUT "X"; X
```

is executed, the program waits for a data value to be entered.

```
X? XYZ
%Data format error at line 120
X?
```

As shown above, if a non-numeric value (XYZ) is typed, an error message is printed and the program pauses for data entry again. If line 120 contained a READ statement, the same error would result if the corresponding DATA statement value was non-numeric. However, in this case, program execution would be terminated.

Program logic errors are caused by mistakes in the logical organization of your program (e.g., program statements are not in the proper sequence or the wrong statements are used). Many of these errors can be avoided if a careful, reasoned approach is taken to problem solving and program development. Logic errors that do occur can often be diagnosed more easily if some care and discipline have been applied in the design and writing of the program. It is our intention to provide, through numerous examples, some useful guidelines for problem solving and program writing.

Exercise 1.9: Find the errors in each line of the following BASIC-PLUS program. There may be more than one error per line.

```
100 READ, HOURS, RATE
    DATA 5.0 25.0
110 LET RATE = 1.5 RATE
120 LET GROSS = HOUR * RATE
130 LET GROSS = NET
140 LET NET - 25.0 = NET
    PRINT HOURS: RATE
150 PRINT "GROSS = ," GROSS
```

1.7   Summary

You have been introduced to the basic components of the computer; the memory, the central processor unit, and the input and output units. A summary of important facts about computers that you should remember follows.

1. A memory cell is never empty.
2. The current contents of a memory cell are destroyed whenever new information is placed in that cell (via an assignment, READ or INPUT statement).

3. Programs must be placed in the memory of the computer before they can be executed.
4. Data may not be manipulated by the computer without first being stored in memory.
5. The computer cannot think for itself. It must be instructed to perform a task in a precise and unambiguous manner, using a programming language.
6. Programming a computer can be fun—if you are patient, organized, and careful.

You have also seen how to use the BASIC-PLUS programming language to perform some very fundamental operations. You have learned how to instruct the computer to read information into memory, perform some simple computations and print the results of the computation. All of this has been done using symbols (punctuation marks, variable names and special operators such as *, – and +) that are familiar, easy to remember, and easy to use. In Table 1.4, we have provided a summary of the BASIC-PLUS statements introduced in this chapter. An example of the use of

Table 1.4 Summary of BASIC-PLUS Statements ✗

Feature	Effect
Assignment	

```100 LET GROSS = HOURS * RATE```
```110 LET SUM = X1 + X2 + X3```
```120 LET TAX = 25```
	Assigns the value of the expression on the right of the equal sign to the variable named on the left.

READ–DATA	

```100 READ HOURS, RATE```
```110 DATA 35, 3.5```
```120 READ PERCENT```
```130 DATA 12.5```
	Reads the value 35 into HOURS, 3.5 into RATE, and 12.5 into PERCENT

INPUT	
```100 INPUT "ENTER A NUMBER"; N```	Prints a prompting message ending with a "?" and reads the data item typed into N.
PRINT	
```100 PRINT "GROSS ="; GROSS```	Prints the string "GROSS =" followed by the value of GROSS.
END	
```350 END```	Terminates program execution.

each statement is also given. You should use these examples as guides to ensure that you are using the correct syntax in the program statements that you write. These statements can also be found inside the front cover of the book.

The small amount of BASIC-PLUS that you have seen is sufficient to enable you to solve many problems using the computer. However, many problems cannot be solved with just this limited BASIC-PLUS subset. The more you learn about BASIC-PLUS, the easier it will be for you to write programs to solve more complicated problems on the computer.

We also introduced several system commands that are used to communicate with the BASIC-PLUS system. These commands are summarized in Table 1.5 and in Appendixes A, B, and inside the back cover of the book.

Table 1.5 Summary of BASIC-PLUS System Commands

Command	Effect
EXTEND	Switches to EXTEND mode of BASIC-PLUS.
NEW PAY1	Creates a new file named PAY1 in the work area.
OLD PAYROL	Copies the permanent file named PAYROL to the work area.
SAVE PAY1	Saves the file in the work area as a permanent file named PAY1.
REPLACE PAYROL	Replaces an existing permanent file with the version in the work area.
NAME "PAY1.BAS" AS "PAY2.BAS"	Changes the name of permanent file PAY1 to PAY2.
RENAME NEWPAY	Changes the work area name to NEWPAY.
UNSAVE PAYROL	Removes permanent file PAYROL from disk storage.
LIST(NH)	Lists (with No Heading) the current work area.
RUN(NH)	Executes (with No Heading) the program in the work area.
DELETE 100-140	Deletes lines 100–140 of the work area.
CAT	Lists all permanent files saved on disk for your account.
BYE	Begins the log out procedure.
CTRL/C	Suspends execution of a program.
CTRL/S (NO SCROLL)	Suspends the output display.
CTRL/Q (NO SCROLL)	Resumes the output display.

In the remainder of the text we will introduce you to more of the features of the BASIC-PLUS language and provide precise descriptions of the rules for using these features. You must remember throughout that, unlike the rules of English, the rules of BASIC-PLUS are quite precise and allow no exceptions. BASIC-PLUS instructions formed in violation of these rules will cause syntax errors in your programs.

You should find the mastery of the rules of BASIC-PLUS relatively easy. By far the most challenging aspect of your work will be the formulation of the logic and organization of your programs. For this reason, we will introduce you to a methodology for problem solving with a computer in the next chapter and continue to emphasize this methodology throughout the remainder of the book.

Programming Problems

1B Write a program to read in the weight (in pounds) of an object, and compute and print its weight in kilograms and grams. [*Hint*: one pound is equal to 0.453592 kilograms or 453.59237 grams.]

1C A cyclist coasting on a level road slows from a speed of 10 miles/hr. to 2.5 miles/hr. in one minute. Write a computer program that calculates the cyclist's constant rate of acceleration and determines how long it will take the cyclist to come to rest, given his original speed of 10 miles/hr.
[*Hint*: Use the equation

$$a = \frac{v_f - v_i}{t}$$

where a is acceleration, t is time, v_i is initial velocity, and v_f is the final velocity.]

1D Write a program to read three data items into variables X, Y, and Z, and find and print their product and sum.

1E Eight track stars entered the mile race at the Penn Relays. Write a program that will read in the race time in minutes and seconds for any one of these runners, and compute and print the speed in feet per second and in meters per second. [*Hints*: There are 5280 feet in one mile and one meter equals 3.282 feet.] Test your program on one of the times (minutes and seconds) given below.

3.0 minutes 52.83 seconds	3.0 minutes 56.22 seconds	3.0 minutes 59.83 seconds
4.0 minutes 00.03 seconds	4.0 minutes 16.22 seconds	4.0 minutes 19.00 seconds
4.0 minutes 19.89 seconds	4.0 minutes 21.21 seconds	

1F   You are planning to rent a car to drive from Boston to Philadelphia. Cost is no consideration, but you want to be certain that you can make the trip on one tankful of gas. Write a program to read in the miles-per-gallon and tank size in gallons for a particular rent-a-car, and print out the distance that can be traveled on one tank. Test your program for the following data:

miles-per-gallon	tank size (*gallons*)
10.0	15.0
40.5	20.0
22.5	12.0
10.0	9.0

1G   Write a program that prints your initials in large block letters. (*Hint*: Use a 6×6 grid for each letter and print six messages. Each message should consist of a row of *'s interspersed with blanks.)

2

Problem Solving with the Computer

In this chapter, we will develop a methodology for solving problems. The data table will be introduced as a means of identifying and describing the use of each variable needed in the problem solution. The general outline, or algorithm, for solving a problem will consist of a list of subtasks. We will add detail to the algorithm through a process called stepwise refinement.

In addition, we will show how to instruct the computer to make decisions and how to specify the repetition of a group of operations through the use of a loop. Finally, we will illustrate how to trace through an algorithm to verify that it is correct and how to implement simple decisions and loops in BASIC-PLUS.

2.1 Problem Analysis

Problem Subtasks

Now that you have been introduced to the computer—what it is, how it works, and what it can do—it is time to turn our attention to learning how to use the computer to solve problems.

Using the computer for problem solving is similar to trying to put a man on the moon in the late 1950's and 1960's. In both instances, there is a problem to be solved and a final "program" for solving it.

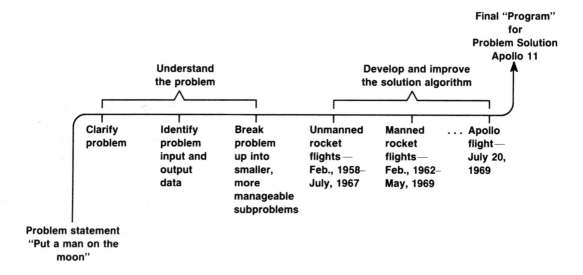

In the moon effort, the final goal was not achieved directly. Rather, it was brought about through the careful planning and organization of subtasks, each of which had to be completed successfully before the Apollo 11 flight could even be attempted.

Programming also requires careful planning and organization. It is rare, indeed, to see an error-free computer program written directly from the original statement of a problem. Usually, the final program is achieved only after a number of steps have been followed. These steps are the subject of this chapter.

Representation and Manipulation of Data

We stated earlier that the computer is a tool that can be used to represent and manipulate data. It is, therefore, not too surprising that the first two tasks in solving a problem on the computer require the definition of the data to be represented in the computer memory, and the formulation of an *algorithm*—a list of steps that describes the desired manipulation of these data.

These two tasks are not entirely unrelated. Decisions that we make in defining the data may be changed when we formulate the algorithm. Nevertheless we should perform the data definition as completely and carefully as possible before constructing the algorithm. Careless errors, or errors in judgment in deciding what information is to be represented, and what form this information is to take, can result in numerous difficulties later. Such mistakes can make the algorithm formulation extremely difficult and sometimes even impossible.

Once the definition of the information to be represented in the computer has been made and a precise statement of the problem is available, the algorithm for solving the problem can be formulated.

Understanding the Problem

The definition of the data to be represented in the computer memory requires a clear understanding of the stated problem. First we must determine what information is to be computed and printed by the computer. Then it is necessary to identify the information that is to be given as input to the computer. Once the input and output data have been identified, we must ask if sufficient information is available to compute the required output from the given input. If the answer to this question is no, we must determine what additional information is needed and how this information can be provided to the program.

When identifying the data items associated with the problem, it is helpful to assign to each item a descriptive variable name that can be used to represent the computer memory cell containing the data item. Recall from Chapter 1 that we need not be concerned with the address of the actual memory cell associated with each variable name. The translator will assign a unique memory cell to each variable name and it will handle all bookkeeping details necessary to retain this correspondence.

To see how this process works, we will apply it to a specific problem.

Problem 2A   Write a program to compute and print the sum and average of two numbers.

Discussion: The first step is to make certain that we understand the problem and to identify the input and output data for the problem. Then we can obtain a more precise formulation of the problem in terms of these input and output items.

All items of information to be used to solve a given problem should be listed in a *data table*, along with a description of the variable used to represent each data item. The data table for Problem 2A is given next. The entries shown describe the input and output data for the problem.

Input Variables		Program Variables	Output Variables	
NUMB1:	First number to be used in computation		SUM:	Sum of two numbers
NUMB2:	Second number to be used in computation		AVERAGE:	Average of two numbers

There are clearly two items of information required as output for this problem. They are the sum and the average of two numbers. In order to compute these values, we must first enter and store in memory the data items to be summed and averaged. In this example, we will use the variables NUMB1 and NUMB2 to represent these two input data items.

The table form just illustrated will be used for all data tables in the text. Variables whose values are entered through READ statements are listed as input variables; variables whose values represent final computational results required by the problem statement are listed as output variables. Other variables that may be used to store intermediate computational results are listed as program variables. Often, program variables are added to the data table as the algorithm develops. There are no program variables as yet in the data table for Problem 2A. In all cases, it is important to include in the data table a short, concise description of how each variable is to be used in the program.

The data table is valuable not only during algorithm development but also as a piece of *program documentation*. It is a convenient reference document for associating variable names and their uses in the program. You should always prepare a data table, pay close attention to it during the algorithm development process, and save it along with your program listing. The data table may subsequently turn out to be your only reminder of how the variables in your program are being used.

A more precise formulation of Problem 2A is now possible: we must read two data items into the variables NUMB1 and NUMB2, find the sum and the average of these two items, and print the values of the sum and the average.

 ## Description of the Problem Solution

Developing an Algorithm

At this point we should have a clear understanding of what is required for the solution of Problem 2A. We can now proceed to organize the problem formulation into a carefully constructed list of steps—the algorithm—that will describe the sequence of manipulations to be performed in carrying out the problem solution.

Algorithm for Problem 2A (Level One)	Step 1 Read the data items into the variables NUMB1 and NUMB2.
	Step 2 Compute the sum of the data items in NUMB1 and NUMB2 and store the result in the variable SUM.
	Step 3 Compute the average of the data items in NUMB1 and NUMB2 and store the result in the variable AVERAGE.
	Step 4 Print the values of the variables SUM and AVERAGE.

Algorithm Refinement

Note that this sequence of events closely mirrors the problem formulation given earlier. This is as it should be! If the problem formulation is complete, it should provide us with a general outline of what must be done to solve the problem. The purpose of the algorithm formulation is to provide a detailed and precise description of the individual steps to be carried out by the computer in solving the problem. The algorithm is essentially a *refinement* of the general outline provided by the original problem formulation. It is often the case that several *levels of refinement* of the general outline are required before the algorithm is complete.

The key question in deciding whether or not further refinement of an algorithm step is required is this:

Is it precisely clear which BASIC-PLUS instructions are necessary in order to tell the computer how to carry out the step?

If it is not immediately obvious what the BASIC-PLUS instructions are, then the algorithm step should be refined further.

What is obvious to some programmers may not be at all clear to others. The refinement of an algorithm is, therefore, a personal matter to some extent. As you gain experience in developing algorithms and converting them to BASIC-PLUS programs, you may discover that you are doing less and less algorithm refinement. This may also happen as you become more familiar with the BASIC-PLUS language.

If we examine the level one algorithm for Problem 2A, we see that only Step 3 may require further refinement. We already know how to write BASIC-PLUS instructions for reading, printing, and adding two numbers. However, we may not know how to tell the computer to find the average of two numbers.

| REFINEMENT OF STEP 3 | Step 3.1 Divide the sum (stored in SUM) by the number of items (2) and store the result in the variable AVERAGE. |

We now have an algorithm that is refined to a level of detail that is sufficient for us to write the BASIC-PLUS representation of the steps required to solve Problem 2A (see Fig. 2.1). We do this by implementing the algorithm on a step-by-step basis using the variable names provided in the data table.

The program consists of the BASIC-PLUS implementation of each of the algorithm steps in sequence. If an algorithm step is refined, then the refinement is implemented instead.

```
100 !COMPUTE THE SUM AND AVERAGE OF TWO NUMBERS
110 !
120 !READ AND PRINT DATA ITEMS
130     READ NUMB1, NUMB2
140     DATA 33, 55
150     PRINT "NUMB1 ="; NUMB1, "NUMB2 ="; NUMB2
155 !
160 !COMPUTE THE SUM OF THE DATA
170     LET SUM = NUMB1 + NUMB2
175 !
180 !COMPUTE THE AVERAGE
190     LET AVERAGE = SUM / 2
200 !
210 !PRINT RESULTS
220     PRINT "SUM ="; SUM, "AVERAGE ="; AVERAGE
230 !
240     END
```

```
RUNNH
NUMB1 = 33          NUMB2 = 55
SUM = 88            AVERAGE = 44
```

Fig. 2.1 Program and sample run for Problem 2A.

The lines in Fig. 2.1 that start with the symbol "!" are descriptive *comments*. They are neither translated nor executed but are listed with the program to identify or document the purpose of each section of the program. The program statements that are not comments are indented so that they stand out. The indentation may be performed most easily by pressing the TAB key after typing the statement line number. Guidelines for the use of comments are provided next.

Program Style

Use of comments

All programs should start with a section of comments describing the purpose of the program and the nature of the algorithm. It is also a good practice to list and describe the major variables used in the program, to identify the programmer, and to record the date of creation and last modification of the program, as shown next.

```
100 !COMPUTE THE SUM AND AVERAGE OF TWO NUMBERS
110 !
120 !PROGRAMMER - ELLIOT KOFFMAN
130 !INSTRUCTOR - FRIEDMAN
140 !COURSE - CIS2, SECTION 3
150 !ASSIGNMENT #4
160 !DATE CREATED - JAN 3, 1984
170 !LAST MODIFIED - JAN 15, 1984
```

```
180 !
190 !MAJOR VARIABLES
200 !   NUMB1, NUMB2 - NUMBERS BEING ADDED
210 !   SUM - SUM OF NUMB1, NUMB2
220 !   AVERAGE - AVERAGE OF NUMB1, NUMB2
```

Since the major variables and the algorithm generally will be described in the text, we will confine ourselves to a brief comment summarizing the purpose of each program as in line 100.

Each comment line within the program in Fig. 2.1 describes the purpose of the program statements that follow it. There should be enough comments to clarify the intent of each step of your program; however, too many comments can clutter the program and make it difficult to read. A good rule of thumb is to use a comment to identify the BASIC-PLUS implementation of each step in the level one algorithm as well as any other steps requiring further refinement. In this way, the correspondence between the algorithm and its BASIC-PLUS implementation becomes obvious. Also, we have used blank comment lines between program steps.

Comments should be carefully worded. One suggestion is to use an abbreviated form of the corresponding algorithm step description. For example, the comment in the program segment

```
180 !COMPUTE THE AVERAGE
190    LET AVERAGE = SUM / 2
```

conveys more information and, hence, is better than the comment

```
180 !DIVIDE SUM BY 2
```

which is simply an English description of the BASIC-PLUS statement that follows the comment.

The reserved word REM may also be used to introduce a comment. Lines beginning with REM are called *remarks*. Line 160 in Fig. 2.1 could also be written as

```
160 REM COMPUTE THE SUM OF THE DATA
```

Although we generally shall not do this, it is possible to add comments (but not remarks) at the end of a statement. Line 170 below

```
170    LET SUM = NUMB1 + NUMB2      !ADD THE DATA
```

consists of a BASIC-PLUS assignment statement followed by a comment. It is not possible to follow a comment with a BASIC-PLUS statement. Line 170 below

```
170 !ADD THE DATA      LET SUM = NUMB1 + NUMB2
```

would be treated as one long comment.

Program Style

Exercise 2.1: Rewrite the "READ AND PRINT DATA ITEMS" section of the sum and average program (Fig. 2.1) to provide prompting messages for interactive execution.

Exercise 2.2: Write a data table and an algorithm for computing the sum and average of four real numbers.

Flow Diagram Representation of Algorithms

As problems become more complicated, precise English descriptions of algorithms for solving these problems become more complex and difficult to follow. It is, therefore, helpful if some kind of notation can be used to specify an algorithm. We will use one such descriptive notation, called a *flow diagram*, throughout this text.

Not everyone in the computer field believes that flow diagrams are useful and many experienced programmers do not always use them. However, we believe that flow diagrams are helpful because they provide a graphical, two-dimensional representation of an algorithm. Consistent use of the special flow diagram symbols and forms shown in the text will make algorithms easy to write, easy to refine, and still easier to follow.

Flow diagram representations of two levels of the algorithm for Problem 2A are shown in Fig. 2.2. They contain a number of symbols that should be noted.

1. Ovals are used to indicate the starting and stopping points of an algorithm.
2. Rectangular boxes are used to indicate the manipulation of information in the memory of the computer.
3. A box in the shape of a computer card (with one corner cut off) is used to indicate the reading of information into the computer.
4. A box with a wavy bottom is used to indicate the printing of information stored in the computer memory.

5. Solid arrows are used to indicate the "flow of control" of an algorithm from one step to another.
6. Dashed arrows indicate refinements of algorithm steps.

You will find it convenient to represent all levels of algorithms with flow diagrams. Often, the first level will be quite general. It will contain a summary, usually written in English, of the basic steps of an algorithm, as shown on the left side of Fig. 2.2. In some cases, usually when the step is very simple, these summaries may be precise and detailed. However, in other cases, one or more levels of refinement will be necessary before a sufficiently detailed diagram is completed. Such refinements are illustrated on the right side of Fig. 2.2. The dashed arrows point to the refinements of Steps 1, 2, 3, and 4; the solid arrows indicate flow of control from one step to the next. Remember that refinements are for your benefit; they should be used when additional detail is needed to clarify what must be done to complete an algorithm step. (The refinements for all steps are not necessary; we have shown them to illustrate the different flow diagram symbols.)

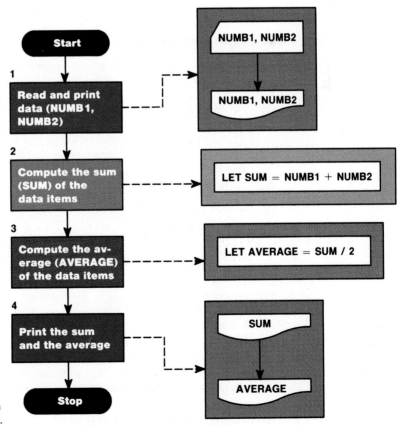

Fig. 2.2 Level one flow diagram and refinements for Problem 2A.

Program Style

In Fig. 2.2, the background color for the refinement of Step 1 is a lighter shade of the color used in Step 1. This is true for Steps 2–4 as well and will be true throughout the text. Each of the individual steps in a refinement has a white background. Any step that is to be refined further will have a colored background instead of white.

Lines 120–150 of Fig. 2.1 implement Step 1 of the flow diagram (Fig. 2.2). These program lines have a background screen that is a lighter shade of the color used in Step 1. This practice also will be followed throughout the text and should help you recognize the program implementation of an algorithm step. The output lines that are generated by program lines 120–150 also have this same color background.

Generally we will use the color red to indicate the major input step in an algorithm, and the color blue will indicate the major output step. Also, in data tables, input variables and output variables will have red and blue backgrounds, respectively. A background color of tan will be used to indicate the major processing step in an algorithm and as a background screen for program variables in data tables.

Problem Solving Principles

Up to now we have presented a few suggestions for solving problems on the computer. These suggestions are summarized below.

1. Understand what you are being asked to do.
2. Identify all problem input and output data. Assign a variable name to each input or output item and list it in the data table.
3. Formulate a precise statement of the problem in terms of the input and output data and make certain there are sufficient input items provided to complete the solution.
4. State clearly the sequence of steps necessary to produce the desired problem output; i.e., develop the algorithm and represent it as a flow diagram.
5. Refine this flow diagram until it can be implemented easily in the programming language to be used. List any additional variables required in the data table.
6. Transform the flow diagram to a program.

Steps 4 and 5 are really the most difficult of the steps listed; they are the only truly creative part of this process. People differ in their ability to formulate solutions to problems. Some find it easy to develop algorithms for the most complex problem, while others must work diligently to produce an algorithm for solving a simple problem.

The ability to solve problems is fundamental to computer programming. The transformation of the refined algorithm to a working program (Step 6) is a highly skilled clerical task that requires a thorough knowledge of the programming language available. This detailed knowledge normally can be acquired by anyone willing to devote the necessary effort. However, a flow diagram that correctly represents the necessary problem-solving operations and their relationships should first be developed.

In this book, we will provide detailed solutions to many sample problems. Examining the text solutions carefully should enable you to become more adept at formulating your own solutions, because the techniques used for one problem may frequently be applied in a slightly different way to solve another. Often, new problems are simply expansions or modifications of old ones.

The process of outlining and refining problem solutions can be used to break a complex problem up into more manageable subproblems that can be solved individually. This technique will be illustrated in all of the problems solved in the text. We suggest you practice it in developing your own solutions to the programming problems.

2.3 Algorithms Involving Decisions

Decision Steps and Conditions

Normally, the steps of an algorithm are performed in the order in which they are listed. In many algorithms, however, the sequence of steps to be performed is determined by the input data. In such cases, decisions must be made, based upon the values of certain variables, as to which sequence of steps is to be performed. Such decisions require the evaluation of a condition that is expressed in terms of the relevant variables. The result of the evaluation determines which algorithm steps will be executed next. An example of this is illustrated in the following problem, which is a modification of the payroll problem discussed in Chapter 1.

Problem 2B *Modified payroll problem.* Compute the gross salary and net pay for an employee of a company, given the number of hours worked and the employee's hourly wage rate. Deduct a tax amount of $25, but only if the employee's gross salary exceeds $100.

Discussion: The data table for this problem is shown below. The flow diagrams are drawn in Fig. 2.3.

DATA TABLE FOR PROBLEM 2B

Input Variables		Output Variables	
HOURS:	Number of hours worked	GROSS:	Gross salary
RATE:	Hourly wage rate	NET:	Net pay

In numbering flow diagrams and their refinements, we will use a scheme that is analogous to the numbering of sections in this text. For example, the refinements of Step 3 are numbered 3.1, 3.2, 3.3. However, if Step 3.1 were to be refined further, its refinements would be numbered 3.1.1, 3.1.2, etc. All steps in a level one flow diagram will be numbered. Normally only those refinement steps that are referred to in the text narrative will be numbered.

As shown in the flow diagram refinement of Step 3 (see Fig. 2.3), the *decision step* (3.1) describes a *logical condition* (GROSS>100) that is evaluated in order to determine which algorithm step should be executed next. If the condition is true, Step 3.2 (deduct tax) is performed next, as indicated by the arrow labeled T (for True). Otherwise, Step 3.3 (LET NET = GROSS) is performed, as indicated by the arrow labeled F (for False). In either case, Step 4 will be carried out following the completion of the chosen step.

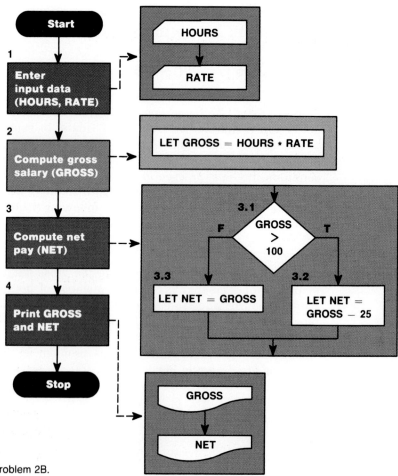

Fig. 2.3 Flow diagrams for Problem 2B.

As illustrated in Fig. 2.3, a logical condition describes a particular relationship between a pair of variables, or a variable and a constant. The value of the condition is true if the specified relation holds for the current variable values; otherwise, the condition value is false. Examples of conditions are shown in Table 2.1. The *relational operators* that may be used in writing logical conditions are summarized in Table 2.2.

The decision step (Step 3.1) used in Problem 2B involves a choice between two alternatives—a sequence of one or more steps to be executed if the condition is true (the True Task) and a sequence to be executed if the condition is false (the False Task). Such a decision step is called a *double-alternative decision step*. The general flow diagram pattern for this step is shown in Fig. 2.4.

Quite often, a decision step in an algorithm will involve only one alternative: a sequence of one or more steps that will be carried out if the given condition is true, but skipped if the condition is false. The flow diagram pattern for this *single-alternative decision step* is shown in Fig. 2.5.

Table 2.1 Examples of BASIC-PLUS Conditions

Condition	BASIC-PLUS form
G greater than MAX	G > MAX
X equal to SUM	X = SUM
X not equal to 0	X <> 0
G less than or equal to 10	G <= 10

Table 2.2 BASIC-PLUS Relational Operators

Relational Operator	Meaning
=	equal to
< >	not equal to
<	less than
>	greater than
< =	less than or equal to
> =	greater than or equal to

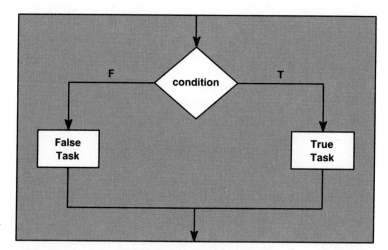

Fig. 2.4 Flow diagram pattern for the double-alternative decision step.

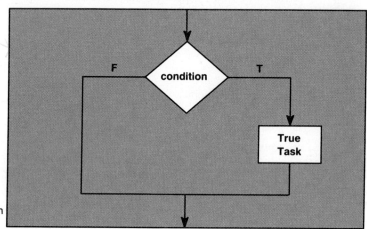

Fig. 2.5 Flow diagram pattern for the single-alternative decision step.

Exercise 2.3: Let A and B have the values −3.5 and 6.2, respectively. Indicate the values (true or false) for each of the following conditions.

a) A <> B
b) A > B
c) B <= A
d) B = 6.2

Exercise 2.4: Write the flow diagram pattern to represent the following English descriptions:

a) If ITEM is not equal to ZERO, then multiply PRODUCT by ITEM. Otherwise, skip this step. In either case, then print the value of PRODUCT.
b) If ITEM exceeds LARGER, store the value of ITEM in LARGER. Otherwise, skip this step. In either case, then print the value of ITEM.
c) If X is larger than 0, add X to SUM.POS. Otherwise, if X is smaller than 0, add X to SUM.NEG. Otherwise, if X = 0, add one to NUM.ZERO.

Exercise 2.5: What values would be printed by the algorithm in Fig. 2.3 if HOURS is 37.5 and RATE is 3.75? If HOURS is 20 and RATE is 4? "Execute" the program yourself to determine the results.

The Largest Value Problem

In the next problem, we illustrate the use of both the single- and double-alternative decisive steps.

Problem 2C   Enter three numbers and find and print the largest of these numbers.

Discussion: The data table for Problem 2C follows, the flow diagrams are drawn in Fig. 2.6

DATA TABLE FOR PROBLEM 2C

Input Variables		Output Variables	
N1:	First Number	LARGEST:	The largest number found at any point in the program
N2:	Second Number		
N3:	Third number		

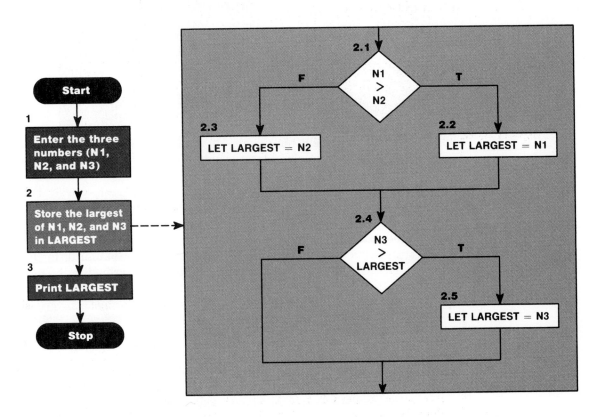

Fig. 2.6 Flow diagrams for Problem 2C.

As shown in Fig. 2.6, once the data are entered into N1, N2, and N3 (Step 1), the double-alternative decision step (2.1–2.3) is used to store the larger of N1 and N2 in LARGEST. The single-alternative decision step (2.4–2.5) is used to compare N3 to this value, and copy N3 into LARGEST if N3 is larger. If LARGEST is already greater than or equal to N3, Step 2.5 is skipped.

In the next section, we will see how to express decision steps in BASIC-PLUS. We will see that it is relatively easy to go from a flow diagram to a program statement.

Exercise 2.6: What happens in Fig. 2.6 if N1 is equal to N2 or N3 is equal to LARGEST? Does the algorithm work for these cases?

Exercise 2.7: Modify the flow diagrams for Problem 2C to find the largest of four numbers.

Exercise 2.8: Draw a flow diagram for an algorithm that computes the absolute difference between two numbers. If X is greater than Y, the absolute difference is X−Y; if Y is greater than X, the absolute difference is Y−X.

Implementing Decisions in BASIC-PLUS

We can implement the algorithms in the previous sections quite easily in BASIC-PLUS through the use of the IF–THEN and IF–THEN–ELSE statements. The IF–THEN–ELSE statement

```
170 IF N1 > N2 THEN LET LARGEST = N1      &
         ELSE LET LARGEST = N2
```

could be used to implement the double-alternative decision in Fig. 2.6. The ampersand (&) will be explained later in this section. The IF–THEN statement

```
200 IF N3 > LARGEST THEN LET LARGEST = N3
```

could be used to implement the single-alternative decision.

These statements will be discussed more formally in Chapter 3; for the time being, however, we will use the restricted forms described in the next displays.

IF-THEN-ELSE Statement (restricted form)

IF *condition* THEN *true statement* ELSE *false statement*

Interpretation: If the *condition* is true, then the *true statement* is executed; otherwise, the *false statement* is executed.

IF-THEN Statement (restricted form)

IF *condition* THEN *true statement*

Interpretation: If the *condition* is true, then the *true statement* is executed. The *true statement* is not executed when the *condition* is false.

The BASIC-PLUS implementation of the modified payroll problem (Fig. 2.3) is shown in Fig. 2.7; and the largest of three numbers problem (Fig. 2.6) is shown in Fig. 2.8. You should compare each program with its corresponding flow diagram representation.

```
100 !MODIFIED PAYROLL PROBLEM -
105 !CONDITIONAL TAX DEDUCTION
110 !
120 !ENTER DATA
130     INPUT "HOURS WORKED"; HOURS
140     INPUT "HOURLY RATE"; RATE
150 !
160 !COMPUTE GROSS SALARY
170     LET GROSS = HOURS * RATE
180 !
190 !COMPUTE NET SALARY
200     IF GROSS > 100 THEN LET NET = GROSS - 25 &
            ELSE LET NET = GROSS
210 !
220 !PRINT RESULTS
230     PRINT "GROSS = $"; GROSS
240     PRINT "NET = $"; NET
250 !
260     END

RUNNH
HOURS WORKED? 35
HOURLY RATE? 7.75
GROSS = $ 271.25
NET = $ 246.25
```

Fig. 2.7 Program and sample run for Problem 2B.

```
100 !FIND THE LARGEST OF THREE NUMBERS
110 !
120 !ENTER DATA
130     PRINT "ENTER THREE NUMBERS"
140     INPUT N1, N2, N3
145 !
```

(continued)

```
150 !STORE THE LARGEST NUMBER IN LARGEST
160 !FIND THE LARGER OF N1, N2
170     IF N1 > N2 THEN LET LARGEST = N1      &
            ELSE LET LARGEST = N2
180 !
190 !FIND THE LARGER OF N3, LARGEST
200     IF N3 > LARGEST THEN LET LARGEST = N3
210 !
220 !PRINT RESULTS
230     PRINT "LARGEST NUMBER ="; LARGEST
240 !
250     END

RUNNH
ENTER THREE NUMBERS
? 31, 45, 15.5
LARGEST NUMBER = 45
```

Fig. 2.8 Program and sample run for Problem 2C.

These programs show that it is possible to continue a long BASIC-PLUS statement on the next line simply by typing the symbol "&" at the end of the current line (see line 200 of Fig. 2.7 and line 170 of Fig. 2.8). The next line must not have a line number.

Program Constants

The following problem provides an illustration of some of the points discussed thus far in this chapter and introduces the use of *program constants* to associate names with special values.

Problem 2D

Write a program to read an employee's salary and compute the Social Security tax due. The Social Security tax is 6.65 percent of an employee's gross salary. Only the first $29,700 earned is taxable. (This means that all employees earning $29,700 or more pay the same tax.)

In the data table for Problem 2D that follows, we introduce the program constants SS.RATE and SS.MAX to represent the special values .0665 (6.65%) and 29700, respectively. Assignment statements that initialize each program constant to its associated value should be placed at the beginning of the program. The flow diagrams for Problem 2D are drawn in Figs. 2.9a and b.

DATA TABLE FOR PROBLEM 2D

Program Constants
SS.RATE = .0665: the Social Security tax rate
SS.MAX = 29700: the maximum salary for Social Security tax computations

Input Variables	Output Variables
SALARY: Employee's salary	TAX: Social Security Tax

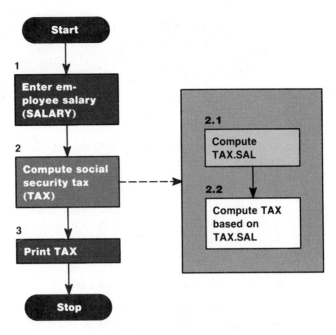

Fig. 2.9a Level one and two flow diagrams for Problem 2D.

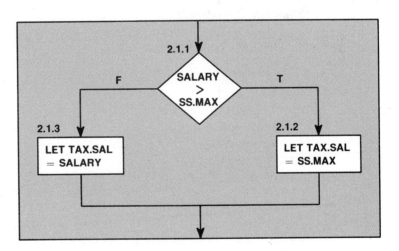

Fig. 2.9b Level three refinement of Step 2.1.

In order to refine Step 2, a new variable, TAX.SAL, is introduced to represent the portion of SALARY on which the Social Security tax will be computed. Since TAX.SAL is neither given as input data nor requested as output, but is instead the result of an intermediate computation, we should list it as a *program variable* in the data table.

Program Variables
TAX.SAL: The portion of SALARY for which TAX is computed.

The level three refinement of Step 2 is shown in Fig. 2.9b. The program for Problem 2D is shown in Fig. 2.10.

```
100 !MODIFIED PAYROLL PROBLEM -
105 !WITH SOCIAL SECURITY TAX DEDUCTION
110 !
120 !INITIALIZE PROGRAM CONSTANTS
130     LET SS.RATE = .0665
140     LET SS.MAX = 29700
150 !
160 !READ SALARY
170     INPUT "EMPLOYEE SALARY"; SALARY
180 !
190 !COMPUTE SOCIAL SECURITY TAX
195 !BASED ON TAXABLE SALARY
200     IF SALARY > SS.MAX THEN LET TAX.SAL = SS.MAX &
            ELSE LET TAX.SAL = SALARY
210     LET TAX = SS.RATE * TAX.SAL
220 !
230 !PRINT SOCIAL SECURITY TAX
240     PRINT "SOCIAL SECURITY TAX = $"; TAX
250 !
260     END
```

```
RUNNH
EMPLOYEE SALARY? 23456.78
SOCIAL SECURITY TAX = $ 1559.88
```

Fig. 2.10 Program and sample run for Problem 2D.

Program Style

Use of program constants

Values such as the tax rate (.0665) and maximum salary (29700), which have a special meaning in a problem and change infrequently should be associated with program constants. Any program constants should be initialized at the beginning of the program (see lines 130, 140 of Fig. 2.10).

One advantage of introducing program constants is to make the program more readable. For example, the line

```
210 LET TAX = SS.RATE * TAX.SAL
```

uses the descriptive name SS.RATE. This conveys more information than

```
210 LET TAX = .0665 * TAX.SAL
```

in which a nondescript value (.0665) appears *in-line*.

Also, if we wish to modify a value associated with a program constant, we need only modify the assignment statement that initializes the program constant. If the value was used in-line, then we would have to redo all statements that manipulate it. This can become a tedious task in a large program with multiple references to a special value.

Program Style

Choosing names for variables and program constants

The names TAX.SAL and SS.RATE include a period. The period helps us to designate meaningful names for our data items. It also ensures that the name used in the program does not match a reserved keyword.

Exercise 2.9: Implement your solutions to Exercise 2.7 and 2.8 in BASIC-PLUS.

2.4 Algorithms Involving Loops

The Motivation for Loops

The algorithm for finding the sum and average of two numbers works quite well. Suppose, however, that we are asked to solve a different problem.

Problem 2E   Write a program to compute and print the sum and average of 100 data items.

Discussion: The first question to be answered now concerns whether or not the approach previously taken will be satisfactory for this problem too. The answer is clearly no ! It is not that the approach won't work, but rather that no reasonable person is likely to have the patience to carry out this solution for 100 numbers. Our difficulties would begin in attempting to produce a data table listing differently named variables for each of the 100 items involved.

DATA TABLE FOR PROBLEM 2E

Input Variables			*Output Variables*	
NR1:	First data item		SUM:	Sum of 100 data items
NR2:	Second data item		AVERAGE:	Average of the 100 data items
NR3:	Third data item			
.				
.				
.				
NR100:	100th data item			

This in itself is a horrendous task. Then assuming we could finally name all 100 variables, we would have quite a boring task in describing the algorithm for solving the problem. Not even little children enjoy drawing pictures that much !

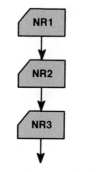

etcetera, etcetera, etcetera

A new approach is needed in order to solve this problem. Regardless of what this new approach involves, it still will be necessary to tell the computer to read in and add together 100 numbers. The essence of the problem is to find a way to do this without writing separate instructions for the reading and the addition of each of the 100 data items needed to compute the sum. It would be ideal if we could write one step for reading and one step for accumulating the sum, and then repeat these two steps for each of the 100 items as shown at the top of next page.

It happens that we can achieve this goal quite easily. All that is necessary is to

• solve the problem of naming each data item,

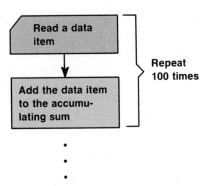

Repeat 100 times

.
.
.

- learn how to describe a repeated sequence of steps in a flow diagram and
- learn how to specify the repetition of a sequence of steps in BASIC-PLUS.

The solution to the naming problem rests upon the following realization:

Once a data item has been read into the computer memory and added to the sum, it is no longer needed in the computer memory.

Thus each input data item can be read into the same variable. After each item is entered, the value of this variable can be added to SUM, and the next data item can be read into the same variable. This, of course, destroys the previous data item, but it is no longer needed for the computation.

To see how this works, consider what happens if we try to carry out an algorithm consisting solely of the repetition of the steps

1. Read a data item into the variable named ITEM.
2. Add the value of ITEM to the value of SUM and store the result in SUM.

To begin, the memory cells ITEM and SUM appear as shown below. The initial value of SUM must be zero; otherwise, the final result will be incorrect by an amount equal to whatever was initially stored in SUM.

Let us assume that the first three data items are the numbers 10, 11, and 6. After Steps (1) and (2) are performed the first time, the variables ITEM and SUM will be defined as

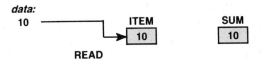

where the new value of SUM (10) equals the old value (0) plus the value of ITEM (10).

Now that the number 10 has been incorporated into the sum that we are computing, it is no longer required for this problem. We may, therefore, read the next data item into the variable ITEM. After the second execution of (1) and (2), we have:

where the new value of SUM (21) equals the old value (10) plus the current value of ITEM (11). After completion of the third execution of (1) and (2), we obtain:

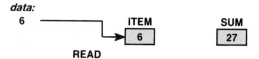

This process continues for all 100 data items. With each execution of Steps 1 and 2, the data item just read in is used as required by the problem and can be replaced in memory by the next data item.

With this solution to the naming problem, the data table for Problem 2E can be rewritten relatively easily.

REVISED DATA TABLE FOR PROBLEM 2E

Input Variables		Output Variables	
ITEM:	Contains each data item as it is being processed	SUM:	Used to accumulate the sum of the data items
		AVERAGE:	Average of all data items

We can also write a level one version of the flow diagram for our algorithm (Fig. 2.11). This diagram reflects the three phases of an algorithm, the *initialization phase*, the *data manipulation phase* and the *output phase*.

From this diagram, it is clear what is required in the initialization and output phases (Steps 1 and 4) of the algorithm. However, part of the computation phase (Step 2) requires further refinement before the program can be written.

In order to refine algorithm Step 2, we need to have a flow diagram representation for a sequence of repeated steps. This representation, shown in Fig. 2.12, is called a *loop*.

The loop is always entered through a box containing the *loop control step*. The *loop body* is the sequence of steps that is to be repeated. It is connected to the rest of the flow diagram by an arrow drawn to the right of the box

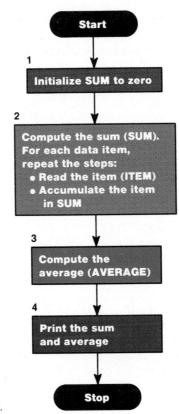

Fig. 2.11 Level one flow diagram for Problem 2E.

containing the loop control step. The arrow labeled *Exit* always points to the first step in the algorithm that is to be carried out upon completion of the loop. The dashed line in Fig. 2.12 (labeled NEXT) serves as a reminder that

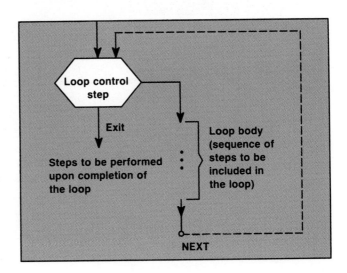

Fig. 2.12 Flow diagram pattern for a loop.

control returns to the loop control step each time the loop body is executed. (We will omit this dashed line in later chapters.)

How do we know when the loop is completed? More importantly, how can we tell the computer when it has completed the execution of the loop? A person might do it 10 or 100 times and then ask, "Am I done yet?". However, we are developing an algorithm that will eventually take the form of a sequence of steps to be performed by a computer—and the computer cannot think. Therefore if we want to tell it to repeat a sequence of steps, it is not enough to tell it what those steps are. We must also tell the computer when to stop performing these steps. This information is provided by the loop control step.

For this problem, the loop control step should specify that 100 repetitions of the loop are to be performed. We can guarantee the correct number of loop repetitions by introducing a new program variable that functions as a *repetition counter*. The counter is used to control loop repetition by counting the number of loop repetitions that are performed. The counter must be

- Initialized to a value of 1 just before the first loop execution.
- Incremented (increased) by 1 after each loop repetition.
- Tested before each loop repetition. If the counter value is still less than or equal to 100, the loop body should be repeated; otherwise, the loop exit should occur.

The flow diagram pattern for this *counter-controlled loop* is illustrated in Fig. 2.13. This is the refinement of Step 2 in the level one flow diagram (Fig. 2.11).

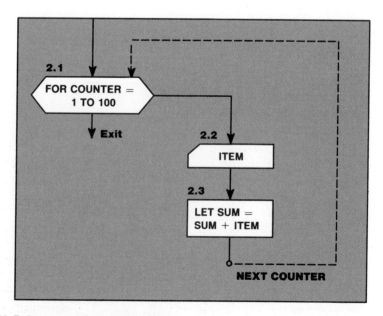

Fig. 2.13 Refinement of Step 2 in Fig 2.11.

The variable COUNTER in the loop control step (2.1) is the repetition counter. This step specifies that the loop is to be executed once for each integer value of COUNTER between 1 and 100 inclusive; hence, the loop body (Steps 2.2 and 2.3) will be repeated exactly 100 times as required, once for each data item. The label, NEXT COUNTER, indicates that COUNTER will be incremented and tested before the next loop repetition begins. With this refinement, the flow diagrams for Problem 2E are complete.

ADDITIONAL DATA TABLE ENTRY FOR PROBLEM 2E

Program Variables	
COUNTER:	Counts the number of loop repetitions

Exercise 2.10:

a) Draw a flow diagram for a counter-controlled loop that computes the sum of the first 10 integers.
b) Draw a flow diagram for a counter-controlled loop that computes the product of the first 10 integers.

Exercise 2.11: Follow the steps shown in Figs. 2.11 and 2.13 to find the sum of the four data items 8.2, −6.1, 0, and 2.4.

2.5 Implementing a Flow Diagram

Tracing a Flow Diagram

Once the algorithm and data table for a problem are complete, it is important to verify that the algorithm specifies the correct sequence of steps required to produce the desired results. This algorithm verification can be carried out by manually *simulating* or *tracing* the sequence of steps indicated by the algorithm. Such traces can often lead to the discovery of a number of logical errors in the flow diagram. The correction of these errors prior to writing the BASIC-PLUS instructions can save considerable effort during the final checkout, or *debugging*, of the BASIC-PLUS program.

We will now provide an illustration of an algorithm trace for the flow diagrams shown in Figs. 2.11 and 2.13. It is clear that we cannot trace the algorithm for all 100 data items. However, we can perform a meaningful, informative trace for three items. If the algorithm works properly for this limited case, it should work for 100 data items as well.

The trace table is shown in Table 2.3. The algorithm step numbers are from the flow diagrams. Only the new value of the variable affected by an algorithm step is shown to the right of each step. All other variable values are unchanged. The values of all variables are considered undefined at the start of execution as shown in the first line. The data items being tested are 12.5, 15 and −3.5.

The trace table shows that the loop is executed exactly three times. The final value accumulated in SUM is 24; the average, stored in AVERAGE, is 8. Note that AVERAGE remains undefined until after the loop is exited. (Even though BASIC-PLUS initializes all numeric variables to 0, we will consider AVERAGE undefined as we have not explicitly given it a value.)

Algorithm traces must be done diligently or they are of little use. The flow diagram must be traced carefully, on a step-by-step basis, without making any assumptions about what is happening. Changes in variable values must be noted at each step and compared to the expected results of the algorithm. This should be done for at least one carefully chosen set of test data for which the intermediate and final results are easily determined. If an algorithm contains decision steps, then extra sets of test data should be used to ensure that all paths through the algorithm are traced.

Table 2.3 Trace Table for Algorithm in Figs. 2.11 and 2.13

Algorithm Step		SUM	COUNTER	ITEM	AVERAGE
		?	?	?	?
	1	0			
1st loop repetition	2.1		1		
	2.2			12.5	
	2.3	12.5			
2nd loop repetition	2.1		2		
	2.2			15	
	2.3	27.5			
3rd loop repetition	2.1		3		
	2.2			−3.5	
	2.3	24			
	3				8

Example 2.1

The flow diagram for Problem 2C (the largest value problem) is redrawn in Fig. 2.14. Since there is a true path (T) and false path (F) out of each condition, there are four distinct paths through the algorithm:

Path 1: Step 2.1 - T, Step 2.4 - T (Execute Steps 2.2 and 2.5)
Path 2: Step 2.1 - T, Step 2.4 - F (Execute Step 2.2)
Path 3: Step 2.1 - F, Step 2.4 - T (Execute Steps 2.3 and 2.5)
Path 4: Step 2.1 - F, Step 2.4 - F (Execute Step 2.3)

The actual path traced depends on the test data. Table 2.4 illustrates the trace for the three data items: 3, 6, and 10. Steps 2.3 and 2.5 change the value of LARGEST to 6 and 10, respectively. If a program step does

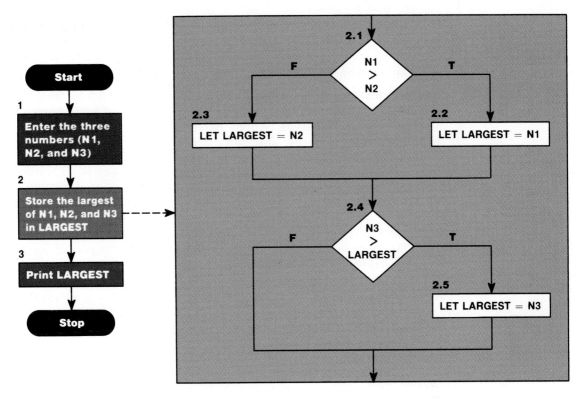

Fig. 2.14 Flow diagram for Problem 2C, redrawn.

something other than change a variable value (Steps 2.1 and 2.4), then its effect is indicated in the rightmost column of Table 2.4.

The trace shown in Table 2.4 follows path 3 (Step 2.1 - F, Step 2.4 - T). To verify the algorithm is correct, you should provide additional test data that causes the three remaining paths to be traced.

Table 2.4 Trace Table for Algorithm in Fig. 2.14

Algorithm Step	Variable Changed				Effect
	N1	N2	N3	LARGEST	
	?	?	?	?	
1	3	6	10		
2.1					3 > 6 is false— execute Step 2.3
2.3				6	
2.4					10 > 6 is true— execute Step 2.5
2.5				10	
3					Print 10

Program Style

The algorithm trace may seem like an unnecessary step and there is often a temptation to implement the algorithm without performing a trace. However, if a trace is done carefully, it may reveal errors in logic that are more easily corrected in the algorithm design stage, before the program is written. After the program is written, correcting logic errors is a very tedious and time-consuming process.

Exercise 2.12: Carry out a complete trace of the flow diagrams shown in Figs. 2.11 and 2.13 for the data items

```
-12.5, 8.25, 0, -16.5, .25
```

Exercise 2.13:

a) Trace the algorithm for the largest of three numbers problem for N1, N2, and N3 equal to 5, 20, and 15, respectively. Which of the four paths described in Example 2.1 did you follow?

b) Assign three values to N1, N2, and N3 that take you through path 1 as defined in Example 2.1. Does the algorithm produce the correct answer for these data?

c) If $N1 = 16$, $N2 = -20$, and $N3 = 0$, which of the four paths of Example 2.1 are followed? Does this test, combined with those of Example 2.1 and parts a) and b) of this exercise adequately test the algorithm? Explain.

Exercise 2.14: Will the algorithm for the largest of three numbers problem (Fig. 2.14) work if two of the numbers have the same value? If all three numbers have the same value? Justify your answer.

Implementing a Loop in BASIC-PLUS

BASIC-PLUS provides a special looping structure (called the *FOR loop*) for implementing counter-controlled loops. The BASIC-PLUS implementation of the flow diagrams in Figs. 2.11 and 2.13 is shown in Fig. 2.15.

Lines 150 through 200 form a program unit called a *control structure*. We will introduce a number of control structures in the text for implementing flow diagram patterns such as loops. Each control structure will consist of an easily recognizable first and last line (the *header* and *terminator* statements, respectively). Although it is not required, the body of the structure will be indented to aid in its recognition and to enhance program readability.

Line 150 is the *loop header* statement. It specifies that the loop will be executed 100 times—or once for each integer value of COUNTER between 1 and 100 inclusive. The *loop body* is represented by lines 160–190. Line 200 is the *loop terminator*; it simply marks the end of the loop with repetition counter COUNTER. A restricted version of the BASIC-PLUS FOR loop (the counter-controlled loop) is summarized in the next display; we will describe the general form of the FOR loop in the next chapter.

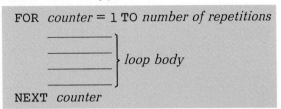

Counter-Controlled Loop (restricted form of the BASIC-PLUS FOR loop)

FOR *counter* = 1 TO *number of repetitions*

$\left.\begin{array}{l}\underline{\hspace{3cm}}\\\underline{\hspace{3cm}}\\\underline{\hspace{3cm}}\\\underline{\hspace{3cm}}\end{array}\right\}$ *loop body*

NEXT *counter*

Interpretation: The loop repetition is controlled by the variable *counter*. The *number of repetitions* may be specified as a whole number or variable. After the required number of loop repetitions have been performed, execution continues with the first statement following NEXT *counter*.

In Fig. 2.15, the input data for the program are found in DATA statements that follow the loop (lines 230–320). The data are also echo printed

```
100 !FIND THE SUM AND AVERAGE OF 100 DATA ITEMS
105 !
110 !INITIALIZE SUM
120     LET SUM = 0
125 !
130 !READ EACH DATA ITEM AND ADD IT TO THE SUM
140     PRINT "LIST OF DATA"
150     FOR COUNTER = 1 TO 100
160         !READ AND PROCESS NEXT ITEM
170         READ ITEM
180         PRINT ITEM;
190         LET SUM = SUM + ITEM
200     NEXT COUNTER
210     PRINT
215 !
220 !DATA READ DURING LOOP EXECUTION
230     DATA 52,52,85,87,79,42,8,254,345,898,57,4
240     DATA 575,896,242,404,56,85,254,589,1578,699
250     DATA 1245,2010,5999,1529,103,884,21,936,12
260     DATA 12,99,45,159,458,2340,588,1259,9230
270     DATA 2019,2012,4581,203,723,6444,286,1,73
280     DATA 209,202,411,33,78,95,8714,12,315,78421
290     DATA 4576,65,97,21,654,7415,5487,545,5354
300     DATA 64435,78,65,123,585,47,78, 54,25,20,32
310     DATA 85,99,412,5420,578,54,75,32,12,100,69,65
```

(continued)

```
320     DATA 87,9624,1105,2103,335,5794,585,330,865
330  !
340  !COMPUTE AVERAGE
350     LET AVERAGE = SUM / 100
355  !
360  !PRINT RESULTS
365     PRINT
370     PRINT "SUM ="; SUM
380     PRINT "AVERAGE ="; AVERAGE
390  !
400     END
```

```
RUNNH
LIST OF DATA
52  52  85  87  79  42  8  254  345  898  57  4
575  896  242  404  56  85  254  589  1578  699
1245  2010  5999  1529  103  884  21  936  12
12  99  45  159  458  2340  588  1259  9230
2019  2012  4581  203  723  6444  286  1  73
209  202  411  33  78  95  8714  12  315  78421
4576  65  97  21  654  7415  5487  545  5354
64435  78  65  123  585  47  78  54  25  20  32
85  99  412  5420  578  54  75  32  12  100  69  65
87  9624  1105  2103  335  5794  585  330  865

SUM = 250026
AVERAGE = 2500.26
```

Fig. 2.15 Program for Problem 2E.

during program execution (line 180). The PRINT statement that precedes the loop (line 140) is used to print the message "LIST OF DATA".

Program Style

Indenting the loop body

In Fig. 2.15, the statements that are repeated (the loop body) are indented (using the TAB key) to clarify the structure of the program. This practice will be followed throughout the text.

Exercise 2.15: Write the flow diagram for a loop to read in a collection of seven data items, compute the product of all nonzero items in the collection, and print the final product. Trace your flow diagram to verify that it is correct. Implement it in BASIC-PLUS. (*Hint:* The product should be initialized to 1.)

Writing General Programs

Data Collections of Arbitrary Size

Suppose that you are asked to solve Problem 2E for 2000 data items instead of 100, for 1966 items, or for 10 items. Will the approach just taken work here too? The answer, of course, is yes; however, the loop control step must be changed for each case before the program can be run. Consequently, the algorithm given is not very general.

Algorithms and programs should be written so that any reasonable variation of a problem can be solved without altering the program. A general program for Problem 2E would compute the sum for an arbitrary, but prespecified, number of data items. To accomplish this, the number of data items should be treated as an input variable (rather than a constant) to be read in by the program at the beginning of execution. In this way, any collection of data may be processed by the same program as long as the first item entered is the number of items in this data collection. The additional input variable required, NUM.ITEMS, should be added to the data table as shown next.

REVISED DATA TABLE FOR PROBLEM 2E

Input Variables		Program Variables		Output Variables	
ITEM:	Contains each data item as it is being processed	COUNTER:	Counts the number of loop repetitions	SUM:	Used to accumulate the sum of the data items.
NUM.ITEMS:	The number of data items to be processed.			AVERAGE:	Average of all data items.

The number of data items to be processed should be read into NUM.ITEMS as the first step in the algorithm. The revised level one algorithm for Problem 2E is shown in Fig. 2.16.

NUM.ITEMS should be used instead of the constant 100 in lines 150 and 350 of Fig. 2.15. The general version of the program for finding the sum and average of a collection of data items is shown in Fig. 2.17, along with the output for a sample run. The data were provided interactively during program execution.

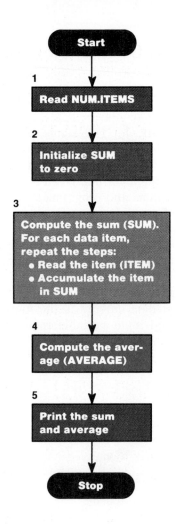

Fig. 2.16 Revised level one algorithm for Problem 2E.

```
100  !GENERAL PROGRAM TO FIND SUM AND AVERAGE
110  !
120  !ENTER NUMBER OF ITEMS
130     INPUT "NUMBER OF ITEMS"; NUM.ITEMS
135  !
140  !INITIALIZE SUM
150     LET SUM = 0
155  !
160  !ENTER EACH ITEM AND ADD IT TO THE SUM
170     PRINT "ENTER ONE ITEM PER LINE"
180     FOR COUNTER = 1 TO NUM.ITEMS
190        !READ AND PROCESS NEXT ITEM
200         INPUT ITEM
210         LET SUM = SUM + ITEM
220     NEXT COUNTER
```

(continued)

```
230  !
235  !COMPUTE AVERAGE
240      LET AVERAGE = SUM / NUM.ITEMS
245  !
250  !PRINT RESULTS
260      PRINT
270      PRINT "SUM ="; SUM
280      PRINT "AVERAGE ="; AVERAGE
290  !
300      END
```

```
RUNNH
NUMBER OF ITEMS? 5
ENTER ONE ITEM PER LINE
? 26
? 45
? 78
? 90
? 15

SUM = 254
AVERAGE = 50.8
```

Fig. 2.17 Revised program and sample run for Problem 2E.

Exercise 2.16:   What data would be required if you wished to use the program in Fig. 2.17 to find the sum and average of all multiples of 10 in the range of 10 to 100?

Exercise 2.17:   Write the flow diagram and program to read in a collection of data items, compute the product of all nonzero items in the collection, and print the final product.

2.7   Summary

In the first part of this chapter we outlined a method for solving problems on the computer. This method stresses six points:

1. Understand the problem given.
2. Identify the input and output data for the problem as well as other relevant data.
3. Formulate a precise statement of the problem.
4. Develop an algorithm.
5. Refine the algorithm.
6. Implement the algorithm in BASIC-PLUS.

In the remainder of the chapter, we introduced the flow diagram representation of the various steps in an algorithm. Flow diagrams provide a graphical representation of an algorithm consisting of a number of specially shaped boxes and arrows as well as several *patterns* of boxes and arrows used to describe decision steps and loops. These boxes and patterns are summarized in Fig. 2.18.

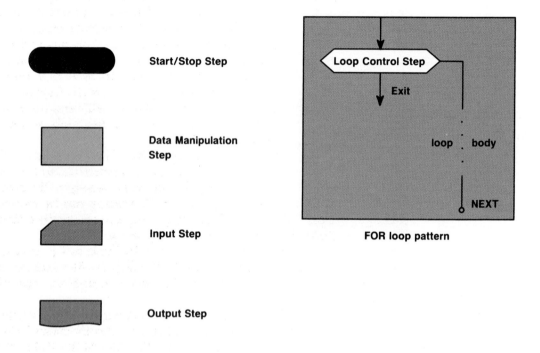

Start/Stop Step

Data Manipulation Step

Input Step

Output Step

FOR loop pattern

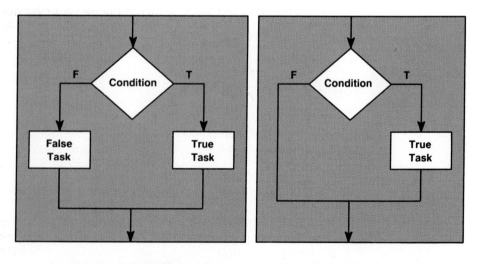

Fig. 2.18 Flow diagram patterns.

Double-Alternative Decision Step

Single-Alternative Decision Step

There was much discussion in this chapter of *program documentation* and good *programming style*. Guidelines for using program comments were presented. Well placed and carefully worded comments, combined with a complete and concise data table, will provide much of the documentation necessary for a program. The flow diagrams are also part of the program documentation as well as an integral step in the design process.

The major points of programming style that were emphasized involved echo printing (or prompting) all input data values, indenting the body of a loop, the use of comments, and the use of program constants to identify special values. We believe that the issues of documentation and style are extremely important as they contribute to making programs and programming systems easier to read, *debug* (locate and correct errors), and *maintain* (keep up-to-date). We urge you to pay particular attention to the documentation and style that you develop; they are as important as the BASIC-PLUS structures and programs that you will learn to write. You will find that complete documentation and consistent style will save you considerable time in the long run.

The algorithms that were developed in this chapter consisted of three major parts: data entry, data manipulation (computation), and the display of results. Of these, the data manipulation phase usually is the most complicated and requires the most attention. This phase can be started once the input data and desired problem output have been clearly defined and a precise understanding of the problem has been achieved.

Often additional entries are made to the data table as the data manipulation phase progresses. For example, in Problem 2E the need for the program variable COUNTER was not readily apparent until the algorithm for manipulating the data was chosen.

Some new features of BASIC-PLUS were introduced in this chapter: the use of the symbol ! (or the keyword REM) to identify comment lines (or remarks); and three control statements, the IF–THEN–ELSE, the IF–THEN, and the FOR loop (see Table 2.5). In the next chapter we will illustrate further the use of these features in implementing flow diagram steps. This will enable us to solve some relatively complex problems using programs that clearly reflect the careful planning and organization used in our algorithm development.

Table 2.5 Summary of BASIC-PLUS Features in Chapter 2

Feature	Effect
comment or remark	
`100 !THIS IS A COMMENT` `100 REM THIS IS A REMARK`	Includes comment (remark) lines with the program.

(continued)

Table 2.5 Summary of BASIC-PLUS Features in Chapter 2 (*continued*)

Feature	Effect
IF-THEN-ELSE *statement*	
`200 IF X >= 0 THEN LET POS = POS + 1 &` `        ELSE LET NEG = NEG + 1`	Increments POS if X is positive (X >= 0); increments NEG if X is negative (X < 0).
IF-THEN *statement*	
`300 IF X > 5 THEN PRINT X`	Prints the value of X if X is greater than 5.
FOR *loop*	

`400 SUM = 0`
`410 FOR I = 1 TO 5`
`420     LET SUM = SUM + I`
`430 NEXT I`
	Accumulates the sum of the first 5 integers (1+2+3+4+5) in SUM.

Programming Problems

For all problems, a data table and flow diagram are required.

2F Given the bank balance in your checking account for the past month and all the transactions against your account for the current month, write a program for an algorithm to compute and print your checking account balance at the end of the current month. You may assume that the total number of transactions for the current month is known ahead of time. (*Hint*: Your first data item should be your checking account balance at the end of last month. The second item should be the number of transactions for the current month. All subsequent items should represent the amount of each transaction for the current month.)

2G *Continuation of Problem 2F.* Modify your data table, algorithm and program for Problem 2F to compute and print the number of deposits and the number of withdrawals.

2H Write a program to simulate a state police radar gun. The program should read a single automobile speed and print the message "OK" if the speed is less than or equal to 55 mph, or "SPEEDING" if the speed exceeds 55 mph.

2I *Continuation of Problem 2H.* Modify your data table, algorithm and program for Problem 2H to do the following:

a) Read in a collection of 10 automobile speeds.
b) Count the number of speeds less than or equal to 55 mph and the number in excess of 55 mph.
c) After all 10 speeds have been processed, print the counts.

2J Write a program to read in a value X and print a message indicating if "X IS POSITIVE", "X IS NEGATIVE", or "X IS ZERO".

2K *Continuation of Problem 2J.* Modify the data table, flow diagram, and program for Problem 2J to read 100 values and count the number of positive values, the number of negative values, and the number of zeros.

2L Write a program for an algorithm to compute the factorial, N!, of a single arbitrary integer N. (N! = N × (N − 1) × . . . 2 × 1). Your program should read and print the value of N and print N! when done.

2M If N contains an integer, then we can compute X^N for any X, simply by initializing a variable POWER to 1 and multiplying it by X a total of N times. Write a program to read in a value of X and a value of N, and compute X^N via repeated multiplications. Check your program for

```
X = 6, N = 4
X = 2.5, N = 6
X = -8, N = 5
```

2N *Continuation of Problem 2M.* a) How many multiplications are required in your program for Problem 2M in order to compute X^9? Can you figure out a way of computing X^9 in fewer multiplications?

b) Can you generalize your algorithm for computing X^9 to compute X^N for any positive N?

c) Can you use your algorithm in part (b) to compute X^{-N} for any positive N? How?

2O Compute and print a table showing the first 15 powers of 2.

2P Redo the payroll program of Chapter 1 (Problem 1A) so that a prespecified number of employees can be processed in a single run.

2Q Redo Problem 1E so that all cases are processed in a single program run.

2R Redo Problem 1F so that all cases are processed in a single program run.

3

Fundamental
Control Structures

3.1 Introduction

Control Structures

In Chapter 2, we introduced flow diagram patterns for decision structures and loops. We also introduced the IF-THEN and IF-THEN-ELSE statements and a restricted form of the FOR loop. In this chapter we will discuss how general control structure patterns may be implemented and provide several examples of their use.

As you learn more of the features of BASIC-PLUS, you will find it easier to solve more complicated problems. You will also see that the process of translating the flow diagram representation of an algorithm into a BASIC-PLUS program will become easier because fewer levels of flow diagram refinement will be required for you to write your programs.

We will show that the development of correct, precise algorithms is an important part of using the computer to solve problems. Furthermore the English descriptions of these algorithms are most critical, for if these descriptions are incorrect or imprecise, all further refinements, as well as the resulting programs, will reflect these maladies. Therefore as we introduce new features of BASIC-PLUS, we will continue to emphasize algorithm development through the use of the flow diagram.

Multiple-Statement Lines and Statement Groups

Before describing the control structures of BASIC-PLUS, we shall discuss combinations of statements that are likely to appear in BASIC-PLUS. In BASIC-PLUS, it is permissible to write multiple statements on a single line. For example, the two PRINT statements on lines 365 and 370 of Fig. 2.15 could be written as

```
370 PRINT \ PRINT "SUM ="; SUM
```

Line 370 is a *multiple-statement line* in that it consists of two BASIC-PLUS statements separated by the symbol "\". (The symbol ":" may also be used as a separator.) Only one line number is needed for these two statements.

For now there seems to be no particular advantage to combining these two statements on a single line, except possibly the elimination of one line number. In the next sections we use multiple-statement lines to implement True and False Tasks of decision structures. A multiple-statement line that is used in this way is called a *statement group*.

3.2 IF-THEN Statement

Single-Alternative Decisions

We begin our study of control structures by discussing how to implement a more general form of the single-alternative decision pattern described earlier. For the single-alternative decision pattern (Fig. 3.1), there is no task to be carried out if the indicated condition is false. However, if the condition is true, the True Task is executed. In either case, the algorithm continues at the point indicated by the arrow at the bottom of the diagram.

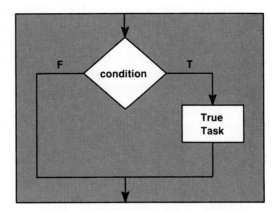

Fig. 3.1 The single-alternative decision pattern.

In Fig. 2.8, we used the `IF-THEN` statement

```
200     IF N3 > LARGEST THEN LET LARGEST = N3
```

to implement a single-alternative decision with a single-statement True Task. We consider more complicated True Tasks next.

Example 3.1 The decision pattern in Fig. 3.2 has a True Task that consists of multiple steps; consequently, we shall implement it using an `IF-THEN` statement with a *true statement group* (multiple-statement line). The general form of the decision structure is

```
IF  condition THEN  true statement group
```

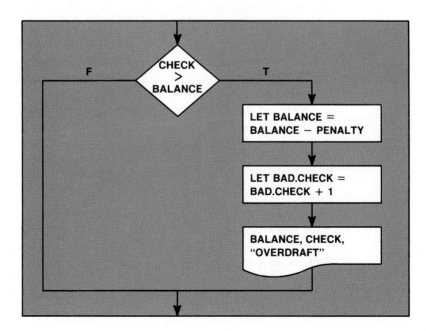

Fig. 3.2 True Task with multiple steps.

The IF-THEN statement corresponding to Fig. 3.2 can be written as

```
200 IF CHECK > BALANCE THEN              &
        LET BALANCE = BALANCE - PENALTY  &
        \LET BAD.CHECK = BAD.CHECK + 1   &
        \PRINT BALANCE, CHECK, "OVERDRAFT"
```

In line 200 above, if the condition CHECK > BALANCE is true, then the true statement group (the last three lines above) is executed; otherwise the true statement group is skipped. Since line 200 consists of one long IF-THEN statement continued over four lines, only the first line is numbered. The "&" symbol must be used at the end of each line that is continued. (The carriage return is pressed after each line is entered.)

The three statements of the true statement group above are shown on separate lines, although they could be combined on fewer lines. The only requirement is that the symbol "\" (or ":") must be used as a separator between these statements.

The statement with line number 200 is considered a single IF-THEN statement even though it extends over four lines. Consequently it may be necessary to retype the entire IF-THEN statement in order to modify just one line or to change a single statement in the true statement group. Using a special program called an *editor* will make it easier to modify your programs. The general form of the IF-THEN statement is shown in the next display.

IF-THEN Statement

```
IF condition THEN        &
    true statement group
```

Interpretation: The *condition* is evaluated. If the *condition* is true, the *true statement group* is executed. If the condition is false, the *true statement group* is not executed. The *true statement group* may be any single executable BASIC-PLUS statement (including another IF-THEN or IF-THEN-ELSE statement) or a multiple-statement line. *Note*: The symbol "&" must be used at the end of each line that is continued. The symbol "\" must be used to separate executable statements of the *true statement group*.

Comment lines may also be inserted in a statement group. Each comment line must begin with the symbol "!". A comment line should always be followed by the symbol "&" unless it is the last line of the statement group. Since a comment is not considered an executable statement, there is no need to separate it using the symbol "\". In the segment below, we have inserted a comment line at the beginning of the true statement group.

```
200 IF CHECK > BALANCE THEN                    &
       !PROCESS BAD CHECK                      &
       LET BALANCE = BALANCE - PENALTY         &
       \LET BAD.CHECK = BAD.CHECK + 1          &
       \PRINT BALANCE, CHECK, "OVERDRAFT"
```

Program Style

Typing the IF-THEN Statement

The sample IF-THEN statement shown above illustrates the style conventions we will use in our programs. Each statement in the true statement group will be indented to emphasize the meaning of the IF-THEN statement and to enhance program readability. Each statement in the group, except the first one, will be preceded by the symbol "\". Generally we will align the continuation symbols "&".

More than one executable statement may be typed on any line provided the statements are separated by the symbol "\". Although this flexibility exists, we recommend that you follow the conventions illustrated in the text.

Application of the IF-THEN Statement

In the next problem, we illustrate the use of the single-alternative decision structure.

Problem 3A
Read two numbers into the variables X and Y and compare them. Place the larger in X and the smaller in Y.

DATA TABLE FOR PROBLEM 3A

Input Variables		Output Variables	
X, Y: Items to be compared		X:	Larger item
		Y:	Smaller item

Discussion: The flow diagram for this program is shown in Fig. 3.3. Note that the contents of variables X and Y are exchanged only if the condition "Y greater than X" is true. In the completed program for this problem (shown in Fig. 3.4), this exchange is implemented using an additional variable, TEMP, in which a copy of the initial value of X is saved.

Program Variable	
TEMP:	Temporary variable used in exchange

To verify the need for TEMP we trace the program execution for the data values 3.5 and 7.2 in Table 3.1.

Table 3.1 Trace of Program in Fig. 3.4

Program Statement	Variables Changed		
	X	Y	TEMP
	?	?	?
INPUT X, Y	3.5	7.2	
LET TEMP = X			3.5
LET X = Y	7.2		
LET Y = TEMP		3.5	

As indicated in the trace, after the assignment statement

    LET X = Y

is executed, the value 3.5 is no longer available in X. Copying X into TEMP first, prevents this value from being lost.

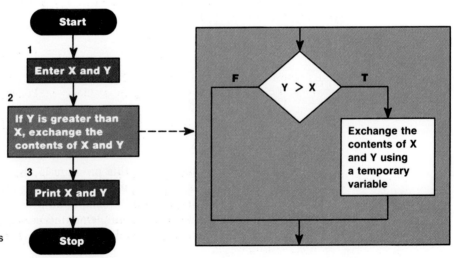

Fig. 3.3 Flow diagrams for Problem 3A.

```
100 !FIND LARGER AND SMALLER OF TWO NUMBERS
110 !
120 !ENTER DATA
130     PRINT "ENTER TWO NUMBERS";
140     INPUT X, Y
160 !
170 !COMPARE X AND Y AND SWITCH IF NECESSARY
180     IF Y > X THEN          &
            LET TEMP = X        &
            \LET X = Y          &
            \LET Y = TEMP
190 !
200 !PRINT RESULTS
210     PRINT
220     PRINT "LARGER =";  X,
230     PRINT "SMALLER =";  Y
240 !
250     END
```

```
RUNNH
ENTER TWO NUMBERS? 3.5, 7.2

LARGER = 7.2 SMALLER = 3.5
```

Fig. 3.4 Program for Problem 3A.

Exercise 3.1:   The True Task in the decision structure of the program for Problem 3A contains three statements and uses an additional variable TEMP. Could we have accomplished the same task performed by this group with either of the statement groups below?

a)   LET X = Y \ LET Y = X
b)   LET TEMP = Y \ LET X = TEMP \ LET Y = X

What values would be stored in X and Y after these statement groups execute? Rearrange the order of statement group (b) so that it works properly.

Exercise 3.2:   Convert the following English descriptions of algorithms to flow diagrams and BASIC-PLUS statements using the single-alternative decision pattern and the IF-THEN statement.

a)   If the remainder (REMAIN) is equal to zero, then print N.
b)   If the product (PROD) is equal to N, then print the contents of the variable DIV and read a new value into N.
c)   If the number of traffic lights (NUM.LIGHT) exceeds 25, then compute the gallons required (GAL.REQ) as total miles (MlLES) divided by 14 and print "CITY DRIVING".

IF-THEN-ELSE Statement

Double-Alternative Decisions

In this section, we discuss the BASIC-PLUS statements needed to represent the double-alternative flow diagram pattern. In the double-alternative decision pattern (Fig. 3.5), if the indicated condition is true the algorithm steps representing the True Task are carried out; otherwise the steps representing the False Task are performed. Exactly one of the paths from the condition test is taken. Execution then continues at the point indicated by the arrow at the bottom of the diagram.

The True and False Tasks may each consist of a number of different boxes and flow diagram patterns. In general, however, it is a good idea to keep these task descriptions simple and refine them in a separate diagram if additional details are needed.

In Fig. 2.7 we used the `IF-THEN-ELSE` statement

```
200 IF GROSS > 100 THEN LET NET = GROSS - 25   &
            ELSE LET NET = GROSS
```

to implement a double-alternative decision. A formal description of this statement is given in the next display.

IF-THEN-ELSE Statement

```
IF  condition THEN          &
        true statement      &
ELSE                        &
        false statement group
```

Interpretation: The *condition* is evaluated. If the *condition* is true, then the *true statement* is executed. If the *condition* is false, then the *false statement group* is executed instead. The *true statement* may be any single executable BASIC-PLUS statement (including another `IF-THEN` or `IF-THEN-ELSE` statement). The *false statement group* may be any single executable BASIC-PLUS statement (including another `IF-THEN` or `IF-THEN-ELSE` statement) or a multiple-statement line.

Note: The symbol `"&"` must be used at the end of each line that is continued. The symbol `"\"` must be used to separate executable statements of the *false statement group*.

As indicated above, the *false statement group* may be a multiple-statement line but the *true statement* can be a single statement only. (BASIC-PLUS-2 and VAX-11 users see *IF-THEN-ELSE statement* in Appendix H and the first sample program in Appendix J.)

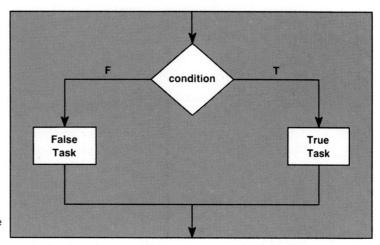

Fig. 3.5 The double-alternative decision pattern.

Example 3.2   The decision pattern in Fig. 3.6 is based on the one shown in Fig. 3.2 except that it processes valid checks as well as overdrafts. Note that the condition (CHECK <= BALANCE) used in Fig. 3.6 is the *complement* or logical opposite of the condition (CHECK > BALANCE) used in Fig. 3.2. (Condition complements are discussed in Chapter 5.) The IF-THEN-ELSE statement that implements the pattern in Fig. 3.6 is shown on the next page.

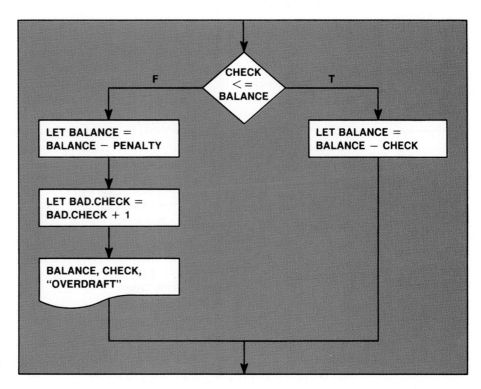

Fig. 3.6 False Task with multiple steps.

```
300 IF CHECK <= BALANCE THEN                        &
        LET BALANCE = BALANCE - CHECK               &
    ELSE                                            &
        !PROCESS BAD CHECK                          &
        LET BALANCE = BALANCE - PENALTY             &
        \LET BAD.CHECK = BAD.CHECK + 1              &
        \PRINT BALANCE, CHECK, "OVERDRAFT"
```

In the IF-THEN-ELSE statement at line 300, the symbol "\" separates the three executable statements of the false statement group. Each line except the last one is terminated by the continuation symbol "&". Note that it is not possible to include a statement that increments a variable GOOD.CHECK for each valid check. (The value of GOOD.CHECK could be determined eventually by subtracting BAD.CHECK from the total number of checks processed.) We shall see how to implement multiple-step True Tasks in Section 3.4.

Application of the IF-THEN-ELSE Statement

The next problem illustrates the use of the IF-THEN-ELSE statement to implement a double-alternative decision.

Problem 3B Read two numbers into the variables X and Y and compute and print the quotient (X / Y).

Discussion: This is a problem that looks quite straightforward, but it has the potential for disaster hidden between the lines of the problem statement. In this case as in many others, the potential trouble spot is due to unanticipated values of input data—values for which one or more of the data manipulations required by the problem are not defined.

In this problem, the quotient X / Y is not defined mathematically if Y equals 0. If we instruct the computer to perform the calculation X / Y in this case, it will not be able to complete the operation and will provide the programmer with a diagnostic message.

```
%Division by zero
```

In order to avoid the problem entirely, we will have our program test for a divisor of zero and print a message of its own if this situation should occur. The data table is provided next; the flow diagrams and program for this problem are shown in Figs. 3.7 and 3.8.

DATA TABLE FOR PROBLEM 3B

Input Variables	Output Variables
X: Dividend	QUOTIENT: Quotient of X and Y
Y: Divisor	

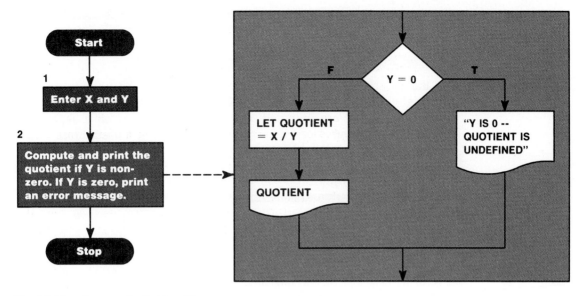

Fig. 3.7 Flow diagrams for Problem 3B.

```
100 !QUOTIENT PROBLEM
110 !
120 !ENTER DATA
130     INPUT "DIVIDEND"; X
140     INPUT "DIVISOR"; Y
150 !
160 !COMPUTE QUOTIENT IF Y IS NON-ZERO
170     IF Y = 0 THEN                                          &
            PRINT "Y IS 0 -- QUOTIENT IS UNDEFINED" &
        ELSE                                                   &
            !QUOTIENT IS DEFINED                               &
            LET QUOTIENT = X / Y                               &
            \PRINT "QUOTIENT ="; QUOTIENT
180 !
190     END


RUNNH
DIVIDEND? 12
DIVISOR? 3
QUOTIENT = 4


RUNNH
DIVIDEND? 356
DIVISOR? 0
Y IS 0 -- QUOTIENT IS UNDEFINED
```

Fig. 3.8 Program for Problem 3B.

Exercise 3.3: Write the BASIC-PLUS form of the decisions stated below.

a) Read a number into the variable `ITEM`. If this number is positive, add one to the contents of NPOS. If the number is not positive, add one to the contents of NNEG.

b) Read a number into `ITEM`. If `ITEM` is zero, add one to the contents of NZERO.

c) *A combination of (a) and (b)*. Read a number into `ITEM`. If `ITEM` is positive, add one to NPOS; if `ITEM` is negative, add one to NNEG; and if `ITEM` is zero, add one to NZERO. *Hint*: The false statement group should be another `IF-THEN-ELSE` statement.

Exercise 3.4: Redraw the decision pattern below so that it can be implemented using the `IF-THEN-ELSE` statement. Write the statement. *Hint*: Use the condition X < 0, which is the complement of the condition X >= 0.

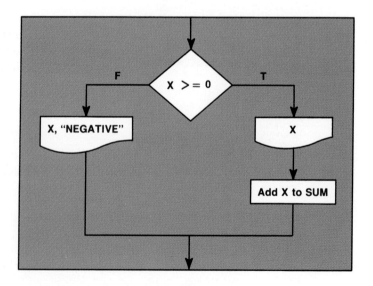

3.4 Subroutines

Limitations of IF-THEN and IF-THEN-ELSE Statements

In earlier sections, we used an IF-THEN or IF-THEN-ELSE statement to implement a single- or double-alternative decision. We saw that such statements could be difficult to enter without error and also difficult to modify. Another major problem was due to the fact that BASIC-PLUS does not permit the use of multiple statements in the True Task of an IF-THEN-ELSE statement. For these reasons it is often preferable (and sometimes even necessary) to use the BASIC-PLUS subroutine to implement decisions as described next.

The GOSUB Statement

A *subroutine* in BASIC-PLUS is a sequence of statements grouped together as a separate unit within a BASIC-PLUS program. The *entry*, or transfer of control, to a subroutine is accomplished through the execution of a *subroutine call* or *GOSUB statement*. For example, the statement

```
100 GOSUB 1000
```

transfers control to the subroutine at line 1000.
   The GOSUB statement is described in the next display.

GOSUB Statement

```
GOSUB sub line
```

Interpretation: The GOSUB statement transfers control to the subroutine starting at line *sub line*. It should be impossible to reach line *sub line* except through the execution of a GOSUB statement.

The RETURN Statement

Once a subroutine has been executed, it is necessary to transfer control back to the first statement following the one that called it. This is accomplished by the RETURN statement. For example if the statement

```
100 GOSUB 1000
110 . . .
```

is used to call the subroutine starting at line 1000

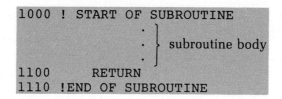

```
1000 ! START OF SUBROUTINE
        .  ⎤
        .  ⎬ subroutine body
        .  ⎦
1100       RETURN
1110 !END OF SUBROUTINE
```

then the statement

```
1100       RETURN
```

would transfer control back to line 110 (the first statement after the GOSUB) following execution of the subroutine body. The effect of the subroutine call and return is diagrammed in Fig. 3.9.

Before transferring to a subroutine, BASIC-PLUS always records the next line number after the GOSUB statement. The RETURN statement causes BASIC-PLUS to transfer control back to the statement with the line number that was saved.

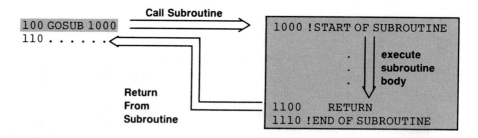

Fig. 3.9 Subroutine call and return.

RETURN Statement

```
RETURN
```

Interpretation: After entering (through execution of a prior GOSUB) and executing a subroutine, the RETURN statement transfers control back to the statement following the GOSUB. If a RETURN is executed without a prior GOSUB, the error message

```
?RETURN without GOSUB
```

will be printed and program execution will terminate.

Implementing Double-Alternative Decisions with Subroutines

The use of subroutines will enable us to implement general double-alternative decisions. By using a GOSUB as the true statement, we can implement True Tasks with multiple steps. This technique is illustrated next.

Example 3.3 The double-alternative decision pattern shown in Fig. 3.6 is revised in Fig. 3.10. In the revised pattern both the True and False Tasks consist of multiple steps. The revised decision pattern is implemented in Fig. 3.11.

If the condition CHECK <= BALANCE at line 300 is true, then the subroutine starting at line 1000 is executed; otherwise the subroutine starting at line 2000 is executed instead. After either subroutine is executed, control is transferred back to line 310.

As shown in Fig. 3.11, the two subroutines are placed at the end of the program, followed by the END statement (line 2070). If the first subroutine is called (CHECK <= BALANCE is true), the statement

```
1050 RETURN
```

would transfer control back to line 310; it also serves to isolate the first subroutine from the second subroutine (lines 2000–2040). If the second subroutine is called instead (CHECK <= BALANCE is false), the statement

```
2040 RETURN
```

would transfer control back to line 310.

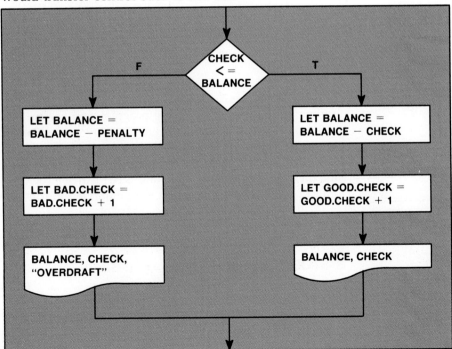

Fig. 3.10 Double-alternative decision with multiple step tasks.

```
300       IF CHECK <= BALANCE THEN GOSUB 1000 &
          ELSE GOSUB 2000
310                    .
                       .
                       .
970       STOP
980    !
990    !
1000   !SUBROUTINES FOR IF-THEN-ELSE AT LINE 300
1010   !IF CHECK <= BALANCE THEN PROCESS GOOD CHECK
1020       LET BALANCE = BALANCE - CHECK
1030       LET GOOD.CHECK = GOOD.CHECK + 1
1040       PRINT BALANCE, CHECK
1050       RETURN
2000   !ELSE PROCESS BAD CHECK
2010       LET BALANCE = BALANCE - PENALTY
2020       LET BAD.CHECK = BAD.CHECK + 1
2030       PRINT BALANCE, CHECK, "OVERDRAFT"
2040       RETURN
2050   !END OF SUBROUTINES FOR IF-THEN-ELSE AT LINE 300
2060   !
2070       END
```

Fig. 3.11 Implementing True Tasks and False Tasks as subroutines.

A subroutine is a separate program unit that should only be entered through the execution of a GOSUB statement. The statement

970 STOP

terminates the execution of the program and serves to isolate the subroutines from the rest of the program. A STOP statement is similar to an END statement in that it terminates program execution. However, a STOP may be placed anywhere in the program (an END must be the last statement) and there may be more than one STOP in a program (only one END is allowed). The STOP statement is summarized in the following display.

STOP Statement

STOP

Interpretation: The STOP terminates or suspends execution of a program. There may be more than one STOP in a program.

Program Style

It is relatively easy to enter and modify individual statements in a subroutine since each statement has its own line number. Consequently True and False Tasks that are implemented as subroutines are also easy to enter and modify. For this reason we will adopt the convention of using subroutines to implement IF-THEN-ELSE statements when either the True Task or False Task consists of a multiple statement group.

All subroutines will appear at the end of the program and must be isolated from the rest of the program. For this reason the line numbers used in subroutines will start at 1000 and all other program statements will have line numbers less than 1000. The first subroutine in a program will start at line 1000, the second subroutine at line 2000, etc. A STOP statement will always precede the first subroutine; an END statement will always follow the last subroutine.

Program Style

Format for decision step subroutines

In writing subroutines to implement True and False Tasks for decision steps, we will follow the format below.

```
1000 !SUBROUTINES FOR IF-THEN-ELSE AT LINE...
1010 !IF condition THEN true task comment
        .⎫
        .⎬ True Task
        .⎭
1090    RETURN
2000 !ELSE false task comment
        .⎫
        .⎬ False Task
        .⎭
2090    RETURN
2100 !END OF SUBROUTINES FOR IF-THEN-ELSE AT...
```

There will be a comment line at the beginning (line 1000) and end (line 2100) of the subroutines indicating the *line number* of the associated IF-THEN-ELSE statement. Each subroutine will begin with a comment line (lines 1010, 2000) and end with a RETURN (lines 1090, 2090). Remember, the comments are not executable statements and are intended solely for documentation purposes; the RETURN statements transfer control back to the first statement allowing the IF-THEN-ELSE statement at line *line number*.

Exercise 3.5: Indicate what is wrong with the program segment below. What happens when the condition is true? When it is false?

add 215 stop to prevent the program from "flowing" into the subroutine

```
200      IF X >= 0 THEN GOSUB 220 &
             ELSE GOSUB 300
220 !SUBROUTINES FOR IF-THEN-ELSE AT LINE 200
230 !IF X >= 0 THEN PROCESS POSITIVE NUMBER
240      PRINT X, "POSITIVE"
250      LET POS.SUM = POS.SUM + X
260      RETURN
300 !ELSE PROCESS NEGATIVE NUMBER
310      PRINT X, "NEGATIVE"
320      LET NEG.SUM = NEG.SUM - X
330      RETURN
340 !END OF SUBROUTINES FOR IF-THEN-ELSE AT LINE 200
```

Exercise 3.6: Implement the decision pattern drawn in Fig. 3.7 using subroutines for the True and False Tasks.

3.5 Nested Decisions and IF-THEN-ELSE Statements

All the examples we have seen so far have involved decisions with only two alternatives. It is not difficult to imagine situations in which you (or a program) may have to choose between several alternatives rather than just two. We shall discuss the whole issue of multiple-alternative decisions in Chapter 7, but for the time being it will be useful to consider a situation that involves three different alternatives.

Example 3.4   We wish to determine a tax rate for a given salary based on data in Table 3.2.

The decision structure in Fig. 3.12a differentiates between salaries that are in the first row of Table 3.2 and all other salaries. Step 1.2 assigns the lowest tax rate for a salary that is in the first row. Step 1.3 processes a

Table 3.2 Table of Salaries and Tax Rates

Salary Greater Than	But Not Over	Tax Rate
0	100	5%
100	250	15%
250	—	20%

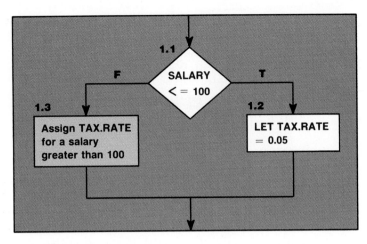

Fig. 3.12a Decision structure for Table 3.2.

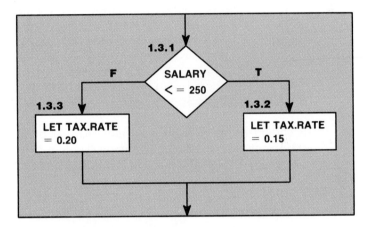

Fig. 3.12b Refinement of Step 1.3 of Fig. 3.12a.

salary that is not in the first row; its refinement is shown in Fig. 3.12b. The decision structures shown in Figs. 3.12a,b are called *nested decision structures* since the second decision structure (Fig. 3.12b) is nested or wholly contained within the first decision structure (Fig. 3.12a).

We can implement the nested decision structure using subroutines for Steps 1.2 and 1.3 of Fig. 3.12a as shown below.

```
120        IF SALARY <= 100 THEN GOSUB 1000 &
           ELSE GOSUB 2000
130                     .
                        .
                        .
970        STOP
980    !
990    !
```

(continued)

```
1000 !SUBROUTINES FOR IF-THEN-ELSE AT LINE 120
1010 !IF SALARY <= 100 THEN ASSIGN LOWEST TAX RATE
1020     LET TAX.RATE = 0.05
1030     RETURN
2000 !ELSE SALARY > 100 ASSIGN A HIGHER TAX RATE
2010     IF SALARY <= 250 THEN LET TAX.RATE = 0.15 &
             ELSE LET TAX.RATE = 0.20
2020     RETURN
2030 !END OF SUBROUTINES FOR IF-THEN-ELSE AT LINE 120
2040 !
2050     END
```

Since the True and False Tasks above are implemented using single statements (lines 1020 and 2010), there is no need to use subroutines. We can implement the nested decision structure using a *nested* IF-THEN-ELSE *statement*. The nested IF-THEN-ELSE statement below has a false statement that is itself an IF-THEN-ELSE statement.

```
120 IF SALARY <= 100 THEN                                       &
        LET TAX.RATE = 0.5                                      &
    ELSE                                                        &
        IF SALARY <= 250 THEN LET TAX.RATE = 0.15               &
            ELSE LET TAX.RATE = 0.20
```

It should be clear from a careful reading of the nested IF-THEN-ELSE statement that it also implements Table 3.2. We can rewrite the nested IF-THEN-ELSE statement in the more compact (and more readable) form below.

```
120 IF SALARY <= 100 THEN LET TAX.RATE = 0.5              &
        ELSE IF SALARY <= 250 THEN LET TAX.RATE = .15     &
            ELSE LET TAX.RATE = 0.20
```

Program Style

Nesting decisions in false tasks

When refining algorithms, you should try to nest each new decision structure in the False Task of an existing decision structure as illustrated in Figs. 3.12a,b. This will enable you to use a nested IF-THEN-ELSE statement like the one preceding this display to implement the decision structure. This technique can be used to implement decisions with more than three alternative categories as will be shown in Chapter 7.

An IF–THEN–ELSE statement may also be used as the true statement of another IF–THEN–ELSE. In most cases this kind of nested IF–THEN–ELSE statement is more difficult to understand, and we shall avoid its use.

Exercise 3.7: Trace the flow diagrams in Figs. 3.12a,b for the following values of SALARY: 0, 75, 100, 125, 200 and 300.

Exercise 3.8: Draw two more sets of flow diagrams that implement Table 3.2. Write them in BASIC-PLUS.

Exercise 3.9: Implement the following table using a nested IF–THEN–ELSE statement.

Salary Greater Than	But Not Over	Tax Rate
0	50	1%
50	150	10%
150	300	15%
300	500	20%
500	—	30%

Exercise 3.10: Draw flow diagrams corresponding to the following nested IF–THEN–ELSE statement

```
IF A > B THEN                                    &
         IF B > C THEN PRINT "A > B > C"         &
              ELSE PRINT "A > B"                 &
   ELSE IF C > B THEN PRINT "C > B >= A"         &
         ELSE PRINT "B >= A and C"
```

The FOR Loop

General Form of the FOR Loop

In Section 2.6 we introduced a restricted form of the FOR loop and used it to implement the flow diagram pattern below.

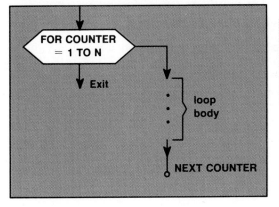

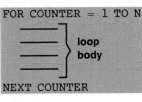

This loop is called a counter-controlled loop. The *loop control variable*, COUNTER, is initialized to one prior to the first execution of the loop body and increased by one after each loop repetition. The loop body is executed N times, once for each value of COUNTER between 1 and N inclusive.

In general the initial value and final value for the loop control variable may be any legal BASIC-PLUS expression (not just constants or variables). As we shall see it is even possible for the loop control variable to decrease in value after each repetition. The BASIC-PLUS FOR loop and its properties are described in the displays that follow; these properties will be illustrated in the next sections.

FOR Loop (unrestricted form)

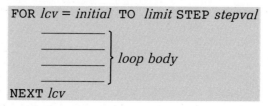

FOR *lcv* = *initial* TO *limit* STEP *stepval*

> loop body

NEXT *lcv*

Interpretation: The loop control variable (*lcv*) must be a variable name. The *loop parameters initial, limit,* and *stepval* may be constants, variables, or expressions. The loop body is executed once for each value of *lcv*, starting with *lcv* equal to the value of *initial*, and continuing in steps specified by *stepval* until *lcv* passes the *limit* value. When the *limit* value is passed, execution continues with the first statement after the loop terminator (NEXT *lcv*). The variable *lcv* will be assigned the last value used inside the loop after loop execution is completed.

Note: If *stepval* is one, the STEP 1 may be omitted from the loop header. If *stepval* is negative, then the value of *lcv* is decreased after each execution of the loop body.

Properties of the FOR Loop

1. Loop execution is terminated when the value of the *loop control variable* (*lcv*) passes the limit value. If the loop header were

        FOR I = 3 TO 8 STEP 2

   the loop would be executed for values of I equal to 3, 5, and 7, and I would have the value 7 after loop execution. If the loop header were

        FOR J = 8 TO 3 STEP −2

the loop would be executed for values of J equal to 8, 6, and 4, and J would have the value 4 after loop execution.

2. If the loop parameters are such that the value of *initial* has already passed the value of *limit*, the loop will not be executed at all. An example is:

```
FOR I = 6 TO 4 STEP 1
```

This means that if *stepval* >= 0, then the loop will execute only if *initial* <= *limit*. If *stepval* < 0, then the loop will execute only if *initial* >= *limit*.

3. If *stepval* is 0 (or undefined), then an *infinite loop* will result. An infinite loop does not terminate until the program runs out of time or is aborted by the programmer (by pressing CTRL/C).

4. The expressions for *initial, limit,* and *stepval* are evaluated before execution begins. This means that changing the value of a variable in a loop parameter expression inside the loop will not affect the number of loop repetitions. However, changing the value of the *loop control variable* inside the loop will affect the number of loop repetitions.

Applications of the FOR Loop

In this section we illustrate several examples of the use of the FOR loop.

Example 3.5   In Fig. 3.13, the first loop computes the sum (SUM, initial value 0) of all odd integers less than or equal to N. After this value is printed, the second loop is used to compute the product (PRODUCT, initial value 1) of all even integers less than or equal to N.

In the first loop, ODD is used as the loop control variable, the limit value expression is N, and the step value is 2. ODD is also used as an operand in the computation performed in the loop (line 180).

```
100 !COMPUTES SUM OF ODD INTEGERS AND PRODUCT OF
110 !EVEN INTEGERS LESS THAN OR EQUAL TO 10
120 !
130     LET N = 10
135 !
140 !COMPUTE SUM OF ODD INTEGERS
150     LET SUM = 0
155     PRINT "ODD INTEGERS <="; N
160     FOR ODD = 1 TO N STEP 2
170         PRINT ODD; "   ";
180             LET SUM = SUM + ODD
190     NEXT ODD
200 !
```

(continued)

```
210        PRINT \ PRINT "SUM OF ODD INTEGERS <=";
230        PRINT N; "IS"; SUM
240        PRINT
250 !
260 !COMPUTE PRODUCT OF EVEN INTEGERS
270        LET PRODUCT = 1
275        PRINT "EVEN INTEGERS <="; N
280        FOR EVEN = 2 TO N STEP 2
290           PRINT EVEN; " ";
300           LET PRODUCT = PRODUCT * EVEN
310        NEXT EVEN
320 !
340        PRINT \ PRINT "PRODUCT OF EVEN INTEGERS <=";
350        PRINT N; "IS"; PRODUCT
360 !
370        END
```

```
RUNNH
ODD INTEGERS <= 10
 1     3     5     7     9
SUM OF ODD INTEGERS <= 10 IS 25

EVEN INTEGERS <= 10
 2     4     6     8     10
PRODUCT OF EVEN INTEGERS <= 10 IS 3840
```

Fig. 3.13 Program for Example 3.5.

Since the value of N is 10, the first loop executes for values of ODD equal to 1, 3, 5, 7, and 9, and the sum (25) is printed. The second loop executes for values of EVEN equal to 2, 4, 6, 8, and 10, and the product (3840) is printed. You should trace both of these loops and verify that they indeed perform as described.

Example 3.6   The program in Fig. 3.14 computes and prints a table showing the conversion from degrees Celsius to degrees Fahrenheit for temperatures ranging from 0°C (value of INIT.CEL) to 100°C (value of LIM.CEL) in steps of 10°C (value of INC.CEL). The forumla

$$\text{Fahrenheit} = 1.8 \times \text{Celsius} + 32$$

is used to compute the equivalent Fahrenheit temperature, FAHREN, for each value of the loop control variable CELSIUS. This program can generate a conversion table for any desired range of Celsius values; all that is required is to change the values of INIT.CEL, LIM.CEL, and INC.CEL entered as data. The data table is shown next.

DATA TABLE FOR EXAMPLE 3.6

Input Variables		Program Variables		Output Variables	
INIT.CEL:	Initial Celsius temperature	CELSIUS:	Loop control variable — temperature in Celsius degrees	FAHREN:	Temperature in Fahrenheit degrees
LIM.CEL:	Final Celsius temperature.				
INC.CEL:	Increment in Celsius degrees				

```
100 !PROGRAM TO PRINT A TABLE OF CELSIUS TO
110 !FAHRENHEIT CONVERSIONS
120 !
130     INPUT "INITIAL CELSIUS TEMPERATURE"; INIT.CEL
140     INPUT "HIGHEST TEMPERATURE"; LIM.CEL
150     INPUT "INCREMENT VALUE"; INC.CEL
155 !
160     PRINT \ PRINT "CELSIUS", "FAHRENHEIT"
170     FOR CELSIUS = INIT.CEL TO LIM.CEL STEP INC.CEL
180        LET FAHREN = 1.8 * CELSIUS + 32
190        PRINT CELSIUS, FAHREN
200     NEXT CELSIUS
210 !
220     END
```

```
RUNNH
INITIAL CELSIUS TEMPERATURE? 0
HIGHEST TEMPERATURE? 100
INCREMENT VALUE? 10

CELSIUS         FAHRENHEIT
 0                 32
 10                50
 20                68
 30                86
 40                104
 50                122
 60                140
 70                158
 80                176
 90                194
 100               212
```

Fig. 3.14 Program for Example 3.6.

In Fig. 3.14, the multiple-statement line

```
160    PRINT \ PRINT "CELSIUS", "FAHRENHEIT"
```

is used to print a table heading. The first PRINT statements prints a blank line. The second PRINT statement prints two strings across a line.

The first string begins in column 1 and the second string begins in column 15 (the start of the second print zone). These strings serve as headings for the table that follows.

The statement

```
190    PRINT CELSIUS, FAHREN
```

is used in the FOR loop to print a table consisting of two columns of numbers. The first character (a blank) printed for each number is aligned under its respective column heading.

Example 3.7   The program in Fig. 3.15 prints a table showing the number of gallons of oil available at the start of each week assuming a fixed usage amount per week. The value of the oil supply is also printed. The initial oil supply and usage amount are entered as data. The data table is shown below.

DATA TABLE FOR EXAMPLE 3.7

Input Variables		Output Variables	
START.OIL:	Starting amount of oil	OIL.SUPPLY:	Amount of oil available at the start of each week
OIL.USE:	Weekly usage of oil	WEEK:	The week number
GAL.COST:	Cost of a gallon of oil	OIL.VALUE:	The value of the oil supply

The FOR loop in Fig. 3.15 begins with the statement

```
200 FOR OIL.SUPPLY = START.OIL TO 0 STEP -OIL.USE
```

This statement initializes OIL.SUPPLY to the value of START.OIL and causes OIL.SUPPLY to be decreased by OIL.USAGE after each loop execution. The variable WEEK is used in the loop to count the number of weeks that oil is used, but it is not used to control loop repetition. WEEK is initialized to 0 (line 190) before the loop begins and WEEK is incremented by 1 (line 210) during each execution of the loop.

```
100 !PRINTS A TABLE SHOWING OIL SUPPLY AND ITS VALUE
110 !ASSUMING A FIXED WEEKLY USAGE OF OIL
120 !
130     INPUT "INITIAL OIL SUPPLY"; START.OIL
140     INPUT "WEEKLY USAGE"; OIL.USE
150     INPUT "COST PER GALLON"; GAL.COST
160 !
170 !PRINT TABLE OF AVAILABLE OIL
180     PRINT \ PRINT "WEEK","OIL SUPPLY","OIL VALUE"
190     LET WEEK = 0
200     FOR OIL.SUPPLY = START.OIL TO 0 STEP -OIL.USE
210         LET WEEK = WEEK + 1
220         LET OIL.VALUE = OIL.SUPPLY * GAL.COST
230         PRINT WEEK, OIL.SUPPLY, OIL.VALUE
240     NEXT OIL.SUPPLY
250 !
260     PRINT \ PRINT OIL.USE - OIL.SUPPLY;           &
            "MORE GALLONS ARE NEEDED FOR WEEK"; WEEK
270 !
280     END
```

```
RUNNH
INITIAL OIL SUPPLY? 2000
WEEKLY USAGE? 215
COST PER GALLON? 1.25

WEEK         OIL SUPPLY         OIL VALUE
1            2000               2500
2            1785               2231.25
3            1570               1962.5
4            1355               1693.75
5            1140               1425
6            925                1156.25
7            710                887.5
8            495                618.75
9            280                350
10           65                 81.25

150 MORE GALLONS ARE NEEDED FOR WEEK 10
```

Fig. 3.15 Program for Example 3.7.

The table of output will be completed when the value of OIL.SUPPLY is less than OIL.USE. The number of extra gallons needed to finish the last week are computed and printed by line 260 following the table. Line 260 shows that it is possible to use an expression in an output list although, normally, we will not do so.

The following problem provides another illustration of the FOR loop.

Problem 3C   The banks in your area all advertise different interest rates for various kinds of long-term savings certificates. Usually the advertisements state the minimum investment period (four years, six years, etc.) for the certificate and the yearly interest rate. Given an investment term (TERM) in years, a yearly interest rate (RATE) in percent, and an amount of deposit (DEPOSIT) in dollars and cents, we will write an interactive program that will compute and print the yearly interest amount (INTEREST) and the value of the certificate (CERT.VAL) at the end of each year of the investment period.

Discussion: An initial data table for this problem is shown next. The level one flow diagram appears on the left in Fig. 3.16.

DATA TABLE FOR
PROBLEM 3C

Input Variables		Program Variables		Output Variables	
TERM:	Investment period (years)	DEC.RATE:	Decimal value of RATE	INTEREST:	Interest amount computed at the end of each year
RATE:	Yearly interest rate (percent)				
DEPOSIT:	Initial deposit (initial value of certificate)			CERT.VAL:	Certificate value at the end of each year

From the level one flow diagram it is clear that a repetition of a short sequence of steps is needed in the refinement of Step 2. The repetition can be controlled easily by using a counter YEAR that takes on successive integer values from 1 (first year) through TERM (last year).

ADDITIONAL
DATA TABLE
ENTRY FOR
PROBLEM 3C

Program Variables	
YEAR:	Loop control variable of FOR loop; initial value, 1, final value, TERM

The refinement of Step 2 is shown on the right in Fig. 3.16 and the BASIC-PLUS program is given in Fig. 3.17, along with sample output for TERM = 10 years, RATE = 10.5 percent and DEPOSIT = $3000.

In the program the interest rate (10.5%) is stored in DEC.RATE as the fraction 0.105 (line 165). The first statement in the loop (line 280) computes the interest for the current year; the next statement increases the certificate value by the interest amount.

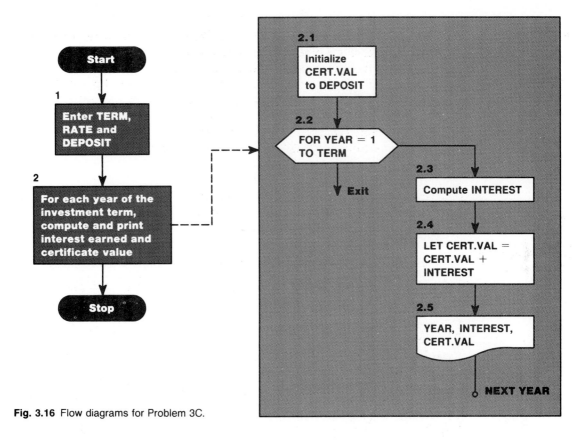

Fig. 3.16 Flow diagrams for Problem 3C.

```
100 !BANK CERTIFICATE PROBLEM
120 !
130 !ENTER DEPOSIT, TERM, AND RATE
140    INPUT "AMOUNT (IN DOLLARS)"; DEPOSIT
150    INPUT "TERM (IN YEARS)"; TERM
160    INPUT "RATE (IN PERCENT)"; RATE
165    LET DEC.RATE = RATE / 100
170 !
220 !PRINT TABLE HEADING
230    PRINT \ PRINT "YEAR", "INTEREST", "VALUE"
250 !
255 !COMPUTE AND PRINT INTEREST AND CERTIFICATE
260 !VALUE AFTER EACH YEAR OF THE TERM
265    LET CERT.VAL = DEPOSIT
270    FOR YEAR = 1 TO TERM
280       LET INTEREST = CERT.VAL * DEC.RATE
290       LET CERT.VAL = CERT.VAL + INTEREST
300       PRINT YEAR, INTEREST, CERT.VAL
310    NEXT YEAR
320 !
330    END
```

(continued)

```
RUNNH
AMOUNT (IN DOLLARS)? 3000
TERM (IN YEARS)? 10
RATE (IN PERCENT)? 10.5

YEAR          INTEREST           VALUE
1             315                3315
2             348.075            3663.08
3             384.623            4047.7
4             425.008            4472.71
5             469.634            4942.34
6             518.946            5461.29
7             573.435            6034.72
8             633.646            6668.37
9             700.179            7368.55
10            773.697            8142.24
```

Fig. 3.17 Program and sample output for Problem 3C.

Exercise 3.11: Modify Fig. 3.13 so that a single FOR loop is used to perform the sum and product computation.

Exercise 3.12:
 a) Modify the temperature-conversion program (Fig. 3.14) so that it will convert Fahrenheit temperatures to Celsius. Print out a table of conversions for temperatures ranging from 210°F down to −30°F in steps of −10°F.
 b) Modify the program to print a conversion table from Fahrenheit to Celsius degrees in steps of 20°F from 32°F to 212°F.

Exercise 3.13: Write a FOR loop that computes the factorial of a positive integer. The factorial of N(N!) is defined as the product of all integers less than or equal to N (e.g., 3! = 3 × 2 × 1 = 6). Use a step value of −1 in your loop.

Exercise 3.14: Write a FOR loop to compute and print a table of square roots of positive integers between 1 and 50. (*Hint*: the square root of an integer K written as $\sqrt{K}$ or $K^{1/2}$ may be computed in BASIC-PLUS as K ^ .5 where the symbol ^ indicates *exponentiation* or "*raised to the power of.*")

Exercise 3.15: Modify the program for Problem 3C to read in the starting year of the certificate (e.g., 1984) as a fourth input value and to print the actual years of the certificate life (e.g., 1984, 1985, . . . 1990) rather than the integers 1, 2, . . . 10.

3.7   The Widget Inventory Control Problem

We now turn our attention to the solution of a problem that illustrates the use of many of the statements introduced in the chapter.

Problem 3D　　The Widget Manufacturing Company needs a simple program to help control the manufacturing and shipping of widgets. Specifically, the program is to process each order for widgets and check to see whether or not there is sufficient inventory to fill the order. The message "FILLED" or "NOT FILLED" should be printed next to each order. After all orders have been processed, the program should print out the final value of the inventory, the number of widgets shipped, and the number of additional widgets that must be manufactured to fill all outstanding orders. The program data must start with the initial inventory value followed by the number of orders and the actual widget orders.

Discussion:　A loop will be needed to process all orders. After each order is read in, it must be compared to the widget inventory and will be either filled or not filled. The data table follows.

DATA TABLE FOR PROBLEM 3D

Input Variables		Output Variables	
OLD.INV:	Initial inventory at start of processing	CUR.INV:	Used to keep track of inventory as orders are processed
NUM.ORDER:	Number of orders to be processed	ADD.WID:	Additional widgets required to fill outstanding orders
ORDER:	Contains each order as it is being processed	SHIP:	Number of widgets shipped

　　　The input information for this problem is the initial inventory (OLD.INV), the number of orders (NUM.ORDER) and each widget order (ORDER). The output information will be the current widget inventory (CUR.INV), the total number of additional widgets required to fill the outstanding orders (ADD.WID) and the number of widgets shipped (SHIP). The value of SHIP can be computed easily as the difference of OLD.INV and the final value of CUR.INV. The flow diagrams are drawn in Fig. 3.18a; additional variables are introduced next.

ADDITIONAL DATA TABLE ENTRIES FOR PROBLEM 3D

Program Variables	
COUNT.ORDER:	Loop control variable— value indicates how many orders have been processed so far.
NOT.FILL:	Used to keep track of the number of widgets in orders that cannot be filled.

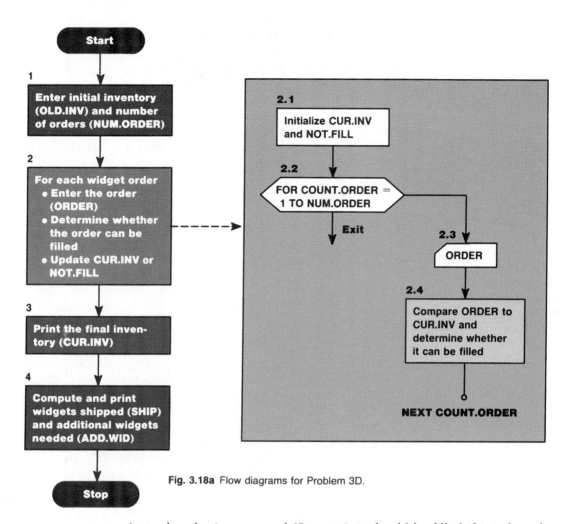

Fig. 3.18a Flow diagrams for Problem 3D.

As each order is processed (Step 2.4), it should be filled if it is less than or equal to the current inventory (CUR.INV) and the value of CUR.INV must be decreased by the amount of the order (ORDER). If the order cannot be completely filled, the order amount should be added to NOT.FILL. Before entering the loop, CUR.INV should be initialized to the starting inventory value (OLD.INV) and NOT.FILL must be initialized to zero. If NOT.FILL does not remain zero, then more widgets are needed. This amount is determined by subtracting the final value of CUR.INV (after all orders are processed) from NOT.FILL. The refinements of Steps 2.4 and 4 are shown in Figs. 3.18b and c. The program and a sample run are shown in Fig. 3.19.

The last line of the program output shown in Fig. 3.19 is

Stop at line 380

A message similar to this will be printed whenever a STOP statement is executed. It simply informs the program user of the reason that program execution was suspended.

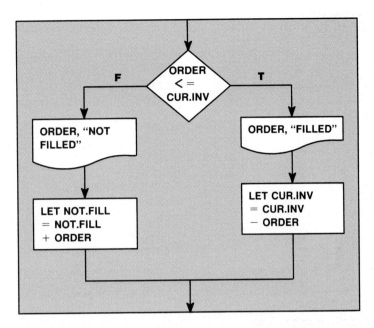

Fig. 3.18b Refinement of Step 2.4 in Fig. 3.18a.

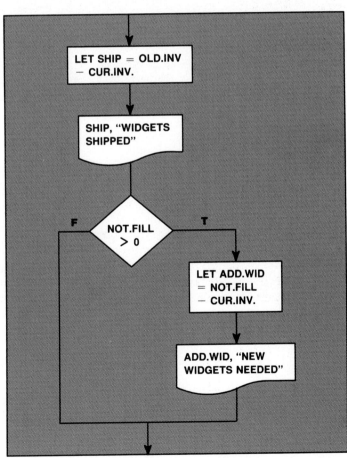

Fig. 3.18c Refinement of Step 4 in Fig. 3.18a.

```
100 !WIDGET INVENTORY CONTROL PROBLEM
110 !
120 !ENTER OLD INVENTORY AND NUMBER OF ORDERS
130     INPUT "ENTER OLD INVENTORY"; OLD.INV
140     INPUT "ENTER NUMBER OF ORDERS"; NUM.ORDER
145     PRINT
150 !
160 !READ AND PROCESS EACH ORDER
170     LET CUR.INV = OLD.INV
180     LET NOT.FILL = 0
190     FOR COUNT.ORDER = 1 TO NUM.ORDER
200        INPUT "ORDER"; ORDER
210        !DECIDE IF ORDER CAN BE FILLED
250        IF ORDER <= CUR.INV THEN GOSUB 1000 &
                 ELSE GOSUB 2000
260     NEXT COUNT.ORDER
270 !
280 !PRINT FINAL INVENTORY COUNT
290     PRINT \ PRINT "FINAL INVENTORY ="; CUR.INV
310 !
320 !COMPUTE AND PRINT NUMBER SHIPPED (SHIP)
330 !AND ADDITIONAL WIDGETS (ADD.WID) IF NEEDED
340     LET SHIP = OLD.INV - CUR.INV
350     PRINT SHIP; "WIDGETS SHIPPED"
360     IF NOT.FILL > 0 THEN                            &
            !ADDITIONAL WIDGETS NEEDED                  &
            LET ADD.WID = NOT.FILL - CUR.INV            &
            \PRINT ADD.WID; "NEW WIDGETS NEEDED"
370 !
380     STOP
390 !
400 !
1000 !SUBROUTINES FOR IF-THEN-ELSE AT LINE 250
1010 !IF ORDER <= CUR.INV THEN FILL ORDER
1020     PRINT , ORDER; "FILLED"
1030     LET CUR.INV = CUR.INV - ORDER
1050     RETURN
2000 !ELSE ORDER NOT FILLED (EXCEEDS INVENTORY)
2010     PRINT , ORDER; "NOT FILLED"
2020     LET NOT.FILL = NOT.FILL + ORDER
2040     RETURN
2050 !END OF SUBROUTINES FOR IF-THEN-ELSE AT LINE 250
2060 !
2070     END  !WIDGET PROGRAM


RUNNH
ENTER OLD INVENTORY? 150
ENTER NUMBER OF ORDERS? 5
```

(continued)

```
ORDER? 55
                55 FILLED
ORDER? 45
                45 FILLED
ORDER? 60
                60 NOT FILLED
ORDER? 30
                30 FILLED
ORDER? 30
                30 NOT FILLED

FINAL INVENTORY = 20
 130 WIDGETS SHIPPED
 70 NEW WIDGETS NEEDED
Stop at line 380
```

Fig. 3.19 Program and sample output for Problem 3D.

Program Style

Correlating algorithms with programs

If you follow the suggestions for algorithm design presented in this chapter and Chapter 2, your level one flow diagrams will consist of a sequence of major steps. Some of these steps may be refined as decision steps and still others may be refined as loops. When your algorithm is translated into BASIC-PLUS, there will be a group of program statements or a *control structure* (decision statement or loop) corresponding to each algorithm step or its refinement in the flow diagram. These statements and structures will be in the same order as their corresponding flow diagram steps. We will use color coding to help you associate each algorithm step with its BASIC-PLUS implementation.

Occasionally one control structure will be nested or wholly contained in another. This will happen if the refinement of a step in a control structure is itself a control structure. An example of this is the refinement of Step 2.4 as a decision structure (see Fig. 3.18b). Since Step 2.4 is part of the loop body, the IF–THEN–ELSE statement (line 250) corresponding to Step 2.4 is nested in the FOR loop as shown in Fig. 3.19. This means that the IF–THEN–ELSE statement is executed during each repetition of the loop and the message "FILLED" or "NOT FILLED" is printed.

The true and false statements for this IF–THEN–ELSE are implemented as separate subroutines (starting at lines 1000 and 2000); consequently, they appear after the main program body. The background color for these subroutines is the same color as the loop.

Exercise 3.16: Explain the purpose of the first " , " in the PRINT statements at lines 1020 and 2010.

3.8

3.8 Debugging Programs

Introduction

It is rare that a program runs correctly the first time. Often one spends a considerable amount of time in removing errors or *bugs* from programs.

The process of locating and removing errors from a program is called *debugging*. You will find that a substantial portion of your time is spent debugging. The debugging time can be reduced if you follow the algorithm and program development steps illustrated in the text without taking any shortcuts.

This approach requires a careful analysis of the problem description, the identification in a data table of the input and output data for the problem, and the careful development of the algorithm for the problem solution. The algorithm development should proceed on a step-by-step basis, beginning with an outline of the algorithm in the form of a level one list of subtasks. Additional algorithm detail (refinements) should be provided as needed, until enough detail has been added so that writing the program is virtually a mechanical process. The data table should be updated during the refinement process, so that all variables introduced in the algorithm are listed and clearly defined in the table.

Once the algorithm and data table are complete, a systematic hand simulation (or trace) of the algorithm, using one or two representative sets of data, can help eliminate many errors in logic before they show up as bugs during the execution of your program. When the hand trace is complete, the program may be written using the data table and the algorithm refinements.

There are three general categories of errors that you may encounter when running programs:

- syntax errors
- run-time errors
- logic errors

Syntax Errors

We discussed syntax errors in Chapter 1. A syntax error results when an illegal statement is present in the program. If a statement cannot be translated because it does not follow the syntax rules, BASIC-PLUS will print a diagnostic message indicating the type of error.

Unfortunately the diagnostic messages printed by BASIC-PLUS often seem vague or confusing. Sometimes careful interpretation and clever detective work are needed to correlate the message with the actual error. There is greater opportunity for making syntax errors when a multiple-statement line is typed; unfortunately the penalty is also more severe as the entire statement must be retyped—not just the line containing the error. Remember to type the symbol "&" at the end of each line that is continued and to insert the symbol "\" between executable statements in a statement group. After all syntax errors have been eliminated, the program can be executed, although it may still contain bugs.

Run-time Errors

Errors that occur during program execution (*run-time errors*) are normally the result of programmer carelessness or errors in logic. They will not prevent the program from being translated; however, they will prevent the program from executing correctly. Depending on the severity of the error, program execution may be terminated.

A common run-time error is caused by referencing a variable before its value has been defined. For example, the assignment statement

```
200 LET X = Y * Z
```

cannot be executed in a meaningful manner unless the values of Y and Z have been previously defined. If Z is not defined, the statement

```
220 LET X = Y / Z
```

will result in the diagnostic message

```
%Division by zero
```

as numeric variables are automatically initialized to zero.

Another example of a run-time error is the failure to provide enough data values in the DATA statements for a program. After the last data value is read, a diagnostic message of the form

```
?Out of data at line 300
```

would be printed if another READ statement (at line 300) is reached. This type of message would also be printed if a loop containing a READ statement did not terminate when expected. In this case the loop would continue to execute and attempt to enter data after all data values had been processed. This diagnostic message is often the only symptom of an improper loop control step.

Logic Errors

If your program executes without error but doesn't produce the desired results, there may be an error in logic. If there was not enough output information printed in your first run, it is often worthwhile to make an extra debugging run in which all pertinent variable values are printed at different steps in the execution of your program.

The PRINT statements used for debugging should be added with some care and thought. Since your program is organized as a linear sequence of steps, it is desirable to print the values of variables that are changed in each step before and after execution of that step. You should carefully simulate the execution of each step to verify that the values printed are correct.

Often the first debugging run will do no more than tell you what step is in error. At this point you should concentrate on that step and insert additional PRINT statements to trace its execution. Be careful when inserting extra PRINT statements in a loop as a new set of values will be printed with each repetition of the loop. This may waste considerable paper and time. If a loop is used to accumulate a result, it is useful to print the accumulated value just after loop exit.

The loop in Fig. 3.20 is supposed to compute the sum of the first 10 integers. However, the value printed for SUM (line 160) is 25 instead of 55.

```
100 !COMPUTE SUM OF FIRST TEN INTEGERS
110 LET SUM = 0
120 FOR I = 1 TO 10
130    LET SUM = SUM + I
140     LET I = I + 1
150 NEXT I
160 PRINT "SUM = ", SUM
170 END

RUNNH
SUM = 25
```

Fig. 3.20 FOR loop with extra statement at line 140

One way to determine what is wrong is to insert the statement

```
135 PRINT "I ="; I, "SUM ="; SUM
```

in the FOR loop. This causes the diagnostic output below.

```
I = 1           SUM = 1
I = 3           SUM = 4
I = 5           SUM = 9
I = 7           SUM = 16
I = 9           SUM = 25
SUM = 25
```

This output shows that the increment for I is 2, not 1, and, therefore, line 140 should be deleted (i.e., it is incorrect to increment I inside the FOR loop).

For decision steps it is a good idea to print the values of variables involved in the conditional test. These values should be printed just before execution of the test and will indicate which decision path was followed. For example, if the decision begins with

```
320 IF X < Y THEN                    &
```

then you might insert the statement

```
315 PRINT "X ="; X, "Y ="; Y
```

just before the condition. You should check that these are the values expected.

Once you have located an error, go back to your algorithm, modify the steps that you believe are in error, and then completely retrace the modified algorithm. This last step is extremely important and one that is often overlooked. Each algorithm change may have important side effects that are difficult to anticipate. Making what seems to be an obvious correction in one step of the algorithm may introduce new errors into other algorithm steps. The only way to establish that there are no side effects is to retrace the revised algorithm.

Once the revised algorithm has been carefully checked out, write the new program statements that are needed, and correct and rerun your program.

Immediate Mode Debugging

It is possible to use a special feature of BASIC-PLUS to obtain diagnostic information after temporarily suspending program execution. If the statement

```
145 STOP
```

were inserted in the program segment in Fig. 3.20, the computer would print

```
STOP at line 145
```

and suspend program execution after each loop repetition. The program user could then examine the current variable values simply by typing an unnumbered PRINT statement such as

```
PRINT "I ="; I, "SUM ="; SUM
```

This statement would be executed immediately, thereby displaying the current value of I and SUM. In order to resume program execution, the program user should type in the system command

```
CONT
```

causing program execution to continue until the next execution of a STOP statement or the program END is reached.

An unnumbered statement such as the PRINT above is not saved in a program but is executed immediately, or in *immediate mode*. It is also possible to assign the value of a variable using an assignment or INPUT statement in immediate mode. Certain statements (e.g., DATA, FOR, NEXT) make no sense when used in immediate mode and would generate the diagnostic message

    ?Illegal in immediate mode

STOP statements can be inserted at key points in a program just like diagnostic PRINT statements. Each time program execution is suspended, temporary results may be checked against hand calculations by using immediate mode PRINT statements to display these results.

It is also possible to suspend a running program by typing CTRL/C. (This would be necessary if your program were stuck in an *infinite loop*— a loop that cannot terminate.) The immediate mode statement

    PRINT LINE

would print out the line number of the statement that was being executed when the program stopped (LINE is a reserved keyword). Other immediate mode statements could be used to obtain diagnostic information. Typing the system command

    CONT

would resume program execution.

 ## 3.9 Testing Programs

Preparing Test Data Sets

Once all errors have been removed and the program has executed to normal completion, the program should be tested as thoroughly as possible. In Section 2.6 we discussed tracing an algorithm and suggested that enough sets of test data be provided to ensure that all paths through the algorithm are traced.

In a similar way the final program should be tested with a variety of data. For example, to test the widget inventory program (Fig. 3.19) one data set should be provided that contains orders that are not filled as well as orders that are filled. This data set should be prepared so that some later orders are filled, even though earlier orders were not. A second data set should also be provided that contains only orders that are filled. (Why?)

Handling the Exceptions

As you get more experienced in programming you will begin to write programs that not only handle all "normal" situations, but also the unexpected. For example, what would the widget inventory program do if the initial inventory value or any widget order happened to be negative? As the algorithm is currently written, all negative orders would automatically be filled. A better solution would be to ignore a negative order and print an "error message" indicating that an invalid order was received.

You are right if you are thinking that no reasonable person would request a negative order; however, users of programs often do not know what is reasonable and what is not. This is particularly true if the program user is not the program designer. Consequently experienced programmers practice *defensive programming* so that their programs will behave in a reasonable way even when the data are unreasonable.

Wherever possible, your programs should test for the occurrence of unusual data values and print an error message when they occur. Very often, these unusual values will eventually result in a run-time error. Whether this happens or not, your program should print an error message to warn the user of a potential problem and its source.

3.10 Common Programming Errors

If you are using multiple-line IF-THEN or IF-THEN-ELSE statements to implement decision structures, remember to insert the continuation symbol "&" and separator symbol "\" where needed. Most errors in decision statements will be detected immediately as syntax errors. Remember that only a single executable statement may be used as the true statement in an IF-THEN-ELSE statement.

A common error in using loop structures involves the specification of too many or too few loop repetitions. You should check carefully that the initial, step and limit values of all loop control variables are specified correctly. BASIC-PLUS FOR loops that cause too few or too many repetitions of the loop body are usually caused by incorrect limit values. Also, when variables or expressions used as loop parameters are incorrectly defined prior to loop entry, the loop will not execute as expected. Changing the loop control variable in the loop body will also lead to errors. Printing critical loop parameter values often can be quite helpful during program debugging. Remember to end all FOR loops with a NEXT statement that includes the name of the loop control variable.

When using subroutines you must ensure that the subroutine is isolated from the rest of the program (by a STOP or RETURN) so that the only way it can be executed is through a GOSUB statement. Failure to do this will result in the diagnostic message

```
?RETURN without GOSUB
```

after the subroutine is executed and its RETURN statement is reached.

3.11 Summary

In this chapter we discussed some of the control structures that are available in BASIC-PLUS. Decision structures, the FOR loop structure and subroutines were described.

Terminator statements serve as end markers, indicating to BASIC-PLUS where the physical end of a structure is in the program. The terminator NEXT *lcv* marks the end of a loop; the terminator RETURN indicates the end of a subroutine.

We also introduced the BASIC-PLUS subroutine that is called through the execution of a GOSUB statement. The line number in the GOSUB indicates which subroutine is being called. The RETURN statement always returns control to the statement following the one that called the subroutine.

In formulating your solution to a programming problem, it is essential that you think in terms of the structures and their functions. The emphasis should be on how the structures affect what is to be done and not on the various transfers of control that are implied.

The features introduced in this chapter are summarized in Table 3.3.

Table 3.3 Summary of BASIC-PLUS Features

Feature	Effect
IF-THEN *statement*	

`100 IF X > 0 THEN        &`
`    LET SUM = SUM + X     &`
`    \PRINT X              &`
`    \LET COUNT = COUNT + 1`
	If X is positive, then add X to SUM, print X, and increment COUNT by 1.

IF-THEN-ELSE *statement*	

`200 IF X < 0 THEN           &`
`    PRINT X; "NEGATIVE"     &`
`  ELSE                      &`
`    LET SUM = SUM + X       &`
`    \PRINT X; "POSITIVE"`
	If X is negative, print X; otherwise, add X to SUM and print X.

Nested **IF-THEN-ELSE**	

`320 IF X < -10 THEN LET LOW = LOW + 1           &`
`    ELSE IF X < 10 THEN LET MID = MID + 1      &`
`        ELSE LET HIGH = HIGH + 1`
	If X is less than -10, then add 1 to LOW; otherwise, if X is less than 10, then add 1 to MID; otherwise, add 1 to HIGH.

Table 3.3 Summary of BASIC-PLUS Features (*continued*)

Feature	Effect
Subroutine CALL	

```
100 GOSUB 1000
```

Calls the subroutine starting at line 1000.

Subroutine RETURN

```
1100 RETURN
```

Returns control from a subroutine. The next statement executed is the one following the GOSUB that called the subroutine.

IF-THEN-ELSE *with subroutines*

```
100 IF X < 0 THEN GOSUB 1000                            &
          ELSE GOSUB 2000
110 PRINT "NEW X ="; X
                .
                .
                .
1000 !SUBROUTINES FOR IF-THEN-ELSE AT LINE 100
1010 !IF X < 0 THEN PROCESS NEGATIVE X
1020      PRINT X; "NEGATIVE"
1030      LET X = -X
1040      RETURN
1050 !ELSE PROCESS POSITIVE X
1060      PRINT X; "POSITIVE"
1070      LET X = X + X
1080      RETURN
1090 !END OF SUBROUTINES FOR LINE 100
```

(Handwritten margin annotations renumbering lines: 2000→1050, 2010→1060, 2020→1070, 2030→1080, 2040→1090)

If X is negative, X and "NEGATIVE" are printed and X is changed to a positive number; otherwise X and "POSITIVE" are printed and X is doubled. The new value of X is printed (line 110) upon return from either subroutine.

FOR *loop*

```
300 FOR I = 1 TO 5 STEP 2
310    LET SUM = SUM + I
320    PRINT "I"; I, "SUM"; SUM
330 NEXT I
```

Add 1, 3, and 5 to SUM. Print each odd integer and the accumulating sum (SUM).

STOP *statement*

```
500 STOP
```

Suspends execution of a program.

CONT *Command*

```
CONT
```

A system command that causes a suspended program to resume execution.

We recommend the use of the structures introduced in this chapter whenever possible in the formulation and implementation of algorithms. Careful use of the structures will pay off in programs that are easier to write and have fewer errors. Subroutines will be discussed again in Chapter 5 and multiple-alternative decisions in Chapter 7.

Programming Problems

3E Write a program to read in a list of integer data items and find and print the index of the first occurrence of the number 12. Your program should print an index value of 0 if the number is not found. (The index is the sequence number of the data item 12. For example, if the 8th data item read in is 12, then the index value 8 should be printed.)

3F Write a program to read in a collection of exam scores ranging in value from 1 to 100. Your program should count and print the number of outstanding scores (90–100), the number of satisfactory scores (60–89), and the number of unsatisfactory scores (1–59). Test your program on the following data:

63	75	72
72	78	67
80	63	75
90	89	43
59	99	82
12	100	

In addition, print each exam score and its category.

3G (*Expanded payroll problem.*) Write a program to process weekly employee time cards for all employees of an organization. Each employee will have three data items indicating an identification number, the hourly wage rate, and the number of hours worked during a given week. Each employee is to be paid time-and-a-half for all hours worked over 40. A tax amount of 3.625 percent of gross salary will be deducted. The program output should show the employee's number and net pay.

3H Suppose you own a beer distributorship that sells Lite (ID number 1), Coors (ID number 2), Bud (ID number 3) and Iron City (ID number 4) by the case. Write a program to (a) read in the case inventory for each brand for the start of the week; (b) process all weekly sales and purchase records for each brand; and (c) print out the final inventory. Each case transaction will consist of two data items. The first item will be the brand identification number (an integer). The second will be the amount purchased (a positive integer value) or the amount sold (a negative integer value). The weekly inventory for each brand (for the start of the week) will also consist of two data items —the identification and initial inventory—for that brand. For now, you may assume that you always have sufficient foresight to prevent depletion of your inventory for any brand.

3I   Write a program to read in an integer N and compute

$$\text{SLOW} = \sum_{i=1}^{N} i = 1 + 2 + 3 + 4 \ldots + N$$

(the sum of all integers from 1 to N, inclusive). Then compute FAST = (N × (N + 1))/2 and compare FAST and SLOW. Your program should print both SLOW and FAST and indicate whether or not they are equal. (You will need a loop to compute SLOW.) Which computation method is preferable?

    To verify your hypothesis of the relationship between SLOW and FAST, modify your program so that it will process a collection of numbers.

3J   Write a program to find the largest value in a collection of N numbers, where the value of N will be the first data item read into the program.

3K   Write a program to process a collection of checking account transactions (deposits or withdrawals) for Mr. Shelley's account. Your program should begin by reading in the previous account balance and the number of transactions, and then process each transaction, computing the new balance. Test your program with the following data.

```
Old balance = 325.5
Transactions: 25, -79.25, -60, 16.75, -259.47, 42,
              -5.5
```

3L   Modify the data table, flow diagram, and program of Problem 3K to compute and print the following additional information: (a) The number of withdrawals; (b) the number of deposits; (c) the number of transactions; (d) the total sum of all withdrawals; (e) the total sum of all deposits.

3M   Following the processing of the transaction −259.47 in Problem 3K (or 3L), the new balance was negative, indicating that Mr. Shelley's account was overdrawn. Modify your data table, flow diagram, and program so that the resulting new program will test for withdrawal amounts that are not covered. Have your program completely skip processing each such withdrawal and, instead, use a PRINT statement to indicate an overdrawn account. The balance should not be altered by withdrawals that are not covered. Your program should count the number of such withdrawals and print a total at the end of execution. (Note that in Problem 3K or 3L Mr. Shelley's final balance was positive. This indicates that he made a deposit during the current time period to cover the $259.47 withdrawal. What could be done to prevent such a transaction from being considered overdrawn as long as the final account balance for the current period is positive?)

3N   Write a program to compute and print the successive powers of one-half (1/2, 1/4, 1/8, 1/16, . . .) in decimal form. Your program should print two columns of information, as shown below:

Power	Fraction
1	0.5
2	0.25
3	0.125
4	0.0625
.	.
.	.
.	.

3O Modify the program for Problem 3N to accumulate and print the sum of the fractions computed at each step. Add a third column of output containing the accumulated sum.

Sum
0.5
0.75
0.875
0.9375
.
.
.

3P The trustees of a small college are considering voting a pay raise for the 12 full-time faculty members. They want to grant a 7½ percent pay raise. However, before doing so, they want to know how much this will cost the college. Write a program that will provide this information. Test your program for the following salaries:

$12,500	$14,029.50
$16,000	$13,250
$15,500	$12,800
$20,000.50	$18,900
$13,780	$17,300
$14,120.25	$14,100

Have your program print the initial salary, raise, and final salary for each faculty member as well as the total amounts for all faculty.

3Q Modify your solution to 3P so that faculty earning $14,000 or less receive a raise of 7 percent; faculty earning $14,000–$16,500 receive a raise of 7½ percent; and faculty earning more than $16,500 receive a raise of 8 percent.

3R The assessor in the local township has estimated the value of all 14 properties in the township. Properties are assessed a flat tax rate of 125 mils per $100 of assessed value, and each property is assessed at only 28 percent of its estimated value. Write a program to compute the total amount of taxes that will be collected on the 14 properties in the township. (A mil is equal to 0.1 of a penny). The estimated values of the properties are:

$50,000	$48,000
$45,500	$67,000
$37,600	$47,100
$65,000	$53,350
$28,000	$58,000
$52,250	$48,000
$56,500	$43,700

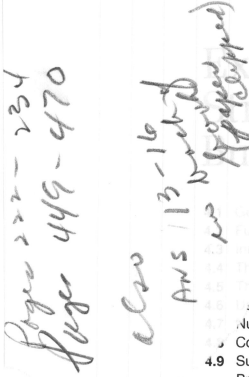

4

Expressions, Strings, and Built-in Functions

While writing earlier programs you may have thought about, and perhaps even written, BASIC-PLUS assignment statements containing parentheses and more than one arithmetic operator. Also, you may have wondered whether or not BASIC-PLUS could be used to instruct the computer to manipulate something other than numbers and, if so, how?

In this chapter, we shall see that BASIC-PLUS can be used to manipulate strings of characters as well as numeric information. We will learn how to form BASIC-PLUS assignment statements of greater complexity than those used so far in order to specify numeric computations and we will introduce some simple character-string manipulations. All of these features will make it still more convenient to program in BASIC-PLUS.

4.1 Generalizing the Assignment Statement

Multiple Operators and Operands

In the first three chapters of the text, we used simple assignment statements containing expressions with one arithmetic operator (+, −, *, /). Obviously the BASIC-PLUS language would have a very limited mathematical capability if only expressions with a single operator were allowed. In fact, it is possible to represent most mathematical formulas in BASIC-PLUS using expressions with multiple operators and parentheses. For example, expressions such as

```
HOURS * RATE - TAX
B * B - 4 * A * C
(40 + 1.5 * (HOURS - 40)) * RATE
(N / DIV) * DIV
```

are all legal in BASIC-PLUS. The major difficulty in writing such expressions is to ensure that the specified operations are carried out (*evaluated*) in the desired order.

Example 4.1   The BASIC-PLUS assignment statement

```
200 LET X = A / (B + C)
```

is evaluated assuming the variable values given below. (X is initially undefined.)

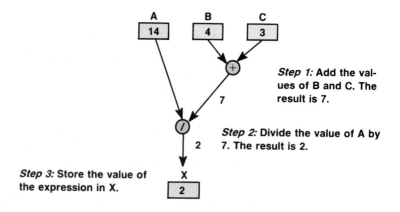

Step 1: Add the values of B and C. The result is 7.

Step 2: Divide the value of A by 7. The result is 2.

Step 3: Store the value of the expression in X.

As shown, the parenthesized *subexpression* (B + C) is evaluated first, followed by the division. The result, A / (B + C), is then assigned to the variable X.

Example 4.2   In addition to the arithmetic operators described in Table 1.1 (+, −, *, /), there is one additional BASIC-PLUS operator, ^, which is called a circumflex. This is the exponentiation operator and it raises its first operand to the power indicated by the second operand. The operands can be variables, constants, or expressions. (You may also use double asterisks, **, to denote exponentiation. However, the circumflex is preferred because it is the standard BASIC-PLUS symbol for exponentiation.) In the assignment statement

```
210 LET Z = X ^ 2
```

X ^ 2 is the BASIC-PLUS representation of X^2 (X raised to the power of 2) or X multiplied by itself. If the value of X were 5, the number 25 would be assigned to Z.

Evaluating BASIC-PLUS Expressions

In order to be certain that the BASIC-PLUS expressions we write produce the desired results, we must understand the way expressions are evaluated in BASIC-PLUS. For example, in the expression A + B * C, is the multiplication performed before the addition or vice versa? Unfortunately, the algorithms used by BASIC-PLUS to analyze an expression and specify the list of operations indicated by the expression are beyond the scope of this text. However, we can formulate a set of *rules of evaluation of BASIC-PLUS expressions*. These rules, which are based upon the algebraic rules of *operator precedence*, are summarized next.

Rules of Expression Evaluation

a) All parenthesized subexpressions must be evaluated first. Nested parenthesized subexpressions must be evaluated inside-out, with the innermost subexpression evaluated first.

b) Operators in the same subexpression are evaluated in the following hierarchy:

- exponentiation, ^ or **   first (highest precedence)
- multiplication and division, *, / next
- addition and subtraction, +, −   last (lowest precedence)

(This is really just an extension of the familiar rule "multiplication and division before addition and subtraction".)

c) Operators in the same subexpression and at the same hierarchy level (such as + and −) are evaluated from left to right.

To illustrate the application of the rules for expression evaluation, we provide diagrams like the one shown next.

Example 4.3   The formula for computing the area of a triangle given its base and height is written in BASIC-PLUS as

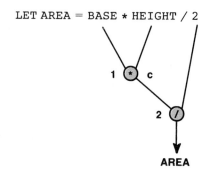

As illustrated in the diagram, each operator is enclosed in a circle. The order of operator evaluation and the rule applied at each step (rule a, b, or c) are indicated alongside the operator. If BASE = 8 and HEIGHT = 10, then the expression value would be 8 * 10 / 2 = 80 / 2 = 40.

Example 4.4   The formula for the area of a circle, $a = \pi r^2$, may be written in BASIC-PLUS as

    220 LET AREA = 3.14159 * RADIUS ^ 2

where π is represented by the constant 3.14159. The evaluation of this formula is shown below.

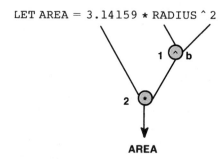

If R is 4, then A is 3.14159 * 4 ^ 2 = 3.14159 * 16 = 50.2654.

Example 4.5   The formula for computing the amount on deposit in a savings account after n days is given by

   $$amount = deposit \times (1 + rate/365)^n$$

where deposit is the initial deposit, rate is the yearly interest rate, and interest is computed on a daily basis. This formula is written and evaluated in BASIC-PLUS as

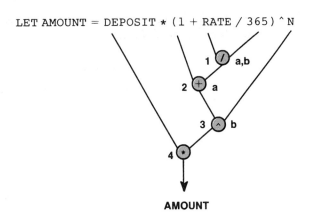

LET AMOUNT = DEPOSIT * (1 + RATE / 365) ^ N

AMOUNT

Example 4.6   The expression

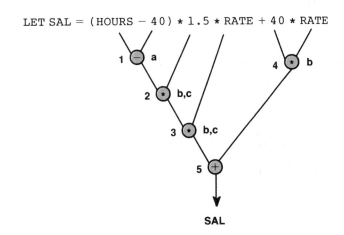

LET SAL = (HOURS − 40) * 1.5 * RATE + 40 * RATE

SAL

could be used to calculate the salary for an employee who has worked more than 40 hours and is paid time-and-a-half for all hours worked over 40. The subexpression in parentheses is evaluated first, according to rule (a). All multiplications are performed before the addition because of rule (b). The multiplications are performed from left to right as required by rule (c). Finally, the addition is performed and the assignment carried out.

It should be clear that inserting parentheses in an expression will affect the order of operator evaluation. If you are in doubt as to the order of evaluation that will be followed by BASIC-PLUS, you should use parentheses freely to clearly specify the intended order of evaluation.

Example 4.7   The diagrams that follow show how parentheses affect the order of operator evaluation and, thus, the value of the expression. Without parentheses, rule b would dictate the evaluation sequence shown in the diagram on the left; the insertion of parentheses would result in the evaluation sequence shown on the right. If X were 3, the value of the expression without parentheses would be 10; the value of the expression with parentheses would be 0.1.

$$1/1 + X^2$$

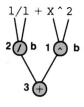

$$1/(1 + X^2)$$

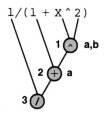

Equivalent mathematical formula:

$$1 + X^2$$

Equivalent mathematical formula:

$$\frac{1}{1 + X^2}$$

Exercise 4.1   Write the mathematical equivalents of the following BASIC-PLUS expressions:

a) (W + X) / (Y + Z)
b) G * H - F * W
c) A ^ (B ^ 2)
d) (B ^ 2 - 4 * A * C) ^ .5
e) (X * X - Y * Y) ^ .5
f) X * 2 + R / 365 ^ N
g) P2 - P1 / T2 - T1

Exercise 4.2:   Let X = 2, Y = 3, and Z = 5. What are the values of the following BASIC-PLUS expressions?

a) (X + Y) / (X + Z)
b) X + Z / X / Z
c) X + Y * Z
d) X / Y * Z
e) X ^ (Y - Z)
f) X ^ Y - Z

Exercise 4.3:   Show by example that (X/Y) * Z and X/(Y * Z) do indeed compute different values. What interpretation does BASIC-PLUS give to the expression X/Y * Z, i.e., is X/Y * Z equal to (X/Y) * Z, or is it equal to X/(Y * Z)?

Rules for Writing BASIC-PLUS Expressions

There are two inherent difficulties in representing a mathematical formula in BASIC-PLUS; one concerns multiplication, and the other concerns division. Multiplication can often be implied in a mathematical formula by writing the two items to be multiplied next to each other; e.g., a = bc. In

BASIC-PLUS, however, the * operator must always be used to indicate multiplication as in

```
240 LET A = B * C
```

The second difficulty arises in formulas involving division. We normally write these with the numerator and denominator on separate lines:

$$m = \frac{y - b}{x - a}$$

In BASIC-PLUS, all assignment statements must be written on a single line; consequently, parentheses are often needed to separate the numerator from the denominator, and to indicate clearly the order of evaluation of the operators in the expression. The formula above would be written as

```
250 LET M = (Y - B) / (X - A)
```

Example 4.8   This example illustrates how several mathematical formulas can be implemented in BASIC-PLUS using expressions involving multiple operators and parentheses.

Mathematical formula	BASIC-PLUS expression
$b^2 - 4ac$	`B ^ 2 - 4 * A * C`
$a + b - c$	`A + B - C`
$\dfrac{a + b}{c + d}$	`(A + B) / (C + D)`
a^b	`A ^ B`
$\dfrac{1}{1 + X^2}$	`1 / (1 + X ^ 2)`
$xy - \dfrac{a}{d^5}$	`X * Y - A / D ^ 5`
$1 + X^{-t}$	`1 + X ^ (-T)`

Example 4.9   The general formula for computing compound interest on a given principal investment is

$$t = p\left(1 + \frac{r}{f}\right)^{f \cdot N}$$

where
    t = the total amount of principal plus interest
    p = the initial principal investment
    r = the interest rate
    f = the frequency with which interest is compounded each year
    N = the number of years (term of investment)

In BASIC-PLUS we can write this formula as the assignment statement

```
LET TOTAL = PRINCIPAL * (1 + RATE / FREQ) ^ (FREQ * N)
```

This is a more general illustration of the interest formula in Example 4.5. The order of evaluation of this formula is shown next.

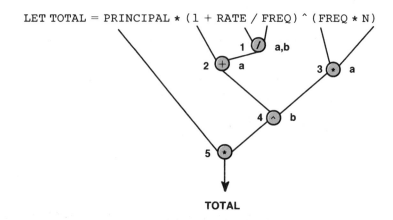

The points just illustrated are summarized in the following display.

Rules for Forming Expressions

1. Always specify multiplication and exponentiation explicitly by using the operator * or ^ where needed.
2. Use parentheses when required to control the order of operator evaluation.

Exercise 4.4: Write BASIC-PLUS assignment statements for the following:

a) $c = (a^2 + b^2)^{1/2}$
b) $y = 3x^4 + 2x^2 - 4$
c) $z = 3k^4 (7k + 4) - k^3$
d) $x = \dfrac{a^2(b^2 - c^2)}{bc}$
e) $d = (a^2 + b^2 + c^2)^{1/2}$
f) $z = \pi r^2$ (use $\pi = 3.14159$)
g) $r = 6.27 \times 10^{45}S$
h) $p = c_0 + c_1 x - c_2 x^2 - c_3 x^3 - c_4 x^4$
i) $b = a^{-5}$

Exercise 4.5: The formula for the monthly payment on an installment purchase is given by

$$\text{payment} = \frac{(\text{total price} - \text{down payment}) \times (\text{rate} - \text{temp})}{(\text{rate} - \text{temp})^{\text{months}}}$$

where

$$\text{temp} = \frac{12}{12 + \text{rate}}$$

Write the BASIC-PLUS assignment statements needed to compute this payment.

Exercise 4.6: Write the following formula in BASIC-PLUS and draw a diagram indicating its order of evaluation.

$$A = C + \frac{S}{Q} + \frac{H \times Q}{2.75 \times R}$$

Getting Complicated Expressions Correct—Using Immediate Mode

BASIC-PLUS permits the execution of an assignment statement in immediate mode without requiring the execution of an entire program. This feature can be extremely useful, especially for verifying the correctness of complicated expressions such as the ones used in Examples 4.6 and 4.9.

To use immediate mode, you simply type the statement (without a line number) that you wish executed. In the example below, the assignment and PRINT statements are executed in immediate mode, causing 1307.99 to be printed.

```
Ready

LET TOTAL = 1000 * (1 + .135 / 12) ^ (12 * 2)

Ready

PRINT TOTAL
   1307.99

Ready
```

These two statements can be used together to help double check the compound interest formula (see Example 4.9) for a principal of $1000 and an interest rate of 13.5% compounded monthly for a two-year term.

Expressions in PRINT Statements

We could have simplified our illustration of the use of immediate mode by taking advantage of a feature of BASIC-PLUS that permits the use of expressions in PRINT statements. Thus the statement

```
PRINT 1000 * (1 + .135 / 12) ^ (12 * 2)
```

could have been used in immediate mode in place of the two statements just shown. Expressions used in PRINT statements are evaluated according to the rules discussed earlier, then the result is printed.

Scientific Notation

As we have already seen, constants written with or without a decimal point may be used as operands anywhere in an expression. Constants also may be written in scientific notation. For example, the constant .0000053 (5.3×10^{-6} in scientific notation) may be written in BASIC-PLUS as 5.3E-6 where the letter E indicates multiplication times the base 10 raised to the indicated power. (The number after the E indicates the direction and the number of positions to move the decimal point. Thus, E-4 indicates that the decimal point is to be moved left four positions; E+3 indicates that the decimal point is to be moved right three positions.) The indicated power must always be written without a decimal point. Commas are not allowed in constants. BASIC-PLUS uses scientific notation in printing output values that fall outside a specified range. Therefore it is important that you understand how to read numbers that are expressed in scientific notation.

4.2 Functions

The *function* is a feature of the BASIC-PLUS language that is of considerable help in specifying numerically oriented computations that produce a single result. Functions are referenced directly in an expression; the value computed by the function is then substituted for the function reference.

Example 4.10 SQR is the name of a function that computes the square root of a non-negative value. Consider the BASIC-PLUS statement

```
300 LET Y = 5.5 + SQR(20.25)
```

The value computed by the function reference SQR(20.25) is 4.5; the result of the evaluation of the addition operation is 10 (5.5 + 4.5), which is stored in the variable Y.

BASIC-PLUS provides a number of standard mathematical functions, such as SQR, that may be referenced by the programmer. The names and descriptions of these functions are given in Table 4.1. The function name is usually followed by its *argument* enclosed in parentheses as shown in Example 4.10 (the argument is 20.25). Any legal BASIC-PLUS expressions, including numeric constants and variables, may be used as arguments for these functions. The function PI should not have an argument.

Table 4.1 BASIC-PLUS Mathematical Functions

Name	Description of the Result Returned
ABS	Absolute value of the argument
INT	The value of the largest integer less than or equal to the argument
FIX	The integer value (with fractional part removed) of the argument
EXP	The value of *e* raised to the power of the argument
LOG	The logarithm (to the base *e*) of the argument
	(see Exercise 4.9)
LOG10	The logarithm (to the base 10) of the argument
RND	A random number between 0 and 1. RND may be called with or without an argument. Either way you call it, you get the same result
SQR	The positive square root of the argument
SGN	The sign of the argument (+1 if the argument is positive; 0 if the argument is 0; −1 if the argument is negative)
ATN	The arctangent of the argument
COS	The cosine of the argument
SIN	The sine of the argument
TAN	The tangent of the argument
	The argument must be expressed in radians (see Examples 4.12 and 4.13)
PI	The constant 3.14159 (cannot have an argument)

The following examples illustrate the use of some of the functions in Table 4.1.

Example 4.11   The following program illustrates the use of the square root (SQR), absolute value (ABS), and integer (INT) functions.

```
100 !AN ILLUSTRATION OF SQR, ABS, AND INT
110 !
120    PRINT " X", " ABS(X)", "SQR(ABS(X))", "INT(X)"
130    FOR I = 1 TO 5
140        READ X
150        PRINT X, ABS(X), SQR(ABS(X)), INT(X)
160    NEXT I
170 !
```

(continued)

```
180     DATA -6.3, 0, -19, 7, 20.25
190 !
200     END
```

RUNNH

X	ABS(X)	SQR(ABS(X))	INT(X)
-6.3	6.3	2.50998	-7
0	0	0	0
-19	19	4.3589	-19
7	7	2.64575	7
20.25	20.25	4.5	20

Each line of the printout shows the value of X and three basic functions of X. In line 150, we see that it is permissible to include a function reference in the output list of a PRINT statement. (Actually, as we indicated earlier, any valid BASIC-PLUS expression can appear in an output list.)

The third item in the output list of line 150, SQR(ABS(X)), is an example of a nested function reference. Since the square root of a negative number is mathematically undefined, we should first determine the absolute value of X before computing the square root.

The INT function determines the largest integer that is less than or equal to its argument; hence, the INT function simply *truncates* or removes the fractional part of a positive argument (INT(20.25) = 20). However, for a negative argument like -6.3, the integer formed by truncating the fractional part, -6, would be larger than the argument. Thus the value of INT (-6.3) is -7, the "largest integer less than or equal to" -6.3. The value of FIX(-6.3) would be -6. FIX and INT always compute the same value for a positive argument.

Example 4.12   The following program illustrates the use of the sine (SIN) and cosine (COS) functions.

```
100 !AN ILLUSTRATION OF SIN AND COS
120 !
130     PRINT "X(IN DEGREES)", " SIN(X)", " COS(X)"
140 !
150     FOR X = 0 TO 180 STEP 15
160         LET SIN.X = SIN(X * PI / 180)
170         LET COS.X = COS(X * PI / 180)
180         PRINT X, SIN.X, COS.X
190     NEXT X
200 !
210     END
```

```
RUNNH
X(IN DEGREES)      SIN(X)          COS(X)
 0                 0               1
 15               .258819         .965926
 30               .5              .866025
 45               .707107         .707107
 60               .866025         .5
 75               .965926         .258819
 90               1               0
 105              .965926        -.258819
 120              .866025        -.5
 135              .707107        -.707107
 150              .5             -.866025
 165              .258819        -.965926
 180              .277556E-16    -1
```

It is important to remember that the input argument to the trigonometric functions SIN, COS, TAN, and ATN must be expressed in radians. To convert from degrees, a measure familiar to most of us, we take advantage of the fact that π radians is equal to 180 degrees. Using the BASIC-PLUS constant function PI (which has no arguments and always returns the value 3.14159) to represent π we have

$$1 \text{ degree} = \text{PI}/180 \text{ radians}$$
$$X \text{ degrees} = X \times \text{PI}/180 \text{ radians}$$

as shown in the above program.

Example 4.12 uses an expression (X * PI / 180) as the argument of a function. The value of the expression is computed first and then the function is applied to this value. Since the expression is evaluated twice inside the loop (lines 160 and 170) it would be more efficient to assign the value PI / 180 to a variable RADIANS before entering the loop, and to compute Y = X * RADIANS as the first step in the loop body. This is left as an exercise (Exercise 4.7).

If you look closely at the output from the program for Example 4.12, you will see that the sine of 180 degrees was not computed to be exactly zero. This is due to a loss of accuracy in the computation. Loss of accuracy is discussed in more detail in Section 4.7.

The next example illustrates the conversion of formulas from physics into BASIC-PLUS statements. You need not be concerned if the formulas are unfamiliar. The main point of the example is to illustrate their application in a BASIC-PLUS program.

Example 4.13 Prince Valiant is trying to rescue Rapunzel by shooting an arrow with a rope attached through her tower window, which is 100 feet off the ground. We will assume that the arrow travels at a constant velocity. The time it takes to reach the tower is given by the formula

$$t = \frac{d}{v \cos \theta}$$

where d is the distance Prince Valiant is standing from the tower, v is the velocity of the arrow, and θ is its angle of elevation.

Our task is to determine whether or not the Prince's arrow goes through the window by computing its distance off the ground when it reaches the tower, as given by the formula

$$h = vt \sin \theta - \frac{gt^2}{2}$$

where g is the gravitational constant. For the arrow to go through the window, h should be between 100 and 110 feet. We will print out an appropriate message to help Prince Valiant correct his aim.

The program and a sample run are shown in Fig. 4.1. The program contains a nested IF–THEN–ELSE statement (line 450). The flow diagram corresponding to this statement is shown in Fig. 4.2 (see p. 142). We implemented the nested decision in a slightly different form than shown in Chapter 3, so that each line would fit. We will discuss this form further in Section 7.1.

```
110 !PRINCE VALIANT TAKES AIM AT RAPUNZEL
120 !
130 !PRINT INTRODUCTORY REMARKS
140     PRINT "DEAR PRINCE,"
150     PRINT "RAPUNZEL, LESS HER GOLDEN TRESSES,"
160     PRINT "IS LOCKED INSIDE THE HIGH TOWER"
170     PRINT "BY THE WICKED WITCH."
180     PRINT "YOUR MISSION, PRINCE, IS TO"
190     PRINT "SHOOT AN ARROW WITH ROPE"
200     PRINT "ATTACHED, AT SUCH AN ANGLE"
210     PRINT "AND SUCH A SPEED AS TO SECURE"
220     PRINT "THE FAIR MAIDEN'S DESCENT."
230     PRINT
235 !
240 !INITIALIZE PROGRAM CONSTANT
250     !G IS GRAVITATIONAL CONSTANT (IN FT/SEC2)
260     LET G = 32.17
270 !
280 !REQUEST ENTRY OF DISTANCE (D), VELOCITY (V) AND
290 !ANGLE OF ELEVATION (THETA) FOR ARROW
300     INPUT "ENTER DISTANCE (IN FEET)"; D
310     INPUT "ENTER SPEED OF ARROW (IN FEET/SEC)"; V
320     INPUT "ENTER ANGLE (IN DEGREES)"; THETA
330     PRINT
340 !
350 !CONVERT DEGREES TO RADIANS
360     LET RADIANS = THETA * PI / 180
370 !
380 !COMPUTE TRAVEL TIME (T) AND HEIGHT (H) OF ARROW
390     LET T = D / (V * COS(RADIANS))
400     LET H = V * T * SIN(RADIANS) - (G * T ^ 2) / 2
410 !
```

(continued)

```
420  !CHECK TO SEE IF ARROW HEIGHT AT TOWER
430  !IS BETWEEN 100 AND 110 FEET
440  !PRINT APPROPRIATE MESSAGE
450     IF H < 0 THEN                                        &
            PRINT "BAD SHOT, ARROW FELL SHORT"               &
        ELSE IF H < 100 THEN                                 &
            PRINT "ARROW TOO LOW, HEIGHT WAS"; H             &
        ELSE IF H <= 110 THEN                                &
            PRINT "BULL'S EYE PRINCE!"                       &
        ELSE                                                 &
            PRINT "ARROW TOO HIGH. HEIGHT WAS"; H
460  !
470     END


RUNNH
DEAR PRINCE,
RAPUNZEL, LESS HER GOLDEN TRESSES,
IS LOCKED INSIDE THE HIGH TOWER
BY THE WICKED WITCH.
YOUR MISSION, PRINCE, IS TO
SHOOT AN ARROW WITH ROPE
ATTACHED, AT SUCH AN ANGLE
AND SUCH A SPEED AS TO SECURE
THE FAIR MAIDEN'S DESCENT.

ENTER DISTANCE (IN FEET)? 100
ENTER SPEED OF ARROW (IN FEET/SEC)? 500
ENTER ANGLE (IN DEGREES)? 47

BULL'S EYE PRINCE!
```

Fig. 4.1 Program and sample output for Example 4.13.

Example 4.14   There is one additional BASIC-PLUS function, TAB, that appears only in PRINT statements and is used to control spacing across an output line. Whenever TAB is referenced, the value of its argument determines the column in which the next item to be printed begins. The PRINT statement at line 110 below would display the values of A1, A2, and A3 in three zones of width 10 (A2 starts in column 11 and A3 starts in column 21). In the second PRINT statement, the width of each zone depends on the value of N.

```
110 PRINT A1; TAB(11); A2; TAB(21); A3
120 PRINT A1; TAB(N); A2; TAB(2 * N); A3
```

Example 4.15   The random number function RND can be important in programming computer simulations of real events (see, for example, Problem 4N). The function returns a *random number* between 0 and 1 (including 0, but not 1).

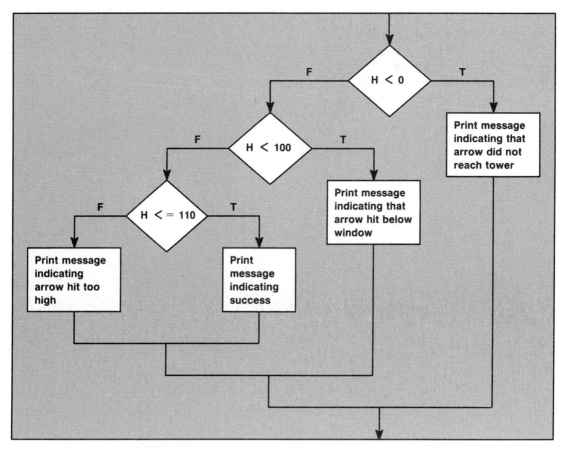

Fig. 4.2 Flow diagram for nested decision structure in Example 4.13.

The following example generates 10 random numbers displayed to six decimal places. How many of these numbers would you expect to be greater than or equal to 0.5? How many were, in fact, greater than or equal to 0.5?

```
100 PRINT "TABLE OF TEN RANDOM NUMBERS"
110 FOR I = 1 TO 10
120     PRINT RND,
130     NEXT I
140 END
```

```
RUNNH
TABLE OF TEN RANDOM NUMBERS
 .204       .2581      .533074     .132211     .995
 .783713    .741854    .313        .709588     .6711
```

One word of caution is in order here: If you run the above program (Example 4.15) again, you will get the same set of random numbers. If you wish to have a different set of random numbers for each run, you should insert the following statement in your program:

```
90 RANDOMIZE
```

This statement may be abbreviated as RANDOM and should be placed before the first call to RND in your program.

Exercise 4.7: (*For the more mathematically inclined student*) Rewrite the program shown in Example 4.12. Compute and print the value of RADIANS = PI/180 before entering the loop. (This value is the decimal representation of the number of radians in one degree.) Then compute Y = X * RADIANS inside the loop and use Y as the argument of the functions SIN and COS. Compare your output to the results shown in Example 4.12. Which results are more accurate? Do you have any idea why?

Exercise 4.8: (*Quadratic equations*) The roots of an equation of the form

$$y = ax^2 + bx + c$$

where a, b, and c are real numbers may be computed as follows.

$$r1 = \frac{-b + \sqrt{b^2 - 4ac}}{2a}$$

$$r2 = \frac{-b - \sqrt{b^2 - 4ac}}{2a}$$

Write a program to read in three values a, b, and c, and determine and print r1 and r2. Test your program with the following values for a, b and c.

a	b	c
1	1	-6
1	-8	16
1	0	-1
1	0	1
15	-2	-1
0	0	0

For each set of three values, a, b, and c, your program should test the value of the *discriminant* $d = b^2 - 4ac$. If d is negative, print the message "NO REAL ROOTS" and omit the remaining computation for the current values of a, b, and c.

Exercise 4.9: The numeric constant *e* is known as Euler's Number. It has had an established place in mathematics alongside the Archimedean number π for over 200 years. The approximate value of *e* (accurate to five decimal places) is 2.71828. Write a BASIC-PLUS program that prints EXP(X) and LOG(X) for integer values of X from 1 to 10.

Exercise 4.10: (*For the more mathematically inclined student*) Let N = 1000. Write a program to compute $P = 0.1 * N$ and $S = \sum_{i=1}^{N} 0.1$ (where $\sum_{i=1}^{N} 0.1$

is equal to 0.1 added to itself 1000 times). You will need a loop to compute S. Following the loop your program should print the values of S and P and also print an appropriate message indicating whether or not S and P are equal.

Exercise 4.11: The formula for the velocity of a body dropped from rest is v = gt, where g is the acceleration due to gravity and t is time (air resistance is ignored here). Write a loop to compute v at five-second intervals (starting with t = 0) for a pickle dropped from a building that is 600 meters tall, with g = 9.81 meters/second.[2] (*Hint*: Use the formula $t = \sqrt{2s/g}$ to determine the time, TGROUND, it takes for the pickle to hit the ground (s equals 600). Use TGROUND to limit the number of repetitions of the loop that produces the table.)

Exercise 4.12: Modify the Prince and Rapunzel program (Fig. 4.1) so that the velocity of the arrow will be increased automatically by 10 feet/second if the arrow is too low, and decreased by 8 feet/second if the arrow is too high. You will need a loop which terminates when the arrow enters the window.

Exercise 4.13: The *modulus* of two positive integers i and j is defined to be the remainder obtained from dividing i by j. For example, if i is 5 and j is 3, then the modulus of 5 and 3, written mod(5, 3), is 2. Similarly, mod(9, 3) = 0. Use the INT function to write a BASIC-PLUS statement to compute the modulus of any two positive integers i and j.

Exercise 4.14: Using the INT function, write a BASIC-PLUS statement to round any positive real value X to the nearest two decimal places. (*Hint*: If the third decimal digit in X is between 0 and 4, then round down by truncating all digits to the right of the second digit. If the third digit is between 5 and 9, round up.)

Exercise 4.15: Write a program that will accept a distance measurement (specified in feet and inches) and print this measurement and its equivalent in inches, yards, and meters. Both input items should be integers. The output should be a five column table with two columns used for the input values and three columns for the output. Test your program on 10 measurements of your own choice. Use a FOR loop. (*Hint*: One meter = 39.37 inches.)

4.3 Integer and String Data in BASIC-PLUS

In all our programming so far, we have manipulated only numeric information. In fact, we have manipulated only one kind of numeric data—*real numbers* (numbers that can have a fractional part). In this section, we introduce two additional BASIC-PLUS data types, *integers* (numbers that cannot have a fractional part) and *strings*. VAX-11 BASIC users should refer to the DECLARE statement in Appendixes I and J.

In order to illustrate the differences among these data types, we have provided an example in which all three types are used. The program shown in Fig. 4.3 is similar to the program for Problem 3C (the Bank Certificate Problem), except that the string variable HOLDER.NAME$ (an input variable used to contain the name of the certificate holder) has been added. We have also used two integer variables, YEAR% and TERM%, in this program.

```
100 !BANK CERTIFICATE PROBLEM
110 !
140 !ENTER THE NAME OF THE CERTIFICATE HOLDER
150     INPUT "ENTER NAME OF CERTIFICATE HOLDER";    &
               HOLDER.NAME$
160 !ENTER DEPOSIT, TERM, AND RATE
165     INPUT "AMOUNT (IN DOLLARS)"; DEPOSIT
170     INPUT "TERM (IN YEARS)"; TERM%
180     INPUT "RATE (IN PERCENT)"; RATE
185     LET DEC.RATE = RATE / 100
210 !
220 !COMPUTE AND PRINT INTEREST AND CERTIFICATE VALUE
230 !AFTER EACH YEAR OF THE TERM
235     PRINT
240     PRINT "CERTIFICATE VALUE FOR "; HOLDER.NAME$
255     PRINT \ PRINT "YEAR", "INTEREST", "VALUE"
260     LET CERT.VAL = DEPOSIT
270     FOR YEAR% = 1 TO TERM%
280        LET INTEREST = CERT.VAL * DEC.RATE
290        LET CERT.VAL = CERT.VAL + INTEREST
300        PRINT YEAR%, INTEREST, CERT.VAL
310     NEXT YEAR%
320 !
330     END
```

```
RUNNH
ENTER NAME OF CERTIFICATE HOLDER? "EMMYLOU HARRIS"
AMOUNT (IN DOLLARS)? 3150.75
TERM (IN YEARS)? 10
RATE (IN PERCENT)? 12.5

CERTIFICATE VALUE FOR EMMYLOU HARRIS

YEAR         INTEREST        VALUE
 1            393.84         3544.59
 2            443.07         3987.66
 3            498.46         4486.12
 4            560.77         5046.89
 5            630.86         5677.75
 6            709.72         6387.47
 7            798.43         7185.90
 8            898.24         8084.14
 9           1010.52         9094.66
10           1136.85        10231.49
```

Fig. 4.3 An illustration of the use of real, integer, and string data.

A brief study of this program will aid your understanding of the differences among the data types. The input to the program consisted of the string

    "EMMYLOU HARRIS"

the integer

    10

and the real data

    12.5
    3150.75

These data illustrate the differences in the *external representations* of integer, real, and string data. A numeric (real or integer) data item consists of a string of decimal digits possibly preceded by a sign (+ or −). Numeric data (such as 12.5 and 3150.75) containing a decimal point are treated as real numbers and are stored with a fractional part. Numeric data (such as 10 and 1) not containing a decimal point are treated as integers; these numbers do not have a fractional part. String data items such as "EMMYLOU HARRIS" consist of a string of characters enclosed in quotation marks. Any character in the BASIC-PLUS character set may be included in the string. There is a special string, called the *null string*, which contains no characters and is written as two consecutive quote symbols " ".

Integer Data and Variables

The percent sign is added to integer variables (such as TERM% and YEAR%) to distinguish them from real variables. Only integer constants can be stored in integer variables. The percent sign may also be used in programs to distinguish integer constants from reals, but this is not required. The percent sign must not be used with integer values entered as program data via a READ or INPUT statement.

Example 4.16   The READ–DATA statements

    100 READ X, I%, Y, J%
    110 DATA 25.7, 10, 35.2, 30

assign the real data 25.7 and 35.2 to the real variables X and Y, respectively. The integer data 10 and 30 are assigned to the integer variables I% and J%.

The main advantages to using integers in BASIC-PLUS programs relate to issues of program efficiency. Integer arithmetic is faster than arithmetic involving real data and integers take up less memory space than reals (integers may range in value from −32768 to +32767, whereas reals range from 10^{-38} to 10^{38}). Integers are especially good for use as counters in loops. Counters (such as YEAR% in the Bank Certificate Example) normally do not have fractional parts; the efficiency resulting from the use of integer counters can be important in programs containing loops with thousands of repetitions.

The next example illustrates a number of important points about working with integer data.

Example 4.17
a) −12% and −12 are legal integer constants.
b) −12.0 is a legal real constant.
c) −12.0% is illegal (the percent sign may not be used with a constant that contains a decimal point).
d) 40677% is illegal (40677 is too large to be an integer).
e) 62E+2% is illegal (scientific notation cannot be used with integers).
f) LET TRUNC% = −25.4 (stores the truncated value −25 in TRUNC%).
g) LET X = 20% / 6% (stores the value 3 in X).

As shown in part (f), any attempt to store a real value (with a fractional part) in an integer variable results in the *truncation* (chopping off) of the fraction—the fractional part is lost. Similarly, as shown in part (g), the result of dividing one integer variable or constant by another is still an integer—the fractional part again is lost. Note that this truncation will occur only if both operands have a percent sign attached.

Program Style

Errors caused by missing "%"

We will not use integer variables too often in this text, since there is little that can be done with them that cannot also be done with real variables. In addition, use of integer variables introduces another potential source of error—forgetting to consistently attach the symbol "%" to integer variable names. As ITEM and ITEM% are considered different variables in a BASIC-PLUS program, failure to attach the symbol "%" will result in the use of the wrong variable (ITEM instead of ITEM%) in a computation. This will not be detected as an error by BASIC-PLUS, but will cause erroneous results. It also may be extremely difficult to diagnose such an error in all but the shortest programs. For these reasons we will use integer variables only in cases where considerable time or memory may be saved. Such examples will be illustrated later in the text.

Exercise 4.16: Let A = 7.5, B = 2.5, I% = 3, and K% = 2. Carry out the computations indicated by the following BASIC-PLUS assignment statements. Show all work.

a) LET Q = A / 3 * 2
b) LET M% = I% + K% * 4
c) LET M% = I% / K% * 5%
d) LET Q = I% / K% - 1
e) LET M% = A / 3 + 7
f) LET Q = A + B / .5 ^ 2

String Data and Variables

In the first three chapters of the text we made considerable use of *string constants* (strings of characters enclosed in quotes) for annotating program output. In the program in Figure 4.3 we also used the BASIC-PLUS *string variable* (first introduced in Example 1.1). String variables are distinguished from numeric variables by the use of the symbol "$" after the name of a variable. Any BASIC-PLUS identifier followed by a dollar sign is a legal string variable, for example, A$, CITY$, HOLDER.NAME$. Simple assignment statements may be used to store string data in string variables.

```
400 LET CITY$ = "BALTIMORE"
410 LET MY.NAME$ = "FRANK"
420 LET SSNO$ = "219-40-8677"
430 LET CHILD$ = "FRANK'S KID"
```

String data may be read using data entry statements such as

```
440 READ CITY$
450 INPUT CHILD$
```

Character string constants appearing in PRINT or assignment statements must be enclosed in either single or double quotes. However, string data that are entered via READ or INPUT statements do not have to be enclosed in quotes. If quotes are not used, leading or trailing blanks will be ignored. Note that if double quotes are used to enclose a string, a single quote may be used within the string (and vice versa). It is not permissible to enter string data containing a comma unless quotes are used. String and numeric data may be entered using the same data entry statements.

Example 4.18   The READ–DATA statements

```
100 READ X, TREE$, Y, FRUIT$
110 DATA 25.7, "TREE, APPLE", 9.37, MY BANANAS
```

would result in the following assignment of values:

X	TREE$	Y	FRUIT$
25.7	TREE, ☐ APPLE	9.37	MY ☐ BANANAS

where the symbol ☐ denotes the blank character. Note that the first string in line 110 must be enclosed in quotes, since it contains a comma.

Numeric operations on strings are not allowed in BASIC-PLUS; however, it is permissible to compare strings. This means that statements such as

```
200 IF ANSWER$ = "YES" THEN PRINT "CONTINUE"
210 IF A$ <> S$ THEN PRINT "UNEQUAL STRINGS"
```

are allowed. The first condition evaluates to true if the string constant "YES" is stored in the string variable ANSWER$; the second condition evaluates to true if the string variables A$ and S$ have different values.

In BASIC-PLUS, order comparisons on string variables can be performed using the relational operators =, <, <=, >, >=, <> and ==. The results of the order comparisons depend upon the *alphabetical (lexical)* ordering of the strings. The rules that apply in all string comparisons are summarized in Table 4.2.

The alphabetical ordering of strings in BASIC-PLUS is based on the *collating sequence* (ordering) of the BASIC-PLUS characters. This ordering is given in the ASCII (American Scientific Code for Information Interchange) Character Code provided in Appendix F. Note that according to this table,

" " < "$" < "%" < "(" < ")" < "." < "0" <
    "1" < . . .   < "9" < "A" < "B" . . .   < "Z" < "^"
    < "a" < "b" < . . .   < "z"

Table 4.2 BASIC-PLUS String Comparison Operators

Operator	Example	Description
=	A$ = B$	The strings A$ and B$ are equal except for possible trailing blanks
<	A$ < B$	The string A$ precedes B$ in alphabetical (lexical) order
<=	A$ <= B$	The string A$ is equal to or precedes B$
>	A$ > B$	The string A$ follows B$
>=	A$ >= B$	The string A$ is equal to or follows B$
<>	A$ <> B$	The strings A$ and B$ are not equal
==	A$ == B$	The strings A$ and B$ are identical, i.e., they have the same length and the same characters. == is the same as = except that == also considers trailing blanks

Thus the digits and letters are ordered as we would expect and the blank precedes all letters, digits, and special characters. Furthermore lower case letters ("a", "b", etc.) follow upper case letters ("A", "B", etc.).

Example 4.19 We can use the information in Table 4.2 and Appendix F to determine the results of the following string comparisons.

	Condition	Value	Explanation
a)	`"A" < "B"`	TRUE	`"A"` precedes `"B"`
b)	`"BART" < "BARTH"`	TRUE	`"BART"` precedes `"BARTH"`
c)	`"*" > ")"`	TRUE	`"*"` follows `")"`
d)	`"12" <= "14"`	TRUE	`"2"` precedes `"4"` (< also holds)
e)	`"12" <= "2"`	TRUE	`"1"` precedes `"2"`
f)	`"BART" = "BART "`	TRUE	The strings are equal except for trailing blanks
g)	`"BART" == "BART "`	FALSE	The strings are not identical
h)	`"BART" <> "BART "`	FALSE	The strings are equal except for trailing blanks which are ignored when comparing for equality using = or <>
i)	`"FRIEDMAN" >= "FRIED"`	TRUE	`"FRIEDMAN"` is longer than `"FRIED"` (> also holds)
j)	`" " < "1"`	TRUE	The blank precedes all characters in the collating sequence
k)	`"    " = ""`	TRUE	The strings differ only by the blanks in the string on the left (the string on the right is the null string which contains no characters)

Keep in mind that string comparison in BASIC-PLUS proceeds from left to right, character by character, until a difference is found. As shown in part (b) of Example 4.19, if one string is longer than another but otherwise the same, the shorter string is said to precede the longer one unless all extra characters are blank. In the latter case the two strings are considered *equal* ("=", see part f), but not *identical* ("==", see part g). Thus the null string, "" is equal (but not identical) to any string of all blanks, no matter how long (see part k).

Also remember that comparison of numbers in string form is not the same as numeric comparison. Thus as shown in Example 4.19e, `"12" < "2"` is true since `"1"` precedes `"2"` lexically; yet numerically, 12 > 2.

BASIC-PLUS also allows the use of the string operator "+" for the concatenation (joining together) of string data. This operator is discussed in more detail in Chapter 9.

Exercise 4.17: Let A$ = "KOFF", B$ = "KOFFMAN", and C$ = "1234". Indicate which of the following conditions are true and which are false.

a) A$ < B$
b) "KOFF " = A$
c) "1234" = "4321"
d) "5" > C$
e) "KOFF " == A$
f) A$ < C$
g) "KOFF " > "KOFF"
h) C$ >= "12345"
i) "1234" == "4321"
j) C$ > "1234 "

Exercise 4.18: Indicate the effect of the following groups of statements; identify any illegal statements.

a) 100 READ SSNO$, HOUR, RATE
    110 DATA "033-30-0785", 40, 5.63
    120 PRINT "SOCIAL SECURITY NUMBER", SSNO$
b) 100 READ SSNO, HOUR, RATE
    110 DATA 033-30-0785, 40, 5.63
    120 PRINT "SOCIAL SECURITY NUMBER", SSNO
c) 100 READ X$, Y$
    110 LET S = X$
    120 LET T = S + X$
    130 DATA "AB", "35"

INPUT LINE Statement

As we indicated earlier, strings entered via an INPUT statement may not contain commas or semicolons unless the string is enclosed in quotes. The INPUT LINE statement can be used to enter and store an arbitrary string of characters (including quotation marks, spaces, and punctuation characters) without enclosing the characters in quotes. The INPUT LINE statement accepts and stores all characters typed after the prompt symbol "?" up to and including the line terminator (normally <RETURN>).

Example 4.20   The following program reads and prints two strings using INPUT LINE.

```
100 PRINT "ENTER AWARD WINNER NAME";
110 INPUT LINE AWARD.WINNER$
120 PRINT "ENTER STREET ADDRESS OF WINNER";
130 INPUT LINE ADDRESS$
140 PRINT AWARD.WINNER$
150 PRINT ADDRESS$
160 PRINT "END OF LIST"
170 END
```

```
RUNNH
ENTER AWARD WINNER NAME? Felice Hymson
ENTER STREET ADDRESS OF WINNER? 135 Lynford St.
Felice Hymson

135 Lynford St.

END OF LIST
```

In examining the output for this problem, we should note that the return key was pressed after the entry of each of the two data lines. This return terminates each entered line and is itself entered and stored by INPUT LINE as part of the input strings AWARD.WINNER$ and ADDRESS$. When these strings are printed the return at the end causes an extra line feed, thereby producing the line spaces between each of the three output lines.

The effect of the INPUT LINE statement is summarized in the following display.

The INPUT LINE Statement

INPUT LINE *string-variable*

Interpretation: The INPUT LINE statement may be used to enter a string of characters (including quotes, spaces, and punctuations) up to and including the line terminator (<RETURN>, <LINE FEED>, <ESCAPE>). As many as 132 characters may be typed after the prompt symbol "?". Only one string (hence only one *string-variable*) may be entered at a time through this statement.

 ## 4.4 The Registered Voters List

The following problem illustrates the manipulation of string data.

Problem 4A For the local election next Tuesday, town officials have decided to use three clerks, Abraham, Martin, and John, to verify that each resident wishing to vote is legally registered and, of course, votes only once. The officials decided that in order to distribute the registered voters fairly evenly among the three clerks, they would assign Abraham to check voters with last names beginning with A through I, Martin to check the voters with last names beginning with J through R, and John to check voters with last names beginning with S through Z.

We will write a program to print a complete voter list with the correct clerk assignment for each voter. The program should read the voter name, house number, and street name for each registered voter in the township. The program will then print a master list with the house number and street name printed first, followed by the voter name, with the clerk assigned to the voter printed last. We will assume that all names are entered correctly, with the last names entered first. The number of voters assigned to each clerk should be printed at the end.

Discussion: The flow diagrams for this problem are drawn in Figs. 4.4a and b, followed by the data table.

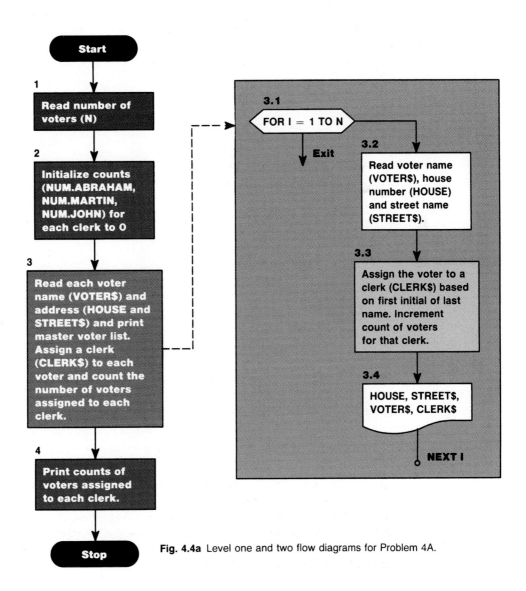

Fig. 4.4a Level one and two flow diagrams for Problem 4A.

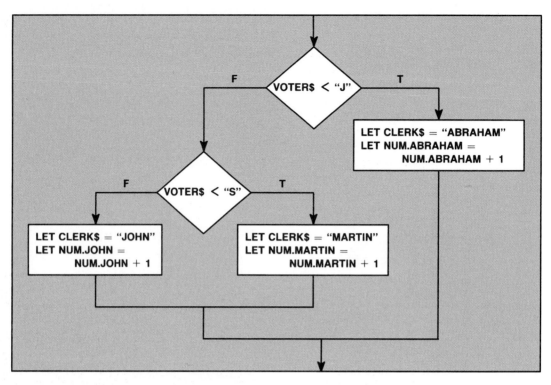

Fig. 4.4b Refinement of Step 3.3 of Problem 4A.

DATA TABLE FOR PROBLEM 4A	Input Variables		Program Variables		Output Variables	
	N:	Number of voters	I:	Loop control variable	CLERK$:	Clerk assigned to a voter
	VOTER$:	Voter name			NUM.ABRAHAM, NUM.MARTIN, NUM.JOHN:	Counts of voters assigned to Abraham, Martin, and John, respectively
	HOUSE:	House number for voter				
	STREET$:	Street name for voter				

NUM.ABRAHAM, NUM.MARTIN, and NUM.JOHN represent the counts of voters assigned to each of the three clerks and they must be initialized to zero (Step 2 of Fig. 4.4a). Step 3 is the only step of the level one flow diagram needing refinement; its refinement consists of a loop in which the data for each voter are entered and the clerk is determined. The latter operation is performed by Step 3.3, which is refined in Figure 4.4b. Figure 4.4b shows a nested decision structure. The first condition (VOTER$ < "J") separates out all voter names that begin with the letters A–I; the second condition (VOTER$ < "S") separates all other names into the remaining two categories (J–R) or (S–Z). The program and a sample run are shown in Fig. 4.5. The nested decision (line 290) is implemented using subroutines since each alternative task consists of two steps.

```
100 !TOWNSHIP VOTER/CLERK ASSIGNMENT LIST
110 !
120 !PRINTS MASTER VOTER LIST AND ASSIGNED CLERK
130 !ALSO COUNTS NUMBER OF VOTERS FOR EACH CLERK
140 !   VOTERS A-I ASSIGNED TO CLERK ABRAHAM
150 !   VOTERS J-R ASSIGNED TO CLERK MARTIN
160 !   VOTERS S-Z ASSIGNED TO CLERK JOHN
165 !
170 !READ AND PRINT NUMBER OF REGISTERED VOTERS
175     READ N
180     PRINT "THE NUMBER OF REGISTERED VOTERS IS"; N
185 !
190 !INITIALIZE COUNTS
200     LET NUM.ABRAHAM = 0
210     LET NUM.MARTIN = 0
220     LET NUM.JOHN = 0
230 !
240 !READ VOTER NAME (VOTER$), HOUSE ADDRESS (HOUSE),
245 !AND STREET NAME (STREET$) FOR EACH VOTER. ASSIGN
250 !CLERK (CLERK$) TO EACH VOTER; UPDATE COUNTER FOR
255 !THE CLERK; PRINT HOUSE, STREET$, VOTER$, CLERK$
260     PRINT \ PRINT "VOTER ADDRESS";
265     PRINT TAB(30); "NAME"; TAB(45); "CLERK"
270     FOR I = 1 TO N
280         READ VOTER$, HOUSE, STREET$
290         IF VOTER$ < "J" THEN GOSUB 1000           &
                ELSE IF VOTER$ < "S" THEN GOSUB 2000 &
                ELSE GOSUB 3000
300         PRINT HOUSE; STREET$; TAB(26); VOTER$;  &
                TAB(44); CLERK$
310     NEXT I
320 !
480 !PRINT COUNTS
485     PRINT
490     PRINT "NUMBER ASSIGNED TO ABRAHAM IS"; &
                NUM.ABRAHAM
500     PRINT "NUMBER ASSIGNED TO MARTIN IS";  &
                NUM.MARTIN
510     PRINT "NUMBER ASSIGNED TO JOHN IS";    &
                NUM.JOHN
```

(continued)

```
520 !
530 !INITIAL VOTER LIST
535     DATA 6
540     DATA "ADAMS, JOHN",  125, "ABBOT ST."
550     DATA "ADAMS, MARY",  129, "ABBOT ST."
560     DATA "YOUNG, ALEX",  137, "VERNON AVE."
570     DATA "KING, MARTIN", 270, "PEACHTREE LANE"
580     DATA "JONES, BILLY", 112, "XAVIER RD."
590     DATA "ICEMAN, JOE",  286, "ZOO AVE."
600 !
610     STOP
620 !
630 !
1000 !SUBROUTINES FOR NESTED IF-THEN-ELSE AT LINE 290
1010 !IF VOTER$ < "J" THEN CLERK IS ABRAHAM
1020     LET CLERK$ = "ABRAHAM"
1030     LET NUM.ABRAHAM = NUM.ABRAHAM + 1
1040     RETURN
2000 !ELSE IF VOTER$ < "S" THEN CLERK IS MARTIN
2010     LET CLERK$ = "MARTIN"
2020     LET NUM.MARTIN = NUM.MARTIN + 1
2030     RETURN
3000 !ELSE CLERK IS JOHN
3010     LET CLERK$ = "JOHN"
3020     LET NUM.JOHN = NUM.JOHN + 1
3030     RETURN
3040 !END OF SUBROUTINES FOR NESTED IF AT LINE 290
3050 !
3060     END    !VOTER PROGRAM
```

```
RUNNH
THE NUMBER OF REGISTERED VOTERS IS 6

VOTER ADDRESS              NAME           CLERK
 125 ABBOT ST.         ADAMS, JOHN     ABRAHAM
 129 ABBOT ST.         ADAMS, MARY     ABRAHAM
 137 VERNON AVE.       YOUNG, ALEX     JOHN
 270 PEACHTREE LANE    KING, MARTIN    MARTIN
 112 XAVIER RD.        JONES, BILLY    MARTIN
 286 ZOO AVE.          ICEMAN, JOE     ABRAHAM


NUMBER ASSIGNED TO ABRAHAM IS 3
NUMBER ASSIGNED TO MARTIN IS 2
NUMBER ASSIGNED TO JOHN IS 1
Stop at line 610
```

Fig. 4.5 Program and sample run for Problem 4A.

4.5 The Prime Number Problem

The prime numbers have been studied by mathematicians for many years. A *prime number* is an integer that has no divisors other than 1 and itself. In order to demonstrate that a number is not prime, we have to identify one or more divisors. In solving this problem we shall introduce the use of a string variable as a program flag. We will treat all numeric data for this problem as type integer and make use of the remainder truncation resulting from integer division.

Problem 4B   Find and print all exact divisors of an integer N% other than 1 and N% it-self. If there are no divisors, print a message indicating that N% is prime. The value of N% will be provided as a data item to be read in by the program.

Discussion: The approach we will take is to see whether we can find an integer, DIVISOR%, which evenly divides N% (with no remainder). We shall print any exact divisors.

   The initial data table for this problem is shown next. The level one flow diagram is shown in Fig. 4.6a.

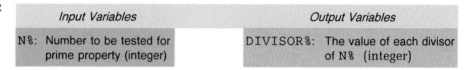

DATA TABLE FOR PROBLEM 4B	Input Variables	Output Variables
	N%: Number to be tested for prime property (integer)	DIVISOR%: The value of each divisor of N% (integer)

Step 3 of the level one diagram requires additional refinement. In carrying out Step 4, we need to know whether any divisors were found in Step 3. Consequently, Step 3 must test each integer between 2 and N% − 1 to see whether it divides N%. We will use a string variable N.PRIME$ to

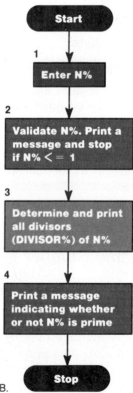

Fig. 4.6a Flow diagram for Problem 4B.

summarize the results of this test. The value of N.PRIME$ will indicate whether N% is still considered a prime number (N.PRIME$ equals "TRUE") or is known to be not prime (N.PRIME$ equals "FALSE"). The additional data table entry for N.PRIME$ is shown below. The refinement of Step 3 is drawn in Fig. 4.6b.

Program Variables	
N.PRIME$:	Indicates whether N% is considered prime, i.e., whether a divisor was found

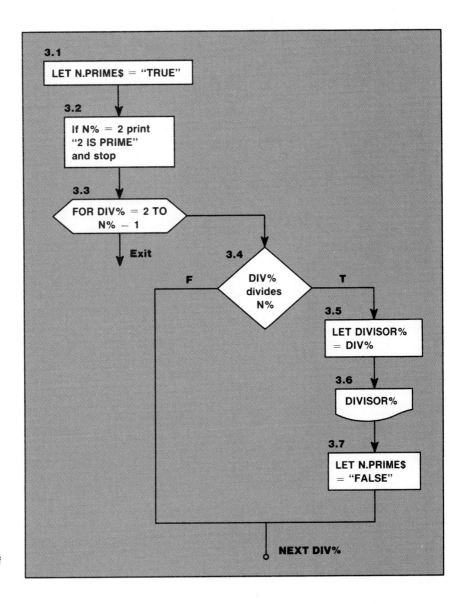

Fig. 4.6b Refinement of Step 3 of Problem 4B.

In Fig. 4.6b, a FOR loop is used to check all integers between 2 and N%-1 inclusive as possible divisors of N%. The integer variable DIV% is the loop control variable for this loop. If N% is the integer 2, the loop would not be executed as N% − 1 is less than 2. Step 3.2 handles this special case (See the Program Style display following Fig. 4.7).

ADDITIONAL DATA TABLE ENTRY FOR PROBLEM 4B

Program Variables

DIV%: Represents each integer tested as a divisor of N%

Step 3.4, the divisibility test, is performed by evaluating the condition

(N% / DIV%) * DIV% = N%

The first step is to calculate the quotient of N% divided by DIV%. If there is no remainder (i.e., if DIV% is a divisor of N%), then when the quotient is multiplied by DIV%, the result should be equal to N%. This computation is illustrated below for N% = 4%, DIV% = 2%.

(4% / 2%) * 2% = 2% * 2% = 4%

If DIV% does not divide N% exactly, the remainder is lost (remember, all of the variables involved in this computation are integers). Consequently, when the quotient is multiplied by DIV%, the result will be less than N% as shown below for N% = 5%, DIV% = 2%.

(5% / 2%) * 2% = 2% * 2% = 4% <> 5%.

As shown in Fig. 4.6b, the string variable N.PRIME$ is used as a *program flag*. A program flag is a variable that is used to communicate to one program step the result of computations performed in another step. Initially we will consider N% to be prime and set N.PRIME$ to an initial value of "TRUE". If a divisor is found in Step 3, N.PRIME$ will be reset to "FALSE". The program will test N.PRIME$ in Step 4 and print a message indicating whether or not N% is still considered prime. The refinement of Step 4 is shown in Fig. 4.6c. The program for Problem 4B is shown in Fig. 4.7.

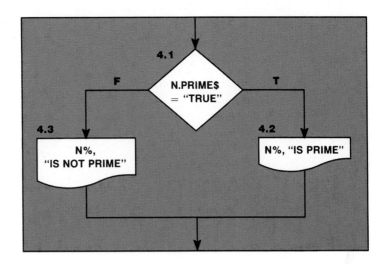

Fig. 4.6c Refinement of Step 4 of Problem 4B.

```
100  !PRIME NUMBER PROBLEM
110  !
160  !ENTER A NUMBER (N%) TO BE TESTED
170      INPUT "ENTER A CANDIDATE PRIME NUMBER"; N%
175  !
180  !VALIDATE N%
190      IF N% <= 1 THEN                                          &
             PRINT "N% <= 1"                                      &
             \PRINT "PROGRAM EXECUTION TERMINATED"                &
             \STOP
195  !
200  !TEST FOR ALL POSSIBLE DIVISORS OF N% --
205  !PRINT ANY THAT ARE FOUND
210      IF N% = 2 THEN        &
             PRINT "2 IS PRIME" &
             \STOP
215  !
220  !INITIALLY ASSUME THAT N% IS PRIME
230      LET N.PRIME$ = "TRUE"
240      PRINT "LIST OF DIVISORS"
250      FOR DIV% = 2 TO N% - 1
260        IF (N% / DIV%) * DIV% = N% THEN   &
               !DIVISOR FOUND                &
               LET DIVISOR% = DIV%           &
               \PRINT DIVISOR%               &
               \LET N.PRIME$ = "FALSE"
270      NEXT DIV%
280  !
290  !INDICATE WHETHER OR NOT N% IS PRIME
310      IF N.PRIME$ ="TRUE" THEN PRINT N%;"IS PRIME" &
             ELSE PRINT N%; "IS NOT PRIME"
320  !
330      END
```

(continued)

```
RUNNH
ENTER A CANDIDATE PRIME NUMBER? 60
LIST OF DIVISORS
  2
  3
  4
  5
  6
 10
 12
 15
 20
 30

 60 IS NOT PRIME
```

```
RUNNH
ENTER A CANDIDATE PRIME NUMBER? 5
LIST OF DIVISORS

 5 IS PRIME
```

Fig. 4.7 Program for Problem 4B.

Program Style

Validating input data

In Fig. 4.7 a decision structure has been inserted that prints an error message if N% is less than or equal to one. Values of N% satisfying this condition are considered to be invalid as the prime number property is not defined for these values. The FOR loop in Fig. 4.7 will not be executed for invalid data values as the program terminates before reaching it (STOP at line 190). (If the program did not terminate, these values would be classified incorrectly as prime numbers.) It is always a good idea to test for invalid input data whether or not this is requested in the problem statement.

Program Style

Validating FOR loop parameters

The second decision in Fig. 4.7 tests whether N% is equal to 2, the first prime number. If so, a prime message is printed and the program is terminated (STOP at line 210). If this test were omitted, the FOR loop body would not be executed anyway since the value of N% - 1 (the FOR loop limit parameter) would be less than 2 (the FOR loop initial parameter). In this case the program would correctly indicate that 2 was prime. Even though our program would work without an explicit test for N% = 2, we have included this test. It is generally a good idea to verify that FOR loop parameters make sense, e.g., for a positive step value, the initial parameter always should be less than or equal to the limit parameter.

4.6 Using Integer Variables to Represent Logical Data

BASIC-PLUS provides integer variables with one additional capability—the representation of logical data. For example, instead of using the string variable N.PRIME\$ in Problem 4B, we could have substituted the integer variable N.PRIME%.

The statement

```
230 LET N.PRIME% = -1%        !N.PRIME% is true
```

could be used to assign N.PRIME% an initial logical value of true (-1% represents true). Then the statement

```
\LET N.PRIME% = 0%            !N.PRIME% is false
```

could be used in line 260 to reset N.PRIME% to false (0% represents false) if a divisor of N% is found. Finally the IF-THEN-ELSE statement

```
310 IF N.PRIME% THEN PRINT N%; "IS PRIME" &
      ELSE PRINT N%; "IS NOT PRIME"
```

could be used to print an appropriate message at the end of the program. The message "IS PRIME" would be printed if the value of N.PRIME% is still -1% (N.PRIME% is true). The message "IS NOT PRIME" would be printed if N.PRIME% were reset to 0% (N.PRIME% is false).

Although this capability exists, we will make limited use of it as we feel that it is confusing to use one data type (integer) to represent another data type (logical).

Exercise 4.19: (*For the more mathematically inclined*) The program shown in Fig. 4.7 tests all integer values between 2 and N% − 1 inclusive to see if any of them divide N%. This is, in fact, quite inefficient, for we need not test all of these values. Revise the algorithm shown in Figs. 4.6a and b to minimize the number of possible divisors of N% that must be tested to determine whether or not N% is prime. Print only the first divisor of N% that is found (if any). Make certain that your improved algorithm still works. *Hints*: If 2 does not divide N%, no other even number will divide N%. If no integer value between 2 and N% / 2 divides N%, then no integer value between N% / 2 + 1 and N% − 1 will divide N%. (In fact, we can even compute a smaller maximum test value than N% / 2. What is it?)

Numerical Errors*

All of the errors discussed in earlier chapters have been programmer errors. However, even if a program is correct, it still may compute the wrong answer, especially if extensive numerical computation is involved. The cause of error is the inherent inaccuracy in the internal representation of data having fractional parts (*real* values as opposed to *integer* values).

For most computers, data are represented using the binary number system (base 2), rather than the decimal system (base 10). Thus the representation of information in the memory of the computer is in terms of binary digits (0's and 1's), rather than decimal digits (0–9). However, as shown in the next example, many real decimal numbers do not have precise binary equivalents and, therefore, only can be approximated in the binary number system.

Example 4.21

This example lists several binary approximations of the decimal number 0.1. The precise decimal equivalent of the binary number being represented and the numerical error are also shown.

Number of Binary Digits	Binary Approximation	Decimal Equivalent	Numerical Error
4	.0001	0.0625	0.0375
5–8	.00011	0.09375	0.00625
9	.000110001	0.09765625	0.00234375
10	.0001100011	0.099609375	0.000390625

We can see from this example that as the number of binary digits used to represent 0.1 is increased, the precise decimal equivalent represented by the binary number gets closer to 0.1. However, it is impossible to obtain an exact binary representation of 0.1, no matter how many digits are used. Unfortunately, the number of binary digits that can be used to represent a real number in the memory of the computer is limited by the size of a memory cell. The larger the cell, the larger the number of binary digits and the greater the degree of accuracy that can be achieved. (Is it possible to represent the fraction 1/3 exactly in the decimal number system?)

The effect of a small error can become magnified when a long sequence of computations is performed. For example, in determining the sine or cosine of an angle, many operations are performed on real numbers by the

*This section may be omitted.

computer (see Example 4.12). The repeated execution of a relatively simple computation may also cause a magnification of round-off error as the inaccuracy in each individual computation is accumulated (see Exercise 4.10). Such magnification can sometimes be diminished through the use of special functions or a reordering of the computations.

Example 4.22   a) The computation

```
SQR(X)
```

is likely to produce more accurate results than X ^ .5 since most square root functions produce more accurate results than the computations required to evaluate X ^ .5.

b) If we have two real numbers A and B, whose difference is very small, and a third number C that is relatively large (compared with A − B), then the calculation

```
(A - B) * C
```

may produce results that are less accurate than

```
A * C - B * C
```

This is because the percentage of error is greater in a very small number such as (A − B), and additional inaccuracy is introduced when a very small number is multiplied by one that is much larger.

4.8   Common Programming Errors

A good deal of care is required when working with complicated expressions. Some of the more common programming errors involving expressions and assignment statements are listed below, along with their solutions. The BASIC-PLUS diagnostics for these errors are shown. In some cases the error may not be detected, since it may result in a legal statement, although not the one intended.

1. *Errors caused by mismatched or unbalanced parentheses.* The statement in error should be carefully scanned, and left and right parentheses matched in pairs, inside-out, until the mis-match becomes apparent. This error is often caused by a missing parenthesis at the end of an expression. To correct this error, carefully count the number of left and right parentheses and make sure you have a matching right parenthesis for each left one in the expression. Usually a missing right parenthesis will produce the error message

```
?Illegal expression
```

A missing left parenthesis may produce one of two messages:

```
?Modifier error
?Illegal verb
```

2. *Missing operator in an expression.* This error is often caused by a missing multiplication operator, *. The expression in error must be scanned carefully, and the missing operator inserted in the appropriate position. The error messages

```
?Illegal expression
?Modifier error
```

may be produced when a missing operator is detected.

3. *String data used with arithmetic operator.* These errors are examples of *mixed expressions* in which operators that can manipulate data of one type are being used with data of another type. These errors produce the message

```
?Illegal mode mixing
```

It is senseless and illegal to do arithmetic on string operands. Attempts to assign string data to numeric variables (and vice versa) will also result in

```
?Illegal mode mixing
```

errors. Attempts to read data of one type into a variable of different type will cause the message

```
?Data format error
```

to be printed.

4. *Illegal number or Division by Zero.* Another type of numerical error is caused by attempts to manipulate very large real numbers or numbers that are very close in value to zero. For example, dividing by a number that is almost zero may produce a number that is too large to be represented

```
?Floating point error
```

You should check that the correct variable is being used as a divisor and that it has the proper value. If a divisor of zero is used, the message

```
%Division by 0
```

is printed and the result is 0.

One type of programming error that can't be detected by BASIC-PLUS involves the writing of expressions that are syntactically correct, but do not accurately represent the computation called for in the problem statement. All expressions, especially long ones, must be checked carefully for accuracy. Often this involves the decomposition of complicated expressions into simpler subexpressions producing intermediate results. The intermediate results should be printed and compared with hand calculations for a simple, but representative data sample.

Care should be taken to ensure that the standard mathematical functions are not given illegal input arguments. The actual arguments that are accepted by these functions may vary according to the function involved. For example, taking the square root or logarithm of a negative value will produce a warning message indicating that an error occurred and the line number of the error. The program will then continue to execute using some value returned by the function (e.g., SQR applied to a negative argument returns the square root of the absolute value of the argument).

Remember that string variable names must end with a dollar sign, $, and that all strings used in a program must be enclosed in quotes. If you forget the closing quotation mark (on the right), your string will run on beyond its intended limit. Similarly, integer variable names must end with a percent sign, %. Note that it is possible to use three different variables named A, A$, and A% (for real, string, and integer data, respectively) in the same BASIC-PLUS program. We do not encourage this practice, however, since it is easy to make mistakes (for example, omitting the $ or % symbols). Some of these mistakes may not be detected by BASIC-PLUS, but will result in incorrect program execution.

4.9 Summary

The specification of multi-operator arithmetic assignment statements and the use of integer and string data have been discussed. The rules for forming and evaluating arithmetic expressions were summarized. The operations of addition (+), subtraction (−), multiplication (*), division (/) and exponentiation (^) may be combined according to these rules to form complicated arithmetic expressions. These expressions may be used in assignment statements on the right-hand side of the assignment operator (=), in the list portion of a PRINT statement, and as arguments in function references. None of these arithmetic operators may be used with string operands, although strings may be compared for equality and for lexical order. Character strings may also be stored in string variables using READ, IN-PUT, or assignment statement.

Fourteen standard mathematical functions provided by BASIC-PLUS, as well as the TAB function for carriage control have been described. The mathematical functions were summarized in Table 4.1. Additional functions are described in Appendix E. Table 4.3 provides a summary of the new BASIC-PLUS statements introduced in this chapter.

Table 4.3 Summary of New BASIC-PLUS Features Introduced in Chapter 4

Feature	Effect
General arithmetic assignment statement	
`110 LET AREA = PI * RADIUS ^ 2`	Assigns the result of the numeric computation `PI * RADIUS ^ 2` to the variable AREA where PI = 3.14159.
String assignment statement	
`120 LET ANIMAL$ = "CAT"` `130 LET NAMES$ = ANIMAL$`	The string constant (or variable) appearing on the right of the assignment operator, "=", is assigned to the string variable at the left.
Integer assignment	
`140 LET YEAR% = 1967%`	The integer constant `1967%` is assigned to the integer variable `YEAR%`.
String comparison	
`180 IF VOTER$ < "S" THEN GOSUB 3000    &` `    ELSE GOSUB 4000`	If the value of the string variable VOTER$ is less than "S" then execute the subroutine at line 3000. Otherwise, execute the subroutine at line 4000.

`200 IF SSNO$ = "219-40-0677" THEN       &`
`        PRINT "THE NUMBER WAS FOUND"    &`
`    ELSE                                 &`
`        PRINT "THE NUMBER IS NOT YET FOUND"`
	If the string variable SSNO$ contains the string "219-40-0677", then the first message is printed. Otherwise the second message is printed.

Reading strings and integers	
`300 READ NAMES$, AGE%` `310 DATA "JOE", 25`	Enter the string "JOE" into NAMES$ and the integer 25 into AGE%. (The quotes around JOE are not required.)

Table 4.3 Summary of New BASIC-PLUS Features Introduced in Chapter 4 (*continued*)

Feature	Effect
`500 INPUT LINE A$`	Enter all characters (including blanks and any punctuation) typed after the prompt "?" into A$.
Printing strings, integers, and expressions	
`110 PRINT PRIME$, JOE%`	Prints the string value stored in PRIME$ and the integer stored in JOE%.
`110 PRINT "AREA =", PI * RADIUS ^ 2`	Prints the string "AREA =", followed by the value of the indicated expression.
Referencing functions	
`110 LET I = FIX(20.25)`	Removes the fractional part of 20.25 and stores the result, 20, in I.
`110 LET HYPOT = SQR(A ^ 2 + B ^ 2)`	Stores the square root of A^2 plus B^2 in HYPOT.

Programming Problems

4C Write a program to compute the sum $1 + 2 + 3 + 4 + \ldots + N$ for any positive integer N; use a FOR loop to accumulate this sum (SUM1). Then compute the value SUM2 using the formula

$$SUM2 = \frac{(N + 1)N}{2}$$

Have your program print both SUM1 and SUM2, compare them, and print a message indicating whether or not they are equal. Test your program for values of N = 1, 7, and 25.

4D The Hoidy Toidy baby furniture company has 10 employees, many of whom work overtime (more than 40 hours) each week. They want a payroll program that reads the weekly time records (containing employee name, hourly rate (rate) and hours worked (hours) for each employee) and computes the gross salary and net pay as follows:

$$\text{gross salary} = \begin{cases} \text{hours} \times \text{rate (if hours} <= 40) \\ 1.5 \times \text{rate} \times (\text{hours} - 40) + \text{rate} \times 40 \text{ (if hours} > 40) \end{cases}$$

$$\text{net pay} = \begin{cases} \text{gross salary (if gross salary} <= \$65) \\ \text{gross salary} \times (15 + .045 \times \text{gross salary}) \text{ (if gross salary} > \$65) \end{cases}$$

The program should print a five column table listing each employee's name, hourly rate, hours worked, gross salary, and net pay. The total amount of the payroll should be printed at the end. It can be computed by summing the gross salaries for all employees. Test your program on the following data:

Name	Rate	Hours
IVORY HUNTER	3.50	35
TRACK STAR	4.50	40
SMOKEY BEAR	3.25	80
OSCAR GROUCH	6.80	10
THREE BEARS	1.50	16
POKEY PUPPY	2.65	25
FAT EDDIE	2.00	40
PUMPKIN PIE	2.65	35
SARA LEE	5.00	40
HUMAN ERASER	6.25	52

4E Write a program to read in a collection of integers and determine whether each is a prime number. Test your program with the four integers 7, 17, 35, and 96.

4F Let n be a positive integer consisting of up to 10 digits, $d_{10}d_9 \ldots d_1$. Write a program to list in one column each of the digits in the number n. The rightmost digit d_1 should be listed at the top of the column. [*Hint:* If n = 3704, what is the value of digit as computed according to the following formula?

$$\text{digit} = n - \text{INT}(n/10) \times 10$$

Test your program for values of n equal to 6, 3704, and 170498.]

4G Each month a customer deposits $50 in a money market account. The account earns 12.5 percent interest, calculated on a quarterly basis (one-fourth of 12.5 percent each quarter). Write a program to compute the total investment, total amount in the account and the interest accrued for each of 120 months of a 10-year period. You may assume that the rate is applied to all funds in the account at the end of a quarter regardless of when the deposits were made.

The table printed by your program should begin as follows:

MONTH	INVESTMENT	NEW AMOUNT	INTEREST	TOTAL SAVINGS
1	50.00	50.00	0.00	50.00
2	100.00	100.00	0.00	100.00
3	150.00	150.00	4.69	154.69
4	200.00	204.69	0.00	204.69
5	250.00	254.69	0.00	254.69
6	300.00	304.69	9.45	314.14
7	350.00	364.14	0.00	364.14

How would you modify your program if interest were computed on a daily basis?

4H Write a program to compute a table of values of $X/(1 + X^2)$ for values of $X = 1,2,3,...,50$. Your table of values should begin as follows:

X	$X/(1 + X^2)$
1	.5
2	.4
3	.3
4	.235294
5	.192308
.	.
.	.
.	.

4I The interest paid on a savings account is compounded daily. This means that if you start with X dollars in the bank, then at the end of the first day you will have a balance of

$$X \times (1 + rate/365)$$

dollars, where rate is the annual interest rate (0.06 if the annual rate is 6 percent). At the end of the second day, you will have

$$X \times (1 + rate/365) \times (1 + rate/365)$$

dollars, and at the end of N days you will have

$$X \times (1 + rate/365)^N$$

dollars. Write a program that will process a set of data records, each of which contains values for X, rate and N and compute the final account balance. Round your interest computation to the nearest two decimal places.

4J Write a program to solve this problem. Compute the monthly payment and the total payment for a bank loan, given:

a) the amount of the loan
b) the duration of the loan in months
c) the interest rate for the loan (as a percent)

Your program should read in one line of data at a time (each containing a loan value, months value, and rate value), perform the required computation, and print the values of the loan, months, rate, monthly payment and total payment.

Test your program with at least the following data (and more if you want).

Loan	Months	Rate
16000	300	6.50
24000	360	7.50
30000	300	9.50
42000	360	8.50
22000	300	9.50
300000	240	9.25

Don't forget to first read in a value indicating how many data records you have.

Notes.

• The formula for computing monthly payments is

$$\text{mpaymt} = \left[\frac{\text{rate}}{1200} \times \left(1 + \frac{\text{rate}}{1200} \right)^{\text{months}} \times \text{loan} \right] \Big/ \left[\left(1 + \frac{\text{rate}}{1200} \right)^{\text{months}} - 1 \right]$$

• The formula for computing the total payment is

$$\text{totpmt} = \text{mpaymt} \times \text{months}$$

Also, you may find it helpful to introduce the additional variables defined below in order to simplify the computation of the monthly payment. You can print the values of ratem and expm to see whether your program's computations are accurate.

$\text{ratem} = \text{rate}/1200$

$\text{expm} = (1 + \text{ratem})^{\text{months}}$

4K The rate of radioactive decay of an isotope is usually given in terms of the half-life, HL (the time lapse required for the isotope to decay to one-half of its original mass). For the strontium 90 isotope (one of the products of nuclear fission), the rate of decay is approximately .60/HL. The half-life of the strontium 90 isotope is 28 years. Compute and print, in table form, the amount remaining after each year for up to 50 years from an initial point at which 50 grams are present. [*Hint*: For each year, the amount of isotope remaining can be computed using the formula

$$r = \text{amount} * C^{(\text{Year}/\text{HL})}$$

where amount is 50 grams (the initial amount), and C is the constant $e^{-0.693}$ ($e = 2.71828$).]

4L   You are to write a program that begins by reading two English words and storing them in the string variables FIRST\$ and LAST\$ (the string stored in FIRST\$ must precede LAST\$). The program will then read additional words one at a time and print them according to the following rules:

- if the word read is less than FIRST\$, print the word in field 1 (at the first TAB position)

- if the word is greater than LAST\$, print the word in field 3 (at the third TAB position)

- if the word falls between FIRST\$ and LAST\$ (inclusive), print it in field 2 (at the second TAB position). Your output might appear as follows:

```
FIRST$ = GOOFY

LAST$ = PLUTO

BEFORE FIRST$        IN BETWEEN        AFTER LAST$
DOC
                     MICKEY
                                       SNOW WHITE
                     GRUMPY
                                       SNEEZY
DUMBO
```

4M   An examination with nine questions is given to a group of 28 students. The exam is worth 10 points and everyone turning in an answer sheet receives at least one point. Each problem is graded on a no credit, half credit, full credit basis. An exam score (SCORE) and name (NAMES\$) are entered for each student. Write a program to determine the rank for each score and print a three column list containing the name, score, and rank of each student. The ranks are determined as follows:

Score	Rank
9–10	GOOD
6–8.5	FAIR
1–5.5	POOR

The program should also print the number of scores in each rank.

4N   Write a program to simulate the tossing of a coin. Use the random number generator RND, and consider any number less than 0.5 to represent tails, and any number greater than or equal to 0.5 to represent heads. Print the number produced by RND and its representation (heads or tails). (*Hint:* Repeat the call to RND 50 or 100 times. At the end print a count of the number of heads versus the number of tails.)

40 Ms. Nichols needs to rent a car to drive from Philadelphia to Orlando (1200 miles). She cannot afford to spend more than $225 in car rental (including gas) but she must have a car that has air conditioning. If gas is $1.25 per gallon and the trip takes three days, write a program that will print the manufacturer, car model number, and trip cost for all cars that will suit her needs. Use the data below to test your program.

Manufacturer	Model ID	Tank Size	MPG	Rental Charge/Day	Rate/Mile	Air
Audi	Fox	15	32	$50	$.10	Y
Cadillac	Seville	30	18	50	.06	Y
Chevrolet	Citation	16	28	20	.09	N
Datsun	B210	14	33	12	.06	N
Dodge	Aries	20	20	15	.10	N
Dodge	Colt	12	35	24	.09	Y
Fiat	Strada	20	33	22	.06	N
Ford	Escort	12	31	20	.06	Y
Honda	Civic	15	40	44	.07	Y
Toyota	Celica	18	35	36	.09	Y

Conditional Loops, Step-wise Programming, and Subroutines

5

One of the most fundamental ideas of computer programming and problem solving concerns the subdivision of large and complicated problems into smaller, simpler, and more manageable subproblems. Once these smaller tasks have been identified, the solution to the original problem can be specified in terms of these tasks; and the algorithms and programs for the smaller tasks can be developed separately.

We have tried to emphasize this technique of programming in all earlier examples through the use of algorithm refinement. In this process, each major part of a problem was identified in a level one flow diagram, and then broken down further into smaller problems during successive stages of refinement. A number of special control structures were introduced that enabled us to implement the solution to each of these subproblems in terms of clearly defined groups of BASIC-PLUS statements or structures.

One of these structures, the FOR loop, has been used extensively to specify the repetition of a group of statements where the repetition is controlled by a counter. Yet there are many programming problems requiring the use of loops in which the repetition can't be controlled conveniently by a counter. For this reason, BASIC-PLUS supports more general loop constructs as extensions of the FOR loop. These structures, often called *conditional loop structures*, are described in the first part of this chapter.

BASIC-PLUS has still another feature called a subroutine, which facilitates solving problems in terms of their more manageable parts. We introduced the subroutine in Chapter 3 as a means of specifying the True and False Tasks in a decision structure. In this chapter we show how the subroutine may be used to write BASIC-PLUS programs in much the same way as we refine flow diagrams. That is, we list the sequence of tasks that must be performed at a particular level, and then provide the implementation details for tasks requiring extensive refinement in separate subroutines. This use of the subroutine in the step-wise approach to programming is the subject of the second portion of this chapter. The step-wise technique will be illustrated in two problems.

5.1 Conditional Loop Structures

Introduction

There is a large collection of programming problems that can be solved using loops that are not conveniently controlled by a counter. For some of these loops, repetition is controlled through the use of a condition involving a test of one or more values that are computed in the body of the loop. For example, many problems of numerical approximation require the repetition of a computation until the difference between two consecutive computed values becomes nearly zero.

A second kind of loop control involves the use of a special input data value, called a *sentinel value*, as a signal to terminate loop repetition. In this case, loop repetition continues as long as the sentinel value has not yet been read.

Both of the above cases are characterized by the fact that the number of loop repetitions required is not known beforehand. Thus a counter could not be used to control the repetition. In the next section we present two BASIC-PLUS *conditional loop structures*, the FOR–WHILE and the FOR–UNTIL, in which the loop repetition test is independent of a counter. After a discussion of these structures we will present two problems in which these structures are used. Then, in Section 5.3, we will introduce several additional BASIC-PLUS loop features, including the WHILE and UNTIL loop structures and the loop statement modifier.

The FOR-WHILE and FOR-UNTIL Loop Structures

We begin our discussion of the FOR-WHILE and FOR-UNTIL loop structures with two examples. The first of these illustrates the use of a condition involving a test of one or more values that are computed in the body of the loop. The second example illustrates the use of a sentinel value for loop control.

Example 5.1 The FOR-WHILE loop in Fig. 5.1 prints a table of powers of two. The loop is repeated as long as (WHILE) the condition POWER < 1000 is true. Each time the loop is repeated, POWER (initial value 1) is multiplied by 2, and the variable X (initial value 0) is automatically incremented by the default step amount of 1.

Note that the simple FOR loop that we have been using so far cannot be used in this situation because we do not know beforehand how many loop repetitions are required. We also do not know the final value of X for which the loop body is to be executed. Therefore, we had to use POWER as the loop control variable (*lcv*) instead of X. (The variable X still serves as a counter, but it is not used for loop control.)

```
100 !USING THE BASIC-PLUS FOR-WHILE LOOP
110 !
120     PRINT "POWERS OF TWO THAT ARE LESS THAN 1000"
130     PRINT \ PRINT " X", " 2^X"
150     LET POWER = 1
160     FOR X = 0 WHILE POWER < 1000
170         PRINT X, POWER
180         LET POWER = POWER * 2
190     NEXT X
200 !
210     END
```

```
RUNNH
POWERS OF TWO THAT ARE LESS THAN 1000

   X                2^X
   0                1
   1                2
   2                4
   3                8
   4                16
   5                32
   6                64
   7                128
   8                256
   9                512
```

Fig. 5.1 An illustration of the FOR-WHILE loop.

The use of the *lcv* POWER in this example is typical of all FOR–WHILE and FOR–UNTIL loop control variables. The *lcv* POWER is tested before each execution of the loop body. The *lcv* must be initialized (see line 150) prior to loop entry and then recomputed each time the loop body is executed (line 180). In this case, initialization accomplishes two goals: it ensures that the assignment statement (line 180) will work correctly and that the loop repetition test (line 160) is meaningful before the first execution of the loop body.

Example 5.2   The FOR–UNTIL loop in Fig. 5.2 reads a list of character strings one at a time, UNTIL the null string is read. When a null string or a string of blanks is read, the program exits from the loop and prints the message "INPUT IS COMPLETE" and the value of COUNTER (the number of strings read). The variable SENTENCE.PART$ is the loop control variable in this FOR–UNTIL loop.

In this example, the null string is used as a *sentinel value* to *signal the end of our data*. The condition

```
SENTENCE.PART$ = ""
```

will be false as long as the string read into SENTENCE.PART$ contains

```
100 !USING THE BASIC-PLUS FOR-UNTIL LOOP
110 !
120    INPUT "ENTER A WORD OR PRESS RETURN"; &
            SENTENCE.PART$
140    FOR COUNTER = 0 UNTIL SENTENCE.PART$ = ""
150       INPUT "NEXT WORD"; SENTENCE.PART$
170    NEXT COUNTER
180 !
190    PRINT \ PRINT "INPUT IS COMPLETE"
210    PRINT "THE NUMBER OF PARTS READ IS"; COUNTER
230 !
240    END
```

```
RUNNH
ENTER A WORD OR PRESS RETURN? THE
NEXT WORD? EARLY
NEXT WORD? BIRD
NEXT WORD? CATCHES
NEXT WORD? THE
NEXT WORD? FROG
NEXT WORD?

INPUT IS COMPLETE
THE NUMBER OF PARTS READ IS 6
```

Fig. 5.2 An illustration of the FOR-UNTIL loop.

at least one nonblank; thus loop repetition will continue as long as nonblank strings are read. To terminate the loop, you simply press the return key after the prompt "NEXT WORD?" appears.

The INPUT statement (line 120) is needed to initialize the loop control variable, SENTENCE.PART$, so that the loop will execute correctly the first time through. The next INPUT statement (line 150) provides all subsequent values for SENTENCE.PART$.

COUNTER is used as a variable for counting and not for loop control. It is increased by the default step amount of 1 each time NEXT COUNTER is executed. It therefore serves to count the number of data items read and printed, which is always useful information to have. Note that COUNTER is incremented to 6 just before loop exit; it retains this value rather than its value (5) during the last execution of the loop body. This is different from the situation described earlier for FOR loop control variables (see Sec. 3.6).

FOR-WHILE and FOR-UNTIL Loop Descriptions

The flow diagram patterns for the FOR–WHILE and FOR–UNTIL loop structures are shown in Fig. 5.3. The labels T (True) and F (False) represent the value of the *condition* in the loop control step (Step 2).

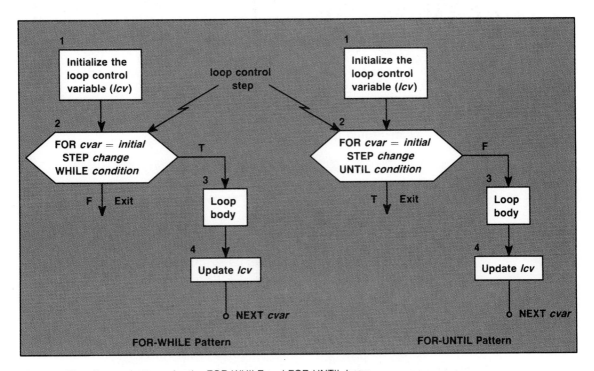

Fig. 5.3 Flow diagram patterns for the FOR-WHILE and FOR-UNTIL loops.

The variable *cvar* shown in these diagrams is initialized (at loop entry) and updated by the value of *change* (when the NEXT *cvar* statement is executed) in much the same way as the loop control variable (*lcv*) is manipulated in the FOR loop. Usually, however, *cvar* is not involved in loop control because we do not know beforehand how many loop repetitions are required. Instead, another variable such as POWER (Example 5.1) or SENTENCE.PART$ (Example 5.2) is used as the *lcv*.

The flow diagram patterns in Fig. 5.3 illustrate how the *lcv* is used. As shown, the behavior of the FOR-WHILE or FOR-UNTIL *lcv* is similar to that of the FOR loop *lcv*; specifically, this variable is

- set to an initial value (Step 1),
- tested before each loop repetition (as part of the *condition* in Step 2),
- updated after each repetition (Step 4).

However, unlike the FOR loop, these loop control steps must be explicitly included in the FOR-WHILE or FOR-UNTIL loop flow diagram, and in the program.

The mechanics of the FOR-UNTIL and FOR-WHILE are summarized in the following displays; the only difference between them is that the condition for one is the *complement* or logical opposite of the condition for the other. Thus the loop header

```
160 FOR X = 0 UNTIL POWER >= 1000
```

could be substituted for

```
160 FOR X = 0 WHILE POWER < 1000
```

in Fig. 5.1 (>= is the complement of <). Similarly, the loop header

```
140 FOR COUNTER = 0 WHILE SENTENCE.PART$ <> ""
```

could be substituted for

```
140 FOR COUNTER = 0 UNTIL SENTENCE.PART$ = ""
```

in Fig. 5.2 (<> is the complement of =). We will have more to say about condition complements in Section 5.4.

FOR-WHILE Loop Structure

```
FOR    cvar = initial STEP  change WHILE  condition
       ———
       ———  } loop body
       ———
NEXT cvar
```

Interpretation: The counter variable, *cvar*, is initialized to the value of *initial* when the loop is entered, and is updated by the value of *change* at the end of each repetition. The loop will execute once for each value of *cvar*, starting at *initial* and continuing WHILE *condition* is true. When *condition* becomes false, execution continues with the first statement following the loop terminator (NEXT *cvar*). For the loop body to be executed at all, *condition* must be true upon entry to the loop.

Note: The header statement is called the FOR-WHILE statement. The FOR-WHILE rules for *cvar*, *initial* and *change* are the same as for the FOR loop. If *change* is one, the step specification (STEP 1) may be omitted.

FOR-UNTIL Loop Structure

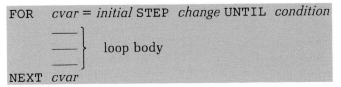

FOR   *cvar* = *initial* STEP *change* UNTIL *condition*

} loop body

NEXT *cvar*

Interpretation: The counter variable, *cvar*, is initialized to the value of *initial* when the loop is entered and is updated by the value of *change* at the end of each loop repetition. The loop will execute once for each value of cvar, starting at *initial* and continuing UNTIL *condition* becomes true. When *condition* becomes true, execution continues with the first statement following the loop terminator (NEXT *cvar*). If *condition* is true upon entry to the loop, the loop body will not be executed at all.

Note: The header statement is called the FOR-UNTIL *statement*. The FOR-UNTIL rules for *cvar, initial*, and *change* are the same as the FOR loop. If *change* is one, the step specification (STEP 1) may be omitted.

In Section 5.2 we will illustrate the design and implementation of algorithms involving the use of the FOR-WHILE and FOR-UNTIL loop structures. Two problems are presented: one illustrates the use of a sentinel value for loop control; the other shows how values computed in the loop body may be used to control loop repetition.

Program Style

Loop body indentation

We have continued the practice of indenting the body of all loops in order to clearly indicate the scope of control of the loop control step.

We suggest that you indent all decision and loop structures in a consistent manner to make your programs easier to read and understand.

Exercise 5.1: List the values printed as the loops below are executed.

```
a)  FOR I = 5 TO -5 STEP -2
        PRINT I
    NEXT I
b)  READ PART$
    FOR I = 1 WHILE PART$ <> "ME"
        PRINT I, PART$
        READ PART$
    NEXT I
    DATA "I", "HIM", "HER", "IT", "YOU", "ME"
c)  LET N = 77
    FOR DIVISOR = 3 STEP 2 UNTIL DIVISOR > SQR(N)
        PRINT DIVISOR
    NEXT DIVISOR
```

Exercise 5.2: Write a FOR–WHILE loop to read a collection of character strings into the string variable C$ and print C$ if it begins with the letters A–H. Loop repetition should continue as long as C$ is not equal to ".".

Exercise 5.3: Use a FOR–UNTIL loop structure and write the flow diagram and program for a loop that will find the largest cumulative product of the numbers 1, 2, 3, 4, . . . that is smaller than 10000.

5.2 Algorithm Development Using Conditional Loops

Use of the Sentinel Value

In Example 5.2 we illustrated the use of a sentinel value to control the repetition of a loop. The sentinel value was used to signal the program that all of the data items had been read into the computer memory and processed.

A sentinel value is a number or string that would not normally occur as a data item for the program. When that value is read, it can be recognized by the program as an indication that all of the actual data items have been processed.

The concept of a sentinel value can be incorporated in the FOR–UNTIL loop pattern as shown in Fig. 5.4. The variable into which each data item is read acts as a loop control variable. It must be initialized using a read step (Step 1) prior to the first test of the repeat condition and its value must be updated during each execution of the loop body using a second read (Step 4). This is normally the last step in the loop and is executed after all other processing of the current value has been performed. These and other points concerning the use of the sentinel value are illustrated in the following problem.

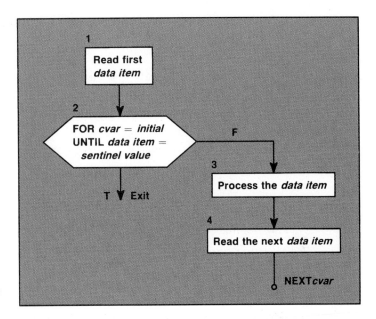

Fig. 5.4 Use of the sentinel value in
FOR–UNTIL loop pattern.

Problem 5A   Write a program that will read all of the scores (all larger than or equal to
0) for a course examination and compute and print the largest of these
scores as well as the number of scores processed. A sentinel value of −1
will be used to mark the end of the data.

Discussion: In order to gain some insight into a solution of this problem,
we should consider how we would go about finding the largest of a long
list of numbers without the computer. Most likely we would read down
the list of numbers one at a time and remember or "keep track of" the
largest number that we had found at each point. If, at some point in the
list, we should encounter a number, SCORE, that is larger than the largest
number found prior to that point, then we would make SCORE the new
largest number, and remember it rather than the previously found number.
An example of how this might proceed is shown in Table 5.1 (see next
page).

   We can use this procedure as a model for constructing an algorithm for
solving Problem 5A on the computer. We will instruct the computer to process a single score at a time and save the largest score it has processed at
any given point during the execution of the program in the variable LARG-
EST.

   In order to terminate the loop repetition, we will use a sentinel value of
−1, which is not within the possible range of scores for the exam. The use
of the sentinel value is required since we do not know how many test
scores are to be processed. The sentinel value is associated with the program constant SENTINEL.

Table 5.1 Finding the Largest of a Collection of Positive Numbers

Test Scores	Effect of Each Score
35	"Since 35 is the first number, we will consider it to be the largest number initially."
12	"12 is smaller than 35, so 35 is still largest."
68	"68 is larger than 35. Therefore, 35 cannot be the largest item. Forget it and remember 68."
8	"8 is smaller than 68, so 68 is still the largest."
–1	"–1 is the sentinel value. There are no more numbers, so 68 is the largest value."

In addition, since we wish to keep track of the number of scores processed (always a good idea if this number is not known beforehand), we must introduce an output variable, COUNTER, for this purpose. COUNTER must be initialized to zero and increased by one after each score is processed. The data table is shown next; the flow diagrams appear in Fig. 5.5a.

DATA TABLE FOR PROBLEM 5A

Program Constant

SENTINEL = −1: sentinel value

Input Variable		*Output Variables*
SCORE: Contains the exam score currently being processed		LARGEST: Contains the value of the largest of all scores processed at any point
		COUNTER: The count of the number of scores processed at any point

From the refinement of Step 1, we see that SCORE is the variable used to control the loop repetition (this should be noted in the data table entry for SCORE). Each time a score is read in, it first must be compared to the sentinel value in order to determine whether loop repetition is to terminate. The condition tested is SCORE = SENTINEL. Prior to performing this test for the first time, we must initialize the loop control variable SCORE by entering the first score (Step 1.1). Finally, at the end of the loop, we must update SCORE by entering the next score (Step 1.5).

Step 1.4 may be refined as the single-alternative decision shown in Fig. 5.5b. In order for the condition SCORE > LARGEST to be meaningful, LARGEST must be defined before the loop is entered. Since exam scores

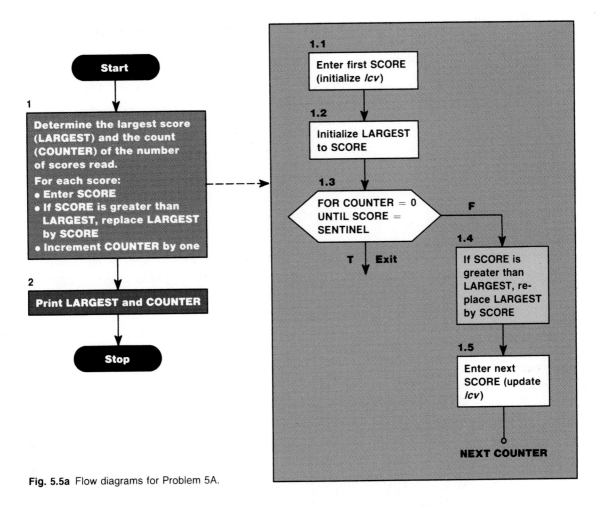

Fig. 5.5a Flow diagrams for Problem 5A.

are normally positive, we could initialize LARGEST to 0; however, the algorithm will be more general if we initialize LARGEST to the first exam score, as done in Step 1.2 of Fig. 5.5a.

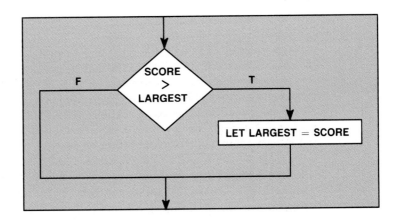

Fig. 5.5b Refinement of Step 1.4.

The program for Problem 5A is shown in Fig. 5.6.

```
100 !FIND THE LARGEST OF A COLLECTION OF EXAM SCORES
120 !
130 !PROGRAM CONSTANT
140     LET SENTINEL = -1
150 !
160 !INITIALIZE LARGEST TO FIRST SCORE
180     INPUT "ENTER FIRST SCORE"; SCORE
200     LET LARGEST = SCORE
210 !
220 !DETERMINE THE LARGEST SCORE AND COUNT THE SCORES
230     FOR COUNTER = 0 UNTIL SCORE = SENTINEL
240         IF SCORE > LARGEST THEN LET LARGEST = SCORE
250         INPUT "NEXT SCORE OR -1"; SCORE
270     NEXT COUNTER
280 !
290 !ALL SCORES PROCESSED. PRINT LARGEST AND COUNT
300     PRINT \ PRINT "LARGEST EXAM SCORE ="; LARGEST
320     PRINT "THE NUMBER OF SCORES IS"; COUNTER
330 !
340     END
```

```
RUNNH
ENTER FIRST SCORE? 76
NEXT SCORE OR -1? 45
NEXT SCORE OR -1? 89
NEXT SCORE OR -1? 96
NEXT SCORE OR -1? 76
NEXT SCORE OR -1? -1

LARGEST EXAM SCORE = 96
THE NUMBER OF SCORES IS 5
```

Fig. 5.6 Program and sample output for Problem 5A.

Exercise 5.4:

a) What would happen in the execution of the program in Fig. 5.6 if we acciden-
    tally omitted all data except the sentinel value?
b) What would happen if COUNTER had been started at 1 instead of 0?

Exercise 5.5: In Problem 5A, we could have initialized LARGEST to 0 instead
of the first exam score; however, initializing LARGEST to 0 would not always
work. Provide a sample set of data for which initializing LARGEST to 0 would
cause the program to produce the wrong answer.

Exercise 5.6: Modify the Problem 5A flow diagrams and data table so that the
smallest score (SMALLEST) and the largest score are found and printed. Also
compute the range, RANGE, of the scores (RANGE = LARGEST - SMALLEST).

Controlling Loop Repetition with Computational Results

The FOR-WHILE and FOR-UNTIL loop structures are well suited for loops in which the repetition condition involves a test of values that are computed in the loop body. For example, in processing checking account transactions, we might want to continue processing transactions as long as the account balance is positive or zero, and stop and print a message when the balance becomes negative.

In problems of this sort, the loop control variable serves a dual purpose: it is used for storage of a computational result as well as for controlling loop repetition. Occasionally, more than one computed value will be involved in the repetition test, as illustrated in the following problem.

Problem 5B

Two cyclists are involved in a race. The first has a head start because the second cyclist is capable of a faster pace. We will write a program that given the average speeds, SPEED1 and SPEED2, of each cyclist, prints out the distance from the starting line that each cyclist has traveled. These distances will be printed for each half hour of the race, beginning when the second cyclist departs and continuing until the second cyclist catches up with the first cyclist.

Discussion: This problem illustrates the use of the computer to *simulate* what would happen in a real world situation. We can get an estimate of the progress of the cyclists before the race even begins and perhaps use this information to set up monitoring or aid stations. The data table follows and the level one flow diagram and refinements are shown in Fig. 5.7.

DATA TABLE FOR PROBLEM 5B

Program Constant

TIME.INTERVAL = 0.5: time interval (one half hour)

Input Variables		*Output Variables*	
SPEED1:	Average speed of first cyclist in mph	ELAPSED.TIME:	Elapsed time from start of second cyclist in hours
SPEED2:	Average speed of second cyclist in mph	DISTANCE1:	Distance traveled by first cyclist
HEAD.START:	Headstart expressed in hours	DISTANCE2:	Distance traveled by second cyclist

We might have used the variable TIME in place of either TIME.INTERVAL or ELAPSED.TIME. However, TIME is a reserved keyword in BASIC-PLUS and cannot be used as a variable name. TIME.INTERVAL and ELAPSED.TIME are also preferred because they are far more descriptive names than TIME.

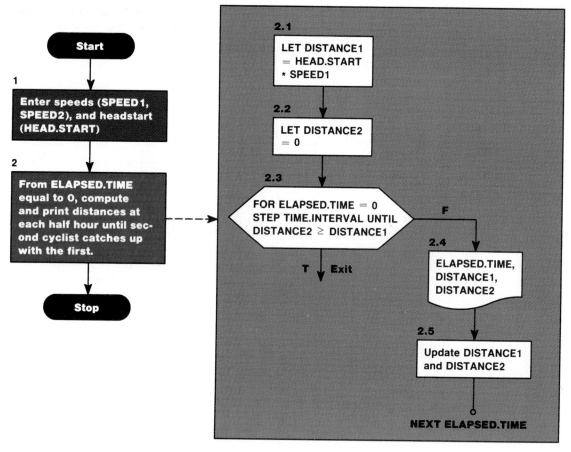

Fig. 5.7 Flow diagrams for Problem 5B.

The loop-repetition test will involve a comparison of the total distances traveled by each cyclist. Hence both DISTANCE1 and DISTANCE2 are considered as loop control variables here. We will make use of the formula

$$\text{distance} = \text{speed} \times \text{elapsed time}$$

in the computation of distance traveled. We will have to compute the distance traveled by the first cyclist before the second cyclist departs and the incremental distance traveled by each cyclist during each subsequent half hour.

The initial value of DISTANCE1 (first cyclist's headstart) is computed as the product of speed (SPEED1) and the duration of the headstart (HEAD.START). The value of DISTANCE2 is initially zero. The loop control test (Step 2.3) involves a comparison of two output variables DIS-TANCE1 and DISTANCE2, both of which are updated at the end of the loop (Step 2.5).

To refine Step 2.5, we must compute the incremental distance traveled in each time interval and add it to the distance traveled prior to the current time interval. This computation can be described as

distance = distance + incremental distance

where

incremental distance = speed × time interval

To carry out these computations for each cyclist, we introduce two program variables I1 and I2.

Program Variables
I1: Incremental distance for first cyclist
I2: Incremental distance for second cyclist

Given these variables, we can refine Step 2.5 as follows:

```
LET I1 = SPEED1 * TIME.INTERVAL
LET DISTANCE1 = DISTANCE1 + I1
LET I2 = SPEED2 * TIME.INTERVAL
LET DISTANCE2 = DISTANCE2 + I2
```

The program for Problem 5B is shown in Fig. 5.8.

```
100 !CYCLE RACE PROBLEM
110 !
120 !PROGRAM CONSTANT
130     LET TIME.INTERVAL = 0.5
140 !
150 !ENTER DATA ITEMS
190     INPUT "FIRST CYCLIST SPEED "; SPEED1
210     INPUT "SECOND CYCLIST SPEED "; SPEED2
230     INPUT "FIRST CYCLIST'S HEADSTART IN HOURS"; &
                HEAD.START
250 !
260 !COMPUTE DISTANCE INCREMENTS
270     LET I1 = SPEED1 * TIME.INTERVAL
280     LET I2 = SPEED2 * TIME.INTERVAL
290 !
300 !PRINT TABLE HEADING
310     PRINT \ PRINT "TIME", "DISTANCE1", "DISTANCE2"
330 !
```

(continued)

```
340 !COMPUTE AND PRINT DISTANCES AT EACH HALF HOUR
350 !WHILE FIRST CYCLIST IS AHEAD
360     LET DISTANCE1 = SPEED1 * HEAD.START
370     LET DISTANCE2 = 0
380     FOR ELAPSED.TIME = 0 STEP TIME.INTERVAL &
        UNTIL DISTANCE2 >= DISTANCE1
390         PRINT ELAPSED.TIME, DISTANCE1, DISTANCE2
400         LET DISTANCE1 = DISTANCE1 + I1
410         LET DISTANCE2 = DISTANCE2 + I2
420     NEXT ELAPSED.TIME
430 !
440     PRINT "CYCLIST 2 PASSES 1 IN NEXT INTERVAL"
450 !
460     END
```

```
RUNNH
FIRST CYCLIST SPEED ? 12.5
SECOND CYCLIST SPEED ? 17
FIRST CYCLIST'S HEADSTART IN HOURS? 1.5

TIME          DISTANCE1          DISTANCE2
 0             18.75              0
 .5            25                 8.5
 1             31.25              17
 1.5           37.5               25.5
 2             43.75              34
 2.5           50                 42.5
 3             56.25              51
 3.5           62.5               59.5
 4             68.75              68
CYCLIST 2 PASSES 1 IN NEXT INTERVAL
```

Fig. 5.8 Program and sample output for Problem 5B.

Program Style

Removing nonvarying computations from a loop

We should note that the values of I1 and I2 will never vary while
the loop is repeated. They remain the same because SPEED1 and
SPEED2 never change and TIME.INTERVAL is a program constant. Consequently, there is no reason to continually recompute the
values of I1 and I2 for each execution of the loop. This pair of
computations should be removed from the loop and performed immediately after SPEED1 and SPEED2 have been computed.

This change in the algorithm is reflected in the final program for Problem 5B shown in Fig. 5.8. The computation of I1 and I2 immediately follows the definition of the variables SPEED1 and SPEED2. The technique of removing computations from the body of a loop yields a faster-executing program because the multiplications required to compute I1 and I2 are performed only once, instead of many times. In general, any computations producing the same result for each repetition of a loop should be removed from the loop in this manner.

Program Style

Program constants revisited

The real constant, 0.5, representing the time interval between measurements could easily have been written in-line whenever it was referenced. For example, we could have written

```
270 LET I1 = SPEED1 * 0.5
```

rather than

```
270 LET I1 = SPEED1 * TIME.INTERVAL
```

However, we used a program constant, TIME.INTERVAL, to represent this parameter in order to make any subsequent program modifications easier. If we later decide to take measurements every 20 minutes (one-third of an hour), we need only change one line

```
130 LET TIME.INTERVAL = 1/3
```

instead of all lines that use the value of TIME.INTERVAL (lines 270, 280 and 380).

Exercise 5.7: Perhaps a more natural way of computing the distances in the loop in Fig. 5.8 (see lines 400 and 410) would be to use the usual formula for distance:

distance = speed × time

where time is the elapsed time since the race began. Rewrite lines 260–420 in the program in Fig. 5.8 to use this formula for computing DISTANCE1 and DIS-TANCE2.

Exercise 5.8: How would you modify the program in Fig. 5.8 to continue printing up to and including the first time period in which the second cyclist is past the first?

A Postscript on Using the FOR-WHILE and FOR-UNTIL Loops

The flow diagram patterns for the FOR-WHILE and FOR-UNTIL loops used in Problems 5A and 5B are based on the patterns shown in Fig. 5.3. The steps leading to the construction of these loops are the same.

Steps for Constructing FOR-WHILE and FOR-UNTIL Loops

1. Complete a description of what must be done in the loop (the loop body).
2. Identify the loop control variable. This variable may already be a part of the loop body such as SCORE in Problem 5A or it may need to be added for the specific purpose of loop control.
3. Set up the loop control variable test to be performed before each execution of the loop.
4. Initialize the loop control variable just prior to the test.
5. Update the loop control variable as the last step of the loop.
6. Identify the counter variable to be used in the FOR part of the loop. This variable is normally distinct from the loop control variable and is often required for counting purposes within the loop, e.g., COUNTER in Problem 5A and ELAPSED.TIME in Problem 5B.

Exercise 5.9: On January 1, the water supply tank for the town of Death Valley contained 10,000 gallons of water. The town used 183 gallons of water a week and it expected no rain in the near future. Write a loop to compute and print the amount of water remaining in the tank at the end of each week. Your loop should terminate when there is insufficient water to last a week.

5.3 Additional Features of Loop Control

The WHILE and UNTIL Loop Structures

In addition to the FOR-WHILE and FOR-UNTIL structures, BASIC-PLUS provides two simpler forms of conditional loop structures, the WHILE and UNTIL loops. These structures are useful in writing general conditional loops that do not involve the use of a counter variable, as illustrated in the following two examples.

Example 5.3 The WHILE loop in Fig. 5.9 computes and prints the largest power of 2 that is less than 1000. This loop is similar to the one shown in Example 5.1 (Fig. 5.1), except that a table of powers of two is not required, and the counter variable, X, is not needed.

When POWER is greater than 1000, loop exit occurs and the previous value of POWER (saved in OLD.POWER) is printed (line 160). If we had

```
100 !USING THE BASIC-PLUS WHILE LOOP
110 !
120      LET POWER = 1
130      WHILE POWER < 1000
135          LET OLD.POWER = POWER
140          LET POWER = POWER * 2
150      NEXT     !WHILE
160      PRINT "THE LARGEST POWER OF 2 THAT IS"
165      PRINT "LESS THAN 1000 IS"; OLD.POWER
170 !
180      END
```

```
RUNNH
THE LARGEST POWER OF 2 THAT IS
LESS THAN 1000 IS 512
```

Fig. 5.9 An illustration of the WHILE loop.

printed POWER at this point, we would end up printing the smallest power of 2 that is larger than 1000, which is not what the problem asked for.

In Example 5.3, the loop control variable POWER was explicitly initialized to 1 prior to loop entry, and recomputed each time through the loop. A FOR loop could not be used here since we did not know beforehand how many loop repetitions were involved. Since no counter was needed in this example, there was also little point to using the FOR-WHILE loop structure. The WHILE loop provides an easy-to-use feature for writing loops without counters.

Example 5.4 The UNTIL loop in Fig. 5.10 is virtually identical to the loop shown in Example 5.2 (Fig. 5.2), except that no counter is used. In this case, when a null string or blank string (the sentinel value) is read, loop exit occurs and the message "INPUT IS COMPLETE" is printed.

The flow diagram patterns for the WHILE and UNTIL loop structures are shown in Fig. 5.11. The steps leading to the construction of these loops are summarized in the display at the bottom of page 194.

```
100 !USING THE BASIC-PLUS UNTIL LOOP
110 !
120      PRINT "ENTER A WORD OR PRESS RETURN";
130      INPUT SENTENCE.PART$
140      UNTIL SENTENCE.PART$ = ""
160          INPUT "NEXT WORD"; SENTENCE.PART$
170      NEXT     !UNTIL
180      PRINT
190      PRINT "INPUT IS COMPLETE"
200 !
210      END
```

(continued)

```
RUNNH
ENTER A WORD OR PRESS RETURN? THE
NEXT WORD? EARLY
NEXT WORD? BIRD
NEXT WORD? CATCHES
NEXT WORD? THE
NEXT WORD? FROG
NEXT WORD?

INPUT IS COMPLETE
```

Fig. 5.10 An illustration of the UNTIL loop.

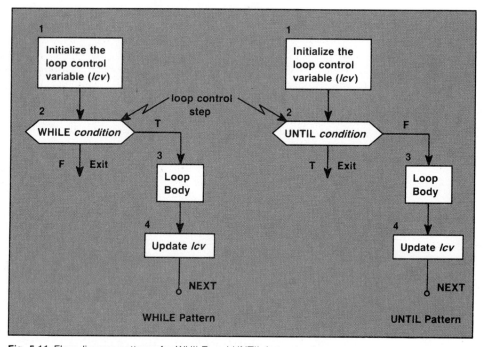

Fig. 5.11 Flow diagram patterns for WHILE and UNTIL loop structures.

Steps for Constructing WHILE and UNTIL Loops

1. Complete a description of what must be done in the loop (the loop body).
2. Identify the *loop control variable*. This variable may already be a part of the loop body (such as POWER or SENTENCE.PART$), or it may need to be added.
3. Set up the *loop control step* (the WHILE or UNTIL statement) at the head of the loop body.
4. Initialize the loop control variable just prior to the loop control step.
5. Update the loop control variable as the last step of the loop.

The general forms for the WHILE and UNTIL loops are described in the following two displays.

WHILE Loop Structure

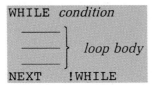

Interpretation: The *condition* is evaluated prior to loop entry and again before each loop repetition. As long as (WHILE) the condition is true, the loop body is executed. If *condition* evaluates to false, execution continues with the first statement following the NEXT statement (loop terminator). The statement

WHILE *condition*

is called the BASIC-PLUS WHILE statement. Since there is no counter variable associated with this loop, no variable is named in the NEXT statement.

UNTIL Loop Structure

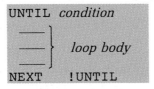

Interpretation: The *condition* is evaluated prior to loop entry and again before each loop repetition. UNTIL *condition* evaluates to true, the loop body will be executed. Once the *condition* becomes true, execution continues with the first statement following the NEXT statement (loop terminator). The statement

UNTIL *condition*

is called the BASIC-PLUS UNTIL statement. Since there is no counter variable associated with this loop, there is no variable named in the NEXT statement.

Exercise 5.10:   List the values printed as the loops below are executed.

```
a)  100 FOR I = 1 TO 10
    110    PRINT I
    120 NEXT I
b)  100 LET I = 1
    110 WHILE I <= 10
    120    PRINT I
    130    LET I = I + 1
    140 NEXT
c)  100 LET I = 1
    110 UNTIL I > 10
    120    PRINT I
    130    LET I = I + 1
    140 NEXT
```

Exercise 5.11:   Write a WHILE or UNTIL loop that computes the end of year dollar value of a savings account (which starts with $10,000) when interest is compounded annually (at 12.5%). Your program should stop executing once the deposit has reached or passed $20,000.

Exercise 5.12:   How would you change Fig. 5.9 to use an UNTIL loop? How would you change Fig. 5.10 to use a WHILE loop?

Loop Statement Modifiers

There are a number of situations in which the body of a loop will consist of a single statement only. In such cases, these loops may be written on one line in BASIC-PLUS, as illustrated in the following examples.

Example 5.5   a) The statement

```
200 PRINT FOR NUM.LINE = 1 TO 3
```

can be used to produce a triple line feed.
b) The statements

```
220 INPUT "ENTER A POSITIVE INTEGER"; N UNTIL N > 0
```

or

```
220 INPUT "ENTER A POSITIVE INTEGER"; N WHILE N <= 0
```

repeatedly print a prompting message and read an integer value until a positive value is entered. These statements can be used to automatically validate a data value since they will continually request a value until a positive number is entered. Since the condition is tested before the first

INPUT operation is performed, it would be a good idea to initialize N to a negative value or zero.

c) The statements

```
240 PRINT X; 2 ^ X FOR X = 0 WHILE 2 ^ X < 1000
```

or

```
240 PRINT X; 2 ^ X FOR X = 0 UNTIL 2 ^ X >= 1000
```

can be used to print a table of powers of 2 similar to the table shown in Fig. 5.1. All powers of 2 less than 1000 will be printed.

As shown in Example 5.5, all of the loop statement headers discussed in the text (FOR, FOR-WHILE, FOR-UNTIL, WHILE, and UNTIL) may be used as loop statement modifiers.

Exercise 5.13: Rewrite the first loop in Example 5.5b and the second loop in Example 5.5c using the long loop forms.

5.4   Using Logical Operators

The Logical Operators AND, OR, XOR, and NOT

There are many situations in which the execution of a task in a decision structure or a loop structure is dependent upon combinations of two or more conditions rather than just a single condition. Several examples of such situations are provided next.

Example 5.6   The condition

```
(SCORE >= 0) AND (SCORE <= 100)
```

can be used to determine whether or not an examination score that has just been entered into a program is within a meaningful range, 0 to 100 inclusive. This condition will have the value true if both SCORE >= 0 and SCORE <= 100 are true. Otherwise the condition will be false. Note that the condition

```
SCORE >= 0 AND <= 100
```

is illegal; the variable SCORE must be an operand of both relational operators, >= and <=. Conditions involving the *logical operator* AND are true if and only if both of the conditions *connected* by the AND are true.

On the other hand, conditions involving the OR operator are true if either one or both of the conditions specified are true. The condition

```
(SCORE < 0) OR (SCORE > 100)
```

would be true if the value of SCORE was illegal (outside the range 0 to 100). The parentheses shown above are not necessary.

Example 5.7

The FOR–UNTIL loop shown in Fig. 5.12 reads a list of numbers until either a sentinel value of 0 is entered or 10 values are read. The *logical operator* OR is used to construct a more complicated condition from two simpler ones, thereby enabling us to specify a loop that will execute repeatedly until either condition (or both) become(s) true. The count of items read so far is printed (line 160) after each data item is entered. If the sentinel 0 is entered, it will be included in the final count that is printed (line 190).

While it might be tempting to use either of the statements

```
150 FOR COUNTER = 1 UNTIL 10 OR X = 0
```

or

```
150 FOR COUNTER = 1 TO 10 UNTIL X = 0
```

to achieve the same effect in Fig. 5.12, these statements are not legal in BASIC-PLUS.

The complement of a condition is true when the condition is false and vice versa. For example, the complement of the condition SCORE >= 0 would be SCORE < 0. The complements of the relational operators are shown in Table 5.2. The logical operator NOT can be used to complement a condition as shown next.

```
100 !USING THE LOGICAL OPERATOR OR
110 !
120     PRINT "ENTER A NUMBER AFTER EACH PROMPT '?'"
130     PRINT "ENTER 0 TO STOP"
140     INPUT X
150     FOR COUNTER = 1 UNTIL X = 0 OR      &
                        COUNTER = 10
160        PRINT "NUMBER"; COUNTER; "IS"; X
170        INPUT X
180     NEXT COUNTER
190     PRINT COUNTER; "ITEMS READ"
```

Fig. 5.12 Using the logical operator OR to control loop repetition.

Table 5.2 Complements of the Relational Operators

Operator	Complement	Example
<	>=	NOT (X < Y) is the same as X >= Y
>	<=	NOT (X > Y) is the same as X <= Y
=	<>	NOT (X = Y) is the same as X <> Y
>=	<	NOT (X >= Y) is the same as X < Y
<=	>	NOT (X <= Y) is the same as X > Y
<>	=	NOT (X <> Y) is the same as X = Y

Example 5.8   The condition

```
NOT (KEY = ITEM)
```

is true when KEY and ITEM contain different values; it is logically equivalent to the condition

```
KEY <> ITEM
```

NOT is a logical operator with one logical operand; the NOT operator complements its operand. In most instances you will find it more convenient to use the complement of a relational operator instead of using the NOT operator.

The AND, OR, and NOT operators are described along with one other BASIC-PLUS operator, XOR (exclusive or), in Table 5.3.

Table 5.3 The Logical Operators AND, OR, XOR, NOT

Operator	Example	Meaning
AND	(X < Y) AND (Y < Z)	The entire condition is true only if both conditions X < Y and Y < Z are true.
OR	(X < Y) OR (Y < Z)	The entire condition is true if either X < Y or Y < Z (or both) are true.
XOR	(X < Y) XOR (Y < Z)	The entire condition is true if X < Y is true or if Y < Z is true. If both X < Y and Y < Z are true or if both are false, the entire condition is false.

(continued)

Table 5.3 The Logical Operators AND, OR, XOR, NOT (*continued*)

Operator	Example	Meaning
NOT	NOT (X < Y)	The condition is true when X < Y is false; it is false when X < Y is true.

The only difference between the logical operators OR and XOR is that the entire condition is false when the two conditions connected by XOR are true. Thus if W = 25.5, the condition

    (W >= 20) XOR (W < 30)

will be false; whereas the condition

    (W >= 20) OR (W < 30)

will be true.

The Precedence of Arithmetic, Logical, and Relational Operators

In Section 4.1 we discussed how to write correct BASIC-PLUS arithmetic expressions. As part of that discussion we introduced the rules of *operator precedence* for the arithmetic operators. According to these rules, the exponentiation operator was placed at the highest precedence level, followed by multiplication and division, and then addition and subtraction. We now expand this operator precedence relation to include all relational and logical operators. This expanded "ordering" of operators is shown in Table 5.4.

All operators introduced in the text to this point are shown in this table. The table indicates the order in which these operators are evaluated when they appear in the same subexpression. This ordering is illustrated in the next example.

Table 5.4 Precedence of Arithmetic, Relational and Logical Operators

Arithmetic operators	exponentiation, ^ multiplication and division, *, / addition and subtraction, +, −	*Highest precedence*
Relational operators	<, =, <=, >, >=, <>, ==	
Logical operators	logical complement, NOT logical and, AND logical or and exclusive or, OR, XOR	Lowest precedence

Example 5.9   This example illustrates operator precedence (the order of operator evaluation). We assume that X = 3, Y = 7, and Z = 1.
a) The condition

    NOT X < Y

evaluates to false, since X < Y is true (3 < 7), and NOT applied to true yields a value of false.
b) The condition

    NOT X < Y AND Z < X

evaluates to false. According to Table 5.3, we evaluate the relational operators first, yielding

    NOT true AND true

We then evaluate the NOT operator (NOT appears above AND in Table 5.3), yielding

    false AND true

Since one operand of the AND operator is false, the entire condition is false. Note that

    NOT (X < Y AND Z < X)

also evaluates to false, although the evaluation is quite different:

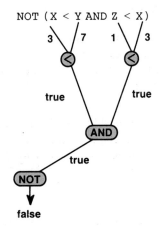

c) The following expression illustrates the evaluation order for an expression containing arithmetic, relational and logical operators. We have inserted some parentheses to clarify the expression.

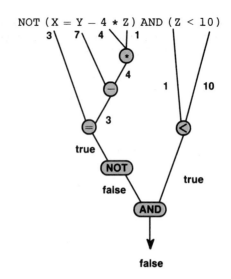

NOT (X = Y − 4 * Z) AND (Z < 10)

Remember that arithmetic operators are always evaluated before the relational operators, which in turn are evaluated before the logical operators. To change this ordering or when in doubt, use parentheses.

Exercise 5.14: Hand trace the program in Fig. 5.12 for the following sets of data:

a) `6   12   −18   −22   15   −6   0`
b) `8   −10   5   −7   68   42   30   18   −1.8   12   0`

What are the values of X and COUNTER after loop execution?

Exercise 5.15: Write the BASIC-PLUS condition (using the AND and OR logical operators) for each of the following:
a) age (AGE) is greater than 0 and less than 120.
b) year of birth (BIRTH.YEAR) is greater than 1912 and less than or equal to 1984.
c) car mileage (CAR.MILES) is greater than 0 and less than or equal to 7500.
d) the number of gerbil babies (GERBIL.BABY) is either less than 6 or more than 22.
e) total income (INCOME) is between $10,000 and $20,000 per year.

Exercise 5.16: Rewrite the loop header statement in Fig. 5.12 using a FOR–WHILE statement rather than a FOR–UNTIL.

Exercise 5.17: Write a FOR loop to read 100 pairs of data items, each containing a person's name and age, and print the names and ages of those between the ages of 25 and 35, inclusive.

Exercise 5.18: Write a FOR–UNTIL or FOR–WHILE loop to read and print a maximum of 100 pairs of data items, each containing a person's name and age. The loop should terminate after 100 items have been processed or whenever an age that is outside the range 0 to 120 has been read.

Exercise 5.19: Let A = 15 and B = 25. Indicate which of the conditions below are true and which are false. Justify your answers by indicating the value (true or false) of each simple condition.

a) A < 13 AND B = 25
b) A >= 13 AND B > 25
c) A < B XOR B < 100
d) A > B OR B = 15
e) A > B XOR B <= 20
f) A <= B OR B < A
g) A < B AND B < A

5.5 Step-wise Programming and Subroutines

Up to now the logic, or flow, of control in the sample programs was relatively straightforward and easy to follow. Most programs consisted of short sequences of structures with little or no nesting. We now have the tools and the skills to write more complex programs involving several levels of nesting. Such programs can become quite cumbersome and difficult to follow unless proper procedures are followed in their design and implementation.

Early in Chapter 2, we indicated that a desirable goal in problem solving was to break a complicated problem into independent subproblems and work on these subproblems separately. We have practiced this technique of problem decomposition throughout the text by drawing a level one flow diagram outlining the subproblems to be solved. We have then separately refined each of these subproblems to fill in the details of an algorithm, subdividing each subproblem still further when necessary. This technique of specifying algorithms through successive refinement is often referred to as *step-wise programming*.

Unfortunately, we have not yet carried this step-wise design process through to the implementation of our programs. What we would like to do is implement a program in the same manner in which the flow diagram was designed. This involves writing an initial program segment (the *main program*) that looks much like a level one flow diagram. Within the main program, each of the subproblems to be solved may be referenced by a unique identifier (either a line number or a name). The specific program statements corresponding to each subproblem are written together as a special *program module* that is provided separately from the main program. If further problem subdivision is necessary, each of these modules may be written in a step-wise manner as well.

To be able to write programs in the manner just described, we must have a structure available for designating sequences of statements that are to be treated as separate modules. We must also have a statement that can be used to request the execution of these modules.

In BASIC-PLUS, there are two different structures available for writing separate modules. One of these structures, the subroutine, is already familiar to us; the other is the *user-defined function*. In the next section we will describe and illustrate the use of the BASIC-PLUS subroutine; in Chapter 8 we will provide an in-depth discussion of user-defined functions.

Use of Subroutines in Step-wise Programming

In order to illustrate the step-wise approach to programming and the use of subroutines, we will re-examine the widget inventory control problem from Chapter 3 (Problem 3D). The level one flow diagram from Fig. 3.18a is redrawn in Fig. 5.13 and the main program is shown in Fig. 5.14a.

The main program parallels the level one flow diagram in that it lists the sequence in which the major subtasks of the program are to be carried

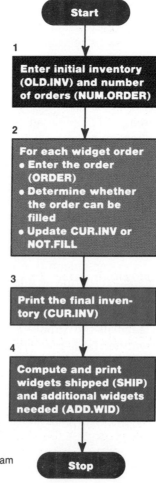

Fig. 5.13 Level one flow diagram for Problem 3D.

```
100  !WIDGET INVENTORY CONTROL PROBLEM
110  !(WITH SUBROUTINES)
120  !
130  !ENTER OLD INVENTORY AND NUMBER OF ORDERS
140      INPUT "ENTER OLD INVENTORY"; OLD.INV
150      INPUT "ENTER NUMBER OF ORDERS"; NUM.ORDER
160      PRINT
220  !
230  !READ AND PROCESS EACH ORDER
240      GOSUB 1000
250  !
260  !PRINT FINAL INVENTORY COUNT
270      PRINT \ PRINT "FINAL INVENTORY ="; CUR.INV
290  !
300  !COMPUTE AND PRINT NUMBER SHIPPED (SHIP)
310  !AND ADDITIONAL WIDGETS (ADD.WID) IF NEEDED
320      LET SHIP = OLD.INV - CUR.INV
330      PRINT SHIP; "WIDGETS SHIPPED"
340      IF NOT.FILL > 0 THEN                           &
             !ADDITIONAL WIDGETS NEEDED                 &
             LET ADD.WID = NOT.FILL - CUR.INV           &
             \PRINT ADD.WID; "NEW WIDGETS NEEDED"
350  !
360      STOP
370  !
380  !
```

Fig. 5.14a Main program with subroutine call for Problem 3D.

out. Each of these subtasks is either written as part of the main program (Steps 1, 3, and 4) or implemented as a separate subroutine (Step 2) and referenced or called in the main program. Normally only subtasks that are complicated enough to require refinement are implemented as subroutines.

Review of Subroutines in BASIC-PLUS

Recall that a subroutine in BASIC-PLUS is a sequence of statements grouped together as a separate unit. The *entry*, or transfer of control to a subroutine, is accomplished through the execution of a *subroutine call* or GOSUB statement (line 240 of Fig. 5.14a). The line number (1000) indicated in the GOSUB statement specifies the location of the first statement of the subroutine. After the subroutine is executed, control is returned to the first statement in the main program following the subroutine call (line 250).

The subroutines for the new version of the widget inventory problem are provided in Fig. 5.14b. These statements should be typed immediately following the statements in Fig. 5.14a since they are part of the same BASIC-PLUS program. You should compare the new program (Figs. 5.14a and b) with the original program (Fig. 3.19) and the flow diagrams from which it was derived (Figs. 3.18a and b).

```
1000  !SUBROUTINE TO READ AND PROCESS EACH ORDER
1010  !AND FILL ORDER IF INVENTORY SUFFICIENT;
1020  !OTHERWISE INDICATE NOT FILLED
1025  !
1030      LET CUR.INV = OLD.INV
1035      LET NOT.FILL = 0
1040      !READ AND PROCESS EACH ORDER
1050      FOR ORDER.COUNT = 1 TO NUM.ORDER
1060        INPUT "ORDER"; ORDER
1070         !DECIDE IF THE ORDER CAN BE FILLED
1080         IF ORDER <= CUR.INV THEN GOSUB 2000 &
                 ELSE GOSUB 3000
1090      NEXT ORDER.COUNT
1100  !
1110      RETURN
1120  !END OF SUBROUTINE TO PROCESS EACH ORDER
1125  !
1130  !
2000  !SUBROUTINES FOR IF-THEN-ELSE AT LINE 1080
2010  !IF ORDER <= CUR.INV THEN FILL ORDER
2020      PRINT , ORDER; "FILLED"
2030      LET CUR.INV = CUR.INV - ORDER
2040      RETURN
3000  !ELSE ORDER NOT FILLED (EXCEEDS INVENTORY)
3010      PRINT , ORDER; "NOT FILLED"
3020      LET NOT.FILL = NOT.FILL + ORDER
3030      RETURN
3035  !END OF SUBROUTINES FOR IF AT LINE 1080
3040  !
3050      END      !WIDGET PROGRAM
```

Fig. 5.14b Subroutines needed for main program in Fig. 5.14a.

As illustrated in Fig. 5.14b, a BASIC-PLUS subroutine must be terminated by a RETURN statement. The group of statements from the first line of a subroutine (line 1000) through the statement

```
1110 RETURN
```

constitutes the *subroutine definition*. We suggest that you explicitly mark the physical end of a subroutine with an appropriate comment as done in line 1120 of Fig. 5.14b.

The statement GOSUB 1000 (at line 240) causes an immediate transfer of control to the subroutine at line 1000. Following this transfer, the subroutine is executed. The RETURN at line 1110 transfers control back to line 250 of the main program.

The actual sequence of statement execution in the program is listed below and illustrated in Fig. 5.15.

1. Main program, lines 100–240: Step 1 of the flow diagram (Fig. 5.13) is performed and the subroutine is called.

2. Subroutine, lines 1000–1110: Step 2 of the flow diagram is performed and control is returned to the main program.

3. Main program, lines 250–360: Steps 3 and 4 of the flow diagram are performed. Program execution is terminated at line 360.

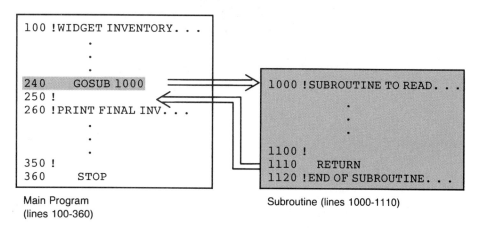

```
100 !WIDGET INVENTORY. . .
        .
        .
        .
240      GOSUB 1000
250 !
260 !PRINT FINAL INV. . .
        .
        .
        .
350 !
360      STOP
```

Main Program
(lines 100-360)

```
1000 !SUBROUTINE TO READ. . .
        .
        .
        .
1100 !
1110     RETURN
1120 !END OF SUBROUTINE. . .
```

Subroutine (lines 1000-1110)

Fig. 5.15 Illustration of subroutine call and returns.

If we look more closely at Step 2 in the list, we will see that each time the FOR loop in the subroutine is executed, the IF–THEN–ELSE at line 1080 calls either the subroutine at line 2000 (the True Task) or the subroutine at line 3000 (the False Task). After this subroutine is executed, its RETURN statement transfers control back to line 1090 and the original subroutine continues execution.

This example shows that subroutine calls may be nested. Each time a subroutine is called, BASIC-PLUS records the line number of the next statement following the subroutine call. When a RETURN statement is executed, BASIC-PLUS transfers control to the most recently recorded line number that has not already been used.

In Fig. 5.14b, the END statement is the last statement in the program as always. However, in this case the END statement only marks the end of the program; the STOP statement in the main program (line 360) actually terminates program execution.

The rules for defining and referencing a subroutine are summarized in the following display.

Subroutine: Definition, Entry, and Exit

Subroutine definition

A group of BASIC-PLUS statements that is entered only through the use of a GOSUB statement and exited only through the use of a RE-TURN. The first statement of the subroutine must be preceded by a STOP or RETURN, which serves to isolate the subroutine from the rest of the program.

GOSUB *line*

This statement causes an immediate transfer of control to the indicated *line*, the first statement in the subroutine.

RETURN

This statement causes an immediate transfer of control to the first statement following the GOSUB that was used for subroutine entry.

Programming with Subroutines

The use of subroutines enables us to implement a flow diagram in a modular fashion. Each subtask requiring refinement may be implemented as a separate subroutine that is called in the main program. The decision as to whether a subtask in the level one flow diagram should be included as part of the main program or implemented separately as a subroutine depends on the complexity of the refinement. Step 2 of Fig. 5.13 was implemented as a subroutine since its refinement consisted of a FOR loop with an IF-THEN-ELSE nested in the loop body; Step 4 was implemented directly in the main program since its refinement is a relatively straightforward decision step; however, it would be quite reasonable to implement Step 4 as a subroutine.

Subroutines may be placed anywhere in a BASIC-PLUS program. However, as we indicated earlier, each subroutine is a separate program module that may only be entered through execution of a GOSUB statement. Consequently, all subroutines must be preceded by a STOP or RETURN statement. Failure to adhere to this requirement could result in the accidental execution of a subroutine as part of a main program or another subroutine. BASIC-PLUS cannot recognize the beginning of a subroutine (there is no beginning marker), but it will provide an error message if a RETURN is executed without previous execution of a corresponding GOSUB. The first statement of each subroutine definition will follow the last statement of the main program or the preceding subroutine definition. The END statement comes after the last subroutine RETURN statement.

Exercise 5.20: Implement Problem 5B (see Fig. 5.8) using the step-wise approach. Implement Step 2 in the level one flow diagram (Fig. 5.7) as a subroutine.

5.6 Application of Step-wise Programming

In this section, we will further illustrate step-wise programming and the use of subroutines by studying a sample program.

Example 5.10 *A Simple Computer-Aided Instruction (CAI) Program.* Figures 5.16a and b show an example of a program that provides an interactive question and

```
100 !A CAI PROGRAM FOR MULTIPLICATION DRILL
105 !
110     PRINT "THIS IS A PROGRAM TO IMPROVE"
120     PRINT "YOUR MULTIPLICATION SKILLS"
130     PRINT
140     PRINT "YOU WILL BE ASKED TO MULTIPLY TWO"
150     PRINT "INTEGERS BETWEEN 0 AND 99. IF YOUR"
160     PRINT "ANSWER IS WRONG, THE COMPUTER"
170     PRINT "WILL GIVE YOU THE CORRECT ANSWER."
180     PRINT
190     PRINT "TYPE 'YES' TO CONTINUE, 'NO' TO STOP."
210     PRINT
220 !
230 !REPEAT THE DRILL AS LONG AS REQUESTED
235     LET CORRECT.COUNT = 0
240     LET WRONG.COUNT = 0
250     INPUT "DO YOU WISH TO CONTINUE"; GO.AHEAD$
260     FOR COUNTER = 0 WHILE GO.AHEAD$ = "YES"
270        !DETERMINE NUMBERS TO BE MULTIPLIED
280        LET M1 = INT (100 * RND)
290        LET M2 = INT (100 * RND)
300        !PRINT OUT NUMBERS AND GET STUDENT RESPONSE
310        PRINT "WHAT IS THE VALUE OF"; M1; "*"; M2;
320        INPUT RESPONSE
325        !
330        !COMPUTE M1 * M2 AND COMPARE TO RESPONSE
340        GOSUB 1000
350        !ASK TO CONTINUE OR NOT
360        PRINT
370        INPUT "DO YOU WISH TO CONTINUE"; GO.AHEAD$
380     NEXT COUNTER
390 !
400     PRINT "YOU ANSWERED"; COUNTER; "QUESTIONS."
410     PRINT COUNTER - WRONG.COUNT; "CORRECTLY"
420     PRINT WRONG.COUNT; "INCORRECTLY"
430     PRINT
440     PRINT "END OF DRILL. BYE NOW."
450 !
460     STOP
470 !
480 !
```

Fig. 5.16a Main program for Example 5.10.

```
1000  !SUBROUTINE TO COMPUTE ACTUAL ANSWER
1010  !COMPARE ANSWER TO STUDENT RESPONSE AND
1020  !INDICATE IF RESPONSE IS CORRECT
1030  !
1040      LET ANSWER = M1 * M2
1050      IF ANSWER = RESPONSE THEN GOSUB 2000 &
              ELSE GOSUB 3000
1060  !
1070      RETURN
1080  !END OF SUBROUTINE TO COMPUTE ACTUAL ANSWER
1090  !
1095  !
2000  !SUBROUTINES FOR THE IF-THEN-ELSE AT LINE 1050
2010  !IF ANSWER = RESPONSE THEN ANSWER IS CORRECT
2020      LET CORRECT.COUNT = CORRECT.COUNT + 1
2030      PRINT "CORRECT"
2040      RETURN
3000  !ELSE ANSWER IS WRONG
3010      LET WRONG.COUNT = WRONG.COUNT + 1
3020      PRINT "INCORRECT."; M1; "*"; M2; "="; ANSWER
3030      RETURN
3035  !END OF SUBRROUTINES FOR LINE 1050
3040  !
9000      END     !CAI PROGRAM
```

Fig. 5.16b Subroutine for Example 5.10.

answer facility for students practicing multiplication. A FOR–WHILE loop (loop control variable GO.AHEAD$) is used to control loop repetition. In this program, the INT and random number (RND) functions are used to generate two random integers (M1 and M2) between 0 and 99 (see lines 280 and 290). (Recall that RND produces a random value between 0 and 1 including 0, but not 1. Multiplying by 100 moves the decimal point two positions to the right and INT removes the fractional part of a positive number.) These integers are then printed at the terminal; the student is asked to compute and type in the product of these integers (RESPONSE). The subroutine at line 1000 (called by line 340) then computes the actual answer (ANSWER), compares it to RESPONSE, and informs the student whether or not the response (RESPONSE) is correct. A sample run is shown in Fig. 5.16c.

Programs such as this, which provide computer-aided instruction (CAI), can be effective tools for classroom use in any educational environment requiring the development of fundamental skills through repetitive drill.

Exercise 5.21: Revise the subroutine shown in Fig. 5.16b to give the student three chances to produce the correct answer. For each incorrect answer, have the program give the student a prompting message indicating that the answer was "TOO LARGE" or "TOO SMALL" and encourage the student to try again.

```
RUNNH
THIS IS A PROGRAM TO IMPROVE
YOUR MULTIPLICATION SKILLS

YOU WILL BE ASKED TO MULTIPLY TWO
INTEGERS BETWEEN 0 AND 99. IF YOUR
ANSWER IS WRONG, THE COMPUTER
WILL GIVE YOU THE CORRECT ANSWER.

TYPE 'YES' TO CONTINUE, 'NO' TO STOP.

DO YOU WISH TO CONTINUE? YES
WHAT IS THE VALUE OF 20 * 22 ? 440
CORRECT

DO YOU WISH TO CONTINUE? YES
WHAT IS THE VALUE OF 53 * 13 ? 699
INCORRECT. 53 * 13 = 689

DO YOU WISH TO CONTINUE? YES
WHAT IS THE VALUE OF 99 * 78 ? 9342
INCORRECT. 99 * 78 = 7722

DO YOU WISH TO CONTINUE? NO
YOU ANSWERED 3 QUESTIONS.
1 CORRECTLY
2 INCORRECTLY

END OF DRILL. BYE NOW.
Stop at line 460
```

Fig. 5.16c Sample output for Example 5.10.

After the third try, print the correct answer. Ensure that the variable WRONG.COUNT is incremented by 1 if and only if the first of the three answers is incorrect.

5.7 Common Programming Errors

The most common errors in writing loops are syntax errors in the header statement, failure to provide the proper terminator statement (NEXT), or failure to initialize or update the loop control variable (*lcv*).

You must always be certain that your loop header and terminator statements conform to the BASIC-PLUS syntax rules. The syntax of the FOR-WHILE and FOR-UNTIL statements is somewhat more complicated than the simple WHILE or UNTIL, but the FOR-UNTIL and FOR-WHILE are extremely convenient and should be mastered.

Failure to initialize and update an *lcv* will not be detected by BASIC-PLUS and may cause the loop to be skipped entirely. Failure to update the *lcv* will likely cause the loop to execute "forever"; that is, until your program runs out of data or exceeds a time limit or some other system constraint causing the loop to stop execution.

You can determine that a program is stuck in an *infinite loop* by pressing CTRL/C to suspend the program. The immediate mode statement

```
PRINT LINE
```

will print the line number that was being executed when the program was suspended. If this line number is inside the loop, then resume the program (command CONT) and repeat this process two or three more times with a small wait between them. If the line number printed is still in the loop, then it is likely that your loop will execute "forever".

A common error that occurs in using the logical operators OR, AND, and XOR involves the omission of one of the operands of a relational operator (<, >=, etc.). For example, the condition

```
SCORE >= 0 AND <= 100
```

is incorrect. It should be written as

```
SCORE >= 0 AND SCORE <= 100
```

When writing subroutines in BASIC-PLUS, it is essential to ensure that all of these modules are properly terminated and that the only means of entry to a module is through an explicit call or reference using a GOSUB statement. Remember that subroutines must terminate with a RETURN and that subroutines may be defined anywhere in a BASIC-PLUS program. However, they must be immediately preceded by a STOP or a RETURN, in order to guarantee entry through explicit reference only. Otherwise your program may accidentally "fall into" a subroutine, eventually causing a run-time error

```
%RETURN without GOSUB
```

when a RETURN is executed. This could happen, for example, in the Widget Program (Fig. 5.14a, b) if the STOP statement (line 360) were omitted.

5.8 Summary

We have introduced and illustrated the use of four conditional loops (FOR–UNTIL, FOR–WHILE, UNTIL, and WHILE), loop statement modifiers, and the BASIC-PLUS subroutine. These constructs are of considerable help in implementing programs in a modular fashion, consistent with the step-wise algorithm development process. The FOR-WHILE and FOR-UNTIL will likely be of more use than the WHILE and UNTIL because they automatically initialize and update a counter variable in addition to performing their loop control function.

Subroutines are an important feature in the practice of step-wise programming techniques. Although we have not shown it in the chapter, they are also helpful in writing programs in which certain operations are performed more than once. These operations can be specified once as a subroutine and then referenced as often as needed in the program. In Chapter 8 we will study the additional, more powerful feature of the user-defined function that can be used in the same way as the subroutine, but with greater flexibility. A summary of the new BASIC-PLUS features introduced in this chapter is given in Table 5.5.

Table 5.5 Summary of New Control Structures Introduced in Chapter 5

Feature	Effect
Subroutine call or reference	
`110 GOSUB 1000`	Transfers control to the subroutine starting at line 1000.
Subroutine terminator	
`1110 RETURN`	Indicates the end of a BASIC-PLUS subroutine. Transfers control to the first statement following the subroutine reference (GOSUB) in the calling program.
FOR-WHILE *loop*	

`110 LET POWER = 1`
`120 FOR X = 0 WHILE POWER < 1000`
`130    PRINT X, POWER`
`140    LET POWER = POWER * 2`
`150 NEXT X`
	The loop body is repeated WHILE POWER is less than 1000. The counter variable X is automatically initialized (to 0) at loop entry, and updated (by 1) after each loop repetition. When POWER becomes greater than or equal to 1000, the first statement following the loop terminator is executed.

FOR-UNTIL *loop*	

`110 LET POWER = 1`
`120 FOR X = 0 UNTIL POWER >= 1000`
`130    PRINT X, POWER`
`140    LET POWER = POWER * 2`
`150 NEXT X`
	The loop body is repeated UNTIL POWER becomes greater than or equal to 1000. The counter variable X is treated in the same manner as described for the FOR-WHILE loop. When POWER becomes greater than or equal to 1000, the first statement following the loop terminator is executed.

(continued)

Table 5.5 Summary of New Control Structures Introduced in Chapter 5. (*continued*)

Feature	Effect
WHILE *loop*	
| ```
110 LET POWER = 1
120 WHILE POWER < 1000
130     PRINT POWER
140     LET POWER = POWER * 2
150 NEXT   !WHILE
``` | The loop body is repeated WHILE POWER is less than 1000. When POW-ER becomes greater than or equal to 1000, the first statement following the loop terminator is executed. |
| UNTIL *loop* | |
| ```
110 LET POWER = 1
120 UNTIL POWER >= 1000
130     PRINT POWER
140     LET POWER = POWER * 2
150 NEXT    !UNTIL
``` | The loop body is repeated UNTIL POWER becomes greater than or equal to 1000, at which time the first statement following the loop terminator (NEXT) is executed. |

In addition to the major loop and subroutine structures introduced, loops with a single statement body, and the logical operators AND, OR, NOT, and XOR were described in this chapter. These features are illustrated in Table 5.6.

Table 5.6 Additional BASIC-PLUS Features Introduced in Chapter 5

Feature	Effect
Loops with a single-statement body (loop statement modifiers)	
| ```
110 PRINT I FOR I = 1 TO 100
110 PRINT I FOR I = 1 WHILE I <= 100
110 PRINT I FOR I = 1 UNTIL I > 100
``` | The values of I ranging from 1 to 100 (in steps of 1) are printed on separate lines. |
| ```
110 LET X = X * 2 WHILE X < 1000
110 LET X = X * 2 UNTIL X >= 1000
``` | X is repeatedly doubled in value as long as it is less than 1000. |
Sample conditions	
(X < Y) AND (Y < Z)	This condition is true only if both X < Y and Y < Z are true.
(X < Y) OR (Y < Z)	This condition is true if either X < Y or Y < Z (or both) are true.
(X < Y) XOR (Y < Z)	This condition is true if either X < Y or Y < Z (but *not* both) are true.
NOT (X < Y)	This condition is true if X < Y is false. Otherwise the condition is false.

Programming Problems

5C   Do Problem 4J using a sentinel value to determine when all of the data have been read and processed.

5D   Do Problem 4M for a class whose size is unknown. Use a sentinel value to mark the end of the input.

5E   Write a program that will read in a positive real number and determine and print the number of digits to the left of the decimal point. (*Hint*: See Problem 4F. Repeatedly divide the number of 10 until it becomes less than 1.) Test the program with the following data:

```
4703.62          0.01
   0.47        5764
  10.12        40000
```

5F   Write a program that uses subroutines to find the range (largest value − smallest value) and the mean value in a collection of data.

5G   The function SIN(X) begins to increase in value starting at X = 0 radians. Then, at some value of X greater than 0, SIN(X) begins to get smaller. Write a program to determine the value of X for which SIN(X) begins to decrease. (*Hint*: Calculate the value of SIN(X) beginning at X = 0 for intervals of .01 radians and watch for a decrease.) Print a two-column table of X and SIN(X) as long as the increase continues. At the point of decrease, simply print X and SIN(X) and stop.

5H   The Small Time Company has three employees, all of whom earn $4 an hour. The company keeps a daily record of the hours worked by each employee. Write a program to read the daily time records for each employee, and compute the total hours worked and gross pay for the employee. For each employee, print a three-column table entry containing employee name, total hours, and gross pay (gross pay = $4 × hours worked). At the end, print the total hours and the total gross pay. Test your program on the following data. (Assume that the time records for each employee are entered consecutively.)

```
SMALL FRY        8
SMALL FRY        8
SMALL FRY        6
SMALL FRY        4
SMALL FRY        8
SHORT PERSON     8
SHORT PERSON     8
SHORT PERSON     6
THIN MAN         8
THIN MAN         8
THIN MAN         2
THIN MAN         8
THIN MAN         8
THIN MAN         5
```

5I The Norecall Auto Company keeps sales records for each employee. Each time an automobile is sold the following data are entered into the record:

name of salesperson   make of car   date of sale   amount of sale

For example:

```
LITTLE NELL      CADILLAC      6/6      9532.67
```

Each month the company must collect the sales records for each employee, count the number of sales, add up the sales amount, and compute the employee commission as follows:

For sales up to $30,000,	five percent commission
For sales between $30,000–$50,000,	five percent commission on first $30,000 eight percent commission on the rest
For sales over $50,000,	five percent of first $30,000 eight percent of next $20,000 fifteen percent of the rest

Write a program to perform these computations. For each employee, your program should print employee name, total sales count, total dollar amount of sales, and total commission. At the end, print grand totals of sales count, dollar amount, and commissions. Use a subroutine to compute the commission. Test your program on the following data.

LITTLE NELL	CADILLAC	6/6	4500.00
LITTLE NELL	BUICK	6/7	3200.00
LITTLE NELL	CADILLAC	6/9	5200.00
LITTLE NELL	BUICK	6/12	3900.00
LITTLE NELL	BUICK	6/12	3700.00
LITTLE NELL	CADILLAC	6/18	5100.00
LITTLE NELL	CADILLAC	6/24	6000.00
BIG SIS	BUICK	6/8	3800.00
BIG SIS	BUICK	6/20	4100.00
BIG SIS	OLDS	6/30	4900.00
MODERN MILLIE	CADILLAC	6/1	6500.00
MODERN MILLIE	CADILLAC	6/3	7300.00
MODERN MILLIE	CADILLAC	6/4	5200.00
MODERN MILLIE	CADILLAC	6/8	7800.00
MODERN MILLIE	BUICK	6/12	3200.00
MODERN MILLIE	OLDS	6/14	4200.00
MODERN MILLIE	CADILLAC	6/15	5200.00
MODERN MILLIE	CADILLAC	6/18	4700.00
MODERN MILLIE	BUICK	6/20	5500.00
MODERN MILLIE	OLDS	6/22	4900.00

As in Problem 5H, assume that sales records for each employee are entered consecutively.

5J Extend the CAI program (Figs. 5.16a and b) to provide drills for addition, subtraction, and division, as well as multiplication. Write three additional subroutines similar to the multiplication subroutine (see Fig. 5.16b) to compute the actual answer for subtraction, addition, and division drills, respectively. (*Hint*: Each time the student decides to continue, your main program should ask if the next drill is to be subtraction ("SUB"), addition ("ADD"), division ("DIV") or multiplication ("MUL"), and then call the appropriate subroutine to check the student solution.) Make certain that you test all cases in your program with a variety of different input, including input containing errors. Print an appropriate message when errors are detected.

5K Write a program to read in a collection of positive integers and print all divisors of each, except for 1 and the number itself. If the number has no divisors, print a message indicating that it is prime. Use a subroutine to determine all of the divisors of each integer read. This subroutine should set a flag to indicate whether or not an integer is prime. The main program should test the flag to decide whether or not to print the prime message (see Problem 4B). Use a sentinel value of 0 to terminate the execution of the loop that reads each data item.

5L Do Problem 5H using a subroutine to process each employee time record. Include computation and output steps for each employee in the subroutine.

5M Write an interactive program that will cause your terminal to behave like a simple calculator on which the user can type a number, an operator (+, −, *, or /) and another number (each separated by a comma) and receive back at the terminal the answer to the indicated computation. The calculator should automatically shut off if either number entered is a zero. The operator should be treated as a string variable. If an incorrect operator is entered, the user should be asked to retype the calculation required. Examples of your input might be

```
 7, +, 12.2
16, −,  8.1
 9, /, 12.7
```

Note that the operator need not be enclosed in quotes.

5N A class of students in an introductory BASIC-PLUS course took six exams during the semester. The third exam counted double weight (twice as much as exams 1, 2, 4, and 5) and the sixth exam (the final) counted triple weight (three times as much as exams 1, 2, 4, and 5). Write a program to compute the weighted average of all exam scores for each student. Use the data below, print each student's name and exam scores, as well as the weighted average. Ensure that all exam scores lie between 0 and 100 inclusive (skip, with an appropriate message, any student record not satisfying this constraint) and use the name "ZZ" as a sentinel value.

Test Data

Name	Exam scores					
Elliot	45	50	10	0	20	30
Dave	60	50	75	70	55	57
Mike	88	83	92	79	87	91
Nancy	40	30	46	52	72	37

(continued)

Test Data

Name			Exam scores			
Frank	0	5	5	0	10	15
Judy	90	95	100	87	93	98
Phil	71	57	62	-6	42	38
Billie	125	0	125	0	125	0
Aaron	35	50	52	57	48	51
Georgio	85	93	88	90	88	95
Gene	91	90	95	100	97	89
Len	67	71	69	73	77	70
Jim	57	49	52	37	35	38
ZZ	0	0	0	0	0	0

The last input line (the sentinel line) must have a data value for every item in your INPUT statement list, even though only "ZZ" is actually tested as the sentinel value.

Arrays and Subscripts

In all of the problems that we have examined so far, we needed only a few memory cells to process relatively large amounts of data. This is because we have been able to process each data item and then reuse the memory cell which contained that item.

For example, in Problem 5A we computed the maximum value of a set of exam scores. Each score was read into the same memory cell, named SCORE, and then completely processed. This score was then destroyed when the next score was read for processing. This approach allowed us to process a large number of scores without having to allocate a separate memory cell for each one. However, once a score was processed it was impossible to reexamine it later.

Yet there are many applications in which we must save data items for subsequent reprocessing. For example, we may need to write a program that computes and prints the average of a set of exam scores and also the difference between each score and the average. In this case, all scores must be processed and the average computed before we can calculate the differences requested. We must, therefore, be able to examine the list of student exam scores twice, first to compute the average and then to compute the differences. Since we would rather not read the exam scores twice, we should save all of the scores in memory during the first step for reuse in the second step.

In processing each data item, it would be extremely tedious to have to reference each memory cell by a different name. If there were 100 exam scores to process, we would need 100 different variables, each of which would have to be used in the input list of a READ statement. Then we would need 100 assignment statements to determine the difference between each score and the average.

In this chapter we will learn how to use another feature of BASIC-PLUS, called an *array*, for storing a collection of related data items. Use of the array simplifies naming and referencing the individual items in the collection. With arrays, we can enter an entire collection of data items using a single READ statement enclosed in a loop. Once the collection is stored in memory, we can reference any of these items as often as we wish without ever having to reenter the item into memory.

6.1 Declaring Arrays

In all programming discussed thus far, each variable name in a program has been used for storing a single data item. An array is a collection of two or more memory cells, called *array elements*, associated with a single variable name. In BASIC-PLUS, whenever we wish to associate two or more memory cells with a single name, we must use an *array declaration statement* to indicate the *name* and the *size* (number of elements) of the array.

For example, the array declaration statement

```
110 DIM X(8)
```

instructs BASIC-PLUS to associate eight memory cells, designated as X(1), X(2), X(3), . . . , X(7), and X(8), with the name X (see Fig. 6.1). The array X is considered to be of size 8—i.e., to consist of 8 elements. Each of the elements may contain a number, as shown in Fig. 6.1.

The *subscripted variable* X(1) can be used to reference the first element of the array X, X(2) references the second element, and X(8) the eighth element. The integer enclosed in parentheses is the *array subscript*.

Array X

X(1)	X(2)	X(3)	X(4)	X(5)	X(6)	X(7)	X(8)
16	12	6	−2	−12	−24	−38	−54

First · Second · Third · · · Eighth
element · element · element · · · element

Fig. 6.1 The eight elements of the array X.

Example 6.1 Let X be the array shown in Fig. 6.1 and let SUM be a variable containing the value 34 (the sum of the first three elements of X). Then the statement

```
130 LET SUM = SUM + X(4)
```

causes the value −2 (the contents of the memory cell designated by $X(4)$) to be added to SUM, yielding a result of 32. An array name must always be used with a subscript in an assignment statement, unless matrix operations are involved (see Chapter 10).

In the next section we study subscripts in more detail; we will see that integer constants are not the only form of a subscript that is allowed in BASIC-PLUS. However, first we describe the BASIC-PLUS array declaration statement.

Array Declaration

```
DIM name(size)
```

Interpretation: A collection of memory cells (array elements) is associated with the variable indicated by *name*. The individual array elements will be referenced by the subscripted variables *name(1)*, *name(2)*, . . . , *name(size)* where the largest legal subscript value is *size*. The number *size* must be a non-negative integer constant. Real, integer, and string arrays are allowed in BASIC-PLUS.

Notes: BASIC-PLUS actually assigns one additional element, the *zero element* (having a subscript of zero) to each array used in a program. We will ignore this element in all subsequent discussions, but you should remember that each array is one element larger than is specified by *size*.

Any array that is referenced but not declared in a program is automatically assigned a *size* of 10 as a default (11 including the zero element). Nonetheless, we encourage you always to declare the arrays that you use. For the sake of program readability and maintenance, this declaration should be placed at the beginning of a program.

Example 6.2   More than one array may appear in a declaration statement. The declaration

```
120 DIM CACTUS(5), NEEDLE(12), PINS(6)
```

will cause memory to be set aside for three arrays: CACTUS (with a maximum subscript of 5), NEEDLE (with a maximum subscript of 12), and PINS (with a maximum subscript of 6).

The statement

```
130 DIM FIRST.NAME$(20), AGE%(20)
```

will allocate memory for the string array FIRST.NAME$ and the integer array AGE% (maximum subscript of 20 in each case).

Exercise 6.1: Draw pictures similar to the one shown in Fig. 6.1 (complete with sample data) for the following arrays.

a) DIM TEAM$(6)
b) DIM RUNS(6), HITS(6), RBI(6)
c) DIM BA(6)

What is the legal range of subscript values for these arrays?

6.2 Array Subscripts

In the preceding section we introduced the array subscript as a means of differentiating among the individual elements of an array. We showed that an array element can be referenced by specifying the name of the array followed by a subscript enclosed in parentheses.

BASIC-PLUS allows an arithmetic expression to be used as the subscript for an array. BASIC-PLUS evaluates the *subscript expression* and then uses the result of this evaluation to indicate the element to be referenced. The rules for the specification and evaluation of array subscripts are summarized next.

Array Subscripts

name (subscript)

Interpretation: The *subscript* may be any arithmetic expression. The range of permissible subscript values is between 0 and the maximum subscript value for that array (as specified in the array declaration). *Notes:* The use of integer-valued expressions is encouraged since any

---

subscripts with fractional parts will be truncated before the array is referenced. If a subscript expression is not within the declared array range, the error message

```
?Subscript out of range
```

will be printed.

Example 6.3 Let ISUB be a variable containing the value 3 and let X be an array consisting of ten elements, X(1)...X(10). Then:
X(ISUB) refers to the third element of the array X;
X(4) refers to the fourth element of the array X;
X(2*ISUB) refers to the sixth element of the array X;
X(5*ISUB−6) refers to the ninth element of the array X.

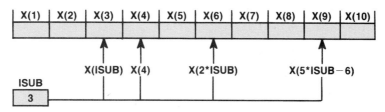

Array X

Example 6.4 a) The program segment

```
100 DIM BALANCE(12)
110 READ BALANCE(I) FOR I = 1 TO 12
120 DATA 5, 100, -15, 10, 25, 10, -25, 50, 10, 10
130 DATA 0, 35
```

declares an array, BALANCE, and enters data into this array as shown below.

Array BALANCE

(1)	(2)	(3)	(4)	(5)	(6)	(7)	(8)	(9)	(10)	(11)	(12)
5	100	−15	10	25	10	−25	50	10	10	0	35

The READ operation in line 110 is performed once for each value of the loop control variable I, starting with I = 1 and continuing until I = 12. Thus each data value in line 120 is stored in a different element of the array BALANCE, starting with BALANCE(1).

b) The following program segment can be used to print the 12 values stored in BALANCE in a single column.

```
200 PRINT "LIST OF BANK BALANCES"
210 FOR I = 1 TO 12
220    PRINT BALANCE(I)
230 NEXT I
```

This loop executes once for each value of the loop control variable I, starting with I = 1 and continuing until I = 12. Thus one array element value will be printed for each execution of the loop.

c) The following program segment can be used to compute and print the SUM of the elements of BALANCE.

```
300 LET SUM = 0
310 FOR I = 1 TO 12
320     LET SUM = SUM + BALANCE(I)
330 NEXT I
340 PRINT "SUM ="; SUM
```

A hand trace for this segment is shown next.

	I	BALANCE(I)	SUM
Prior to loop entry	?	?	0
	1	5	5
	2	100	105
	3	−15	90
	4	10	100
	5	25	125
	6	10	135
	7	−25	110
	8	50	160
	9	10	170
	10	10	180
	11	0	180
	12	35	215
At loop exit	12	35	215(printed)

d) The following program segments use loop statement modifiers to accomplish the same tasks as carried out by the loops in parts b) and c).

b)
```
200 PRINT "LIST OF BANK BALANCES"
210 PRINT BALANCE(I) FOR I = 1 TO 12
```
c)
```
300 LET SUM = 0
310 LET SUM = SUM + BALANCE(I) FOR I = 1 TO 12
320 PRINT "SUM ="; SUM
```

Example 6.5   Let G be an array of 10 elements as shown below.

Array G

G(1)	G(2)	G(3)	G(4)	G(5)	G(6)	G(7)	G(8)	G(9)	G(10)
−11.2	12	−6.1	4.5	8.2	1.3	−.7	8.3	9	−3.3

The following statements can be made about array G:
The contents of the second element (subscript value 2) in the array is 12.
The contents of the fourth element (subscript value 4) is 4.5.
The contents of the tenth element (subscript value 10) is −3.3.

Remember, the subscript value is used to select a particular array element, but does not by itself tell us what is stored in that element.

Exercise 6.2: In Example 6.3, which elements of the array X are referenced if ISUB is equal to 4 rather than 3?

Exercise 6.3: Let I contain the integer 6 and let X be an array of size 10. Which of the following references to elements of X are within the range of legal subscripts for X?

a) `X(I)`
b) `X(3*I-20)`
c) `X(4+I)`
d) `X(I*3-12)`
e) `X(4*I-12)`
f) `X(I-2*1)`
g) `X(30)`
h) `X(I*I-1)`

Exercise 6.4: a) Show the contents of the array SCORES following the execution of the program segment

```
100   DIM SCORES(6)
110   FOR I = 1 TO 6
120      READ SCORES(I)
130      PRINT SCORES(I)
140   NEXT I
150   DATA 100, 42, 85, 70, 58, 65
```

b) Write a program segment to compute and print the sum and average of the values in SCORES as defined in part a. Show a complete trace of the execution of your program. Your trace should include the values of I and the sum at each step, as well as an indication of which element of the array SCORES is being processed at each step (see Example 6.4c).

c) Write a program segment to compute and print the absolute value of the difference between each element of SCORES and the average. Compute and print the sum of these *absolute differences* and the average absolute difference. (*Hint*: The average of the six data items in part a is 70. The "absolute differences" for these six items are therefore 30, 28, 15, 0, 12, and 5.)

6.3 Manipulating Array Elements

Introduction and Examples

Array elements may be manipulated just as other variables are manipulated in BASIC-PLUS statements. In most cases we can only specify the manipulation of one array element at a time. For example, each use of an array name in a BASIC-PLUS assignment statement or a condition must be followed by a subscript indicating the particular array element to be manipulated.

It is important to understand the distinction among the array subscript, the value of the subscript (usually called the *index* to an array), and the contents of the array element. The subscript is enclosed in parentheses following the array name. Its value (the index) is used to select one of the array elements for manipulation. The contents of that array element is used as an operand or modified as a result of executing a BASIC-PLUS statement.

The array G shown below

G(1)	G(2)	G(3)	G(4)	G(5)	G(6)	G(7)	G(8)	G(9)	G(10)
−11.2	12	−6.1	4.5	8.2	1.3	−.7	8.3	9	−3.3

will be used for both Examples 6.6 and 6.7. This array was also used in Example 6.5.

Example 6.6 The six assignment statements below involve the variables M, N, X, and Y and the array G. Assume that M = 2, N = 4, and X = 28.5. Make sure you understand the differences among these statements as shown below.

	Results
110 LET Y = M + N	Y [6]
120 LET Y = G(M+N)	Y [1.3]
130 LET Y = G(M) + G(N)	Y [16.5]
140 LET M + N = X	illegal
150 LET G(M+N) = X	G(6) [28.5]
160 LET G(M) + G(N) = X	illegal

Line 110 assigns the value of M + N, or 6, to Y.

Line 120 uses the expression M+N as a subscript. The value of G(6), which is 1.3, is assigned to Y.

Line 130 computes the sum of array elements G(2) and G(4). This value, 16.5, is assigned to Y.

Line 140 is illegal. (Why?)

Line 150 assigns the value of X to the array element with subscript M+N. The value 28.5 is assigned to G(6); the previous value of G(6), which was 1.3, is destroyed.

Line 160 is illegal. (Why?)

Example 6.7 Let G be the array of size 10 shown before Example 6.6 (and in Example 6.5).

Then the sequence of instructions

```
100 LET J = 1
110 LET I = 4
120 LET G(10) = 10
130 LET G(I) = 400
140 LET G(2*I) = G(I) + G(J)
```

will alter the contents of the 10th, 4th, and 8th elements of G, as shown in Table 6.1; the new contents of array G are shown in Fig. 6.2.

Table 6.1 Manipulating Array G

Statement		Subscript	Value of Subscript	Effect
120 LET G(10) = 10		10	10	Store 10 in G(10)
130 LET G(I) = 400		I	4	Store 400 in G(4)
140 LET G(2*I) =	&	2*I	8	Add contents of G(4)
G(I) + G(J)		I,J	4,1	and G(1), 400 + (−11.2), and store sum (388.8) in G(8)

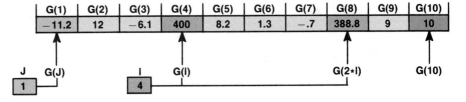

Fig. 6.2 Array G after modifications.

Example 6.8   Let ALPHA be an array declared as

```
110 DIM ALPHA(10)
```

a) The statement

```
120 LET ALPHA(I) = 10 * I FOR I = 1 TO 10
```

will cause the values 10, 20, 30, . . . 100 to be placed in succession in the first, second, third, . . . tenth elements of ALPHA, yielding

Array ALPHA

(1)	(2)	(3)	(4)	(5)	(6)	(7)	(8)	(9)	(10)
10	20	30	40	50	60	70	80	90	100

b) The statement

```
120 LET ALPHA(I) = 0 FOR I = 1 TO 10
```

will cause each element of ALPHA (in order, from the first (I = 1) to the last (I = 10)) to be set to 0.

Example 6.9 In Example 6.4 we wrote program segments to display and sum 12 bank balances. In the program shown in Fig. 6.3, each depositor's name and bank balance are first read and echo printed (lines 220–250). Then the sum and average of all bank balances are computed and displayed (lines 270–330). Finally, the names of all depositors with balances greater than the average are printed (lines 350–400).

In the first loop (lines 220–250), each depositor's name and balance, starting with NAMES$(1) and BALANCE(1) and ending with NAMES$(12) and BALANCE(12), are read. The program reads 12 lines, each containing a character string followed by a number (e.g., HENRY, 6000). The summation of all balances also could be performed in the read loop; however, we preferred to implement this as a separate step (the loop at line 290).

```
100    !SIMPLE BANK BALANCE PROGRAM
110    !
120    !PROGRAM CONSTANT
140        LET MAX.DEPOS = 12   !MAX NUMBER OF DEPOSITORS
150    !
160    !ARRAYS USED
170        DIM NAMES$(12), BALANCE(12)
180    !
190    !READ AND PRINT ALL DEPOSITOR NAMES AND BALANCES
200        PRINT "LIST OF ALL DEPOSITORS"
210        PRINT "  NAME", "BALANCE"
220        FOR I = 1 TO MAX.DEPOS
230            READ NAMES$(I), BALANCE(I)
240            PRINT NAMES$(I), BALANCE(I)
250        NEXT I
260    !
270    !COMPUTE & PRINT SUM AND AVERAGE OF ALL DEPOSITS
280        SUM = 0
290        LET SUM = SUM + BALANCE(I)          &
               FOR I = 1 TO MAX.DEPOS
300        PRINT
310        PRINT "THE SUM OF BALANCES IS"; SUM
320        LET AVERAGE = SUM / MAX.DEPOS
330        PRINT "THE AVERAGE BALANCE IS"; AVERAGE
340    !
350    !PRINT NAMES OF ALL DEPOSITORS WITH
355    !BALANCES OVER AVERAGE
360        PRINT
370        PRINT "LIST OF DEPOSITORS WITH ";          &
               "BALANCES OVER THE AVERAGE"
380        FOR I = 1 TO MAX.DEPOS
390            IF BALANCE(I) > AVERAGE THEN           &
               PRINT NAMES$(I)
400        NEXT I
410    !
```

(continued)

```
420        DATA HENRY, 6000
430        DATA JOHN, 3000
440        DATA STEVE, 1000
450        DATA JACK, 1234.5
460        DATA THURGOOD, 9876.5
470        DATA JUDY, 4568.5
480        DATA FRANK, 5000.25
490        DATA DAVE, 4999.75
500        DATA BOB, 8763.25
510        DATA HARRY, 3215.68
520        DATA ED, 9273.62
530        DATA JOE, 4211.11
540    !
550        END
```

Fig. 6.3 An illustration of simple array manipulations.

In the third loop (lines 380–400), each value stored in the array BAL-ANCE is compared to the average balance, AVERAGE. The program prints the name, NAMES$(I), of each depositor whose balance, BALANCE(I), is greater than AVERAGE.

Note that it is only necessary to read each array element once (line 230). After it is read, an array element may be referenced many times in a program (e.g., lines 240, 290, and 390). A sample run of the program is shown in Fig. 6.4.

```
RUNNH
LIST OF ALL DEPOSITORS
   NAME         BALANCE
HENRY           6000
JOHN            3000
STEVE           1000
JACK            1234.5
THURGOOD        9876.5
JUDY            4568.5
FRANK           5000.25
DAVE            4999.75
BOB             8763.25
HARRY           3215.68
ED              9273.62
JOE             4211.11


THE SUM OF BALANCES IS 61143.2
THE AVERAGE BALANCE IS 5095.26


LIST OF DEPOSITORS WITH BALANCES OVER THE AVERAGE
HENRY
THURGOOD
BOB
ED
```

Fig. 6.4 Sample run of program in Fig. 6.3.

Example 6.9 illustrates a very common programming technique: the use of one array (BALANCE) to select for processing an item from another *parallel array* (NAMES$). In this case, the program prints each name (in NAMES$) that corresponds to a balance (in BALANCE) that exceeds AVERAGE. The arrays NAMES$ and BALANCE are called parallel arrays, since the elements from each array with the same index pertain to the same depositor, as shown below.

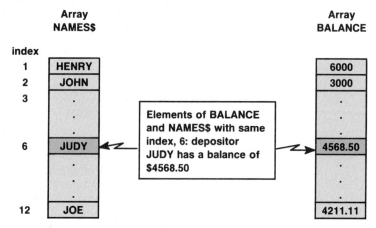

It is important to realize that the loop control variable I in Fig. 6.3 determines which array element is manipulated during each loop repetition. The use of the loop control variable as an array subscript is very common since it allows us to specify easily the sequence in which the elements of an array are to be manipulated. Each time the loop control variable is increased, the next array element is automatically selected. Note also that the same loop control variable is used in all three loops. This is not necessary, but it is permitted since I is reset to 1 each time a loop is entered.

Program Style

Program constants revisited

The maximum number of depositors (MAX.DEPOS = 12) for the Bank Balance Example (Fig. 6.3) is a good example of an important program constant. In this example, this value is used to limit the repetition in all three FOR loops (lines 220, 290, 380).

Program constants such as this should always be given a name in an assignment statement. If the value of the constant is ever changed, then only that assignment statement would require alteration. No other statements (such as lines 220, 290, and 380) would need changing. This approach saves time and greatly reduces the chance of error. Remember, however, not to try to use a program constant name in an array declaration.

Program Style

In all examples in this chapter, we have chosen not to use integer variables (names ending with a % sign) as array subscripts or as FOR loop control variables. Although many programmers prefer to use integer variables for these purposes in order to improve program efficiency, we have chosen not to do so for two reasons:

1. It is far too easy to forget to attach the percent sign in all places where it is needed. This failure can result in errors that are not detected by BASIC-PLUS (as either a syntax or a run-time error) but yet produce incorrect results. Recall that both I and I% may be used as variable names in the same program. If I% were used as a FOR loop control variable in Example 6.9 and I (rather than I%) were used as an array subscript in the loop, BASIC-PLUS would not detect an error. Since all numeric variables are initialized to 0, BASIC-PLUS would manipulate BALANCE(0) and NAMES$(0) each time the loop was repeated.

2. A proliferation of percent signs, in our view, makes a program more difficult to read.

These disadvantages, especially (1), normally will outweigh efficiency considerations except in extreme cases where hundreds or maybe thousands of repetitions are involved. Therefore, we will avoid using integer variables for FOR loop control or subscripting except in these extreme cases.

Exercise 6.5: Given the array G as shown in Fig. 6.2:

a) What is the contents of G(3)?
b) If I = 3, what is the contents of G(2*I−1)?
c) What is printed by the statement

```
100 IF G(I) = 8.2 THEN PRINT "YES"     &
        ELSE PRINT "NO"
```

if I is equal to 3; if I is equal to 5?
d) What will be the value of the string variable FLAG$ after the following statements are executed?

```
100 LET FLAG$ = "FALSE"
110 FOR INDEX = 1 TO 10
120    IF G(INDEX) = −.7 THEN LET FLAG$ = "TRUE"
130 NEXT INDEX
```

e) What will the array G look like after the following loop is executed?

```
200 LET G(IX) = 2 * IX FOR IX = 1 TO 10
```

f) Describe how the original array G would be changed by the following statement sequence.

```
300 READ G(INX) FOR INX = 1 TO 4
310 DATA 12, 18, 22, -9.3
```

Exercise 6.6: Why is it necessary to use arrays in Fig. 6.3? Could we easily avoid the use of arrays in this example? Justify your answer.

Exercise 6.7: If we wished to rewrite the program in Example 6.9 to process a maximum of 100 depositors, what statements would need to be changed? If we had not used MAX.DEPOS as a name for the constant 12, but instead used 12 everywhere MAX.DEPOS appears, what additional work would be required to change the maximum number of depositors to 100 (or any number other than 12)?

Exercise 6.8: Rewrite the program in Example 6.9 using only two loops. Could you write this program using one loop? Explain.

Reading and Printing Array Elements

In Chapter 10, we will introduce some features of BASIC-PLUS that will enable us to fill an entire array with a collection of data using a single READ (or INPUT) statement. These features will also allow us to print an entire array with a single PRINT statement. With the array features currently at our disposal, however, we will have to read and print array elements one at a time using a loop. We will use the loop control variable as a subscript to specify which array element is being defined or printed at any given time.

The program shown in Fig. 6.5 reads two separate arrays of data and prints both arrays in tabular form. The first loop (line 140) reads in all elements of the string array PRES.NAME$, the second loop (line 170) reads in all elements of the array YEAR. In the third loop (line 210), the output list for the PRINT statement references a pair of parallel array elements with subscript I. As the value of I goes from 1 to 5, the contents of these arrays will be printed in two columns, as shown in the output of Fig. 6.5.

If the input data had been prepared so that each president's name was followed by his first year in office, a single FOR loop could be used to enter all data. In this case, the statements that follow would replace lines 140 through 190 of Fig. 6.5.

```
140 READ PRES.NAME$(I), YEAR(I) FOR I = 1 TO SIZE
150 DATA WASHINGTON, 1789
160 DATA ADAMS, 1797
170 DATA JEFFERSON, 1801
180 DATA MADISON, 1809
190 DATA MONROE, 1817
```

```
100    !ILLUSTRATION OF ARRAY READ AND PRINT
105    !
110       LET SIZE = 5
115    !
120       DIM PRES.NAME$(5), YEAR(5)
130    !
140       READ PRES.NAME$(I) FOR I = 1 TO SIZE
150       DATA WASHINGTON, ADAMS, JEFFERSON
155       DATA MADISON, MONROE
160    !
170       READ YEAR(I) FOR I = 1 TO SIZE
180       DATA 1789, 1797, 1801, 1809, 1817
190    !
200       PRINT "NAME", "FIRST YEAR IN OFFICE"
210       PRINT PRES.NAME$(I); TAB(23); YEAR(I) &
              FOR I = 1 TO SIZE
220    !
230       END

RUNNH
NAME                FIRST YEAR IN OFFICE
WASHINGTON                1789
ADAMS                     1797
JEFFERSON                 1801
MADISON                   1809
MONROE                    1817
```

Fig. 6.5 A program and sample output for reading and printing two arrays.

The program in Fig. 6.5 filled all five elements of the two arrays PRES.NAME$ and YEAR with data, and then printed out these elements in pairs. This program used all elements of both arrays. There are numerous problems, however, in which we may want to manipulate only a portion of an array, with the exact number of elements involved determined during each execution of the program. In this case, we should declare the size of the array to be large enough to accomodate the largest expected set of data items. We must also provide our program with information indicating exactly how many data items (how many array elements) will be used in a given program run. We can then use this information to determine the upper subscript limit of the array elements involved in the program computations. This process is illustrated in the following example.

Example 6.10   Because of classroom space limitations, the maximum size of a class at the New University is 100. The students at the University are given a series of achievement examinations and we are asked to write the data entry portion of a program to perform some statistical computations on the exam scores on a class-by-class basis. We will be given the size of each class and a list of the achievement exam scores for the class.

The interactive program segment shown in Fig. 6.6 can be used to enter the input data into computer memory for subsequent processing.

```
100  !READING PART OF AN ARRAY
105  !
110  !PROGRAM CONSTANT
120     LET MAX.SIZE = 100    !MAX DATA ITEMS ALLOWED
140  !
150  !ARRAYS USED
160     DIM SCORES(100)
165  !
170  !READ IN NUMBER OF ITEMS TO BE PROCESSED AND
175  !ENSURE IT IS WITHIN BOUNDS
180     INPUT "ENTER CLASS SIZE"; CLASS.SIZE
190     INPUT "OUT OF RANGE -- REENTER"; CLASS.SIZE &
            UNTIL 1 <= CLASS.SIZE AND                &
                  CLASS.SIZE <= MAX.SIZE
200  !
210  !ENTER SCORES
220     PRINT
230     PRINT "ENTER SCORES, ONE AT A TIME"
250     INPUT SCORES(I) FOR I = 1 TO CLASS.SIZE
```

Fig. 6.6 Reading part of an array.

Program Style

Verifying array bounds

The input variable CLASS.SIZE is an essential part of the program
segment shown in Fig. 6.6. It specifies exactly what portion of the array SCORES is manipulated in the FOR loop (at line 250). If the value
of CLASS.SIZE does not fall within a range of values that is meaningful (1 <= CLASS.SIZE <= MAX.SIZE), the loop will not execute correctly. It is always important to ensure that an input value
such as CLASS.SIZE is displayed during execution (if it is not entered interactively), and to verify that it falls within a meaningful
range of values.

The loop at line 190 in Fig. 6.6 illustrates a very convenient BASIC-
PLUS technique for validating important input values—i.e., ensuring
that these values fall within a meaningful range. This loop will cause
the program to type the "OUT OF RANGE -- REENTER" message
and request a corrected value of CLASS.SIZE, until CLASS.SIZE
falls within the desired range. Note that for the UNTIL test to work
correctly the first time it is encountered, the initial input request for
CLASS.SIZE (line 180) must precede it.

Exercise 6.9: Declare an array PRIME consisting of 10 elements. Prepare a
DATA statement and READ statement for entering the first 10 prime numbers into
the array PRIME.

Exercise 6.10: Write a program segment to display the index and the contents of each element of the array PRIME in the tabular form below. (See Exercise 6.9.)

```
N        PRIME(N)
1            1
2            2
3            3
4            5
.            .
.            .
.            .
10          23
```

Exercise 6.11: Write program segments (using a FOR loop) to:

a) print the contents of the first eight elements of the array PRIME (see Exercise 6.10);

b) print the contents of the middle six elements (the third through the eighth) of PRIME;

c) print the contents of the last four elements of PRIME;

d) print the contents of the first K elements of PRIME, where K is an integer variable.

Initialization of Arrays

BASIC-PLUS will automatically initialize all elements of a numeric array to zero and a string array to blanks (the null string) when the array declaration is processed. However, it is best to initialize all array elements explicitly before they are referenced either through assignment statements or data entry (READ/INPUT) statements. Such initialization can be done most easily by writing FOR loops in which the elements of the array are referenced one-by-one using the loop control variable as a subscript.

Example 6.11
The program segment below initializes all elements of the arrays P and Q to zero and one, respectively.

```
100 DIM P(100), Q(100)
110 FOR I = 1 TO 100
120     LET P(I) = 0
130     LET Q(I) = 1
140 NEXT I
```

The FOR loop is repeated 100 times. Each time, an element of P is set to zero and the corresponding element of Q is set to one; first P(1), Q(1), then P(2), Q(2), and finally P(100), Q(100).

Example 6.12
The program segment at the top of the next page creates an array of squares. The value I^2 is stored in the array element with subscript I.

```
100 DIM SQUARE(10)
110 LET SQUARE(I) = I ^ 2 FOR I = 1 TO 10
```

SQUARE(1)	SQUARE(2)	SQUARE(3)		SQUARE(10)
1	4	9	. . .	100

Example 6.13   The program segment

```
110 DIM X(9)
120 LET X(I) = 200 FOR I = 1 TO 5
130 LET X(I) = 300 FOR I = 6 TO 8
```

initializes the array X as shown below.

X(1)	X(2)	X(3)	X(4)	X(5)	X(6)	X(7)	X(8)	X(9)
200	200	200	200	200	300	300	300	?

Example 6.14   Both of the statement sequences

```
100 DIM AGE.INFO$(4)          100 DIM AGE.INFO$(4)
110 LET AGE.INFO$(1) = "MY"   110 READ AGE.INFO$(I) &
120 LET AGE.INFO$(2) = "AGE"      FOR I = 1 TO 4
130 LET AGE.INFO$(3) = "IS"   120 DATA "MY", "AGE", &
140 LET AGE.INFO$(4) = "97"        "IS", "97"
```

will cause the four elements of the array AGE.INFO$ to be initialized as
shown below.

AGE.INFO$ (1)	AGE.INFO$ (2)	AGE.INFO$ (3)	AGE.INFO$ (4)
MY	AGE	IS	97

Exercise 6.12:   a) Declare and initialize an array called LETTER$ that contains
each letter of the alphabet in consecutive elements.
b)   Declare and initialize an array S of size 10 in which the value of each element is the same as its subscript; i.e., S(1) = 1, S(2) = 2, ... S(10)
= 10.
c)   Declare and initialize an array T of size 10 for which T(1) = 10, T(2)
= 9, ... T(10) = 1.
d)   Declare and initialize an array CUBE of size 10 in which the value of each element is the cube of its subscript; i.e., CUBE(1) = 1; CUBE(2) = 8;
... CUBE(10) = 1000.

Additional Examples of Array Processing

In this section, we provide two additional short examples involving arrays. In the first example (Example 6.15), array input is controlled using a
sentinel value. The second example (Example 6.16) illustrates the use of a
simple *array search* to locate a specified item in an array.

Example 6.15   The program in Fig. 6.7 reads a simple inventory list of items until a sentinel string of one or more blanks is entered. The program prints the entire inventory in a tabular form, along with the total dollar value of each item. It also computes and prints the total value of the inventory. This program provides another illustration of some of the fundamental techniques for manipulating array elements.

The input line for each inventory item consists of the item name, a count of the number of items on hand, and the cost of each item. A WHILE loop is used to store these data triples in successive elements of three parallel arrays. The variables ONE.NAME$, ONE.COUNT and ONE.COST are used as temporary holding places for each data value. In line 250, the program checks that ONE.NAME$ is not the sentinel and that the array is not full (I < MAX.STOCK) before incrementing I and copying each temporary variable value into an array. The use of these variables is not absolutely necessary. It does, however, enable us to keep the sentinel record out of the arrays and it makes it easier to ensure that the subscript I never exceeds MAX.STOCK.

```
100   !SIMPLE INVENTORY CONTROL PROBLEM
110   !
120   !PROGRAM CONSTANTS
130       LET MAX.STOCK = 1000    !MAX NUMBER ALLOWED
140       LET SENTINEL$ = " "     !SENTINEL VALUE
150   !
160   !ARRAYS USED
170       DIM ITEM.NAME$(1000), ON.HAND%(1000)
175       DIM COST(1000)
180   !
190   !READ AND PRINT EACH ITEM AND
195   !ACCUMULATE CASH VALUE OF INVENTORY
200       PRINT "INVENTORY CONTROL" \ PRINT
210       PRINT "ITEM NAME", " ", "ON HAND", &
215            "COST", "TOTAL VALUE"
220       LET INV.VALUE = 0
230       READ ONE.NAME$, ONE.COUNT, ONE.COST
240       LET I = 0
250       WHILE (ONE.NAME$ <> SENTINEL$) AND    &
                 (I < MAX.STOCK)
260          LET I = I + 1
270          LET ITEM.NAME$(I) = ONE.NAME$
280          LET ON.HAND%(I) = ONE.COUNT
290          LET COST(I) = ONE.COST
300          LET ITEM.VALUE = ON.HAND%(I) * COST(I)
310          LET INV.VALUE = INV.VALUE + ITEM.VALUE
320          PRINT ITEM.NAME$(I), ON.HAND%(I),      &
                    COST(I), ITEM.VALUE
330          READ ONE.NAME$, ONE.COUNT, ONE.COST
340       NEXT    !WHILE
350       LET COUNT.ITEMS = I
360   !
```

(continued)

```
370   !PRINT FINAL TOTALS
380      PRINT
390      PRINT COUNT.ITEMS; "ITEMS WERE PROCESSED"
400      PRINT "THE INVENTORY VALUE IS"; INV.VALUE
420      IF ONE.NAME$ <> SENTINEL$ THEN                      &
            PRINT "DATA ITEMS EXCEEDED"; MAX.STOCK;          &
               "ALL EXTRAS WERE LOST!"
425   !
430      DATA "MICE             ", 42, 3.5
440      DATA "MONTREAL YOUPPIE ", 12, 45
450      DATA "BIRD BRAIN       ", 3, 145
460      DATA "SAN DIEGO CHICKEN", 84, 22
470      DATA "PHILLY PHANATIC  ", 147, 8.25
480      DATA "BALTIMORE BIRD   ", 37, 17
490      DATA " ",0, 0
495   !
500      END

RUNNH
INVENTORY CONTROL

ITEM NAME                 ON HAND   COST        TOTAL VALUE
MICE                      42        3.5         147
MONTREAL YOUPPIE          12        45          540
BIRD BRAIN                3         145         435
SAN DIEGO CHICKEN         84        22          1848
PHILLY PHANATIC           147       8.25        1212.75
BALTIMORE BIRD            37        17          629

6 ITEMS WERE PROCESSED
THE INVENTORY VALUE IS 4811.75
```

Fig. 6.7 Illustration of array manipulation techniques.

A simple FOR loop will not work here because we do not know before-hand exactly how many items are to be processed. Although we have a limit on the maximum number of items (1000), it is very likely that fewer items will be processed in most runs of the program. In cases like this, a sentinel value is needed to signal the end of data and the UNTIL or WHILE loop (or FOR–UNTIL or FOR–WHILE) should be used to control repetition.

Program Style

Use of the integer data type for large arrays

The arrays declared in Fig. 6.7 (line 170) are relatively large. In order to minimize the amount of memory space actually used, we defined the count-on-hand array as an integer array (ON.HAND%). This is because an array of 1000 integer values uses only half as much memory as an array of 1000 real values. As indicated earlier, we will only use the integer data type in cases where considerable savings in time or space would result.

Example 6.16   A very common problem in working with arrays involves the need to search an array to determine whether or not a particular value, called a *key*, is in the array. The program segment shown next could be used to search the array ITEM.NAME$ in order to determine if a particular item (the key) is present. If the key, KEYS$, is found, a message is printed and the search is terminated. If the entire array is searched without finding the key, an appropriate message is also printed. The FOR loop illustrated (lines 110, 120) is an example of an empty loop—it contains no statements in the loop body, since all required steps are specified in the loop header.

```
100  !SEARCH ITEM.NAME$ ARRAY FOR AN ITEM (KEYS$)
110     FOR INDEX = 1 UNTIL INDEX = ITEM.COUNT OR      &
                              ITEM.NAME$(INDEX) = KEYS$
120     NEXT INDEX
130     IF ITEM.NAME$(INDEX) = KEYS$ THEN             &
           PRINT "KEY "; KEYS$; " FOUND."             &
        ELSE                                          &
           PRINT "KEY "; KEYS$; " NOT FOUND."
```

Exercise 6.13:
a) Is it necessary to use arrays in writing the program for Example 6.15? Justify your answer.
b) If your answer to (a) is no, how would you change it so that it would still work (without arrays)?
c) Would your answers to (a) and (b) change if the data were entered interactively?
d) Rewrite the loop portion of the program in Fig. 6.7 without using the temporary "hold" variables to initially store each data line that is read. Check your loop carefully to ensure it works. What problems did you encounter in writing a correct loop?

Exercise 6.14:   Explain in detail how you would alter the inventory problem (Example 6.15) if the number of items to be processed were known and could be read in at the beginning of the program.

Exercise 6.15:   Explain in detail how you would alter the bank balance program (Example 6.9) using a sentinel value to mark the end of the data collection.

Exercise 6.16:   Write a program segment to search the array ON.HAND% (Fig. 6.7) to see if there is any item with a zero count-on-hand value. Your program should print the name of the first item with the zero count-on-hand.

Exercise 6.17:   (*Extension of Exercise 6.16*)
a) Alter your program segment in Exercise 6.16 to print the names of all items having a zero count-on-hand value.
b) Extend (a) to also print the indexes (subscripts) of each item with a zero count-on-hand and the total number of such items.

Array Search Applications

Our first example of a simple array search appeared in Example 6.16. In this example, an array of ITEM.COUNT data items was searched in order to determine whether or not a particular item (KEYS$) was present in the array. The need for array searches is very common in computer programming. In variations of the simple search for one occurrence of a key, we might want to know how many times the key is present or where in the array each copy of the key is located (see Exercise 6.17).

In the following problem we use an array search to determine the index of an array element containing a specified key.

Problem 6A

Write an interactive program that could be used by a small bank (maximum of 20 depositor accounts) to process the daily transactions (deposits and withdrawals) against each account and maintain an up-to-date record of the balance for each account.

Discussion: For each depositor account, the bank keeps a record of depositor name, starting balance, and current balance. We will use three parallel arrays (DEP.NAME$ for depositor names, START.BAL for starting balances, and CUR.BAL for current balances) of size 20 to store this data. The initial data for DEP.NAME$ and START.BAL will be read in at the start of the program.

Once the initial account information has been processed, all transactions for the day will be entered at the terminal. Each transaction record will specify the depositor name (TRANS.NAME$) and transaction amount (TRANS.AMOUNT); a positive transaction amount indicates a deposit, and a negative amount indicates a withdrawal. At the end of the day, when there are no more transactions to be processed, the data entry operator at the terminal can obtain a printout of the starting and final balance for each account simply by typing the sentinel name, "*". The data table follows; the flow diagrams are shown in Fig. 6.8.

DATA TABLE FOR PROBLEM 6A

	Program Constants		

NUM.ACCOUNTS = 20: number of accounts to be processed

SENTINEL$ = "*":   the sentinel value for DEP.NAME$

Input Variables		Output Variables	
DEP.NAME$( ):	Array of depositor names (size 20)	CUR.BAL( ):	Array of current balances (size 20)
START.BAL( ):	Array of starting balances (size 20)		
TRANS.NAME$:	Depositor name for current transaction		
TRANS.AMOUNT:	Amount of current transaction		

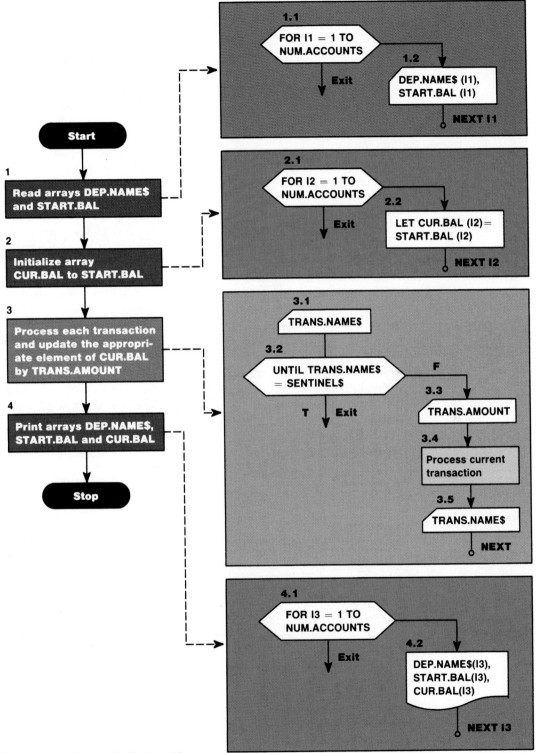

Fig. 6.8 Flow diagrams for Problem 6A.

The array of current balances, CUR.BAL, must be initially the same as the array of starting balances, START.BAL. Hence each individual element of START.BAL should be copied into the corresponding element of CUR.BAL. A FOR loop is used to accomplish this in the refinement of Step 2 (see Fig. 6.8.)

The refinement of Step 3 consists of an UNTIL loop used to process all transactions. Each transaction is completely processed before the next transaction is entered; hence only two variables (TRANS.NAME$ and TRANS.AMOUNT) are needed to store the depositor name and transaction amount for the current transaction. When the sentinel name "*" is entered, the UNTIL loop is exited and execution continues at Step 4. The actual processing of each transaction (Step 3.4) is discussed next.

It is important to realize that the transactions do not follow any particular order and that there may be zero, one, or many transactions during the day for each depositor's account. In order to process the current transaction, each transaction amount, TRANS.AMOUNT, must be added to the current balance for the proper account. In other words, TRANS.AMOUNT must be added to a particular element of the array CUR.BAL—namely, the element containing the current balance for the depositor name, TRANS.NAME$. This is easily accomplished since the arrays are parallel.

The value of TRANS.NAME$ is the key that must be found in DEP.NAME$ (array of depositor names). Each element of DEP.NAME$ is examined in sequence until the element (indicated by KEY.INDEX) that matches the key is found. The corresponding element of CUR.BAL, CUR.BAL(KEY.INDEX), is then updated.

For example, consider the arrays DEP.NAME$ and CUR.BAL and the depositor name TRANS.NAME$ shown below (TRANS.NAME$ equals "KLEIN"). In this case the key is "KLEIN" and the index of the element of DEP.NAME$ that matches the key is 3; hence CUR.BAL(3) should be updated.

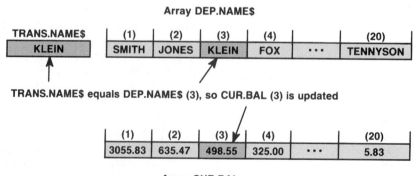

This process of examining each element in DEP.NAME$ to find a key is an array search. The flow diagram for the search is shown in Fig. 6.9. In this diagram, the FOR loop control variable I4 is used to select each element of DEP.NAME$ in sequence.

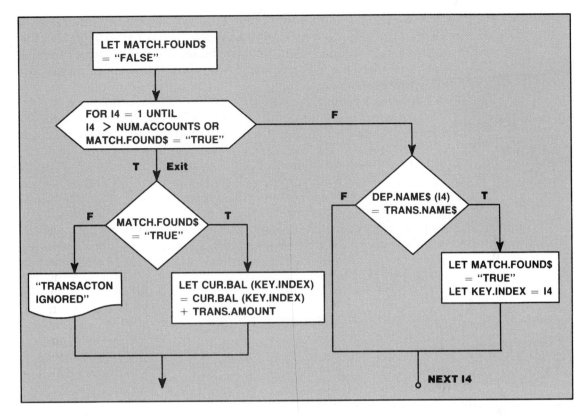

Fig. 6.9 Refinement of Step 3.4 of Problem 6A.

If an array element DEP.NAME$(I4) matches TRANS.NAME$, the found indicator, MATCH.FOUND$, is set to "TRUE" and the index of the key, KEY.INDEX, is set to I4. After loop exit, the transaction amount, TRANS.AMOUNT, is added to CUR.BAL(KEY.INDEX) provided that the key was found in DEP.NAME$ (MATCH.FOUND$ equal to "TRUE"). If MATCH.FOUND$ is equal to "FALSE" (TRANS.NAME$ not found), an error message is printed instead. The additions to the data table follow.

ADDITIONAL DATA TABLE ENTRIES FOR PROBLEM 6A

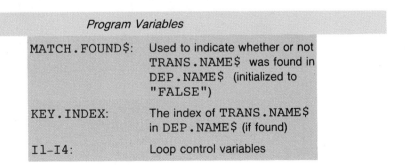

Program Variables	
MATCH.FOUND$:	Used to indicate whether or not TRANS.NAME$ was found in DEP.NAME$ (initialized to "FALSE")
KEY.INDEX:	The index of TRANS.NAME$ in DEP.NAME$ (if found)
I1-I4:	Loop control variables

The program is shown in Fig. 6.10a. As in earlier programs, short refinements (in this case, Steps 2 and 4) were not implemented as separate modules. The longer refinements needed by the main program (to read data—Step 1, and process each transaction—Step 3) are implemented as *level two subroutines* (see Fig. 6.10b). The additional, *level three subroutine* for Step 3.4 is shown in Fig 6.10c.

We have placed the initial account information at the very end of the subroutine that reads this data (lines 1070–1270). These DATA statements will all be processed by the READ statement on line 1030. (In Chapter 11 we will learn how to use another BASIC-PLUS feature, the file, to simplify this process.) None of the transaction data need be provided, since the transactions will be entered interactively as the program executes (lines 2040, 2080 and 2100).

The final output for this program consists of the three columns of summary information for each account, which is produced by line 340 of the main program. A sample run of the program is given in Fig. 6.11.

```
110     !SMALL BANK SAVINGS ACCOUNT UPDATE PROBLEM
120     !
130     !PROGRAM CONSTANTS
140         LET NUM.ACCOUNTS = 20    !MAX ACCOUNTS
150         LET SENTINEL$ = "*"      !SENTINEL VALUE
160     !
170     !ARRAYS USED
180         DIM DEP.NAME$(20), START.BAL(20), CUR.BAL(20)
190     !
200     !READ DATA
210         GOSUB 1000
220     !
230     !INITIALIZE CURRENT BALANCES (CUR.BAL)
235     !TO STARTING BALANCES (START.BAL)
240         LET CUR.BAL(I2) = START.BAL(I2)                &
                FOR I2 = 1 TO NUM.ACCOUNTS
250     !
260     !PROCESS ALL TRANSACTIONS
270         GOSUB 2000
280     !
290     !WHEN TRANSACTION PROCESSING IS COMPLETE,
300     !DISPLAY FINAL RESULTS FOR THE DAY
310         PRINT \ PRINT "TOTALS FOR TODAY"
320         PRINT \ PRINT "ACCOUNT", "START", "FINAL"
330         PRINT "NAME", "BALANCE", "BALANCE" \ PRINT
340         PRINT DEP.NAME$(I3), START.BAL(I3),           &
                CUR.BAL(I3) FOR I3 = 1 TO NUM.ACCOUNTS
350     !
360         STOP
```

Fig. 6.10a Main Program for Problem 6A.

```
1000 !DATA ENTRY SUBROUTINE
1020 !
1030     READ DEP.NAME$(Il), START.BAL(Il)            &
             FOR Il = 1 TO NUM.ACCOUNTS
1040 !
1050     RETURN
1060 !
1070 !ACCOUNT NAMES AND INITIAL BALANCES
1080     DATA "SMITH", 3055.83
1090     DATA "JONES", 635.47
1100     DATA "KLEIN", 498.55
1110     DATA "FOX", 325.00
1120     DATA "O'HARA", 4567.98
1130     DATA "FITZGERALD", 532.76
1140     DATA "FRY", 45.90
1150     DATA "LESSING", 1345.70
1160     DATA "JONG", 789.05
1170     DATA "DATES", 7040.88
1180     DATA "GARDNER", 890.54
1190     DATA "EVERT", 33.99
1200     DATA "ROTH", 668.90
1210     DATA "STEINBECK", 1087.43
1220     DATA "ROSNER", 55.78
1230     DATA "BRONTE", 888.77
1240     DATA "CARMICHAEL", 66.43
1250     DATA "BROWN", 7869.00
1260     DATA "PHILLIPS", 546.88
1270     DATA "TENNYSON", 5.83
1300 !END OF DATA ENTRY SUBROUTINE
1310 !
1320 !
2000 !SUBROUTINE TO PROCESS ALL TRANSACTIONS
2010 !
2020 !ENTER FIRST TRANSACTION
2030     PRINT
2040     INPUT "ENTER NAME OR A '*'"; TRANS.NAME$
2050 !PROCESS TRANSACTIONS UNTIL '*' ENTERED
2060     UNTIL TRANS.NAME$ = SENTINEL$
2065        PRINT "ENTER TRANSACTION AMOUNT"
2070        PRINT "(USE NEGATIVE FOR WITHDRAWAL)";
2080        INPUT TRANS.AMOUNT
2085        !SEARCH FOR TRANS.NAME$ AND UPDATE CUR.BAL
2090        GOSUB 3000
2095        PRINT
2100        INPUT "ENTER NAME OR A '*'"; TRANS.NAME$
2110     NEXT    !UNTIL
2120 !
2130     RETURN
2140 !END OF SUBROUTINE TO PROCESS ALL TRANSACTIONS
```

Fig. 6.10b Level two subroutines for Problem 6A.

```
3000  !SEARCH SUBROUTINE
3005  !FIND TRANS$.NAME IN DEP.NAME$
3010  !IF FOUND, UPDATE CORRESPONDING BALANCE;
3020  !OTHERWISE, PRINT AN ERROR MESSAGE
3030  !
3040  !INITIALIZE MATCH.FOUND$ TO FALSE
3050      LET MATCH.FOUND$ = "FALSE"
3060  !SEARCH FOR TRANS.NAME$ IN DEP.NAME$
3070      FOR I4 = 1 UNTIL I4 > NUM.ACCOUNTS OR      &
                              MATCH.FOUND$ = "TRUE"
3080          IF DEP.NAME$(I4) = TRANS.NAME$ THEN    &
                  !TRANS.NAME$ FOUND AT ELEMENT I4   &
                  LET MATCH.FOUND$ = "TRUE"          &
                  \LET KEY.INDEX = I4
3090      NEXT I4
3100  !
3110  !UPDATE BALANCE IF TRANS.NAME$ FOUND
3120      IF MATCH.FOUND$ = "TRUE" THEN              &
              LET CUR.BAL(KEY.INDEX) =               &
                  CUR.BAL(KEY.INDEX) + TRANS.AMOUNT  &
          ELSE                                       &
              PRINT "TRANSACTION IGNORED -- ";       &
                  "KEY NOT FOUND"
3130  !
3140      RETURN
3150  !END OF SEARCH SUBROUTINE
3160  !
3170      END    !SAVINGS UPDATE
```

Fig. 6.10c Level three subroutine for Problem 6A.

```
ENTER NAME OR A '*'? KLEIN
ENTER TRANSACTION AMOUNT
(USE NEGATIVE FOR WITHDRAWAL)? 88.00

ENTER NAME OR A '*'? FOX
ENTER TRANSACTION AMOUNT
(USE NEGATIVE FOR WITHDRAWAL)? 38.40

ENTER NAME OR A '*'? TENNYSON
ENTER TRANSACTION AMOUNT
(USE NEGATIVE FOR WITHDRAWAL)? -99.00

ENTER NAME OR A '*'? CARMICHAEL
ENTER TRANSACTION AMOUNT
(USE NEGATIVE FOR WITHDRAWAL)? -44.00

ENTER NAME OR A '*'? WILSON
ENTER TRANSACTION AMOUNT
(USE NEGATIVE FOR WITHDRAWAL)? -33.00
TRANSACTION IGNORED -- KEY NOT FOUND
```

(continued)

```
ENTER NAME OR A '*'? BROWN
ENTER TRANSACTION AMOUNT
(USE NEGATIVE FOR WITHDRAWAL)? -1000.00

ENTER NAME OR A '*'? *

TOTALS FOR TODAY

ACCOUNT           START               FINAL
NAME              BALANCE             BALANCE

SMITH             3055.83             3055.83
JONES             635.47              635.47
KLEIN             498.55              586.55
FOX               325                 363.4
O'HARA            4567.98             4567.98
FITZGERALD        532.76              532.76
FRY               45.9                45.9
LESSING           1345.7              1345.7
JONG              789.05              789.05
DATES             7040.88             7040.88
GARDNER           890.54              890.54
EVERT             33.99               33.99
ROTH              668.9               668.9
STEINBECK         1087.43             1087.43
ROSNER            55.78               55.78
BRONTE            888.77              888.77
CARMICHAEL        66.43               22.43
BROWN             7869                6869
PHILLIPS          546.88              546.88
TENNYSON          5.83                -93.17
Stop at line 360
```

Fig. 6.11 Sample run of Problem 6A.

Exercise 6.18: A common error in implementing the search (Fig. 6.10c) is to place the "TRANSACTION IGNORED" message in the false branch of the decision structure inside the loop instead of after the loop exit. Explain what effect this error would have on the program output.

Exercise 6.19: The withdrawal of $99 for Tennyson should not have been allowed as it exceeded the account balance. Modify the search subroutine so this is prevented.

Exercise 6.20: It would be desirable to keep track of the number of deposits and withdrawals for each account during the day as well as the overall total number of deposits and withdrawals. Explain how this information could be determined and displayed.

6.5 Processing Selected Array Elements

In the examples seen so far, the loop control variable of a FOR loop often serves as an array subscript as well. This technique permits us to easily reference the elements of an array in sequential order.

However, there are many programming problems (including Problem 6A) in which only selected elements of an array are to be processed. In these problems, the selection process involves the determination of the index to a specific array element. Usually, the values of one or more input data items are involved in the determination of the index.

Two important techniques for determining the index of the desired array elements are:

- by searching a parallel array (as done in Problem 6A)
- through direct computation using a formula

We will illustrate the use of both techniques in the following problem.

Problem 6B   The IRS has provided us with a tax table (see Table 6.2) that can be used to determine the tax amount for all salaries up to $14,000. We wish to use this table to write a program that computes the tax owed by all graduate students in a university.

Table 6.2 IRS Tax Table for Salaries under $14,000

Tax Bracket	Base Salary	Tax Due on Base	Percentage for Excess over Base
1	$ 0	$ 0	14%
2	$ 500	$ 70	15%
3	$ 1000	$ 145	16%
4	$ 1500	$ 225	17%
5	$ 2000	$ 310	19%
6	$ 4000	$ 690	21%
7	$ 6000	$ 1110	24%
8	$ 8000	$ 1590	25%
9	$ 10000	$ 2090	27%
10	$ 12000	$ 2630	29%

Discussion: Each line of the tax table represents a different tax bracket. For example, all salaries between $1500 and $1999.99 are in tax bracket four. The table shows that the minimum tax for this bracket is $225. In addition, an extra tax amount is owed if the salary is greater than the base salary, $1500. This tax is equal to 17% of the excess salary over the base salary (e.g., for a salary of $1750, the extra tax owed is 0.17 $\times$ $250 or $42.50).

We will use three parallel arrays to store the information in Table 6.2.

	Base salary BASE.SALARY		Base tax due BASE.TAX		Tax percentage for excess amount earned PERCENT
1	0	1	0	1	0.14
2	500	2	70	2	0.15
3	1000	3	145	3	0.16
4	1500	4	225	4	0.17
5	2000	5	310	5	0.19
6	4000	6	690	6	0.21
7	6000	7	1110	7	0.24
8	8000	8	1590	8	0.25
9	10000	9	2090	9	0.27
10	12000	10	2630	10	0.29
11	14000				

Each column of the tax table is stored in a separate array; the relevant data for line i of the table are stored in element i of the arrays BASE.SALARY, BASE.TAX, and PERCENT. The reason for the extra element in BASE.SALARY will be explained later. The data table for the problem follows; the flow diagrams are shown in Figure 6.12a. For the purposes of this problem, we will assume that a student's salary and taxable income are the same.

DATA TABLE FOR PROBLEM 6B

Program Constants

SENTINEL$ = "*": sentinel value for NAMES$

TABLE.SIZE = 10: the number of tax brackets

Input Variables		Program Variables		Output Variables	
SALARY:	The salary earned by each student	BASE.SALARY( ):	The array of base salaries (size 11)	TAX:	The tax owed by each student
NAMES$:	The name of the student being processed	BASE.TAX( ):	The array of base taxes (size 10)		
		PERCENT( ):	The array of tax percentages (size 10)		

Step 1 uses a FOR loop to read in the tax table data to be stored in the three arrays BASE.SALARY, BASE.TAX, and PERCENT. Although the program is designed to run interactively, we will use READ/DATA statements to enter the tax data into these tables, since these data will not often change from one run of the program to the next. The main program and data entry subroutine are shown in Fig. 6.13a.

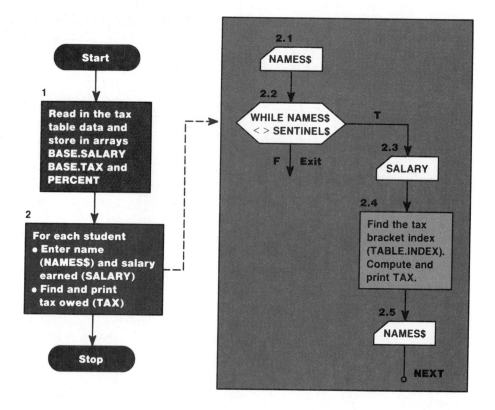

The refinement of Step 2 is shown in Fig. 6.12a. In performing Step 2.4,
the program must first determine whether or not SALARY is within the
range of the tax table. If so, the program flag, FOUND$, is set to "TRUE"
when the tax bracket, TABLE.INDEX, is found. The tax owed can be
computed by using the tax table data for that bracket. The refinement of
Step 2.4 is shown in Fig. 6.12b; the additional data table entries follow.

**ADDITIONAL
DATA TABLE
ENTRIES FOR
PROBLEM 6B**

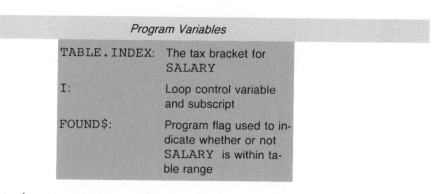

Program Variables	
TABLE.INDEX:	The tax bracket for SALARY
I:	Loop control variable and subscript
FOUND$:	Program flag used to indicate whether or not SALARY is within table range

FOR loop 2.4.2 in Fig. 6.12b must find the tax bracket (a value from 1 to
10) for SALARY. It does this by searching for the pair of elements in array
BASE.SALARY that "bracket" SALARY. In the tax computation subroutine
(see Fig. 6.13b), the condition at line 2090

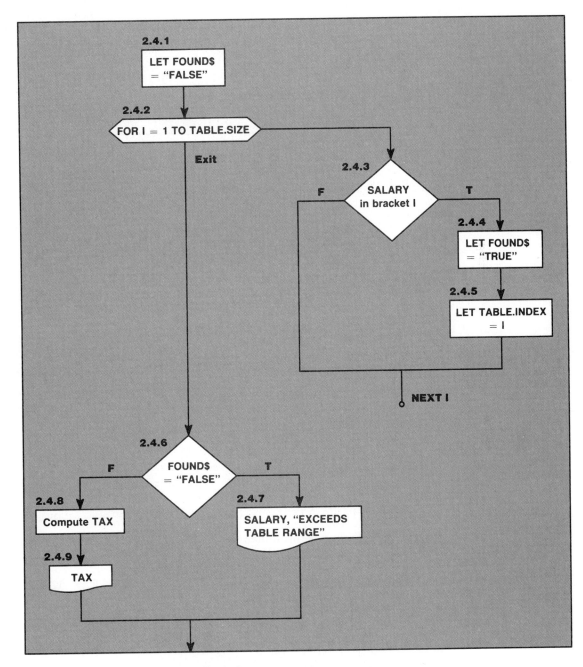

Fig. 6.12b Refinement of Step 2.4 of Fig. 6.12a.

```
SALARY >= BASE.SALARY(I) AND
SALARY < BASE.SALARY(I+1)
```

is true only when SALARY falls between the adjacent array elements BASE.SALARY(I) and BASE.SALARY(I+1). The subscript, I, of the smaller element corresponds to the tax bracket index, `TABLE.INDEX`. As shown below, the value of `TABLE.INDEX` should be set to four for a SALARY of $1750.

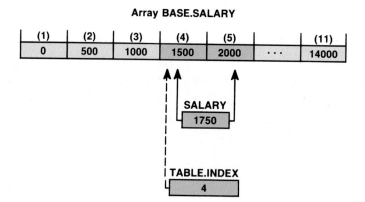

Array BASE.SALARY

Once defined, `TABLE.INDEX` can be used to compute the tax amount owed using the assignment statement

```
3020 LET TAX = BASE.TAX(TABLE.INDEX)                    &
               + PERCENT(TABLE.INDEX)                   &
               * (SALARY - BASE.SALARY(TABLE.INDEX))
```

In the expression above, `TABLE.INDEX` selects the tax computation data from the three parallel arrays `BASE.SALARY`, `BASE.TAX`, and `PERCENT`. This computation is performed below for a SALARY of $1750.

```
TAX =
    BASE.TAX(4)  +  PERCENT(4)  *  (1750-BASE.SALARY(4))
       = 225     +  0.17        *  (1750-1500)
       = 225     +  42.50
       = 267.50
```

The main program and subroutines for Problem 6B are shown in Figs. 6.13a, b. A sample run is shown in Fig. 6.13c.

```
100   !COMPUTE TAX OWED ON EACH SALARY - USE TAX TABLE
110   !
120   !PROGRAM CONSTANTS
130      LET SENTINEL$ = "*"   !SENTINEL VALUE
140      LET TABLE.SIZE = 10   !TABLE SIZE
150   !
160   !TAX TABLE ARRAYS
170      DIM BASE.SALARY(11), BASE.TAX(10)
180      DIM PERCENT(10)
200   !
210   !READ TAX TABLE DATA
220      GOSUB 1000
230   !
```

(continued)

```
240    !FOR EACH TAXPAYER, ENTER NAME AND SALARY,
245    !AND COMPUTE TAX
250        GOSUB 2000
260    !
270        STOP
280    !
290    !
1000   !SUBROUTINE TO READ TAX TABLE DATA
1010   !
1020       PRINT "GRADUATE STUDENT TAX TABLES" \ PRINT
1030       PRINT "BASE SALARY", "BASE TAX", "PERCENT"
1040       FOR I = 1 TO TABLE.SIZE
1050           READ BASE.SALARY(I), BASE.TAX(I),        &
                   PERCENT(I)
1060           PRINT BASE.SALARY(I), BASE.TAX(I)        &
                   PERCENT(I)
1070       NEXT I
1080       READ BASE.SALARY(TABLE.SIZE+1)
1085   !
1090       RETURN
1100   !
1110       DATA 0, 0, 0.14
1120       DATA 500, 70, 0.15
1130       DATA 1000, 145, 0.16
1140       DATA 1500, 225, 0.17
1150       DATA 2000, 310, 0.19
1160       DATA 4000, 690, 0.21
1170       DATA 6000, 1110, 0.24
1180       DATA 8000, 1590, 0.25
1190       DATA 10000, 2090, 0.27
1200       DATA 12000, 2630, 0.29
1210       DATA 14000
1220   !END OF SUBROUTINE TO READ TAX TABLE DATA
```

Fig. 6.13a Main program and data entry subroutine for Problem 6B.

```
2000   !SUBROUTINE TO COMPUTE TAX FOR EACH TAXPAYER
2010   !
2020       PRINT "TAX SUMMARY" \ PRINT
2030       INPUT "ENTER NAME OR A '*'"; NAMES$
2040       WHILE NAMES$ <> SENTINEL$
2050           INPUT "ENTER STUDENT SALARY"; SALARY
2060           !SEARCH TABLE FOR BRACKET INDEX
2070           LET FOUND$ = "FALSE"
2080           FOR I = 1 TO TABLE.SIZE
2090               IF SALARY >= BASE.SALARY(I) AND        &
                       SALARY < BASE.SALARY(I+1) THEN     &
                       LET FOUND$ = "TRUE"                &
                       \LET TABLE.INDEX = I
2100           NEXT I
```

(continued)

```
2105  !
2110          !IF TABLE.INDEX WAS FOUND, COMPUTE TAX
2120          IF FOUND$ = "TRUE" THEN GOSUB 3000           &
                 ELSE PRINT "SALARY EXCEEDS TABLE RANGE"
2130          !READ NEXT NAME
2140          INPUT "ENTER NAME OR A '*'"; NAMES$
2150      NEXT    !WHILE
2155  !
2160      RETURN
2170  !END OF SUBROUTINE TO COMPUTE TAX
2180  !
2190  !
3000  !SUBROUTINE FOR IF-THEN-ELSE AT LINE 2120
3010  !IF FOUND$ = "TRUE" THEN COMPUTE TAX
3020      LET TAX = BASE.TAX(TABLE.INDEX)                  &
                 + PERCENT(TABLE.INDEX)                     &
                 * (SALARY - BASE.SALARY(TABLE.INDEX))
3030      PRINT "THE TAX IS"; TAX \ PRINT
3040      RETURN
3050  !END OF SUBROUTINE FOR IF-THEN-ELSE AT LINE 2120
3060  !
3070      END
```

Fig. 6.13b Tax computation subroutine for Problem 6B

Program Style

Testing subscripts at loop boundary values

The subroutine shown in Fig. 6.13b contains a potential subscript error. When the search loop starting at line 2080 is executed for I = 10, the value of the subscript I+1 of BASE.SALARY will be 11. To ensure that a loop will function as desired, you must focus upon the boundary values (1 and 10 in this case) for the loop control variable. For each array referenced in the loop, you should verify that the values of all subscript expressions are in range and are correct. If correct at the boundaries, they will most likely be correct for all values in between.

However, if such a check indicates an error, then you may have to change the algorithm. To avoid a subscript error, we added an extra array element (BASE.SALARY(11) = 14000). Alternatively, we could have handled the case of a salary in excess of $12,000 separately, prior to loop entry, and could have rewritten the FOR loop header as FOR I = 1 TO TABLE.SIZE −1 rather than FOR I = 1 TO TABLE.SIZE. Of the several solutions, the addition of the extra array element is preferred because it is so simple.

```
RUNNH
GRADUATE STUDENT TAX TABLES

BASE SALARY      BASE TAX       PERCENT
 0                0             .14
 500              70            .15
 1000             145           .16
 1500             225           .17
 2000             310           .19
 4000             690           .21
 6000             1110          .24
 8000             1590          .25
 10000            2090          .27
 12000            2630          .29
TAX SUMMARY

ENTER NAME OR A '*'? Frank
ENTER STUDENT SALARY? 4500
THE TAX IS 795

ENTER NAME OR A '*'? Matthew
ENTER STUDENT SALARY? 9000
THE TAX IS 1840

ENTER NAME OR A '*'? Steve
ENTER STUDENT SALARY? 4000
THE TAX IS 690

ENTER NAME OR A '*'? Amelia
ENTER STUDENT SALARY? 8500
THE TAX IS 1715

ENTER NAME OR A '*'? *
Stop at line 270
```

Fig. 6.13c Sample run for Problem 6B.

Another approach to selecting the tax bracket is to compute the index as shown in Fig. 6.14. This direct computation is more convenient and efficient than an array search if there is a constant increment between table items.

```
IF SALARY < 0 OR SALARY >= BASE.SALARY(11) THEN  &
    PRINT "SALARY", SALARY, "IS OUT OF RANGE."    &
ELSE                                              &
    IF SALARY < 2000 THEN                         &
        LET TABLE.INDEX = INT(SALARY / 500) + 1   &
    ELSE                                          &
        LET TABLE.INDEX = INT(SALARY / 2000) + 4
```

Fig. 6.14 Direct computation of tax bracket index TABLE.INDEX.

In Fig. 6.14 the statement

```
LET TABLE.INDEX = INT(SALARY / 500) + 1
```

computes the index of the tax bracket for all values of SALARY less than $2000 (brackets one through four). There is a constant increment of $500 for the tax table entries in this range. The statement

```
LET TABLE.INDEX = INT(SALARY / 2000) + 4
```

is used for all larger salaries (tax increment of $2000).

For a salary of $1750, the computation would proceed as follows:

```
LET TABLE.INDEX = INT(1750 / 500) + 1
               = INT(3.5) + 1
               = 3 + 1 = 4
```

The value of TABLE.INDEX should always be checked to verify that it is in range since it is used to select array elements.

Exercise 6.21: Verify by hand simulation that the above formulas for TABLE.INDEX are correct. Test the following values of SALARY:

```
$250, $1275, $2750, $4000, $11700, $23000
```

Exercise 6.22: An exam with the grade ranges

> A: 90–100
> B: 80–89
> C: 70–79
> D: 60–69
> F: 0–59

is given to a math class. Write two subroutines to examine a student score (SCORE) and print the student grade. Use the array search technique in one subroutine and the direct computation technique in the other.
Hint: Store the lower grade boundaries in an array LOW.GRADE and the letter grades in an array LETTER$. For the direct computation technique, process the scores 100 and 0 through 49 separately.

Exercise 6.23: In Fig. 6.13b it is really not necessary to continue testing elements of BASE.SALARY once the bracket is found. Explain how to use the program flag to keep this from happening.

Exercise 6.24: Alter the program for Problem 6B (Figs. 6.13a, b) so that it checks to ensure that all salaries that are processed have values that are greater than 0.

6.6 Common Programming Errors

There are two very common programming errors associated with arrays. One involves the failure to declare a name that is to be used to represent an array and the other involves the use of subscripts with values that are too small or too large.

Failure to Declare an Array

The use of a subscript reference with a symbolic name that has not been declared as an array (via a DIM statement) will not cause a syntax error in BASIC-PLUS because BASIC-PLUS permits the "implicit declaration of arrays." However, the largest legal subscript value for all such arrays is always assumed to be 10. If you reference an element with a subscript value greater than 10, you will get a subscript out-of-range error diagnostic as described in the next section. To avoid this problem altogether, we urge you to declare all arrays used in a program and explicitly specify the sizes of each.

Out-of-Range Subscript Values

Out-of-range subscript values (subscripts that are less than zero or exceed the largest legal subscript value for an array) are often caused by errors in subscript computation (such as the computations described in Section 6.5) or by loops that do not terminate properly. Such errors, which are not detected as syntax errors, can cause unpredictable program behavior if they go undetected during program execution.

Fortunately, BASIC-PLUS checks all subscripts during program execution and prints a message indicating an out-of-range subscript, the line number of the program statement at which the error occurred and the value of the subscript. For example, the message

```
?Subscript out of range at line 110
```

indicates that the subscript in the array reference at line 110 is out of range. When such errors occur, the cause of the error must be determined and the statement used to define the value of the subscript must be corrected in order to produce the proper in-range value. To avoid this error in the first place, you should carefully check all subscript calculations to ensure that all results are within the specified range.

6.7 Summary

In this chapter we introduced a special *data structure* called an array, which is a convenient facility for naming and referencing a collection of like items. We discussed how to inform BASIC-PLUS that an array of elements is to be allocated (by using the DIM statement), and we described how to reference an individual array element by placing a parenthetical expression, called a subscript, following the array name. A summary of statements that manipulate arrays is provided in Table 6.3.

Table 6.3 Summary of BASIC-PLUS Statements for Manipulating Arrays

Statement	Effect
Array declaration	
`100 DIM X(15)`	Allocate storage for array elements X(1), X(2), ... X(15) (and also X(0)).
Array read and print	

`100 FOR I = 1 TO 5`
`110    INPUT X(I)`
`120    PRINT X(I)`
`130 NEXT I`
	For loop—reads and prints one item at a time. Each item must be on a separate line; each item is printed on a separate line. Can be used to read or print all or a portion of an array.

Array manipulation	
`100 LET R = X(5) - X(1)`	Assign the difference of X(5) and X(1) to R.
Array assignment	
`100 LET X(I) = X(I-2) + X(I-1)`	Assign to X(I) the sum of the two preceding array element values.
Array search	

`100 FOR I = 1 TO N`
`110    IF X(I) = KEY THEN                  &`
`       LET INDEX = I                      &`
`       \PRINT "INDEX OF KEY IS"; INDEX`
`120 NEXT I`
	Search for KEY in X; print index of all elements of X that equal KEY.

The FOR loop was shown to be a convenient structure for referencing each array element in sequence. We have used this structure to initialize arrays, read and print arrays, and to control the manipulation of array elements.

Referencing Array Elements—Review

In the examples we have seen, there have been two methods used to select an array element for manipulation. The first involves the use of a loop to reference all elements of an array in sequence; the second involves setting an index through a search process or computation in order to select a single array element for update or reference.

In illustrating these methods, we introduced the use of parallel arrays—arrays of data in which all elements with the same index represent the information for a single record of information—e.g., a person's bank account record, or an inventory record for a single item.

The first approach, of sequentially processing the elements of an array, has been used many times in program solutions. We have read information into array elements in sequential order (Example 6.10), and we have searched array elements in sequential order to find a specific data item (Problems 6A and 6B), etc. For each of these operations, a FOR loop was used in which the counter variable also served as the subscript of the array being scanned.

Both approaches were used in Problem 6A and again in 6B. In Problem 6A, the variable I4 was used to scan through an array of depositor names to find a desired name (the key). The location of the key in the name array was used as the index to the parallel array of account balances, in order to select the corresponding account balance for update.

Classifying a Data Item

In Problem 6B, we showed that the problem of *classifying a data item* (determining which of a number of categories or classes an item falls into) could be simplified through the use of arrays. If an ordered list of boundary values for tax brackets is stored in an array, the tax bracket corresponding to a particular salary can be determined easily through an array search. If there is a constant increment between boundary values, direct computation can be used to conveniently determine the appropriate category (tax bracket). Once the bracket is defined, it can be used as an index to select elements from other arrays for further processing in subsequent program steps.

The arrays discussed in this chapter are "one dimensional" in that a single subscript is used to uniquely identify each array element. In Chapter 10, we will examine a more complicated data structure—an array with two dimensions (called a matrix).

Programming Problems

6C Professor J. Nichols has given an exam to a large lecture class of students. The grade scale for the exam is 90–100(A), 80–89(B), 70–79(C), 60–69(D), 0–59(F). Ms. Nichols needs a program to perform the following statistical analysis of the data:

a) Count the number of A's, B's, C's, D's, and F's.
b) Determine the averages of the A, B, C, D, and F scores, computed on an individual basis—i.e., the average A score, the average B score, . . . the average F score.

c) Find the total number of students taking the exam.
d) Compute the average and standard deviation for all of the scores.

Test your program with the following data: 55, 60, 82, 71, 98, 41, 85, 90, 27, 59, 89, 100, 70, −1, where −1 is the sentinel value.

6D Let A be an array consisting of 20 elements. Write a program to read a collection of up to 20 data items into A and then find and print the subscript of the largest item in A. Use any collection of data items you wish.

6E The Department of Traffic Accidents each year receives accident count reports from a number of cities and towns across the country. To summarize these reports, the Department provides a frequency distribution printout that gives the number of cities reporting accident counts in the following ranges: 0–99, 100–199, 200–299, 300–399, 400–499, 500 or above. The Department needs a computer program to read city name/accident count pairs of data and determine the number of cities in each category. After all the data have been processed, the resulting frequency counts are to be printed.

6F Write a program which, given the *taxable income* for a single taxpayer, will compute the income tax for that person. Use Schedule X shown in Fig. 6.15. Assume that "line 34," referenced in this schedule, contains the taxable income.

Example: If the individual's taxable income is $8192, your program should use the tax amount and percent shown in column 3 of line 5 (arrow). The tax in this case is

$$692 + .19 \times (8192 - 6500) = \$1013.48$$

For each individual processed, print the taxable earnings and the total tax. *Hint*: Set up three arrays, one for the base tax (column 3), one for the tax percent and the third for the excess base (column 4). Your program must then compute the correct index to these arrays, given the taxable income.

6G Assume for the moment that your computer has the very limited capability of being able to read and print only single decimal digits at a time; and to add together two integers consisting of one decimal digit each. Write a program to read in two ten-digit integers, add these numbers together, and print the result. Test your program on the following numbers.

```
X = 1487625
Y =    12783


X = 60705202
Y = 30760832


X = 1234567890
Y = 9876543210
```

Hints: Store the numbers X and Y in two arrays XAR, YAR, of size 10, one decimal digit per element. If the number is less than 10 digits in length, enter

Tax Rate Schedule

Schedule X
Single Taxpayers

Use this schedule if you checked **Filing Status Box 1** on Form 1040—

If the amount on Form 1040, line 34 is: Over—	But not Over—	Enter on line 2 of the worksheet on this page:	of the amount over—
$0	$2,300	—0—	
2,300	3,400	. . . . 14%	$2,300
3,400	4,400	$154 + 16%	3,400
4,400	6,500	314 + 18%	4,400
6,500	8,500	692 + 19%	6,500
8,500	10,800	1,072 + 21%	8,500
10,800	12,900	1,555 + 24%	10,800
12,900	15,000	2,059 + 26%	12,900
15,000	18,200	2,605 + 30%	15,000
18,200	23,500	3,565 + 34%	18,200
23,500	28,800	5,367 + 39%	23,500
28,800	34,100	7,434 + 44%	28,800
34,100	41,500	9,766 + 49%	34,100
41,500	55,300	13,392 + 55%	41,500
55,300	81,800	20,982 + 63%	55,300
81,800	108,300	37,677 + 68%	81,800
108,300	. . . . . .	55,697 + 70%	108,300

Fig. 6.15 Schedule X (from IRS Form 1040).

enough *leading zeros* (to the left of the number) to make the number 10 digits long. Thus the first two values for X and Y should be entered as

```
0, 0, 0, 1, 4, 8, 7, 6, 2, 5  (store in XAR)
0, 0, 0, 0, 0, 1, 2, 7, 8, 3  (store in YAR)
```

You will need a loop to add together the digits in the array elements. You must start with the element with subscript value 10 and work toward the left. Do not forget to handle the carry, if there is one.

Use an integer variable, CARRY, to indicate if a carry occurred in adding together XAR(I) and YAR(I). CARRY is set to 1 if a carry occurs here; otherwise, CARRY will be 0.

6H Write a data table, flow diagram, and a program for the following problem. You are given a collection of scores for the last exam in your computer course. You are to compute the average of these scores and then assign grades to each student according to the following rule.

If a student's score, SCORE, is within 10 points (above or below) of the average, assign the student a grade of SATISFACTORY. If SCORE is more

than 10 points higher than the average, assign the student a grade of OUT−
STANDING. If SCORE is more than 10 points below the average, assign the
student a grade of UNSATISFACTORY.

Test your program on the following data:

```
"RICHARD LUGAR", 62
"DONALD SCHAEFFER", 84
"KEVIN WHITE", 93
"JAMES RIEHLE", 74
"ABE BEAME", 70
"TOM BRADLEY", 45
"RICHARD HATCHER", 82
```

The output from your program should consist of a labeled 3-column list containing the name, exam score, and grade of each student.

6I Write a program to read N data items into each of two arrays X and Y of
size 20. Compare each of the elements of X to the corresponding element of
Y. In the corresponding element of a third array Z, store:

$$+1 \text{ if X is larger than Y}$$
$$0 \text{ if X is equal to Y}$$
$$-1 \text{ if X is smaller than Y}$$

Then print a three-column table displaying the contents of the arrays X, Y,
and Z, followed by a count of the number of elements of X that exceed Y,
and a count of the number of elements of X that are less than Y. Make up
your own test data; be sure your program will work with test cases involving
less than 20 data items.

6J The results of a true-false exam given in a class of Computer Science students have been coded for input to a program. The information available
consists of a student identification number and the students' answers to 10
true-false questions. The data entries are as follows:

Student Identification	Answers (1 = true; 0 = false)									
0080	0	1	1	0	1	0	1	1	0	1
0340	0	1	0	1	0	1	1	1	0	0
0401	1	1	0	0	1	0	0	1	1	1
0462	1	1	0	1	1	1	0	0	1	0
0463	1	1	1	1	1	1	1	1	1	1
0464	0	1	0	0	1	0	0	1	0	1
0618	1	1	1	0	0	1	1	0	1	0
0619	0	0	0	0	0	0	0	0	0	0
0687	1	0	1	1	0	1	1	0	1	0
0700	0	1	0	0	1	1	0	0	0	1
0712	0	1	0	1	0	1	0	1	0	1
0837	1	0	1	0	1	1	0	1	0	1
The correct answers are										
	0	1	0	0	1	0	0	1	0	1

Write a program to compute and store the number of correct answers for each student in one array, and store the student ID number in the corresponding element of another array. Determine the best score, BEST. Then print a three-column table displaying the ID number, score, and grade for each student. The grade should be determined as follows: If the score is equal to BEST or BEST − 1, give an A; BEST − 2 or BEST − 3, give a B, BEST − 4 or BEST − 5, give a C. Otherwise, give an F.

6K The results of a survey of the households in your town have been made available. The data for each household include a four-digit integer identification number, the annual income for the household, and the number of members of the household. Write a program to read the survey results into three arrays and perform the following analyses:

a) Count the number of households included in the survey and print a three-column table displaying the data read in. (You may assume that no more than 25 households were surveyed.)

b) Calculate the average household income and list the identification number and income of all households that exceed the average.

c) Determine the percentage of households having incomes below the poverty level. The poverty level income may be computed according to the formula

$$p = \$3750.00 + \$750.00 \times (m - 1)$$

where m is the number of members of each household.
Test your program on the following data.

Identification Number	Annual Income	Household Members
1041	$12,180	4
1062	13,240	3
1327	19,800	2
1483	22,458	8
1900	17,000	2
2112	18,125	7
2345	15,623	2
3210	3,200	6
3600	6,500	5
3601	11,970	2
4725	8,900	3
6217	10,000	2
9280	6,200	1

6L Write a program to read N data items into two arrays X and Y of size 20. Compute the products of the corresponding elements in X and Y and store the results in a third array XY, also of size 20. Print a three-column table displaying the arrays X, Y, and XY. Then compute and print the square root of the sum of the items in XY. Make up your own data; be sure your program will work with test cases involving less than 20 data items.

6M It can be shown that a number is prime if there is no smaller prime number that divides it. Consequently, in order to determine whether N% is prime, it is sufficient to check only the prime numbers less than N% as possible divisors (see Problem 4B). Use this information to write a program that stores the first one hundred prime numbers in an array. Have your program print the array after it is done.

6N Write a program to simulate the tossing of a pair of dice. Use RND and INT to obtain the number on each die:

```
200 LET D1 = INT(6 * RND) + 1
210 LET D2 = INT(6 * RND) + 1
```

and add these two values together.

Repeat the computation until 1000 tosses have been made and print a frequency table containing a list of die values and the number of times each occurred. Do not store all 1000 value pairs in memory. Compare this table to the table of expected frequencies shown below. To obtain different results each time you run your program, use the RANDOMIZE statement (see Section 4.2).

Die Value	Expected Frequency	Die Value	Expected Frequency
2	28	7	167
3	56	8	139
4	83	9	111
5	111	10	83
6	139	11	56
		12	28

6O Let CERT.VALUE be the value of a long-term savings certificate available at your local bank, let CERT.TERM be the term of the certificate (in years) and let INT.RATE be the yearly interest rate. Write a program which, given CERT.VALUE, CERT.TERM, and INT.RATE, will compute and print the interest amount (rounded to two decimal places), and the accumulated certificate value for each of the years of the term. Your program should print out CERT.VALUE, CERT.TERM, and INT.RATE and a three-column table containing the year (1, 2, 3, ... CERT.TERM), the interest for that year, and the accumulated value. Do not print the table until all computations (for the entire term period) have been computed and saved in parallel arrays. Test your program for CERT.VALUE = 5000, CERT.TERM = 10 (years), and INT.RATE = 10.5 (percent).

6P Write a program that plays the game of Hangman. Read each letter of the word to be guessed into successive elements of the string array WORD$ (one letter per array element). The player must guess the letters belonging to WORD$. The program should terminate when either all letters have been guessed correctly (player wins), or a specified number of incorrect guesses have been made (computer wins). Your program should work for words of 10 characters or less. *Hint*: Use a string array, SOLUTION$, to keep track of the solution so far (again, store one character in each element of SOLUTION$). Initialize each element of SOLUTION$ to the symbol "*". Each time a letter in WORD is guessed, replace the corresponding "*" in array SOLUTION$ with that letter. After each guess the player makes, print the array SOLUTION$ on a single line.

7

Nested Structures and Multiple-Alternative Decisions

In Chapters 2, 3, and 5 we introduced some fundamental control structures to be used in computer programming. We presented flow diagram patterns and described several forms of these structures. We illustrated the application of these structures in the solution to a number of problems, some of which utilized nests of control structures.

In this chapter, we will examine the use of nested control structures in some detail and provide some guidelines that should help reduce the potential for error in using nested structures. In addition, several forms of decision structures with multiple (more than two) alternatives will be presented. Throughout the chapter, a number of examples and solved problems illustrating the nesting of structures will be provided.

You may already be applying some of the guidelines discussed in this chapter in your programming. Nonetheless, we believe that a careful consideration of these guidelines will be useful in clearing up any confusion concerning the use of control structures. It might also provide some new insights as to how these structures can be used to solve a variety of problems.

7.1 The Multiple-Alternative Decision Structure

Most decision steps in the problems examined so far have involved only two alternatives. However, there are many situations in which it is necessary to choose from among several alternative courses of action.

As an example, consider a grading problem in which there are five grade categories, A, B, C, D, and F, and where the range of exam scores for each grade category is allowed to vary each time the exam is administered. In solving this problem, we shall use an array, FREQ, with five elements to count the number of exam scores in each grade category. Assuming that the range of all exam scores is between 0 and 100, we can define the four variables listed below to represent the grade boundaries.

LOWA: Lowest score in the A grade category
LOWB: Lowest score in the B grade category
LOWC: Lowest score in the C grade category
LOWD: Lowest score in the D grade category

The only restriction on the values of these variables is that LOWD must be less than LOWC, LOWC less than LOWB, and LOWB less than LOWA.

If the grade boundary values (LOWA, LOWB, etc.) were stored in an array (along with 0 for LOWF), we could use the array search technique described in Section 6.4 to determine the correct grade category of an exam score, SCORE. Although this is the most desirable solution, it is instructive to examine a solution that uses a nest of double-alternative decision structures, as shown in Fig. 7.1.

This is a rather complicated nest of structures that is not particularly easy to follow, much less program. The necessary decisions for this problem can be written more easily and clearly if we generalize the double-alternative decision into a *multiple-alternative decision pattern* so that more than two alternatives may be represented. The flow diagram pattern for the multiple-alternative decision is shown in Fig. 7.2, along with an example of the pattern defined for the new grading problem.

This flow diagram pattern implies the following program action:

• The conditions are evaluated from top to bottom.

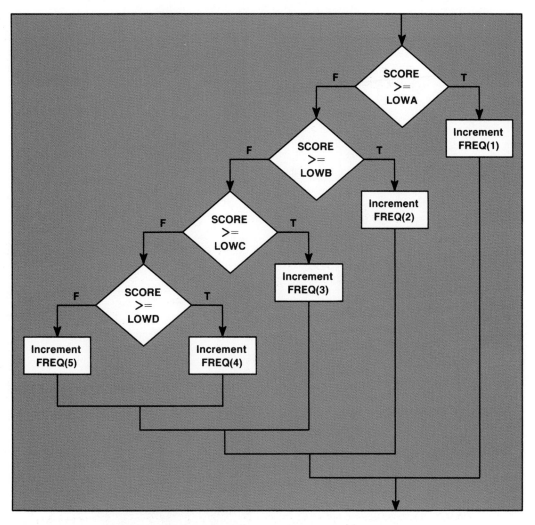

Fig. 7.1 A nest of IF-THEN-ELSE decision patterns.

- The task ($Task_i$) corresponding to the first condition ($condition_i$) that evaluates to true is performed and the pattern is exited immediately.
- If no condition evaluates to true, $Task_E$ is performed.

Thus the steps in exactly one of the tasks will be performed. Although more than one condition may actually be true, only the task associated with the first true condition will be executed. This is because of the top-to-bottom order of evaluation of conditions and the fact that the exit immediately follows the execution of the selected task.

The bottom task, $Task_E$, may be omitted from this pattern. In this case, if all conditions evaluate to false, none of the tasks in the multiple-alternative decision will be performed. The description of the subtasks in a multiple-alternative decision pattern should be kept short, and refined, if necessary, in separate flow diagrams.

General form

Example

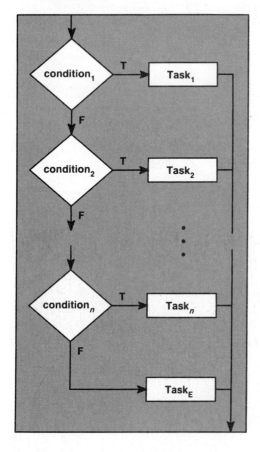

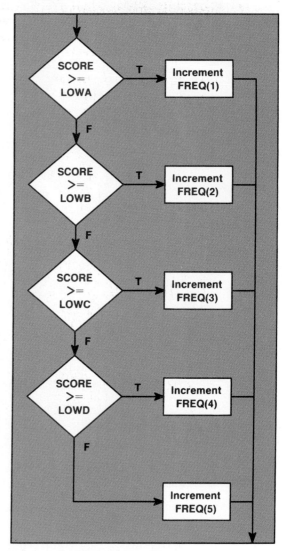

Fig. 7.2 Multiple-alternative decision pattern, general form and example.

Example 7.1   A BASIC-PLUS implementation of the flow diagram shown in Fig. 7.2 follows.

```
200 IF SCORE >= LOWA THEN              &
        LET FREQ(1) = FREQ(1) + 1      &
    ELSE IF SCORE >= LOWB THEN         &
        LET FREQ(2) = FREQ(2) + 1      &
    ELSE IF SCORE >= LOWC THEN         &
        LET FREQ(3) = FREQ(3) + 1      &
    ELSE IF SCORE >= LOWD THEN         &
        LET FREQ(4) = FREQ(4) + 1      &
    ELSE                               &
        LET FREQ(5) = FREQ(5) + 1
```

For a grade of A, all four of the conditions would evaluate to true. However, only the first of these is tested and only FREQ(1) is incremented, as desired.

The general form of the multiple-alternative decision is shown in the next display. VAX-11 BASIC users should also see Appendix J.

Multiple-Alternative Decision

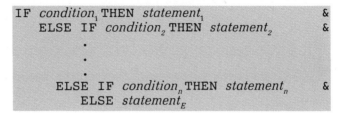

Interpretation: *Condition$_1$, condition$_2$,* etc. are tested in sequence until a condition is reached that evaluates to true. At most, one *statement$_i$* will be executed: if *condition$_i$* is the first condition that is true, then *statement$_i$* is executed. If none of the conditions is true, then *statement$_E$* is executed. Regardless of which statement is executed, control is passed next to the first line following the multiple-alternative decision. Each *statement$_i$* must be a single statement; *statement$_E$* may be a multiple statement group.

Note: The word ELSE and *statement$_E$* may be omitted. In this case, no statement is executed when all conditions are false. If *statement$_E$* is omitted, then *statement$_n$* may be a multiple statement group.

Program Style

Typing the multiple-alternative decision

We will use the simple form of the multiple-alternative decision shown in the display above whenever the *statement$_i$* alternatives are short enough to fit on one line. Otherwise, we will use the expanded form shown in Example 7.1. BASIC-PLUS treats both forms identically.

Program Style

Using statement$_E$ to verify data values

In Example 7.1, the ELSE alternative (*statement$_E$*) is executed by default for all exam scores less than LOWD. Although all exam scores are expected to be positive, it is normally a good idea to use *state-*

$ment_E$ to print an error message in case the "impossible" happens and the value of SCORE is negative, as shown below.

```
200 IF SCORE >= LOWA THEN                &
       LET FREQ(1) = FREQ(1) + 1         &
    ELSE IF SCORE >= LOWB THEN           &
       LET FREQ(2) = FREQ(2) + 1         &
    ELSE IF SCORE >= LOWC THEN           &
       LET FREQ(3) = FREQ(3) + 1         &
    ELSE IF SCORE >= LOWD THEN           &
       LET FREQ(4) = FREQ(4) + 1         &
    ELSE IF SCORE >= 0 THEN              &
       LET FREQ(5) = FREQ(5) + 1         &
    ELSE                                 &
       PRINT SCORE; "IS NEGATIVE"
```

Exercise 7.1: You are writing a program to print grade reports for students at the end of each semester. After computing and printing each student's grade point average (maximum of 4) for the semester, you must use this average to make the following decision:

If the grade point average is 3.5 or above, print "DEAN'S LIST";
If the grade point average is above 1 and less than or equal to 1.99, print "PROBATION WARNING";
If the grade point average is less than or equal to 1, print "ON PROBATION".

Write the BASIC-PLUS program segment for these decisions.

Exercise 7.2: Let MINCAT be an array of size 5 used to store the values of LOWA, LOWB, LOWC, LOWD, and LOWF. Redo the flow diagrams and program segment to search the array MINCAT (see Problem 6B) to determine which element of FREQ to update for a given score.

7.2 Subroutines with Multiple-Alternative Decisions

There are two problems with the multiple-alternative decision structure just described. First, if there are more than three alternative tasks, it becomes increasingly difficult to enter all tasks without a typing error. Second, only the last task may be implemented using a multi-statement group. Both of these problems can be alleviated by using separate subroutines to implement each of the alternative tasks as illustrated next.

Example 7.2   In developing a personal checking account program, it is necessary to distinguish among the following transaction types:

1. Negative transaction amounts
2. Deposits
3. Legitimate checks
4. Rubber checks (insufficient account balance)
5. Unidentifiable transaction type

The multiple-alternative decision pattern shown in Fig. 7.3a distinguishes among four types of transactions (all checks are grouped together). Each transaction is assumed to contain a code (TRANS.CODE$) and a transaction amount (TRANS.AMOUNT). The code may be one of two characters: "C" (for check) and "D" (for deposit). The refinement of Step 2.6 (see Fig. 7.3b) distinguishes between categories 3 and 4 above. An implementation of Figs. 7.3a and b using a multiple-alternative decision structure with subroutines is shown in Fig. 7.4.

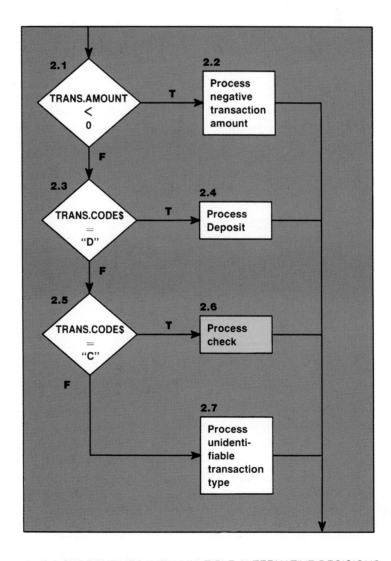

7.3a Decision pattern for Example 7.2.

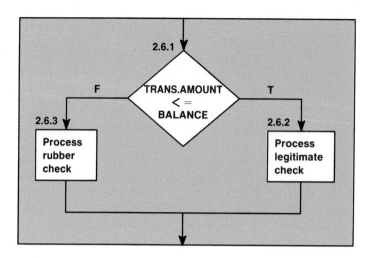

7.3b Refinement of Step 2.6.

As shown in Fig. 7.4, each alternative task is implemented as a separate subroutine (lines 1000, 2000, 3000, 4000). Each GOSUB statement (GOSUB 1000, GOSUB 2000, etc.) in the multiple-alternative decision at line 200 causes one of these subroutines to be executed when its associated condition evaluates to true. Each subroutine begins with a descriptive comment that specifies its associated condition. Each subroutine ends with a RE-TURN statement.

The detailed implementation of each subroutine is not shown in Fig. 7.4 with the exception of the subroutine at line 3000 (process check). This subroutine calls either the subroutine at line 5000 (legitimate check) or the subroutine at line 6000 (rubber check) to process a transaction that is a check. Immediately after returning from any of these subroutines, the statement

    3020 RETURN

would transfer control to line 210.

Implementing Arbitrary Decision Patterns with Subroutines

Sometimes it is difficult to fit a complicated decision into the general multiple-alternative decision pattern shown in Fig. 7.2. It will still be possible to implement any nested decision pattern using subroutines for true and false tasks as illustrated next.

Example 7.3   The flow diagram in Fig. 7.5 has three conditions represented by C1%, C2%, C3%. (Recall that it is legal to use an integer variable to represent a logical condition.) We will use separate subroutines to implement the True and False Tasks associated with each of these conditions (see Fig. 7.6).

```
200       IF TRANS.AMOUNT < 0 THEN                              &
            GOSUB 1000                                          &
          ELSE IF TRANS.CODE$ = "D" THEN                        &
            GOSUB 2000                                          &
          ELSE IF TRANS.CODE$ = "C" THEN                        &
            GOSUB 3000                                          &
          ELSE                                                  &
210         GOSUB 4000
            .
            .
            .
970       STOP
980    !
990    !
1000   !SUBROUTINES FOR MULTIPLE DECISION AT LINE 200
1010   !IF TRANS.AMOUNT < 0 THEN PROCESS NEGATIVE TRANS
            .
            .
            .
1090      RETURN
2000   !ELSE IF TRANS.CODE$ = "D" THEN PROCESS DEPOSIT
            .
            .
            .
          RETURN
3000   !ELSE IF TRANS.CODE$ = "C" THEN PROCESS CHECK
3010      IF TRANS.AMOUNT <= BALANCE THEN GOSUB 5000    &
            ELSE GOSUB 6000
3020      RETURN
4000   !ELSE PROCESS UNIDENTIFIABLE TRANSACTION TYPE
            .
            .
            .
4090      RETURN
4100   !END OF SUBROUTINES FOR DECISION AT LINE 200
4110   !
4120   !
5000   !SUBROUTINES FOR IF-THEN-ELSE AT LINE 3010
5010   !IF TRANS.AMOUNT <= BALANCE PROCESS GOOD CHECK
            .
            .
            .
5090      RETURN
6000   !ELSE PROCESS RUBBER CHECK
            .
            .
            .
          RETURN
6100   !END OF SUBROUTINES FOR LINE 3010
```

Fig. 7.4 Multiple-alternative decision structure for Figs. 7.3a,b.

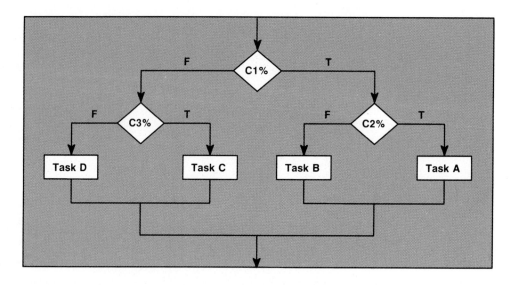

Fig. 7.5 Nested decision pattern.

In Fig. 7.6, the IF-THEN-ELSE at line 300 calls either the subroutine starting at line 1000 (C1% is true) or at line 2000 (C1% is false). If executed, the subroutine at line 1000 would call either the subroutine starting at line 3000 (C1% true, C2% true—perform Task A) or the subroutine at line 4000 (C1% true, C2% false—perform Task B). In a similar manner, the subroutine at line 2000 would call either the subroutine starting at line 5000 (C1% false, C3% true—perform Task C) or the subroutine at line 6000 (C1% false, C3% false—perform Task D). (The subroutines starting at lines 3000, 4000, 5000, and 6000 are not shown.) Control would be immedi-

```
300      IF C1% THEN GOSUB 1000            &
         ELSE GOSUB 2000
310         .
            .
            .
970      STOP
980   !
990   !
1000 !SUBROUTINES FOR IF-THEN-ELSE AT LINE 300
1010 !IF C1% IS TRUE THEN TEST C2%
1020      IF C2% THEN GOSUB 3000            !TASK A &
         ELSE GOSUB 4000            !TASK B
1040     RETURN
2000 !ELSE TEST C3%
2010      IF C3% THEN GOSUB 5000            !TASK C &
         ELSE GOSUB 6000            !TASK D
2020     RETURN
```

(continued)

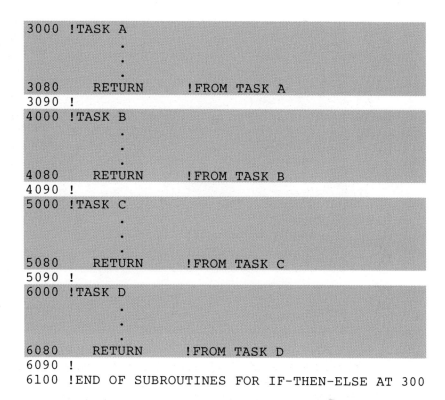

```
3000  !TASK A
         .
         .
         .
3080      RETURN         !FROM TASK A
3090  !
4000  !TASK B
         .
         .
         .
4080      RETURN         !FROM TASK B
4090  !
5000  !TASK C
         .
         .
         .
5080      RETURN         !FROM TASK C
5090  !
6000  !TASK D
         .
         .
         .
6080      RETURN         !FROM TASK D
6090  !
6100  !END OF SUBROUTINES FOR IF-THEN-ELSE AT 300
```

Fig. 7.6 Implementation of decision pattern in Fig. 7.5.

ately returned to line 310 after one of the tasks (A, B, C, or D) is performed.

Exercise 7.3: Provide BASIC-PLUS implementations of the following decision patterns. Use subroutines, as illustrated in this section.

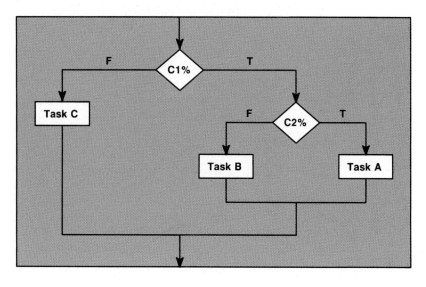

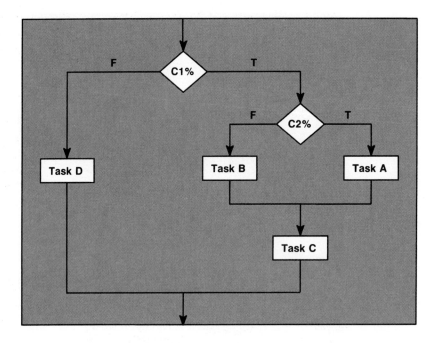

Exercise 7.4: Redraw each of the decision patterns in Exercise 7.3 as a multiple-alternative decision pattern as shown in Fig. 7.2. *Hint*: Use the logical operator AND to form compound conditions.

The Bowling Problem

The next problem makes use of the multiple-alternative decision structure.

Problem 7A: Write a program that will compute a person's ten-pin bowling score for one game, given the number of balls rolled, NUM.BALL, and the number of pins knocked down per ball. Print the score for each frame as well as the cumulative score at the end of each frame.

Discussion: A bowling *game* consists of 10 *frames*. In ten-pin bowling, a maximum of two balls may be rolled in each of the first nine frames and two or three balls may be rolled in frame ten. Each frame is scored according to the following rules.

1. If the first ball rolled in a frame knocks down all 10 pins (called a *strike*), then the score for the frame is equal to 10 + (the total score on the next two balls rolled). Since all 10 pins are down, no other balls are rolled in the current frame.
2. If the two balls rolled in the frame together knock down all 10 pins (called a *spare*), then the score for the frame is equal to 10 + (the score on the next ball rolled).
3. If the two balls rolled knock down fewer than 10 pins (no *mark*), then the frame score is equal to the number of pins knocked down.

The initial data table for this problem is shown next; an example of the array PINS is shown in Fig. 7.7. The array shows that 10 pins were knocked down by the first ball, seven by the second ball, etc.

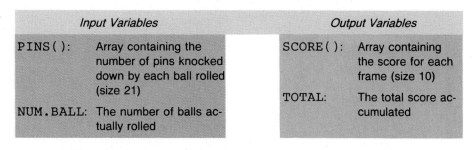

DATA TABLE FOR PROBLEM 7A

Input Variables		Output Variables	
PINS( ):	Array containing the number of pins knocked down by each ball rolled (size 21)	SCORE( ):	Array containing the score for each frame (size 10)
NUM.BALL:	The number of balls actually rolled	TOTAL:	The total score accumulated

Array PINS

(1)	(2)	(3)	(4)	(5)			(21)
10	7	3	5	3	. . .		8

Fig. 7.7 Array of pin counts for each ball.

The level one flow diagram for the problem is shown on the left side of Fig. 7.8a. Steps 2 and 3 in this diagram are refined on the right side of Fig. 7.8a; Step 1 will be implemented using a FOR loop with final value parameter NUM.BALL.

In the refinement for Step 2, the loop control variable FRAME serves to count each frame as it is processed. In the computation of the scores (Step 2.3), the variable FIRST is used as the index to the array PINS to indicate which ball in PINS is the first ball of each frame. The use of FIRST and the computation of the score for each of the first three frames are illustrated in Table 7.1.

Since PINS(1) is 10, a strike was bowled in the first frame. The frame score (20) is determined by computing 10 + PINS(2) + PINS(3); FIRST, which is next used as the index to the first ball of the second frame, is then set to 2 (Step 2.3). In the second frame, balls 2 and 3 are

Table 7.1 Processing the Array PINS

FRAME	FIRST	Frame Score	Effect
1	1	10 + 7 + 3 = 20	Strike: Only one ball rolled in frame 1
2	2	7 + 3 + 5 = 15	Spare: Two balls rolled in frame 2
3	4	5 + 3 = 8	No Mark: Two balls rolled in frame 3
4	6		

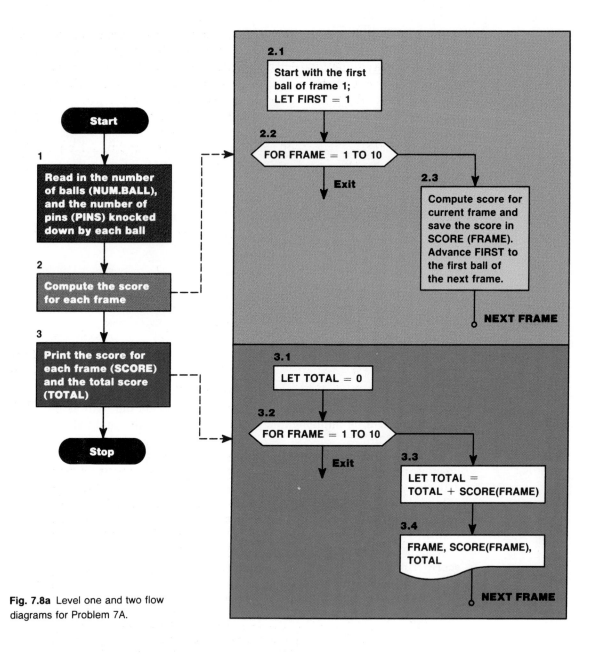

Fig. 7.8a Level one and two flow diagrams for Problem 7A.

needed to knock down all 10 pins (a spare). Adding in the pins knocked down by the next ball, `PINS(4)`, gives a frame score of 15; the index `FIRST` is then set to 4 (the fourth ball is the first one for frame 3). Two balls are rolled in the third frame (balls 4 and 5). The frame score is 8 (`PINS(4) + PINS(5)`), and `FIRST` is set to 6.

Since `FIRST` contains the index to the first ball bowled in each frame, the subscript expressions `FIRST`, `FIRST+1`, and (possibly) `FIRST+2` are used to select the elements of the array `PINS` (the number of pins knocked down by each ball) to be used in each frame score. Thus PINS(1), PINS(2), and PINS(3) are used to compute the score for frame 1; PINS(2), PINS(3), and PINS(4) for frame 2, and so on.

The refinement of the computation step is drawn in Fig. 7.8b. The test for a strike is whether PINS(FIRST) is equal to 10; the test for a spare is whether the sum PINS(FIRST) + PINS(FIRST+1) is equal to 10. FIRST should be incremented by 1 each time a strike is bowled; otherwise, it should be incremented by 2. (Why?) The additional data table entries for the Step 2.3 refinement are listed next.

ADDITIONAL DATA TABLE ENTRIES FOR PROBLEM 7A

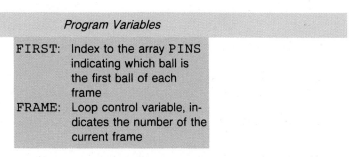

Program Variables	
FIRST:	Index to the array PINS indicating which ball is the first ball of each frame
FRAME:	Loop control variable, indicates the number of the current frame

FRAME is also used as the loop control variable for the Step 3 refinement in which the total score (TOTAL) is accumulated (Step 3.3), and the frame number, frame score, and TOTAL are all printed (Step 3.4)

The program for Problem 7A is shown in Fig. 7.9 and a sample run in Fig. 7.10.

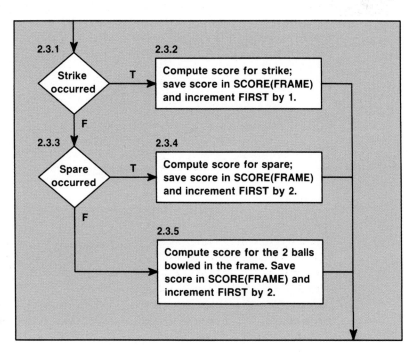

Fig. 7.8b Refinement of Step 2.3 of Fig 7.8a.

```
110  !BOWLING PROBLEM
120  !
130     DIM PINS(21), SCORE(10)
140  !
150  !ENTER NUMBER OF BALLS
155  !AND PINS KNOCKED DOWN BY EACH BALL
160     GOSUB 1000
170  !
180  !COMPUTE SCORE FOR EACH FRAME
190     GOSUB 2000
200  !
210  !COMPUTE TOTAL SCORE AND PRINT RESULTS
220     GOSUB 3000
230  !
240     STOP
250  !
260  !
1000 !SUBROUTINE TO ENTER DATA
1010 !ENTER NUMBER OF BALLS, NUM.BALL, AND PINS
1020 !KNOCKED DOWN BY EACH BALL
1030     INPUT "HOW MANY BALLS WERE BOWLED"; NUM.BALL
1040     PRINT "ENTER PIN COUNTS FOR EACH BALL"
1050     FOR BALL = 1 TO NUM.BALL
1060        PRINT "BALL"; BALL;
1070        INPUT PINS(BALL)
1080     NEXT BALL
1090 !
1100     RETURN
1110 !END OF DATA ENTRY SUBROUTINE
1120 !
1130 !
2000 !SUBROUTINE TO COMPUTE ALL FRAME SCORES
2010 !BALL 1 IS FIRST BALL OF FRAME 1
2020     LET FIRST = 1
2030     FOR FRAME = 1 TO 10
2040        !COMPUTE SCORE FOR FRAME, INCREMENT FIRST
2050        GOSUB 4000
2060     NEXT FRAME
2070 !
2080     RETURN
2090 !END OF SUBROUTINE TO COMPUTE ALL FRAME SCORES
2100 !
2110 !
3000 !SUBROUTINE TO COMPUTE TOTAL AND PRINT RESULTS
3010     LET TOTAL = 0
3020     PRINT "THE FRAME-BY-FRAME SCORES ARE..."
3030     PRINT "FRAME", "SCORE", "TOTAL SCORE"
3040     FOR FRAME = 1 TO 10
3050        !ADD IN SCORE FOR CURRENT FRAME
3060        LET TOTAL = TOTAL + SCORE(FRAME)
3070        PRINT FRAME, SCORE(FRAME), TOTAL
```

(continued)

```
3080      NEXT FRAME
3090 !
3100      RETURN
3110 !END OF SUBROUTINE TO COMPUTE TOTAL SCORE
3120 !
3130 !
4000 !SUBROUTINE TO COMPUTE THE FRAME SCORE
4020 !AND INCREMENT FIRST
4030 !
4040 !CATEGORIZE FRAME AS STRIKE, SPARE OR NO MARK
4050      IF PINS(FIRST) = 10 THEN                      &
              GOSUB 5000                                &
          ELSE IF PINS(FIRST)+PINS(FIRST+1) = 10 THEN &
              GOSUB 6000                                &
          ELSE                                         &
              GOSUB 7000
4060 !
4070      RETURN
4080 !END OF COMPUTE FRAME SCORE SUBROUTINE
4090 !
4100 !
5000 !SUBROUTINES FOR DECISION AT LINE 4050
5010 !IF STRIKE THEN
5020      LET SCORE(FRAME) = 10 + PINS(FIRST+1)          &
                                 + PINS(FIRST+2)
5030      LET FIRST = FIRST + 1
5040      RETURN
6000 !ELSE IF SPARE THEN
6010      LET SCORE(FRAME) = 10 + PINS(FIRST+2)
6020      LET FIRST = FIRST + 2
6030      RETURN
7000 !ELSE NO MARK
7010      LET SCORE(FRAME) = PINS(FIRST)+PINS(FIRST+1)
7020      LET FIRST = FIRST + 2
7030      RETURN
7040 !END OF SUBROUTINES FOR DECISION AT LINE 4050
7050 !
7060      END   !BOWLING PROGRAM
```

Fig. 7.9 Program for Problem 7A.

```
RUNNH
HOW MANY BALLS WERE BOWLED? 20
ENTER PIN COUNTS FOR EACH BALL
BALL 1 ? 4
BALL 2 ? 6
BALL 3 ? 3
BALL 4 ? 5
BALL 5 ? 4
BALL 6 ? 5
BALL 7 ? 7
BALL 8 ? 2
```

(continued)

```
BALL 9 ? 5
BALL 10 ? 5
BALL 11 ? 4
BALL 12 ? 3
BALL 13 ? 10
BALL 14 ? 1
BALL 15 ? 9
BALL 16 ? 1
BALL 17 ? 3
BALL 18 ? 7
BALL 19 ? 3
BALL 20 ? 7
THE FRAME-BY-FRAME SCORES ARE...
FRAME           SCORE           TOTAL SCORE
  1              13                 13
  2               8                 21
  3               9                 30
  4               9                 39
  5              14                 53
  6               7                 60
  7              20                 80
  8              11                 91
  9               4                 95
 10              17                112
```
Stop at line 240

Fig. 7.10 Sample run of Problem 7A.

Exercise 7.5: They do things a little differently in Massachusetts where Dr. Koffman grew up. The bowling pins (called candlepins) are narrow at the top and bottom and wider in the middle. The balls are about the size of a softball. The rules for a strike and a spare are the same; however, the bowler gets to roll a third ball in each frame that is neither a strike nor spare. Modify the bowling program to score a candlepin game. (Any pins that fall on the lane are not cleared away in candlepins. This can help the bowler but should not affect your program).

 The ON-GOSUB and ON-GOTO Statements

ON-GOSUB Statement

There are many situations in which the value of an expression may be used to select a task to be executed from among several alternatives. The ON−GOSUB *statement* may be used to accomplish the selection as shown next.

Example 7.4   We wish to design a CAI (computer-assisted instruction) program to drill students in American History. In order to determine which questions to ask, the subroutine in Fig. 7.11a begins by printing a *menu* (lines 1040–

```
1000 !SUBROUTINE TO PRESENT MENU AND SELECT PERIOD
1010 !
1020 !PRESENT MENU TO STUDENTS
1030 !
1040     PRINT "PERIODS OF AMERICAN HISTORY COVERED"
1050     PRINT "1 -- COLONIAL PERIOD"
1060     PRINT "2 -- PERIOD PRECEDING CIVIL WAR"
1070     PRINT "3 -- CIVIL WAR AND RECONSTRUCTION"
1080     PRINT "4 -- EVENTS LEADING TO WORLD WAR I"
1090     PRINT "5 -- EVENTS LEADING TO WORLD WAR II"
1100     PRINT "6 -- AFTER WORLD WARS"
1110     PRINT
1120 !
1130 !ENTER PERIOD TO BE STUDIED
1140     LET PERIOD = 0
1150     INPUT "ENTER A NUMBER FROM 1 TO 6"; PERIOD    &
             UNTIL PERIOD >= 1 AND PERIOD <= 6
1160     ON PERIOD GOSUB 2000, 5000, 10000, 15000,    &
                  20000, 25000
1170 !
1180     RETURN
1190 !END OF SUBROUTINE TO PRESENT MENU
```

Fig. 7.11a Subroutine for Example 7.4.

1150) or list of choices. Based on the student's response, one of several subroutines (not shown) of our CAI program will be called. The value of PERIOD at line 1160

```
1160 ON PERIOD GOSUB 2000, 5000, 10000, 15000,    &
                  20000, 25000
```

determines which subroutine will be called (i.e., PERIOD = 1—subroutine at line 2000, PERIOD = 2—subroutine at line 5000, etc.). A display of the menu is shown in Fig. 7.11b.

The subroutines referenced at line 1160 are not shown. Each subroutine will consist of a sequence of GOSUB statements followed by a single RE-

```
PERIODS OF AMERICAN HISTORY COVERED
1 -- COLONIAL PERIOD
2 -- PERIOD PRECEDING CIVIL WAR
3 -- CIVIL WAR AND RECONSTRUCTION
4 -- EVENTS LEADING TO WORLD WAR I
5 -- EVENTS LEADING TO WORLD WAR II
6 -- AFTER WORLD WARS

ENTER A NUMBER FROM 1 TO 6?
```

Fig. 7.11b Menu printed by subroutine in Fig. 7.11a.

TURN. Each GOSUB will call another subroutine that asks a question dealing with the specified period of American History as illustrated next.

Example 7.5 Figure 7.12a provides an example of the use of an ON–GOSUB statement to select a meaningful prompting message based on a student answer (ANSWER). The subroutine shown could be part of the CAI program in Example 7.4. It would be called by the subroutine starting at line 5000 (for

```
6000 !SUBROUTINE FOR COTTON GIN QUESTION
6010 !
6020     PRINT "WHO INVENTED THE COTTON GIN?"
6030     PRINT "1 - ROBERT FULTON"
6040     PRINT "2 - GEORGE WASHINGTON"
6050     PRINT "3 - ELI WHITNEY"
6060 !
6070 !VALIDATE STUDENT ANSWER
6080     LET ANSWER = 0
6090     INPUT "ENTER A NUMBER BETWEEN 1 AND 3";      &
             ANSWER  UNTIL ANSWER >= 1 AND ANSWER <= 3
6100 !
6110 !PRINT A MEANINGFUL PROMPT AND RETURN
6120     ON ANSWER GOSUB 6200, 6300, 6400
6125 !
6130     RETURN
6140 !END OF COTTON GIN QUESTION
6150 !
6160 !
6200 !SUBROUTINES FOR ON-GOSUB AT LINE 6120
6210 !ANSWER = 1
6220     PRINT "NO.  HE INVENTED THE STEAM BOAT."
6230     LET WRONG = WRONG + 1
6240     RETURN
6300 !ANSWER = 2
6310     PRINT "NO.  HE WAS THE FIRST PRESIDENT."
6320     LET WRONG = WRONG + 1
6330     RETURN
6400 !ANSWER = 3
6410     PRINT "GOOD!"
6420     LET CORRECT = CORRECT + 1
6430     RETURN
6450 !END OF SUBROUTINES FOR ON-GOSUB AT LINE 6120
```

Fig. 7.12a
ON-GOSUB
in a CAI program.

```
WHO INVENTED THE COTTON GIN?
1 - ROBERT FULTON
2 - GEORGE WASHINGTON
3 - ELI WHITNEY
ENTER A NUMBER BETWEEN 1 AND 3? 3
GOOD!
```

Fig. 7.12b Sample
output for Fig. 7.12a.

period preceding Civil War.) CORRECT and WRONG represent the accumulated number of correct and incorrect answers, respectively.

The multiple-choice question is printed (lines 6020–6050) and the student's answer is read into ANSWER. Line 6090 will execute until a valid value of ANSWER is entered. Depending upon the student's answer (1, 2, or 3), one of the three subroutines (line 6200, 6300, or 6400) will be executed. Each subroutine prints a prompting message and increments CORRECT or WRONG. After returning from one of these subroutines, control will pass to the first executable statement

```
6130 RETURN
```

following the ON–GOSUB statement. This statement will return control to the subroutine starting at line 5000. An output sample is shown in Fig. 7.12b.

If the expression in the ON–GOSUB statement evaluates to a real number, BASIC-PLUS will truncate the fractional part. It is best to do this yourself using the INT or FIX function as illustrated next.

Example 7.6   Ticket prices for seats at the home game for the Klondike Nuggets football team are based on the section in which the seats are located, as indicated in the following table.

Sections	Ticket Prices
100–199	$2.50
200–299	$2.00
300–399	$1.75
400–499	$0.50

The program in Fig. 7.13 can be used to compute the total cost of a group of seats, given the section and the number of seats.

```
100 !PROGRAM TO COMPUTE TICKET COST
110 !
120 !ENTER SECTION NUMBER AND NUMBER OF SEATS
130     LET SECTION = 0
140     INPUT "ENTER SECTION # BETWEEN 100 AND 499";    &
                SECTION UNTIL SECTION >= 100 AND          &
                             SECTION <= 499
150     INPUT "ENTER NUMBER OF SEATS"; NUM.SEAT
160 !
170 !COMPUTE AND PRINT TICKET COST
180     ON INT(SECTION / 100) GOSUB 1000, 2000,          &
                             3000, 4000
190     PRINT "TOTAL TICKET COST = $"; COST
200 !
210     STOP
220 !
230 !
```

(continued)

```
1000 !SUBROUTINES FOR ON-GOSUB AT LINE 180
1010 !SECTIONS 100-199
1020     PRINT "$2.50/TICKET"
1030     LET COST = NUM.SEAT * 2.50
1040     RETURN
2000 !SECTIONS 200-299
2010     PRINT "$2.00/TICKET"
2020     LET COST = NUM.SEAT * 2
2030     RETURN
3000 !SECTIONS 300-399
3010     PRINT "$1.75/TICKET"
3020     LET COST = NUM.SEAT * 1.75
3030     RETURN
4000 !SECTIONS 400-499
4010     PRINT "$0.50/TICKET"
4020     LET COST = NUM.SEAT * 0.50
4030     RETURN
4040 !END OF SUBROUTINES FOR ON-GOSUB AT LINE 180
4050 !
4060     END    !TICKET COST PROGRAM

RUNNH

ENTER SECTION # BETWEEN 100 AND 499? 223
ENTER NUMBER OF SEATS? 3
$2.00/TICKET
TOTAL TICKET COST = $ 6
Stop at line 210
```

Fig. 7.13 Program for Example 7.6.

The ON-GOSUB statement in line 180 calls one of the four subroutines listed (1000, 2000, 3000, or 4000) depending on the value (1, 2, 3, or 4) of the expression INT(SECTION / 100). Each subroutine prints the ticket price for a given section range and computes the total ticket cost. After one of these subroutines executes, control is returned to the statement at line 190 which prints the total ticket cost.

The general form of the ON-GOSUB statement is given in the next display.

ON-GOSUB Statement

ON *expression* GOSUB *line-list*

Interpretation: The *expression* is first evaluated and any fraction is truncated. The expression value is then used to select one line number from the list of line numbers provided in *line-list*. The line numbers are indexed from left to right starting with 1; hence, if the value of *expression* is 3, the subroutine starting at the third line number in *line-list* would be called. After the subroutine RETURN is executed, control is transferred to the first executable statement following the ON–GOSUB statement.

Note: If the value of *expression* is less than 1 or greater than the number of line numbers in line-list, the error message

> ?ON statement out of range

will be printed and program execution will terminate.

Note that we have been careful to ensure that the expression value is in-range whenever the ON–GOSUB statement is reached. If the expression value is not in range, an error will result as described in the display above.

Exercise 7.6: Modify the menu printing subroutine (Fig. 7.11a) for the CAI example so that an additional choice

> 7 -- STOP THE DRILL

is presented. Write a main program that calls this subroutine repeatedly until 7 is chosen.

GOTO and ON-GOTO Statements

There is also an ON–GOTO statement

> ON *expression* GOTO *line-list*

that is similar to the ON–GOSUB except that a transfer of control occurs instead of a subroutine call. The line transferred to is determined by the value of *expression*. In general, it is preferable to use the ON–GOSUB statement (see Program Style display *Transfer instructions (GOTO) considered harmful* following the example).

Example 7.7 The CAI subroutine in Fig. 7.12a is redone in Fig. 7.14a using the ON–GOTO statement

> 6110 ON ANSWER GOTO 6200, 6300, 6400

The lines preceding line 6110 are the same as in Fig. 7.12a.

The ON–GOTO transfers control to line 6200, 6300, or 6400 depending on the value of ANSWER (ANSWER = 1, ANSWER = 2, or ANSWER = 3). Unlike a subroutine call, there is no return point associated with a transfer of control. Hence, the statements

```
6240      GOTO 6460
6330      GOTO 6460
6430      GOTO 6460
```

are used to transfer control to the subroutine RETURN at line 6460.

```
6000 !SUBROUTINE FOR COTTON GIN QUESTION
6010 !
6020     PRINT "WHO INVENTED THE COTTON GIN?"
6030     PRINT "1 - ROBERT FULTON"
6040     PRINT "2 - GEORGE WASHINGTON"
6050     PRINT "3 - ELI WHITNEY"
6060 !
6070 !VALIDATE STUDENT ANSWER
6080     LET ANSWER = 0
6090     INPUT "ENTER A NUMBER BETWEEN 1 AND 3";        &
                 ANSWER UNTIL ANSWER >= 1 AND           &
                              ANSWER <= 3
6095 !
6100 !PRINT A MEANINGFUL PROMPT AND RETURN
6110     ON ANSWER GOTO 6200, 6300, 6400
6120 !
6200 !TASKS FOR ON-GOTO AT LINE 6110
6210 !ANSWER = 1
6220     PRINT "NO, HE INVENTED THE STEAMBOAT."
6230     LET WRONG = WRONG + 1
6240     GOTO 6460
6300 !ANSWER = 2
6310     PRINT "NO, HE WAS THE FIRST PRESIDENT."
6320     LET WRONG = WRONG + 1
6330     GOTO 6460
6400 !ANSWER = 3
6410     PRINT "GOOD"
6420     LET CORRECT = CORRECT + 1
6430     GOTO 6460
6440 !END OF TASKS FOR ON-GOTO AT LINE 6110
6450 !
6460     RETURN
6470 !END OF COTTON GIN QUESTION
```

Fig. 7.14a Example of GOTO and ON-GOTO.

```
WHO INVENTED THE COTTON GIN?
1 - ROBERT FULTON
2 - GEORGE WASHINGTON
3 - ELI WHITNEY
ENTER A NUMBER BETWEEN 1 AND 3? 1
NO, HE INVENTED THE STEAMBOAT
```

Fig. 7.14b Sample output for Fig. 7.14a.

ON-GOTO Statement

ON *expression* GOTO *line-list*

Interpretation: The *expression* is evaluated and any fraction is truncated. The expression value is then used to select one line number from the list of numbers provided in *line-list*. The line numbers are indexed from left to right starting with 1; hence, if the value of *expression* is 3, control is transferred to the third line number in *line-list*.

Note: If the value of expression is less than 1 or greater than the number of line numbers in *line-list*, the error message

?ON statement out of range

will be printed and program execution will terminate.

GOTO Statement (Unconditional Transfer)

GOTO *line*

Interpretation: Control is transferred to the BASIC-PLUS statement at line number *line*.

Note: If there is no statement with number *line*, an execution error will occur.

Program Style

Transfer instructions (GOTO) *considered harmful*

Most computer scientists and experienced programmers avoid using transfer instructions except when absolutely necessary; whereas many unskilled programmers use them with abandon to jump all around in their programs. Overuse of the GOTO leads to programs that are difficult to read and understand. Consequently, you should generally avoid the use of transfer instructions.

Exercise 7.7:
a) If the value of D is three, what line number is transferred to by the statement

```
30 ON 2 * D - 1 GOTO 60, 70, 80, 90, 100, 110
```

What line number is transferred to if D is 1? If D is 0?

b) What subroutines would be called in the execution of the following statements?

```
100 FOR I = 1 TO 5
110     READ X
120       ON X GOSUB 200, 170, 150, 160, 200
130 NEXT I
140 DATA 3, 1, 2, 4, 5
```

Exercise 7.8: Explain why the multiple-alternative decision structure in Fig. 7.3a could not be implemented using the ON–GOSUB statement.

Exercise 7.9: Write an ON–GOSUB statement that would execute a different task for each of the cases listed below and print an error message if X is out-of-range.

Case 1: $0 \leq X < 5$
Case 2: $5 \leq X < 10$
Case 3: $10 \leq X < 15$
Case 4: $15 \leq X < 20$

Exercise 7.10: Assuming that LOWA = 90, LOWB = 80, etc., implement the flow diagram shown in Fig. 7.2 using an ON–GOSUB statement. *Hint:* You will have to pick an expression that computes a value between 1 and 5 for all scores between 50 and 100 (e.g., 90–100 → 1, 80–89 → 2, etc.). Use one subroutine for all scores < 60.

7.4 Structure Nesting, Entry, and Exit

Nested loops are perhaps the most difficult of all nested structures to write, read, and debug. For this reason, we will examine some programs involving nested FOR loops.

Example 7.8   A flow diagram of a pair of nested FOR loops is shown in Fig. 7.15. The refinement of Step 3 is itself a loop. This means that during each repetition of the outer loop, the inner loop must also be entered and executed until

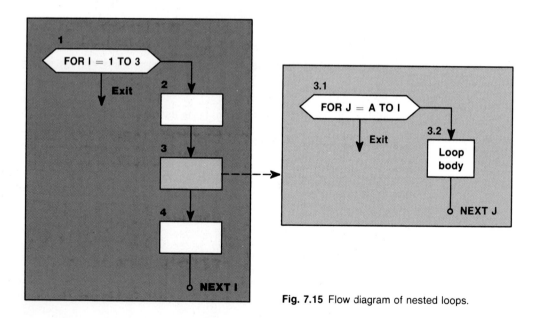

Fig. 7.15 Flow diagram of nested loops.

loop exit occurs. The number of times each loop is repeated depends upon its respective loop control parameters. Each time the inner loop is reentered, its loop control variable (J) is reinitialized. (In this case, it is set to the current value of A.)

As shown, it is permissible to use the loop control variable of the outer loop as a parameter in the initialization, update, or test of an inner loop control variable. However, the same variable should never be used as the loop control variable of both an outer loop and an inner loop in the same nest.

Example 7.9   Fig. 7.16 shows a sample run of a program with two nested FOR loops. The number of repetitions of the inner loop is determined by the value of the outer loop control variable. The loop control steps (lines 140 and 160) correspond to Steps 1 and 3.1 of Fig. 7.15.

```
100   !NESTED FOR LOOPS
110   !
120       LET A = 1
130       PRINT , " I", " J", " A"
140       FOR I = 1 TO 3
150           PRINT "OUTER", I
160           FOR J = A TO I
170               PRINT "INNER", I, J, A
180           NEXT J
190       NEXT I
200   !
210       END
```

RUNNH

	I	J	A
OUTER	1		
INNER	1	1	1
OUTER	2		
INNER	2	1	1
INNER	2	2	1
OUTER	3		
INNER	3	1	1
INNER	3	2	1
INNER	3	3	1

Fig. 7.16 Sample run with nested FOR loops.

The inner loop must be completely contained within the outer loop. Consequently, it would be illegal to attempt to switch the order of the loop terminator statements (lines 180 and 190) in Fig. 7.16 to

```
180           NEXT I
190       NEXT J
```

This would result in *overlapping*, rather than nested, FOR loops as sketched in Fig. 7.17. The error messages

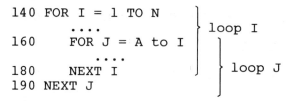

```
140 FOR I = 1 TO N
        ....
160     FOR J = A to I          } loop I
        ....                          } loop J
180     NEXT I
190 NEXT J
```

Fig. 7.17 Improper overlapping of FOR loops.

```
? NEXT without FOR at line 180
? FOR without NEXT at line 140
```

would be printed when the program was executed.

The inner FOR loop in Fig. 7.16 could also be written using a FOR statement modifier. In this case, lines 160–180 would be replaced by

```
160 PRINT "INNER", I, J, A FOR J = A TO I
```

Example 7.10   The subroutine (lines 1000–1180) in Fig. 7.18 plots the contents of the array FREQ in the form of a bar graph. Array FREQ and the data table appear below. The length of each line in the bar graph indicates the number of occurrences, or frequency, of data items in a particular class. For example, the second line of the graph (Fig. 7.18) shows that class three was the most popular with 24 occurrences.

Array to be plotted	FREQ(1)	FREQ(2)	FREQ(3)	FREQ(4)	FREQ(5)
	8	21	24	16	3

Number of items in the array	NUM.FREQ
	5

DATA TABLE FOR EXAMPLE 7.10

Program Constant

STAR$ = "*": Symbol printed on each bar

Input Variables		Program Variables		Output Variables
FREQ( ):	Array to be plotted (size 5)	NUM.BAR:	Loop control variable, serves as index to FREQ	A bar graph representation of array FREQ is printed
NUM.FREQ:	Number of elements of FREQ to be plotted	NUM.STAR:	Inner loop control variable (for printing each bar)	

NUM.BAR is the outer loop control variable and is used to cycle through the elements of the array FREQ. NUM.STAR is the loop control

```
100 !PROGRAM THAT TESTS BAR GRAPH SUBROUTINE
110 !
120     DIM FREQ(5)
125 !
130 !ENTER TEST DATA
140     READ NUM.FREQ
150     DATA 5
160     READ FREQ(I) FOR I = 1 TO NUM.FREQ
170     DATA 8, 21, 24, 16, 3
175 !
180 !PRINT THE BAR GRAPH
190     GOSUB 1000
200 !
210     STOP
215 !
220 !
1000 !SUBROUTINE TO DRAW A BAR GRAPH
1010 !
1020 !PROGRAM CONSTANTS
1030     LET STAR$ = "*"   !BAR GRAPH SYMBOL
1040 !
1050     PRINT "CLASS", "FREQUENCY PLOT";
1060 !
1070     FOR NUM.BAR = 1 TO NUM.FREQ
1080        !START A NEW BAR
1090        PRINT
1100        PRINT "   "; NUM.BAR; " I";
1110        !DRAW FREQ(NUM.BAR) STARS ON CURRENT BAR
1120        PRINT STAR$;                          &
             FOR NUM.STAR = 1 TO FREQ(NUM.BAR)
1130     NEXT NUM.BAR
1140     PRINT
1150     PRINT "      I----I----I----I----I----I----I"
1160 !
1170     RETURN
1180 !END OF BAR GRAPH SUBROUTINE
1190 !
2000     END
```

```
RUNNH
CLASS          FREQUENCY PLOT
    1 I********
    2 I*********************
    3 I************************
    4 I****************
    5 I***
      I----I----I----I----I----I----I
Stop at line 210
```

Fig. 7.18 Program and sample run for Example 7.10.

variable for the inner loop of the nest. Since STAR$ is associated with the symbol "*", the statement

```
1120 PRINT STAR$;                                               &
          FOR NUM.STAR = 1 TO FREQ(NUM.BAR)
```

instructs the computer to print a string of asterisks on an output line. Thus a bar consisting of a row of asterisks will be printed for each element of FREQ. The number of asterisks printed on a line is determined by the value of the element of FREQ being represented, FREQ(NUM.BAR), on that line. No asterisks are printed if the value is zero.

Program Style

Use of driver programs to test subroutines

The program in Fig. 7.18 contains a very brief main program segment (lines 100 through 210) whose sole purpose is to enter test data and call the bar graph printing subroutine. Using a simple *driver program* to test an individual subroutine illustrates an important design technique. After you have verified that the subroutine works properly through such simple, easy to implement tests, you can use it with confidence in more complicated programs.

Exercise 7.11: Write out each line of the printout for the following program fragment.

```
100 FOR I = 1 TO 2
110     PRINT "OUTER", I
120     FOR J = 1 TO 4 STEP 2
130         PRINT "INNER J", I, J
140         PRINT "INNER K", I, K FOR K=2 TO 4 STEP 2
150     NEXT J
160 NEXT I
```

Exercise 7.12 How many times is line 130 below executed? line 150?

```
100 LET A = 0
110 LET B = 0
120 FOR J = 1 TO 1000
130     LET A = A + 4
140     FOR I = 1 TO 50
150         LET B = B + 1
160     NEXT I
170 NEXT J
```

Exercise 7.13: In Fig. 7.16, what would be the effect of inserting the statement

```
175 LET A = A + 1
```

at line 175? What would be the effect of inserting this statement at line 185 instead of line 175? Show the output for each case.

Structure Entry

A control structure should always be entered through the top, i.e., by executing the header statement first. Otherwise it is possible that important initialization steps will be skipped. Consequently, you should never use a GOTO statement to transfer into a FOR loop or a subroutine. In the former case, the loop control parameters may not be initialized properly; in the latter case, no return point will be saved and this will result in a

```
?RETURN without GOSUB error
```

Structure Exit

A control structure should also have only one exit point, the structure terminator (RETURN or NEXT). You should never use the GOTO statement to exit from a subroutine; although, it is permissible to use the GOTO statement to transfer to the subroutine RETURN. As we shall discuss, this is generally preferable to having multiple RETURN statements in a single subroutine.

Normally, the next statement to be executed after loop exit is the statement that follows the loop terminator. Although it is possible to use a GOTO statement to exit to some other point, use of the GOTO statement is not recommended except to exit from within a nest of loops or to transfer to a subroutine RETURN as illustrated next.

Example 7.11 The program segment in Fig. 7.19 uses a GOTO statement (line 1090) to exit from a nest of loops when the first occurrence of a key is found in an array. Line 1090 in the inner FOR loop is used to search for CUR.KEY in the array ITEMS. The outer WHILE loop is used to read in a new key as long as no prior key read was found in the array. This loop executes until a key is found or the sentinel value is read.

The PRINT statement at line 1090 is executed just before loop exit when CUR.KEY is found. If no keys are found, the PRINT statement at line 1160 is executed just after the sentinel value is read. In either case, the subroutine RETURN (line 1190) is executed next.

If the FOR loop is exited normally, the value of the loop control variable (INDEX) will be equal to the limit parameter (NUM.ITEMS). If the FOR loop is exited via the GOTO statement, the value of INDEX will be equal to its value just before loop exit occurs (i.e., the subscript of the element of the array that contains CUR.KEY).

```
1000 !SUBROUTINE TO SEARCH ARRAY ITEMS
1005 !UNTIL A KEY IS FOUND
1010 !
1020 !PROGRAM CONSTANT
1030     LET SENTINEL = -999
1035 !
1040 !READ AND SEARCH FOR EACH KEY
1050     INPUT "NEXT KEY (OR -999)"; CUR.KEY
1060     WHILE CUR.KEY <> SENTINEL
1070        !SEARCH FOR CUR.KEY -- RETURN IF FOUND
1080        FOR INDEX = 1 TO NUM.ITEMS
1090           IF ITEMS(INDEX) = CUR.KEY THEN          &
                    PRINT CUR.KEY; "FOUND AT INDEX";   &
                         INDEX                         &
                    \GOTO 1190     !EXIT LOOP AND RETURN
1100        NEXT INDEX
1105 !
1110        !ARRAY SEARCH COMPLETED, CUR.KEY NOT FOUND
1120        PRINT CUR.KEY; "NOT FOUND"
1125        INPUT "NEXT KEY (OR -999)"; CUR.KEY
1130     NEXT    !WHILE
1140 !
1150 !SENTINEL READ -- NO KEYS WERE FOUND
1160     PRINT "NO KEYS FOUND IN ARRAY"
1170 !
1190     RETURN
1200 !END OF ARRAY SEARCH SUBROUTINE
```

Fig. 7.19 Nested loop exit using a GOTO statement.

Program Style

Multiple returns from a subroutine

It would seem reasonable to consider replacing the GOTO statement
in Fig. 7.19 with a RETURN statement. This would not change the operation of the subroutine in any way and would eliminate the GOTO
statement. However, most computer scientists would not recommend
this as it would provide two distinct exit points from the subroutine.
It is generally preferable to have a single RETURN statement located
at the physical end of each subroutine.

Exercise 7.14: Implement Fig. 7.19 without using the GOTO statement or multiple returns. *Hint*: You should introduce a program flag to remember whether the
last key was found.

7.5 Sorting an Array

The problem that follows is an example of the use of nested loops in *sorting*, or rearranging in order, the data stored in an array. Sorting programs are used in a variety of applications and the program developed here could be modified easily to sort alphabetic data (such as last names) stored in a string array. In this example, we will sort numeric data in ascending numerical order (smallest value first); however, it would be just as easy to sort the data in descending order (largest value first).

Problem 7B   Write a subroutine to sort, in ascending order, an array of numbers.

Discussion: There are many different algorithms for sorting. We will use one of the simplest of these algorithms, the *Bubble Sort*. The Bubble Sort is so named because it has the property of "bubbling" the smallest items to the top of a list. The algorithm proceeds by comparing the values of adjacent elements in the array. If the value of the first of these elements is larger than the value of the second, these values are exchanged, and then the values of the next adjacent pair of elements are compared. This process starts with the pair of elements with indexes 1 and 2 and continues through to the pair of elements with indexes n–1 and n, in an array of size n. Then this sequence of comparisons (called a *pass*) is repeated, starting with the first pair of elements again, until the entire array of elements is compared without an exchange being made. This condition indicates that the array is sorted.

As an example, we will trace through the sort of the array M as shown in Fig. 7.20. In this sequence of diagrams, diagram (1) shows the initial arrangement of the data in the array; the first pair of values are out of order and they are exchanged. The result is shown in diagram (2).

The sequence in Fig. 7.20 shows all exchanges that would be made during each pass through the adjacent pairs of array elements. After pass one, we see that the array is finally ordered except for the value 25. Sub-

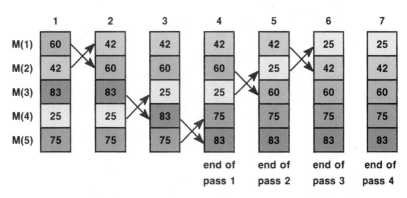

Fig. 7.20 Trace of Bubble Sort on a small array.

sequent passes through the array will "bubble" this value up one array element at a time until the sort is complete. In each pass through M, the elements are compared in the following order: M(1) and M(2); M(2) and M(3); M(3) and M(4); M(4) and M(5). Note that even though the array is sorted at the end of pass 3, it will take one more pass through the array without any exchanges to complete the algorithm.

Now that we have a general idea of how the algorithm works, we can write the initial data table and the flow diagrams for the Bubble Sort. The data table is shown next; the level one and two flow diagrams appear in Fig. 7.21a.

DATA TABLE FOR PROBLEM 7B

Program Constant

M.COUNT = 10: Maximum number of items that can be processed.

Input Variables		Output Variables
M( ): Array containing the data to be sorted (size 10)		M( ): At the conclusion of the subroutine, this array will contain the data sorted in ascending order

The refinement of Step 1 is a loop that processes array M until it becomes sorted. As shown in Fig. 7.21a, the program flag SORT.DONE$ will be used to control repetition of this loop. Step 1.3 sets SORT.DONE$ to "TRUE" before each pass through array M (Step 1.4). If an exchange is made during this pass, the array is not yet sorted, and SORT.DONE$ is reset to "FALSE", causing the outer loop to be repeated. When a pass is made without any exchanges, the value of SORT.DONE$ will remain "TRUE" and the outer loop will be exited upon completion of Step 1.4. Since there must be at least one pass through the array, SORT.DONE$ is initialized to "FALSE" before entering the outer loop (Step 1.1).

Step 1.4 must perform a complete pass through array M; its refinement (see Fig. 7.21b) is a FOR loop. In the FOR loop, adjacent pairs of elements of M are compared. As indicated in Step 1.4.2, if a pair of array elements is out of order, their values are exchanged (Step 1.4.3). A temporary storage cell, TEMP, is used to hold one of these values during the exchange. Note that INDEX, the loop control variable for the Step 1.4 refinement, always points to the first array element of any pair being compared. Consequently, the limit expression for the FOR loop must be M.COUNT - 1.

The data table additions for the algorithm refinements are shown at the top of the next page.

Remember that whenever nested loops are used, the inner loop is executed from start to finish for each iteration of an outer loop. In the program in Fig. 7.22, the inner FOR loop (Step 1.4) will be executed for all values of INDEX between 1 and M.COUNT - 1 for each repetition of the outer loop.

Program Variables	
TEMP:	Temporary storage cell required for the ex-change
SORT.DONE$:	Program flag—a value of "TRUE" at the completion of a pass in-dicates no exchanges were made and the ar-ray is sorted. A value of "FALSE" indicates at least one exchange was made
INDEX:	Loop control variable and array index for inner loop

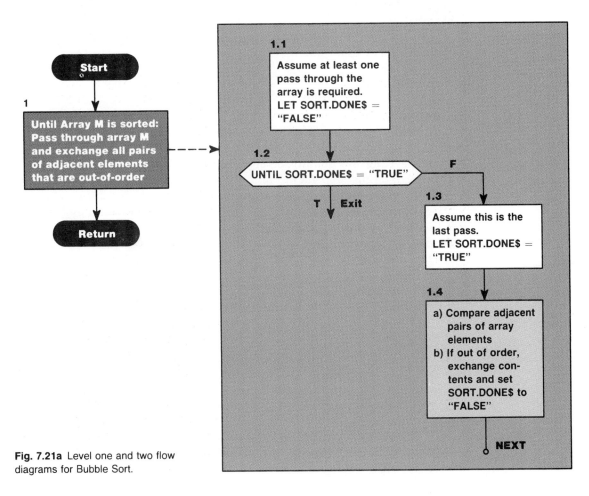

Fig. 7.21a Level one and two flow diagrams for Bubble Sort.

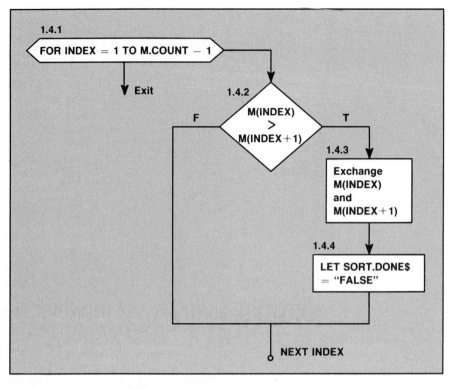

Fig. 7.21b Refinement of Step 1.4 of Fig. 7.21a.

To simplify the representation of nested loops, it is often helpful to outline the logic of each loop separately. This may be accomplished simply by summarizing the activity of any loop nested within another (such as has been done for Step 1.4 in Fig. 7.21a), and then providing the details of execution of the inner loop in a separate diagram (e.g., Fig. 7.21b).

The algorithm is shown as a subroutine in Fig. 7.22. The inner loop is also written as a subroutine (starting at line 3000) and is called by line 2060 during each repetition of the outer loop.

```
2000 !BUBBLE SORT SUBROUTINE
2005 !SORT ARRAY M IN ASCENDING ORDER
2010 !
2020 !REPEATEDLY PASS THROUGH ARRAY M UNTIL SORTED
2030 !ASSUME ARRAY IS INITIALLY UNSORTED
2030     LET SORT.DONE$ = "FALSE"
2050     UNTIL SORT.DONE$ = "TRUE"
2060        GOSUB 3000    !MAKE A SINGLE PASS THROUGH M
2070     NEXT    !UNTIL
2080 !
2090     RETURN
2100 !END OF BUBBLE SORT SUBROUTINE
```

(continued)

```
2110 !
2120 !
3000 !SUBROUTINE TO MAKE ONE PASS THROUGH ARRAY M
3010 !AND EXCHANGE ALL PAIRS OF ADJACENT ELEMENTS
3015 !THAT ARE OUT OF ORDER
3020 !
3030 !ASSUME NO MORE PASSES NEEDED AFTER THIS ONE
3040     LET SORT.DONE$ = "TRUE"
3060 !COMPARE ALL PAIRS OF ADJACENT ELEMENTS,
3070 !FROM FIRST PAIR TO LAST
3080     FOR INDEX = 1 TO M.COUNT - 1
3090        IF M(INDEX) > M(INDEX+1) THEN            &
                !EXCHANGE AND RESET SORT.DONE$        &
                LET TEMP = M(INDEX)                   &
                \LET M(INDEX) = M(INDEX+1)            &
                \LET M(INDEX+1) = TEMP                &
                \LET SORT.DONE$ = "FALSE"
3100     NEXT INDEX
3110 !
3120     RETURN
3130 !END OF A PASS
```

Fig. 7.22 Bubble Sort subroutine.

Exercise 7.15: In Fig. 7.20 note that after pass i, the i largest values are in the correct order in array elements M(M.COUNT−i+1), ... M(M.COUNT). Hence, it is only necessary to examine elements with indexes less than M.COUNT −i+1 during the next pass. Modify the algorithm to take advantage of this.

Exercise 7.16: Modify the subroutine in Fig. 7.22 to sort the array M in descending order (largest number first). Trace the execution of your subroutine on the initial array shown in Fig. 7.20.

Exercise 7.17: Modify the subroutine in Fig. 7.22 so that the median or middle item of the final sorted array is printed out. If M.COUNT is even, the median should be the average of the two middle numbers, i.e., the average of the elements with subscripts M.COUNT/2 and M.COUNT/2+1. If M.COUNT is odd, the median is the array element with subscript INT((M.COUNT/2)+1). A number is even if it is divisible by 2.

Exercise 7.18: A more efficient version of the bubble sort advances the smaller of each pair of elements being exchanged as far up the array as it can go. For this version, the second exchange shown in Fig. 7.20 would not be completed until the value 25 was advanced to the first element of the array. Write this version of the Bubble Sort Subroutine. *Hint*: Replace the single alternative decision with a loop.

Exercise 7.19: A different technique for sorting (the *selection sort*) consists of searching an array of N elements to find the location of the smallest element, and then exchanging the smallest element with the first element. Next, elements 2 through N are searched for the next smallest element which is exchanged with the second array element. This process continues until only elements N − 1 and N are left to search. Flow diagram the algorithm. *Hint*: Use a pair of nested FOR loops.

7.6 Common Programming Errors

Structure Nesting Errors

Structure nesting errors are among the most common programming errors that are made and the most difficult to detect. Such errors are more likely to occur when nested decision structures or multiple-alternative decision structures with lengthy statement groups for each alternative are used.

To aid in obtaining the proper structure nesting, we urge you to faithfully follow the process of flow diagram refinement illustrated in the text. Refine each nested structure as a separate entity, and then carefully implement the refined flow diagram as a BASIC-PLUS program. The use of subroutines and consistent, clear indentation can also help prevent structure nesting errors. To retain the proper structure nesting, go back to the flow diagram when making any nontrivial changes to the algorithm. Rearranging structure components in the program without referring to the flow diagram may introduce unexpected logic errors.

Multiple-Alternative Decision Errors

Care must be taken in listing the conditions to be used in a multiple-alternative decision. If the conditions are not *mutually exclusive* (that is, if more than one of the conditions can be true at the same time), then the condition sequence must be ordered carefully to ensure the desired results.

It is always a good idea to include an ELSE task in every multiple-alternative decision structure. Even if the condition list is constructed so as to "guarantee" that the ELSE task can never be executed, it is still a good practice to print a warning message, should the unexpected happen during the execution of your program.

ON-GOSUB and ON-GOTO Errors

The most common ON−GOSUB or ON−GOTO error is caused by the failure to ensure that the *expression* falls within the range 1 to n, where n is the number of line numbers in the statement

$$\text{ON } expression \text{ GOSUB } line_1, line_2, \ldots, line_n$$
$$\text{or ON } expression \text{ GOTO } line_1, line_2, \ldots, line_n$$

If *expression* is out-of-range, an execution error will occur. You should validate the value of *expression* before reaching the ON−GOSUB or ON−

GOTO statement as shown in Figs. 7.11–7.14. Also, make sure each of the lines, *line₁*, *line₂*, . . . , *lineₙ*, occurs in your program.

Nested Loop Errors

The most common errors in using FOR loops involve the incorrect definition of loop parameters in the header statement. If the parameter expressions used in a FOR loop header are invalid expressions, you will get a diagnostic message. If they are valid but compute the wrong values, you will likely receive no diagnostics. Incorrect expressions will result in the wrong number of loop repetitions being performed. This error, in turn, may cause you to run out of data items and could result in an ?Out of data diagnostic message. If the loop control variable is being used in an array subscript expression, you may get a ?Subscript out of range diagnostic if the loop parameters are incorrect. It is often helpful to print the value of the loop control variable if you suspect it is not being manipulated properly.

Whenever practical, you should completely simulate the execution of each loop to ensure that the number of repetitions is correct. At a minimum, you should test the "boundary conditions"; i.e., verify that the initial and final values of the loop control variable are correct. Furthermore, you should verify that all array references that use the loop control variable in subscript computations are within range at the loop control variable boundary values.

When using nested loops, make sure that the loop terminators are in the correct order so that the loops do not overlap. Also, remember that a different loop control variable must be used with each loop in the nest. This is required even if the inner loop is part of a subroutine called from within the outer loop.

7.7 Summary

In this chapter, we discussed different techniques for implementing decisions with several (more than two) alternatives. Various forms of the multiple-alternative decision structure were introduced and discussed. In special cases where the choice of alternative depends solely upon the value of a single expression, the ON–GOSUB or ON–GOTO statement may be used to select the alternative to be executed instead of a sequence of conditions. Table 7.2 summarizes the new statements introduced in this chapter.

We saw that structures may be nested but may not overlap, and we examined several examples of nested loops. We discussed the use of the GOTO statement to exit from a nest of loops.

Each structure should be entered through its header statement and exited through its terminator, except in special cases where the GOTO may be used for loop exit. Transfers into the middle of a structure are not permitted.

Table 7.2 Summary of New BASIC-PLUS Statements

Statement	Effect

Multiple-alternative decision

```
100 IF SCORE < 60 THEN PRINT "F"          &
        ELSE IF SCORE < 80 THEN PRINT "C" &
            ELSE PRINT "A"
```

If SCORE is less than 60, print F, if SCORE is between 60 and 80, print C; if SCORE is greater than or equal to 80, print A.

Multiple-alternative decision with subroutines

```
100 IF SCORE < 60 THEN GOSUB 1000          &
        ELSE IF SCORE < 80 THEN GOSUB 2000 &
            ELSE  GOSUB 3000

110
              .
              .
              .

1000 !SUBROUTINES FOR NESTED IF AT LINE 100
1010 !IF SCORE < 60 THEN PROCESS F
1020      PRINT "GRADE IS F"
1030      LET F.COUNT = F. COUNT + 1
1040      RETURN
2000 !ELSE IF SCORE < 80 THEN PROCESS C
2010      PRINT "GRADE IS C"
2020      LET C.COUNT = C.COUNT + 1
2030      RETURN
3000 !ELSE PROCESS A
3010      PRINT "GRADE IS A"
3020      LET A.COUNT = A.COUNT + 1
3030      RETURN
3040 !END OF SUBROUTINES FOR AT LINE 100
```

If SCORE is less than 60, a grade of F is assigned and F.COUNT is incremented; if SCORE is between 60 and 80, a grade of C is assigned and C.COUNT is incremented; if SCORE is greater than or equal to 80, a grade of A is assigned and A.COUNT is incremented. Execution resumes with the statement at line 110.

ON-GOSUB statement

```
400 ON I GOSUB 1000, 2000, 3000
```

If I is 1, the subroutine at line 1000 is called; if I is 2, the subroutine at line 2000 is called; if I is 3, the subroutine at line 3000 is called.

ON-GOTO and GOTO statement

```
160      ON ANSWER GOTO 180, 220, 260
170 !
180 !ANSWER EQUAL 1
190      PRINT "NO. HE INVENTED . . ."
200      LET WRONG = WRONG + 1
210      GOTO 290
220 !ANSWER EQUAL 2
230      PRINT "NO. HE WAS THE . . ."
```

If ANSWER is 1, lines 180–210 are executed; if ANSWER is 2, lines 220–250 are executed; if ANSWER is 3, lines 260–280 are executed. In any case, control is transferred to line 290.

(continued)

Table 7.2 Summary of New BASIC-PLUS Statements (*continued*)

Statement	Effect

```
240      LET WRONG = WRONG + 1
250      GOTO 290
260 !ANSWER EQUAL 3
270      PRINT "CORRECT"
280      LET CORRECT = CORRECT + 1
290 !END ON-GOTO
```

Programming Problems

7C *Frequency-distribution problem.* An instructor has just given an exam to a very large class. The grading scale is 90–100 (A), 80–89 (B), 70–79 (C), 60–69 (D), 0–59 (F). The instructor wants to know how many students took the exam, what the average and standard deviation were for the exam, and how many A's, B's, C's, D's, and F's there were. Write a program using a loop and a multiple-alternative decision structure to help the instructor obtain this information. Also, plot the frequency distribution as a bar graph.

7D A tax table is used to determine the tax rate for a company employee, based on weekly gross salary and number of dependents. The tax table has the form shown below. An employee's net pay can be determined by multiplying gross salary times the tax rate and subtracting this product from the gross salary. Write a program to read in the identification number, number of dependents, and gross salary for each employee of a company, and then determine the net salary to be paid to each employee. Your program should also print out a count of the number of employees with gross salary in each of the ranges shown. [*Hint*: Use a multiple-alternative decision structure to "implement" this table. Note that the decrease in rate for each column is constant (0.1 for 0–100, 0.12 for 100–200, 0.13 for ≥ 200.]

Tax Rate Table

		Gross Salary		
		0–100	100–200	≥200
Number of	0	0.2	0.28	0.38
dependents	1	0.1	0.16	0.25
	≥2	0.0	0.04	0.12

7E The equation of the form

$$mx + b = 0$$

(where m and b are real numbers) is called a linear equation in one unknown, x. If we are given the values of both m and b, then the value of x that satisfies this equation may be computed as

$$x = -b/m.$$

Write a program to read in N different sets of values for m and b and compute x. Test your program for the following five sets of values:

m	b
−12.0	3.0
0.0	18.5
100.0	40.0
0.0	0.0
−16.8	0.0

[*Hint*: There are three distinct possibilities concerning the values of x that satisfy the equation mx + b = 0.

1. As long as m ≠ 0, the value of x that satisfies the original equation 1 is given by equation 2.
2. If both b and m are 0, then any real number that we choose satisfies mx + b = 0.
3. If m = 0 and b ≠ 0, then no real number x satisfies this equation.]

7F Each year the legislature of a state rates the productivity of the faculty of each of the state-supported colleges and universities. The rating is based on reports submitted by each faculty member indicating the average number of hours worked per week during the school year. Each faculty member is ranked, and the university also receives an overall rank.

The faculty productivity rank is computed as follows:

a) faculty members averaging over 55 hours per week are considered "highly productive";
b) faculty members averaging between 35 and 55 hours a week, inclusive, are considered "satisfactory";
c) faculty members averaging fewer than 35 hours a week are considered "overpaid".

The productivity rating of each school is determined by first computing the faculty average for the school:

$$\text{Faculty average} = \frac{\Sigma \text{ hours worked per week for all faculty}}{\text{Number of faculty reporting}}$$

and then comparing the faculty average to the category ranges defined in (a), (b), and (c).

Use the multiple-alternative decision structure and write a program to rank the following faculty:

HERM	63
FLO	37
JAKE	20
MO	55
SOL	72
TONY	40
AL	12

Your program should print a three-column table giving the name, hours and productivity rank of each faculty member. It should also compute and print the school's overall productivity ranking.

7G Write a savings account transaction program that will process the following set of data

```
"ADAM",        1054.37  ⎫
"W",             25.00  ⎪
"D",            243.35  ⎬ group 1
"W",            254.55  ⎪
"Z",                 0  ⎭
"EVE",         2008.24  ⎫
"W",             15.55  ⎬ group 2
"Z",                 0  ⎭
"MARY",         128.24  ⎫
"W",             62.48  ⎪
"D",             13.42  ⎬ group 3
"W",             84.60  ⎪
"Z",                 0  ⎭
"SAM",            7.77  ⎫
"Z",                 0  ⎬ group 4
"JOE",           15.27  ⎫
"W",             16.12  ⎬ group 5
"D",             10.00  ⎪
"Z",                 0  ⎭
"BETH",       12900.00  ⎫
"D",           9270.00  ⎬ group 6
"Z",                 0  ⎭
"ZZZZ",              0     (Sentinel for all accounts)
```

The first record in each group gives the name for an account and the starting balance in the account. All subsequent records show the amount of each withdrawal (W) or deposit (D) that was made for that account followed by a sentinel record ("Z", 0). Print out the final balance for each of the accounts processed. If a balance becomes negative, print an appropriate message and take whatever corrective steps you deem proper. If there are no transactions for an account, print a message so indicating.

7H *Variation on the mortgage interest problem—Problem 4J.* Use FOR loops to write a program to print tables of the following form.

Home Loan Mortgage Interest Payment Tables		
Amount _____ Loan duration (Months) _____		
Rate (Percent)	Monthly Payment	Total Payment
6.00		
6.25		
6.50		
6.75		
7.00		
7.25		

(continued)

Your program should produce tables for loans of 30, 40, and 50 thousand dollars, respectively. For each of these three amounts, tables should be produced for loan durations of 240, 300, and 360 months. Thus nine tables of the above form should be produced. Your program should contain three nested loops, some of which may be inside separate subroutines, depending upon your solution. Be careful to remove all redundant computations from inside your loops, especially from inside the innermost loop.

7I *Quadratic-equation problem.* The equation of the form

(1) $ax^2 + bx + c = 0$ (a, b, c real numbers, with a $\neq$ 0)

is called a quadratic equation in x. The real *roots* of this equation are those values of x for which

$ax^2 + bx + c$

evaluates to zero. Thus if a = 1, b = 2, and c = −15, then the real roots of

$x^2 + 2x - 15$

are +3 and −5, since

$(3)^2 + 2(3) - 15 = 9 + 6 - 15 = 0$

and

$(-5)^2 + 2(-5) - 15 = 25 - 10 - 15 = 0$

Quadratic equations of the form (1) have either 2 real different roots, 2 real and equal roots, or no real roots. The determination as to which of these three conditions holds for a given equation can be made by evaluating the discriminant d of the equation, where

$d = b^2 - 4ac.$

There are three distinct possibilities:

a) If d > 0, then the equation has two real and unequal roots.
b) If d = 0, the equation has two real and equal roots.
c) If d < 0, the equation has no real roots.

Write a program to compute and print the real roots of quadratic equations having the following values of a, b, and c.

a	b	c
1.0	2.0	−15.0
1.0	−1.25	−9.375
1.0	0.0	1.0
1.0	−80.0	−900.0
1.0	−6.0	9.0

If the equation has no real roots for a set of a, b, and c, print an appropriate message and read the next set. *Hint*: If the equation has two real and equal roots, then the root values are given by the expression

$$\text{Root } 1 = \text{Root } 2 = -b/2a.$$

If the equation has two real and unequal roots, their values may be computed as

$$\text{Root } 1 = \frac{-b + \sqrt{d}}{2a},$$

$$\text{Root } 2 = \frac{-b - \sqrt{d}}{2a}.$$

7J Write a program to solve the following problem: Read in a collection of N data items, each containing one integer between 0 and 9, and count the number of consecutive pairs of each integer occurring in the data set. Your program should print the number of consecutive pairs of 0's, of 1's, 2's, . . . and the number of consecutive pairs of 9's found in the data.

7K Write a program that will provide change for a dollar for any item purchased that costs less than one dollar. Print out each unit of change (quarters, dimes, nickels, or pennies) provided. Always dispense the biggest-denomination coin possible. For example, if there are 37 cents left in change, dispense a quarter, which leaves 12 cents in change, then dispense a dime, and then two pennies. You may wish to use a multiple-alternative decision structure in solving this problem. However, you can also use a four-element array (to store each denominational value 25, 10, 5, and 1).

7L *Statistical measurements with functions—a simple linear-curve fit problem.* Scientists and engineers frequently perform experiments designed to provide measurements of two variables X and Y. They often compute measures of central tendency (such as the mean) and measures of dispersion (such as the standard deviation) for these variables. They then attempt to decide whether or not there is any relationship between the variables, and, if so, they express this relationship in terms of an equation. If there is a relationship between X and Y that is describable using a linear equation of the form

$$Y = aX + b,$$

the data collected is said to *fit a linear curve*.

For example, the ACE Computing Company recently made a study relating aptitude test scores to programming productivity of new personnel. The six pairs of scores shown below were obtained by testing 6 randomly selected applicants and later measuring their productivity.

Applicant	Aptitude Score (Variable X)	Productivity (Variable Y)
1	$x_1 = 9$	$y_1 = 46$
2	$x_2 = 17$	$y_2 = 70$
3	$x_3 = 20$	$y_3 = 58$
4	$x_4 = 19$	$y_4 = 66$
5	$x_5 = 20$	$y_5 = 86$
6	$x_6 = 23$	$y_6 = 64$

ACE wants to find the equation of the line that they can use to predict the productivity of workers tested in the future. They are also interested in obtaining means and standard deviations for the variables X and Y. The required computations can be performed as follows:

1. Compute SUMX $= \Sigma X$ $= x_1 + x_2 + \cdots + x_6$
   SUMY $= \Sigma Y$ $= y_1 + y_2 + \cdots + y_6$
   SUMXY $= \Sigma X \cdot Y$ $= x_1y_1 + x_2y_2 + \cdots + x_6y_6$
   SUMXSQ $= \Sigma X^2$ $= x_1^2 + x_2^2 + \cdots + x_6^2$
   SUMYSQ $= \Sigma Y^2$ $= y_1^2 + y_2^2 + \cdots + y_6^2$
2. Compute MEANX $=$ SUMX/N where $N = 6$
   MEANY $=$ SUMY/N
3. Compute STDDVX $= \sqrt{\text{SUMXSQ}/N - \text{MEANX}^2}$
   STDDVY $= \sqrt{\text{SUMYSQ}/N - \text{MEANY}^2}$
4. Compute a and b in $Y = aX + b$ using the equation

$$a = \frac{\text{SUMXY} - N \times \text{MEANX} \times \text{MEANY}}{\text{SUMXSQ} - N \times \text{MEANX}^2}$$

$$b = \text{MEANY} - a \times \text{MEANX}$$

Write subroutines to carry out the above computations. Test your program on the aptitude/productivity data just shown.

7M   Write the selection sort described in Exercise 7.19 as a subroutine.

7N   The insertion sort inserts each element of an array in its proper place starting with element 2. If element 1 is bigger than element 2, then element 1 is shifted right and old element 2 is inserted in its place. If elements 1 through K are in order, then element K + 1 can be inserted. This is done by comparing element K + 1 to elements K, K − 1, etc. until a value smaller than element K + 1 is found. The part of the array following this element is shifted right one position and old element K + 1 is inserted. Write an insertion sort subroutine.

User-Defined
Functions and
Program Systems

In Chapter 5 we showed how the subroutine structure of BASIC-PLUS could be used to help construct nicely modularized programs that reflected the step-wise refinement process used in the design of algorithms. We also indicated that subroutines are helpful in writing programs in which it is necessary to perform certain sequences of steps more than once.

BASIC-PLUS provides an additional feature, the *user-defined function*, which facilitates the solution of problems in terms of their more manageable parts.* In the next section, we describe the user-defined function in detail, providing numerous short examples. Following this, we illustrate

---

*A more advanced feature, the *subprogram*, is described in Appendixes I and J for those who have BASIC-PLUS-2 or VAX-11 BASIC.

how user-defined functions and subroutines can be used to implement a reasonably complicated problem involving the computation of several statistical measures.

8.1   User-Defined Functions

Single-Line Functions

In addition to the standard mathematical functions (such as SQR, INT) discussed in Section 4.2, BASIC-PLUS provides a facility for programmers to introduce function definitions of their own. The simplest form of user-defined function is a *single-line function* with a single, numeric argument. However, BASIC-PLUS also allows multiple-line, multiple-argument user-defined functions. We will discuss all of these function forms in this chapter. We will concentrate on the rules of definition for these functions. The techniques for calling or referencing user functions are the same as those for the standard functions (see Section 4.2).

Example 8.1   The single-line function FNFRAC defined as

```
110 DEF* FNFRAC(X) = X - FIX(X)
```

can be used to compute the fractional part of any real number X. FNFRAC is an example of a single-line function with one *function parameter*, X. Single-line functions are defined by prefixing the *function description* with DEF*.

An assignment statement such as

```
120 LET Z = FNFRAC(30.98)
```

may be used to call the function FNFRAC. In this call, the argument 30.98 is substituted for the parameter X in the expression part of the function description and the function result

$$30.98 - FIX(30.98) = 30.98 - 30 = .98$$

is assigned to Z. A function result must always be assigned to a variable if it is to be saved.

Functions may be reused as often as desired, as illustrated in the following program segment.

```
100    LET X = -1.234
110    DEF* FNFRAC(X) = X - FIX(X)
120    PRINT FNFRAC(X), X
130    PRINT FNFRAC(PI), PI
140    END

RUNNH
-.234          -1.234
 .14159         3.14159
```

This segment contains two calls to the function FNFRAC. In the first call (line 120), the value -1.234 of the argument X is substituted for the parameter X, and the result is $-.234$; in the second call (line 130), the value (3.14159) of the function PI is substituted for X and the result is .14159. Note that neither argument, X or PI, is changed as a result of the function execution.

Example 8.2   We can define a single-line function, FNAMOUNT, to compute the amount on deposit in a savings account after N days, given the initial deposit (DEPOSIT) and the interest rate (RATE), compounded daily.

```
130 DEF* FNAMOUNT(DEPOSIT, RATE, N) =                    &
                 DEPOSIT * (1 + RATE / 365) ^ N
```

Use of this function is illustrated in the program shown in Fig. 8.1.

```
100    !VALUE OF DEPOSIT INVESTED AT A FIXED
110    !RATE COMPOUNDED DAILY FOR N DAYS
120    !
130       DEF* FNAMOUNT(DEPOSIT, RATE, N) =             &
                    DEPOSIT * (1 + RATE / 365) ^ N
140    !
150       INPUT "ENTER DEPOSIT (IN DOLLARS)"; DEPOSIT
160       INPUT "ENTER RATE (IN PERCENT)"; RATE
170       INPUT "NUMBER OF DAYS"; N
180    !
190       PRINT "DAY", "AMOUNT"
200       FOR I = 1 TO N
210          PRINT I, FNAMOUNT(DEPOSIT, RATE / 100, I)
220       NEXT I
230    !
240       END

RUNNH
ENTER DEPOSIT (IN DOLLARS)? 3000
ENTER RATE (IN PERCENT)? 9.4
NUMBER OF DAYS? 10
DAY           AMOUNT
 1            3000.77
 2            3001.55
 3            3002.32
 4            3003.09
 5            3003.87
 6            3004.64
 7            3005.41
 8            3006.19
 9            3006.96
10            3007.73
```

Fig. 8.1 Using a single-line function.

The function FNAMOUNT is defined using the DEF* statement on line 130; it has three parameters, DEPOSIT, RATE, and N. The *reference* (call) to the function (line 210) contains three *arguments*, DEPOSIT, RATE/100, and I, each of which corresponds to a parameter in the function definition. Note that the argument names need not be the same as the parameter names. Furthermore, expressions (such as RATE/100) and constants may be used as arguments (but not as parameters). When a function call occurs, the value of each argument is substituted for the corresponding parameter and the function is evaluated.

The definition of a single line function must precede any references to the function. The rules of definition for single-line functions are summarized in the following display.

Single-Line Function Definition

DEF* FN*variable* = *expression*
or DEF* FN*variable* (*parameter list*) = *expression*

Interpretation: FN*variable* is the function name, where *variable* may be any legal BASIC-PLUS variable name. *Integer* or *string functions* (functions that return integer or string values) are permitted and may be specified by placing % or $, respectively, at the end of the variable name. When the function is called, the expression is evaluated and its value is returned. If the function has parameters, the argument values in the calling statement are substituted (in left-to-right order) for the corresponding parameters. The parameters must be simple numeric or string variable names; constants, expressions, array names, or array references are not allowed. The parameter and argument lists must agree in length and the corresponding items must agree in type (numeric or string). Integer and real types may be mixed; BASIC-PLUS does the required conversion.

Notes: A maximum of five parameters is allowed in BASIC-PLUS. The *expression* need not reference all of the parameters and it may manipulate variables not appearing in the parameter list.

Example 8.3   The single-line, single-argument function FNROUNDP defined as

```
120 DEF* FNROUNDP(X) = INT(X * 100 + 0.5) / 100
```

can be used to round any positive real number (represented by X) to the nearest two decimal places. Two examples of the computation performed by FNROUNDP are shown in the next table.

X	Evaluation of FNROUNDP(X)
12.579	INT(12.579 * 100 + 0.5) / 100 =INT(1257.9 + 0.5) / 100 =INT(1258.4) / 100 = 1258 / 100 = 12.58
8.1433	INT(8.1433 * 100 + 0.5) / 100 =INT(814.33 + 0.5) / 100 =INT(814.83) / 100 = 814 / 100 = 8.14

Multiple-Line Functions

BASIC-PLUS also allows the definition of functions that cannot be written in a single line.

Example 8.4   The function in Fig. 8.2 can be used to calculate the tuition charge (in dollars), given the number of credit hours taken during one semester by a resident student at a public university. Full-time students taking 12 hours and over are charged a flat rate of $1150.00. Students taking less than 12 hours are charged $100.00 per credit hour.

In this function, the parameter HOURS represents the number of credit hours taken by a student whose tuition is being computed. For example, if the statement

```
300 LET TUITION = FNCHARGE(10.5)
```

were used to call FNCHARGE, HOURS would be assigned the value of the argument 10.5. The value returned from the call to FNCHARGE would be 10.5 × 100 or 1050; this value would be stored in TUITION.

```
100      DEF* FNCHARGE(HOURS)
110    !
120    !COMPUTES THE TUITION CHARGE GIVEN
125    !THE NUMBER OF HOURS
       !
140    !FUNCTION CONSTANTS
150       LET CHARGE.CREDIT = 100
160       LET CHARGE.SEMESTER = 1150
170       LET CHARGE.FULL = 12
180    !
190    !DEFINE FUNCTION RESULT
200       IF HOURS >= CHARGE.FULL THEN            &
             LET FNCHARGE = CHARGE.SEMESTER        &
          ELSE                                     &
             LET FNCHARGE = CHARGE.CREDIT * HOURS
210    !
220       FNEND    !FNCHARGE
```

Fig. 8.2 Defining a multiple-line function.

As illustrated in this example, the function parameter (HOURS) is defined when the function is called; it does not need to be explicitly assigned or read inside the function.

In a multiple-line function, the DEF* statement starts the definition, and the statement FNEND marks the end of the function definition. The statements between are all considered to be part of the *function description*. The variables listed in the DEF* statement (HOURS in this case) are called the *parameters* of the function.

The IF–THEN–ELSE statement

```
200 IF HOURS >= CHARGE.FULL THEN                                    &
        LET FNCHARGE = CHARGE.SEMESTER                              &
    ELSE                                                            &
        LET FNCHARGE = CHARGE.CREDIT * HOURS
```

in the function description defines the value of the function. At least one statement that assigns a value to the function name must be executed each time the function is called. In this example, the assignment following THEN is executed if the value passed to HOURS is larger than CHARGE.FULL; otherwise the assignment following ELSE is executed.

As another example of a call or reference to FNCHARGE, we could write the statements

```
400 LET HOURS = 0
410 LET HOURS = HOURS + SEM.HOURS(I) FOR I = 1 TO N
420 LET TUITION = FNCHARGE(HOURS)
```

to compute the tuition charge for a student taking N courses in a semester, where N is likely to be between 1 and 7. If SEM.HOURS is an array containing the credit hours for each course, then the FOR loop computes the total credit hours taken. The call to FNCHARGE would return the tuition cost for the total credit hours taken. In this example, the argument is a variable with the same name (HOURS) as the parameter used in the function definition. This is not necessary, but it also causes no difficulties.

The rules of definition for multiple-line functions are summarized in the following display.

Multiple-Line Function Definition

```
    DEF* FNvariable
or  DEF* FNvariable (parameter list)
    - - -
    - - -
    - - - } function description
    - - -
    - - -
    FNEND
```

Interpretation: FN*variable* is the function name, where *variable* may be any legal BASIC-PLUS name. The statements written in the *function description* part are carried out each time the function is called. At least one statement of the form

    LET FN*variable* = expression

in the function description must be executed each time the function is called. (If no such statement is executed, a value of zero is returned for numeric functions; the null string is returned for string functions.) The rules for the use and substitution of arguments for parameters are the same as for single-line functions. The values of the actual arguments in the call of a function are not altered by the function execution.

Notes: Within the function definition, FN*variable* may only appear in the DEF* statement and on the left-hand side of assignment statements. (The only exception to this is in the case of recursion, which is discussed in Section 8.4)

Exercise 8.1: Write single-line functions to compute:

a)   the area of a circle.
b)   the area of a rectangle.
c)   the volume of a sphere.
d)   the volume of a cube.

Exercise 8.2: Write a multiple-line, two-argument function FNMAX to determine the larger of two numeric values. Also write the function FNMAX$, the string version of FNMAX.

Exercise 8.3: Show how the function FNMAX (see Exercise 8.2) could be used to find the largest of four variables, A, B, C, and D. Use a single BASIC-PLUS statement. *Hint*: Remember that function calls may be nested.

Exercise 8.4:

  a) Define a one-argument, multiple-line function FNABSOLUTE that calculates the absolute value of its argument without using the ABS function.
  b) Define a one-argument function FNSIGN that performs the same computation as SGN, but do not use SGN in the definition.
  c) Write a program to check the equivalence of FNABSOLUTE and ABS as well as FNSIGN and SGN.

Exercise 8.5: Write a function FNSUM to compute the sum of two data items.

A Review of Argument/Parameter Correspondence

The parameters appearing in a function definition are used in the description of the action of the function. They serve as place-holders for the actual arguments and are not, themselves, manipulated. Rather, they represent the data that are to be used in the computation. At each call of the function, the values of the arguments appearing in the function reference are substituted for the parameters in the definition. The data manipulation is then performed on the actual argument values and the result is assigned as the value of the function.

Only the function value may be returned by the function; any change made to a function parameter will not affect the value of the corresponding argument. BASIC-PLUS protects the arguments in a function call from being changed, regardless of what is done in the function.

Example 8.5 Let FNADDONE be defined as

```
110 DEF* FNADDONE(X)
120 LET X = X + 1
130 LET FNADDONE = X
140 FNEND
```

If FNADDONE is called using the statement

```
210 LET NEW.Z = FNADDONE(OLD.Z)
```

the value of NEW.Z would be equal to OLD.Z + 1, but OLD.Z (the function argument) would remain unchanged.

Any legal BASIC-PLUS expression may be used as an argument in a function reference. The order and number of the arguments in a function reference must correspond exactly to the order and number of the parameters in the definition. As indicated earlier, string arguments must be used wherever string parameters appear. However, integer arguments may be used interchangeably where real parameters appear in a function definition, and vice versa.

Example 8.6 Let FNMAX(X, Y) be a function that returns the larger of its two values. (You may have already written this function as part of Exercise 8.2, although it is not necessary that you do so to finish this example.)

```
100      DEF* FNMAX(X, Y)
110   !
120   !RETURNS THE LARGER OF X AND Y
130   !
140      IF X > Y THEN LET FNMAX = X        &
              ELSE LET FNMAX = Y
150   !
160      FNEND     !FNMAX
```

a) The value of Z following the execution of the statements

```
210 LET A = 35.5
220 LET Z = FNMAX(A, 30) + 10
```

is 45.5. In the reference to FNMAX, the value of the variable A (35.5) is substituted for X, and 30 is substituted for Y. This correspondence between arguments and parameters is illustrated below.

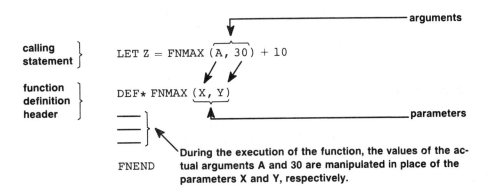

During the execution of the function, the values of the actual arguments A and 30 are manipulated in place of the parameters X and Y, respectively.

b) The value of P following the execution of the statements

```
310 LET A = 22
320 LET P = FNMAX(A + 10, 30)
```

is 32. When the function FNMAX is referenced, the expression A + 10 is evaluated first and the result, 32, is substituted for the parameter X. The value 30 is substituted for the parameter Y.

c) We could use the pair of statements below:

```
330 LET Z1 = FNMAX(A, B)
340 LET Z = FNMAX(Z1, C)
```

to find the largest of three variables A, B, and C. In this example, the larger of A and B is first assigned to Z1, and then the larger of Z1 and C is assigned to Z. In the first function reference, A is substituted for X and B for Y; in the second function reference, Z1 is substituted for X and C for Y.

These two statements could be combined as the single statement:

```
330 LET Z = FNMAX(FNMAX(A, B), C)
```

This statement contains a nested function reference. The value of the first (inner) reference, FNMAX(A, B), is used as an argument in the second (outer) reference.

8.2 Passing Arrays: Global and Local Variables

Global Variables

Unfortunately, BASIC-PLUS does not allow arrays to be passed as function arguments. Because of this, any array to be accessed by a function must be defined *global* to the function, as illustrated in the next example.

Example 8.7   An algorithm for determining the largest of a collection of N (N > 1) data items in an array X is shown in Fig. 8.3.

This algorithm can be implemented as a multiple-line function FNLARGEST (Fig. 8.4). FNLARGEST is a function having one parameter, N, which represents the number of input data items. The array X is a *global variable* used to provide input data to the function. We have described the array X as an *input global variable* (designated by IN in line 320) because it is used only to provide input data to the function (there are no modifications made to X during the execution of the function). If the data to be provided to the function were initially stored in another array, that data would have to be copied into X before FNLARGEST was called.

Note that it is possible for a function to change the values of its global variables (although FNLARGEST did not alter the contents of X). These

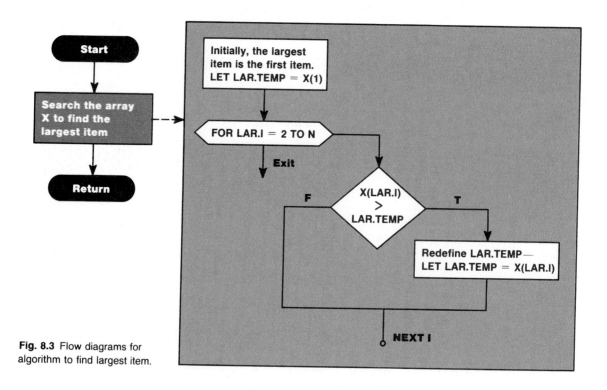

Fig. 8.3 Flow diagrams for algorithm to find largest item.

```
230   !ILLUSTRATION OF THE LARGEST VALUE FUNCTION
235   !
240      DIM X(20)
245   !
250      DEF* FNLARGEST(N)
255   !
260   !FUNCTION TO DETERMINE THE LARGEST OF
265   !N DATA ITEMS IN AN ARRAY X
270   !
280   !PARAMETER DEFINITIONS --
290   !  N - NUMBER OF ITEMS IN X
300   !
310   !GLOBAL VARIABLES
320   !  IN: X( ) - ARRAY TO BE SEARCHED
330   !
340   !LOCAL VARIABLES - LAR.I, LAR.TEMP
350   !
360   !INITIALIZE LARGEST VALUE LAR.TEMP
370      LET LAR.TEMP = X(1)
380   !CHECK FOR LARGER VALUES THAN LAR.TEMP
390      FOR LAR.I = 2 TO N
400         IF X(LAR.I) > LAR.TEMP THEN               &
               !REDEFINE LAR.TEMP                     &
               LET LAR.TEMP = X(LAR.I)
410      NEXT LAR.I
420   !
430      LET FNLARGEST = LAR.TEMP
440   !
450      FNEND    !END OF FUNCTION FNLARGEST
460   !
470   !
480   !MAIN PROGRAM
490   !
500   !READ VALUES FOR N AND ARRAY X
510      READ N
515      DATA 10
520      READ X(I) FOR I = 1 TO N
550      DATA 67, 4, 35, 89, 765, 22, 134, 17, 33, 1
560   !
570   !FIND LARGEST ITEM
580      LET LARGEST = FNLARGEST(N)
590      PRINT "THE LARGEST VALUE IS"; LARGEST
600   !
610      END    !MAIN PROGRAM


RUNNH
THE LARGEST VALUE IS 765
```

Fig. 8.4 The definition and call of a function to compute the largest value in array X.

changes are often called the *side effects* of a function. It is a good idea to avoid side effects whenever possible; any side effects that do occur in a function should be carefully documented with comments.

It is often not easy to avoid side-effects in BASIC-PLUS, because arrays cannot be passed as arguments to functions. It would be most convenient if we could write FNLARGEST as a two-parameter function with the first parameter being the name of the array containing the list of data and the second being the number of items in the list. Then the name of the array in which the data were stored could be specified at each call of FNLARGEST and the array argument would be substituted for the array parameter. Since BASIC-PLUS does not permit the use of arrays as parameters in functions, we were forced to treat X as a global variable to the function FNLARGEST.

The relationships between parameters and global variables are summarized in the following display.

Parameters and Global Variables in Function Definitions

Variables used in a function definition, but not included in the parameter list, are called *global variables*. They are identical to the variables of the same name that appear outside the function definition.

A parameter in a function is distinct from any variable with the same name used outside the function definition. Changes in the parameter value will not affect the values of global variables having the same name.

Local Variables

Multiple-line functions may also have another kind of variable called a *local variable*, which is defined and used only within the function itself. The variables LAR.I and LAR.TEMP in Fig. 8.4 are examples of such local variables.

LAR.I is used as the loop control variable in the FOR loop, and LAR.TEMP is required to store the largest value encountered at any point during execution of the function. Since the function name, FNLARGEST, must be set to the largest value before completing the function (line 430), we might consider using FNLARGEST everywhere in place of LAR.TEMP. However, within the function definition, the name of the function may be used only to the left of the equal sign in an assignment statement (unless we are using recursion—see Section 8.4). Thus FNLARGEST could not have been used (in place of LAR.TEMP) in the IF statement at line 400.

We have explicitly listed both LAR.I and LAR.TEMP as local variables to the function (line 340). This is to document the use of these names within the function, and to remind the function user that the values of these variables might change during function execution. Such changes are side effects of FNLARGEST that could cause unexpected results if LAR.I or LAR.TEMP were used elsewhere in any program that references FNLARGEST.

For a variable to be considered local to a function, its name must be used exclusively within the function. Since BASIC-PLUS does not check to see that you are using local variables properly, it is up to you to be sure that your local variables are indeed used locally and nowhere else. In the following display, we provide some suggested naming conventions for local variables. Following these conventions should help ensure that each local variable name is unique.

Program Style

Naming conventions for local variables

In the program in Fig. 8.4, we attached a prefix tag consisting of LAR to the name of each local variable (TEMP and I) used in function FNLARGEST. We will continue this convention throughout the text and suggest that you do the same. This will help to ensure that these variables are indeed local to the indicated function—i.e., that their names are distinct from those of other variables used outside the function.

The tags that we use will consist of the first three to five letters (after FN) in the function name.

Documentation in Function Definitions

In addition to the naming conventions just described, there are a number of other aspects of function documentation that are extremely important in the writing of good programs. Each of these documentation issues is illustrated in Fig. 8.4 and summarized in the following display.

Program Style

Documentation of function parameters, global and local variables

In the function FNLARGEST illustrated in Fig. 8.4, we were careful to explicitly list all function parameters and global and local variables in comments at the beginning of the function. We urge you to do the same with all functions that you write in order to make debugging easier and to improve the readability of your programs.

The descriptions of *function parameters* should come first; all parameters should be listed, along with a definition of their use in the function (lines 280–300 in Fig. 8.4).

Following the list of parameters, you should have a second section in which all *global variables* are listed along with their definitions (lines 310–330). The list of global variables should be written in two parts: IN—for global variables that are used for input only; OUT—for global variables that are used for output only. Global variables that are used for input and output will be listed in both parts.

Finally, in a third section, you should list the names of all *local variables* to be used in the function (line 340).

Listing global and local variables is extremely important as a means of informing the function user about potential side effects of the function that might have ramifications elsewhere in a program.

The largest value function shown in Fig. 8.4 could be changed easily to return the largest of a collection of string values. The function header should be changed to

```
250 DEF* FNLARGEST$(N)
```

and the variable LAR.TEMP to LAR.TEMP$. The assignment statement at line 430 should be changed to

```
430 LET FNLARGEST$ = LAR.TEMP$
```

Of course, the global array manipulated should be a string array, X$(20).

Exercise 8.6: Let B (an array of size 20) and COUNT.N (a variable) be defined as follows:

COUNT.N

16

Array B

1	2	3	4	5	6	7	8	9	10	11	12	13	14	15	16	17	18	19	20
0	1	1	0	1	0	0	0	1	1	0	1	1	0	1	0	?	?	?	?

a) Consider the following function:

```
100        DEF* FNCOUNT(KEYS, N)
105    !
110        LET COUNTER = 0
120        FOR I = 1 TO N
130            IF B(I) = KEYS THEN                    &
                   LET COUNTER = COUNTER + 1
140        NEXT I
150    !
160        LET FNCOUNT = COUNTER
170    !
180        FNEND      !FNCOUNT
```

What are the global variables used as input in FNCOUNT? Which variables are local to FNCOUNT? Document the function parameters and global and local variables as in Example 8.7.

What is the value of L after execution of the statement

```
210 LET L = FNCOUNT(0, COUNT.N)
```

What is the value of L after execution of the statement

```
220 LET L = FNCOUNT(1, COUNT.N)
```

What are the values of K and L after execution of the statements

```
230 LET K = 5
240 LET L = FNCOUNT(6-K, 12)
```

What is the value of L after execution of the statement

```
250 LET L = FNCOUNT(B(10), B(10)+10)
```

b) Write a sequence of BASIC-PLUS statements that use the function FNCOUNT to count the number of occurrences of a value V in an array X of size 12 containing M elements. You may destroy the contents of B if necessary.

c) Redo (b) for an array Y(12) containing K elements (K <= 12).

d) Write a function FNP of three arguments K, FIRST, and LAST, which counts the number of occurrences of K in the array B between the FIRST and LAST elements of B inclusive. (Assume FIRST is always less than or equal to LAST. FIRST and LAST are indexes to the array B.)

Exercise 8.7: Write a function FNROUND(X, N) of two arguments that will round any value X (positive or negative) to the nearest N decimal places for any integer N greater than or equal to zero (see Example 8.3).

Exercise 8.8: Rewrite Example 4.12 using the function FNROUND (Exercise 8.7) to round both the computed sine and cosine to the nearest three decimal places before printing.

Exercise 8.9:

a) Write an integer function FNMOD%(I%,J%) to compute the remainder in the division of the positive integer I% by the positive integer J%. (See also Exercise 4.13). Rewrite the IF statement (line 260) of the prime number program (Fig. 4.7) to use this function to determine if DIV% is a divisor of N%.

b) Write a function FNTRUNC(X) that truncates (removes) the fractional part of X: FNTRUNC(-27.85) = -27.

c) Write a function FNCEIL(X) that computes the smallest integer that is greater than X: FNCEIL(27.851) = 28, FNCEIL(-27.851) = -27.

Exercise 8.10: Write a function FNSUMN to compute the sum of a collection of N data items stored in an array W.

8.3 Solving a Larger Problem

Program System Charts

As the number of modules used in a program begins to grow, it becomes increasingly important to carefully document the functional relationships and information flow among the modules. In this section we provide the solution to a simple statistics problem, illustrating the use of user-defined functions (hereafter referred to simply as functions) and subroutines. In the process, we illustrate some conventions of programming style and documentation for describing the relationships among program modules and the flow of information into and out of each module of a program.

Problem 8A   Given a collection of N numbers stored in an array, compute the range, mean (average), and median for this collection.

Discussion: The initial data table is shown next; the level one flow diagram for this problem is shown in Fig. 8.5. Each box in the diagram represents a major step in the problem solution. Additional lower level subproblems may be identified within each of Steps 2, 3, and 4. Each of these *subtasks* represents a refinement of a task shown at a higher level.

DATA TABLE FOR PROBLEM 8A

Program Constants		
MAX.ITEMS = 100: Maximum number of items that can be processed		

Input Variables		Output Variables
N: Number of data items to be processed		RANGE: Range of the data (difference between the largest and smallest values)
X( ): Array containing the data (size 100)		MEAN: Mean of the data
		MEDIAN: Median of the data

We can represent the functional relationships among the main problem and all of the subproblems using a *program system chart* (Fig. 8.6). The program system chart identifies the major subproblems of the original problem and illustrates the relationships among them. The solutions to the subproblems shown at one level in the chart can be specified in terms of the connected subproblems at the next lower level. For example, the program system chart indicates that the solution of the subproblem "compute median" may be specified in terms of the solutions to the subproblems "sort data" and "compute middle value of sorted data." Similarly, in order to find the average, we must first solve the subproblem "compute sum."

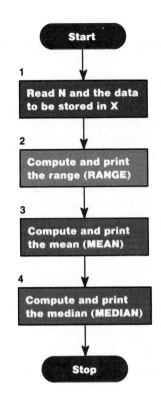

Fig. 8.5 Level one flow diagram for Problem 8A.

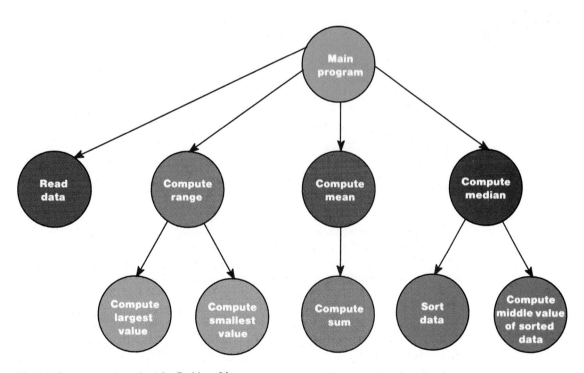

Fig. 8.6 Program system chart for Problem 8A.

Once the data table, level one flow diagram, and program system chart have been completed, we can begin to add data flow information to the program system chart and to work on the lower level refinements shown in the chart. In considering the refinements, it is necessary to decide which subtasks should be implemented as subroutines or functions and which should be implemented as part of the solution of the task above it in the program system chart. In general, a subtask should be implemented using a function or subroutine unless it occurs only once in the program system chart and is rather trivial. The subtasks "compute range", "compute sum", and "compute middle value" fall in the latter category. The "read data" task could be implemented as a subroutine or as part of the main program; we did the latter.

The decision as to whether to write a subroutine or a function normally depends upon the number of values to be returned. Functions are most convenient when a single value is to be computed. Such is the case in the subtasks for computing the largest value, the smallest value, the mean, and the median. The sort task, however, rearranges an entire array of information (it does not compute a single value) and is, therefore, a natural candidate to be written as a subroutine. In BASIC-PLUS, however, the sort module also can be written easily as a function instead of a subroutine. First, we will use a subroutine for the sort for this problem; then we will

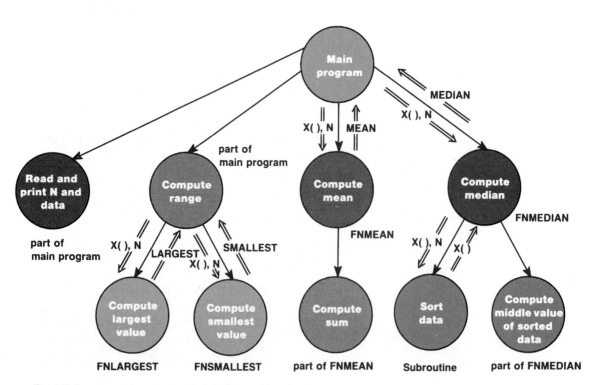

Fig. 8.7 Program system chart with data flow and function designation for Problem 8A.

discuss the use of functions instead of subroutines, and redo the sort as a function.

Fig. 8.7 shows a program system chart (updated from Fig. 8.6) that reflects the decisions just discussed. Also, we have added a description of the information flow between the various program modules. For example, the array X and its size N are provided as input to FNMEDIAN; the median value, MEDIAN, is returned to the main program by FNMEDIAN.

At this point, we are ready to write the main program (Fig. 8.8). As was the case with the largest value function, FNLARGEST (see Example 8.7), we treat FNSMALLEST, FNMEAN, and FNMEDIAN as functions with one argument. Additional input data to all four of these functions is passed through the global array X.

The program in Fig. 8.8 represents the step-by-step implementation of the level one flow diagram for the statistics problem. It is easy to read as each major step stands out and is not obscured by the details required for implementation.

```
100   !STATISTICS PROBLEM - MAIN PROGRAM
120   !
130   !COMPUTE THE RANGE, MEAN AND MEDIAN OF A
140   !COLLECTION OF N DATA ITEMS
150
160   !PROGRAM CONSTANTS
170       LET MAX.ITEMS = 100    !MAX ITEMS ALLOWED
180   !
190   !ARRAYS USED
200       DIM X(100)
210   !
220   !FUNCTIONS REFERENCED -
230   !  FNLARGEST, FNSMALLEST, FNMEDIAN, FNMEAN
240   !
250   !MAIN PROGRAM
260   !ENTER AND VALIDATE N. ENTER DATA IN ARRAY X
270       INPUT "ENTER NUMBER OF ITEMS"; N
280       INPUT "OUT OF RANGE. PLEASE RE-ENTER."; N    &
              UNTIL N >= 1 AND N <= MAX.ITEMS
290       PRINT "ENTER DATA LIST, SEPARATED BY COMMAS."
300       INPUT X(I) FOR I = 1 TO N
310   !
320   !COMPUTE THE RANGE
330       LET RANGE = FNLARGEST(N) - FNSMALLEST(N)
340       PRINT
350       PRINT "THE RANGE IS"; RANGE
360   !
370   !COMPUTE THE MEAN
380       LET MEAN = FNMEAN(N)
390       PRINT
400       PRINT "THE MEAN IS"; MEAN
410   !
```

(continued)

```
420    !DETERMINE THE MEDIAN
430       LET MEDIAN = FNMEDIAN(N)
440       PRINT
450       PRINT "THE MEDIAN IS"; MEDIAN
460    !
470       PRINT "CALCULATIONS COMPLETE"
480    !
490    !FUNCTION DEFINITIONS WILL GO HERE
          .
          .
          .
32767    END    !STATISTICS PROGRAM
```

Fig. 8.8 Main program for Problem 8A.

The functions required will be placed just before the END statement in the program. To complete the data table for this program we should add the loop control variable I (as a program variable) and provide a list of the functions referenced at the bottom of the table.

ADDITIONAL
DATA TABLE
ENTRIES FOR
PROBLEM 8A

Program Variables
I: Loop control variable
Functions Referenced

(In all functions, X is a global input array; N is a parameter.)
FNLARGEST: Computes the largest of a collection of N data items in an array X( ).
FNSMALLEST: Computes the smallest of a collection of N data items in an array X( ).
FNMEAN: Computes the average of a collection of N data items in an array X( ).
FNMEDIAN: Computes the median of a collection of N data items in an array X( ).

Data tables and flow diagrams for each of the functions FNLARGEST, FNSMALLEST, FNMEAN, and FNMEDIAN may now be designed independently of the main program except for the name of the global variable X. The data tables and flow diagrams for FNLARGEST, FNSMALLEST, and FNMEAN are straightforward and are left as exercises (see Exercise 8.12). The function FNLARGEST is shown in Fig. 8.4; FNSMALLEST and FNMEAN should be written as part of Exercise 8.12.

We now can complete the statistics problem by writing the function FNMEDIAN to find the median of a collection of N data items stored in the array X. In the process, we will once again illustrate many of the points made so far in this chapter and provide some additional insights concerning the use of functions in BASIC-PLUS.

Problem 8B   Write a function FNMEDIAN to determine the median of a collection of N data items stored in an array X.

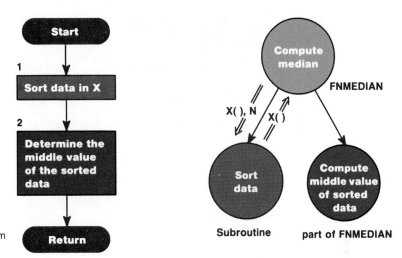

Fig. 8.9 Level one flow diagram and program system chart for Problem 8B.

Discussion: Figure 8.9 shows the portion of the program system chart (Fig. 8.7) that is relevant to the median function, as well as a level one flow diagram for the function.

As is so often the case, the level one flow diagram simply reflects an ordering of the primary steps shown in the program system chart. The information involved in the solution of the problem at this level is shown in the program system chart and in the following data table.

DATA TABLE FOR PROBLEM 8B (FNMEDIAN)

Parameters
N: The number of items in the array X( )

Global Variables
X( ): The array containing the data to be processed (input). Also contains the sorted data at completion of sort (output)

The next step in the solution of the problem is to decide how to implement Steps 1 and 2 in the flow diagram. Since sorting a collection of data is a somewhat complicated task, we will implement the sort as a separate module. Since the sort does not return a value, but rather rearranges a collection of data in a global array, we will use a subroutine instead of a function. Once the data have been sorted, finding the median is rather easy (see Fig. 8.10). This algorithm is based upon the definition of the median as the middle value in an ordered list of data.

We now can write the function FNMEDIAN to find the median (see Fig. 8.11a). One new variable, MED.INDEX, was used in the function FNMEDIAN, and is added to the data table following Fig. 8.10.

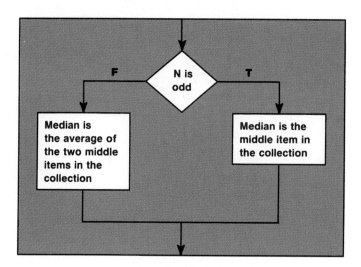

Fig. 8.10 Refinement of Step 2 in Fig. 8.9.

ADDITIONAL
DATA TABLE
ENTRY FOR
PROBLEM 8B
(FNMEDIAN)

Local Variables

MED.INDEX: Index to "middle" element of array X

The sort subroutine shown in Fig. 8.11b is an implementation of the Bubble Sort algorithm (Problem 7B) using X and N instead of M and M.COUNT.

The sort subroutine has two global and three local variables, as shown in the following data table.

DATA TABLE FOR
PROBLEM 8B (SOR-
SUBROUTINE)

Global Variables

X( ): Contains the original array of data before sorting (input)
    Also contains the sorted data at completion of subroutine (output)

N: The number of items to be sorted (input)

Local Variables

SORT.DONE$: Indicates whether or not another pass will be required following the current one. (Loop control variable for the outer sort loop.)

SORT.INDEX: Loop control variable for the inner sort loop—used to make one pass through array

SORT.TEMP: Temporary variable used in exchange of out-of-order data items

```
4000      DEF* FNMEDIAN(N)
4010   !
4020   !FUNCTION TO COMPUTE THE MEDIAN OF N DATA ITEMS
4025   !IN AN ARRAY X
4030   !
4040   !PARAMETER DEFINITIONS --
4050   !  N - NUMBER OF ITEMS IN X
4060   !
4070   !GLOBAL VARIABLES
4080   !  IN:  X( ) - ORIGINAL DATA UNSORTED
4090   !  OUT: X( ) - ORIGINAL DATA SORTED
4100   !
4110   !LOCAL VARIABLES - MED.INDEX
4120   !
4130   !SORT DATA IN ASCENDING ORDER
4140      GOSUB 5000
4150   !
4160   !DETERMINE MEDIAN VALUE
4170   !CHECK IF N IS ODD OR EVEN
4175   !USE MIDDLE ITEM IF N IS ODD
4180   !OTHERWISE, USE AVERAGE OF TWO MIDDLE ITEMS
4190      LET MED.INDEX = INT(N / 2) + 1
4200      IF (INT(N / 2) * 2) <> N THEN                    &
              LET FNMEDIAN = X(MED.INDEX)                  &
          ELSE                                            &
              LET FNMEDIAN = (X(MED.INDEX-1)               &
                             + X(MED.INDEX)) / 2
4210   !
4220      GOTO 9990    !RETURN FROM FNMEDIAN
4230   !
4240   !
5000   !BUBBLE SORT SUBROUTINE WILL GO HERE
          .
          .
          .
9990      FNEND    !FNMEDIAN
```

Fig. 8.11a Function for Problem 8A.

Global and local variables for subroutines should be documented in both data tables and BASIC-PLUS comments with the same care as global and local variables in functions. You should follow the conventions illustrated in the data table and BASIC-PLUS code for the sort subroutine.

The function FNMEDIAN illustrates how subroutines may be defined internally within a function. Such subroutines may only be referenced from within the function, and they return control to a statement inside the function definition. As usual, the subroutine must be entered only through the use of the GOSUB statement (line 4140); the GOTO statement (line 4220) is required to branch around the subroutine definition at the completion of

```
5000    !BUBBLE SORT SUBROUTINE -
5005    !SORT ARRAY X IN ASCENDING ORDER
5010    !
5020    !GLOBAL VARIABLES
5030    !   IN:   X( ) - ORIGINAL DATA UNSORTED
5040    !         N - NUMBER OF ITEMS IN X
5050    !   OUT:  X( ) - ARRAY IN ASCENDING ORDER
5060    !
5070    !LOCAL VARIABLES CHANGED -
5075    !   SORT.TEMP, SORT.DONE$, SORT.INDEX
5080    !
5090    !REPEATEDLY PASS THROUGH ARRAY X UNTIL SORTED
5100    !ASSUME ARRAY IS INITIALLY UNSORTED
5110       LET SORT.DONE$ = "FALSE"
5120       UNTIL SORT.DONE$ = "TRUE"
5130          GOSUB 6000   !MAKE A SINGLE PASS THROUGH X
5140       NEXT    !UNTIL
5150    !
5160       RETURN
5170    !END OF BUBBLE SORT SUBROUTINE
5180    !
5190    !
6000    !SUBROUTINE TO MAKE ONE PASS THRU ARRAY X AND
6010    !EXCHANGE ALL PAIRS OF ADJACENT ELEMENTS THAT
6015    !ARE OUT OF ORDER (PART OF BUBBLE SORT)
6020    !
6030    !ASSUME NO MORE PASSES NEEDED AFTER THIS ONE
6060       LET SORT.DONE$ = "TRUE"
6070    !
6080    !COMPARE ALL PAIRS OF ADJACENT ELEMENTS
6090       FOR SORT.INDEX = 1 TO N - 1
6100          IF X(SORT.INDEX) > X(SORT.INDEX+1) THEN   &
                 !EXCHANGE AND RESET SORT.DONE$          &
                 LET SORT.TEMP = X(SORT.INDEX)          &
                 \LET X(SORT.INDEX) = X(SORT.INDEX+1)   &
                 \LET X(SORT.INDEX+1) = SORT.TEMP       &
                 \LET SORT.DONE$ = "FALSE"
6110       NEXT SORT.INDEX
6120    !
6130       RETURN
6140    !END OF SUBROUTINE FOR EACH PASS
6150    !
9990       FNEND    !FNMEDIAN
```

Fig. 8.11b Bubble Sort subroutine for Problem 8B.

execution of the function FNMEDIAN. (Anytime a subroutine is written inside a function, a transfer around the subroutine is required to prevent "falling into" the subroutine.) The FNEND statement (line 9990) comes after the subroutine, and not before, as the subroutine is part of (nested within) the function definition.

FNMEDIAN is an example of a function with a side effect. It computes not only a single value (the median of the N items in the array X) but also alters the array X by sorting the data in ascending order.

There are additional side effects in that the three local variables for the SORT subroutine (SORT.DONE$, SORT.INDEX, and SORT.TEMP) are assigned new values during the execution of this subroutine. Any prior values assigned to these variables would be destroyed when the subroutine is executed. If these values are critical to the proper execution of some other portion of the program, these side effects could be extremely harmful. As we indicated in Section 8.2, when choosing names of variables used "locally" within a function or subroutine, you must pick names that are not used elsewhere. If this is not possible, at least verify that these names do not contain valuable information prior to execution of the function or subroutine in which they are used.

Exercise 8.11: In the program in Fig. 8.8, there is no reference to the computation of the sum or to the sorting of the data items (see the program system chart, Fig. 8.7). Why not?

Exercise 8.12: Develop data tables and flow diagrams for the functions FNLARGEST, FNSMALLEST, and FNMEAN. Write the functions FNMEAN and FNSMALLEST (complete with documentation) to complete the statistics problem.

Exercise 8.13: If we examine the program system chart for the statistics problem (Fig. 8.7), we can see that the sort subtask does not enter the picture until the third level, where sorting is required to find the median of the data items. Yet the sort could have been quite helpful in the computation of the range. Since sorting is needed anyway, we might just as well have sorted the data in X before we computed the range. Once this has been done, the range could be computed in the main program by the statement

```
330 LET RANGE = X(N) - X(1)
```

and the functions FNLARGEST and FNSMALLEST would no longer be needed. Rewrite the level one flow diagram, program system chart, and main program with the sort done immediately after reading the data.

Using Functions Instead of Subroutines

Although the sort module does not normally return a single value as the result of its computations, it is instructive to examine this module written as a multiple-line, logical function in BASIC-PLUS (see Fig. 8.12).

```
5000     DEF* FNSORT%(N)
5010   !
5020   !FUNCTION TO SORT N DATA ITEMS IN AN
5025   !ARRAY X IN ASCENDING ORDER
```

(continued)

```
5030   !
5040   !PARAMETER DEFINITIONS - -
5050   !  N - NUMBER OF ITEMS IN X
5060   !
5070   !GLOBAL VARIABLES
5080   !  IN:  X( ) - UNSORTED ARRAY
5090   !  OUT: X( ) - ORIGINAL ARRAY SORTED
5100   !
5110   !LOCAL VARIABLES -
5115   !  SORT.TEMP, SORT.INDEX, SORT.DONE$
5120   !
5125   !VALIDATE N
5130      IF N < 1 THEN                                    &
              LET FNSORT% = 0%   !FALSE                     &
              \GOTO 6150          !RETURN FROM FNSORT%
5135   !
5140   !REPEATEDLY PASS THROUGH ARRAY X UNTIL SORTED
5145   !ASSUME ARRAY IS INITIALLY UNSORTED
5150      LET SORT.DONE$ = "FALSE"
5160      UNTIL SORT.DONE$ = "TRUE"
5170         GOSUB 6000 !MAKE A SINGLE PASS THROUGH X
5180      NEXT   !UNTIL
5190   !
5200      LET FNSORT% = -1%     !TRUE
5205   !
5210      GOTO 6150    !RETURN FROM FNSORT%
5220   !
5230   !
6000   !SUBROUTINE TO MAKE ONE PASS THROUGH ARRAY X
6005   !AND EXCHANGE ALL PAIRS OF ADJACENT ELEMENTS
6010   !THAT ARE OUT OF ORDER
6020   !
6030   !ASSUME NO MORE PASSES NEEDED AFTER THIS ONE
6060      LET SORT.DONE$ = "TRUE"
6070   !
6075   !COMPARE ALL PAIRS OF ADJACENT ELEMENTS
6080      FOR SORT.INDEX = 1 TO N - 1
6090         IF X(SORT.INDEX) > X(SORT.INDEX+1) THEN &
                !EXCHANGE AND RESET SORT.STATUS$      &
                LET SORT.TEMP = X(SORT.INDEX)         &
                \LET X(SORT.INDEX) = X(SORT.INDEX+1)  &
                \LET X(SORT.INDEX+1) = SORT.TEMP      &
                \LET SORT.DONE$ = "FALSE"
6100      NEXT SORT.INDEX
6110   !
6120      RETURN
6130   !END OF SUBROUTINE FOR EACH PASS
6140   !
6150      FNEND    !FNSORT%
```

Fig. 8.12 The sort module as a single-argument function.

The function FNSORT% (lines 5000–6150 of Fig. 8.12) would replace the sort subroutine (lines 5000–6140) of Fig. 8.11b. Function definitions cannot be nested, so the statement in Fig. 8.11a that branches around the sort subroutine

```
4220 GOTO 9990    !RETURN FROM FNMEDIAN
```

should be replaced by

```
4220 FNEND   !FNMEDIAN
```

and line 9990 should be deleted from Figs. 8.11a, b.

A comparison of the function (Fig. 8.12) and subroutine (Fig. 8.11b) for the sort module reveals a number of advantages to using the function. Perhaps the most noticeable of these advantages is that the function has a name by which it can be called; it also permits us to explicitly list all input arguments (except arrays) directly in the calling statement. Thus the sort function can be referenced inside FNMEDIAN by writing

```
FNSORT%(N)
```

in an expression at line 4140 (Fig. 8.11a). This provides considerable descriptive improvement over the subroutine reference

```
4140 GOSUB 5000
```

An example of the function call is provided in the next Program Style box.

Functions also have formal header and terminator statements (DEF* and FNEND, respectively), which mark the beginning and end of a function. These statements make it easier for us to ascertain the function's physical scope, even without looking at comments.

The only real problem associated with the function FNSORT% is that it must be called within an expression. The function description should also contain a statement that assigns a value to FNSORT% (if no such assignment is made, a value of zero will be returned). Both of these requirements seem difficult to meet because FNSORT% rearranges an array of data instead of computing a single value. We can circumvent these problems by considering FNSORT% a logical function as explained in the next program style display.

Program Style

Rationale for logical functions

Recall from Section 4.7 that the integer values −1% and 0% can be used to represent the logical values true and false, respectively. If we write functions that do not compute a single value as logical functions, then we can associate the logical value true with successful completion of the function and the logical value false with unsuccessful completion. We can often accomplish this in a meaningful way by inserting a test to validate the function argument upon entry to the function (see line 5130 in Fig. 8.12). If the argument is invalid the function result is defined as 0% (false) and a function return occurs.

If the function argument is valid, function execution continues. Just before returning from the function, the statement

```
5200 LET FNSORT% = -1%    !TRUE
```

in Fig. 8.12 sets the function result to indicate successful completion.

Since the function description guarantees that a value of 0% (false) or -1% (true) will be returned, we can call FNSORT% from FNMEDIAN using a statement such as

```
4140 IF FNSORT%(N) THEN PRINT "SORT COMPLETED"    &
        ELSE PRINT "SORT NOT COMPLETED"
```

(Recall that a logical variable or value may be used by itself as a condition.) If we do not care to signal that the sort completed successfully, then we would use the statement

```
4140 IF NOT FNSORT%(N) THEN            &
        PRINT "SORT NOT COMPLETED"
```

to print an error diagnostic only when the unexpected happens and the function result is 0%.

8.4 Recursion

Introduction to Recursion

Recursion is a powerful tool that is sometimes useful in simplifying a problem solution. Recursive definitions are often encountered in the study of mathematics. For example, the set of natural numbers {1,2,3,4,. . . } may be defined recursively as follows:

1. 1 is a natural number.
2. The successor of a natural number is a natural number where the successor of a number is obtained by adding one to that number.

The power of this recursive definition in mathematics is its ability to define a set consisting of an infinite number of elements using only two statements. In a similar way, in programming, a recursive algorithm can specify a large number of computations using a few program statements and without looping.

The step-wise refinement technique of programming that we have been emphasizing throughout this text is even more important when considering the recursive solution to a problem. Using recursion involves describing the solution of a problem in terms of smaller subproblems, just as is required when formulating nonrecursive solutions. What complicates matters when recursion is involved is that one or more of the subproblems may be the original problem itself! In solving such problems, a rigorous, step-wise approach, using the tools provided earlier in the text (the data table, flow diagram, and the program system chart) is essential.

In the next two sections, we will examine the complete recursive solutions of two problems, the factorial and the binary search. We are by no means suggesting that the recursive solutions to these problems are better than the nonrecursive ones. Rather, we simply wish to illustrate the use of recursion in BASIC-PLUS.

A Recursive Factorial Function

One example of the use of recursion involves the computation of the factorial, $N!$, of a non-negative integer N . The recursive definition of $N!$ is given by

```
N! = 1              (if N = 0)
N! = N × (N - 1)! (if N > 0)
```

Thus $3!$ may be computed as

$$3 \times (2!) = 3 \times (2 \times (1!)) = 3 \times (2 \times (1 \times (0!)))$$
$$= 3 \times (2 \times (1 \times 1)) = 6$$

The recursive algorithm for this problem can be described as follows:

Step S: if $N = 0$, the factorial is defined as 1
Step R: if $N > 0$, the factorial is defined as N times the factorial of $N - 1$

Step S is called the *stopping step* of the algorithm, and Step R is called the *recursion step*. All recursive algorithms may be expressed in terms of a stopping step and a recursion step. Eventually, the recursion step leads to the stopping step, as illustrated in Fig. 8.13, for $N = 3$.

As shown in Fig. 8.13, the repeated application (lines 1, 2, and 3) of the recursion step, R, eventually leads to the stopping step, S (line 4). The stopping step "turns off," or stops, the recursion, producing a result of 1 (the factorial of 0) that can be passed back to the last recursion step, the computation of the factorial of 1 (line 3). At this point, the factorial of 1 can be computed (line 5), and the result (1) returned to the computation of the factorial of 2. This process continues until finally, the factorial of 3 can be computed (line 7).

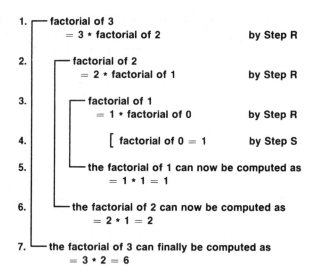

1. ┌── factorial of 3
   │   = 3 * factorial of 2   **by Step R**

2. ┌── factorial of 2
   │   = 2 * factorial of 1   **by Step R**

3. ┌── factorial of 1
   │   = 1 * factorial of 0   **by Step R**

4. [factorial of 0 = 1   **by Step S**

5. └── the factorial of 1 can now be computed as
          = 1 * 1 = 1

6. └── the factorial of 2 can now be computed as
          = 2 * 1 = 2

7. └── the factorial of 3 can finally be computed as
          = 3 * 2 = 6

Fig. 8.13 Recursive computation of the factorial of 3.

The BASIC-PLUS implementation of the recursive algorithm is shown in Fig. 8.14. The function FNFACT returns a value of one if its argument is 0. Otherwise the value returned is determined by the value of the expression N * FNFACT(N−1). Since FNFACT calls itself, it is considered a *recursive function*.

The statement

```
300 LET NEWNUM = FNFACT(3)
```

computes the value of 3!. As illustrated in Fig. 8.15, each new call to FNFACT increases the level of recursion. BASIC-PLUS saves the value of the function's parameter (N) just before each new call. At the time of the call, the expression N−1 is evaluated and assigned as the new value of the parameter N (indicated by arrows pointing downward). Eventually, the argument will be zero and a value of one will be associated with the last

```
100     DEF* FNFACT(N)
110   !
120   !RECURSIVE FUNCTION TO COMPUTE N FACTORIAL (N!)
130   !
140   !PARAMETER DEFINITIONS --
150   !  N - INTEGER FOR WHICH FACTORIAL IS COMPUTED
160   !
170     IF N = 0 THEN LET FNFACT = 1                          &
            ELSE LET FNFACT = N * FNFACT(N-1)
180   !
190     FNEND    !FNFACT
```

Fig. 8.14 Recursive factorial function.

call to FNFACT. Just before returning from each level of recursion, the function computes the value to be returned, (shown at left of Fig. 8.15) by multiplying the argument value saved at this level by the result just returned from the previous level. Each return reduces the level of recursion by one. When the level of recursion is back to zero, the value returned, 6, represents the value of the initial function call and is assigned to NEWNUM.

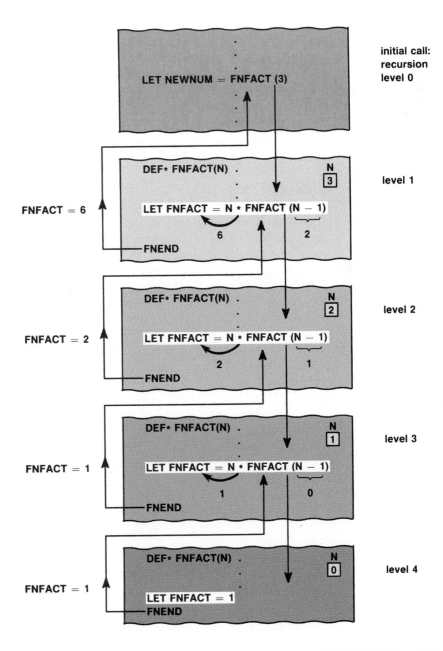

Fig. 8.15 Trace of execution of FNFACT(3).

Binary Search Algorithm

In Chapter 6 (see Example 6.16), we illustrated an algorithm for performing a *linear search* through an array of data items. It can be shown that if each of the items in the array are equally likely to occur as a key, then the expected number of comparisons (probes) needed to find any key is $(N+1)/2$, where N is the number of items in the array. Thus if N is 999, the expected number of probes for a given key is 500. Clearly, there must be a better way of searching.

The *binary search* provides considerable improvement in efficiency over the linear search method. However, it may be used only when the data in the array are ordered. (Of course, ordering data is easier for us now that we have a sort function to assist us.) The binary search algorithm is described in the following problem.

Problem 8C: Write a recursive function to perform a binary search of an ordered array of N elements. The function should return the index (a value between 1 and N) of the key in the search array if the key is found; otherwise it should return a value of 0.

Discussion: The binary search achieves its efficiency by successively eliminating portions of the array that cannot possibly contain the key. The algorithm takes advantage of the fact that the data are sorted and compares the key to the middle item in the array. If the two data items are the same, the search is complete. If the key is larger than the middle value, we ignore the first half of the array and repeat this probing process on only the last half of the array. If the key is smaller than the middle item, we ignore the last half of the array and search the first half. Whichever half was chosen, that half is divided in half again, leaving only one quarter of the array to be searched. This process is continued (recursively) until the item is found or no more divisions are possible.

The process is illustrated at the top of the next page for an array S.LIST of 9 items (N = 9). Three pointers (indexes) to the array are required. FIRST and LAST are used to define the *boundaries* for each probe. FIRST always points to the first item in the part of the array that is to be searched (initially, FIRST = 1). LAST always points to the last item in the portion that is to be searched (initially, LAST = N = 9). To begin the search for the key (37), we compute

```
BIN.MID = INT((FIRST + LAST)/2) = 5
```

and compare the key to S.LIST(5), which has the value 45. Since the key is less than S.LIST(5), we ignore the last half of the array by setting LAST to BIN.MID-1 (value of 4), and repeat the process using the first half of the array. Now with FIRST = 1 and LAST = 4, we recompute BIN.MID and make a second probe, comparing the key to S.LIST(2), which is 35. Since the key is greater than 35, we reset

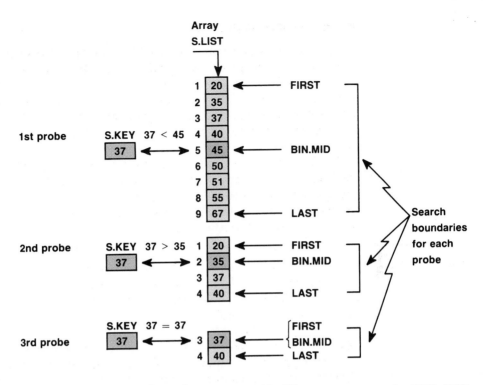

FIRST to 3 (the value of BIN.MID+1). We now recompute BIN.MID again, with FIRST = 3 and LAST = 4. The value of BIN.MID is 3, and the third probe is made at S.LIST(3). In our example, the key is found at this point, after three probes.

It can be shown that for the binary search, the expected number of probes for a key is approximately $\log_2 N$ (assuming that each item in the array can occur as the key with equal probability). If $N = 999$, $\log_2 N$ is approximately equal to 10, a considerable improvement over 500. The data table for this function is shown next and the flow diagrams are shown in Fig. 8.16.

DATA TABLE FOR PROBLEM 8C	Parameters	
S.KEY:	Item to be found	
FIRST:	Always contains the index to the first item in the portion of the array to be searched	
LAST:	Always contains the index of the last item in the portion of the array to be searched	
	Global Variables	
S.LIST( ):	Array to be searched	
	Local Variables	
BIN.MID:	The index of the middle item in the portion of the array to be searched	

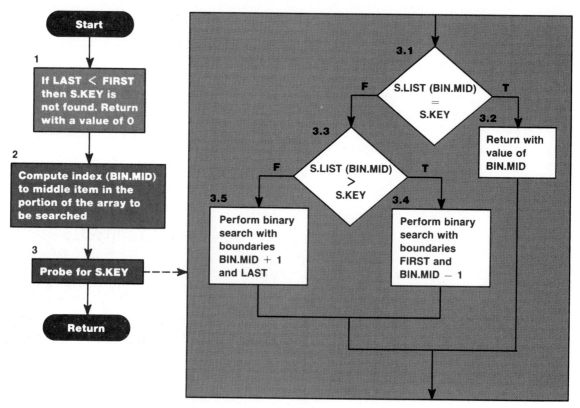

Fig. 8.16 Flow diagrams for Problem 8C.

As shown in the flow diagram, Steps 1 and 3.2 are the stopping steps. In order to implement the recursion steps (3.4 and 3.5), new values must be passed to the parameters FIRST and LAST by the statements that call the procedure recursively. These new values define the search boundaries for the next probe into the array. In the initial call to the recursive procedure, FIRST and LAST should be defined as the first and last elements of the array, respectively. The function FNBIN is shown in Fig. 8.17. The statements

```
500  !SEARCH S.LIST(1) THROUGH S.LIST(20) FOR S.KEY
510     LET INDEX = FNBIN(S.KEY, 1, 20)
520     IF INDEX = 0 THEN PRINT S.KEY; "NOT FOUND" &
            ELSE PRINT S.KEY;"FOUND AT ELEMENT";INDEX
```

could be used to call and print the function result (assigned to INDEX).

```
100          DEF* FNBIN(S.KEY, FIRST, LAST)
110     !
120     !RECURSIVE BINARY SEARCH FUNCTION
130     !
140     !PARAMETER DEFINITIONS --
150     !   S.KEY - ITEM TO BE FOUND
160     !   FIRST - INDEX TO FIRST ITEM IN SEARCH ARRAY
170     !   LAST - INDEX TO LAST ITEM IN SEARCH ARRAY
180     !
190     !GLOBAL VARIABLES
200     !   IN: S.LIST( ) - LIST TO BE SEARCHED
210     !
220     !LOCAL VARIABLES - BIN.MID (INDEX TO MIDDLE ITEM
230     !                               IN SEARCH ARRAY)
240     !
245     !DETERMINE IF FURTHER SEARCHING IS POSSIBLE
250         IF LAST < FIRST THEN                            &
                !S.KEY CANNOT BE FOUND. STOP PROBING        &
                LET FNBIN = 0                               &
                \GOTO 320    !RETURN                        &
255     !
260     !DEFINE INDEX TO MIDDLE ITEM
270         LET BIN.MID = INT((FIRST + LAST) / 2)
280     !
290     !RECURSIVELY PROBE AGAIN
300         IF S.LIST(BIN.MID) = S.KEY THEN                 &
                LET FNBIN = BIN.MID                          &
            ELSE IF S.LIST(BIN.MID) > S.KEY THEN            &
                LET FNBIN =                                 &
                    FNBIN(S.KEY, FIRST, BIN.MID - 1)        &
            ELSE                                            &
                LET FNBIN =                                 &
                    FNBIN(S.KEY, BIN.MID + 1, LAST)
310     !
320         FNEND      !FNBIN
330     !
340         END
```

Fig. 8.17 Recursive binary search function for Problem 8C.

Exercise 8.14: Trace the search of the array S.LIST shown in this section for a key of 40. Specify the values of FIRST, LAST, and BIN.MID for each recursive call.

Exercise 8.15: Implement the binary search algorithm without recursion. Use a loop that is repeated until the key is located or there are no more array elements left to search. *Hint:* FIRST, LAST, and BIN.MID will still be computed as in Fig. 8.17, and then the loop will be repeated, instead of calling the function again.

Exercise 8.16: The Fibonacci Series is defined recursively as follows:

1. The first Fibonacci number is one.
2. The second Fibonacci number is one.
3. Any other Fibonacci number is equal to the sum of the preceding two Fibonacci numbers.

Write a recursive function that computes the Fibonacci number corresponding to its argument, N. Also write the non-recursive Fibonacci function, using a loop.

Exercise 8.17: Try using the binary search technique to locate your name in the phone book.

8.5 Testing a Program System

As the size of a program system grows, the possibility of error also increases. However, if the system is written in terms of small and manageable modules (subroutines or functions), then the possibility of error will increase much more slowly. Also, the limited use of global variables will minimize the likelihood of harmful side effects, and this can help reduce the possibility of errors.

Whenever possible, it is best to test each system module independently before putting the entire package together. This can be done by writing a short driver program (see Example 7.10) consisting of array declarations, initialization of input arguments, and a call to the module being tested. The driver program should also print the results returned by the tested module. A little time spent testing each module independently in this manner should significantly reduce the total time required to debug the entire program system. (An example of a driver program would be the main program for testing FNLARGEST shown in Fig. 8.4.)

If a module being tested calls another, it is often helpful to initially substitute a dummy module, or *stub*, for the second module. The body of the stub should consist only of a PRINT statement indicating that the stub was entered. After the second level module is written and tested, it can be inserted in place of its stub.

After all the modules are tested independently, the entire program system should be tested and debugged. Some suggestions for preventing and detecting errors at this stage follow.

1. Accurate, written descriptions of all parameters and global variables of a function should be maintained. These descriptions should be included as comments in the module definition.
2. Leave a trace of execution by printing the name of each function as it is entered.
3. At least in the early debugging stage, the values of all input arguments and any global variables should be printed upon entry to a module.
4. Whenever possible, the values of input arguments and any global vari-

ables should be checked to see whether or not they fall within a meaningful range. For example, an argument (such as N in the median and sort functions) used to indicate the number of items in an array must always be positive and should not exceed the upper bound for the array. Meaningful diagnostics should be printed and appropriate action taken if the array range is violated.

5. It is often helpful while debugging to print the values of all output global variables immediately after returning from a module.

8.6 Common Programming Errors

Some of the more common errors that can arise in writing user-defined functions are listed in Table 8.1.

All of these errors will be detected by BASIC-PLUS. However, unexpected and undesired side effects in a function, caused by changes in the values of global variables, will not be detected, and can cause program errors that are difficult to correct. You will have to provide your own means of detecting, or better still, preventing such errors. Some suggestions for this are provided in the previous section on program testing. The more care

Table 8.1 Common Errors in Writing Functions

Message	Error
FNEND without a DEF*	An FNEND statement was encountered that has no corresponding DEF* preceding it.
DEF* without FNEND	The FNEND for a DEF* was either omitted or put in the wrong place.
Illegal DEF* nesting	A DEF* statement is found within the definition of a function.
Illegal function name	Function name has incorrect form (for example, it might not start with FN).
Illegal dummy variable	All dummy variables (parameters) must be simple variable names.
Arguments don't match	Arguments in a function call do not match, in number or in type, the parameters used in the function definition.
Inconsistent function usage	The number of actual arguments used in a function call doesn't match the number of parameters in the definition.

you take in maintaining a clear separation between local and global variables, and in minimizing the use (especially the redefinition) of global variables within a function, the better.

8.7 Summary

In this chapter, we introduced a feature of BASIC-PLUS, the *user-defined function*, that can be extremely useful in the practice of step-wise programming. One-line and multiple-line functions of zero or more arguments were described and illustrated. We discussed how to define and reference user-defined functions and we showed how data are communicated between function and subroutine modules and a main program, using arguments and global variables.

The *side effects* caused by the use of global variables were described. Some suggestions were given for documenting the arguments and the global variables used in function and subroutine definitions.

To illustrate the use of user-defined functions and subroutines, we presented the solution to a simple statistics problem. We introduced the program system chart as a tool for describing the functional relationships and information flow among the different modules of a program system. The use of the program system chart is the same regardless of whether the modules used are subroutines or functions. The sort module in the statistics problem was written both as a subroutine and as a function in order to illustrate some of the differences between these two types of modules.

The concept of recursion was discussed and illustrated in two examples. When judiciously applied, recursion can be a most natural, convenient, and efficient tool for solving a wide variety of problems. Formulating the solution to a problem in terms of the solution of the same, albeit "reduced" problem, takes considerable getting used to for most programmers.

The new features introduced in this chapter are illustrated in Table 8.2.

Table 8.2 Summary of Chapter 8 Features

Statement	Effect
Single-line function definition	
`100    DEF* FNFAHREN(C) = (9 / 5) * C + 32`	Defines the function FNFAHREN. This function has a single parameter, C.

(continued)

Table 8.2 Summary of Chapter 8 Features *(continued)*

Statement	Effect
Multi-line function definition	

```
110        DEF* FNDIFF(X, Y)
115     !
120     !PARAMETER DEFINITIONS
130     !  X, Y - INPUT VALUES
140     !
150        IF  X > Y THEN LET FNDIFF = X - Y  &
160            ELSE LET FNDIFF = Y - X
170     !
           FNEND
```

Defines the function FNDIFF with two parameters, X and Y. FNDIFF returns the absolute difference between the argument values.

Function calls

```
290     LET TEMP = FNFAHREN(100)
```

Calls the function FNFAHREN and substitutes the argument, 100, for the parameter C. The value returned, 212, is stored in TEMP.

```
300     LET DIFF = FNDIFF(T1, T2)
```

Calls the function FNDIFF with the arguments T1 and T2. FNDIFF returns their absolute difference which is stored in DIFF.

Programming Problems

Unless otherwise noted, all problems listed can be solved using subroutines and functions. Complete documentation, especially with respect to arguments and global variables (if any), should be included in all cases. Judicious use of global variables is suggested.

8D Given the lengths a, b, c of the sides of a triangle, write a function to compute the area, A, of the triangle; the formula for computing A is given by

$$A = \sqrt{(s-a)(s-b)(s-c)}$$

where s is the semi-perimeter of the triangle:

$$s = \frac{a+b+c}{2}$$

Triangle

Write a program to read in values for a, b, and c and call your function to compute A. Your program should print A, and a, b, and c.

8E   Define a function FNMY.SQR that calculates the square root of a single argument without using SQR. *Hint*: One simple scheme for computing the square root, the Newton-Raphson method, requires that you start with an initial guess of the correct answer and then repeatedly refine this guess, obtaining more accurate ones. The formula for finding a more accurate guess from the old one is

$$\text{new guess} = 1/2(\text{old guess} + \frac{N}{\text{old guess}})$$

where N is the argument whose square root is required. When a new guess is found, it replaces the old guess in the formula, and "another new guess" is computed. This process continues until

$$| \text{ new guess} - \text{old guess} | \leq \text{epsilon}$$

where epsilon is some suitably chosen small value (such as 0.0001). The brackets indicate that the absolute value of the difference between guesses is compared to epsilon.

Write a program to call FNMY.SQR and compare your result to the value computed by SQR. Test your program for the values 3, 9, 50, 99, and 100. Use N/2 as an initial value of old guess.

8F   Two positive integers I and J are considered to be *relatively prime* if there exists no integer greater than 1 that divides them both. Write a function FNPRIME that has two parameters, I and J, and returns a value of 1 if and only if I and J are relatively prime. Otherwise, FNPRIME should return a value of 0.

8G   The greatest common divisor, GCD, of two positive integers I and J is an integer N with the property that N divides both I and J (with 0 remainder), and N is the largest integer dividing both I and J. An algorithm for determining N was devised by the famous mathematician Euclid; a flow diagram description of that algorithm, suitable for direct translation into a BASIC-PLUS function, is provided. In the diagram at the top of the next page, FNMOD is the mod function (Exercise 8.9).

Write a main program to read in four positive integers N1, N2, N3, and N4 and find the GCD of all four numbers. [*Hint*: The GCD of the four integers is the largest integer N that divides all four of them.] Implement the above algorithm as a function and call it as many times as needed to solve the problem.

Note that GCD(N1,N2,N3,N4) = GCD(GCD(N1,N2), GCD (N3,N4)). Print N1, N2, N3, and N4, and the resulting GCD.

8H   Redo Problem 8G but use recursion in writing the GCD function. *Hints*: The stop step occurs when SMALL (the second parameter) is zero. When this happens, you return from FNGCD with FNGCD = LARGE. If SMALL is not zero, then you should try calling FNGCD again with arguments SMALL and FNMOD(LARGE,SMALL). Provide a handwritten trace of your algorithm to show that it works. Compare with the algorithm shown in Problem 8G.

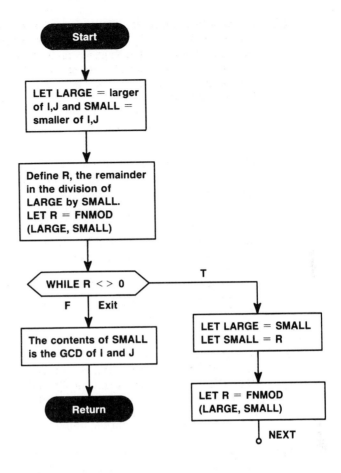

8I The electric company charges its customers as follows:

8 cents a kilowatt-hour (kwh) for electricity used up to the first 300 kwh;
6 cents a kwh for the next 300 kwh (up to 600 kwh);
5 cents a kwh for the next 400 kwh (up to 1000 kwh);
3 cents a kwh for all electricity used over 1000 kwh.

Write a function to compute the total charge for each customer. Write a program to call this function using the following data:

Customer number	Kilowatt-hours used
123	725
205	115
464	600
596	327
601	915
613	1011
722	47

The calling program should print a three-column table listing the customer number, the hours used and the charge for each customer. It should also compute and print the number of customers, total hours and total charges.

8J Each week the employees of a local manufacturing company turn in time cards containing the following information:

a) an identification number (a five-digit integer),
b) hourly pay rate (a real number),
c) time worked Monday, Tuesday, Wednesday, Thursday and Friday (each a four-digit integer of the form HHMM, where HH is hours and MM is minutes).

For example, last week's time cards contained the following data:

Employee Number	*Hourly Rate*	*Time Worked (Hours, Minutes)*				
		Monday	*Tuesday*	*Wednesday*	*Thursday*	*Friday*
16025	4.00	0800	0730	0800	0800	0420
19122	4.50	0615	0800	0800	0800	0800
21061	4.25	0805	0800	0735	0515	0735
45387	3.50	1015	1030	0800	0945	0800
50177	6.15	0800	0415	0800	0545	0600
61111	5.00	0930	0800	0800	1025	0905
88128	4.50	0800	0900	0800	0800	0700

Write a program system that will read the above data and compute for each employee the total hours worked (in hours and minutes), the total hours worked (to the nearest quarter-hour), and the gross salary. Your system should print the data shown above with the total hours (both figures) and gross pay for each employee. You should assume that overtime is paid at 1½ times the normal hourly rate, and that it is computed on a weekly basis (only on the total hours in excess of 40), rather than on a daily basis. Your program system should contain the following modules:

a) A function for computing the sum (in hours and minutes) of two four-digit integers of the form HHMM (*Example*: 0745 + 0335 = 1120);
b) A function for converting hours and minutes (represented as a four-digit integer) into hours, rounded to the nearest quarter hour (*Example*: 1120 = 11.25);
c) A function for computing gross salary given total hours and hourly rate;
d) A function for rounding gross salary accurate to two decimal places.

Test your program system using the data above.

8K An examination has been administered to a class of students, and the scores for each student have been provided as data along with the student's name. Write a program to do the following:

a) Determine and print the class average for the exam.
b) Find the median grade.
c) Scale each student's grade so that the class average will become 75. For example, if the actual class average is 63, add 12 to each student's grade.
d) Assign a letter grade to each student based on the scaled grade: 90–100 (A), 80–89 (B), 70–79 (C), 60–69 (D), 0–59 (F).
e) Print out each student's name in alphabetical order followed by the scaled grade and the letter grade.
f) Count the number of grades in each letter grade category.

8L *Internal Sort/Merge.* Let A and B be two arrays of size 10, and C an array of size 20. Write a program system to read two lists of data, one of size N1 and the other of size N2 (N1, N2 $\leq$ 10) into A and B respectively, sort A and B in ascending order, and then merge A and B into C maintaining the ascending order. The merge process is illustrated below for N1 = 5, N2 = 3. The numbered lines between arrays A and B indicate the order of comparison of the pairs of elements in A and B. The smaller of each pair of numbers is always merged into array C; the larger is then compared with the next entry in the other array (either A or B).

A(1)	A(2)	A(3)	A(4)	A(5)	A(6)	A(7)	A(8)	A(9)	A(10)
−10.5	−1.8	3.5	6.3	7.2	?	?	?	?	?

B(1)	B(2)	B(3)	B(4)	B(5)		B(10)
−2.5	3.1	5.7	?	?	···	?

C(1)	C(2)	C(3)	C(4)	C(5)	C(6)	C(7)	C(8)	C(9)		C(20)
−10.5	−2.5	−1.8	3.1	3.5	5.7	6.3	7.2	?	···	?

When one of the arrays A or B has been exhausted, do not forget to copy the remaining data from the other array into C.

8M Write a nonrecursive function that will compute the factorial, n!, of any small positive integer n.

8N The expression for computing C(n,r), the number of combinations of n items taken r at a time, is

$$C(n,r) = \frac{n!}{r!\,(n-r)!}$$

Assuming that we already have available a function for computing n! (see Fig. 8.14 or Problem 8M), write a function for computing C(n,r). Write a program that will call this function for n = 4, r = 1; n = 5, r = 3; n = 7, r = 7; and n = 6, r = 2.

8O Assume the existence of a main program containing a call to a function FNSEARCH of the form

```
FNSEARCH(N, MY.KEY)
```

and a global array B. Write the function FNSEARCH to compare each of the N elements in the array B to the data item stored in MY.KEY. If a match is found, define the value to be returned as the index of the element in the array B in which the key, MY.KEY, is located. If the key is not found, return a value of 0.

8P There are many ways of determining an approximate value for the number π. Here we describe one such technique.

Consider a quarter of a circle as drawn in Fig. 8.18.

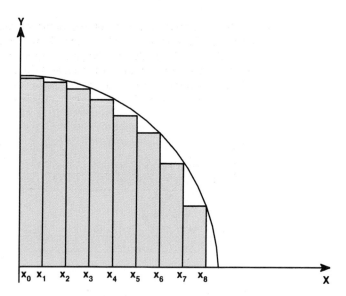

Fig. 8.18 Quarter circle.

The area of this quarter circle is $\frac{1}{4}\pi r^2$ which for $r = 2$ is π. Thus we can obtain an approximation to the value of π by approximating the area under the quarter circle.

To approximate the area under the quarter circle, we *partition* the interval $[0, 2]$ along the X-axis into n *subintervals* $[x_0 = 0, x_1]$, $[x_1, x_2]$, $[x_2, x_3]$ ... $[x_i, x_{i+1}]$, ... $[x_{n-1}, x_n = 2]$. In this figure, the interval has been partitioned into 8 subintervals:

$$[x_0, x_1] = [0, .25],$$
$$[x_1, x_2] = [.25, .50]$$

.
.
.

$$[x_7, x_8] = [1.75, 2.00]$$

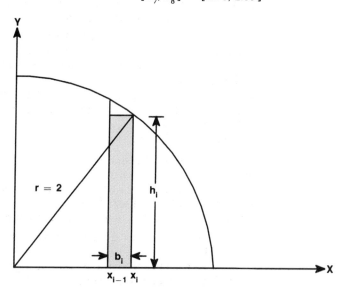

Fig. 8.19 Computing the area of the ith rectangle for Problem 8Q.

We then compute the sum of the areas of the rectangles defined by these partitions. This sum yields the desired approximation. The larger the number of partitions, the better the approximation because there is less area lost. You should try your program for several different partition sizes.

The area underneath each rectangle can be computed as indicated in Fig. 8.19. The area of the ith rectangle is computed as

$$A_i = b_i \times h_i$$

The base of the rectangle has length $b_i = 2/n$, where n is the number of partitions of the interval $[0, 2]$ ($n = 8$ in the example in Fig. 8.18). The height, h_i, of the ith rectangle is computed as follows:

$$r^2 = x_i^2 + h_i^2$$

But $r = 2$; therefore:

$$h_i^2 = 2^2 - x_i^2 \times h_i = \sqrt{4 - x_i^2}$$

Also, $x_i = i \times b_i = i \times \dfrac{2}{n}$, so

$$h_i = 2\sqrt{1 - (i/n)^2}$$

Finally,

$$A_i = b_i \times h_i = \left(\frac{2}{n}\right) \times 2\sqrt{1 - (i/n)^2} = \frac{4}{n}\sqrt{1 - (i/n)^2}$$

The total area of all rectangles (for n partitions) is

$$T = \sum_{i=1}^{n} A_i = \frac{4}{n} \sum_{i=1}^{n} \sqrt{1 - (i/n)^2}$$

8Q A mail order house with the physical facilities for stocking up to 20 items decides that it wants to maintain inventory control records on a small computer. For each stock item, the following data are to be stored on the computer:

1. the stock number (a five-digit integer);
2. a count of the number of items on hand;
3. the total year-to-date sales count (number of items sold);
4. the unit price;
5. the date (a four-digit integer of the form MMDD representing month and day) of the last order placed by the mail order house to the item manufacturer to restock an item.
6. the number of items ordered in 5.

Both items (5) and (6) will be zero if there is no outstanding order for an item.

Design and implement a program system to keep track of the data listed in (1) through (6). You will need six arrays, each of size 20. Your system should contain subroutines and functions to perform the following tasks:

a) change the price of an item (given the item stock number and the new price);
b) add a new item to the inventory list (given the item number, the price and the initial stock on hand);

c) enter information about the date and size of a new order for restocking an item;

d) reset the date and size of a new restock order to zero and update the amount on hand when a new order is received;

e) increase the total sales and decrease the count on hand each time a purchase order is received (if the order cannot be filled, print a message to that effect and reset the counts);

f) search for the array element that corresponds to a given stock number.

The following information should be stored initially in memory. This information should be printed at the start of execution of your program system.

Stock Numbers	On-Hand Count	Price
02421	12	100.00
00801	24	32.49
63921	50	4.99
47447	100	6.99
47448	48	2.25
19012	42	18.18
86932	3	67.20

A set of typical transactions for this inventory system is given below.

Price Changes

Trans no.	Trans ID	Stock no.	New price
2	"PRIC"	19012	18.99
9	"PRIC"	89632	73.90

Add Items

Trans no.	Trans ID	Stock no.	Price	On-hand
4	"ADIT"	47447	14.27	36
5	"ADIT"	56676	.15	1500

New Orders

Trans no.	Trans ID	Stock no.	Date	Volume
3	"NUOR"	00801	1201	18
8	"NUOR"	47446	1116	15

Orders Received

Trans no.	Trans ID	Stock no.	Volume
6	"ORIN"	00801	18

Purchase Orders

Trans no.	Trans ID	Stock no.	Number wanted
11	"PRCH"	00801	30
1	"PRCH"	12345	1
7	"PRCH"	56676	150
10	"PRCH"	86932	4

Note: To obtain a reasonable test of your program, the data should be entered in order by *transaction number*.

Your main program should process the transactions, one at a time, as discussed next.

Each subroutine should print an appropriate informative message for each transaction, indicating whether or not the transaction was processed, and giving other pertinent information about inventory changes that resulted from processing the data.

After the last transaction is processed, all inventory data should be printed in tabular form.

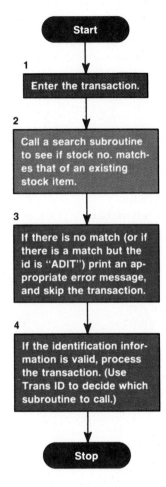

8R Write the Selection Sort algorithm described in Exercise 7.19 as a recursive function. You will also need a function that finds the largest element given the first and last boundary markers of an array.

9

Character String Manipulation

So far, we have seen limited use of character data. Most of our programs manipulated numerical data; string variables were used mainly for storing character strings that were later displayed to identify program output.

Many computer applications are concerned with the manipulation of textual data rather than numerical data. Computer-based *word processing systems* enable a user to compose letters, term papers, newspaper articles, and even books at a computer terminal instead of a typewriter. The advantage of using such a system is that words and sentences can be modified, whole paragraphs can be moved, etc. and then a fresh copy can be printed without mistakes or erasures.

Additional applications include the use of computerized typesetters in the publishing industry; text editors are used to update telephone directories and annual reports on a regular basis; computers are used in the analysis of great works of literature.

In the sections that follow, we will introduce some fundamental operations that can be performed on character data. We will describe how to reference a character substring and how to concatenate (or join) two strings. We will learn how to search for a substring in a larger string, and how to delete a substring or replace it with another.

9.1   The Length of a Character String

In BASIC-PLUS, all string variable names must end with the symbol $ and all string values are enclosed in quotation marks (single or double). String variables are initialized to the null string (denoted as `""` or `' '`) where the null string is a string of length 0. The concept of character string length is important to the discussion of character-type data. We will introduce this concept by defining what is meant by the length of a character string constant and a string variable.

Length of Character String Constants and Variables

1. The length of a character string constant is equal to the number of characters in the constant excluding the quote marks used to delimit the constant.
2. The length of a string variable is equal to the number of characters stored in the variable. The length of a string variable may change when new information is stored in the variable.

In BASIC-PLUS, the maximum allowable length for a character string constant or string variable is limited only by the amount of available memory.

BASIC-PLUS provides a function LEN that can be used to determine the length of its character-string argument. This function is described in the next display.

String Length Function LEN

LEN (*string*)

Interpretation: The argument *string* must be a character string constant, string variable or string expression. The value returned is an integer denoting the number of characters in the argument *string*.

Example 9.1   The program in Fig. 9.1 illustrates the use of the function LEN.

```
100   !ILLUSTRATE FUNCTION LEN
110   !
120       FOR I = 1 TO 4
130         READ STR$
140         PRINT 'LENGTH OF "'; STR$; '" ='; LEN(STR$)
150       NEXT I
160       DATA "ACES"
170       DATA "JOE'S ACES"
180       DATA " "
190       DATA ""
200   !
210       END

RUNNH
LENGTH OF "ACES" = 4
LENGTH OF "JOE'S ACES" = 10
LENGTH OF " " = 1
LENGTH OF "" = 0
```

Fig. 9.1 Using the function LEN.

9.2 Substrings

We frequently need to reference *substrings* of a longer character string. For example, we might want to examine the day "25", in the string "JUNE 25, 1984" or remove the substring "Machinery" from the string "Association for Computing Machinery". In this section, we will see how to use special features of BASIC-PLUS to segment a character string into substrings or to reference part of a longer string.

There are three BASIC-PLUS substring functions. These functions enable the programmer to reference substrings starting at either the beginning (function LEFT), middle (function MID), or end (function RIGHT) of a string.

Function LEFT

LEFT(*string*, *last*)

Interpretation: The argument *string* is a string constant, string variable, or string expression; *last* is a number or numeric expression. The substring referenced starts with the leftmost character (position 1) in *string* and ends with the character in position *last*. *Note*: If *last* is 0 or negative, then the null string is referenced.

Function RIGHT

> RIGHT(*string, start*)

Interpretation: The argument *start* is a number or numeric expression. The substring referenced starts with the character in position *start* of *string* and ends with the rightmost character (position LEN(*string*)) in *string*. *Note*: If *start* is 0 or negative, then it is considered to be 1. If *start* is greater than LEN(*string*), the null string is referenced.

Function MID

> MID(*string, start, length*)

Interpretation: The argument *length* is a number or numeric expression. The substring referenced starts with the character in position *start* of *string* and is exactly *length* characters long (i.e., the substring consisting of all characters in positions *start* through *start* + *length* − 1). *Notes*: If *start* is 0 or negative, then it is considered to be 1. If *start* is greater than LEN(*string*) or if *length* is 0 or negative, the null string is referenced. If *length* is greater than LEN(*string*), then it is considered to be equal to LEN(*string*).

Example 9.2   For the string assignment statement

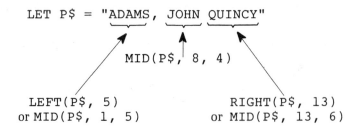

```
LET P$ = "ADAMS, JOHN QUINCY"
                MID(P$, 8, 4)
LEFT(P$, 5)              RIGHT(P$, 13)
or MID(P$, 1, 5)        or MID(P$, 13, 6)
```

some substrings of P$ are indicated in brackets.

Example 9.3   The program segment below reads a social security number and partitions it into three substrings, FIRST$, MIDDLE$, LAST$, as shown.

```
100  READ SOC.NUM$
110  DATA "042-30-0786"
120  LET FIRST$ = LEFT(SOC.NUM$, 3)
130  LET MIDDLE$ = MID(SOC.NUM$, 5, 2)
140  LET LAST$ = RIGHT(SOC.NUM$, 8)
```

SOC.NUM$	FIRST$	MIDDLE$	LAST$
042-30-0786	042	30	0786

Example 9.4   In Fig. 9.2, we use a string array, PRES$(4), for storing substrings. Each substring is 10 characters in length.

The FOR loop shown in this example partitions the string stored in PRES.DATA$ into four substrings of 10 characters each, which are stored in the string array PRES$. (See line 190 in Fig. 9.2).

PRES$(1)	PRES$(2)	PRES$(3)	PRES$(4)
RONALD	REAGAN	MOVIES	CALIFORNIA

```
100 !PROGRAM TO PROCESS PRESIDENTIAL DATA
110     DIM PRES$(4)
120 !
130 !ENTER DATA AS A SINGLE STRING
140     READ PRES.DATA$
150     DATA"RONALD    REAGAN    MOVIES    CALIFORNIA"
160 !
170 !FILL ARRAY PRES$ AND PRINT EACH ARRAY ELEMENT
180     FOR I = 1 TO 4
190         LET PRES$(I) = MID(PRES.DATA$, 10*I-9, 10)
200         PRINT PRES$(I)
210     NEXT I
220 !
230     END
```

```
RUNNH
RONALD
REAGAN
MOVIES
CALIFORNIA
```

Fig. 9.2 Storing substrings in a string array.

Table 9.1 Substrings Referenced in FOR Loop (line 190) for Each Value of I

I	Start of Substring 10*I-9	Length of Substring	PRES$(I)
1	1	10	"RONALD "
2	11	10	"REAGAN "
3	21	10	"MOVIES "
4	31	10	"CALIFORNIA"

Example 9.5   The program in Fig. 9.3 prints each word in the sentence SENT$ on a separate line. It assumes that a single blank occurs between individual words.

The program variable START points to the start of the current word (START is initialized to 1). During each execution of the FOR loop, the condition

```
MID(SENT$, I, 1) = BLANK$
```

```
100 !PRINT EACH WORD IN STRING SENT$
110 !
120 !PROGRAM CONSTANT
130     LET BLANK$ = " "      !SYMBOL BETWEEN WORDS
140 !
150 !ENTER DATA STRING
160     PRINT "ENTER SENTENCE"
165     INPUT LINE SENT$
170 !
180 !PRINT CHARACTERS BETWEEN SUCCESSIVE BLANKS
190 !FIRST WORD STARTS AT POSITION 1
200     LET START = 1
210     PRINT "LIST OF WORDS"
220     FOR I = 1 TO LEN(SENT$)
230        !PRINT A WORD IF NEXT CHARACTER IS A BLANK
240        IF MID(SENT$, I, 1) = BLANK$ THEN          &
               PRINT MID(SENT$, START, I-START)       &
               \LET START = I + 1
250     NEXT I
260 !
270 !PRINT LAST WORD
280     PRINT RIGHT(SENT$, START)
290 !
300     END


RUNNH
ENTER SENTENCE
? Able was I ere I saw Elba
LIST OF WORDS
Able
was
I
ere
I
saw
Elba
```

Fig. 9.3 Printing words in a sentence.

in line 240 tests whether the character in position I of SENT$ is a blank.
If it is a blank, the substring consisting of all characters from the start of
the current word up to the blank (character positions START through I-1)
is printed and START is reset to point to the first character following the
blank. Line 280 prints the last word in the sentence.

Exercise 9.1: Indicate how you could modify the program in Fig. 9.3 to convert a
sentence to a simplified form of Pig Latin. In our simple Pig Latin, the first letter of
each word is moved to the end of the word and is followed by the letters AY. The
Pig Latin form of THE QUICK BROWN FOX JUMPED would be HETAY UICKQAY
ROWNBAY OXFAY UMPEDJAY. *Hint:* It is only necessary to change the PRINT
statements.

Exercise 9.2: Given the string variables P$ and PRES$ (defined in Examples 9.2 and 9.4), list the characters that would be printed by the statements:

```
PRINT LEFT(PRES$(1), 3)
PRINT MID(P$, 6, 13)
PRINT MID(PRES$(4), 3, 7)
PRINT RIGHT(P$, LEN(P$))
PRINT RIGHT(P$, LEN(P$)-5)
PRINT MID(P$, 1, LEN(P$))
```

Exercise 9.3: Explain what would happen in line 240 of Fig. 9.3 if more than one blank occurred between words.

Exercise 9.4: Write a program that reads a string and prints it without blanks (e.g., "A E IO U" would be printed as "AEIOU").

9.3 Concatenation of Strings

The only character string operator in BASIC-PLUS is the operator for *concatenation* (joining strings), written as the symbol "+".

The Concatenation Operator

$string_1 + string_2$

Interpretation: $String_1$ is concatenated with $string_2$. This means $string_2$ is joined to the right end of $string_1$. The length of the resulting string is equal to the sum of the lengths of $string_1$ and $string_2$.

Example 9.6   The concatenation operator is illustrated next.

a) The assignment statement

```
100 LET A$ = "ABC" + "DE"
```

concatenates the strings "ABC" and "DE" together to form one string of length 5, "ABCDE", which is stored in A$.

b) Given the string

```
"ADAMS, JOHN QUINCY"
```

stored in the variable P$ (length 18), the statement

```
200 LET N$ = LEFT(P$, 6) + RIGHT(P$, 12)
```

will result in storage of the string

```
    "ADAMS, QUINCY"
```

in N$ (length 13). The statement

```
300 LET S$ = MID(P$, 8, 5) + LEFT(P$, 5)
```

will assign the string

```
    "JOHN ADAMS"
```

to S$ (length 10).

c) Given the array PRES$ as defined in Example 9.4, the statement

```
400 LET R$ = LEFT(PRES$(2), 6) + ", "       &
             + LEFT(PRES$(1), 6)
```

will cause the string assignment

R$

REAGAN, RONALD

Exercise 9.5: Given P$ and PRES$ as defined in Examples 9.2 and 9.4, evaluate the following

```
MID(P$, 8, 4) + " " + LEFT(PRES$(2), 5)
```

```
LEFT(P$, 5) + MID(P$, 7, 2) + "."       &
             + MID(P$, 13, 1) + "."
```

9.4 String Expressions and Comparisons

String expressions may be used in string assignment statements, as operands of relational operators, and as arguments in function calls. In this section we will describe the rules for the formation and use of string expressions.

String Assignment Statements

The string assignment statement assigns a value to a string variable. The rules of formation of the string assignment statement are summarized below.

String Assignment Statement

```
LET strvar = strexp
```

Interpretation: The variable *strvar* is a string variable and *strexp* is a string expression. A string expression consists of one or more string constants, string variables, string array elements, or substrings connected by the concatenation operator. The length of *strvar* will be equal to the length of *strexp*.

We have used string assignment statements in earlier examples. The statements from Example 9.6

```
100 LET A$ = "ABC" + "DE"
200 LET N$ = LEFT(P$, 6) + RIGHT(P$, 12)
```

are examples of string assignment statements.

String Replacement

We can use the string assignment statement to replace a substring within a string. In this case, substrings of the string variable being assigned will appear in the string expression.

Example 9.7   The string assignment statements

```
300 LET A$ = "ABCDE"
310 LET P$ = LEFT(P$, 6) + A$ + RIGHT(P$, 12)
```

would replace the characters in positions 7 through 11 of the string P$ with the string A$. Given the original string P$

P$

| ADAMS, JOHN QUINCY |

the new string P$ would become

P$

| ADAMS,ABCDE QUINCY |

It is not necessary that A$ be the same length as the substring that it replaces, as the position of the substring RIGHT(P$, 12) would be shifted to follow A$. Given the assignment statements

```
300 LET A$ = "ABC"
310 LET P$ = LEFT(P$, 6) + A$ + RIGHT(P$, 12)
```

the new string P$ would be

P$

| ADAMS,ABC QUINCY |

where the substring " QUINCY" has been shifted to the left (starting at position 10). If the length of A$ was greater than 5, " QUINCY" would be shifted to the right.

Exercise 9.6: Write a program segment that reads the three character strings

```
"THE CHAIRMAN SAID"
"GENTLEMEN-WOULD EVERYONE"
"PLEASE TAKE HIS SEAT"
```

and modifies them to look like:

```
"THE CHAIRPERSON SAID"
"LADIES AND GENTLEMEN-"
"PLEASE BE SEATED"
```

String Comparison

We have already seen examples of string comparisons in earlier chapters. In Section 4.3, the relational operators were used to compare character strings for equality, or for order. The results of these comparisons were always determined by the alphabetical sequence of the operands involved. For example if A$ and B$ contain only upper case letters (or only lower case letters) then the relation A$ < B$ is true if the string in A$ would precede the string in B$ in the dictionary. It is possible to compare arbitrary strings of characters containing not just letters, but also numbers and special characters such as + , − , * , ?, /, etc. The next display reviews how the BASIC-PLUS *collating sequence* (ordering of characters) is used to determine whether or not a string relation is true.

String Comparisons

string₁ relop string₂

Interpretation: *String₁* and *string₂* are string expressions that are evaluated; *relop* is a relational operator. The resulting strings are compared one character at a time, from left to right, until a pair of characters is reached that are different. The value of the string relation depends on the relative positions of these two different characters in the collating sequence (e.g., if *relop* is <, then the relation is true if the character from *string₁* precedes the character from *string₂* in the collating sequence). If one string ends before the other and all characters compared are the same, then the shorter string is considered less than the larger string (e.g., "ACE" < "ACES").

The BASIC-PLUS collating sequence is shown in Appendix F. The following relations among the characters can be observed.

```
" " < "+" < "0" < "9" < "A" < "Z" < "a" < "z"
```

Example 9.8   Given the string variable W$

W$

| PROGRAMS |

the relations below are all true. The reason each relation is true is indicated in parentheses following the relation.

```
W$ > "PROG"                     ("PROGRAMS" is longer than "PROG")
"PROG" < "Prog"      ("R" < "r"–upper case precedes lower case)
LEFT(W$, 4) = "PROG" ("PROG" = "PROG"–all characters match)
LEFT(W$, 4) <> "prog"    ("PROG" <> "prog"–"P" <> "p")
LEFT(W$, 1) < "PR"                      ("P" is shorter than "PR")
LEFT(W$, 4) > "PRANKS"   ("PROG" > "PRANKS"–"O" > "A")
RIGHT(W$, 6) < "A" + "PROG"             ("AMS" < "APROG")
```

Example 9.9   We mentioned that character strings can contain numbers and special symbols as well as letters. Sometimes character comparisons involving these other symbols lead to unexpected results as the dictionary relationship is no longer meaningful. The following relations are true for the BASIC-PLUS collating sequence.

```
"3" > "15"              ("3" > "1")
"1234" < "1236"         ("4" < "6")
"1234" >= "12"          ("3" > "")
"124" > "12398"         ("4" > "3")
"AB398" < "AC25"        ("B" < "C")
"A*B+" <= "A+F$"        ("*" < "+")
"AZ" < "az"             ("A" < "a")
"Aa" > "AZ"             ("a" > "Z")
"ABC" > " abc"          ("A" > " ")
```

Exercise 9.7: For each relation below, write all the relational operators that would yield a value of true.

```
a)  "A" + "35" relop "Z" + "12"
b)  "A*C" relop "A+Z"
c)  "A+35" relop "A" + "35"
d)  "123" relop "12A4"
e)  "345" relop "32896"
f)  "ACE" relop "ace"
g)  "WxYz" relop "wXyZ"
```

Converting Numeric Character Strings to Numbers

There are many applications involving the manipulation of strings or substrings containing only the numeric characters "0", "1", "2", ..., "9" with or without a sign or decimal point (e.g., "-398" or "62.573"). Some of these applications require that these *numeric strings* be manipulated arithmetically, yet in Example 9.9, we saw the rather surprising result that "3" is greater than "15". We also know that expressions such as "3" * "15" are not permitted in BASIC-PLUS since arithmetic operators can't be used with character string operands. (Why is "3" + "15" permitted?) Consequently, if we wish to perform arithmetic manipulations on these strings or to compare them numerically, we must first convert them from string data to numbers.

BASIC-PLUS provides a function VAL to convert numeric character strings into numbers. The functions NUM$ and NUM1$ are also provided that perform the *inverse* (opposite) of the VAL operation. This means that NUM$ and NUM1$ convert a number into a numeric string. The program below stores a numeric string in ANS$ and its numeric value in N and N1.

```
100  !ILLUSTRATE NUM1$ AND VAL
110  !
120      INPUT "ENTER A NUMBER"; N
130      LET ANS$ = NUM1$(N)
140      LET N1 = VAL(ANS$)
150      PRINT "THE STRING " + ANS$          &
                 + " IS THE NUMBER"; N1
160      END
```

```
RUNNH
ENTER A NUMBER? 4.26
THE STRING 4.26 IS THE NUMBER 4.26
```

The statements

```
100 INPUT "ENTER A NUMERIC STRING"; ANS$
110 INPUT "NOT NUMERIC-TRY AGAIN"; ANS$ &
        UNTIL ANS$ = NUM1$(VAL(ANS$))
```

can be used to ensure that the string read into ANS$ is numeric. The condition will be true only when ANS$ is a numeric string as explained next.

The Function VAL (string to number conversion)

VAL(*numeric string*)

Interpretation: VAL returns the numeric value of its *numeric string* argument. *Numeric string* may include digits, a sign, a decimal point, and the letter E if scientific notation is used. *Note*: The error diagnostic

```
?Illegal number
```

is printed if *numeric string* cannot be converted, and execution continues with the function result equal to any partially converted value or to 0.

The Functions NUM$ and NUM1$ (number to string conversion)

> NUM1$ (*expression*)
> or NUM$ (*expression*)

Interpretation: The argument *expression* may be a numeric expression, variable or constant. The *expression* value is converted to a numeric string. If NUM$ is used, the numeric string will be identical to the form in which the *expression* value would be printed by BASIC-PLUS; whereas, if NUM1$ is used, there will not be any blank characters at the beginning and end of the string.

Example 9.10 The string PERSON$ contains a person's name (characters 1 through 10) followed by gross salary (characters 11 through 16) and number of dependents (characters 18 and 19).

PERSON$

JOHANSON   345.62 02

The program in Fig. 9.4a computes taxable salary, TAX.SAL, by deducting $50 for each dependent from gross salary GROSS. Net salary, NET, is 85 percent of the taxable salary. The substrings representing the gross salary and dependents are converted to numbers by use of the function VAL (lines 150 and 160). If either substring is non-numeric, then the diagnostic

```
    ?Illegal number at line 150
or ?Illegal number at line 160
```

will be printed but execution will continue.

```
100 !USING VAL WITH SUBSTRINGS AS ARGUMENTS
110 !
120     READ PERSON$
130     DATA "JOHANSON  345.62 02"
140     LET NAMES$ = LEFT(PERSON$, 10)
150     LET GROSS = VAL(MID(PERSON$, 11, 6))
160     LET DEPEND = VAL(RIGHT(PERSON$, 18))
170     LET TAX.SAL = GROSS - 50 * DEPEND
180     LET NET = .85 * TAX.SAL
190     PRINT NAMES$, "NET SALARY = $"; NET
200     END

RUNNH
JOHANSON        NET SALARY = $ 208.77
```

Fig. 9.4a Converting character strings to numbers.

9.5 Searching for a Substring

In this section, we describe the BASIC-PLUS function INSTR, that searches a string (the *subject string*) for a substring (the *target string*). For example, if SUBJECT$ is the string "WHAT NEXT", we could use the function call

```
INSTR(1, SUBJECT$, "AT")
```

to determine whether or not the target string "AT" appears anywhere in this string. If the target string is found, INSTR returns its starting position (position 3 in the example) in the subject string; otherwise INSTR returns 0. INSTR is described in the next display.

String Search Function

INSTR (*start, subject, target*)

Interpretation: The *subject* string is examined from left to right, starting at position *start*, to determine the location of the next occurrence of the *target* string. If the *target* string is found, the value returned is the position in the *subject* string of the first character of the *target* string (value >= *start*); otherwise the value returned is 0. *Note*: If *start* is less than 1, it is considered to be 1 and the entire *subject* string is searched. If *start* is greater than LEN(*subject*) + 1 the value returned is 0. If *target* is the null string and *start* <= LEN(*subject*) + 1, the value returned is *start*.

Example 9.11   The string search function INSTR is illustrated below.

Function Reference	Value
INSTR(1, "SENTENCE", "E")	2
INSTR(3, "SENTENCE", "E")	5
INSTR(5, "SENTENCE", "E")	5
INSTR(6, "SENTENCE", "E")	8
INSTR(9, "SENTENCE", "E")	0
INSTR(9, "SENTENCE", "")	9
INSTR(10, "SENTENCE", "")	0
INSTR(-3, "SENTENCE", "EN")	2
INSTR(3, "SENTENCE", "EN")	5
INSTR(6, "SENTENCE", "EN")	0
INSTR(1, "SENTENCE", "ACE")	0
INSTR(1, "SENTENCE", "NCE")	6

```
100 !USING INSTR TO LOCATE SUBSTRING DELIMITERS
110 !
120     PRINT "ENTER SALARY, # OF DEPENDENTS, AND NAME"
130     PRINT "USE A COMMA BETWEEN DATA ITEMS"
140     INPUT LINE PERSON$
150     LET POS1 = INSTR(1, PERSON$, ",")
160     LET POS2 = INSTR(POS1+1, PERSON$, ",")
170     LET GROSS = VAL(LEFT(PERSON$, POS1-1))
180     LET DEPEND = VAL(MID(PERSON$, POS1+1,  &
                    POS2-POS1-1))
190     LET NAMES$ = RIGHT(PERSON$, POS2+1)
210     LET TAX.SAL = GROSS - 50 * DEPEND
220     LET NET = .85 * TAX.SAL
230     PRINT NAMES$, "NET SALARY = $"; NET
240     END

RUNNH
ENTER SALARY, # OF DEPENDENTS, AND NAME
USE A COMMA BETWEEN DATA ITEMS
? 345.62, 2, JOHANSON
 JOHANSON
                NET SALARY = $ 208.77
```

Fig. 9.4b Locating and converting numeric strings.

Example 9.12   Fig. 9.4b contains a program that performs the same computation as the program shown in Fig. 9.4a. The data string is read into PERSON$ using an INPUT LINE statement (line 140). Instead of assuming that the three substrings of PERSON$ are in fixed positions, the new program assumes that the symbol "," is used as a separator between the substrings. The function INSTR is used to find the positions, POS1 and POS2, of the separator symbols. Verify for yourself that the expression

```
MID(PERSON$, POS1+1, POS2-POS1-1)
```

references the substring of PERSON$ between the symbols ",".

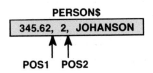

Example 9.13   The program in Fig. 9.5 counts the number of occurrences of the word "AIN'T" in a string and replaces each occurrence with "IS NOT".

Line 170 searches for the first occurrence of the string TARGET$ in SUBJECT$ (starting position is 1). If TARGET$ is found, its location is stored in POS.TARG and the loop is entered. Line 200 replaces the substring TARGET$ ("AIN'T") with REPLAC$ ("IS NOT"). Line 220

```
100  !REPLACE "AIN'T" BY "IS NOT"
110  !
120  !INITIALIZE PROGRAM CONSTANTS AND ENTER DATA
130      LET TARGET$ = "AIN'T"
135      LET REPLAC$ = "IS NOT"
140      PRINT "SUBJECT STRING" \ INPUT LINE SUBJECT$
150  !
160  !FIND EACH OCCURRENCE OF TARGET$
165  !STARTING WITH THE FIRST OCCURENCE
170      LET POS.TARG = INSTR(1, SUBJECT$, TARGET$)
180      FOR COUNT.TARG = 0 UNTIL POS.TARG = 0
190         !REPLACE TARGET$ WITH REPLAC$
200         LET SUBJECT$ = LEFT(SUBJECT$, POS.TARG-1) &
                    + REPLAC$                          &
                    + RIGHT(SUBJECT$, POS.TARG+LEN(TARGET$))
210         !FIND NEXT OCCURRENCE OF TARGET$
220         LET POS.TARG =                             &
                    INSTR(POS.TARG+LEN(REPLAC$),        &
                    SUBJECT$, TARGET$)
230      NEXT COUNT.TARG
240  !
250  !PRINT RESULTS
260      PRINT "NUMBER OF OCCURRENCES OF TARGET ";     &
                TARGET$; " ="; COUNT.TARG
270      PRINT \ PRINT "MODIFIED STRING"
275      PRINT "   "; SUBJECT$
280  !
290      END


RUNNH
SUBJECT STRING
? THIS AIN'T QUITE RIGHT.
NUMBER OF OCCURRENCES OF TARGET AIN'T = 1

MODIFIED STRING
   THIS IS NOT QUITE RIGHT.
```

Fig. 9.5 Replacing "AIN'T" by "IS NOT".

searches for each occurrence of TARGET$ after the initial one; the next search starts at position POS.TARG + LEN(REPLAC$), the first character following the replacement string. After all occurrences of TARGET$ have been replaced, the function INSTR will return a value of zero and the loop will be exited.

Example 9.14   The function INSTR may be used in conjunction with an ON–GOSUB statement to select a subroutine to be executed based on the value of a string variable. The subject string should be a concatenation of all possible values of the string variable being tested. For example, the statement

```
300 ON INSTR(1, "AEIOU", LETTER$)+1 GOSUB 1000,      &
                2000, 3000, 4000, 5000, 6000
```

calls a different subroutine for each vowel as determined by the value of
LETTER$. The subroutine at line 2000 is called if the INSTR function re-
turns a value of 1 (i.e., if LETTER$ is "A"); the subroutine at line 3000
will be called if LETTER$ is "E", etc. The subroutine at line 1000 will be
called if LETTER$ does not contain a vowel (INSTR returns 0).

Example 9.15   Function FNSPAN in Fig. 9.6 is used to skip over consecutive occurrences
of a specified substring (TARGET$) in a second string (SUBJECT$). The
parameter START represents the starting position of the search. If TAR–

```
1000      DEF* FNSPAN(START, SUBJECT$, TARGET$)
1010 !
1020 !PASSES OVER ALL CONSECUTIVE OCCURENCES OF
1025 !SUBSTRING TARGET$
1030 !BEGINNING AT POSITION START OF SUBJECT$ AND
1040 !RETURNS POSITION OF FIRST UNMATCHED CHARACTER.
1050 !IF START IS INVALID, THEN
1060 !THE FUNCTION VALUE IS 0.
1070 !E.G. FNSPAN(1, "ABABCDE", "AB") IS 5
1080 !     FNSPAN(2, "ABABCDE", "AB") IS 2
1090 !
1100 !PARAMETER DEFINITIONS
1110 !   START - STARTING POINT
1120 !   SUBJECT$ - STRING BEING SCANNED
1130 !   TARGET$ - STRING BEING SKIPPED
1135 !
1140 !LOCAL VARIABLE - SPAN.POS
1145 !
1150 !VALIDATE START
1160      IF START < 1 OR START > LEN(SUBJECT$) THEN   &
             LET FNSPAN = 0                            &
             \GOTO 1260    !RETURN FROM FNSPAN
1170 !
1180 !PASS OVER CONSECUTIVE OCCURENCES OF TARGET$
1185 !BEGINNING AT START
1190      LET SPAN.POS = START
1200      WHILE INSTR(SPAN.POS, SUBJECT$, TARGET$) &
                = SPAN.POS
1210         LET SPAN.POS = SPAN.POS + LEN(TARGET$)
1220      NEXT     !WHILE
1225 !
1230 !DEFINE FUNCTION RESULT
1240      LET FNSPAN = SPAN.POS
1250 !
1260      FNEND     !FNSPAN
```

Fig. 9.6 Function FNSPAN.

GET$ does not occur at START, the function result will be START; otherwise the function result will be the position of the first character following the consecutive occurrence of TARGET$ as explained next.

The local variable SPAN.POS is initialized to START, the search start point. Line 1210 of the function advances SPAN.POS past the target substring each time the target substring is found at the current search start point. When the target string is not found, the current search start point is returned as the function result (line 1240). If the initial search start point (START) is out-of-range, the function is exited immediately (GOTO 1260) and a value of 0 is returned.

The statement

```
200 LET POS.LET = FNSPAN(1, SENT$, " ")
```

could be used to skip over any blanks that might occur at the beginning of the string SENT$. The statement

```
200 LET POS.LET = FNSPAN(POS.BLANK, SENT$, " ")
```

could be used to skip over a string of blanks starting at POS.BLANK. In general, the statement

```
300 LET POS.LET =                                      &
        FNSPAN(POS.X, SENT$, MID(SENT$, POS.X, 1))
```

could be used to skip over a string of whatever character is at position POS.X.

Program Style

Returning error indicators

Function FNSPAN in Fig. 9.6 returns a value of 0 when its first argument (the search start point) is out-of-range. A function result of zero could not be computed under normal circumstances, so this special value is used to signal to the calling program that an error occurred. After completion of the function, the calling program could test for this error condition and print an error message. For example, line 300 above could be followed by the statement

```
310 IF POS.LET = 0 THEN                                &
        PRINT "SEARCH START POINT"; POS.X;             &
            "IS OUT-OF-RANGE"
```

A different approach would be to print the error message in the function itself rather than return a special error indicator. This approach is less desirable as there are situations in which we would rather not print an explicit error message. Placing the error message in the function takes away this option.

Exercise 9.8: In Example 9.13, assume that we only want to count the number of occurrences of TARGET$. The statement below has been proposed as a substitute for the FOR loop in Fig. 9.5. Will it work? If not, fix it.

```
180 LET POS.TARG = INSTR(POS.TARG, SUBJECT$,         &
                                    TARGET$)          &
        FOR COUNT.TARG = 0 UNTIL POS.TARG = 0
```

Exercise 9.9: In Example 9.14, we assumed that the target string (LETTER$) contained a single letter only. Assume that the string CODE$ can contain any of the two letter codes: "DE", "RE", "IN", "PR", "FI". Write an ON−GOSUB statement that calls a different subroutine for each value of CODE$.

Exercise 9.10: Redo Example 9.5 using FNSPAN to skip over any extra blanks that might occur at the beginning of SENT$ or between words of SENT$. Also, use INSTR to find the first blank that follows a group of non-blank characters. *Hint*: You will need a loop that alternates calls to each of these functions.

Exercise 9.11: Function FNSPAN will skip only the first of a series of *overlapping* target substrings. For example, if TARGET$ is "ABRA" and SUBJECT$ is "ABRABRACADABRA", the function result will be 5 instead of 8. Define a new function FNOVERSPAN that skips overlapping and non-overlapping substrings.

9.6 Manipulating Individual Characters in a String

ASCII Code

Recall that each BASIC-PLUS character has a unique numeric code that determines its position in the collating sequence for characters. This code is based on the American Standard Code for Information Interchange (ASCII) shown in Table 9.2 and Appendix F. In this section, we shall study some BASIC-PLUS features for converting back and forth from characters to numeric codes.

The Functions ASCII and CHR$

There are two complementary functions in BASIC-PLUS that manipulate the ASCII code: the function ASCII converts a single character to its ASCII equivalent (e.g., the value of ASCII("B") is 66), and the function CHR$ converts an ASCII number to its corresponding character (e.g., the value of CHR$(50) is the character "2"). These functions are described in the next displays.

Table 9.2 Portion of ASCII Code

Character	ASCII Equivalent	Character	ASCII Equivalent	Character	ASCII Equivalent
blank	32	A	65	O	79
+	43	B	66	P	80
−	45	C	67	Q	81
.	46	D	68	R	82
0	48	E	69	S	83
1	49	F	70	T	84
2	50	G	71	U	85
3	51	H	72	V	86
4	52	I	73	W	87
5	53	J	74	X	88
6	54	K	75	Y	89
7	55	L	76	Z	90
8	56	M	77	a	97
9	57	N	78	b	98

Function ASCII

`ASCII(`*string*`)`

Interpretation: The value returned is the number corresponding to the ASCII code for the first character in *string*.

Function CHR$

`CHR$(`*numeric code*`)`

Interpretation: The argument *numeric code* is a non-negative integer. The value returned is the character with *numeric code* as its ASCII equivalent. Generally, *numeric code* will be less than or equal to 127.

Example 9.16   The program in Fig. 9.7 prints each character of TEXT$ followed by its ASCII code. The last three lines of the sample output are due to the line terminator characters at the end of TEXT$. (Recall that the INPUT LINE statement stores the line terminator characters at the end of the data line.) These characters are not displayed; rather, they control the terminal when they are "printed". The carriage return character (code 13) simply returns the carriage or cursor to the left margin; the line feed character (code 10) causes an extra blank line to be inserted in the displayed output.

Example 9.17   The program in Fig. 9.8 counts and prints the number of occurrences of each character in a string (TEXT$). The array CHAR.COUNT (subscripts 0

```
100 !DISPLAY CHARACTERS IN TEXT AND THEIR ASCII CODES
110 !
120 !ENTER DATA
130     PRINT "ENTER TEXT" \ INPUT LINE TEXT$
140 !
150 !PRINT EACH CHARACTER AND ITS CODE
160     PRINT "CHARACTER", "CODE"
170     FOR POS.CHAR = 1 TO LEN(TEXT$)
180         LET NEXT.CHAR$ = MID(TEXT$, POS.CHAR, 1)
190         PRINT NEXT.CHAR$, ASCII(NEXT.CHAR$)
200     NEXT POS.CHAR
210 !
220     END
```

```
RUNNH
ENTER TEXT
? What, now?
CHARACTER        CODE
W                87
h                104
a                97
t                116
,                44
                 32
n                110
o                111
w                119
?                63
                 13

                 10
```

Fig. 9.7 Printing characters and ASCII codes.

through 127) is used to keep track of the number of occurrences of each character. This array is initialized to all zeros.

```
100 !FIND THE NUMBER OF OCCURRENCES OF EACH CHARACTER
110 !
120     DIM CHAR.COUNT(127)    !COUNTS BY ASCII CODE
130 !
140 !INITIALIZE CHAR.COUNT AND ENTER DATA
150     LET CHAR.COUNT(INDEX) = 0 FOR INDEX = 0 TO 127
155     PRINT "ENTER TEXT" \ INPUT LINE TEXT$
165 !
170 !INCREMENT ELEMENT OF CHAR.COUNT CORRESPONDING
175 !TO EACH CHARACTER IN TEXT$
180     FOR POS.CHAR = 1 TO LEN(TEXT$) - 1
190         LET INDEX = ASCII(MID(TEXT$, POS.CHAR, 1))
200         LET CHAR.COUNT(INDEX) =                      &
                CHAR.COUNT(INDEX) + 1
210     NEXT POS.CHAR
220 !
```

(continued)

```
230  !PRINT RESULTS
240      PRINT
245      PRINT "CHARACTER", "CODE", "OCCURRENCES"
250      FOR INDEX = 0 TO 127
260          IF CHAR.COUNT(INDEX) > 0 THEN                    &
                 PRINT CHR$(INDEX), INDEX,                    &
                     CHAR.COUNT(INDEX)
270      NEXT INDEX
280  !
290      END
```

```
RUNNH
ENTER TEXT
? THE QUICK BROWN DOG JUMPED OVER THE LAZY FOX.

CHARACTER        CODE      OCCURRENCES

                  10         1
                  13         1
                  32         8
     .            46         1
 A                65         1
 B                66         1
 C                67         1
 D                68         2
 E                69         4
 F                70         1
 G                71         1
 H                72         2
 I                73         1
 J                74         1
 K                75         1
 L                76         1
 M                77         1
 N                78         1
 O                79         4
 P                80         1
 Q                81         1
 R                82         2
 T                84         2
 U                85         2
 V                86         1
 W                87         1
 X                88         1
 Y                89         1
 Z                90         1
```

Fig. 9.8 Counting occurrences of characters.

The statement

```
190 LET INDEX = ASCII(MID(TEXT$, POS.CHAR, 1))
```

assigns to INDEX a value (from 0 to 127) based on the ASCII code of the character in TEXT$ at position POS.CHAR. The statement

```
200 LET CHAR.COUNT(INDEX) = CHAR.COUNT(INDEX) + 1
```

increments the array element with subscript INDEX. In the second FOR loop (line 250), the statement

```
PRINT CHR$(INDEX), INDEX, CHAR.COUNT(INDEX)
```

prints each character that occurred in TEXT$ followed by its ASCII code (value of INDEX) and the number of occurrences.

The sample run of the program shown in Fig. 9.8 lists the number of occurrences of each letter in the sentence as well as the number of blanks (8) and periods (1). The top three lines of the output table (including the blank line under the heading) are due to the line terminator characters (codes 10 and 13) at the end of TEXT$.

Example 9.18 The program in Fig. 9.9 converts each upper case letter (ASCII codes 65–90) to its equivalent lower case letter (ASCII codes 97–122). All other characters in TEXT$ are unchanged.

The statement

```
180 IF NEXT.CODE>=65 AND NEXT.CODE<=90 THEN        &
        LET TEXT$ = LEFT(TEXT$, POS.CHAR-1)        &
                  + CHR$(NEXT.CODE+32)             &
                  + RIGHT(TEXT$, POS.CHAR+1)
```

```
100 !CONVERT UPPER CASE TO LOWER CASE
110 !
120 !ENTER DATA
130    PRINT "ENTER DATA" \ INPUT LINE TEXT$
140 !
150 !FIND EACH UPPER CASE LETTER IN TEXT$
160    FOR POS.CHAR = 1 TO LEN(TEXT$)
170       LET NEXT.CODE =                          &
             ASCII(MID(TEXT$, POS.CHAR, 1))
175       !SUBSTITUTE LOWER CASE FOR UPPER CASE
180       IF NEXT.CODE>=65 AND NEXT.CODE<=90 THEN &
             LET TEXT$ = LEFT(TEXT$,POS.CHAR-1)    &
                       + CHR$(NEXT.CODE+32)        &
                       + RIGHT(TEXT$,POS.CHAR+1)
190    NEXT POS.CHAR
```

(continued)

```
200 !
210 !PRINT CONVERTED STRING
220    PRINT "CONVERTED TEXT"
230    PRINT "   "; TEXT$
240 !
250    END

RUNNH
ENTER DATA
? Baa Baa Black Sheep, have you any wool?
CONVERTED TEXT
   baa baa black sheep, have you any wool?
```

Fig. 9.9 Converting upper case to lower case.

tests whether the character at position POS.CHAR is an upper case letter
by comparing its ASCII code (NEXT.CODE) to the codes for "A" (65)
and "Z" (90). If so, that character is replaced in TEXT$ with the char-
acter whose code is greater by 32—its lower case equivalent.

Exercise 9.12: Modify the program in Fig. 9.9 to switch the case of every letter
that occurs in TEXT$ (i.e., all upper case letters to lower case and all lower case
letters to upper case).

Exercise 9.13: Rewrite the IF–THEN statement at line 180 of Fig. 9.9 assuming
that you do not know the ASCII code for the letters and the difference between
the codes for corresponding upper and lower case letters. *Hint:* Use the ASCII
function.

The CVT$$ Function

In the last section, we discussed a number of string editing operations
such as removing blanks from a string, changing upper case to lower case,
etc. BASIC-PLUS has a special function, CVT$$, for *converting from string
to string*.

Example 9.19 The first three lines in the sample run shown in Fig. 9.8 are due to the line
terminator characters stored in TEXT$. Inserting the statement

```
160 LET TEXT$ = CVT$$(TEXT$, 4)
```

in Fig. 9.8 would remove the line terminator characters, thereby eliminat-
ing these extraneous lines.

CVT$$ Function

CVT$$(*string, modbit*)

Interpretation: The CVT$$ function manipulates *string* as specified
by *modbit* and generates a new string. *Modbit* may be any power of

2 from 1 (2^0) to 256 (2^8); the operation on *string* prescribed by each value of *modbit* is described next.

1— trim parity bit from each character

2— discard all spaces and tabs

4— discard carriage return (ASCII code 13), line feed (code 10), form feed (code 12), escape (code 27), rubout (code 127), and any fill or null characters (code 0)

8— discard leading spaces and tabs

16— reduce consecutive spaces and tabs to one space

32— convert lower case to upper case

64— convert square brackets to parentheses

128— discard trailing spaces and tabs

256— suppress alteration of characters inside single or double quotes except for parity bit trimming

Note: *Modbit* may also be the sum of one or more values above. In this case, the operations represented by all values in the sum will be performed.

Certainly not all of the operations in the CVT$$ display will be of interest. However, we shall examine some of the more useful ones in the following example.

Example 9.20 We can convert the string STR$

    " AB cd ' [e f'] g"

to the string

    "ABCD'(EF')G"

by the sequence of statements

```
200 LET STR$ = CVT$$(STR$, 2) !ELIMINATE ALL SPACES
210 LET STR$ = CVT$$(STR$, 32)!CONVERT LOWER CASE  &
                              !TO UPPER CASE
220 LET STR$ = CVT$$(STR$, 64)!CONVERT BRACKETS    &
                              !TO PARENTHESES
```

These operations could be specified in a single statement whose *modbit* value is the sum of the individual values of *modbit* above.

```
200 LET STR$ = CVT$$(STR$, 2+32+64)
```

or

```
200 LET STR$ = CVT$$(STR$, 98)
```

If we add 256 to the *modbit* 98, then the operations listed above will not be applied to any characters that are enclosed in single or double quotes within the string. The statement

```
200 LET STR$ = CVT$$(STR$, 2+32+64+256)
```

or

```
200 LET STR$ = CVT$$(STR$, 354)
```

would convert the original string STR$

```
"  AB  cd  '  [e  f']  g"
```

to

```
"ABCD'  [e  f')G"
```

where the substring enclosed in single quotes is unchanged. (*Note*: The double quotes used to enclose the string are not considered part of the string.)

Exercise 9.14: What would be the result of performing the edit operations specified by the function calls listed below? Assume that STR$ is restored to the original value of " AB cd ' [e f'] g" before each call.

```
CVT$$(STR$, 16)
CVT$$(STR$, 80)
CVT$$(STR$, 258)
```

Exercise 9.15: Write your own functions that perform the operations associated with *modbit* values 8 and 32. *Hint*: The horizontal tab has an ASCII code of 9. Therefore, a character that matches CHR$(9) is a horizontal tab. You can subtract 32 from the ASCII code for each lower case letter (codes 97–122) to get the ASCII code for the corresponding upper case letter (codes 65–90).

 ## 9.7 Text Processing Applications

Generating Cryptograms

Now that we have introduced the BASIC-PLUS string manipulation features and provided several examples of their use, we will use these features to solve two sample problems. The first problem is a program for generating cryptograms; the second problem involves the design of a text editor program.

Problem 9A   A cryptogram is a coded message formed by substituting a code character for each letter of an original message. The substitution is performed uniformly throughout the original message, i.e., all A's might be replaced by Z, all B's by Y, etc. We will assume that all punctuation (including blanks between words) remains unchanged.

Discussion: The program must examine each character in a message, MESSAGE$, and substitute the appropriate code for that character in the cryptogram, CRYPTO$. This can be done by using the index in ALPHA-BET$ (the string "AB ... Z") of each character in MESSAGE$ to select a code symbol from the string CODE$ (e.g., the code symbol for the letter "A" should be the first symbol in CODE$; the code symbol for letter "B" should be the second symbol in CODE$, etc.). The data table is shown below; the flow diagrams are drawn in Fig. 9.10.

DATA TABLE FOR PROBLEM 9A

Program Constants
ALPHABET$ = "ABC ... Z": The alphabet string

Input Variables		Program Variables		Output Variables	
CODE$:	Code symbols for the letters	POSIT:	Position of next message character in the string AL-PHABET$	CRYPTO$:	The cryptogram
MESSAGE$:	Original message				
		NEXT.CHAR:	Loop control variable, indicates next character in MESSAGE$ to encode		

The refinement of Step 2 in Fig. 9.10 shows that the index, POSIT, in ALPHABET$ of each message character is first found (Step 2.2). If POSIT is non-zero, the code symbol for that letter is inserted in the string CRYPTO$ (Step 2.4); otherwise, the message character itself is inserted (Step 2.5). The program is shown in Fig. 9.11.

The variable CRYPTO$ is initialized to the null string. The statement

```
250 LET POSIT = INSTR(1, ALPHABET$,                    &
              MID(MESSAGE$, NEXT.CHAR, 1))
```

locates the current message character in the string ALPHABET$. The statement

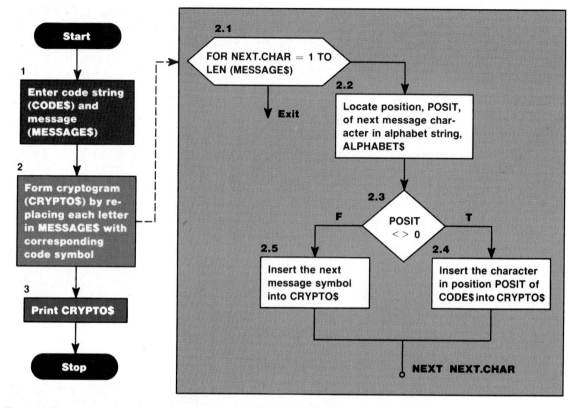

Fig. 9.10 Flow diagrams for Problem 9A.

```
LET CRYPTO$ = CYRPTO$ + MID(CODE$, POSIT, 1)
```

concatenates the corresponding code symbol for a letter to the cryptogram formed so far. The statement

```
LET CRYPTO$ = CRYPTO$ + MID(MESSAGE$, NEXT.CHAR, 1)
```

concatenates the current message character if it is not a letter.

```
100  !CRYPTOGRAM GENERATOR
110  !
120  !INITIALIZE ALPHABET STRING AND CRYPTOGRAM
130     LET ALPHABET$ = "ABCDEFGHIJKLMNOPQRSTUVWXYZ"
140     LET CRYPTO$ = ""
150  !
160  !ENTER CODE SYMBOL FOR EACH LETTER AND MESSAGE
170     PRINT "ENTER CODE SYMBOL UNDER EACH LETTER"
180     PRINT "  "; ALPHABET$
```

(continued)

```
190     INPUT CODE$
200     INPUT "ENTER 26 CHARACTERS"; ALPHABET$            &
            UNTIL LEN(ALPHABET$) = 26
210     PRINT "ENTER MESSAGE";
215     INPUT LINE MESSAGE$
220 !
230 !SUBSTITUTE CODE SYMBOL FOR EACH LETTER
240     FOR NEXT.CHAR = 1 TO LEN(MESSAGE$)
250         LET POSIT = INSTR(1, ALPHABET$,               &
                        MID(MESSAGE$, NEXT.CHAR, 1))
260       IF POSIT <> 0 THEN                              &
              LET CRYPTO$ = CRYPTO$ +                     &
                        MID(CODE$, POSIT, 1)              &
          ELSE                                            &
              LET CRYPTO$ = CRYPTO$ +                     &
                        MID(MESSAGE$, NEXT.CHAR, 1)
270     NEXT NEXT.CHAR
280 !
290 !PRINT RESULTS
300     PRINT "CRYPTOGRAM    : "; CRYPTO$
310 !
320     END
```

```
RUNNH
ENTER CODE SYMBOL UNDER EACH LETTER
ABCDEFGHIJKLMNOPQRSTUVWXYZ
? BCDEFGHIJKLMNOPQRSTUVWXYZA
ENTER MESSAGE? O.K., GO TO THE HEAD OF THE CLASS.
CRYPTOGRAM    : P.L., HP UP UIF IFBE PG UIF DMBTT.
```

Fig. 9.11 Program for Problem 9A.

Text Editor

There are many applications for which it is useful to have a computerized text-editing program. For example, if you are preparing a laboratory report (or a textbook), it would be convenient to edit or modify sections of the report (improve sentence and paragraph structure, change words, correct spelling mistakes, etc.) at a computer terminal and then have a fresh, clean copy of the text typed at the terminal without erasures or mistakes.

Problem 9B   A Text Editor System is a relatively sophisticated system of sub-programs that can be used to instruct the computer to perform virtually any kind of text alteration. As an example, consider the following sentence prepared by an overzealous member of the Addison-Wesley marketing group.

THE BOOK BY KAUFMANN AND ON FRACTURED PROGRAMMING IS GREATT?!

To correct this sentence, we would want to specify the following edit operations:

1. Insert "FRIEDMAN" at position 26 (where "ON" is now)
2. Replace "KAU" in "KAUFMANN" with "KOF"
3. Delete the extra "N" in "KAUFMANN"
4. Replace "FRA" in "FRACTURED" with "STRU"
5. Delete "T?" from "GREATT?!"

The corrected sentence would read:

THE BOOK BY KOFFMAN AND FRIEDMAN ON STRUCTURED PROGRAMMING IS GREAT!

Discussion: The main program for the text editor first will read an input string (TEXT$) and then process each of the edit commands (COMMAND$). The text editor will be able to insert a substring at a specified location, replace one substring with another, delete a substring, locate the first occurrence of a substring, and enter a new string to be edited.

We will write separate functions to perform each of the first three operations. The variables and functions referenced in the main program are listed below.

DATA TABLE FOR PROBLEM 9B (MAIN PROGRAM)

Program Constant

SENTINEL$ = "Q": the sentinel command

Input Variables		*Output Variables*	
TEXT$:	A string to be edited	TEXT$:	The edited string
COMMAND$:	Each edit command	POS.OLD:	The location of a substring found in TEXT$
OLD.STR$:	A substring to be located or deleted or replaced by another		
NEW.STR$:	A substring to be inserted at a specified position or in place of another substring		
WHERE:	The insertion point in TEXT$ of a new substring		

Functions Referenced

FNDELETE%: Deletes a substring OLD.STR$ from TEXT$

FNINSERT%: Inserts substring NEW.STR$ at position WHERE in TEXT$

FNREPLACE%: Replaces substring OLD.STR$ in TEXT$ with NEW.STR$

The main program will call one of the functions above (for insertion, deletion, replacement) or function INSTR to locate a specified substring. There will also be a subroutine in the main program that displays the menu for text editing. The level one flow diagram and program system chart are shown in Fig. 9.12a.

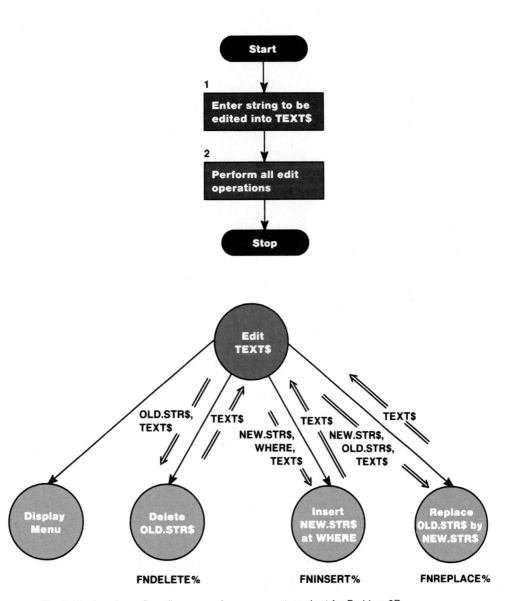

Fig. 9.12a Level one flow diagram and program system chart for Problem 9B.

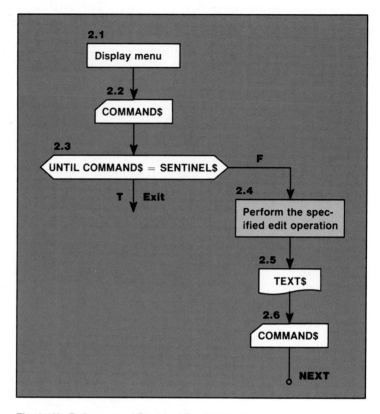

Fig. 9.12b Refinement of Step 2 of Fig. 9.12a.

The refinement of Step 2 is shown in Fig. 9.12b. The refinement of Step 2.4, a multiple-alternative decision, is drawn in Fig. 9.12c.

The main program is shown in Fig. 9.13a. The multiple-alternative decision is implemented using an ON–GOSUB statement; it's subroutines are shown in Fig. 9.13b.

In Fig. 9.13a, the statement

```
240 LET COMMAND$ = LEFT(CVT$$(COMMAND$, 40), 1)
```

uses the CVT$$ function to discard any leading blanks from COMMAND$ and to change all lower case letters to upper case letters (*modbit* = 8 + 32). Then the first nonblank character is assigned to COMMAND$.

The statement

```
250 ON INSTR(1, "DEILRSQ", COMMAND$) + 1                    &
        GOSUB 1000,2000,3000,4000,5000,6000,7000,8000
```

uses this character to determine which subroutine will be executed (2000 if COMMAND$ is "D", 3000 if COMMAND$ is "E", etc.) as explained in Exam-

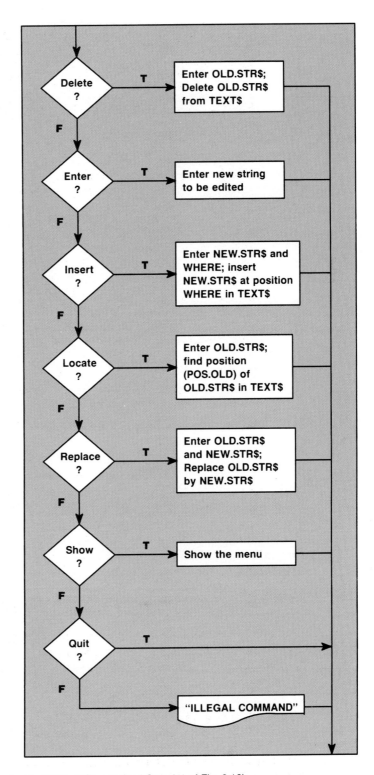

Fig. 9.12c Refinement of Step 2.4 of Fig. 9.12b.

```
100  !TEXT EDITOR PROGRAM
110  !
120  !INITIALIZE PROGRAM CONSTANT
130      LET SENTINEL$ = "Q"
140  !
145  !ENTER STRING TO BE EDITED
150      PRINT "ENTER STRING TO BE EDITED"
160      INPUT LINE TEXT$
170  !
180  !PERFORM ALL EDIT OPERATIONS
190  !FIRST SHOW THE MENU
200      LET COMMAND$ = "S"
210      GOSUB 7000
220      UNTIL COMMAND$ = SENTINEL$
230          INPUT "ENTER EDIT OPERATION OR S(HOW) ";   &
                  "OR Q(UIT)"; COMMAND$
240          LET COMMAND$ = LEFT(CVT$$(COMMAND$, 40), 1)
250          ON INSTR(1, "DEILRSQ", COMMAND$) + 1       &
                  GOSUB 1000, 2000, 3000, 4000,          &
                      5000, 6000, 7000, 8000
260          PRINT TEXT$
280      NEXT    !UNTIL
290  !
300      STOP
```

Fig. 9.13a Main program for Problem 9B.

```
1000  !SUBROUTINES FOR ON-GOSUB AT LINE 250
1010  !COMMAND IS ILLEGAL
1020      PRINT "ILLEGAL COMMAND"
1030      RETURN
2000  !DELETE A SUBSTRING
2005      PRINT "DELETE WHAT STRING";
2010      INPUT LINE OLD.STR$
2015      OLD.STR$ = CVT$$(OLD.STR$, 4)
2020      IF NOT FNDELETE%(OLD.STR$) THEN              &
              PRINT "DELETION NOT PERFORMED"
2030      RETURN
3000  !ENTER A NEW STRING TO BE EDITED
3010      PRINT "ENTER STRING TO BE EDITED"
3020      INPUT LINE TEXT$
3030      RETURN
4000  !INSERT A SUBSTRING AT POSITION WHERE
4005      PRINT "INSERT WHAT STRING";
4010      INPUT LINE NEW.STR$
4015      NEW.STR$ = CVT$$(NEW.STR$, 4)
4020      INPUT "POINT OF INSERTION"; WHERE
4030      IF NOT FNINSERT%(NEW.STR$, WHERE) THEN       &
              PRINT "INSERTION NOT PERFORMED"
4040      RETURN
```

(continued)

```
5000 !LOCATE A SUBSTRING
5005      PRINT "LOCATE WHAT STRING";
5010      INPUT LINE OLD.STR$
5015      OLD.STR$ = CVT$$(OLD.STR$, 4)
5020      LET POS.OLD = INSTR(1, TEXT$, OLD.STR$)
5030      IF POS.OLD <> 0 THEN                              &
              PRINT "FOUND AT POSITION"; POS.OLD            &
          ELSE                                              &
              PRINT "NOT FOUND"
5040      RETURN
6000 !REPLACE ONE SUBSTRING WITH ANOTHER
6005      PRINT "REPLACE WHAT STRING";
6010      INPUT LINE OLD.STR$
6015      OLD.STR$ = CVT$$(OLD.STR$, 4)
6020      PRINT "TO BE REPLACED BY";
6025      INPUT LINE NEW.STR$
6030      NEW.STR$ = CVT$$(NEW.STR$, 4)
6040      IF NOT FNREPLACE%(OLD.STR$, NEW.STR$) THEN   &
              PRINT "REPLACEMENT NOT PERFORMED"
6050      RETURN
7000 !SHOW THE MENU
7005      PRINT
7010      PRINT "ENTER FIRST LETTER OF EDIT COMMAND"
7020      PRINT "THE COMMANDS ARE:"
7030      PRINT "      D(ELETE A SUBSTRING)"
7040      PRINT "      E(NTER NEW STRING TO EDIT)"
7050      PRINT "      I(NSERT A SUBSTRING)"
7060      PRINT "      L(OCATE A SUBSTRING)"
7070      PRINT "      R(EPLACE ONE STRING WITH ANOTHER)"
7080      PRINT "      S(HOW THE MENU)"
7090      PRINT "      Q(UIT)"
7100      PRINT
7110      RETURN
8000 !QUIT
8010      RETURN
8030 !END OF SUBROUTINES FOR ON-GOSUB AT LINE 250
```

Fig. 9.13b Subroutines for ON-GOSUB at line 250 of Fig. 9.13a.

ple 9.14. Each subroutine reads any additional data that may be needed for the desired edit operation and then performs the operation. If COM- MAND$ is "D" or "I" or "R", an IF-THEN statement (see lines 2020, 4030, 6040 of Fig. 9.13b) calls a user-defined function to perform the edit operation. If the operation cannot be performed, the function result will be 0% (false) and an error message will be printed.

The user-defined functions are shown in Figs. 9.13c, d, and e. Each of these functions returns a value of −1% (true) only if the required editing operation is performed. The functions LEFT and RIGHT are used to extract the left and right substrings of TEXT$; the concatenation operator, +, is used to join these substrings as needed. The result of the editing operation is returned to the main program as a function side-effect, i.e., through modification of the global variable TEXT$. This is carefully documented in the comments appearing at the beginning of each function.

As an example, the assignment statement

```
LET TEXT$ = LEFT(TEXT$, DEL.POS-1) +                      &
            RIGHT(TEXT$, DEL.POS+LEN(OLD.STR$))
```

is used in function FNDELETE% (at line 10150) to delete the substring OLD.STR$ which starts at position DEL.POS of TEXT$. If OLD.STR$ is "THIS" then the functions LEFT and RIGHT would concatenate the two substrings of TEXT$ shown below.

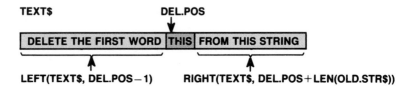

The result would, of course, be

TEXT$

| DELETE THE FIRST WORD   FROM THIS STRING |

A sample run of the text editor program is shown in Fig. 9.13f.

```
10000      DEF* FNDELETE%(OLD.STR$)
10005 !
10010 !DELETES FIRST OCCURRENCE OF OLD.STR$ FROM TEXT$
10020 !RETURNS A VALUE OF 0% (FALSE) IF
10030 !THE DELETION CANNOT BE PERFORMED; OTHERWISE,
10040 !RETURNS -1% (TRUE) AND MODIFIES TEXT$
10045 !
10050 !PARAMETER DEFINITIONS --
10060 !   OLD.STR$ - THE SUBSTRING TO BE DELETED
10070 !GLOBAL VARIABLES
10080 !   TEXT$ - THE STRING BEING EDITED
10090 !LOCAL VARIABLE
10100 !   DEL.POS - FIRST OCCURRENCE OF OLD.STR$
10105 !
```

(continued)

```
10110 !INITIALIZE FUNCTION RESULT TO FALSE
10120     LET FNDELETE% = 0%
10130 !DELETE OLD.STR$ IF FOUND IN TEXT$
10140     LET DEL.POS = INSTR(1, TEXT$, OLD.STR$)
10150     IF DEL.POS <> 0 THEN                            &
              !CONCATENATE SUBSTRING BEFORE OLD.STR$      &
              !WITH SUBSTRING FOLLOWING OLD.STR$          &
              LET TEXT$ = LEFT(TEXT$, DEL.POS-1) +        &
                  RIGHT(TEXT$, DEL.POS+LEN(OLD.STR$))     &
              \LET FNDELETE% = -1%      !TRUE
10210 !
10220     FNEND    !FNDELETE%
```

Fig. 9.13c Function FNDELETE%.

```
20000     DEF* FNINSERT%(NEW.STR$, WHERE)
20005 !
20010 !INSERTS NEW.STR$ AT POSTION WHERE IN TEXT$
20020 !RETURNS A VALUE OF 0% (FALSE) IF
20030 !INSERTION IS NOT PERFORMED; OTHERWISE,
20040 !RETURNS -1% (TRUE) AND MODIFIES TEXT$
20050 !
20060 !PARAMETER DEFINITIONS --
20070 !    NEW.STR$ - THE SUBSTRING TO BE INSERTED
20080 !    WHERE - DESIRED POSTION OF NEW.STR$
20090 !GLOBAL VARIABLES
20100 !    TEXT$ - THE STRING BEING EDITED
20110 !
20120 !INITIALIZE FUNCTION RESULT TO FALSE
20130     LET FNINSERT% = 0%        !FALSE
20140 !
20150 !INSERT NEW.STR$ IF WHERE IS IN RANGE
20160     IF WHERE >= 1 AND                              &
              WHERE <= LEN(TEXT$) + 1 THEN               &
              !CONCATENATE SUBSTRING PRECEDING           &
              !INSERTION POINT WHERE WITH NEW.STR$       &
              !AND WITH SUBSTRING STARTING AT WHERE      &
              LET TEXT$ = LEFT (TEXT$, WHERE-1)          &
                      + NEW.STR$                         &
                      + RIGHT(TEXT$, WHERE)              &
              \LET FNINSERT% = -1%     !TRUE
20170 !
20180     FNEND    !FNINSERT%
```

Fig. 9.13d Function FNINSERT%.

```
30000      DEF* FNREPLACE%(OLD.STR$, NEW.STR$)
30005 !
30010 !REPLACES FIRST OCCURRENCE OF OLD.STR$ WITH
30020 !NEW.STR$.  RETURNS A VALUE OF 0% (FALSE) IF
30030 !REPLACEMENT CANNOT BE PERFORMED; OTHERWISE,
30040 !RETURNS -1% (TRUE) AND MODIFIES TEXT$
30050 !
30060 !PARAMETER DEFINITIONS --
30070 !    OLD.STR$ - THE SUBSTRING BEING REPLACED
30080 !    NEW.STR$ - THE SUBSTRING BEING INSERTED
30090 !GLOBAL VARIABLE
30100 !    TEXT$ - THE STRING BEING EDITED
30105 !LOCAL VARIABLES
30110 !    REP.POS - FIRST OCCURRENCE OF OLD.STR$
30115 !
30120 !INITIALIZE FUNCTION RESULT TO FALSE
30130      LET FNREPLACE% = 0%          !FALSE
30140 !
30150 !REPLACE OLD.STR$ WITH NEW.STR$ IF FOUND
30160      LET REP.POS = INSTR (1, TEXT$, OLD.STR$)
30170      IF REP.POS <> 0 THEN                          &
               !INSERT NEW.STR$ AT POSITION REP.POS    &
               LET TEXT$ = LEFT(TEXT$, REP.POS-1) +    &
                 NEW.STR$ +                            &
                 RIGHT(TEXT$, REP.POS+LEN(OLD.STR$)) &
               \LET FNREPLACE% = -1%     !TRUE
30230 !
30240      FNEND     !FNREPLACE%
30250 !
32767      END    !TEXT EDITOR
```

Fig. 9.13e Function FNREPLACE%.

```
RUNNH
ENTER STRING TO BE EDITED
? Today is the first day of the new semester.

ENTER FIRST LETTER OF EDIT COMMAND
THE COMMANDS ARE:
    D(ELETE A SUBSTRING)
    E(NTER NEW STRING TO EDIT)
    I(NSERT A SUBSTRING)
    L(OCATE A SUBSTRING)
    R(EPLACE ONE STRING WITH ANOTHER)
    S(HOW THE MENU)
    Q(UIT)

ENTER EDIT OPERATION OR S(HOW) OR Q(UIT)? D
DELETE WHAT STRING?  new
Today is the first day of the semester.
```

(continued)

```
ENTER EDIT OPERATION OR S(HOW) OR Q(UIT)? I
INSERT WHAT STRING? Hooray!
POINT OF INSERTION? 1
Hooray! Today is the first day of the semester.

ENTER EDIT OPERATION OR S(HOW) OR Q(UIT)? R
REPLACE WHAT STRING? first
TO BE REPLACED BY? last
Hooray! Today is the last day of the semester.

ENTER EDIT OPERATION OR S(HOW) OR Q(UIT)? L
LOCATE WHAT STRING? last
FOUND AT POSITION 22
Hooray! Today is the last day of the semester.

ENTER EDIT OPERATION OR S(HOW) OR Q(UIT)? Q
Hooray! Today is the last day of the semester.
```

Stop at line 300

Fig. 9.13f Sample run for Problem 9B.

Program Style

Initializing and resetting logical function results

Each of the logical functions used in the text editor program begins by initializing the function result to 0% (false). The function result is not reset to −1% (true) until after the required editing operation is performed. In the event a function cannot perform its required operation or returns with an error for some unanticipated reason, the calling program would be able to detect this simply by testing whether a value of 0% (false) was returned. We recommend that you follow this procedure for initializing and resetting the value returned by a logical function.

Exercise 9.16: Indicate how you would use the text editor program to replace all occurrences of one substring with another.

Exercise 9.17: Write a subroutine that could be called to replace all occurrences of one substring by another when the command "A" (for "ALL") was entered.

Exercise 9.18: Discuss how you might utilize an index or pointer to the position of the last edit operation so that all edit operations would be performed on the substring of TEXT\$ starting at the pointer. The pointer should be initialized to 1. There should be commands that reset the pointer to 1 or move it forward or backward a specified number of characters.

9.8 Common Programming Errors

Now that we know how to manipulate different types of data, we must be especially careful not to misuse these data types in expressions. Character strings can be operands of the concatenation operator, +, and relational operators only. Remember that string variables and character string constants can be manipulated only with other string variables and constants.

The string manipulation functions introduced in this chapter require string expressions as well as numeric expressions as arguments. Make sure that your arguments are in the proper order and that string arguments are not used in place of numeric arguments (or vice versa), as attempts to use these functions with incorrect argument types will cause errors. In user-defined functions, if the parameter is a string variable, indicated by a $ in its name, then the matching argument must be a string expression.

In using substrings, care must be taken to ensure that the numeric expressions indicating the starting position and length of a substring are correct. If they are not correct, the wrong substring will be referenced. Normally, BASIC-PLUS will not detect incorrect values for these numeric expressions; consequently, it is advisable to double check them yourself and print their values if you are in doubt.

9.9 Summary

In this chapter, we reviewed earlier work with character strings and introduced several new functions (LEN, INSTR, MID, LEFT, RIGHT, VAL, NUM$, NUM1$, CHR$, ASCII, CVT$$) and a new operator, +, for concatenation. Table 9.3 summarizes these new features.

Many examples of these new features for manipulating character strings were presented. We have used these features to generate cryptograms and to design a text editor.

These kinds of problems are called non-numerical problems and they are among the most challenging in computer science. This is because the computer is a numerical device and, consequently, is well suited for use as a tool for manipulating numerical data. However, many of the concepts that interest us most are not quantitative or numerical; hence, we are often unable to apply the computer effectively in solving these problems. The techniques presented in this chapter should give you a better idea of how to use the computer to solve non-numerical problems.

Programming Problems

9C Let FIRST$ contain the string "DINGBAT" and LAST$ the string "WOMBAT". Write a program to read in a set of words and determine whether or not each word falls between FIRST$ and LAST$. Print

Table 9.3 Summary of New Statements and Functions

Statement	Effect
Concatenation	
`"ABC" + "DE"`	Forms the string `"ABCDE"`
String functions	
`LEN("ABCDE")`	value is 5 (length of `"ABCDE"`)
`LEFT("ABCDE", 2)`	value is `"AB"` (left substring ending with second character)
`RIGHT("ABCDE", 2)`	value is `"BCDE"` (right substring starting with second character)
`MID("ABCDE", 2, 3)`	value is `"BCD"` (substring of length 3 starting with second character)
`INSTR(2, "ABCDE", "DE")`	value is 4 (`"DE"` starts at fourth character of `"ABCDE"`)
`INSTR(2, "ABCDE", "AE")`	value is 0 (`"AE"` not found in substring `"BCDE"`)
Conversion between strings and numbers	
`VAL("12E-1")`	value is the real number `1.2`
`NUM1$(15.5)`	value is the string `"15.5"`
`NUM$(15.5)`	value is the string `" 15.5 "`
`ASCII("4")`	value is the number 52 (ASCII code for character `"4"`)
`CHR$(43)`	value is the character `"+"` (ASCII code is 43)
String editing	
`CVT$$("A b'c D' e", 34)`	value is `"AB'CD'E"` (modbit 32+2)
`CVT$$("A b'c D' e", 290)`	value is `"AB'c D'E"` (modbit 256+32+2)

FIRST$ and LAST$ and print each word read in (except the last) along with the message "BETWEEN" or "NOT BETWEEN", whichever applies. Use the following data.

```
HELP
ME
STIFLE
THE
DINGBAT
AND
THE
WOMBATS
BEFORE
IT
IS
TOO
LATE
```

9D Assume a set of sentences is to be processed. Each sentence consists of a sequence of words, separated by one or more blank spaces. Write a program that will read these sentences and count the number of words with one letter, two letters, etc., up to 10 letters.

9E Write a program that will scan a sentence and replace all multiple occurrences of a blank with a single occurrence of a blank.

9F Write a program to read in a collection of character strings of arbitrary length. For each string read, your program should do the following:

a) print the length of the string;
b) count the number of occurrences of four letter words in each string;
c) replace each four letter word with a string of four asterisks and print the new string.

9G Write a program that removes all of the blanks from a character string and "compacts" all nonblank characters in the string. You should only have to scan the input string once from left to right. (Do not use CVT$$.)

9H Write an arithmetic expression translator that "translates" fully-parenthesized arithmetic expressions involving the operators ∗ , /, + , and − . For example, given the input string

```
"((A+(B∗C))-(D/E))"
```

the translator would print out:

```
Z = (B∗C)
Y = (A+Z)
X = (D/E)
W = (Y−X)
```

Assume only the letters A through F can be used as variable names. *Hint:* Find the first right parenthesis. Remove it and the four characters preceding it and replace them with the next unused letter at the end of the alphabet. Print out the assignment statement used. For example, the following is a summary of the sequence of steps required to process the input string above. The arrow points to the first right parenthesis at each step.

expression status	*print*
"((A+(B∗C))-(D/E))" ↑	Z = (B∗C)
"((A+Z)-(D/E))" ↑	Y = (A+Z)
"(Y-(D/E))" ↑	X = (D/E)
"(Y−X)" ↑	W = (Y−X)

9I Write a program to read in a string of up to 10 characters representing a number in the form of a Roman numeral. Print the Roman numeral form and then convert to Arabic form (an integer). The character values for Roman numerals are

M	1000
D	500
C	100
L	50
X	10
V	5
I	1

Test your program on the following input.

```
LXXXVII              87
CCXIX               219
MCCCLIV            1354
MMDCLXXIII         2673
MDCDLXXVI             ?
```

9J   Shown below is the layout of a string that the registrar uses as input for a program to print the end-of-the-semester final grade report for each student.

Positions	Data description
1–6	Student number
7–19	Last name
20–27	First name
28	Middle initial
29	Academic year:
	1 = Fr, 2 = So, 3 = Jr, 4 = Sr
30–32	First course—Department ID (3 letters)
33–35	First course—Number (3 digits)
36	First course—Grade A, B, C, D, or F
37	First course—Number of credits: 0–7
40–42	
43–45	
46	Second course: data as described above
47	
50–52	
53–55	
56	Third course data
57	
60–62	
63–65	
66	Fourth course data
67	
70–72	
73–75	
76	Fifth course data
77	

Write a data table, flow diagram and program to print the following grade report sheet for each student.

```
Line  1              MAD RIVER COLLEGE
Line  2             YELLOW GULCH, OHIO
Line  3
Line  4        GRADE REPORT, SPRING SEMESTER
Line  5
Line  6 (student number)  (year)  (student name)
        ------------------  -----  --------------

Line  7
Line  8                  GRADE SUMMARY
Line  9          COURSE
Line 10      DEPT     NMBR     CREDITS      GRADE
Line 11  1. ____.    ____.       __          __
Line 12  2. ____.    ____.       __          __
Line 13  3. ____.    ____.       __          __
Line 14  4. ____.    ____.       __          __
Line 15  5. ____.    ____.       __          __
Line 16
Line 17 SEMESTER GRADE POINT AVERAGE = _.__
```

Compute the grade point average as follows:

a) Use 4 points for an A, 3 for a B, 2 for a C, 1 for a D, and 0 for an F
b) Compute the product of points times credits for each course
c) Add together the products computed in (b)
d) Add together the total number of course credits
e) Divide (c) by (d) and print the result.

Your program should work for students taking anywhere from one to five courses. You will have to determine the number of courses taken by a student from the input data.

9K Write a data table, flow diagram and program that will process the employee records described in Table 9.4 (each record is represented as a character string) and perform the following tasks:

a) For each employee compute the gross pay:
    Gross pay = hours worked $*$ hourly pay +
                     overtime hours worked $*$ hourly pay $*$ 1.5
b) For each employee compute the net pay as follows:
    Net pay = gross pay − deductions

Deductions are computed as follows:

Federal Tax = (gross pay − 13 $*$ no. of dependents) $*$ .14

FICA = gross pay $*$ .052

City Tax = $\begin{cases} \$0.00 \text{ if employee works in the suburbs} \\ 4\% \text{ of gross pay if employee works in city} \end{cases}$

Union Dues = $\begin{cases} 0.00 \text{ if employee not a union member} \\ 6.75\% \text{ of gross pay otherwise} \end{cases}$

For each employee, print one or more lines of output containing:

1. Employee number
2. First and last name
3. Number of hours worked
4. Hourly pay rate
5. Overtime hours
6. Gross pay
7. Federal tax
8. FICA
9. City wage tax (if any)
10. Union dues (if any)
11. Net pay

Also compute and print:

1. Number of employees processed
2. Total gross pay
3. Total federal tax withheld
4. Total hours worked
5. Total overtime hours worked

Table 9.4 Employee Record String for Problem 9K

Positions	Data Description
1–6	Employee number (an integer)
7–19	Employee last name
20–27	Employee first name
28–32	Number of hours worked (to the nearest ½ hour) for this employee
33–37	Hourly pay rate for this employee
38	Contains a C if employee works in the City Office and an S if employee works in the Suburban Office
39	Contains an M if the employee is a union member
40–41	Number of dependents
42–46	Number of overtime hours worked (also to the nearest ½ hour)

9L Do the hangman problem (Problem 6P) using character strings instead of string arrays to hold the word to be guessed and the solution so far.

9M Write a text editor that will edit a "page" of text. Store each line of the page in a separate element of a string array. Enter an empty line (null string) to indicate the end of the page. You should maintain a pointer (index) to the current line of the text. Provide commands that move the index to the top of the page, the bottom of the page, or up or down a specified number of lines. All editing operations should be performed on the section of the page beginning with the current line. *Hint:* See Problem 9B and Exercise 9.18.

10

Two-Dimensional Arrays and Matrixes

In previous chapters, we have written programs that manipulate both numeric and string data. In addition, we have used one data structure, the array, for identifying and referencing a collection of data items of the same type. The array enables us to save a list of related data items in memory. All of these data items are referred to by the same name, and the array subscript is used to distinguish among the individual array elements.

In this chapter, the use of the array will be extended to facilitate the organization of related data items into tables of two dimensions. These tables provide a very natural form of representation of certain kinds of information. For example, a two-dimensional array with three rows and

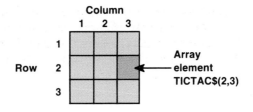

Fig. 10.1 Representation of a tic-tac-toe board as a two-dimensional array.

three columns can be used to represent a tic-tac-toe board. This array has nine elements, each of which can be referenced by specifying the *row subscript* (1, 2, or 3) and *column subscript* (1, 2, or 3), as shown in Fig. 10.1.

10.1 Declaration of Two-Dimensional Arrays

The general form of an array declaration can be expanded to handle arrays of two dimensions, as shown in the next display.

Two-Dimensional Array Declaration

`DIM name (row size, column size)`

Interpretation: *Row size* and *column size* are non-negative integer constants representing the largest legal values for the row subscript (number of rows) and column subscript (number of columns) respectively. The legal subscripts are

1,2,. . .,*row size*   row subscript
1,2,. . .,*column size*   column subscript

Notes: Two-dimensional numeric arrays are initialized to all zeros; string arrays are initialized to null strings.

BASIC-PLUS actually has a zero value for the row subscript and the column subscript. We will ignore these zero values throughout most of the chapter, but you should remember that the size of a two-dimensional array is actually given by the product (*row size* +1) $\times$ (*column size* +1) rather than *row size* $\times$ *column size*.

If a two-dimensional array *name* is referenced, but not declared in a DIM statement, BASIC-PLUS automatically creates a 10×10 array (11×11 including the zero subscript).

Example 10.1   The statement

`DIM TICTAC$(3,3), REC(7,5)`

illustrates the declaratiom of two-dimensional arrays. The string array TICTAC$ consists of three rows and three columns. In the array REC, the first subscript may take on values from 1 to 7; the second, from 1 to 5. There are a total of 7 × 5 or 35 elements in the array, excluding the elements having a zero row or column subscript.

10.2 Manipulation of Two-Dimensional Arrays

Manipulation of Individual Array Elements

We may reference the individual elements of a two-dimensional array using two subscripts, as shown next.

Array Subscripts (Two-dimensional Arrays)

name (*subscript₁*, *subscript₂*)

Interpretation: *Subscript₁* and *subscript₂* are subscript expressions. The forms permitted are the same as those discussed in Section 6.2 for one-dimensional arrays.

In the case of two-dimensional arrays, the first subscript of an array reference is considered the row subscript and the second subscript the column subscript. Consequently, the subscripted array reference

```
TICTAC$(2,3)
```

selects the element in row 2, column 3 of the array TICTAC shown in Fig. 10.1. This row/column convention is derived from the area of mathematics called *matrix algebra*. A *matrix* M is a two-dimensional arrangement of numbers. Each element in M is referred to by the symbol M_{ij}, where i is the number of its row and j is the number of its column.

Example 10.2   Consider the array M drawn below.

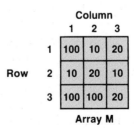

Array M

This array (or matrix) consists of three elements containing the value 10 (M(1,2), M(2,1), M(2,3)), three elements with value 100 (M(1,1), M(3,1), M(3,2)), and three elements with value 20 (M(1,3), M(2,2), M(3,3)).

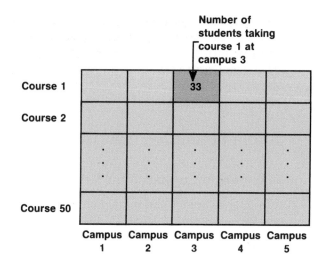

Number of
students taking
course 1 at
campus 3

Course 1   33

Course 2

Course 50

Campus Campus Campus Campus Campus
   1   2   3   4   5

Fig. 10.2 Two-dimensional array
of course enrollments, ENROLL.

Example 10.3   A university offers 50 courses at each of five campuses. We can conveniently store the enrollments of these courses in an array declared by

```
110 DIM ENROLL(50,5)
```

This array consists of 250 elements; ENROLL(I,J) represents the number of students in course I at campus J.

The program segment below could be used to find the total number of students enrolled in course 3 at all campuses.

```
200     LET COURSE = 3
210     LET NUM.STUDENTS = 0
220 !ADD UP ALL STUDENTS IN SPECIFIED COURSE
230     LET NUM.STUDENTS =                          &
            NUM.STUDENTS + ENROLL(COURSE,CAMPUS)    &
            FOR CAMPUS = 1 TO 5
240     PRINT "NUMBER OF STUDENTS IN COURSE";       &
            COURSE; "="; NUM.STUDENTS
```

We might also be interested in determining the total number of students enrolled in all courses at all campuses. To accomplish this, a pair of nested FOR loops is required.

```
310     LET NUM.STUDENTS = 0
320 !ACCUMULATE IN NUM.STUDENTS THE SUM OF
325 !ALL ELEMENTS OF ENROLL
330 !PROCESS ONE ROW AT A TIME
340     FOR COURSE = 1 TO 50
350        !ADD IN THE ELEMENTS FOR EACH COURSE
360        LET NUM.STUDENTS =                       &
               NUM.STUDENTS + ENROLL(COURSE,CAMPUS)&
               FOR CAMPUS = 1 TO 5
370     NEXT COURSE
380     PRINT "TOTAL NUMBER OF STUDENTS =";
            NUM.STUDENTS
```

This program segment accumulates the sum of all elements of the array ENROLL in NUM.STUDENTS. It starts with the five elements of row 1 (ENROLL(1,1). . . ENROLL(1,5)), followed by the five elements of row 2 (ENROLL(2,1). . . ENROLL(2,5)) until it finally adds in the five elements of row 50 (ENROLL(50,1). . . ENROLL(50,5)).

Exercise 10.1:

a) For the array ENROLL in Fig. 10.2, write a program segment to count the number of students in all courses at campus 3. Students will be counted once for each course in which they are enrolled.

b) For the array ENROLL in Fig. 10.2, write a program segment that will count the total number of 0's (courses with no students).

Relationship between Loop Control Variables and Array Subscripts

Sequential referencing of array elements is frequently required when working with two-dimensional arrays. This process often requires the use of nested loops, since more than one subscript must be incremented in order to process all or a portion of the array elements. It is very easy to become confused in this situation and interchange subscripts, or nest the loops improperly. If you are in doubt as to whether or not your loops and subscripts are properly synchronized, you should include extra PRINT statements to display the subscript and array element values.

Example 10.3 and Exercise 10.1(b) provide some examples of writing nested loops to process two-dimensional arrays. The following problem, which processes the array TICTAC$, provides further illustration.

Problem 10A   Write a function that will be used after each move is made in a computerized tic-tac-toe game to see if the game is over. The function will indicate whether or not the game is over, and return the winning player or the fact that the game ended in a draw.

Discussion: We will use a 3 × 3 string array TICTAC$ to represent the tic-tac-toe board. The letters "X" and "O" will represent player moves; all memory cells in TICTAC$ initially will be blank. To see whether a player has won, the function must check each row, column, and diagonal on the board to determine if all three squares are occupied by the same player. A draw occurs when all squares on the board are occupied but neither player has won. The logical function FNOVER% will return a value of −1% (true) when the game is over and a value of 0%(false) when it is not over. The flow diagrams for this problem are shown in Fig. 10.3. The data table follows.

Global Input Variables		Global Output Variables	
TICTAC$(,):	The current state of the tic-tac-toe board after each move (size 3 × 3)	WINNER$:	An indicator used to define the winner of the game ("X", "O", or "D" for draw) when the game is over

Local Function Variables	
OVER.ROW:	Row subscript for array TICTAC$; used as loop control variable
OVER.COL:	Column subscript for array TICTAC$; used as loop control variable

The refinement of Step 3 of Fig. 10.3 would be similar to Step 2 except that the three columns of array TICTAC$ would be examined. Step 2.2 and Steps 3 and 4 all involve the same operation—a comparison of the contents of three elements of the array TICTAC$ to see whether they are identical. In Step 4 there are two diagonals to be checked. To perform these comparisons, we will use a logical function FNSAME% that will return a value of −1%(true) if the three array elements are the same (and not blank), and will return 0%(false) otherwise. The input arguments for FNSAME% will be the three elements of TICTAC$ that are to be compared. With this lowest-level detail now handled, we can write the function for Problem 10A (see Fig. 10.4). Additional data table entries are shown below.

Functions Referenced by FNOVER%	
FNSAME% (logical function):	Tests a row, column, or diagonal; returns a value of −1% (true) if all three elements are the same ("X" or "O") and not blank; otherwise, returns a value of 0% (false)
Arguments 1,2,3	The arguments are the elements of a row, column, or diagonal of TICTAC$. The order in which these elements are specified is immaterial.

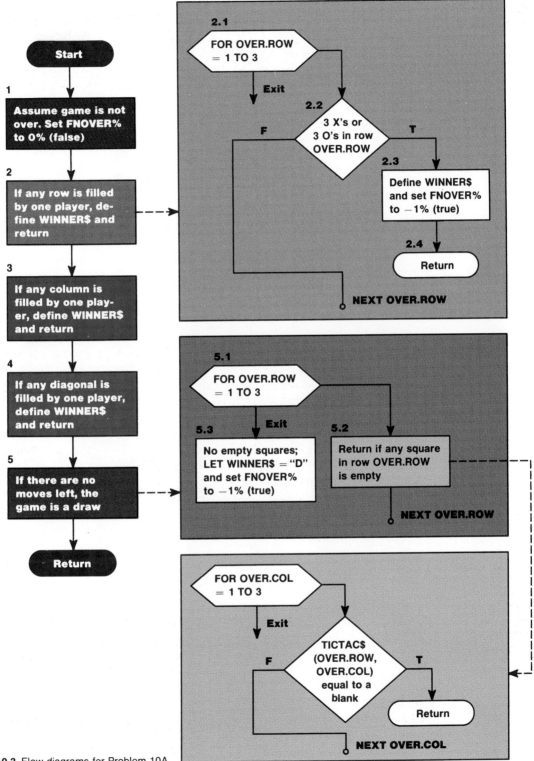

Fig. 10.3 Flow diagrams for Problem 10A.

```
1000    DEF* FNOVER%
1010 !
1020 !FUNCTION TO CHECK IF TIC-TAC-TOE GAME IS OVER
1030 !AND DETERMINE WINNER (IF ANY)
1040 !
1050 !GLOBAL VARIABLES
1060 !  IN:  TICTAC$( , ) - CURRENT STATE OF GAME
1080 !  OUT: WINNER$ - INDICATES WINNER
1085 !                 ("X" OR "O") OR DRAW ("D")
1090 !
1100 !LOCAL VARIABLES CHANGED - OVER.ROW, OVER.COL
1110 !
1120 !FUNCTIONS CALLED - FNSAME%
1130 !
1140 !ASSUME THAT THE GAME IS NOT OVER
1150     LET FNOVER% = 0%    !FALSE
1160 !
1170 !CHECK FOR WINNER BY ROWS
1180     FOR OVER.ROW = 1 TO 3
1190        IF FNSAME%(TICTAC$(OVER.ROW,1),          &
                      TICTAC$(OVER.ROW,2),          &
                      TICTAC$(OVER.ROW,3)) THEN     &
             !WIN IN ROW OVER.ROW                   &
             !SET WINNER$ AND RETURN                &
             LET WINNER$ = TICTAC$(OVER.ROW,1)      &
             \LET FNOVER% = -1%    !TRUE            &
             \GOTO 1500    !RETURN FROM FNOVER%
1200     NEXT OVER.ROW
1210 !
1220 !NO WINNER BY ROWS -- CHECK COLUMNS
1230     FOR OVER.COL = 1 TO 3
1240        IF FNSAME%(TICTAC$(1,OVER.COL),          &
                      TICTAC$(2,OVER.COL),          &
                      TICTAC$(3,OVER.COL)) THEN     &
             !WIN IN COLUMN OVER.COL.               &
             !SET WINNER$ AND RETURN                &
             LET WINNER$ = TICTAC$(1,OVER.COL)      &
             \LET FNOVER% = -1%    !TRUE            &
             \GOTO 1500    !RETURN FROM FNOVER%
1245     NEXT OVER.COL
1250 !
1260 !NO WINNER BY ROWS OR COLUMNS -- CHECK DIAGONALS
1270     IF FNSAME%(TICTAC$(1,1),                         &
                   TICTAC$(2,2), TICTAC$(3,3)) OR         &
           FNSAME%(TICTAC$(1,3),                          &
                   TICTAC$(2,2), TICTAC$(3,1)) THEN       &
             !WIN IN DIAGONAL. SET WINNER$ AND RETURN     &
             LET WINNER$ = TICTAC$(2,2)                   &
             \LET FNOVER% = -1%    !TRUE                  &
             \GOTO 1500    !RETURN FROM FNOVER%
1280 !
```

(continued)

```
1290 !NO WINNER.  SEE IF GAME IS A DRAW
1300 !LOOK FOR AN EMPTY CELL
1310     FOR OVER.ROW = 1 TO 3
1320        FOR OVER.COL = 1 TO 3
1330           IF TICTAC$(OVER.ROW,OVER.COL)=" " THEN &
                !EMPTY CELL FOUND. GAME NOT OVER      &
                GOTO 1500     !RETURN FROM FNOVER%
1340        NEXT OVER.COL
1350     NEXT OVER.ROW
1360 !
1370 !NO EMPTY SPACES -- GAME IS A DRAW
1380     LET WINNER$ = "D"
1390     LET FNOVER% = -1%     !TRUE
1400 !
1500     FNEND     !FNOVER%
```

Fig. 10.4 Function for Problem 10A.

The function FNSAME% is called in lines 1190, 1240, and 1270 of Fig. 10.4. The arguments listed in each call are all elements of the array TIC-TAC$. Each argument is a subscripted variable consisting of the array name (TICTAC$) followed by a pair of subscripts. If the header statement in the definition of function FNSAME% had the form

```
DEF* FNSAME%(P1$, P2$, P3$)
```

a different set of array elements would be associated with the parameters P1$, P2$, P3$ each time FNSAME% was called.

The use of the GOTO statement in lines 1190, 1240, 1270, and 1330 is required in order to return from the function; BASIC-PLUS only allows function returns through the FNEND statement (line 1500).

Exercise 10.2: Write the function FNSAME%.
Note: Make sure FNSAME% properly handles the situation in which all three items being compared are blank; the value returned should be −1% (true) only if all three items are "X" or all three are "O".

10.3 Matrix Input and Output Operations

As we have seen, the manipulation of two-dimensional arrays or matrixes often requires a pair of nested loops. In order to make it easier to program some of the more common matrix manipulations, BASIC-PLUS provides some special matrix operators. These include operators for reading and printing matrixes, matrix initialization, matrix addition, subtraction, multiplication, and inversion. These operations are described in the next few sections.

Reading and Printing Matrixes

In this section, we illustrate the BASIC-PLUS matrix input and output statements, MAT READ, MAT INPUT, and MAT PRINT.

Example 10.4   The program in Fig. 10.5 enters data into matrixes A and B and prints their contents.

```
100     DIM  A(4,4), B(3,2)
105 !
110     MAT READ A
115     DATA 100, 200, 30, 40, 20, 300, 40, 50
120     DATA 30, 40, 500, 600, 400, 50, 60, 70
130 !
140     PRINT "THE VALUES OF NUM AND NUM2 FOR "; &
                "MATRIX A ARE"; NUM; NUM2
145     PRINT "THE MATRIX A IS"
150     MAT PRINT A;   !PRINT A IN PACKED FORMAT
160     PRINT
165 !
170     MAT READ B
175     DATA 1, 2, 3, 4, 5, 6
180     PRINT "THE VALUES OF NUM AND NUM2 FOR "; &
                "MATRIX B ARE"; NUM; NUM2
190     PRINT "THE MATRIX B IS"
200     MAT PRINT B,   !PRINT B IN ZONED FORMAT
210 !
240     END

RUNNH
THE VALUES OF NUM AND NUM2 FOR MATRIX A ARE 4    4
THE MATRIX A IS
 100   200   30   40

 20   300   40   50

 30   40   500   600

 400   50   60   70


THE VALUES OF NUM AND NUM2 FOR MATRIX B ARE 3    2
THE MATRIX B IS
 1                 2

 3                 4

 5                 6
```

Fig. 10.5 Illustration of MAT READ and MAT PRINT.

Observe the difference in output format resulting from the use of the semicolon as a separator versus the comma. Note that column alignment is not preserved when the semicolon is used unless all output values are the same width.

The program in Fig. 10.5 also illustrates the use of the BASIC-PLUS *system variables* NUM and NUM2. These variables are assigned values whenever a MAT READ or MAT INPUT statement is executed. NUM is assigned the row subscript of the last array element processed; NUM2 is assigned the column subscript. It is illegal to attempt to assign values to NUM or NUM2 in any other way.

The matrix input and output operations can be performed with one-dimensional arrays as well as two-dimensional arrays. In this case, NUM is assigned the subscript of the last array element processed and NUM2 is set to zero. Any array used with MAT READ, MAT INPUT, or MAT PRINT must be declared in a DIM statement.

Example 10.5 The program segment in Fig. 10.6 uses the MAT READ and MAT PRINT statements with a one-dimensional array. The extra data values in line 120 are ignored. The array A is printed on one line.

```
100      DIM A(5)
110      MAT READ A
120      DATA 1, 2, 3, 4, 5, 6, 7, 8
130      MAT PRINT A;
140      PRINT "NUM ="; NUM,  "NUM2 ="; NUM2
150      END
```

```
RUNNH
 1   2   3   4   5

NUM = 5        NUM2 = 0
```

Fig. 10.6 Using MAT READ and MAT PRINT with a one-dimensional array.

The MAT READ and MAT PRINT operators are shown in the following displays.

Matrix Read

MAT READ *list of arrays*

Interpretation: The *list of arrays* is a list of array names. The data are stored in each array on a row-by-row basis: the first set of values is stored in row 1 of the first array, the next set in row 2 of the first array, etc. The first array will be filled before any data are stored in the second array. The MAT READ does not change row 0 or column 0 of any of the listed arrays. Excess data items in the DATA statement for a MAT READ will not be read until the next READ or MAT READ is encountered. If there is an insufficient number of data items, the remaining array elements will not be changed, an "out of data" error message will be printed and the program will stop.

Note: A one-dimensional array may be included in the *list of arrays*. The row subscript of the last array element read is assigned to NUM; the column subscript is assigned to NUM2 (0 for one-dimensional arrays).

Matrix Print

`MAT PRINT` *array separator*

Interpretation: The values of *array* will be printed in row order. MAT PRINT will not print any elements in row 0 or column 0 of *array*. The *separator* in the `MAT PRINT` statement determines the output format, as follows:

a) `MAT PRINT A;`
   The semicolon character causes array elements to be separated with a single space. Each row is started on a new line. A blank line is inserted between rows.
b) `MAT PRINT A,`
   The comma causes each array element to print in a new zone. Each row is started on a new line. A blank line is inserted between rows.
c) `MAT PRINT A`
   Prints each array element on a new line.

Note: BASIC-PLUS allows only one array to be printed in a single `MAT PRINT` statement. This may be a one-dimensional or two-dimensional array. The `MAT PRINT` statement always resets NUM and NUM2 equal to the current size of *array*. Thus if NUM and NUM2 are to be used as indicators of how many data items were entered into *array* via a `MAT READ` or `MAT INPUT`, they should be checked prior to the next `MAT PRINT` *array* statement.

BASIC-PLUS also provides a `MAT INPUT` statement for interactive entry of array data.

Example 10.6   The program in Fig. 10.7 uses the `MAT INPUT` statement to enter string data into the array A$. The data items are typed following the prompt symbol "?". A comma should be inserted between all data items entered. If the list of data items requires more than one line, then LINE FEED should be used to terminate each line except for the last one. RETURN should be used to terminate the last data line.

As illustrated in this program, array elements that do not receive data are not altered (recall that string arrays are initialized to the null string).

```
100       DIM A$(2,4)
110       PRINT "ENTER ARRAY A$"
120       MAT INPUT A$
130       PRINT "NUM ="; NUM, "NUM2 ="; NUM2
140       PRINT \ MAT PRINT A$,
150       PRINT "NUM ="; NUM, "NUM2 ="; NUM2
160       END

RUNNH
ENTER ARRAY A$
? YOU, ARE, LUCKY, TO BE, A STUDENT, HERE
NUM = 2          NUM2 = 2


YOU              ARE             LUCKY          TO BE

A STUDENT        HERE

NUM = 2          NUM2 = 4
```

Fig. 10.7 Illustration of MAT INPUT.

Note too, that the MAT PRINT at line 140 resets the values of NUM and
NUM2 back to the current size of the array A$ (2×4). This point is illus-
trated again in Example 10.8.

Matrix Reading from a Terminal

`MAT INPUT` *array*

Interpretation: MAT INPUT enters data from a terminal into *array*.
The items read must be the same type as *array*.
Notes: All data items entered on one line must be separated by commas. LINE FEED terminates a line of data; RETURN terminates the
data entry operation.

The assignment of input data to array elements is done on a row-
by-row basis, beginning with element *array*(1,1). Row 1 is completely filled before row 2 is begun. If there are fewer data items
than there are array elements, the remaining array elements are not
changed. This situation can easily be detected by examining the values of NUM and NUM2 (see next paragraph). If there are more data
elements than will fit in the array, the extra are ignored.

The MAT INPUT statement assigns values to the system variables
NUM and NUM2 in the same way as the MAT READ. NUM is
assigned the row subscript of the last array element read; NUM2 is
assigned the column subscript of the last array element read.

Subscripts in Matrix Input/Output—Redimensioning Matrixes

When writing MAT READ, PRINT, and INPUT statements, it is permissible to specify subscripts after any array listed in the statement. The subscripts indicate the last element of the array to be processed. It is very important to note that for MAT READ and INPUT statements, if the subscripts differ from the array dimension, BASIC-PLUS will redimension the array to the specified size. However, BASIC-PLUS cannot increase the total number of elements. If the subscripts indicate such an increase, the error message

```
?Subscript out of range
```

will be printed. This redimensioning only occurs with MAT READ and MAT INPUT. Redimensioning is not done in a MAT PRINT, even when subscripts are specified.

Example 10.7   The program shown in Fig. 10.8 (with its output) causes a redimensioning of the matrix A, from a 10 × 10 matrix to a 4 × 3. Element A(4,3) will be the last element to receive data (it will receive the data item 14), and matrix A becomes a 4 × 3 matrix.

```
100     DIM A(10,10)
110     MAT INPUT A(4,3)
120     PRINT
140     MAT PRINT A,   !PRINTS A IN ZONED FORMAT
150     END

RUNNH
? 3, 4, 5, 6, 7, 8, 9, 10, 11, 12, 13, 14, 15

 3              4              5

 6              7              8

 9             10             11

12             13             14
```

Fig. 10.8 Redimensioning a matrix.

For this example (with A dimensioned as a 10 × 10 array), the statement

```
MAT INPUT A(15,6)
```

is permissible because it redimensions A to a total size less than 100 ($15 \times 6 = 90$). The statement

```
MAT INPUT A(20,5)
```

is also legal, but

```
MAT INPUT A(20,6)
```

is not, because it attempts to redimension A to 120 (20×6) elements, which is larger than the original size of A.

Example 10.8 The BASIC-PLUS system variables NUM and NUM2 can be used, as illustrated in Fig. 10.9, to indicate whether or not there were sufficient data for a MAT READ or INPUT operation. However, upon execution of the MAT PRINT (line 160), NUM and NUM2 are reset back to the current size of A (2×3).

```
100   DIM A(10,10)
110     PRINT "ENTER MATRIX DIMENSIONS ";
115     INPUT "(MAX OF 100 ELEMENTS)"; N, M
120     PRINT "ENTER ELEMENTS SEPARATED BY COMMAS"
130     MAT INPUT A(N,M)
140     PRINT "NUM ="; NUM,  "NUM2 ="; NUM2
150     IF NUM * NUM2 = N * M THEN                        &
            PRINT "MATRIX FILLED"                         &
        ELSE                                              &
            PRINT "MATRIX NOT FILLED. ";                  &
                  "REMAINING ELEMENTS UNCHANGED"
160     MAT PRINT A(N,M)
170     PRINT \ PRINT "NUM AND NUM2 NOW RESET TO ";       &
                      "CURRENT SIZE OF A"
180     PRINT "NUM IS NOW ="; NUM
190     PRINT "NUM2 IS NOW ="; NUM2
200   END
```

```
RUNNH
ENTER MATRIX DIMENSIONS (MAX OF 100 ELEMENTS)? 2, 3
ENTER ELEMENTS SEPARATED BY COMMAS
? 1, 2, 3, 4
NUM = 2        NUM2 = 1
MATRIX NOT FILLED. REMAINING ELEMENTS UNCHANGED
 1              2              3
 4              0              0

NUM AND NUM2 NOW RESET TO CURRENT SIZE OF A
NUM IS NOW = 2
NUM2 IS NOW = 3
```

Fig. 10.9 More on matrix input and output.

Matrix Initialization and Arithmetic Operations

Matrix Initialization

BASIC-PLUS also provides special operations for initializing matrixes to all zeros, all ones, or to the identity matrix. These operations are described next.

Matrix Initialization Statements

```
MAT array = ZER
MAT array = CON
MAT array = IDN
```

Interpretation: The indicated *array* is initialized. ZER causes *array* to be initialized to all zeros, CON to all ones, and IDN to the identity matrix.

Notes: The identity matrix contains ones along its major diagonal (upper left corner to lower right corner) and zeros everywhere else. If dimensions appear after ZER, CON, or IDN, matrix redimensioning will occur, subject to the same rules listed in the previous section. If a one-dimensional array is initialized to IDN, the array will be reset to all zeros.

Example 10.9 The program in Fig. 10.10 illustrates the effect of the matrix initialization statements.

```
100     DIM A(2,2), B(2,4), C(3,3)
120     MAT A = ZER
130     MAT B = CON
140     MAT C = IDN
150     MAT PRINT A,
160     MAT PRINT B,
170     MAT PRINT C,
180     END

RUNNH
 0              0

 0              0


 1              1              1              1

 1              1              1              1
```

(continued)

1	0	0
0	1	0
0	0	1

Fig. 10.10 Effect of matrix initialization statements.

Matrix Arithmetic Operations*

BASIC-PLUS provides some more operators to simplify the programming of matrix arithmetic. Statements using these operators all begin with the word MAT; they are listed in Table 10.1.

Table 10.1 Matrix Arithmetic Operators

Statement	*Effect*
MAT C = A	Copy matrix A into matrix C
MAT C = A + B	Add matrix A to matrix B—store the sum in matrix C
MAT C = A − B	Subtract matrix B from matrix A—store the difference in matrix C
MAT C = A * B	Multiply matrix A by matrix B—store the product in matrix C
MAT C = (*expr*) * A	Multiply each element of matrix A by *expr* (an arithmetic expression) and store the result (scalar product) in matrix C. The parentheses around *expr* are required.
MAT C = TRN(A)	Store the transpose of matrix A in matrix C
MAT C = INV(A)	Store the inverse of matrix A in matrix C
LET W = DET	Store the determinant of the most recently inverted matrix in the variable W.

For the operations of copy, addition, subtraction, and scalar multiplication, each element of the result matrix, C, is determined by the values of the corresponding elements of the operand matrix (or matrixes) as shown below:

Copy:	$C(i,j) = A(i,j)$
Addition:	$C(i,j) = A(i,j) + B(i,j)$
Subtraction:	$C(i,j) = A(i,j) - B(i,j)$
Scalar Multiplication:	$C(i,j) = (expr) * A(i,j)$

If there are two operand matrixes, they must have the same dimensions. The result matrix, C, will always have the same dimensions as the operand matrix (or matrixes). The result matrix C will be redimensioned (if

---

*This section is optional.

necessary) to the dimensions of the operand matrix (or matrixes). This may result in a

?Subscript out-of-range

error message if array C has fewer elements than needed.

The matrix multiplication operation, however, is somewhat more complicated. The product of two matrixes (A × B) is defined only when matrix A has the same number of columns as matrix B has rows. If A is a matrix with M rows and N columns (M × N matrix) and B is a matrix with N rows and P columns (N × P matrix), the result matrix will have M rows and P columns (M × P matrix).

Each element, C(i,j), of the result matrix is determined by forming the *dot-product* of row i of matrix A with column j of matrix B. The formula for the dot-product is shown below where N is the number of columns of matrix A and the number of rows of matrix B:

$$C(i,j) = A(i,1) \times B(1,j) + A(i,2) \times B(2,j) + \ldots + A(i,N) \times B(N,j)$$

or

$$C(i,j) = \sum_{k=1}^{N} A(i,k) \times B(k,j)$$

In the example below, a matrix with 2 rows and 3 columns (2 × 3 matrix) is multiplied by a matrix with 3 rows and 2 columns (3 × 2 matrix); the result is a matrix with 2 rows and 2 columns (2 × 2 matrix).

$$\begin{vmatrix} 6 & 8 & 7 \\ 3 & 4 & 5 \end{vmatrix} \times \begin{vmatrix} 1 & 2 \\ 2 & 1 \\ -1 & 0 \end{vmatrix} = \begin{vmatrix} 15 & 20 \\ 6 & 10 \end{vmatrix}$$

A(2 × 3) B(3 × 2) C(2 × 2)

Element	Dot-Product of Row (in A) × Column (in B)		Computation
C(1,1)	1	1	6×1+8×2+7×(−1)=15
C(1,2)	1	2	6×2+8×1+7×0=20
C(2,1)	2	1	3×1+4×2+5×(−1)=6
C(2,2)	2	2	3×2+4×1+5×0=10

As shown above, C(1,1) is computed by first multiplying corresponding elements of row 1 of A (values 6, 8, 7) and column 1 of B (values 1, 2, −1), and then adding these three products together.

In the next example, a 2 × 3 matrix is multiplied by a 3 × 1 matrix. The result is a 2 × 1 matrix (2 rows, 1 column). A matrix with a single column is called a *column vector*. A column vector with N rows is the same as a one-dimensional array with N elements.

$$
\underbrace{\begin{vmatrix} 6 & 8 & 7 \\ 3 & 4 & 5 \end{vmatrix}}_{A(2\times 3)} \times \underbrace{\begin{vmatrix} 2 \\ 1 \\ 0 \end{vmatrix}}_{B(3\times 1)} = \underbrace{\begin{vmatrix} 20 \\ 10 \end{vmatrix}}_{C(2\times 1)}
$$

Element	Row (in A) $\times$	Dot-Product of Column (in B)	Computation
C(1,1)	1	1	$6\times 2+8\times 1+7\times 0=20$
C(2,1)	2	1	$3\times 2+4\times 1+5\times 0=10$

Problem 10B A businessman owns three stores; each store carries the same five items of merchandise. He has kept a record of the number of items sold at each store for the four quarters of the current year, and now needs to compute the annual gross sales for each store and the total gross for all three stores.

Discussion: The quarterly sales figures for each store and each item are shown below.

	Quarter 1 Item					Quarter 2 Item					Quarter 3 Item					Quarter 4 Item				
	1	2	3	4	5	1	2	3	4	5	1	2	3	4	5	1	2	3	4	5
Store 1	18	20	30	40	55	25	33	40	60	77	37	20	55	65	70	25	28	42	53	60
Store 2	60	90	80	55	23	30	100	60	45	15	50	80	40	33	20	75	85	93	90	80
Store 3	40	37	62	15	10	38	45	90	20	8	60	70	60	55	18	60	73	82	91	25

Sales data are entered one quarter at a time. For each quarter, the sales data for all three stores and all five items are first read into the 3 × 5 matrix QUARTER.SALES, and then accumulated in the 3 × 5 matrix ANNUAL.SALES. QUARTER.SALES(i,j) will contain the quantity of item j sold at store i during a quarter. After all four quarters of data have been read and accumulated, the matrix ANNUAL.SALES will contain the annual sales figures for each of five items in each of three stores.

We can next multiply this entire matrix by the column vector ITEM.PRICE (provided as input data) in order to obtain the dollar sales volume for each store (stored in a column vector, STORE.VOLUME). This multiplication is illustrated on the next page where a_{ij} represents ANNUAL.SALES(i,j) and p_k represents ITEM.PRICE(k).

$$
\begin{array}{c}
\text{Items} \\
\begin{array}{ccccc}
1 & 2 & 3 & 4 & 5
\end{array}
\end{array}
$$

$$
\begin{array}{l}
\text{Store 1} \\
\text{Store 2} \\
\text{Store 3}
\end{array}
\begin{vmatrix}
a_{11} & a_{12} & a_{13} & a_{14} & a_{15} \\
a_{21} & a_{22} & a_{23} & a_{24} & a_{25} \\
a_{31} & a_{32} & a_{33} & a_{34} & a_{35}
\end{vmatrix}
\times
\begin{vmatrix}
p_1 \\
p_2 \\
p_3 \\
p_4 \\
p_5
\end{vmatrix}
=
\begin{vmatrix}
v_1 \\
v_2 \\
v_3
\end{vmatrix}
$$

ANNUAL.SALES(3×5) STORE.VOLUME (3×1)

ITEM.PRICE(5×1)

where:
$$
\begin{aligned}
v_1 &= a_{11}p_1 + a_{12}p_2 + a_{13}p_3 + a_{14}p_4 + a_{15}p_5 \\
v_2 &= a_{21}p_1 + a_{22}p_2 + a_{23}p_3 + a_{24}p_4 + a_{25}p_5 \\
v_3 &= a_{31}p_1 + a_{32}p_2 + a_{33}p_3 + a_{34}p_4 + a_{35}p_5
\end{aligned}
$$

The product v_1 above represents STORE.VOLUME(1). The elements of the column vector STORE.VOLUME must be summed to find the total gross volume, GROSS.VOLUME, for the business. The data table is shown below; the flow diagrams are drawn in Fig. 10.11 and the program is listed in Fig. 10.12.

DATA TABLE FOR PROBLEM 10B

Input Variables		Program Variables		Output Variables	
QUARTER. SALES(,):	Matrix of quarterly sales figures (size 3×5)	ANNUAL. SALES(,):	Matrix of annual sales figures (size 3×5)	STORE. VOLUME( ):	Vector of annual sales volume for each store (size 3)
ITEM. PRICE( ):	Vector of item prices (size 5)	I:	Loop control variable	GROSS. VOLUME:	Total gross volume

In the program of Fig. 10.12, each of the first four DATA statements contains 15 numbers representing the sales figures for all items and all stores for one quarter. The first five numbers in each DATA statement are stored in the first row of matrix QUARTER.SALES; they represent the sales for Store 1 for that quarter. The last five numbers in each statement are stored in the third row of QUARTER.SALES, and represent the sales for Store 3 for that quarter. The last number in each of these DATA statements would be read into QUARTER.SALES(3,5) and accumulated in ANNUAL.SALES(3,5); the resulting sum represents the quantity of item 5 sold at store 3 over the entire year. The last DATA statement provides the prices for all items (stored in ITEM.PRICE). For the data provided, the initial contents of matrix QUARTER.SALES and the column vector ITEM.PRICE are shown below:

$$
\begin{array}{c}
\text{Items} \\
\begin{array}{ccccc}
1 & 2 & 3 & 4 & 5
\end{array}
\end{array}
$$

	1	2	3	4	5			
Store 1	18	20	30	40	55		15.5	Price of item 1
Store 2	60	90	80	55	23		37.83	Price of item 2
Store 3	40	37	62	15	10		42.55	Price of item 3
							95.63	Price of item 4
							110.87	Price of item 5

QUARTER.SALES(3×5)   ITEM.PRICE(5×1)

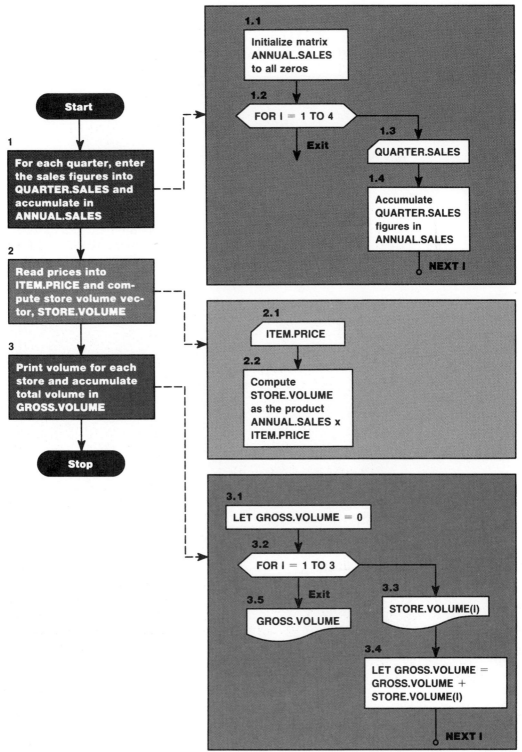

Fig. 10.11 Flow diagrams for Problem 10B.

```
100  !DETERMINE GROSS SALES VOLUME
110  !
120      DIM QUARTER.SALES(3,5), ANNUAL.SALES(3,5)
130      DIM ITEM.PRICE(5), STORE.VOLUME(3)
135  !
140  !ACCUMULATE ANNUAL SALES FIGURES
150      MAT ANNUAL.SALES = ZER
160      FOR I = 1 TO 4
170          MAT READ QUARTER.SALES
180          MAT ANNUAL.SALES = ANNUAL.SALES              &
                            + QUARTER.SALES
185      NEXT I
190      DATA 18, 20, 30, 40, 55, 60, 90, 80, 55,        &
             23, 40, 37, 62, 15, 10
200      DATA 25, 33, 40, 60, 77, 30, 100, 60, 45,       &
             15, 38, 45, 90, 20, 8
210      DATA 37, 20, 55, 65, 70, 50, 80, 40, 33,        &
             20, 60, 70, 60, 55, 18
220      DATA 25, 28, 42, 53, 60, 75, 85, 93, 90,        &
             80, 60, 73, 82, 91, 25
230  !
240  !ENTER PRICES AND COMPUTE VOLUME FOR EACH STORE
250      MAT READ ITEM.PRICE
260      DATA 15.50, 37.83, 42.55, 95.63, 110.87
270      MAT STORE.VOLUME = ANNUAL.SALES * ITEM.PRICE
280  !
290  !COMPUTE TOTAL GROSS VOLUME AND
300  !DISPLAY ANNUAL VOLUME FOR EACH STORE
310      LET GROSS.VOLUME = 0
320      FOR I = 1 TO 3
330          PRINT "GROSS VOLUME AT STORE"; I;          &
                 "= $"; STORE.VOLUME(I)
340          LET GROSS.VOLUME = GROSS.VOLUME            &
                            + STORE.VOLUME(I)
350      NEXT I
360  !
370      PRINT "TOTAL GROSS = $"; GROSS.VOLUME
380  !
390      END
```

```
RUNNH
GROSS VOLUME AT STORE 1 = $ 62449.5
GROSS VOLUME AT STORE 2 = $ 65003.9
GROSS VOLUME AT STORE 3 = $ 48162.6
TOTAL GROSS = $ 175616
```

Fig. 10.12 Program for Problem 10B.

Exercise 10.3: Indicate what changes would be necessary to the program and data of Fig. 10.12 if we wished to compute and display the annual dollar volume by item instead of store. [*Hint*: Multiplying a row vector by a rectangular matrix yields a row vector.]

Exercise 10.4: Indicate what changes would be necessary to the program and data of Fig. 10.12 if the price of each item changed quarterly and we desired to compute the gross volume for each store on a quarterly basis as well as an annual basis.

Exercise 10.5: Test your understanding of the MAT operations of * and + by:
   a) using a calculator and handchecking the computation performed by the program in Fig. 10.12 (use the data provided in this program too).
   b) writing the necessary FOR loops to carry out (simulate) matrix multiply and add.

Exercise 10.6: Let A be a 3 × 5 matrix similar to the annual sales array, ANNUAL.SALES, in Problem 10B, and let P be an array similar to the ITEM.PRICES array. Write the BASIC-PLUS statements to produce the following output.

Annual Sales Matrix
Items

	1	2	3	4	5
Store 1	——	——	——	——	——
Store 2	——	——	——	——	——
Store 3	——	——	——	——	——

Prices Vector

1	2	3	4	5
——	——	——	——	——

The precise spacing of the output is not important, but the general form should be adhered to. *Hint*: You will need nested loops to print out matrix A in the form indicated.

Matrix Transpose, Inverse, and Determinant*

The last three operations listed in Table 10.1 are matrix transpose, inverse, and determinant. The *transpose of a matrix* is a new matrix with rows and columns interchanged. Hence, if matrix A has M rows and N columns, its transpose will have N rows and M columns. Row i of matrix A will be identical to column i of its transpose as shown below.

$$\begin{vmatrix} 6 & 8 & 7 \\ 3 & 4 & 5 \end{vmatrix} \qquad \begin{vmatrix} 6 & 3 \\ 8 & 4 \\ 7 & 5 \end{vmatrix}$$

Matrix A (2×3)   Matrix B (3×2)

The *inverse of a square matrix* is defined to be that matrix which, when multiplied by the original matrix, yields the identity matrix. A *square matrix* has the same number of rows as columns. The inverse of matrix A is represented mathematically as A^{-1}; hence, A^{-1} times A equals I (the identity matrix). This property of matrixes is used in solving systems of simultaneous equations as illustrated in the next example. (*Note*: Not all

---

*This section is optional.

square matrixes have inverses. Those that do not are called *singular matrixes*.) If you attempt to invert a matrix A for which A^{-1} is not defined, BASIC-PLUS will print the diagnostic.

```
?Can't invert matrix
```

Due to the method used by BASIC-PLUS to compute the inverse, the statement MAT A = INV(A) is illegal.

When BASIC-PLUS inverts a matrix A, it automatically computes the *determinant*, |A|, as a byproduct of the inversion. The DET function retrieves this numeric value. If there is no value (because INV has not been called or was called to invert a singular matrix), then DET returns a value of 0. The mathematical definition of |A| is beyond the scope of this text.

Example 10.10 The BASIC-PLUS statements below cause the inverse of the square matrix A to be stored in B and the determinant of A to be stored in the variable X.

```
300 MAT B = INV(A)
310 LET X = DET
```

Example 10.11 In many scientific and engineering problems, it is necessary to find a set of values that satisfy several constraints expressed in the form of a set of *linear equations*. In the following example, a set of linear equations is solved for values of x_1, x_2, and x_3.

$$3x_1 + 2x_2 + x_3 = 7$$
$$x_1 + 3x_2 - 7x_3 = -8$$
$$-2x_1 + x_2 + 5x_3 = 11$$

This set of equations can be represented by the matrix equation

1) AX = B

where A is the coefficient matrix, X is the solution vector of unknowns and B is the constant vector.

$$A = \begin{vmatrix} 3 & 2 & 1 \\ 1 & 3 & -7 \\ -2 & 1 & 5 \end{vmatrix} \quad X = \begin{vmatrix} x_1 \\ x_2 \\ x_3 \end{vmatrix} \quad B = \begin{vmatrix} 7 \\ -8 \\ 11 \end{vmatrix}$$

Multiplying both sides of matrix equation (1) by A^{-1} (inverse of A), we get

$$A^{-1}AX = A^{-1}B$$

or

$$IX = A^{-1}B$$

where I is the identity matrix. Since IX equals X, the product of A^{-1} and B is a vector that represents the values of x_1, x_2 and x_3, which satisfy the original set of equations. The program for computing X is listed in Fig. 10.13.

```
100    !PROGRAM TO SOLVE A SET OF SIMULTANEOUS
110    !EQUATIONS IN 3 UNKNOWNS
120    !
130        DIM A(3,3), X(3), B(3), V(3,3)
140    !
150        MAT READ A
160        DATA 3, 2, 1
180        DATA 1, 3, -7
190        DATA -2, 1, 5
200        PRINT "COEFFICIENT MATRIX"
220        MAT PRINT A,
230    !
240        MAT READ B
250        DATA 7, -8, 11
260        PRINT "VECTOR OF CONSTANTS"
270        MAT PRINT B
280    !
290    !INVERT MATRIX A
300        MAT V = INV(A)
310        PRINT "INVERSE OF THE COEFFICIENT MATRIX IS"
320        MAT PRINT V,
330    !
340    !SOLVE FOR UNKNOWNS X
350        MAT X = V * B
360        PRINT "SOLUTION VECTOR -- X"
370        MAT PRINT X
380    !
390        END

RUNNH
COEFFICIENT MATRIX
 3              2              1

 1              3              -7

-2              1              5

VECTOR OF CONSTANTS
 7
-8
11

INVERSE OF THE COEFFICIENT MATRIX IS
.241758        -.989011E-1    -.186813

.989011E-1     .186813        .241758

.769231E-1     -.769231E-1    .769231E-1

SOLUTION VECTOR -- X
.428571
1.85714
2
```

Fig. 10.13 Program for Example 10.11.

Exercise 10.7: Modify the program and data in Fig. 10.13 to solve the pair of equations:

$$3x_1 + 2x_2 = 14$$
$$x_1 - x_2 = 2$$

 Application of Two-Dimensional Arrays

To further illustrate the use of the two-dimensional array (or matrix), we will present a solved problem in which this data structure plays a central role.

Problem 10C

The little red high school building in Sunflower, Indiana, has three floors, each with five classrooms of various sizes. Each semester the high school runs 15 classes that must be scheduled for the 15 rooms in the building. We will write a program which, given the capacity of each room in the building and the size of each class, will attempt to find a satisfactory room assignment that will accommodate all 15 classes. For those classes that can't be satisfactorily placed, the program will print a "NO ROOM AVAILABLE" message.

Discussion: As part of the data table definition, we must decide how the table of room capacities is to be represented in the memory of the computer. Since the building may be pictured as a two-dimensional structure with three floors (vertical dimension) and five rooms (horizontal dimension), a two-dimensional array should be a convenient structure for representing the capacities of each room in the building. We will read the room capacities into a 3 x 5 array ROOM.CAP.

By using a two-dimensional array, we will be able to determine the number of the room assigned to each class directly from the indexes of the array element that represents that room. For example, if a class is placed in a room with capacity given by ROOM.CAP(2,4), we know that the number of this room is 204. In general, ROOM.CAP(i,j) represents the capacity of the room whose number is the value of the expression

```
i * 100 + j
```

The level one flow diagram for this problem is shown in Fig. 10.14 along with the program system chart. We will handle Steps 1 and 3 through the use of a subroutine (starting at line 1000) that, given the room capacity table and its dimensions, will print the table in a readable form. Step 2 will be performed by a subroutine, (starting at line 2000), which will read and process room requests and print the room assigned, if any. For the purpose of this discussion, we will name these two subroutines PRINTCAP and PROCESS, respectively, even though these names cannot be used in BASIC-PLUS. The data table for the main programs follows; the program is shown in Fig. 10.15.

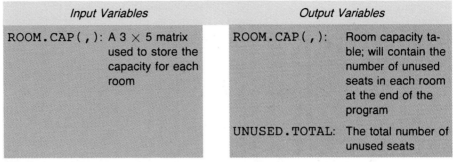

Program Constants

NUM.ROWS = 3: Number of floors

NUM.COLS = 5: Number of rooms per floor

Input Variables		Output Variables	
ROOM.CAP(,):	A 3 × 5 matrix used to store the capacity for each room	ROOM.CAP(,):	Room capacity table; will contain the number of unused seats in each room at the end of the program
		UNUSED.TOTAL:	The total number of unused seats

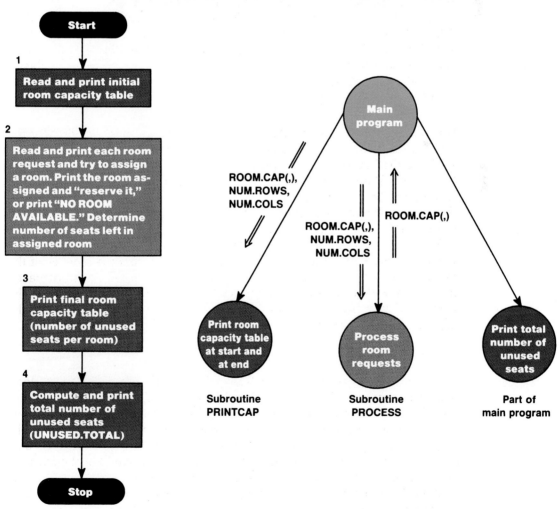

Start

1 Read and print initial room capacity table

2 Read and print each room request and try to assign a room. Print the room assigned and "reserve it," or print "NO ROOM AVAILABLE." Determine number of seats left in assigned room

3 Print final room capacity table (number of unused seats per room)

4 Compute and print total number of unused seats (UNUSED.TOTAL)

Stop

Main program

ROOM.CAP(),
NUM.ROWS,
NUM.COLS

ROOM.CAP(),
NUM.ROWS,
NUM.COLS

ROOM.CAP()

Print room capacity table at start and at end

Process room requests

Print total number of unused seats

Subroutine
PRINTCAP

Subroutine
PROCESS

Part of
main program

Fig. 10.14 Level one flow diagram and program system chart for Problem 10C.

```
110   !ROOM SCHEDULING PROBLEM
120   !
130   !PROGRAM CONSTANTS
140      LET NUM.ROWS = 3      !NUMBER OF FLOORS
150      LET NUM.COLS = 5      !NUMBER OF ROOMS
160   !
170   !ARRAYS USED
180      DIM ROOM.CAP(3,5)
185   !
190   !ENTER ROOM CAPACITIES TABLE
200      MAT READ ROOM.CAP
210      DATA 30, 30, 15, 30, 40
220      DATA 25, 30, 25, 10, 110
230      DATA 62, 30, 40, 40, 30
240   !
250   !PRINT ROOM CAPACITY TABLE
255      PRINT "INITIAL TABLE OF ROOM CAPACITIES"
260      PRINT
265      GOSUB 1000    !CALL PRINT.CAP
270      PRINT
280   !
290   !SET UP HEADING FOR ROOM ASSIGNMENT TABLE
300      PRINT "ROOM ASSIGNMENT TABLE"
310      PRINT "CLASS ID", "CLASS SIZE",
320      PRINT "ROOM", "CAPACITY"
340   !
350   !PRINT AND PROCESS EACH ROOM REQUEST
360      GOSUB 2000    !CALL PROCESS
365      PRINT
370   !
380   !PRINT FINAL ROOM CAPACITY TABLE
390      PRINT "TABLE OF UNUSED SEATS IN EACH ROOM"
395      PRINT
400      GOSUB 1000    !CALL PRINT.CAP
410   !
420   !COMPUTE AND PRINT TOTAL NUMBER OF UNUSED SEATS
430      LET UNUSED.TOTAL = 0
440      FOR I = 1 TO NUM.ROWS
450         LET UNUSED.TOTAL = UNUSED.TOTAL              &
                             + ABS(ROOM.CAP(I,J))       &
            FOR J = 1 TO NUM.COLS
460      NEXT I
470      PRINT
475      PRINT "THE TOTAL NUMBER OF UNUSED ";           &
               "SEATS IS"; UNUSED.TOTAL
480   !
490      STOP
```

Fig. 10.15 Main program for Problem 10C.

Subroutines Referenced by Main Program

PRINTCAP (line 1000): Used to print the contents of the two-dimensional array ROOM.CAP (left as an exercise)

PROCESS (line 2000): Reads and processes each room request consisting of a class ID and a class size. Determines the room number to be assigned (if one is available) and prints the number

For each room request, subroutine PROCESS will read a pair of data items representing the class identification (CLASS.ID$) and class size (CLASS.SIZE). Subroutine PROCESS should find a room that is large enough to hold each class if one is available. (The ideal situation would be to find a room whose capacity exactly matches the class size.) For each class, PROCESS will print, in tabular form, the class ID and size and the room number (CLASS.ROOM) and capacity of the room assigned to the class. The flow diagrams for PROCESS are shown in Fig. 10.16 along with a third level addition to the program system chart. The data table for PROCESS follows.

DATA TABLE FOR SUBROUTINE PROCESS (LINE 2000)

Subroutine Constant

NUM.CLASSES = 15:   Number of classes

Global Variables

ROOM.CAP(,):   Room capacity table (input and output)
NUM.ROWS, NUM.COLS: Dimensions of ROOM.CAP (input)

Local Input Variables	Local Subroutine Variables	Local Output Variables
CLASS.ID$: Identification code for each class	CLASS.I: Loop control variable for loop to process each class	CLASS.ROOM: Number of the room assigned to each class
CLASS.SIZE: Size of each class		Also required as output is the capacity of the room assigned

A third level module, the function FNASSIGN% will be called by PROCESS to perform Step 1.3 in Fig. 10.16. This function will search the room capacity table, ROOM.CAP, to find a room of size CLASS.SIZE or greater. It will determine the subscripts CLASS.FL.IX and CLASS.RM.IX of an assigned room, if one is found, and indicate success or failure by returning a logical value (-1% for success, 0% for failure). The additional data table entries for PROCESS are shown next along with a description of function FNASSIGN%.

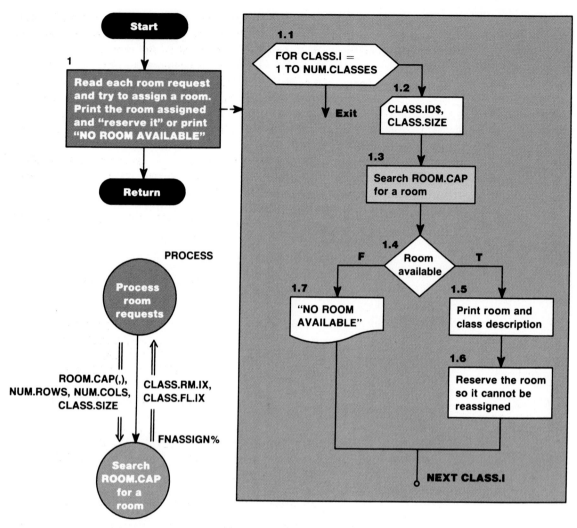

Fig. 10.16 Flow diagrams and program system chart for PROCESS.

ADDITIONAL DATA TABLE ENTRIES FOR PROCESS		
	Local Subroutine Variables	
	`CLASS.FL.IX,` `CLASS.RM.IX:`	Indexes specifying room to be assigned to a class; returned by `FNASSIGN%` if a room is found
	Function Referenced by PROCESS	
	`FNASSIGN%:`	Searches the two-dimensional array, `ROOM.CAP`, to find the indexes, `CLASS.FL.IX` and `CLASS.RM.IX` of a room that is greater than or equal to a specified class size, `CLASS.SIZE`. If such a room is found, a value of -1% (true) is returned; otherwise 0%(false) is returned.

There are probably many ways to resolve the problem indicated in Step 1.6 of the flow diagram for PROCESS (Fig. 10.16). When a room is assigned, the program will compute the number of unused seats in the room. To ensure that this room cannot be reassigned to another class, the program will negate this value when the assignment is made. Exactly why this works will become clearer when function FNASSIGN% is written. We can now write subroutine PROCESS (see Fig. 10.17). An additional local variable, CLASS.TEMP, is used to eliminate unnecessary references to ROOM.CAP.

The only task remaining is the specification of function FNASSIGN%. The algorithm that we will use to find a room for a class size, CLASS.SIZE, may be summarized as follows:

Search ROOM.CAP and find the smallest room that is greater than or equal to CLASS.SIZE and is still not assigned.

```
2000  !SUBROUTINE TO PROCESS EACH ROOM REQUEST
2020  !
2030  !GLOBAL VARIABLES
2040  !   IN:   ROOM.CAP( , ) - ROOM CAPACITY TABLE
2050  !         NUM.ROWS, NUM.COLS - DIMENSION OF
2060  !                          ROOM.CAP
2070  !   OUT:  ROOM.CAP( , ) - CAPACITY TABLE WITH
2075  !                          SEATS LEFT IN EACH
2080  !                          ROOM (NEGATED VALUES)
2090  !
2100  !LOCAL VARIABLES CHANGED - CLASS.ID$,
2105  !      CLASS.SIZE, CLASS.I, CLASS.ROOM
2110  !      CLASS.FL.IX, CLASS.RM.IX, CLASS.TEMP
2120  !
2130  !SUBROUTINE CONSTANT
2140     LET NUM.CLASSES = 15   !NUMBER OF CLASSES
2150  !
2160  !READ AND PROCESS EACH ROOM REQUEST
2170     FOR CLASS.I = 1 TO NUM.CLASSES
2180        READ CLASS.ID$, CLASS.SIZE
2190        !SEARCH FOR A ROOM USING FNASSIGN%
2200        IF FNASSIGN%(CLASS.SIZE) THEN GOSUB 3000 &
                ELSE GOSUB 4000
2210     NEXT CLASS.I
2220  !
2230     DATA CIS1,37, CIS2,55, CIS3,100, CIS10,26
2240     DATA CIS11,26, CIS25,39, CIS30,30, CIS31,56
2250     DATA CIS101,20, CIS120,15, CIS203,22
2260     DATA CIS301,10, CIS302,5, CIS324,28
2265     DATA CIS330,25
2270  !
2275     RETURN
2280  !END OF SUBROUTINE PROCESS
```

(continued)

```
2290  !
2300  !
3000  !SUBROUTINES FOR IF-THEN-ELSE AT LINE 2200
3010  !IF CLASS ASSIGNED THEN
3020  !COMPUTE ROOM NUMBER AND RESERVE IT
3030      LET CLASS.ROOM = CLASS.FL.IX * 100         &
                          + CLASS.RM.IX
3040      LET CLASS.TEMP =                           &
              ROOM.CAP(CLASS.FL.IX,CLASS.RM.IX)
3050      PRINT CLASS.ID$, CLASS.SIZE, CLASS.ROOM,   &
              CLASS.TEMP
3060      LET ROOM.CAP(CLASS.FL.IX,CLASS.RM.IX) =    &
                          -(CLASS.TEMP - CLASS.SIZE)
3070      RETURN
4000  !ELSE NO ROOM AVAILABLE
4010      PRINT "NO ROOM AVAILABLE FOR "; CLASS.ID$
4020      RETURN
4030  !END OF SUBROUTINES FOR IF-THEN-ELSE (LINE 2200)
```

Fig. 10.17 PROCESS subroutine for Problem 10C.

This is called the *best fit* algorithm because the unassigned room with the least excess capacity is chosen for each class. (The ideal situation is to find a room that fits exactly.) This algorithm assigns as many classes to suitable rooms as is physically possible without later juggling room assignments. The implementation of this search requires two nested loops with loop control variables AS.I and AS.J. The flow diagrams for FNASSIGN% are drawn in Fig. 10.18. The data table follows.

DATA TABLE FOR FUNCTION FNASSIGN%

Parameters	
CLASS.SIZE: Size of class to be assigned a room	

Global Variables	
ROOM.CAP(,):	Room capacity table (input)
NUM.ROWS,NUM.COLS:	Dimensions of ROOM.CAP (input)
CLASS.FL.IX,CLASS.RM.IX:	Indexes of assigned room (output)

Local Function Variables	
AS.I:	Outer loop control variable (row subscript)
AS.J:	Inner loop control variable (column subscript)

As shown in Fig. 10.18, function FNASSIGN% uses the following criteria to locate the room with smallest capacity that is larger than CLASS.SIZE.

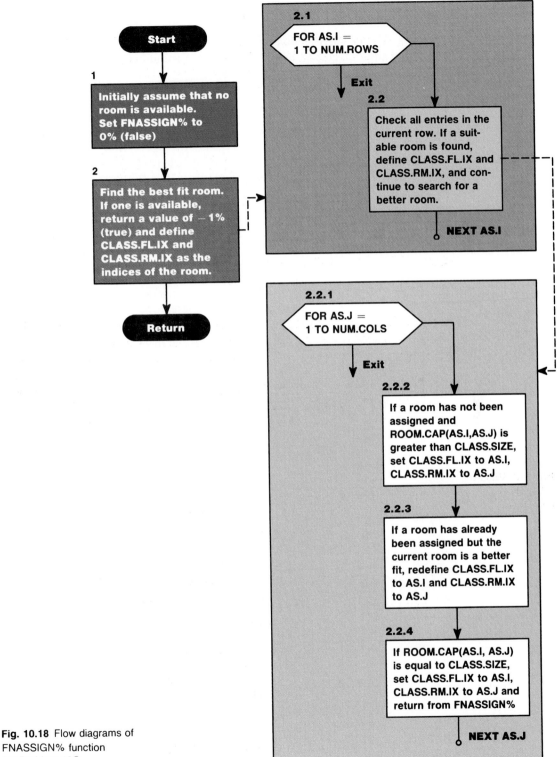

Fig. 10.18 Flow diagrams of
FNASSIGN% function
for Problem 10C.

1. When the first room with capacity larger than CLASS.SIZE is found, it is chosen (perhaps temporarily) to be the best-fit room (Step 2.2.2).
2. If, subsequently, a room of sufficient capacity is located that is smaller than the current best-fit room, the new room becomes the best-fit room (Step 2.2.3).
3. If a room is found with a capacity equal to CLASS.SIZE, this room is chosen as the best-fit room and the search is complete (Step 2.2.4).

We will implement these steps using a multiple-alternative decision structure. The implementation of function FNASSIGN% is shown in Fig. 10.19 and a sample run of the complete program is shown in Fig. 10.20. Three additional variables needed to write the function are described in the following data table section.

ADDITIONAL DATA TABLE ENTRIES FOR FNASSIGN%

	Local Function Variables
AS.SIZE:	Used to save the size of the current room being checked as a candidate. This variable eliminates four references to a two-dimensional array inside the multiple alternative decision structure.
AS.FOUND%:	Program flag used to indicate whether or not a successful room assignment has been made for the current CLASS.SIZE.

```
5000     DEF* FNASSIGN%(CLASS.SIZE)
5010 !
5020 !FUNCTION TO ASSIGN A ROOM TO A CLASS
5030 !
5040 !PARAMETER DEFINITIONS --
5050 !   CLASS.SIZE - SIZE OF CLASS TO BE ASSIGNED
5060 !
5070 !GLOBAL VARIABLES
5080 !   IN:  ROOM.CAP( , ), NUM.ROWS, NUM.COLS -
5090 !        ROOM CAPACITY TABLE AND DIMENSIONS
5100 !   OUT: CLASS.FL.IX, CLASS.RM.IX - INDEXES OF
5105 !        ASSIGNED ROOM
5110 !
5120 !LOCAL VARIABLES CHANGED - AS.I, AS.J, AS.SIZE,
5125 !                          AS.FOUND%
5130 !
5140 !ASSUME NO ROOM AVAILABLE
5150     LET FNASSIGN% = 0%     !FALSE
5160     LET AS.FOUND% = 0%     !FALSE
5165 !
5170 !FIND THE BEST FIT ROOM
```

(continued)

```
5180    !OUTER LOOP, CHECK EACH FLOOR
5190        FOR AS.I = 1 TO NUM.ROWS
5200          !INNER LOOP, CHECK EACH ROOM ON FLOOR
5210          FOR AS.J = 1 TO NUM.COLS
5220            LET AS.SIZE = ROOM.CAP(AS.I,AS.J)
5230            IF AS.SIZE > CLASS.SIZE AND            &
                    NOT AS.FOUND% THEN                 &
                    !FIRST FIT-                        &
                    !MAKE ASSIGNMENT BUT KEEP LOOKING  &
                    GOSUB 6000                         &
                ELSE IF AS.SIZE > CLASS.SIZE AND       &
                        AS.SIZE < ROOM.CAP(CLASS.FL.IX,&
                            CLASS.RM.IX) THEN          &
                    !BETTER FIT-                       &
                    !MAKE ASSIGNMENT BUT KEEP LOOKING  &
                    GOSUB 6000                         &
                ELSE IF AS.SIZE = CLASS.SIZE THEN      &
                    !PERFECT FIT-                      &
                    !MAKE ASSIGNMENT AND STOP LOOKING  &
                    GOSUB 6000                         &
                    \LET FNASSIGN% = -1%    !TRUE      &
                    \GOTO 6070   !EXIT LOOP, RETURN
5250          NEXT AS.J
5260        NEXT AS.I
5270    !
5280    !ALL FLOORS HAVE BEEN SEARCHED
5290        LET FNASSIGN% = AS.FOUND%
5300        GOTO 6070    !RETURN FROM FNASSIGN%
5310    !
5320    !
6000    !SUBROUTINE TO MAKE ROOM ASSIGNMENT TO CLASS
6010        LET CLASS.FL.IX = AS.I
6020        LET CLASS.RM.IX = AS.J
6030        LET AS.FOUND% = -1%    !TRUE
6040        RETURN
6050    !END OF SUBROUTINE TO MAKE ROOM ASSIGNMENT
6060    !
6070        FNEND    !FNASSIGN%
6080    !
6090        END    !ROOM SCHEDULING PROGRAM
```

Fig. 10.19 Function FNASSIGN% for Problem 10C.

INITIAL TABLE OF ROOM CAPACITIES

| | ROOM NUMBER | | | | |
FLOOR	01	02	03	04	05
1	30	30	15	30	40
2	25	30	25	10	110
3	62	30	40	40	30

(continued)

```
ROOM ASSIGNMENT TABLE
CLASS ID          CLASS SIZE      ROOM            CAPACITY
CIS1              37              105             40
CIS2              55              301             62
CIS3              100             205             110
CIS10             26              101             30
CIS11             26              102             30
CIS25             39              303             40
CIS30             30              104             30
NO ROOM AVAILABLE FOR CIS31
CIS101            20              201             25
CIS120            15              103             15
CIS203            22              203             25
CIS301            10              204             10
CIS302            5               202             30
CIS324            28              302             30
CIS330            25              305             30


TABLE OF UNUSED SEATS IN EACH ROOM


                            ROOM NUMBER
FLOOR           01          02          03          04          05
-----           --          --          --          --          --
  1             4           4           0           0           3
  2             5           25          3           0           10
  3             7           2           1           40          5

THE TOTAL NUMBER OF UNUSED SEATS IS 109
Stop at line 490
```

Fig. 10.20 Sample run of problem 10C.

Program Style

Use of "logical" variables as program flags

In earlier programs, we used string variables and the string values
"TRUE" and "FALSE" to implement program flags. In function
FNASSIGN%, the "logical" variable AS.FOUND% and the "logical"
values -1% (true) and 0% (false) are used instead. We did this to be
consistent with the use of FNASSIGN% as a "logical" function.

Exercise 10.8: Complete the program system for Problem 10C by writing the
subroutine PRINTCAP. Your subroutine output should be similar to the tables in
Fig. 10.20.

Exercise 10.9: The algorithm used in function FNASSIGN% is called a best-fit
algorithm, because the room having the capacity that was closest to the class size
was assigned to each class. Another algorithm that might have been used is called
a *first-fit* algorithm. In this algorithm, the first room having a capacity greater than
or equal to the class size is assigned to the class (no further searching for a room
is carried out). Modify the flow diagram (Fig. 10.18) and program (Fig. 10.19) to re-

flect the first-fit algorithm. (You will see that this algorithm is simpler than best-fit.) Apply both algorithms using the room capacities shown in the program in Fig. 10.15, and the following 15 class sizes: 38, 41, 6, 26, 28, 21, 25, 97, 12, 36, 28, 27, 29, 30, 18. Exactly what is the problem with the first-fit algorithm?

10.6 Common Programming Errors

The errors encountered using two-dimensional arrays are similar to those encountered in processing one-dimensional arrays. The most frequent errors are likely to be subscript range errors. These errors may be more common now because two subscripts are involved in an array reference, introducing added complexity and confusion. BASIC-PLUS will check each subscript to see whether it is within range. Nevertheless, it is good practice for you to verify for yourself that all subscripts are correct by printing any suspect subscript values during program testing.

Other kinds of errors arise because of the complex nesting of FOR loops when they are used to manipulate two-dimensional arrays. Care must be taken to ensure that the subscript order is consistent with the nesting structure of the loops. Inconsistent usage may not result in an error diagnostic but will likely produce incorrect program results. You should also be careful not to confuse the row and column subscripts in an array.

As illustrated in Problem 10C, use of two-dimensional arrays can result in rather complicated and long statements. It is wise to shorten such statements whenever possible by using additional, temporary variables (such as AS.SIZE in FNASSIGN%, and CLASS.TEMP in subroutine PROCESS) to save intermediate results or simply to eliminate multiple references to the same matrix element (CLASS.TEMP = ROOM.CAP(CLASS.FL.IX, CLASS.RM.IX)). This will not only help reduce typing errors, but also may make your program more efficient.

10.7 Summary

In this chapter, we have introduced a more general form of the array. This form is useful in representing data that are most naturally thought of in terms of tables or other two-dimensional structures. The two-dimensional array is convenient for representing rectangular tables of information such as matrixes, game-board patterns and business-related tables.

We have seen examples of the manipulation of individual array elements through the use of nests of FOR loops. The correspondence between the loop control variables and the array subscripts determines the order in which the array elements are processed.

Special matrix operators for reading, printing, and initializing two-dimensional arrays were also described in this chapter; the matrix arithmetic operators and the inverse, transpose, and determinant operators were introduced. The use of the matrix operators was illustrated in several small examples and in two problems. A summary of the statements and operators introduced in this chapter is given in Table 10.2.

Table 10.2 Summary of BASIC Features Introduced in this Chapter

Statement	Effect
Matrix declaration	
`DIM A(4,2), B(3,3), C$(2,5)`	Declares A to be a matrix with four rows and two columns; B has three rows and three columns; C$ has two rows and five columns.
Matrix read	

`MAT READ A, B, C$`
`MAT INPUT A`
`MAT INPUT B`
`MAT INPUT C$`
	The MAT READ and MAT INPUT statements read the first eight data items into matrix A, the next nine data items into matrix B, and ten string data items into matrix C$. Only one array may be specified in a MAT INPUT statement.

Matrix print	

`MAT PRINT A,`
`MAT PRINT A;`
`MAT PRINT A`
	Prints the eight elements of matrix A in four rows and two columns. All output is zoned if a comma is used and packed if a semicolon is used. Output is printed in a single column if neither the comma nor semicolon is used.

Matrix initialization	

`MAT A = ZER`
`MAT A = CON`
`MAT A = IDN`
	Initializes A to all zeros.
	Initializes A to all ones.
	Initializes A to the identity matrix.

Matrix arithmetic	
`MAT C = A`	Copy matrix A into matrix C.
`MAT C = A + B`	Add matrix A to matrix B—store the sum in matrix C.
`MAT C = A - B`	Subtract matrix B from matrix A—store the difference in matrix C.
`MAT C = A * B`	Multiply matrix A by matrix B—store the product in matrix C.
`MAT C = (2) * A`	Multiply each element of matrix A by 2 and store the result (scalar product) in matrix C.
`MAT C = TRN(A)`	Store the transpose of matrix A in matrix C.
`MAT C = INV(A)`	Store the inverse of square matrix A in matrix C.
`W = LET`	Stores the determinant of the most recently inverted matrix in the variable W.

Programming Problems

10D Write a program that reads in a tic-tac-toe board and determines the best move for player X. Use the following strategy: Consider all squares that are empty and evaluate potential moves into them. If the move fills the third square in a row, column, or diagonal that already has two X's, add 50 to the score; if it fills the third square in a row, column, or diagonal with two O's, add 25 to the score. For each row, column, or diagonal containing this move that will have two X's and one blank, add 10 to the score; add eight for each row, column, or diagonal containing this move that will have one O, one X, and one blank; add four for each row, column, or diagonal which will have one X and the rest blanks. Select the move that scores the highest.

The possible moves for the board below are numbered. Their scores are shown to the right of the board. Move 5 is selected.

1	O	X
2	X	3
O	4	5

1: 10 + 8 = 18
2: 10 + 8 = 18
3: 10 + 10 = 20
4: 8
5: 10 + 10 + 8 = 28

10E Each card of a poker hand will be represented by a pair of integers: the first integer represents the suit; the second integer represents the value of the card. For example: 4, 10 would be the 10 of spades; 3, 11 the jack of hearts; 2, 12 the queen of diamonds; 1, 13 the king of clubs; 4, 1 the ace of spades. Read in the pairs for five cards of a poker hand and represent them in a 4 × 13 array. A one should be placed in the five array elements with row and column indexes corresponding to the cards entered. Evaluate the poker hand. Provide subroutines or functions to determine whether the hand is a flush (all one suit), a straight (five consecutive cards of different suits), a straight flush (five consecutive cards of one suit), 4 of a kind, a full house (3 of one kind, 2 of another), 3 of a kind, 2 pair, or 1 pair.

10F Represent the cards of a bridge hand by a pair of integers, as described in Problem 10E. Read the 13 cards of a bridge hand into a 4 × 13 array. Compute the number of points in the hand. Score 4 for each ace, 3 for a king, 2 for a queen, 1 for a jack. Also, add 3 points for any suit not represented, 2 for any suit with only one card that is not a face card (jack or higher), 1 for any suit with only two cards, neither of which is a face card.

10G *Continuation of Problem 10C.* If, in the room scheduling problem (10C), we removed the restriction of a single building, and wished to write the program to accommodate an entire campus of buildings, each with varying numbers of floors and varying numbers of available rooms on each floor, the choice of a two-dimensional array for storing room capacities may prove inconvenient. Instead, we would have to use two *parallel arrays*, ROOM.ID$ and ROOM.CAP, to store the identification of each room (building and number) and its size. Write a program, with appropriate subroutines, to solve the room scheduling problem using the 15 class sizes given in Exercise 10.9, and the campus room table shown next.

Room ID		
Building	*Number*	*Room size*
HUMA	1003	30
MATH	11	25
MUSI	2	62
LANG	701	30
MATH	12	30
ART	2	30
EDUC	61	15
HUMA	1005	25
ART	1	40
ENG	101	30
MATH	3	10
EDUC	63	40
LANG	702	40
MUSI	5	110
HUMA	1002	30

10H The results from the mayor's race have been reported by each precinct as follows, one input card per precinct:

Precinct	Candidate A	Candidate B	Candidate C	Candidate D
1	192	48	206	37
2	147	90	312	21
3	186	12	121	38
4	114	21	408	39
5	267	13	382	29

Write a program to do the following:

a) Print out the table with appropriate headings for the rows and columns.
b) Compute and print the total number of votes received by each candidate and the percent of the total votes cast.
c) If any one candidate received over 50% of the votes, the program should print a message declaring that candidate the winner.
d) If no candidate received over 50% of the votes, the program should print a message declaring a run-off between the two candidates receiving the largest number of votes; the two candidates should be identified by their letter names.
e) Run the program once with the above data and once with candidate C receiving only 108 votes in precinct 4.

The input for this program might consist of five DATA statements, each containing a precinct number and the vote totals in that precinct for all candidates.

10I The game of Life, invented by John H. Conway, is supposed to model the genetic laws for birth, survival, and death. (See *Scientific American*, October 1970, p. 120.) We will play it on a board consisting of 25 squares in the horizontal and vertical directions. Each square can be empty or contain an X indicating the presence of an organism. Every square (except the border squares) has eight neighbors. The small square shown in the segment of the board drawn below connects the neighbors of the organism in row 3, column 3.

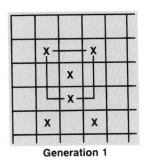

Generation 1

The next generation of organisms is determined according to the following criteria:

1. *Birth*: An organism will be born in each empty location that has exactly three neighbors.
2. *Death*: An organism with four or more organisms as neighbors will die from overcrowding. An organism with fewer than two neighbors will die from loneliness.
3. *Survival*: An organism with two or three neighbors will survive to the next generation.

Generations 2 and 3 for the previous sample are shown below.

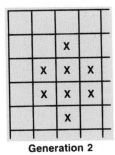

Generation 2

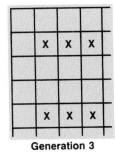

Generation 3

Read in an initial configuration of organisms and print the original game array. Calculate the next generation of organisms in a new array, copy the new array into the original game array, and repeat the cycle for as many generations as you wish. Provide a program system chart. *Hint*: Assume that the borders of the game array are infertile regions where organisms can neither survive nor be born; you will not have to process the border squares.

10J Another approach to solving the room scheduling program would be to first read all class requests into an array and then sort the requests in decreasing order by size. Then apply the first-fit algorithm described in Exercise 10.8. Provide a program system corresponding to this solution.

Formatted Output and Files

In this chapter, we describe two additional features of input and output in BASIC-PLUS: formatted output and files. Formatted output features enable us to specify explicitly the appearance of a program output line by using special symbols and codes.

As we have seen already, programs may be stored as files on a secondary storage device (e.g., a disk). These files may be transferred into memory and then executed. In this chapter we will learn how to use files for the storage and organization of data, as well as programs.

Formatting Output with PRINT USING Statements

The PRINT USING Statement

BASIC-PLUS follows certain conventions for displaying output list items in a PRINT statement. For example, numbers are printed with a single trailing blank and a leading blank or minus sign; strings are printed without leading or trailing blanks. If a comma is used as a separator between two output list items, the second output value is printed at the start of the next print zone where print zones begin at columns 1, 15, 29, 43, etc. In this section, we learn how to override these conventions and provide our own control of the *format* or appearance of a program output line with a PRINT USING statement.

Example 11.1 A PRINT USING statement and the output it generates (in immediate mode) are shown next.

```
LET X = -15.5462
PRINT USING "###.## ###.### #####.", X, X, X
-15.55 -15.546    -16.
```

In this example, the reserved word USING is followed by an *image string* that contains three *fields* (separated by blanks). Each field contains a single decimal point and one or more "#" symbols that represent digits. The output list (X, X, X) specifies that the value of X is to be printed three times (using each field once).

The first field (###.##) specifies that the value of X (-15.5462) is to be printed using only two decimal places; the value of X is *rounded* to -15.55 and printed. The next field specifies that X should be printed using three decimal places; a blank space separates these two values as there is a blank space between the corresponding fields in the image string. The last field specifies that X should be rounded to the nearest whole number (-16.) and printed. There are two more "#" symbols in this field than digits (including the "-"sign); consequently, two extra blank spaces precede the value printed.

In PRINT USING statements, it makes no difference whether the output list items are separated by commas or semicolons since the spacing between fields determines the relative positions of the output values. However, a comma or semicolon at the end of an output list will suppress the normal carriage return/line feed at the end of the printed line just as with an ordinary PRINT statement.

PRINT USING Statement

PRINT USING *image, output list*

Interpretation: The *image* is a string variable, constant or expression that specifies the format of the output line. The *output list* is a list of items to be printed. The fields in the *image* and the items in the *output list* are associated in left-to-right order. If there are not enough fields in the image, then all or part of the *image* will be reused until the output list is exhausted.

Note: Each numeric field in the *image* must contain enough "#" symbols to the left of the decimal point to accommodate all the digits required and a "-" sign if the number is negative. If there are not enough "#" symbols to the left of the decimal point, a "%" symbol is printed followed by the number in normal or unformatted form. If there are fewer "#" symbols than digits to the right of the decimal point, the output value will be rounded before it is printed.

Other Formatting Symbol for Numeric Fields

Besides the symbol "#", there are several other characters that have special meaning in a numeric field. These include the circumflex "^", asterisk "*" , minus sign "-", dollar sign "$", and comma ",".

Example 11.2 The PRINT USING statements below illustrate the meaning of the symbols "*" and "-" in the image string. All three output list items are printed using the same field.

```
PRINT USING "**##.##-", 11.123, -1.05, 155.6
**11.12
***1.05-
*155.60
```

As shown above, if a numeric field begins with two asterisks, then any unused spaces to the left of the decimal point are filled with asterisks instead of blanks.

Negative numbers cannot be printed with leading asterisks unless the minus sign is printed after the number. This is prescribed by appending the "-" sign to the end of the associated field.

This example also shows that it is not necessary for the number of fields in an image to be the same as the number of output list items. If there are fewer fields than output list items, then the image will be reused. Each time it is reused, a new output line is started. If there are more fields than images, then the extra fields will be ignored.

Example 11.3 Image fields may also be used to print the symbol "$" before a number or to insert the symbol "," making large numbers more readable.

```
PRINT USING "$$#,###.##-", 11504.5, 1504.5, -504
$11,504.50
 $1,504.50
    $504.00-
```

As shown above, a "$" symbol is printed to the left of the first digit if the field begins with two "$" symbols. The comma will be printed only when four or five digits precede the decimal points. Note that the decimal points are all aligned. The "−" sign must follow a negative number that begins with a "$" symbol.

Example 11.4 The symbol "^" is used in an image field to prescribe exponential format (scientific notation).

```
PRINT USING "##^^^^", -10000, 1.535, .0123
-1E 04
15E-01
12E-03

PRINT USING "#.##^^^^", -10000, 1.535, .0123
%-10000
1.54E 00
1.23E-02
```

Four "^" symbols are required at the end of each field to indicate scientific notation. The remaining portion of the field specifies how the *mantissa* of the number will be printed. If this portion of the field cannot accommodate all of the digits, the most significant ones are rounded and printed; the exponent is adjusted accordingly. Note that −10000 cannot be printed in exponential format using the second image above, as both the "−" sign and the digit 1 must precede the decimal point and there is only space for one character.

Table 11.1 provides a summary of the symbols that may appear in a numeric field.

Table 11.1 Table of Numeric Symbols for PRINT USING

Data to be Printed	Image Field	Printed Value
-4567.35	"#####.#"	-4567.4
-4567.35	"#####.###"	-4567.350
-4567.35	"####.##-"	4567.35-
-4567.35	"$$#,###.##-"	$4,567.35-
-4567.35	"**#,###.##-"	**4,567.35-
-4567.35	"####^^^^"	-457E 01
-4567.35	"##.##^^^^"	-4.57E 03

Example 11.5 Besides the special characters discussed above, it is possible to include any other character in an image. These characters are printed exactly as they appear. It is also possible to assign an image string to a string variable and reference this variable in a PRINT USING statement as shown next.

```
LET IM$ = "X = ##.### Y = ###.#"
PRINT USING IM$, 13.86, 210.582
X = 13.860 Y = 210.6
```

The strings "X = " and "Y = " are inserted in the output line above in the positions prescribed by the image string assigned to IM$.

String Fields

So far we have described the use of numeric fields only. There are also fields that specify the format of string values. These fields use the characters "!" and "\" (backslash).

Example 11.6 The exclamation point "!" is used to prescribe a single character field.

```
PRINT USING "! !!", "AB", "CD", "EF"
A CE
```

As shown above, only the first character of each string value is printed; the rest are ignored. A space is printed between the first two string values as prescribed by the image "! !!".

Example 11.7 A pair of backslash symbols "\" is used to specify a string field longer than one character. The string field specified includes the two symbols "\" and the spaces between them as indicated below.

```
LET ST$ = "ABCD"
PRINT USING "\ \ \\ \   \", ST$, ST$, ST$
ABCD AB ABCD
```

The backslash pairs in the image above specify fields of length 4, 2, and 5, respectively. Each string is printed left justified in its field and a space is left between strings. If the spaces between backslash pairs were removed, the string values would be printed without spaces between them.

Example 11.8 It is, of course, permissible to mix string and numeric fields in the same image string as shown next.

```
PRINT USING "\ \ ###", "JOSEPH", 155
JOSE 155
```

Example 11.9 PRINT USING statements can be used to align table headings and output values. Two string fields of length 10 are specified in the image string at line 120; the image string at line 130 describes two numeric fields of length 6, with two decimal places each. The numeric fields are centered under each string field.

```
120 LET HEAD$ =    "\         \     \         \"
130 LET TAB.VAL$ = "  ###.##          ###.##"
```

The statement

```
140 PRINT USING HEAD$, "FAHRENHEIT", "CENTIGRADE"
```

would cause each output string to be printed in one of the string fields. The statement

```
230 PRINT USING TAB.VAL$, FAHREN, CENT
```

could be used in a loop to center a list of temperature values under each of the column headings printed by line 140. A portion of a sample output table is shown below.

```
FAHRENHEIT        CENTIGRADE
    32.00             0.00
    44.50             6.94
    57.00            13.89
      .                 .
      .                 .
      .                 .
```

Example 11.10   The PRINT and PRINT USING statements

```
130 PRINT USING "\    \ #      ", "VALUE", I;                     &
        FOR I = 1 TO 5
135 PRINT
140 PRINT USING "####.##      ", PRICE(I);                       &
        FOR I = 1 TO 5
145 PRINT
```

would create the table format

```
VALUE 1      VALUE 2      VALUE 3      VALUE 4      VALUE 5
####.##      ####.##      ####.##      ####.##      ####.##
```

where line 140 causes an element of array PRICE to be printed in each field ####.## above. The FOR statement modifier in line 130 causes the PRINT USING statement to be repeated five times; each time the string "VALUE" is printed followed by a space and the value of I. If the semicolon preceding the word FOR in line 130 were omitted, each output pair would be printed on a separate line (Why?). Lines 135 and 145 are needed to terminate each output line.

Exercise 11.1: For each set of variable values below, write the output line printed by the statements

```
150 LET F$ = "\   \ ###.# SECONDS"
160 PRINT USING F$, L$, X
```

where there are three spaces between the backslash characters.

a) L$ = "FABIAN" and X = 62.5
b) L$ = "THE DOCTOR" and X = 125.27
c) L$ = "HOSS" and X = 1026.2
d) L$ = "ACE" and X = -41

Exercise 11.2: Consider the variable definitions shown below.

S1	S2	S3	L$	F$	H	R	P
219	40	1677	DOG	HOT	40	4.5	180

Write the PRINT USING statements required to produce the following output:

```
Line 1    SOCIAL SECURITY NUMBER 219-40-1677
Line 2
Line 3    DOG, HOT
Line 4
Line 5    HOURS RATE PAY
Line 6    40.00 4.50 180.00
```

Exercise 11.3: Show the output produced by the statement

```
PRINT USING IM$, -1158.45
```

for each of the values of IMAGE$ below.

```
a)  LET IM$ = "#####"
b)  LET IM$ = "##,###.##"
c)  LET IM$ = "##,###.##-"
d)  LET IM$ = "**#####.#-"
e)  LET IM$ = "$$###,###.##-"
f)  LET IM$ = "##.##^^^^"
```

Exercise 11.4: Provide the PRINT USING statements necessary to print a table with the format shown below.

```
HORSES        GIRAFFES    TIGERS        MONKEYS
#####         #####       #####         #####
```

There are five spaces between HORSES and GIRAFFES and between TIGERS and MONKEYS and only three spaces between GIRAFFES and TIGERS. Assume these column headings are stored in the array ANIMAL$.

11.2 Introduction to Sequential and Random Access Files

All of the examples and problems that we have examined so far share the limitation that the input data must be typed in with the program (in DATA statements) or entered interactively as the program executes. In problems involving large amounts of data, this approach is not very practical.

There is also little sense of "permanency" for the data that we have used in our programs. Data items appearing in DATA statements may be saved with the program, but these data can't be used by other programs. Data items entered interactively (via INPUT statements) are processed immediately and can't normally be reused.

In addition, all output results are printed on the terminal, but are not saved in main or secondary memory. This means that it is impossible to process the "data" generated by a program after that program has executed. In the next sections, we shall learn how to create and retrieve *data files* in secondary storage in much the same way that we save program files. This will enable us to read data that are stored on one or more data files and also to create new data files for future processing.

We shall study two types of data files: *formatted ASCII* files and *virtual arrays*. Formatted ASCII files are also called *sequential files* because the file *records* (or lines) must be processed serially, starting with the first. At any time, the next record to be processed is always the record that physically follows the one being processed.

Virtual arrays are arrays that are stored in secondary storage. They are analogous to conventional arrays that are stored in main memory in that it is possible to reference any element of a virtual array at any time. Virtual arrays are called *random access files* because the records can be accessed in random order.

Creating and Listing ASCII Files at the Terminal

Before describing how to access files from within a program, it will be useful to see how ASCII files can be created and listed at a terminal. The data entry subroutine for the savings account update program in Fig. 6.10b contained the list of DATA statements

```
1070   !ACCOUNT NAMES AND INITIAL BALANCES
1080       DATA "SMITH", 3055.83
1090       DATA "JONES",  635.47
1100       DATA "KLEIN",  498.55
                    .
                    .
                    .
```

It would be very convenient to remove the DATA statements from the program and prepare an ASCII file that could be read by this program or another program. This can be accomplished using a *system editor*. Each pair of data values (e.g., "SMITH", 3055.83) should become a separate unnumbered line in the file created by the editor. We will use the extension .DAT to indicate an ASCII file and name this file BANK.DAT.

An ASCII file cannot be listed using OLD and LIST since it is not a BASIC-PLUS program. However, it can be listed using the system file transfer program PIP (*Peripheral Interchange Program*) as shown next.

```
PIP BANK.DAT
"SMITH", 3055.83
"JONES",  635.47
"KLEIN",  498.55
        .
        .
        .
```

Be careful when using the PIP command as the contents of the work area will be lost when BANK.DAT is transferred into the work area.

The permanent file BANK.DAT can be deleted from disk storage using the command

```
UNSAVE BANK.DAT
```

Our main goal is, of course, to be able to create and read data files under program control. The data entry subroutine from Fig. 6.10b is rewritten in Fig. 11.1 to read data from the ASCII file BANK.DAT. The statements OPEN, CLOSE and INPUT # will be described in the sections that follow. Note that the DATA statements are no longer needed.

```
1000  !DATA ENTRY SUBROUTINE
1010  !
1020       OPEN "BANK.DAT" FOR INPUT AS FILE #1
1030       INPUT #1 DEP.NAME(I1), START.BAL(I1)        &
             FOR I1 = 1 TO NUM.ACCOUNTS
1040       CLOSE #1
1050  !
1060       RETURN
1070  !END OF DATA ENTRY SUBROUTINE
```

Fig. 11.1 Reading data from ASCII file BANK.DAT

Accessing a File from a Program

In order to access any file, it is necessary to be able to transfer data between disk storage and main memory. A special *buffer area* in main memory must be allocated for temporary storage of file data. This is done using the BASIC-PLUS OPEN statement, which identifies a permanent file to be accessed and an associated *channel number*. The channel number is an integer from 1 to 12 that will be used in other program statements (e.g., INPUT, PRINT) to identify the file.

Example 11.11   The OPEN statements

```
100 OPEN "OLD.DAT" FOR INPUT AS FILE #2
110 OPEN "NEW.DAT" FOR OUTPUT AS FILE #1
```

allocate buffer areas for two files. One of these files, OLD.DAT (associated with channel number 2) should be an existing file already saved in disk storage since it is opened FOR INPUT. The other file, NEW.DAT (associated with channel number 1), may or may not exist. If NEW.DAT already exists, BASIC-PLUS will erase, or delete, its contents. In either case, an empty file named NEW.DAT will be created since NEW.DAT is opened FOR OUTPUT.

In most cases, a file that is to be read will be opened FOR INPUT and a file that is to be written or created will be opened FOR OUTPUT. Each opened file must be associated with a unique channel number. The BASIC-PLUS OPEN statement is described next. (VAX-11 BASIC users see Appendixes H and J.)

OPEN Statement

```
OPEN filename FOR INPUT AS FILE channel number
OPEN filename FOR OUTPUT AS FILE channel number
OPEN filename AS FILE channel number
```

Interpretation: The OPEN statement makes file *filename* (a string) available for input/output and associates it with the specified *channel number*. The *channel number* must be an integer expression (preceded by the symbol "#") with value 1 through 12. A buffer area (large enough to hold 512 characters) is allocated for file *filename*. OPEN FOR INPUT is used when an existing permanent file is to be read. An error diagnostic is printed if *filename* does not exist or cannot be accessed.

OPEN FOR OUTPUT is used when a file is to be created. Any existing file named *filename* is deleted. A new file named *filename* that is initially empty (zero records) is created. OPEN (without FOR. . .) first attempts to access a permanent file named *filename*. If none exists, the system creates an empty file named *filename*.

After a file has been processed, you should "disconnect" or *close* it before your program terminates. If you wish to read a new file that was just created, or read a file a second time, your program should first close the file and then reopen it for INPUT.

CLOSE Statement

```
CLOSE list of channel numbers
```

Interpretation: Each file identified in the *list of channel numbers* is closed. A closed file cannot be accessed unless it is reopened. Each channel number must be an integer expression (preceded by the symbol "#"). Commas are used between channel numbers.

11.3 Processing ASCII Files under Program Control

Creating a Sequential File

Formatted ASCII files are files whose *records* (elements) are individual lines. Each line is a collection of ASCII characters; the line format is defined by the PRINT statement that writes it in a manner similar to the way lines printed at the terminal are defined.

Example 11.12   The program in Fig. 11.2 creates a file that represents the inventory of a bookstore. Each record of this file consists of a stock number, author name (string), title (string), book price, and quantity on hand. These data are first read interactively (lines 180 through 220) and are written as a file record (line 240) on file INVEN.DAT which is associated with channel number 1 (line 130).

```
100 !CREATE A BOOK STORE INVENTORY
110 !
120 !PREPARE FILE INVEN FOR OUTPUT
130     OPEN "INVEN.DAT" FOR OUTPUT AS FILE #1
140 !
150 !READ ALL BOOK DATA AND CREATE INVENTORY FILE
160     INPUT "MORE RECORDS (YES OR NO)"; MORE$
170     WHILE CVT$$(MORE$, 2 + 32) = "YES"
180         INPUT "STOCK #"; STOCK.NUM
190         INPUT "AUTHOR"; AUTHOR$
200         INPUT "TITLE"; TITLE$
210         INPUT "PRICE"; PRICE
220         INPUT "QUANTITY"; QUANTITY
230         !COPY RECORD TO FILE INVEN
240         PRINT #1, STOCK.NUM; ","; AUTHOR$; ","; &
                TITLE$; ","; PRICE; ","; QUANTITY
250         INPUT "MORE RECORDS (YES OR NO)"; MORE$
260     NEXT   !WHILE
270 !
280 !CLOSE INVENTORY FILE
290     PRINT "FILE INVEN CREATED"
300     CLOSE #1
310 !
320     END

RUNNH
MORE RECORDS (YES OR NO)? YES
STOCK #? 1
AUTHOR? TY COBB
TITLE? NO PLACE LIKE HOME
PRICE? 5.95
QUANTITY? 60
MORE RECORDS (YES OR NO)? YES
STOCK #? 2
AUTHOR? PETE ROSE
TITLE? GREATEST HITS
PRICE? 6.34
QUANTITY? 20
MORE RECORDS (YES OR NO)? NO
FILE INVEN CREATED
```

Fig. 11.2 File creation program for Example 11.12.

The order of the records written on file INVEN.DAT will correspond to the order in which they are entered at the terminal. Each execution of the PRINT # statement at line 240 will cause a new record to be written at the end of the file INVEN.DAT. The length (number of characters) of each record will vary depending on the input data. The PRINT # statement is described next.

PRINT # Statement

PRINT # *channel number, output list*

Interpretation: Each execution of a PRINT # statement writes the data specified by *output list* at the end of the file indicated by *channel number*.

The output list items in line 240 are separated by the symbols ; ","; which cause the data separator symbol "," to be written between data items of each record. This enables the individual data items of file INVEN.DAT to be read separately at a later date. As with regular PRINT statements, each record will automatically be terminated with carriage return/line feed characters unless the output list ends with a semicolon.

The file created by the sample run shown in Fig. 11.2 is listed below using PIP.

```
PIP INVEN.DAT
  1 ,TY COBB,NO PLACE LIKE HOME, 5.95 , 60
  2 ,PETE ROSE,GREATEST HITS, 6.34 , 20
```

Even though the records above may not be very readable to us, BASIC-PLUS would have no difficulty in reading the individual data items since they are separated by commas. For this reason, the strings for AUTHOR$ and TITLE$ should not contain commas. This restriction could be removed if these strings were enclosed in quotes. (See Exercise 11.6.)

Exercise 11.5: Explain what would happen if the semicolons in line 240 of Fig. 11.2 were replaced by commas. Why is this not recommended?

Exercise 11.6: Modify the PRINT # statement in line 240 so that the strings in AUTHOR$ and TITLE$ will be enclosed in quotes.

Exercise 11.7: Write a program that reads a name and a list of three exam scores for each student in a class and copies this information to file GRADES.DAT.

Reading a Sequential File and Testing for End of File

We mentioned earlier that one motivation for files was to enable the output generated by one program to be used as input data for another. This process is illustrated next.

Example 11.13 The program in Fig. 11.3 reads a file similar to the one created by the execution of the program in Fig. 11.2 and echo prints each file record on the terminal. The INPUT # statement (line 250) that reads each file record

```
100    !PRINTING THE DATA ON AN INVENTORY FILE
110    !
120        ON ERROR GOTO 1000
125    !
130    !OPEN FILE FOR INPUT
140        INPUT "ENTER NAME OF INVENTORY FILE"; &
                FILE.NAME$
150        OPEN FILE.NAME$ FOR INPUT AS FILE #1
160    !
170    !DEFINE IMAGE STRINGS AND PRINT TABLE HEADING
190        LET HEADING$ = "STOCK #    AUTHOR            " &
                + "     TITLE          PRICE  QUANTITY"
200        LET TABLE$   = "  ####    \             \  " &
                + "\           \  ##.##        ###"
210        PRINT HEADING$
215    !
220    !ECHO PRINT EACH FILE RECORD
225    !UNTIL END OF FILE IS REACHED
230        LET TOTAL = 0
240        FOR REC.NUM = 0 WHILE -1%    !TRUE
250            INPUT #1, STOCK.NUM, AUTHOR$, TITLE$,   &
                    PRICE, QUANTITY
260            PRINT USING TABLE$, STOCK.NUM,          &
                    AUTHOR$, TITLE$, PRICE, QUANTITY
270           LET TOTAL = TOTAL + QUANTITY
280        NEXT REC.NUM
285    !
290        PRINT "INVENTORY FILE IS PROCESSED"
300        PRINT REC.NUM; "RECORDS WERE PRINTED"
310        PRINT "TOTAL NUMBER OF BOOKS ="; TOTAL
320    !
330    !CLOSE FILE AND STOP
340        CLOSE #1
345    !
350        STOP
360    !
370    !
1000   !ERROR PROCESSING ROUTINE
1010   !CHECK FOR END OF FILE ERROR AT LINE 250
1020       IF ERR = 11 AND ERL = 250 THEN RESUME 290 &
                ELSE ON ERROR GOTO 0
1030   !END OF ERROR PROCESSING ROUTINE
1035   !
1040       END
```

(continued)

```
ENTER NAME OF INVENTORY FILE? INVEN.DAT
STOCK #     AUTHOR            TITLE         PRICE QUANTITY
      1   TY COBB      NO PLACE LIKE HOME    5.95       60
      2   PETE ROSE    GREATEST HITS         6.34       20
INVENTORY FILE IS PROCESSED
 2 RECORDS WERE PRINTED
TOTAL NUMBER OF BOOKS = 80
Stop at line 350
```

Fig. 11.3 File print program for Example 11.13.

corresponds to the PRINT # statement (line 240 of Fig. 11.2) that wrote each record as described below. The name of the ASCII file to be read and printed is read into FILE.NAME\$ (line 140). A PRINT USING statement (line 260) is used to format the data displayed on the terminal. The program also counts and prints the number of titles inventoried and the total number of books on hand (saved in REC.NUM and TOTAL, respectively).

INPUT # Statement

INPUT # *channel number, variable list*

Interpretation: Each execution of an INPUT # statement causes the next record of the file identified by *channel number* to be read. The *variable list* for the INPUT # statement must correspond to the output list used in the PRINT # statement that created the file, i.e., the type of each variable in the INPUT # statement must match the type of its corresponding output list item in the PRINT # statement. *Note*: READ # cannot be used to read data files.

The statement

```
120 ON ERROR GOTO 1000
```

is a special BASIC-PLUS statement that enables a program to process certain errors and attempt to recover from them. If an error occurs anytime after this statement is executed, BASIC-PLUS transfers control to the *error processing routine* at line 1000 instead of printing an error diagnostic and terminating execution.

When an error does occur, the variable ERR (a reserved word) takes on one of the values listed in Appendix G and the variable ERL is assigned the number of the line causing the error. After testing these values in the error processing routine, the program can take appropriate action to recover from certain errors.

The FOR loop repetition test (WHILE -1%) is always true so the loop cannot terminate except through an error. This should happen when the INPUT # statement (line 250) is repeated after the last file record is processed. This *end of file error* is indicated by a value of ERR = 11 and ERL = 250 and is handled by the error processing routine as discussed next.

As soon as an error occurs, control is transferred to line 1000 (the error processing routine). If the error results because the end of file INVEN.DAT has been reached, the IF-THEN-ELSE statement

```
1020 IF ERR = 11 AND ERL = 250 THEN RESUME 290 &
     ELSE ON ERROR GOTO 0
```

will detect this and cause program execution to continue at line 290 where the final program results will be printed.

If the transfer is not due to the end of file INVEN.DAT being reached, the statement ON ERROR GOTO 0 returns control of error handling to the BASIC-PLUS system (instead of the program) causing BASIC-PLUS to generate an appropriate diagnostic message and suspend program execution.

A RETURN statement must not be used to return control from an error processing routine. Note that the statement

```
350 STOP
```

prevents the program from falling into the error routine.

The statements used for error processing are described next.

ON ERROR Statement

ON ERROR GOTO *line number*

Interpretation: If an error occurs after the ON ERROR statement is executed, control is transferred to the specified *line number*. If *line number* is 0 (or omitted), the error processing routine is disabled and BASIC-PLUS processes the error.

RESUME Statement

RESUME *line number*

Interpretation: Program execution continues at the statement with the specified *line number*. If *line number* is 0 (or omitted), program execution continues at the line where the error occurred.

Exercise 11.8: Write a program to read and echo print the file GRADES.DAT described in Exercise 11.7.

The INPUT LINE # Statement

The INPUT LINE # statement may also be used to read an ASCII file as described next.

INPUT LINE # Statement

INPUT LINE # *channel number, string variable*

Interpretation: Each execution of an INPUT LINE # statement causes the next record of the file identified by *channel number* to be read into *string variable*.

The entire record (line) of the specified file is read as a unit up to and including the carriage return/line feed characters. The string extraction functions MID, LEFT and RIGHT may be used to reference substrings of a record entered in this way.

11.4 File Update and Merge

Appending Data to a File

It is very rare that a file is not changed in some way after it is created. For example, we may wish to add new items to our inventory file or perhaps modify some of its records. We shall illustrate how to add data to an existing file in the next example.

Example 11.14   Our bookstore has received a new shipment of books and we would like to add the new titles to the end of our inventory file. The safest way to accomplish this is to read each record of the existing file and then copy it to a new file. After the last record of the existing file is copied, any new records should be appended to the end of the new file.

This approach is illustrated in Fig. 11.4. The main program contains a loop that reads (line 180) an entire record from file INVEN.DAT and copies it (line 190) to file NEWINV.DAT. The string variable NEX.REC$ provides temporary storage for each record. The ";" at the end of line 190 prevents the insertion of a redundant pair of carriage return/line feed characters at the end of each record of NEWINV.DAT.

The error processing routine at line 1000 is called after all records are copied. It returns control to line 220 of the main program, which echo prints the last record. The main program then calls the subroutine at line 2000 (not shown) to append any additional records to NEWINV.DAT; this subroutine should contain the loop shown in Fig. 11.2 (lines 170–260).

```
100    !EXTEND AN EXISTING FILE
110    !
120        ON ERROR GOTO 1000
130    !
140        OPEN "INVEN.DAT" FOR INPUT AS FILE #1
145        OPEN "NEWINV.DAT" FOR OUTPUT AS FILE #2
150    !
160    !COPY FILE INVEN.DAT TO NEWINV.DAT
170        FOR REC.NUM = 0 WHILE -1%    !TRUE
180            INPUT LINE #1, NEX.REC$
190            PRINT #2, NEX.REC$;
200        NEXT REC.NUM
205    !
210    !ADD MORE RECORDS AFTER END OF FILE IS REACHED
220        PRINT REC.NUM; "RECORDS COPIED"
225        PRINT "LAST RECORD COPIED:"
230        PRINT NEX.REC$
240    !
250    !APPEND ANY ADDITIONAL RECORDS
260        GOSUB 2000
270    !
280    !CLOSE FILES AND STOP
290        CLOSE #1, #2
300    !
310        STOP
320    !
330    !
1000   !ERROR PROCESSING ROUTINE
1010   !CHECK FOR END OF FILE AT LINE 180
1020       IF ERR = 11 AND ERL = 180 THEN RESUME 220 &
               ELSE ON ERROR GOTO 0
1025   !END OF ERROR PROCESSING ROUTINE
1030   !
1040   !
2000       !SUBROUTINE TO APPEND MORE RECORDS GOES HERE


                       .
                       .
                       .


2040       RETURN
2050   !END OF APPEND SUBROUTINE
2060   !
2070       END
```

```
RUNNH
 2 RECORDS COPIED
LAST RECORD COPIED:
 2 ,PETE ROSE,GREATEST HITS, 6.34 , 20
```

Fig. 11.4 File update program for Example 11.14.

Exercise 11.9: Write the subroutine at line 2000 of Fig. 11.4. It should be possible not to add any additional records to the file.

Exercise 11.10: Write a program that adds a fourth exam score to each component of the file GRADES.DAT created in Exercise 11.7. It will be necessary to create a new file with a record for each student on the original file. You should read each record from the original file to retrieve the first three scores and read the fourth score from the terminal before writing a record to the new file.

Merging Two Sequential Files

A common problem when working with files is to update one file (master file) by merging in information from a second file (update file). This process is illustrated in the following problem.

Problem 11A   The Junk Mail Company has recently received a new mailing list (file UPDATE.DAT) that it wishes to merge with its master file (file OLDMST.DAT). Each of these files is in alphabetical order by name. The company wishes to produce a new master file (NEWMST.DAT) that is also in alphabetical order.

Discussion: Each client name and address on either mailing list is represented by four character strings as shown below:

```
SANTA CLAUS
1 STAR LANE
NORTH POLE
ALASKA, 99999
```

There is a sentinel name and address at the end of each of the files UPDATE.DAT and OLDMST.DAT. The sentinel entry is the same for both files and consists of four strings containing all Z's. We shall assume that there are no names that appear on both files OLDMST.DAT and UPDATE.DAT. The files information is summarized in the data table shown below.

**DATA TABLE FOR
PROBLEM 11A**

Input Files		Output Files	
OLDMST.DAT:	The original mailing list in alphabetical order by name.	NEWMST.DAT:	The final mailing list, formed by merging OLDMST.DAT and NEWMST.DAT.
UPDATE.DAT:	The additions to be made to OLDMST.DAT, also in alphabetical order by name.		

The level one flow diagram is shown in Fig. 11.5a. The program must read one name and address entry at a time from each input file. These two entries are compared and the one that comes first alphabetically is copied to the output file (NEWMST.DAT). Another entry is then read from the file containing the entry just copied and the comparison process is repeated.

When the end of one of the input files (OLDMST.DAT or UPDATE.DAT) is reached, the program will copy the remaining information from the other input file to NEWMST.DAT and then write the sentinel record.

To simplify the implementation of the algorithm, we will use two string arrays, OLD.CLIENT\$ and UP.CLIENT\$, to hold the current client data from OLDMST.DAT and UPDATE.DAT, respectively. The layout of these arrays is shown below.

(1)	(2)	(3)	(4)
$name_1$	$street_1$	$city_1$	$state_1$ & zip_1

OLD.CLIENT\$ (from OLDMST.DAT)

(1)	(2)	(3)	(4)
$name_2$	$street_2$	$city_2$	$state_2$ & zip_2

UP.CLIENT\$ (from UPDATE.DAT)

The additional data table entries are shown on the next page. The refinement of Step 2 of Fig. 11.5a is shown in Fig. 11.5b.

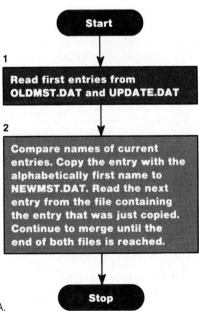

Fig. 11.5a Level one flow diagram for Problem 11A.

Input Variables	
OLD.CLIENT$( ):	String array to hold current client data from OLDMST.DAT (size 4)
UP.CLIENT$( ):	String array to hold current client data from UPDATE.DAT (size 4)

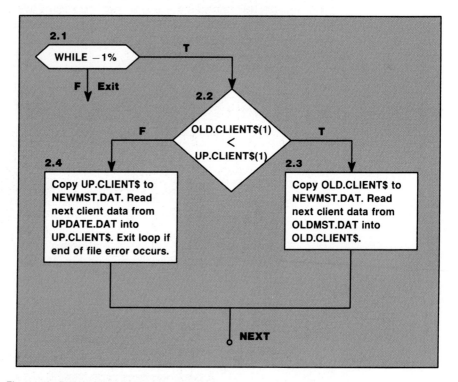

Fig. 11.5b Refinement of Step 2 of Fig. 11.5a.

It is important to verify that all the remaining data on one file will be copied into NEWMST.DAT when the end of the other file has been reached. Just before reaching the end of file UPDATE.DAT (or OLDMST.DAT), the sentinel record will be read into UP.CLIENT$ (or OLD.CLIENT$). Since the sentinel name (all Z's) alphabetically follows any other client name, the remaining client data on the unfinished file will be copied to NEWMST.DAT as desired. Loop repetition cannot terminate until both OLD.CLIENT$ and UP.CLIENT$ contain the sentinel record.

After the sentinel records of both files are read, the sentinel record will be copied to file NEWMST.DAT (Step 2.4). An end of file error will occur when BASIC-PLUS attempts to read the next file record. Since OLD.CLIENT$(1) = UP.CLIENT$(1) at this point, the error will be caused by the INPUT LINE # statement at line 2020 of Fig. 11.6.

```
100  !PROGRAM TO MERGE TWO FILES
110  !
120      ON ERROR GOTO 3000
130  !
140      DIM OLD.CLIENT$(4), UP.CLIENT$(4)
145  !
150  !PREPARE OLDMST.DAT AND UPDATE.DAT FOR INPUT
160  !AND NEWMST.DAT FOR OUTPUT
170  !
180      OPEN "OLDMST.DAT" FOR INPUT AS FILE #1
190      OPEN "UPDATE.DAT" FOR INPUT AS FILE #2
200      OPEN "NEWMST.DAT" FOR OUTPUT AS FILE #3
210  !
220  !GET FIRST RECORD FROM EACH INPUT FILE
230      INPUT LINE #1, OLD.CLIENT$(I)      &
             FOR I = 1 TO 4
240      INPUT LINE #2, UP.CLIENT$(I)       &
             FOR I = 1 TO 4
250  !
260  !MERGE OLDMST.DAT AND UPDATE.DAT TO NEWMST.DAT
270      WHILE -1%    !TRUE
280         !COPY ALPHABETICALLY FIRST NAME
290         IF OLD.CLIENT$(1) < UP.CLIENT$(1) THEN    &
                GOSUB 1000                            &
             ELSE                                     &
                GOSUB 2000
300      NEXT    !WHILE
305  !
310  !CLOSE FILES AND STOP
320      CLOSE #1, #2, #3
325  !
330      STOP
340  !
350  !
1000 !SUBROUTINES FOR IF-THEN-ELSE AT LINE 290
1010 !IF OLD.CLIENT$(1) < UP.CLIENT$(1) THEN
1015 !COPY OLD.CLIENT$ TO NEWMST.DAT
1020     PRINT #3, OLD.CLIENT$(I);           &
             FOR I = 1 TO 4
1030     INPUT LINE #1, OLD.CLIENT$(I)       &
             FOR I = 1 TO 4
1040     RETURN
2000 !ELSE COPY UP.CLIENT$ TO NEWMST.DAT
2010     PRINT #3, UP.CLIENT$(I);            &
             FOR I = 1 TO 4
2020     INPUT LINE #2, UP.CLIENT$(I)        &
             FOR I = 1 TO 4
2030     RETURN
2035 !END OF SUBROUTINES FOR LINE 290
2040 !
2050 !
```

(continued)

```
3000  !ERROR PROCESSING ROUTINE
3010  !CHECK FOR END OF FILE ERROR AT LINE 2020
3020      IF ERR = 11 AND ERL = 2020 THEN      &
              RESUME 320                        &
          ELSE                                  &
              ON ERROR GOTO 0
3025  !END OF ERROR PROCESSING ROUTINE
3030  !
3040      END    !FILE MERGE PROGRAM
```

Fig. 11.6 Program for Problem 11A.

Exercise 11.11: Modify the program for Problem 11A to handle the situation in which the UPDATE.DAT file may contain some of the same names as file OLDMST.DAT. In this case only one address should appear on file NEWMST.DAT; the address in file UPDATE.DAT should be used as it is more recent. Also, print a count of the number of file entries in each of the three files.

Exercise 11.12: Let FILEA.DAT and FILEB.DAT be two files containing the name and identification number of the students in two different programming classes. Assume that these files are arranged in ascending order by student number and that no student is in both classes. Write a program to read the information on FILEA.DAT and FILEB.DAT, and merge them onto a third file (FILEC.DAT) retaining the ascending order.

11.5 Virtual Arrays

The formatted ASCII files that we have been using are sequential files. In many applications, it is necessary to reference records of a file in arbitrary or random order, rather than in sequential or serial order. The array is a data structure that permits *random access* to its elements; the *virtual array* is a file structure that permits random access to its records.

Virtual Arrays and Arrays in Main Memory

A virtual array is an array that is stored on disk rather than in main memory; hence, processing a virtual array is similar to processing an array that is stored in main memory. There are some important differences, however, and they are described next.

Virtual Arrays and Main Memory Arrays

- A virtual array is stored on disk; consequently, it can be much larger than an array that is stored in main memory.

- A virtual array is saved as a permanent file; consequently, it remains in disk storage after it is processed. The space allocated to an array in main memory is reused after the program that processes the array is terminated.
- Each element of a virtual array uses the same amount of storage space on disk. Consequently, the maximum string length for a virtual string array must be specified when the array is declared. A string array that is stored in main memory may contain strings of different lengths and there is no maximum length other than memory space limitations.
- All elements of a numeric array in main memory are initialized to zero; all elements of a string array are initialized to the null string. Virtual array elements are not initialized when space is allocated to them on disk.
- The efficiency of a program that processes a virtual array may vary depending on the order in which the array elements are accessed; the efficiency of a program that manipulates an array in main memory is unaffected by the order in which the elements are accessed.

All of these points will be illustrated in the sections that follow.

Declaring a Virtual Array

Before a virtual array may be processed in a program, its organization must be described using a DIM # statement.

Example 11.15 The statements

```
100 DIM #1, X(9999)
110 OPEN "X.VIR" AS FILE #1
```

indicate that a virtual array X is associated with the virtual array file X.VIR on channel number 1. (We will use the extension .VIR to indicate a virtual array.) Subscripts ranging in value from 0 to 9999 may be used to reference elements of the virtual array X.

It is not necessary that the virtual array name and channel number be the same in each program that processes a virtual array file. The data in file X.VIR are associated with a virtual array named Y (on channel number 2) in the program segment that begins with

```
100 DIM #2, Y(9999)
110 OPEN "X.VIR" FOR INPUT AS FILE #2
```

The same file name, X.VIR, must be used in both OPEN statements and the virtual array size (9999) should be the same in both DIM # statements. The DIM # statement for declaring virtual arrays is described next.

DIM # Statement

> DIM # *channel number*, *list of virtual arrays*

Interpretation: The DIM # statement describes the virtual arrays associated with the indicated *channel number*. The name and dimensions of each virtual array are specified in the *list of virtual arrays* using the form

>   *array*(*size*)
> or *array*$(*size*) = length

where *size* represents the largest subscript value. The second form above should be used for string arrays where *length* represents the number of characters in each string element. The string *length* should be a power of two between 2 and 512 (i.e., 2, 4, 8, 16, 32, 64, 128, 256, 512). If string *length* is not specified, BASIC-PLUS will assume a string *length* of 16 characters.

Example 11.16 In order to create a new virtual array, a virtual array file should be opened for OUTPUT. The program segment in Fig. 11.7 creates a virtual array RANDOM.VIR that consists of 500 random integers with values between 0 and 99. The PRINT # statement cannot be used to write data into a virtual array; instead the assignment statement

```
200 LET RAND.INT(I) = RND * MAX.RAND              &
        FOR I = SIZE TO 1 STEP -1
```

```
100 !CREATE A VIRTUAL ARRAY
105 !OF RANDOM NUMBERS BETWEEN 0 AND 100
110 !
120 !PROGRAM CONSTANTS
130     LET MAX.RAND = 100
140     LET SIZE = 500
150 !
160     OPEN "RANDOM.VIR" FOR OUTPUT AS FILE #1
170     DIM #1, RAND.INT(500)
180 !
190 !STORE 500 RANDOM NUMBERS
200     LET RAND.INT(I) = RND * MAX.RAND       &
            FOR I = SIZE TO 1 STEP -1
210 !
220     CLOSE #1
230 !
240     END
```

Fig. 11.7 Program for Example 11.16

actually stores the random numbers in the virtual array. Because of the way BASIC-PLUS allocates disk space to a new virtual array, it is better to start with the last array element, RAND.INT(SIZE), as shown.

Example 11.17   The statements

```
140 DIM #1, MAIL.LABEL$(20000) = 64
150 OPEN "MAIL.VIR" FOR INPUT AS FILE #1
```

in Fig. 11.8 associate the virtual string array MAIL.LABEL$ with the virtual array file MAIL.VIR on channel number 1. The string array has elements with subscripts ranging from 0 to 20000.

Each element of the virtual string array contains exactly 64 characters. If a string assigned to a virtual array element is shorter than the maximum length (64 characters), null characters are appended to the right end of the string. These extra null characters will be ignored after the string is retrieved from the virtual array.

The program in Fig. 11.8 prints every 100th string that is stored in the virtual array MAIL.LABEL$ and the actual string length (minus the extra null characters). Each time the PRINT statement

```
190 PRINT MAIL.LABEL$(REC.NUM),           &
        LEN(MAIL.LABEL$(REC.NUM))
```

is executed, an element of the virtual array MAIL.LABEL$ is copied from disk to a buffer area in main memory and then printed. Note that it is not possible to use an INPUT # statement to read the virtual array data. Rather, this data is accessed in the same way as data in regular arrays.

```
100 !PRINT EVERY 100TH STRING AND ITS LENGTH
110 !
115 !PROGRAM CONSTANTS
120     LET SIZE = 20000
130     LET GAP = 100
135 !
140     DIM #1, MAIL.LABEL$(20000) = 64
150     OPEN "MAIL.VIR" FOR INPUT AS FILE #1
160 !
170 !PERFORM SELECTIVE PRINT
180     FOR REC.NUM = 1 TO SIZE STEP GAP
190         PRINT MAIL.LABEL$(REC.NUM),        &
                LEN(MAIL.LABEL$(REC.NUM))
200     NEXT REC.NUM
210 !
220     CLOSE #1
230 !
240     END
```

Fig. 11.8 Program for Example 11.17

Example 11.18 The statements below describe a two-dimensional virtual array.

```
150 DIM #2, SALES(4,20)
160 OPEN "SALES.VIR" AS FILE #2
```

The virtual array SALES associated with channel number 2 has five rows and 21 columns (including row 0 and column 0). The layout of the virtual array is shown in Fig. 11.9. The OPEN statement above associates SALES with the permanent file SALES.VIR; if SALES.VIR does not exist, a new file will be allocated for storage of the virtual array SALES.

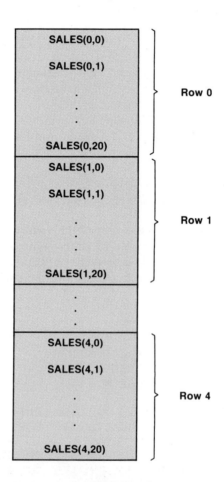

Fig. 11.9 Layout of virtual array SALES in Example 11.18.

Program Style

Sequential access to virtual arrays

Because of the way BASIC-PLUS transfers virtual array data between disk storage and main memory, it turns out that it is more efficient to access the elements of a virtual array in sequential rather than random order. Consequently, whenever possible, it would be preferable to process the elements of array SALES one row at a time rather than one column at a time. This is illustrated in the program of Fig. 11.10 that sets all array elements to 0.

The matrix manipulation statements described in Chapter 10 may also be used with virtual arrays. The statement

```
190 MAT SALES = ZER
```

could replace the FOR loop in Fig. 11.10.

```
100 !ZERO OUT ALL ELEMENTS OF VIRTUAL ARRAY SALES
110 !
120 !PROGRAM CONSTANTS
130     LET MAX.ROW = 4
140     LET MAX.COL = 20
145 !
150     DIM #2, SALES(4,20)
160     OPEN "SALES.VIR" FOR OUTPUT AS FILE #2
170 !
180 !ZERO-OUT ALL ARRAY ELEMENTS ONE ROW AT A TIME
190     FOR ROW = MAX.ROW TO 1 STEP -1
200         LET SALES(ROW,COLUMN) = 0               &
                FOR COLUMN = MAX.COL TO 1 STEP -1
210     NEXT ROW
220 !
230     CLOSE #2
240 !
250     END
```

Fig. 11.10 Program for Example 11.18.

Example 11.19 The statements

```
120 DIM #3, NAMES$(1000) = 32,                      &
             BIRTH.MONTH$(1000) = 16, AGE%(1000)
130 OPEN "PERSON.VIR" AS FILE #3
```

associate channel number 3 with a virtual array file PERSON.VIR, that contains three "parallel" virtual arrays. The layout of the virtual array file is shown in Fig. 11.11.

We have used an integer array AGE% in order to conserve some disk space. Nevertheless, the virtual array file PERSON.VIR uses considerable disk storage. You should delete a virtual array (using UNSAVE) after you are finished processing it.

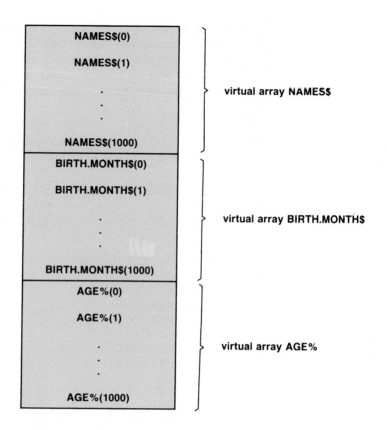

Fig. 11.11 Layout of virtual arrays in Example 11.19.

The program in Fig. 11.12 updates an existing file named PERSON.VIR by adding 1 to selected elements of the virtual array AGE%. An element of array AGE% is incremented if the corresponding element of array BIRTH.MONTH$ has the same value as CUR.MONTH$.

Although this program is correct, it is not very efficient. This is because BASIC-PLUS transfers one *block* of 512 bytes into main memory each time a virtual array is referenced unless the element referenced is already in main memory. Since there are more than 512 bytes (characters) between corresponding elements of arrays AGE% and BIRTH.MONTH$, it would be necessary to transfer a block from virtual array AGE% into the buffer area before updating that array. The data from AGE% would overwrite the data previously transferred from virtual array BIRTH.MONTH$; so, it may be necessary to transfer that block back in after AGE% is updated.

Unfortunately, each transfer operation is relatively time-consuming; consequently, one goal in using virtual arrays is to eliminate needless transfers from secondary storage to main storage. It would be more efficient to store all data regarding each person as a single element of a virtual string array. The string manipulation functions described in Chapter 9 could be used to examine and modify selected substrings as illustrated in the next section.

```
100  !INCREASE AGE OF EVERY PERSON
105  !BORN IN CURRENT MONTH
110  !
120     DIM #3, NAMES$(1000) = 32,                        &
               BIRTH.MONTH$(1000) = 16, AGE%(1000)
130     OPEN "PERSON.VIR" AS FILE #3
135  !
140  !READ CURRENT MONTH
150     INPUT "ENTER CURRENT MONTH"; CUR.MONTH$
160  !
170  !ADD ONE TO THE AGE OF EVERY PERSON BORN IN
175  !CURRENT MONTH. PRINT THE NAME AND NEW AGE.
180     PRINT "          NAME"; TAB(33); "AGE"
190     FOR I = 1 TO 1000
200        IF BIRTH.MONTH$(I) = CUR.MONTH$ THEN     &
              LET AGE%(I) = AGE%(I) + 1              &
              \PRINT NAMES$(I); TAB(33); AGE%(I)
210     NEXT I
220  !
230     PRINT \ PRINT "FILE UPDATE COMPLETE"
235  !
240     CLOSE #3
250  !
260     END

RUNNH
ENTER CURRENT MONTH? JAN
           NAME                        AGE
DEBORAH AMY KOFFMAN                     16
JOSEPH MICHAEL SIBLEY                   3
JENNIFER MILDRED HOLZBAUR               2

FILE UPDATE COMPLETE
```

Fig. 11.12 Program for Example 11.19.

Exercise 11.13: Write a program that reads the virtual array file RANDOM.VIR (see Example 11.16) and counts and prints the number of random values in each decile (i.e., 0–9, 10–19, etc.).

11.6 Manipulating Virtual Arrays

Virtual Array Update

We stated earlier that a major advantage of virtual array files is that the file records may be accessed in random or arbitrary order, although the order may affect the processing speed. A second advantage is that a record in the middle of a virtual array may be modified without disturbing the rest of the file. For this reason, virtual array files should be used when selected records of a file are likely to be updated. Sequential (ASCII) files may be used when most, or all, of the records are likely to be updated in serial order.

Problem 11B A program is needed to update our bookstore inventory file at the end of each day. The input data for the program consists of the stock number (STOCK.NUM) and amount sold (ORDER) for each book that is purchased. These data are not arranged in any special order.

Discussion: Considering the random nature of the input data, a virtual array should be used. We will assume that all inventory records contain the same information about a book as the records shown in Example 11.12 (stock number, title, author, price, quantity). This information will be stored in the virtual string array BOOK$. The string length declared for array BOOK$ should be greater than or equal to the length of the longest string to be stored. We shall pick a maximum length of 64. (This may require some abbreviation of long titles, but the next larger length, 128, could result in too much wasted space.) A sample record is shown below.

```
1 ,TY COBB*NO PLACE LIKE HOME $5.95 \ 60
```

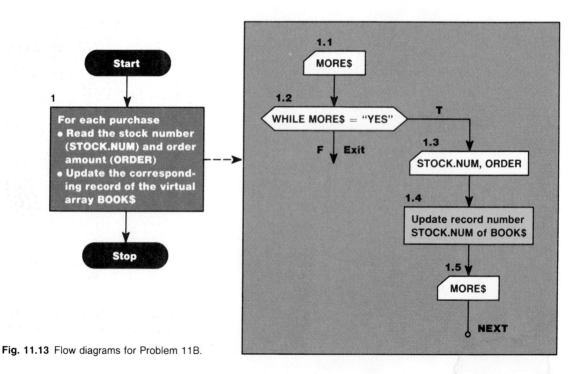

Fig. 11.13 Flow diagrams for Problem 11B.

Since each record is stored as a single character string, we can use the string manipulation functions described in Chapter 9 to reference and modify substrings of a record. To simplify this process, the symbols ",", "*", "$", and "\" are used as *delimiters* (separators) between substrings.

The substring terminated by the comma is the stock number of the record. The virtual array file (INV.VIR) will be organized so that the subscript of each array element that contains a record will match the record's stock number (an integer between 1 and 1000). The last substring (preceded by "\") of each record, represents the quantity on hand and is the substring that must be modified.

With this file organization in mind, we can proceed with the design of the algorithm. As each purchase is entered, the corresponding record of BOOK$ will be referenced and updated provided the record data are correct. The flow diagram for the main program is shown in Fig. 11.13; the data table follows.

DATA TABLE FOR PROBLEM 11B

Program Constants

MAX.STOCK = 1000: Largest stock number

Input-Output File

INV.VIR: Virtual array file for bookstore inventory

Input Variables		Output Variables
BOOK$ ( ): The virtual array being updated (size 1000, string length 64)		BOOK$ ( ): The updated virtual array
STOCK.NUM: The stock number of book purchased		
ORDER: The quantity purchased		
MORE$: Indicates whether there are more purchases		

Functions Referenced

FNUPDATE%: Updates record number STOCK.NUM of virtual array BOOK$

The main program (shown in Fig. 11.14) reads in the purchase data and calls (line 230) function FNUPDATE% to update each record of the virtual array BOOK$ that corresponds to a purchase.

```
100  !UPDATE OF VIRTUAL ARRAY FILE
110  !
120  !PROGRAM CONSTANT
130     LET MAX.STOCK = 1000      !MAX STOCK NUMBER
140  !
150     DIM #1, BOOK$(1000) = 64
160     OPEN "INV.VIR" AS FILE #1
170  !
175  !PROCESS EACH VALID UPDATE REQUEST
180     INPUT "MORE ORDERS (YES OR NO)"; MORE$
190     WHILE CVT$$(MORE$, 2 + 32) = "YES"
200        INPUT "STOCK NUMBER";STOCK.NUM
210        INPUT "OUT-OF-RANGE, TRY AGAIN";STOCK.NUM   &
              UNTIL STOCK.NUM > 0 AND                   &
                 STOCK.NUM <= MAX.STOCK
220        INPUT "ORDER"; ORDER
230        IF FNUPDATE%(STOCK.NUM, ORDER) THEN          &
              PRINT "UPDATED RECORD:";                  &
                 BOOK$(STOCK.NUM)                       &
           ELSE                                         &
              PRINT "CURRENT RECORD:";                  &
                 BOOK$(STOCK.NUM)                       &
                 \PRINT "BAD UPDATE DATA FOR ABOVE RECORD"
240        INPUT "MORE ORDERS (YES OR NO)"; MORE$
250     NEXT     !WHILE
260  !
270     PRINT "FILE UPDATE COMPLETED"
280  !
290  !CLOSE FILE
300     CLOSE #1
```

Fig. 11.14 Main program to Problem 11B.

Before updating the record, FNUPDATE% must extract its associated stock number and quantity-on-hand and verify that all data are valid. The flow diagrams for FNUPDATE% are shown in Fig. 11.15; the data table for FNUPDATE% follows.

DATA TABLE FOR FUNCTION FNUPDATE%	
Function Parameters	
STOCK.NUM:	The stock number of the record being updated
ORDER:	The order amount
Function Constants	
UP.DELIM1$ = ",":	symbol following stock number
UP.DELIM2$ = "\":	symbol preceding quantity-on-hand
Global Variables	
BOOK$( ):	The virtual array being updated

(continued)

`UP.POS1:`	Position of first delimiter
`UP.POS2:`	Position of second delimiter
`UP.STOCK$:`	The stock number substring
`UP.QUANT$:`	The quantity substring

Steps 3.2 and 3.4 in Fig. 11.15 are used to define the function result as 0% (false) or −1% (true), respectively. The main program either prints the updated record (result is true) or an error message and the original record (result is false). Function FNUPDATE% is shown in Fig. 11.16a. A sample run is shown in Fig. 11.16b.

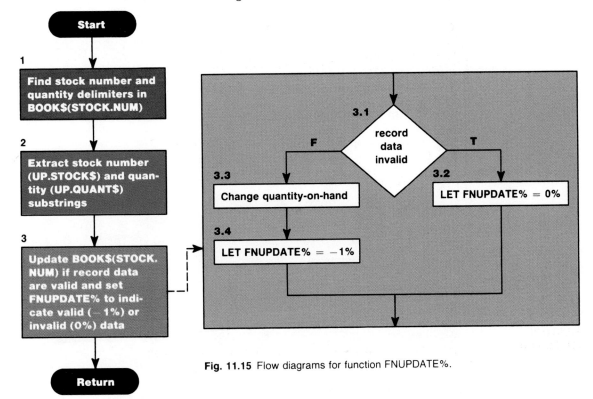

Fig. 11.15 Flow diagrams for function FNUPDATE%.

Program Style

Validating a file record

Line 1190 of function FNUPDATE% performs several tests for invalid data in the virtual array BOOK$. First, the function tests whether the delimiters are properly placed in the record being examined. Next, the stock number substring of the record is compared to STOCK.NUM (the array subscript) in order to verify that the correct record was accessed. Finally, the program verifies that the new quantity-on-hand will be positive before updating the virtual array.

Since many programmers may have access to a file these error checks are vital to ensure that the virtual array file is maintained properly and to warn file users if the integrity of the file data becomes suspect.

```
1000     DEF* FNUPDATE% (STOCK.NUM, ORDER)
1010 !
1020 !UPDATE RECORD STOCK.NUM OF VIRTUAL ARRAY BOOK$
1030 !
1040 !PARAMETER DEFINITIONS
1050 !   STOCK.NUM - STOCK NUMBER OF ITEM PURCHASED
1060 !   ORDER - PURCHASE AMOUNT
1065 !GLOBAL VARIABLES
1070 !   BOOK$( ) - VIRTUAL ARRAY BEING UPDATED
1075 !LOCAL VARIABLES
1080 !   UP.POS1, UP.POS2, UP.STOCK$, UP.QUANT$
1085 !
1090 !FUNCTION CONSTANTS
1095     LET UP.DELIM1$ =","     !STOCK.NUM DELIMITER
1100     LET UP.DELIM2$ ="\"     !QUANTITY DELIMITER
1105 !
1110 !FIND DELIMITERS FOR STOCK.NUM AND QUANTITY
1120     LET UP.POS1 =                                &
            INSTR(1, BOOK$(STOCK.NUM), UP.DELIM1$)
1130     LET UP.POS2 =                                &
            INSTR(1, BOOK$(STOCK.NUM), UP.DELIM2$)
1135 !
1140 !EXTRACT STOCK NUMBER AND QUANTITY
1145 !SUBSTRINGS OF BOOK$(STOCK.NUM)
1150     LET UP.STOCK$ =                              &
            LEFT(BOOK$(STOCK.NUM), UP.POS1-1)
1160     LET UP.QUANT$ =                              &
            RIGHT(BOOK$(STOCK.NUM), UP.POS2+1)
1170 !
1180 !UPDATE RECORD DATA IF VALID AND SET FNUPDATE%
1190     IF UP.POS1 = 0 OR UP.POS2 = 0               &
            OR UP.POS1 > UP.POS2                     &
            OR VAL(UP.STOCK$) <> STOCK.NUM           &
            OR ORDER > VAL(UP.QUANT$) THEN           &
            GOSUB 2000                               &
        ELSE                                         &
            GOSUB 3000
```

(continued)

```
1200 !
1220     GOTO 3070    !RETURN FROM FNUPDATE%
1230 !
1240 !
2000 !SUBROUTINES FOR IF-THEN-ELSE AT LINE 1190
2010 !IF DATA IS INVALID THEN SET FNUPDATE% TO FALSE
2020     LET FNUPDATE% = 0%     !FALSE
2030     RETURN
3000 !ELSE UPDATE QUANTITY OF BOOK$(STOCK.NUM)
3010     LET UP.QUANT$ = NUM1$(VAL(UP.QUANT$)-ORDER)
3015     !JOIN NEW QUANTITY TO REST OF STRING
3020     LET BOOK$(STOCK.NUM) =                          &
             LEFT(BOOK$(STOCK.NUM),UP.POS2) + UP.QUANT$
3030     LET FNUPDATE%= -1%     !TRUE
3040     RETURN
3050 !END OF SUBROUTINES FOR LINE 1190
3060 !
3070     FNEND      !FNUPDATE%
3080 !
3090     END        !RANDOM ACCESS UPDATE
```

Fig. 11.16a Program for function FNUPDATE%.

```
RUNNH
MORE ORDERS (YES OR NO)? YES
STOCK NUMBER? 2
ORDER? 20
UPDATED RECORD: 2,PETE ROSE*GREATEST HITS$6.50\15
MORE ORDERS (YES OR NO)? YES
STOCK NUMBER? 1
ORDER? 80
CURRENT RECORD: 1,TY COBB*NO PLACE LIKE HOME$5.95\60
BAD UPDATE DATA FOR ABOVE RECORD
MORE ORDERS (YES OR NO)? YES
STOCK NUMBER? 1
ORDER? 30
UPDATED RECORD: 1,TY COBB*NO PLACE LIKE HOME$5.95\30
MORE ORDERS (YES OR NO)? YES
STOCK NUMBER? 2
ORDER? 15
UPDATED RECORD: 2,PETE ROSE*GREATEST HITS$6.50\0
MORE ORDERS (YES OR NO)? YES
STOCK NUMBER? -5
OUT-OF-RANGE, TRY AGAIN? 1
ORDER? 5
UPDATED RECORD: 1,TY COBB*NO PLACE LIKE HOME$5.95\25
MORE ORDERS (YES OR NO)? NO
FILE UPDATE COMPLETED
```

Fig. 11.16b Sample run of program for Problem 11B.

Creating Virtual Arrays from ASCII Files

It is important to realize that the virtual array file INV.VIR and the sequential file INVEN.DAT (created in Example 11.12) cannot be used interchangeably. A different program would be required to create the original virtual array file. This program must read each record field entered at the terminal (or from a sequential file like INVEN.DAT) and then construct a string by concatenating these fields and inserting the appropriate delimiters as illustrated next.

```
200 LET BOOK$(STOCK.NUM)  = NUM1$(STOCK.NUM) + ","    &
                          + AUTHOR$ + "*" + TITLE$     &
                          + "$" + NUM1$(PRICE) + "\" &
                          + NUM1$(QUANTITY)
```

Recall that the function NUM1$ converts each numeric argument to a character string. The stock number field (STOCK.NUM) determines which virtual array element is used for storing each record. If there are gaps between stock numbers, this will present no problem. However, the corresponding array elements will contain whatever characters happen to be stored on the disk. It would be advisable to initialize each element of the virtual array file to a string of blanks to simplify the recognition of missing records. It will always be possible to insert new records at a later time (i.e., to replace the blank strings with actual data).

Exercise 11.14: Write a program to create the virtual array file INV.VIR for Problem 11B. Assume that a sequential inventory file, INVEN.DAT, already exists and is used as the basis for the new file (i.e., read from INVEN.DAT to create INV.VIR).

Exercise 11.15: Write a program to perform the "inverse" of Exercise 11.14 (i.e., start with a virtual array file and create a sequential file).

11.7 Chaining Programs

BASIC-PLUS provides an additional feature, the CHAIN statement, which enables a long program to be divided into more manageable segments. This feature allows each segment to be designed relatively independently. Once the segments are completed, they can be executed serially (one after the other) without programmer intervention to complete the desired programming task.

The CHAIN Statement

CHAIN *next program*

Interpretation: The CHAIN statement initiates the execution of the program specified by *next program*. *Next program* is a string expression designating the name of the file containing the program to be executed.

When chaining is used, there is complete independence between the names of variables and arrays used in the current program and those used in the new program. No information is transferred from one program of a chain to another except through files. Hence, it is impossible for variables altered in one program to have any effect upon the values of variables in the other program, even if these variables have the same name. The CHAIN feature is, therefore, an important aid in the construction, debugging, and maintenance of large program systems. In BASIC-PLUS, chaining is the only means of segmenting a large-scale system into a set of compact, independent modules.

When the CHAIN statement is executed, the new program segment is placed in memory and begins execution. Any files used in common by several programs should be closed before each CHAIN statement is executed and opened again in the called program. If virtual arrays are used, the dimensions should be the same in all programs.

Example 11.20 The two programs shown in Fig. 11.17 are chained together via the statement

```
330 CHAIN "PRNTCK"
```

where PRNTCK is the name of the file containing the second program. The first program reads file PAYROL.DAT (channel number 1) containing payroll data for all employees. It then computes each employee's pay, PAY, and writes it on file CHECKS.DAT (channel number 5), along with the employee's name.

The second program (contained on file PRNTCK) reads file CHECKS.DAT and prints it at the terminal. The first record of each data file is the number of employees processed.

It is important to remember that there is no transfer of data between these two programs except as provided through file CHECKS.DAT. The variable names used in the second program have no connection with the variable names used in the first program. In fact, we have used different names in each program to refer to the number of employees and the amount paid.

```
100 !CREATES PAYROLL FILE FOR PROGRAM PRNTCK
110 !
120    OPEN "PAYROL.DAT" FOR INPUT AS FILE #1
130    OPEN "CHECKS.DAT" FOR OUTPUT AS FILE #5
140 !
150 !READ AND PRINT NUMBER OF EMPLOYEES
160 !SAVE NUMBER ON FILE CHECKS.DAT
170    INPUT #1, NUM.EMP
180    PRINT "NUMBER OF EMPLOYEES IS"; NUM.EMP
190    PRINT #5, NUM.EMP
200 !
```

(continued)

```
210 !READ NAME, HOURS, AND RATE FOR EACH EMPLOYEE
220 !SAVE EMPLOYEE NAME AND PAY ON FILE CHECKS.DAT
240    FOR I = 1 TO NUM.EMP
250        INPUT #1, EMP.NAME$, HOURS, RATE
260        LET PAY = HOURS * RATE
270        PRINT #5, EMP.NAME$; ","; PAY
280    NEXT I
290 !
295 !CLOSE FILES
300    CLOSE #1, #5
310 !
320 !PRINT PAYROLL FILE (CHECKS.DAT)
330    CHAIN "PRNTCK"
340 !
350    END


100 !PRINT PAYROLL FILE (CHECKS.DAT)
120 !
130    OPEN "CHECKS.DAT" FOR INPUT AS FILE #5
140 !
150 !READ THE COUNT OF EMPLOYEES ON CHECKS.DAT
160    INPUT #5, N
165 !
170 !PRINT THE NAME AND SALARY SAVED ON CHECKS.DAT
175    PRINT "NAME", "AMOUNT PAID"
180    FOR I = 1 TO N
190        INPUT #5, EMP.NAME$, GROSS
200        PRINT EMP.NAME$, GROSS
210    NEXT I
220 !
225 !CLOSE PAYROLL FILE
230    CLOSE #5
240 !
250    END

RUNNH
NUMBER OF EMPLOYEES IS 3
NAME            AMOUNT PAID
ANDERSON           213.75
JONES              140
HOLZBAUR           390
```

Fig. 11.17 Chained programs for Example 11.20.

11.8 Common Programming Errors

The most common error with PRINT USING statements is specifying an image field that is too small to accommodate the value being printed. This will result in a number being printed in standard format preceded by a % sign. Remember to leave space for the minus sign of a negative number. If a string is larger than its corresponding field, the string will be truncated and only the left-most characters will be printed.

Another common error is a type mismatch between the image field and the output list item. For example, attempting to print a string in a numeric field will cause a

```
?Print using format error
```

There are many errors that may arise when working with files, some of which are beyond the control of the programmer. For example, the BASIC-PLUS system may be unable to read a particular record of an existing file. This will result in the diagnostic

```
?Data error on device
```

being printed. It is possible that the record may be read at a later time.

You may be prevented from accessing a file for a variety of reasons. If you do not have the privilege code necessary to read or write to a file, the error diagnostic

```
?Protection violation
```

will be printed when the OPEN statement is executed. This message may also be printed if someone else has write access to the file at the time you try to open it.

If either your file directory or the disk is full, the diagnostic

```
?No room for user on device
```

will be printed. It may help to delete any unused files.

If an OPEN statement contains an invalid channel number (outside the range 1 to 12), the diagnostic

```
?Illegal I/O Channel
```

will be printed. If the same channel number is used in two OPEN statements, the diagnostic

```
?I/O channel already open
```

will result.

An invalid file name in an OPEN statement will be indicated by the diagnostic

```
?Illegal file name
```

If a file name is misspelled in an OPEN FOR INPUT statement, the message

```
?Can't find file or account
```

will be printed. A list of all OPEN statement errors is provided in Table 11.2 along with the value assigned to the variable ERR when each error occurs.

One error that will not be detected is opening FOR OUTPUT a file whose name is the same as a file currently in your file directory. This will cause the existing file to be deleted. Obviously, the consequences may be quite serious if this was not your intention.

When writing records to a formatted ASCII file, make sure that the separator symbol "," is inserted between individual data fields; otherwise it may be difficult to read these data items. When creating a virtual array file that may contain gaps between records (i.e., unused subscripts), make sure that the file is first initialized to null strings (or zeros); otherwise it will be difficult to determine whether a valid record was referenced at a later time.

Table 11.2 OPEN Statement Errors

Value of ERR	Message	Explanation
2	?Illegal file name	The file name specified is not acceptable. It contains unacceptable characters, or else it violates the file specification format.
4	?No room for user on device	The directory space of your device is exceeded, or the device is too full to accept further data.
5	?Can't find file or account	The file or account number is not found on the specified device.
6	?Not a valid device	The device specification is not valid for one of the following reasons: • The unit number or its type is not in the system configuration. • The logical name has no associated physical device and is thus untranslatable.

(continued)

Table 11.2 OPEN Statement Errors (*continued*)

Value of ERR	Message	Explanation
8	`?Device not available`	The specified device exists on the system, but you cannot assign or open it for one of the following reasons: • The device is reserved for another job. • You lack necessary access privileges for the device. • The device is disabled. • The device is a keyboard line for pseudo keyboard use only.
10	`?Protection violation`	You do not have access privileges for the file.
14	`?Device hung or write-locked`	Check the hardware condition of the device you requested. Possible causes of this error include a line printer out of paper or a high-speed reader off-line.
17	`?Too many open files on unit`	The system permits only one open output file per DECtape drive and only one open file per magnetic tape drive.
32	`?No buffer space available`	You accessed a file and the monitor requires one small buffer to complete the request. No small buffer is available.
39	`?Magtape select error`	When you attempted to access a magnetic tape drive, it was off-line.
46	`?Illegal I/O channel`	You specified an I/O channel number outside the range of integers 1 through 12.

Summary

This chapter described the use of PRINT USING statements to specify the appearance or format of an output line. A PRINT USING statement has the form

```
100 PRINT USING image string, output list
```

We described the meaning of various symbols that might be found in an *image string*. Some of these symbols are illustrated in Table 11.3.

We also described the use of formatted ASCII files and virtual array files. Many new BASIC-PLUS statements were introduced to enable us to manipulate files; these new statements are summarized in Table 11.4.

The use of both types of files was illustrated in this chapter. When using a formatted ASCII file, the file records must always be accessed in serial or sequential order, starting with the first record. An ASCII file may be created (or listed) using an editor (or PIP), or processed under program control. Normally, a program performs one operation at a time (read or write) on all the records of a formatted ASCII file. We illustrated how to merge the data on two input files to create a third output file.

We saw that processing a virtual array file on disk was analogous to manipulating an array in main memory. When using virtual array files, it is possible to access the file records in random or arbitrary order. This enables us to update selected items without affecting neighboring records. Also, we can retrieve old values and assign new values simultaneously when processing a virtual array. A virtual array may not be created or listed using an editor.

Finally, we described the use of the CHAIN statement as a means of separating large program systems into smaller program files. Each execution of a CHAIN statement initiates the program on the specified program file. Data may be communicated between program segments only by using data files.

Table 11.3 Summary of Image Fields

Data Value	Field	Output String
-1.3456		
	##.#	-1.3
	###.###	-1.346
	##.##-	1.35-
	**##.##-	***1.35-
	#.##	%-1.3456
	###.#^^^^	-13.5E-01
"ABCDE"	!	A
	/ /	ABC
	/ /	ABCDE

Table 11.4 Summary of File Features

Example	Effect
OPEN *statement*	
`OPEN "ERZA.VIR" AS FILE #1`	Opens a file named `ERZA.VIR` on channel number 1. If `ERZA.VIR` does not exist, a new file with 0 records is created.
`OPEN "MIS.DAT" FOR INPUT AS FILE #2`	Opens a file named `MIS.DAT` on channel number 2. If `MIS.DAT` is not in the file directory, a diagnostic is printed.
`OPEN "STUFF.DAT" FOR OUTPUT AS FILE #3`	Creates a new file named `STUFF.DAT` on channel number 3. If `STUFF.DAT` is already in the file directory, the existing file will be deleted.
CLOSE *statement*	
`CLOSE #1, #2, #3`	Disconnects or closes the files on channel numbers 1, 2, and 3.
PRINT # *statement*	
`PRINT #1, A; ","; B`	Writes a record consisting of the values of A and B (separated by " , ") to the end of the file associated with channel number 1.
INPUT # *statement*	
`INPUT #1, A, B`	Reads the first two data items from the next record of the file associated with channel number 1. These data must be numeric or an error will result.
DIM # *statement*	
`DIM #1, W(100), B$(100) = 32`	Associates two virtual arrays with the file connected to channel number 1. Both arrays have subscripts ranging from 0 to 100. The first array is numeric; the second array contains strings of length 32.

(continued)

Table 11.4 Summary of File Features (*continued*)

Example	Effect
Virtual array reference	
`LET W(30) = 46`	Assigns the value 46 to the element of virtual array W with subscript 30.
`PRINT B$(30), LEN(B$(30))`	Prints the string stored in the element with subscript 30 of virtual array B$. The actual length of this string (ignoring null characters at the end) is also printed.
`CHAIN` *statement*	
`CHAIN "PAYROL"`	Causes execution of the program on file PAYROL to be initiated. Any data files used by this program must be opened before they may be accessed.

Programming Problems

11C Assume that the table below reflects the current market value of six well-known stocks:

```
LEAVEM COLD ELEC CO., 13.66
WE FLEECEM GAS CO., 19.27
US THIEVES SUGAR CO., 8.01
TAINTED COFFEE INC., 6.45
DRYWELL OIL OF MAINE, 27.42
HOT PRODUCTS INC., 2.82
```

Write an interactive program to read the above table from a sequential file and write a sequential file containing three entries for each stock: company name, number of shares, and market value per share. Allow the user to enter the number of shares of each of the stocks at the terminal.

11D Write a program that reads the file created in Problem 11C and prints the following table:

CORPORATION NAME	STOCK VALUE PER SHARE	NO. OF SHARES	TOTAL VALUE
XX . . . X (allow for a max of 25 characters)	XXX.XX	XXXX	XXXXXXX.XX
.	.	.	.
.	.	.	.
.	.	.	.
XX . . . X	XXX.XX	XXXX	XXXXXXX.XX
TOTALS		XXXXX	XXXXXXX.XX

Use the PRINT USING statements to obtain the table.

11E A local music school has the following payroll data on a file called PAYROL.DAT.

Employee Name	Year-to-Date Earnings	YTD Federal Tax	YTD Social Security
BEETHOVEN	9132.83	913.28	657.56
MOZART	7781.35	778.14	560.26
ROSSINI	1847.51	184.75	133.02
GERSHWIN	7951.38	759.14	572.50
PACHELBEL	5699.16	569.92	410.34
BALIN	6222.81	622.28	448.04
CLIBURN	4995.88	499.59	359.70

The weekly payroll figures are:

Name	Hours	Rate
BEETHOVEN	40	8.50
MOZART	44	6.45
ROSSINI	36	4.75
GERSHWIN	35.5	8.50
PACHELBEL	50	6.00
BALIN	16.5	20.00
CLIBURN	0	2.90

Write an interactive program to read and update the payroll file. Federal tax is computed as a straight 10 percent of earnings. The Social Security tax is computed as 7.2 percent of earnings up to a maximum tax of $2500 a year. List the updated file after the program is run.

11F Revise the program in Problem 11E to read the updated payroll file and print a table containing employee name, earnings, Federal tax, Social Security tax, and net pay. Use PRINT USING statements.

11G a) Write a program with PRINT USING statements to print N copies of the questionnaire in Fig. 11.18, where N is read interactively from the terminal.

b) Write a program that will read in the responses to the questionnaire for all students in your class and tabulate the results as follows:

• Compute and print the total number of responses and a breakdown according to class and according to age: less than 18; 18–22; over 22.

• Compute and print the number of Yes and No answers to each of questions 4–10 for all students.

Label all output appropriately, and use PRINT USING statements for all output.

POLITICS AS USUAL—A PREFERENCE POLL

1. NAME: _____, _____ ____

                 Last   First   M.I.

2. Academic year: ____ ____
   (Fr, So, Jr, Sr, Use "O" for other)

3. Age ____ ____

   For items 4. through 10., answer yes (Y) or no (N).

4. Have you ever voted in a presidential election?   ____

5. Do you think that most politicians are honest?   ____

6. Do you think that most politicians are responsive to the needs of their constituents?   ____

7. Do you think that the Federal government has taken sufficient steps to prevent another Watergate?   ____

8. Have you ever taken a Political Science course?   ____

9. Are you very interested in national politics?   ____

10. Have you ever paid any Federal income taxes?   ____

Fig. 11.18 Questionnaire for Problem 11G.

11H In Example 11.12, we assumed that the entries on an inventory file were in sequence according to stock number, ordered from 1, 2, and so on. Write a program to read from the terminal the stock entries for a dozen or so inventory items and build a sequential file containing these items. (You are not to make any assumptions concerning the ordering of the stock numbers of these items.)

11I Write a program to read the sequential file created in Problem 11H, sort the file in ascending order according to stock number and write the results on a new file. You may assume that the entire sequential file will fit in memory at once (Use arrays large enough to accommodate the sequential file entries that you made in Problem 11H).

11J Chain together the programs for Problems 11H and 11I. Then chain a third program to read the resulting sequential file and print it at the terminal with the appropriate PRINT USING and image features.

11K Create a sequential file SALMEN containing the salaries of 10 men, and a second sequential file SALWOM containing the salaries of 10 women. For each employee on these files, there is an employee number (four digits), an employee name (a string) and an employee salary. Each file is arranged in ascending order by employee number. Write a program that will read each of these files and merge the contents onto a third file, SALARY, retaining the ascending order of employee numbers. For each employee written to the file SALARY, write an "M" (for male) or an "F" (for female) following the employee number.

11L Write a program to read and print the file SALARY and compute the average salary for all employees. Chain together this program and the program from Problem 11K. Use the PRINT USING statement with appropriately designed images.

11M Do Problem 9J with the PRINT USING statement.

11N Do Problem 9K with the PRINT USING statement.

11O Do Problem 11K using virtual arrays. Use each employee number as an array subscript.

11P Do Problem 11L using a virtual array.

Appendixes

Appendix A*
System Command Summary

Command	Description
APPEND	Merges the contents of a previously saved source program with the current program.
BYE	Logs you out; closes and saves any open files. After you type BYE and press the RETURN key, the system displays the word Confirm: You have five options: ? Displays help on valid responses to the "Confirm" prompt. Y Normal logout. N No logout; cancels the BYE command. I Delete files individually before logging out. F Fast logout. To request one of these options in the BYE command, type BYE, a slash, and one of the valid responses (BYE/F, for example).
CATALOG or CAT	Displays your file directory. The default device is the system disk, but you can specify another device after the word CAT or CATALOG.
COMPILE	Saves a translated image of the current program in a disk file. The default file name is the current program name; the default file type is .BAC.
CONT	Continues execution of the current program after execution of a STOP statement.
DELETE DELETE 10,20 DELETE 10-50	Removes one or more lines from the program in memory. After the word DE-LETE, type the line number of the line to be deleted or type two line numbers separated by a dash (to delete a range of lines). You can specify several single lines or ranges of lines. Use commas to separate line numbers or line number ranges. Typing DELETE with no line numbers deletes all lines from your current program.
EXTEND	Puts BASIC-PLUS in EXTEND mode. You can write and run programs that include EXTEND mode features.
HELLO	Tells RSTS/E that you want to log in. The system prompts you for a project-programmer number and password. You can also use HELLO to attach a detached job to the terminal or change accounts without logging out.
LENGTH	Returns the length of your current program in 1K increments, along with its maximum allowed size. For example, if the current program is between 6K and 7K and the maximum size is 16K, BASIC-PLUS displays: 7(16)K of memory used

*The material in all of these appendixes has been adapted in part from copyrighted publications of Digital Equipment Corporation. This material is the sole responsibility of the authors.

Command	Description
LIST LIST 100,200 LIST 200-250	Displays all or part of the program currently in memory. The word LIST by itself displays your entire program. LIST followed by one line number displays that line; LIST followed by two line numbers separated by a dash displays the lines between and including the indicated lines. You can display several single lines or ranges of lines. Use commas to separate line numbers or line number ranges.
LISTNH	Same as LIST, but does not print the header that contains the program name and current date and time.
NAME f1 as f2	Rename permanent file f1 (include extension) as f2.
NEW	Clears your memory area, names a new program, and lets you enter a new program at the terminal. The default program name is NONAME.
NOEXTEND	Puts BASIC-PLUS in NOEXTEND mode. EXTEND mode features are no longer available unless the program contains an EXTEND statement.
OLD	Retrieves a saved source program from disk and places it in memory. By default, OLD retrieves NONAME.BAS in your account on the public structure.
RENAME	Changes the name of the program currently in memory.
REPLACE	Copies the source program currently in memory into a disk file. The default file name is the current program name; the default file type is .BAS. Unlike the SAVE command, REPLACE replaces an existing file with the same name.
RUN	Executes the program in memory. If you type a file specification after the word RUN, the system loads the file from disk, and executes it.
RUNNH	Executes the current program in memory without printing the header that contains the program name and current date and time.
SAVE	Copies the source program currently in memory into a disk file. The default file name is the current program name; the default file type is .BAS. SAVE does not replace an existing file with the same name.
UNSAVE	Deletes a file from a directory. The default file name is your current program name; the default file type is .BAS.

Additional VAX-11 System Commands

BASIC	Switches from DCL mode to BASIC language mode.
EDIT 20/I/IX/	Replaces first occurrence of I at line 20 by IX.
EDIT 30/,/"/2	Replaces second comma at line 30 with ".
EDIT 40/**/	Deletes first occurrence of ** at line 40.
EXIT	Switches from BASIC language mode to DCL mode.
HELP	Describes the BASIC command listed after HELP.
LOGOUT	Used in DCL mode to terminate the session.

Appendix B
Control Characters and Terminal Keys

Key	Function
CTRL/C	Halts execution of the current program and returns control to the job keyboard monitor. Echoes on the terminal as "^C".
CTRL/O	Stops and restarts terminal output while a program is running.
CTRL/Q	Resumes terminal output suspended by CTRL/S while a program is running. You can use CTRL/Q only if the terminal STALL characteristic is set.
CTRL/R	Redisplays the current terminal line.
CTRL/S	Suspends terminal output while a program is running. You can use CTRL/S only if the terminal STALL characteristic is set.
CTRL/U	Deletes the current terminal line. CTRL/U does not erase characters from the screen. Instead, it echoes "^U" and moves the cursor to the next line.
CTRL/Z	Is an end-of-file marker.
DELETE	Erases the last character typed.
ESCAPE ALTMODE	Sends a typed line to the system for processing. Echoes on your terminal as a "$" and does not perform a carriage return/line feed.
FORM FEED CTRL/L	Sends a typed line to the system for processing. Performs a form feed operation on the terminal.
LINE FEED	Continues the current program line on another terminal line. Performs a line feed/carriage return operation. It is recommended that you use the ampersand (&)/RETURN key combination instead of the LINE FEED key to continue the current program line on another terminal line. You can use the ampersand/RETURN key combination only in EXTEND mode.
NO SCROLL	Performs the same function as CTRL/S and CTRL/Q on a VT100 terminal. The terminal STALL characteristic must be set.
RETURN	Sends a typed line to the system for processing. Performs a carriage return/line feed operation on the terminal.
RUBOUT	Erases the last character typed and echoes erased characters inside backslashes.
TAB	Moves the cursor to the next tab stop on the terminal line. By default, tab stops are eight spaces apart.

Appendix C
Reserved Keywords

All names listed in Table C.1 below are *reserved keywords* in BASIC-PLUS, BASIC-PLUS-2, and VAX-11 BASIC. You cannot use any of these names as variable, array, or function names. The additional names in Table C.2 are reserved keywords only in VAX-11 BASIC.

Table C.1 Reserved Keywords

ABS	CVT$$	FILL$	LOG
ABS%	CVT$%	FILL%	LOG10
ACCESS	CVT$F	FIND	LSET
ALLOW	CVT%$	FIX	MAGTAPE
ALTERNATE	CVTF$	FIXED	MAP
AND	DATA	FNEND	MAT
APPEND	DATE$	FNEXIT	MID
AS	DEF	FOR	MID$
ASCII	DELETE	FORMAT$	MODE
ATN	DENSITY	FROM	MODIFY
BACK	DESC	FSP$	MOVE
BEL	DET	FSS$	NAME
BLOCK	DIF$	GE	NEXT
BLOCKSIZE	DIM	GET	NOCHANGES
BS	DIMENSION	GO	NODUPLICATES
BUCKETSIZE	DUPLICATES	GOSUB	NOECHO
BUFFER	ECHO	GOTO	NOEXTEND
BUFSIZ	EDIT$	GT	NONE
BY	ELSE	HT	NOREWIND
CALL	END	IDN	NOSPAN
CCPOS	EQ	IF	NOT
CHAIN	EQV	IMP	NUL$
CHANGE	ERL	INDEXED	NUM
CHANGES	ERN$	INPUT	NUM$
CHR$	ERR	INSTR	NUM1$
CLOSE	ERROR	INT	NUM2
CLUSTERSIZE	ERT$	INV	ON
COM	ESC	KEY	ONECHR
COMMON	EXIT	KILL	ONERROR
COMP%	EXP	LEFT	OPEN
CON	EXTEND	LEFT$	OR
CONNECT	FF	LEN	ORGANIZATION
CONTIGUOUS	FIELD	LET	OUTPUT
COS	FILE	LF	PEEK
COUNT	FILE$	LINE	PI
CR	FILESIZE	LINPUT	PLACE$
CTRLC	FILL	LOC	POS

PRIMARY	RIGHT	STREAM	UNLOCK
PRINT	RIGHT$	STRING$	UNTIL
PROD$	RND	SUB	UPDATE
PUT	RSET	SUBEND	USEROPEN
QUO$	SCRATCH	SUBEXIT	USING
RAD$	SEG%	SUM$	VAL
RANDOM	SEQUENTIAL	SWAP%	VAL%
RANDOMIZE	SGN	SYS	VALUE
RCTRLC	SI	TAB	VARIABLE
RCTRLO	SIN	TAN	VIRTUAL
READ	SLEEP	TAPE	VT
RECORD	SO	TASK	WAIT
RECORDSIZE	SP	TEMPORARY	WHILE
RECOUNT	SPACE$	THEN	WINDOWSIZE
REF	SPAN	TIME	WRITE
RELATIVE	SPEC	TIME$	WRKMAP
REM	SQR	TO	XLATE
RESET	STATUS	TRM$	XOR
RESTORE	STEP	TRN	ZER
RESUME	STOP	UNDEFINED	
RETURN	STR$	UNLESS	

Table C.2 Additional reserved keywords for VAX-11 BASIC

ABORT	ENDIF	LONG	REAL
ALIGNED	EXTENDSIZE	LSA	RECORDATTR
ALL	EXTERNAL	MAR	RECORDTYPE
ANY	FLUSH	MAR%	SEG$
ASC	FORCEIN	MARGIN	SHIFT
ATN2	FORTRAN	MAX	SINGLE
BIN$	FREE	MIN	SQRT
BINARY	FSP$	MOD	SUBROUTINE
BIT	FSS$	MOD%	TERMINAL
BROADCAST	FUNCTION	MSGMAP	TIM
BUFSIZ	FUNCTIONEND	NODATA	TST
CALLR	FUNCTIONEXIT	NOMARGIN	TSTEND
CLK$	HANGUP	NOPAGE	TYP
CONSTANT	HEX	NOQUOTE	TYPE
COT	HEX$	NOTAPE	TYPE$
DAT	IFMORE	OCT$	UNALIGNED
DAT$	IMAGE	ONENDFILE	USEAGE
DECLARE	INIMAGE	PAGE	USEAGE$
DEF*	INVALID	POKE	USR
DEFAULTNAME	JSB	POS%	USR$
DEL	LINO	PPS%	VFC
DELIMIT	LIST	PRN	VPS%
DOUBLE	LOCK	QUOTE	WITH
DOUBLEBUF	LOF	RAD%	WORD

Appendix D
Summary of Operators

Type	Operator	Operates Upon
Arithmetic	− Unary minus ^ or ** Exponentiation *,/ Multiplication, division +,− Addition, subtraction	Numeric variables and constants
Relational	= Equal to < Less than <= Less than or equal to > Greater than >= Greater than or equal to <> Not equal to == Approximately equal to (numbers) Identically equal to (strings)	String or numeric variables and constants
Logical	NOT Logical negation AND Logical product OR Logical sum XOR Logical exclusive or IMP Logical implication EQV Logical equivalence	Relational expressions composed of string or numeric elements, integer variables or integer valued expressions
String	+ Concatenation	String constants and variables
Matrix	+,− Addition and subtraction of matrices of equal dimensions, one operator per statement * Multiplication of conformable matrices * Scalar multiplication of a matrix	Array or matrix variables

Appendix E
Summary of BASIC-PLUS Functions

Under the column headed "Function", the functions are shown as

$$Y = function(arguments)$$

where the characters % and $ are appended to Y if the value returned is an integer or a character string, respectively.

An argument specified as a real value (X) can always be replaced by an integer value. An integer value (N%) can always be replaced by a real value (an implied FIX is done) except in the CVT%$ function, where the symbol I% indicates the need for an integer value.

We have listed many BASIC-PLUS functions not covered in the text.

Type	Function	Explanation
Mathematical	Y=ABS(X)	Returns the absolute value of X.
	Y=ATN(X)	Returns the arctangent (in radians) of X.
	Y=COS(X)	Returns the cosine of X where X is in radians.
	Y=EXP(X)	Returns the value of e^X, where e=2.71828 . . .
	Y=FIX(X)	Returns the truncated value of X, SGN(X) * INT(ABS(X)).
	Y=INT(X)	Returns the greatest integer in X which is less than or equal to X.
	Y=LOG(X)	Returns the natural logarithm of X, $\log_e X$.
	Y=LOG10(X)	Returns the common logarithm of X, $\log_{10} X$.
	Y=PI	Returns the constant 3.14159 . . .
	Y=RND	Returns a random number between 0 and 1.
	Y=RND(X)	Returns a random number between 0 and 1 (including 0, but not 1).
	Y=SGN(X)	Returns the sign function of X; +1 if positive, 0 if zero, −1 if negative.
	Y=SIN(X)	Returns the sine of X where X is in radians.
	Y=SQR(X)	Returns the square root of X.
	Y=TAN(X)	Returns the tangent of X where X is in radians.
Print	Y%=POS(X%)	Returns the current position of the print head for I/O channel X%. X% = 0 indicates the user's Teletype.
	TAB(X%)	Moves print head to position X% in the current print record, or is disregarded if the current position is beyond X%. (The first position is counted as 0.)
String	Y%=ASCII(A$)	Returns the ASCII value of the first character in the string A$.

Type	Function	Explanation
	`Y$=CHR$(X%)`	Returns a character string having the ASCII value of X%. Only one character is generated.
	`Y$=CVT%$(I%)`	Maps integer into 2-character string.
	`Y$=CVTF$(X)`	Maps floating-point number into 4- or 8-character string.
	`Y%=CVT$%(A$)`	Maps first two characters of string A$ into an integer.
	`Y=CVT$F(A$)`	Maps first four or eight characters of string A$ into a floating-point number.
	`Y$=CVT$$(A$,I%)`	Converts string A$ to string Y$ according to value of I%.
	`Y$=RAD$(N%)`	Converts an integer value to a 3-character string and is used to convert from Radix-50 format back to ASCII.
	`Y%=SWAP%(N%)`	Causes a byte swap operation on the two bytes in the integer variable N%.
	`Y$=STRING$(N1,N2)`	Creates string Y$ of length N1, composed of characters whose ASCII decimal value is N2.
	`Y$=LEFT(A$,N)`	Returns a substring of the string A$ from the first character to the Nth character (the leftmost N characters).
	`Y$=RIGHT(A$,N)`	Returns a substring of the string A$ from the Nth to the last character; the rightmost characters of the string starting with the Nth character.
	`Y$=MID(A$,N1,N2)`	Returns a substring (N2 characters long) of the string A$, starting with the N1st character (the characters between and including the N1 to N1+N2−1 characters).
	`Y%=LEN(A$)`	Returns the number of characters in the string A$, including trailing blanks.
	`Y%=INSTR(N1,A$,B$)`	Indicates a search for the substring B$ within the string A$ beginning at character position N1. Returns a value 0 if B$ is not in A$, and the position of the first character of B$ if B$ is found in A$ (the position is measured from the start of A$).
	`Y$=SPACE$(N)`	Indicates a string of N spaces, used to insert spaces within a character string.
	`Y$=NUM$(N)`	Indicates a string of numeric characters representing the value of N as it would be output by a PRINT statement. For example: NUM$(1.0000)= (space)1(space) and NUM$(−1.0000)= −1(space).
	`Y$=NUM1$(N)`	Returns a string of characters representing the value of N. This is similar to the function NUM$, except that it does not return spaces or E-format results.
	`Y=VAL(A$)`	Computes the numeric value of the string of numeric characters A$. If A$ contains any character not acceptable as numeric input with the INPUT statement, an error results. For example: VAL("15")=15

Type	Function	Explanation
	Y$=XLATE(A$,B$)	Translate A$ to the new string Y$ by means of the table string B$.
	Y$=SUM$(A$,B$)	Returns a numeric string equal to the arithmetic sum of numeric strings A$ and B$.
	Y$=DIFF$(A$,B$)	Returns a numeric string equal to the arithmetic difference A$−B$ of numeric strings A$ and B$.
	Y$=PROD$(A$,B$,P%)	Returns a numeric string equal to the product of numeric strings A$ and B$, rounded or truncated to P% places.
	Y=QUO$(A$,B$,P%)	Returns a numeric string equal to the arithmetic quotient A$/B$ of numeric strings A$ and B$, rounded or truncated to P% places.
	Y=PLACE$(A$,P%)	Returns a numeric string equal to the numeric string A, rounded or truncated to P% places.
	T%=COMP%(A$,B$)	Returns a value reflecting the result of an arithmetic comparison between numeric strings A$ and B$; T%=−1 for A<B, 0 for A=B and 1 for A>B.
System	Y$=DATE$(0%)	Returns the current date in the following format: 02-Mar-71
	Y$=DATE$(N%)	Returns a character string corresponding to a calendar date as follows: N=(day of year)+[(number of years since 1970)∗1000] DATE$(1) ="01-Jan-70" DATE$(125)="05-May-70"
	Y$=TIME$(0%)	Returns the current time of day as a character string as follows: TIME$(0)="05:30 PM" or "17:30 "
	Y$=TIME$(N%)	Returns a string corresponding to the time at N minutes before midnight. For example: TIME$(1)="11:59 PM" or "23:59 " TIME$(1440)="12:00 AM" or "00:00 " TIME$(721)="11:59 AM" or "11:59 "
	Y=TIME(0%)	Returns the clock time in seconds since midnight, as a floating-point number.
	Y=TIME(1%)	Returns the central processor time used by the current job in tenths of seconds.
	Y=TIME(2%)	Returns the connect time (during which the user is logged into the system) for the current job in minutes.
	Y=TIME(3%)	Returns to Y the decimal number of kilocore ticks (KCT's) used by this job.

Type	Function	Explanation
	`Y=TIME(4%)`	Returns to `Y` the decimal number of minutes of device time used by this job.
	`Y%=STATUS`	Returns to `Y%` the status of the OPEN statement executed most recently.
	`Y%=BUFSIZ(N)`	Returns to `Y%` the buffer size of the device or file open on channel `N`.
	`Y%=LINE`	Returns to `Y%` the line number of the statement being executed at the time of an interrupt.
	`Y%=ERR`	Returns value associated with the last encountered error if an ON ERROR GOTO statement appears in the program.
	`Y%=ERL`	Returns the line number at which the last error occurred if an ON ERROR GOTO statement appears in the program.
Matrix Functions and Variables	`MAT Y=TRN(X)`	Returns the transpose of the matrix `X`.
	`MAT Y=INV(X)`	Returns the inverse of the matrix `X`.
	`Y=DET`	Following an `INV(X)` function evaluation, the variable `DET` is equivalent to the determinant of `X`.
	`Y%=NUM`	Following input of a matrix, `NUM` contains the number of rows input or, in the case of a one-dimensional matrix, the number of elements entered.
	`Y%=NUM2`	Following input of a matrix, `NUM2` contains the number of elements entered in the last row read.
Input/Output	`Y%=RECOUNT`	Returns the number of characters read following an input operation. Used primarily with non-file-structured devices.

Appendix F
ASCII Character Codes

A list of ASCII codes follows. The codes at the beginning (0–31) are used for special control characters. Only those that are relevant to the text are listed.

Decimal Code	Character	Decimal Code	Character
0	Null	60	<
3	End of text	61	=
8	Backspace	62	>
9	Horizontal tab	63	?
10	Line feed	64	@
11	Vertical tab	65	A
12	Form feed	66	B
13	Carriage return	67	C
27	Escape	68	D
32	Space	69	E
33	!	70	F
34	"	71	G
35	#	72	H
36	$	73	I
37	%	74	J
38	&	75	K
39	'	76	L
40	(	77	M
41	)	78	N
42	*	79	O
43	+	80	P
44	,	81	Q
45	—	82	R
46	.	83	S
47	/	84	T
48	0	85	U
49	1	86	V
50	2	87	W
51	3	88	X
52	4	89	Y
53	5	90	Z
54	6	91	[
55	7	92	\
56	8	93	]
57	9	94	^
58	:	95	_
59	;	96	'

Decimal Code	Character	Decimal Code	Character
97	a	113	q
98	b	114	r
99	c	115	s
100	d	116	t
101	e	117	u
102	f	118	v
103	g	119	w
104	h	120	x
105	i	121	y
106	j	122	z
107	k	123	{
108	l	124	|
109	m	125	}
110	n	126	~
111	o	127	Delete
112	p		

Appendix G
BASIC-PLUS Error Messages

Because a BASIC-PLUS program can recover from certain errors, this appendix lists errors in two categories—*recoverable* and *nonrecoverable*. The recoverable error messages are in ascending order of their error numbers. A program can use these error numbers to differentiate errors. Nonrecoverable errors are in alphabetical order without error numbers because a program cannot use these numbers in an error handling routine. The first character position of each message indicates the severity of the error. Table G.1 describes this standard.

Table G.1 Severity Standard in Error Messages*

Character	Severity	Meaning
%	Warning	Execution of the program can continue but may generate the expected results.
?	Fatal	Execution cannot continue unless you remove the cause of the error. No space or tab is allowed after the question mark.
	Information	A message beginning with neither a question mark nor a percent sign is for information only.

*Notes: 1. The letters CCL stand for Command Control Language.
2. The letters KB stand for Keyboard.
3. The letters FFP stand for Floating Point Processor.

Table G.2 User-Recoverable Error Messages

ERR	Message Printed	Meaning
0	(system installation name)	The error code 0 is associated with the system installation name. System programs use this to print identification lines.
1	?Bad directory for device	1. The directory of the device referenced is in an unreadable format. 2. The magnetic tape label format on tape differs from the system-wide default format, the current job default format, or the format specified in the OPEN statement. Use the ASSIGN command to set the correct format default or change the format specification in the MODE option of the OPEN statement.
2	?Illegal file name	1. The file name or type specified is not acceptable. It contains unacceptable characters or violates the file specification format. 2. The CCL command to be added begins with a number or contains a character other than A through Z, 0 through 9, or at sign (@).
3	?Account or device in use	1. The account to be deleted has one or more files and must be zeroed before being deleted. 2. Reassigning or dismounting of the device cannot be done because the device is open or has one or more open files. 3. The run-time system to be deleted is in use. 4. Output to a pseudo keyboard cannot be done unless the device is in KB wait state. 5. An echo control field cannot be declared while another field is active. 6. The CCL command to be added already exists.
4	?No room for user on device	You have already used the allowed storage space; the device as a whole is too full to accept further data.
5	?Can't find file or account	Either the file or account number specified was not found on the device specified, or the CCL command to be deleted does not exist.
6	?Not a valid device	The device specification supplied is not valid for one of the following reasons: 1. The unit number or its type is not configured on the system.

Table G.2 User-Recoverable Error Messages (*continued*)

ERR	Message Printed	Meaning
		2. The specification is untranslatable because a physical device is not associated with it.
7	?I/O channel already open	You tried to open one of the twelve I/O channels that the program had already opened.
8	?Device not available	The specified device exists on the system, but you cannot assign or open it for one of the following reasons: 1. The device is currently reserved by another job. 2. The device requires privileges for ownership that you do not have. 3. The system manager has disabled the device or its controller. 4. The device is a keyboard line for pseudo keyboard use only.
9	?I/O channel not open	You tried to perform I/O on one of the twelve channels that the program has not previously opened.
10	?Protection violation	You cannot perform the requested operation because the operation is illegal (such as input from a line printer) or because you do not have the privileges necessary (such as deleting a protected file).
11	?End of file on device	You tried to perform input beyond the end of a data file, or a BASIC-PLUS source file is called into memory that does not contain an END statement.
12	?Fatal system I/O failure	An I/O error has occurred on the system level. You have no guarantee that the last operation has been performed. This error is caused by a hardware condition. Report such occurrences to the system manager.
13	?Data error on device	One or more characters may have been transmitted incorrectly due to a parity error, bad punch combination on a card, or similar error.
14	?Device hung or write locked	Check the hardware condition of the device you are requesting. Possible causes of this error include a line printer out of paper or high-speed reader being off-line.
15	?Keyboard WAIT exhausted	Time that the WAIT statement requests has been exhausted with no input received from the specified keyboard.

Table G.2 User-Recoverable Error Messages (*continued*)

ERR	Message Printed	Meaning
16	?Name or account now exists	Either you tried to rename a file with the name of a file that already exists, or the system manager tried to insert an account number that is already in the system.
17	?Too many open files on unit	Only one open DECtape output file is permitted per DECtape drive. Only one open file per magnetic tape drive is permitted.
18	?Illegal SYS() usage	Illegal use of the SYS system function.
19	?Disk block is interlocked	The requested disk block segment is already in use (locked) by some other user.
20	?Pack IDs don't match	The identification code for the specified disk pack does not match the identification code already on the pack.
21	?Disk pack is not mounted	No disk pack is mounted on the specified disk drive.
22	?Disk pack is locked out	The disk pack specified is mounted but is temporarily disabled.
23	?Illegal cluster size	The specified cluster size is unacceptable. The cluster size must be a power of 2. For a *file* cluster, the size must be equal to or greater than the pack cluster size and must not be greater than 256. For a *pack* cluster, the size must be equal to or greater than the device cluster size and must not be greater than 16. The device cluster size is fixed by type.
24	?Disk pack is private	You do not have access to the specified private disk pack.
25	?Disk pack needs 'CLEANing'	Nonfatal disk mounting error; run the ONLCLN system program.
26	?Fatal disk pack mount error	Fatal disk mounting error. Disk cannot be successfully mounted.
27	?I/O to detached keyboard	I/O was attempted to a hung-up dataset or to the previous, but now detached, console keyboard for the job.
28	?Programmable ^C trap	A CTRL/C was typed while an ON ERROR GOTO statement was in effect and programmable CTRL/C trapping was enabled.
29	?Corrupted file structure	Fatal error in CLEAN operation.

Table G.2 User-Recoverable Error Messages (*continued*)

ERR	Message Printed	Meaning
30	?Device not file structured	An attempt is made to access a device other than a disk, DECtape, or magnetic tape device as a file-structured device. This error occurs, for example, when you attempt to get a directory listing of a nondirectory device.
31	?Illegal byte count for I/O	This error has two possible causes: 1. The buffer size you specified in the RECORDSIZE option of the OPEN statement or the COUNT option of the PUT statement is not a multiple of the block size of the device you are using for I/O, or is illegal for the device. 2. You tried to run a compiled file that has improper size due to incorrect transfer procedure.
32	?No buffer space available	You accessed a file and the monitor required one small buffer to complete the request, but there is no buffer available. If the program is sending messages, two conditions are possible. The first occurs when a program sends a message and the receiving program has exceeded the pending message limit. The second occurs when a sending program attempts to send a message and a small buffer is not available for the operation.
33	?Odd address trap	This error occurs when you attempt to address nonexistent memory or an odd address with the PEEK function. If you get this error for any other reason, report it to your system manager.
34	?Reserved instruction trap	An attempt is made to execute an illegal or reserved instruction or an FPP instruction when floating-point hardware is not available.
35	?Memory management violation	You specified an illegal monitor address in the PEEK function. If you get this error for any other reason, report it to your system manager.
36	?SP stack overflow	An attempt was made to extend the hardware stack beyond its legal size.
37	?Disk error during swap	A hardware error occurs when your job is swapped into or out of memory. The contents of your job area are lost, but the job remains logged into the system and is reinitialized to run the NONAME program. Report such occurrences to the system manager.

Table G.2 User-Recoverable Error Messages (*continued*)

ERR	Message Printed	Meaning
38	?Memory parity failure	A parity error was detected in the memory occupied by this job.
39	?Magtape select error	When access to a magnetic tape drive was attempted, the selected unit was found to be off line.
40	?Magtape record length error	When performing input from magnetic tape, the record on magnetic tape was longer than the buffer designated to handle the record.
41	?Non-res run-time system	The run-time system referenced has not been loaded into memory and is therefore nonresident.
42	?Virtual buffer too large	Virtual array buffers must be 512 bytes long.
43	?Virtual array not on disk	A nondisk device is open on the channel on which the virtual array is referenced.
44	?Matrix or array too big	Memory array size is too large.
45	?Virtual array not yet open	You tried to use a virtual array before opening the corresponding disk file.
46	?Illegal I/O channel	You tried to open a file on an I/O channel outside the range of the integer numbers 1 to 12.
47	?Line too long	The buffer overflows because of an attempt to input a line longer than 255 characters. (This includes any line terminator.)
48	%Floating point error	You tried to use a computed floating-point number outside the range 1E–38 < n < 1E38 excluding zero. If no transfer to an error handling routine is made, zero is returned as the floating-point value; your program will continue executing.
49	%Argument too large in EXP	Acceptable arguments are within the approximate range −89 < arg < +88. The value returned is zero; your program will continue executing.
50	%Data format error	A READ or INPUT statement detected data in an illegal format. E.g., 1..2 is an improperly formed number; 1.3 is an improperly formed integer; "HELLO" "THERE" is an illegal string; your program will continue executing.
51	%Integer error	You tried to use a computed integer outside the range −32768 < n < 32767. For example, you tried to assign to an integer variable a floating-point number outside the integer range.

Table G.2 User-Recoverable Error Messages (*continued*)

ERR	Message Printed	Meaning
		If no transfer to an error handling routine is made, zero is returned as the integer value; your program will continue executing.
52	?Illegal number	Integer overflow or underflow, or floating-point overflow. The integer range is −32768 to +32767; for floating-point numbers, the upper limit is 1E38. (For floating-point underflow, the "%Floating point error" (ERR=4 8) is generated.)
53	%Illegal argument in LOG	Negative or zero argument to LOG function. Value returned is the argument passed to the function; your program will continue executing.
54	%Imaginary square roots	You tried to take the square root of a number less than zero. The value returned is the square root of the absolute value of the argument; your program will continue executing.
55	?Subscript out of range	You tried to reference an array element beyond the number of elements created for the array when it was dimensioned.
56	?Can't invert matrix	You tried to invert a singular or nearly singular matrix.
57	?Out of data	The DATA list was exhausted and a READ requested additional data.
58	?ON statement out of range	The index value in an ON−GOTO or ON−GOSUB statement is less than one or is greater than the number of line numbers in the list.
59	?Not enough data in record	An INPUT statement did not find enough data in one line to satisfy all the specified variables.
60	?Integer overflow, FOR loop	The integer index in a FOR loop attempted to go beyond 32766 or below −32767.
61	%Division by 0	Attempt in your program to divide some quantity by zero. If no transfer is made to an error handling routine, the result is 0, and your program will continue to execute.
62	?No run−time system	The run-time system referenced has not been added to the system list of run-time systems.
63	?FIELD overflows buffer	You tried to use FIELD to allocate more space than exists in the specified buffer.

Table G.2 User-Recoverable Error Messages (*continued*)

ERR	Message Printed	Meaning
64	?Not a random access device	You tried to perform random access I/O to a nonrandom access device.
65	?Illegal MAGTAPE() usage	Improper use of the MAGTAPE function.
66	?Missing special feature	Your program uses a BASIC-PLUS feature not present on the given installation.
67	?Illegal switch usage	This error has two possible causes: 1. A CCL command contains an error in an otherwise valid CCL switch. (For example, use of the /SI:n switch without a value for n or a colon; or specification of more than one of the same type of CCL switch.) 2. A file specification switch is not the last element in a file specification or is missing a colon or an argument.

Table G.3 Nonrecoverable Error Messages

Message Printed	Meaning
?Arguments don't match	Arguments in a function call do not match, in number or in type, the arguments defined for the function.
?Bad line number pair	Line numbers specified in a LIST or DELETE command were formatted incorrectly.
?Bad number in PRINT-USING	Format specified in the PRINT-USING string cannot be used to print one or more values.
?Can't CONTinue	Program was stopped or ended at a spot from which execution cannot be resumed with CONT or CCONT.
?Data type error	Incorrect usage of floating-point, integer, or string variable or constant where some other data type was necessary.
?DEF without FNEND	A second DEF statement was encountered in the processing of a user function without an FNEND.
?End of statement not seen	Statement contains too many elements to be processed correctly.

Table G.3 Nonrecoverable Error Messages (*continued*)

Message Printed	Meaning
?Error text lookup failure	An I/O error occurred while the system was attempting to retrieve an error message. Possible cause could be that the device containing the system error file (ERR.SYS) is off-line or the system error file contains a bad block.
?Execute only file	Attempt was made to add, delete, or list a statement in a translated (.BAC) file.
?Expression too complicated	This error usually occurs when parentheses have been nested too deeply. The depth allowed depends on the individual expression.
?File exists-RENAME/REPLACE	A file of the name specified in a SAVE command already exists. To save the program with the name specified, use REPLACE, or use RENAME followed by SAVE.
?FNEND without DEF	A FNEND statement was encountered in your program before a DEF statement was seen.
?FNEND without function call	An FNEND statement was encountered in your program before a function call was executed.
?FOR without NEXT	A FOR statement was encountered in your program without a corresponding NEXT statement to terminate the loop.
?Illegal conditional clause	Incorrectly formatted conditional expression.
?Illegal DEF nesting	The range of one function definition crosses the range of another function definition.
?Illegal dummy variable	One of the variables in the dummy variable list of user-defined functions is not a legal variable name.
?Illegal expression	Double operators, missing operators, mismatched parentheses, or some similar error was found in an expression.
?Illegal FIELD variable	The FIELD variable specified is unacceptable.

Table G.3 Nonrecoverable Error Messages (*continued*)

Message Printed	Meaning
?Illegal FN redefinition	Attempt was made to redefine a user function.
?Illegal function name	Attempt was made to define a function with a function name of incorrect format.
?Illegal IF statement	Incorrectly formatted IF statement.
?Illegal in immediate mode	You entered a statement in immediate mode that can only be executed as part of a program.
?Illegal line number(s)	Line number reference outside the range $1 < n < 32767$.
?Illegal mode mixing	String and numeric operations cannot be mixed.
?Illegal statement	Attempt was made to execute a statement that did not translate without errors.
?Illegal symbol	An unrecognizable character was encountered. For example, a line consisting of a # character.
?Illegal verb	The verb portion of the statement cannot be recognized.
%Inconsistent function usage	A function is defined with a certain number of arguments but is referenced elsewhere with a different number of arguments. Fix the reference to match the definition and reload the program to reset the function definition.
%Inconsistent subscript use	A subscripted variable is being used with a different number of dimensions from the number with which it was originally defined.
?Literal string needed	A variable name was used where a numeric or character string was necessary.
?Matrix dimension error	Attempt was made to dimension a matrix to more than two dimensions, or an error was made in the syntax of a DIM statement.

Table G.3 Nonrecoverable Error Messages (*continued*)

Message Printed	Meaning
?Matrix or array without DIM	A matrix or array element was referenced beyond the range of an implicitly dimensioned matrix.
?Maximum memory exceeded	This error has two possible causes: 1. During an OLD operation, the job's private memory size maximum was reached. 2. While running a program, the system required more memory for string or I/O buffer space, and the job's private memory size maximum or the system maximum (16K words for BASIC-PLUS) was reached.
?Modifier error	This error has two possible causes: 1. Attempt was made to use one of the statement modifiers (FOR, WHILE, UNTIL, IF, or UNLESS) incorrectly. 2. An OPEN statement modifier, such as a RECORDSIZE, CLUSTERSIZE, FILESIZE, or MODE option, is not in the correct order.
?NEXT without FOR	A NEXT statement was encountered in your program without a previous FOR statement.
?No logins	Message printed if the system is full and cannot accept additional users, or if further logins are disabled by the system manager.
?Not enough available memory	An attempt was made to load a nonprivileged compiled program that is too large to run given the job's private memory size maximum. The program must be made privileged in order to expand above a private memory size maximum, or the system manager must increase the job's private memory size maximum to accommodate the program.
?Number is needed	A character string or variable name was used where a number was necessary.

Table G.3 Nonrecoverable Error Messages (*continued*)

Message Printed	Meaning
?1 or 2 dimensions only	Attempt was made to dimension a matrix to more than two dimensions.
?ON statement needs GOTO	A statement beginning with ON does not contain a GOTO or GOSUB clause.
Please say HELLO	Message printed by the LOGIN system program. A user who was not logged into the system has typed something other than a legal, command.
?Please use the RUN command	A transfer of control (as in a GOTO, GOSUB, or IF–GOTO statement) cannot be performed from immediate mode.
?PRINT-USING buffer overflow	Format specified contains a field too large to be manipulated by the PRINT-USING statement.
?PRINT-USING format error	An error was made in the construction of the string used to supply the output format in a PRINT-USING statement.
?Program lost-Sorry	A fatal system error caused your program to be lost. This error can indicate hardware problems or use of an improperly compiled program.
?Redimensioned array	Usage of an array or matrix within your program has caused BASIC-PLUS to redimension the array implicitly.
?RESUME and no error	A RESUME statement was encountered where no error had occurred to cause a transfer into an error handling routine with the ON ERROR GOTO statement.
?RETURN without GOSUB	RETURN statement is encountered in your program when a previous GOSUB statement was not executed.

Table G.3 Nonrecoverable Error Messages (*continued*)

Message Printed	Meaning
%SCALE factor interlock	1. You set a new scale factor and then executed a program that was translated using a different scale factor. The program runs, but BASIC-PLUS uses the scale factor in effect when the program was translated. To cause BASIC-PLUS to translate the program with the new scale factor, use REPLACE and OLD. 2. You set a new scale factor and then entered an immediate mode statement. Immediate mode statements are always translated using the current scale factor. The new scale factor will take effect when you use the NEW or OLD command or run a program from its source file.
?Statement not found	Reference is made in the program to a line number that is not in the program.
Stop	STOP statement was executed. You can usually continue program execution by typing CONT and the RETURN key.
?String is needed	A number or variable name was used where a character string was necessary.
?Syntax error	BASIC-PLUS statement was incorrectly formatted.
?Too few arguments	The function has been called with a number of arguments not equal to the number defined for the function.
?Too many arguments	A user-defined function can have up to five arguments only.
?Undefined function called	BASIC-PLUS interpreted some statement component as a function call for which there is no defined function (system or user).
?What?	You entered a command or immediate mode statement that BASIC-PLUS cannot process. Illegal verb or improper format error most likely.

Table G.3 Nonrecoverable Error Messages (*continued*)

Message Printed	Meaning
`?Wrong math package`	Program was compiled on a system with either the two-word or four-word math package, and an attempt is made to run the program on a system with the opposite math package. Recompile the program using the math package of the system on which it will be run.

Appendix H
Some Differences Between BASIC-PLUS, BASIC-PLUS-2, and VAX-11 BASIC

This appendix contains a summary of the differences between BASIC-PLUS, BASIC-PLUS-2, and VAX-11 BASIC. This summary only covers language differences related to features that are described in the text.

NOEXTEND Mode

In VAX-11 BASIC and BASIC-PLUS-2, all variable names may be multicharacter names. The NOEXTEND mode does not exist.

IF-THEN-ELSE Statement

The true statement of an IF–THEN–ELSE may be a multiple-statement line in VAX-11 BASIC and BASIC-PLUS-2.

```
100    IF X < 0 THEN                            &
            LET POS.SUM = POS.SUM + X           &
            \PRINT X; "POSITIVE"                &
        ELSE                                    &
            LET NEG.SUM = NEG.SUM + X           &
            \PRINT X; "NEGATIVE"
```

The DIM Statement

The DIM statement may be placed anywhere in a BASIC-PLUS or BASIC-PLUS-2 program, although we recommend placing all DIM statements at or near the beginning of a program. In VAX-11 BASIC, you must declare an array (using a DIM statement) before you can reference it.

The DEF Statement

Either

    DEF
or DEF*

may be used to begin a function definition in VAX-11 BASIC and BASIC-PLUS-2. You cannot transfer control into or out of a multiple line function beginning with DEF in VAX-11 BASIC. In all versions, you can transfer control into or out of a multiple line function beginning with DEF*, although this is a bad programming practice and should not be done.

Reserved Keywords in VAX-11 BASIC

There are many more reserved keywords in VAX-11 BASIC. They are listed in Appendix C, Table C.2.

Multiple Statement Lines in VAX-11 BASIC

Individual statements of a statement group or multiple statement line may be typed one per line, without the & at the end of each line or the \ between statements. Each new statement in the group must be preceded by at least one blank space. A single statement that extends over more than one line must be indicated by the use of the & symbol at the end of each line that is continued.

```
200     PRINT "X = "; X
        PRINT "Y = "; Y
        PRINT "THIS IS ONE LONG STRING"; ST1$;        &
               "CONTINUED OVER TWO LINES"
```

Function Arguments

BASIC-PLUS allows a maximum of five arguments in a function. BASIC-PLUS-2 and VAX-11 BASIC allow up to eight arguments.

Handling of Numeric Errors

The handling of numeric errors such as arithmetic overflow, division by zero, square root of a negative number, etc. differs in BASIC-PLUS-2 and VAX-11 BASIC from what is discussed in Chapter 4 for BASIC-PLUS. In general, VAX-11 BASIC returns more informative diagnostics for these errors than either BASIC-PLUS or BASIC-PLUS-2. Many of these errors are fatal to execution in VAX-11 BASIC, but not in BASIC-PLUS or BASIC-PLUS-2.

The PRINT Statement

The standard print formats used with BASIC-PLUS-2 are different than those used in VAX-11 BASIC and BASIC-PLUS. Specifically, a small real value such as .000123456 would be printed exactly as it appears in BASIC-PLUS-2, but would be printed as .123456E-3 in VAX-11 BASIC or BASIC-PLUS. In BASIC-PLUS-2, an output item at the end of a print line is automatically split and continued on the next line if it will not fit on the current line. VAX-11 BASIC and BASIC-PLUS are more restrictive and will not automatically split all output items.

PRINT USING Statement

Leading zeros in an exponential image field are printed as spaces in VAX-11 BASIC and BASIC-PLUS; they are printed as zeros in BASIC-PLUS-2. BASIC-PLUS-2 also follows different rounding conventions for numeric output items than does VAX-11 BASIC and BASIC PLUS. BASIC-PLUS-2 first rounds each number to six significant digits and then rounds a second time as specified by the image field; VAX-11 BASIC and BASIC-PLUS only round once—as specified by the image field.

String Functions POS and SEG$

BASIC-PLUS-2 and VAX-11 BASIC support a function called POS that searches a string for a substring. They also support a function called SEG$ that extracts a substring from the middle of a string. These functions may be used in place of their BASIC-PLUS counterparts, INSTR and MID, respectively.

File Features

BASIC-PLUS-2 and VAX-11 BASIC support a number of different file types in addition to ASCII files and virtual arrays. These file types are beyond the scope of this text. In BASIC-PLUS-2, the symbol "#" must always be used when specifying a decimal number in an OPEN or CLOSE statement. Also, the integer 0 must appear in the statement

```
ON ERROR GOTO 0
```
that disables an error processing routine. The separator symbol ";" must appear between output list items in PRINT, PRINT USING, and PRINT# statements in BASIC-PLUS-2. VAX-11 BASIC requires the specification of file organization (sequential or virtual) with the OPEN statement.

CHAIN Statement

In BASIC-PLUS-2, the word LINE must be used in a CHAIN statement to specify a starting point other than the first program line.

```
CHAIN "CHECKS" LINE 350
```

The word LINE is optional in BASIC-PLUS. The LINE option is not supported in VAX-11 BASIC.

Appendix I
Extensions to BASIC-PLUS Found in BASIC-PLUS-2 and VAX-11 BASIC

DECLARE Statement (VAX-11 BASIC Only)

The DECLARE statement (available only in VAX-11 BASIC) can be used to associate a data type with a variable regardless of the variable name. Thus variables with names not ending with a $ (or %) may be associated with string (or integer) values. The following three statements illustrate the use of the DECLARE statement.

```
DECLARE STRING MY.NAME, CITY
DECLARE INTEGER COUNT
DECLARE REAL ALPHA, BETA
```

The general form of the VAX-11 BASIC DECLARE statement is shown in the following display.

DECLARE Statement (VAX-11 BASIC only)

DECLARE *data-type variable-list*

Interpretation: *Data-type* may be either INTEGER, REAL, STRING, or any other valid VAX-11 BASIC data type. One or more variable names may appear in the *variable-list* (the comma is used as a separator) and these variables will be treated as being of the declared type (*data type*). The variable names cannot end with a $ or a %. DECLARE statements should be placed at the beginning of a program, before any of the executable program statements.

Using the DECLARE Statement to Declare Program Constants (VAX-11 BASIC)

In VAX-11 BASIC, important *program constants* may be associated with names using the DECLARE statement, rather than assignment statements, as shown in the text. For example, the statements

```
DECLARE REAL CONSTANT GRAVITY = 32.17
DECLARE INTEGER CONSTANT MONTHS = 30
DECLARE STRING CONSTANT ALPHABET =        &
    "ABCDEFGHIJKLMNOPQRSTUVWXYZ"
```

may be used instead of the statements

```
LET GRAVITY = 32.17
LET MONTHS% = 30%
LET ALPHABET$ = "ABCDEFGHIJKLMNOPQRSTUVWXYZ"
```

to specify the data type and constant value associated with each variable name listed. Only one such name-constant pair is permitted per declaration. Note that the symbols "%" and "$" are not needed to identify integer and string constants or variables.

Subprograms

The subprogram is a feature of BASIC-PLUS-2 and VAX-11 BASIC that is extremely useful in implementing nicely modularized programs. Subprograms overcome the major shortcoming of the BASIC-PLUS function and subroutine—i.e., the fact that neither provides the degree of *module independence* that is so important in the implementation of large program systems.

A reasonable degree of independence between modules can be achieved only through the use of programming language features that permit complete control of the *information flow interface* between these modules. The fundamental requirements of any such language features are:

1. that all information to be communicated between two modules can be passed through the use of argument/parameter lists (in a manner similar to the use of argument/parameter lists for user-defined functions).
2. that all other variables and arrays referenced in the module must be local to the module—i.e., distinct from data objects with the same name which appear outside the module.

Unfortunately, neither user-defined functions nor subroutines meet either of these two requirements. Subroutines do not have arguments; the user-defined functions allow only simple variables (and not arrays) to be used as arguments. User-defined functions also allow for the return from the function of only a single computed value. Furthermore, any variable used in a function or subroutine module and not listed as a parameter is considered global to the module. This means that changes in the value of such a variable within the module are not confined to the module, but will propagate outside the module (side effects).

The subprogram feature of BASIC-PLUS-2 and VAX-11 BASIC satisfies the two requirements of module independence listed above. We will illustrate the use of the subprogram feature by rewriting the median for the Simple Statistics Problem (Problem 8A) as an independent subprogram. The new main program and subprogram are shown in Figs. I.1. and I.2.

```
100 !STATISTICS PROBLEM - MAIN PROGRAM
120 !
130 !COMPUTE THE RANGE, MEAN AND MEDIAN OF A
140 !COLLECTION OF N DATA ITEMS
150 !
160 !PROGRAM CONSTANTS
180     LET MAX.ITEMS = 100    !MAX ITEMS ALLOWED
190 !
200 !ARRAYS USED
210     DIM X(100)
220 !
230 !FUNCTIONS REFERENCED -
240 !   FNLARGEST, FNSMALLEST, FNMEAN
250 !
260 !MAIN PROGRAM
270 !ENTER AND VALIDATE N. ENTER ALL DATA IN ARRAY X
280     INPUT "ENTER NUMBER OF ITEMS"; N
290     INPUT "OUT OF RANGE. PLEASE RE-ENTER."; N          &
            UNTIL N >= 1 AND N <= MAX.ITEMS
295     PRINT "ENTER DATA LIST, SEPARATED BY COMMAS"
300     INPUT X(I) FOR I = 1 TO N
310 !
320 !COMPUTE THE RANGE
330     LET RANGE = FNLARGEST(N) - FNSMALLEST(N)
340     PRINT
350     PRINT "THE RANGE IS"; RANGE
360 !
370 !COMPUTE THE MEAN
380     LET MEAN = FNMEAN(N)
390     PRINT
400     PRINT "THE MEAN IS"; MEAN
410 !
420 !DETERMINE THE MEDIAN BY CALLING A SUBPROGRAM
430     CALL FINDMED (X( ), N, MEDIAN)
440     PRINT
```

```
450     PRINT "THE MEDIAN IS"; MEDIAN
460 !
470     PRINT "CALCULATIONS COMPLETE"
480 !
490 !DEFINITION OF FUNCTIONS FNLARGEST, FNSMALLEST,
500 !AND FNMEAN GO HERE
                .
                .
                .
3990    END    !MAIN PROGRAM
```

Fig. I.1 Main Program for Problem 8A using subprogram FINDMED.

```
4000    SUB FINDMED (X( ), N, MEDIAN)
4010 !
4020 !SUBPROGRAM TO COMPUTE THE MEDIAN OF N DATA
4030 !ITEMS IN AN ARRAY
4040 !
4050 !PARAMETER DEFINITIONS --
4060 !  IN:  N - NUMBER OF ITEMS IN X
4070 !  OUT: MEDIAN - MEDIAN OF THE DATA
4080 !  IN/OUT: X( ) - ARRAY TO BE PROCESSED. WHEN
4090 !                 FINDMED ENDS, X( ) IS SORTED
4100 !
4110 !LOCAL VARIABLES - MED.INDEX
4120 !
4130 !SORT DATA IN ASCENDING ORDER
4140    CALL SORT(X( ), N)
4150 !
4160 !DETERMINE MIDDLE VALUE.
4170 !CHECK IF N IS ODD OR EVEN.
4180 !USE MIDDLE ITEM IF N IS ODD;
4190 !OTHERWISE, USE AVERAGE OF TWO MIDDLE ITEMS.
4200    LET MED.INDEX = N / 2 + 1
4210    IF INT(N / 2) * 2 <> N THEN        &
            LET MEDIAN = X(MED.INDEX)      &
        ELSE                               &
            LET MEDIAN = (X(MED.INDEX-1) &
                    + X(MED.INDEX)) / 2
4220 !
4230    SUBEND
```

Fig. I.2 Subprogram FINDMED.

The subprograms are independent program modules and should come
after the END statement of the main program. As illustrated in Fig. I.2, the
name of a subprogram appears in the subprogram header statement (line
4000) between the keyword SUB and the subprogram parameter list. The
parentheses after the parameter X indicate that X is an array argument.
The SUBEND statement (line 4230) terminates a subprogram definition.

Some of the advantages and major features of subprograms are clearly demonstrated in Figs. I.1 and I.2. The sort and median subprograms have unique names which appear in their headers and calls. They are completely separated from each other and from the main program. Array variables are allowed as subprogram arguments, and all variables involved in the communication between subprograms are clearly indicated in the subprogram calls

```
430 CALL FINDMED(X( ), N, MEDIAN)   (in the main program)
```

and

```
4140 CALL SORT(X( ), N)   (in subprogram FINDMED)
```

At each call, information is provided to a subprogram via the *input arguments* (X( ) and N, in this case); all results are returned through the *output arguments* (e.g., MEDIAN). Unlike a function, a subprogram may change the value of an argument; an argument whose value is changed is called an output argument. Any number of values may be returned, such as the median value, MEDIAN (returned by FINDMED), and the sorted array X (returned by SORT).

Some subprogram parameters, such as X, are used for both input and output; some, such as N, are used just for input; others, such as MEDIAN in FINDMED, are used solely for output purposes. When preparing a data table for a subprogram, you should carefully note which parameters are used for input, which for output, and which are used for both.

As with functions, the names used in the argument list of a subprogram call are completely independent of the names used in the parameter list of the subprogram definition. Thus, subprograms can be called with different arguments in the same program or in different programs. Each argument must, however, agree in number and type (numeric variable, string variable, or array) with the corresponding subprogram parameter. This means that we could use FINDMED to determine the median value, MX, of a sorted array A with 10 elements, by using the call

```
CALL FINDMED (A( ), 10, MX)
```

Aside from the argument/parameter interface, subprogram modules are completely independent of one another. There can be no side effects, because there are no global variables. Variables such as MED.INDEX are all local to the subprograms in which they appear. Changes to these variables have no effect outside the subprograms. Hence, they can be used freely in more than one module without causing harmful interaction.

Because of this independence, the various subprograms required for a program system can easily be written and used by different programmers. *Libraries* of subprograms can be created, thereby making the subprograms available to large numbers of users. The only information about a subprogram that a user needs to know is its name, a brief description of what it does, but not how it does it, and a complete description of the subprogram parameters.

All of these factors make the subprogram a far more powerful tool for programming than either the function or the subroutine. The displays that follow summarize the definition and call of subprograms in BASIC-PLUS-2 and VAX-11 BASIC.

Subprogram Definition (BASIC-PLUS-2 and VAX-11 BASIC)

SUB *name* (*parameter list*)

} subprogram description

SUBEND

Interpretation: The subprogram *name* may be one to six characters in length. The *parameter list* consists of the names of simple variables or arrays. All communication between the subprogram and the calling program (or calling subprogram) is through the parameter list. Any other names used in the subprogram are considered local. The SUBEND statement terminates the subprogram definition and causes a return to the calling program during execution.

Notes: An array parameter is indicated by a pair of parentheses following the array name. A maximum of eight parameters is allowed in BASIC-PLUS-2. Thirty-two parameters are permitted in VAX-11 BASIC. Transfers into or out of a subprogram are not permitted except through the use of the CALL and SUBEND statements, respectively.

The SUBEND not only marks the physical end of a subprogram, but also causes a return to the calling module during execution. Returns from points other than the end of a subprogram may be specified using the statement

SUBEXIT

which transfers control to the SUBEND statement. Note that it is not possible to follow a SUBEND statement with a comment.

If a subprogram argument is an expression (not a variable, array, or array element), the value of the expression is passed as input only to the subprogram; any changes in the associated parameter are not returned to the calling program. If the argument is a variable, array, or array element, any changes in the associated parameter will be returned to the calling program. (The argument itself changes in value.)

Appendix J
VAX-11 BASIC Programs

This appendix contains four programs that illustrate some important features of VAX-11 BASIC that are not available in BASIC-PLUS. These features include the VAX-11 DECLARE statement, VAX-11 versions of the IF–THEN, IF–THEN–ELSE statements, and the VAX-11 Subprogram feature. The example programs are modified versions of programs presented in the text. These new programs are listed, with a summary of the VAX-11 features illustrated, in the order in which they originally appear in the text. The programs that are redone here are Problem 4A, Registered Voters List; Problem 9B, Text Editor; Problem 10C, Room Scheduling; Problem 11B, Updating a Virtual Array.

Problem 4A illustrates the DECLARE statement and the VAX-11 IF-THEN and IF-THEN-ELSE statements. The remaining problems illustrate the use of subprograms and would execute in BASIC-PLUS-2 as well as VAX-11 BASIC. We would recommend using the DECLARE statement in these programs as well; we chose not to so that the programs would be compatible with BASIC-PLUS-2.

Problem 4A: Registered Voters List

All variables in this progam are listed in DECLARE statements (lines 150–165) as either integer or string variables. Note that no dollar sign or percent sign is needed (in fact these symbols are prohibited) with declared integer and string variables. The DECLARE statement is also used in this problem to assign a name to a constant as in lines 165 and 170.

The VAX-11 BASIC IF-THEN and IF-THEN-ELSE statements are identical to the BASIC-PLUS versions with the added feature that the THEN alternative of the VAX-11 IF-THEN-ELSE may be a statement group (see line 290).

```
100 !TOWNSHIP VOTER/CLERK ASSIGNMENT LIST
105 !PRINTS MASTER LIST OF VOTER AND ASSIGNED CLERK
110 !ALSO COUNTS VOTERS ASSIGNED TO EACH CLERK
115 !    VOTERS A-I ASSIGNED TO CLERK ABRAHAM
120 !           (COUNT IN NUM.ABRAHAM)
125 !    VOTERS J-R ASSIGNED TO CLERK MARTIN
130 !           (COUNT IN NUM.MARTIN)
135 !    VOTERS S-Z ASSIGNED TO CLERK JOHN
140 !           (COUNT IN NUM.JOHN)
145 !
150 !VARIABLE DECLARATIONS
155    DECLARE INTEGER NUM.ABRAHAM, NUM.MARTIN,     &
                        NUM.JOHN, HOUSE, N
160    DECLARE STRING VOTER, CLERK, STREET
165    DECLARE STRING CONSTANT FIRST.MARTIN = 'J'
170    DECLARE STRING CONSTANT FIRST.JOHN = 'S'
172 !
175 !READ IN AND PRINT NUMBER OF REGISTERED VOTERS.
180 !INITIALIZE COUNTS
185    READ N
190    PRINT "THE NUMBER OF REGISTERED VOTERS IS"; N
200    LET NUM.ABRAHAM = 0
210    LET NUM.MARTIN = 0
220    LET NUM.JOHN = 0
230 !
240 !READ VOTER NAME (VOTER), ADDRESS (HOUSE),
245 !STREET NAME (STREET) FOR EACH VOTER. ASSIGN
250 !CLERK (CLERK) TO EACH VOTER, UPDATE COUNTER FOR
```

(continued)

```
250 !CLERK (CLERK) TO EACH VOTER, UPDATE COUNTER FOR
255 !CLERK. PRINT HOUSE, STREET, VOTER, CLERK.
260     PRINT \ PRINT "REGISTERED VOTER ADDRESS";
265     PRINT TAB(35); "NAME"; TAB(60); "CLERK"
270     FOR I = 1 TO N
280         READ VOTER, HOUSE, STREET
290         IF VOTER < FIRST.MARTIN THEN          &
                LET CLERK = 'ABRAHAM'             &
                \LET NUM.ABRAHAM = NUM.ABRAHAM + 1 &
            ELSE                                  &
                IF VOTER < FIRST.JOHN THEN        &
                    LET CLERK = 'MARTIN'          &
                    \LET NUM.MARTIN = NUM.MARTIN + 1 &
                ELSE                              &
                    \LET CLERK = 'JOHN'           &
                LET NUM.JOHN = NUM.JOHN + 1
300         PRINT HOUSE; STREET; TAB(31); VOTER; &
                TAB(59); CLERK
310     NEXT I
320 !
480 !PRINT COUNTS
485     PRINT
490     PRINT "NUMBER ASSIGNED TO ABRAHAM IS"; &
                NUM.ABRAHAM
500     PRINT "NUMBER ASSIGNED TO MARTIN IS"; &
                NUM.MARTIN
510     PRINT "NUMBER ASSIGNED TO JOHN IS"; &
                NUM.JOHN
520 !
530 !INITIAL VOTER LIST
535     DATA 6
540     DATA "ADAMS, JOHN         ", 125, "ABBOT ST.          "
550     DATA "ADAMS, MARY         ", 129, "ABBOT ST.          "
560     DATA "WASHINGTON, GEORGE", 137, "MOUNT VERNON AVE."
570     DATA "KING, MARTIN        ", 270, "PEACHTREE LANE     "
580     DATA "JONES, BILLY        ", 112, "XAVIER RD.         "
590     DATA "ICEMAN, JOE         ", 286, "ZOO AVE.           "
600 !
610     END    !VOTER PROGRAM
```

Problem 9B: Text Editor

This program uses separate subprograms (starting at lines 10000, 20000, and 30000) to perform the delete, insert, and replace operations. Each subprogram is called in the main program (lines 2020, 4030, and 6040). The string TEXT$ is passed as an input/output argument to each subprogram and is modified by the subprogram.

The last parameter of each subprogram is an output parameter that is used to signal whether or not the edit operation was performed. The corresponding argument is tested immediately after returning from a subprogram (lines 2030, 4040, and 6050).

```
100 !TEXT EDITOR PROGRAM
110 !
120 !INITIALIZE PROGRAM CONSTANT
130    LET SENTINEL$ = "Q"
140 !
145 !ENTER STRING TO BE EDITED
150    PRINT "ENTER STRING TO BE EDITED"
160    INPUT LINE TEXT$
170 !
180 !PERFORM ALL EDIT OPERATIONS
190 !FIRST SHOW THE MENU
200    LET COMMAND$ = "S"
210    GOSUB 7000
220    UNTIL COMMAND$ = SENTINEL$
230       PRINT "ENTER EDIT OPERATION OR";
235       INPUT "S(HOW)OR Q(UIT) "; COMMAND$
240       LET COMMAND$ = LEFT(CVT$$(COMMAND$, 8+32), 1)
250       ON INSTR(1, "DEILRSQ", COMMAND$) + 1                    &
             GOSUB 1000, 2000, 3000, 4000,                       &
                   5000, 6000, 7000, 8000
260       PRINT TEXT$
280    NEXT    !UNTIL
290 !
300    STOP
310 !
320 !
1000 !SUBROUTINES FOR ON-GOSUB AT LINE 250
1010 !COMMAND IS ILLEGAL
1020    PRINT "ILLEGAL COMMAND"
1030    RETURN
2000 !DELETE A SUBSTRING
2005    PRINT "DELETE WHAT STRING";
2010    INPUT LINE OLD.STR$
2015    OLD.STR$ = CVT$$(OLD.STR$, 4)
2020    CALL EDIT.DEL(TEXT$, OLD.STR$, DEL.DONE%)
2030    IF NOT DEL.DONE% THEN                                    &
             PRINT "DELETION NOT PERFORMED"
2040    RETURN
3000 !ENTER A NEW STRING TO BE EDITED
3010    PRINT "ENTER STRING TO BE EDITED"
3020    INPUT LINE TEXT$
3030    RETURN
4000 !INSERT A SUBSTRING AT POSITION WHERE
4005    PRINT "INSERT WHAT STRING";
4010    INPUT LINE NEW.STR$
4015    NEW.STR$ = CVT$$(NEW.STR$, 4)
4020    INPUT "POINT OF INSERTION"; WHERE
4030    CALL EDIT.INS(TEXT$,NEW.STR$,WHERE,INS.DONE%)
4040    IF NOT INS.DONE% THEN                                    &
             PRINT "INSERTION NOT PERFORMED"
4050    RETURN
```

(continued)

```
5000  !LOCATE A SUBSTRING
5005      PRINT "LOCATE WHAT STRING";
5010      INPUT LINE OLD.STR$
5015      OLD.STR$ = CVT$$(OLD.STR$, 4)
5020      LET POS.OLD = INSTR(1, TEXT$, OLD.STR$)
5030      IF POS.OLD <> 0 THEN                                    &
              PRINT "FOUND AT POSITION"; POS.OLD                  &
          ELSE                                                    &
              PRINT "NOT FOUND"
5040      RETURN
6000  !REPLACE ONE SUBSTRING WITH ANOTHER
6005      PRINT "REPLACE WHAT STRING";
6010      INPUT LINE OLD.STR$
6015      OLD.STR$ = CVT$$(OLD.STR$, 4)
6020      PRINT "TO BE REPLACED BY";
6025      INPUT LINE NEW.STR$
6030      NEW.STR$ = CVT$$(NEW.STR$, 4)
6040      CALL EDIT.REP(TEXT$, OLD.STR$,                          &
                        NEW.STR$, REP.DONE%)
6050      IF NOT REP.DONE% THEN                                   &
              PRINT "REPLACEMENT NOT PERFORMED"
6060      RETURN
7000  !SHOW THE MENU
7005      PRINT
7010      PRINT "ENTER FIRST LETTER OF EDIT COMMAND"
7020      PRINT "THE COMMANDS ARE:"
7030      PRINT "    D(ELETE A SUBSTRING)"
7040      PRINT "    E(NTER NEW STRING TO EDIT)"
7050      PRINT "    I(NSERT A SUBSTRING)"
7060      PRINT "    L(OCATE A SUBSTRING)"
7070      PRINT "    R(EPLACE ONE STRING WITH ANOTHER)"
7080      PRINT "    S(HOW THE MENU)"
7090      PRINT "    Q(UIT)"
7100      PRINT
7110      RETURN
8000  !QUIT
8010      RETURN
8030  !END OF SUBROUTINES FOR ON-GOSUB AT LINE 250
8040  !
8050      END    !TEXT EDITOR MAIN PROGRAM

10000     SUB EDIT.DEL (TEXT$, OLD.STR$, DEL.DONE%)
10010 !
10020 !DELETES FIRST OCCURRENCE OF OLD.STR$ FROM TEXT$
10030 !
10040 !PARAMETER DEFINITIONS --
10045 !   IN: OLD.STR$ - THE SUBSTRING TO BE DELETED
10050 !   OUT: DEL.DONE% - INDICATES WHETHER OR NOT
10060 !                        DELETION WAS PERFORMED
10070 !   IN/OUT: TEXT$ - THE STRING BEING EDITED
10075 !
```

```
10080 !LOCAL VARIABLE
10090 !    DEL.POS - FIRST OCCURRENCE OF OLD.STR$
10100 !
10110 !ASSUME DELETION CANNOT BE PERFORMED
10120     LET DEL.DONE% = 0%    !FALSE
10130 !DELETE OLD.STR$ IF FOUND IN TEXT$
10140     LET DEL.POS = INSTR(1, TEXT$, OLD.STR$)
10150     IF DEL.POS <> 0 THEN                               &
              !CONCATENATE SUBSTRING BEFORE OLD.STR$         &
              !WITH SUBSTRING FOLLOWING OLD.STR$             &
              LET TEXT$ = LEFT(TEXT$, DEL.POS-1) +           &
                  RIGHT(TEXT$, DEL.POS+LEN(OLD.STR$))        &
              \LET DEL.DONE% = -1%    !TRUE
10210 !
10220     SUBEND


20000     SUB EDIT.INS(TEXT$,NEW.STR$,WHERE,INS.DONE%)
20010 !
20020 !INSERTS NEW.STR$ AT POSTION WHERE IN TEXT$
20030 !
20040 !PARAMETER DEFINITIONS --
20050 !    IN: NEW.STR$ - THE SUBSTRING TO BE INSERTED
20060 !        WHERE - DESIRED POSTION OF NEW.STR$
20070 !    OUT: INS.DONE% - INDICATES WHETHER OR NOT
20080 !                       INSERTION WAS PERFORMED
20085 !    IN/OUT: TEXT$ - THE STRING BEING EDITED
20090 !
20100 !ASSUME INSERTION CANNOT BE PERFORMED
20130     LET INS.DONE% = 0% !FALSE
20140 !
20150 !INSERT NEW.STR$ IF WHERE IS IN RANGE
20160     IF WHERE >= 1 AND                                  &
              WHERE <= LEN(TEXT$) + 1 THEN                   &
              !CONCATENATE SUBSTRING PRECEDING               &
              !INSERTION POINT WHERE WITH NEW.STR$           &
              !AND WITH SUBSTRING STARTING AT WHERE          &
              LET TEXT$ = LEFT (TEXT$, WHERE-1)              &
                    + NEW.STR$                               &
                    + RIGHT(TEXT$, WHERE)                    &
              \LET INS.DONE% = -1%    !TRUE
20170 !
20180     SUBEND


30000     SUB EDIT.REP (TEXT$, OLD.STR$,                     &
                        NEW.STR$, REP.DONE%)
30010 !
30020 !REPLACES FIRST OCCURRENCE OF OLD.STR$
30030 !WITH NEW.STR$
30040 !
```

(continued)

```
30050 !PARAMETER DEFINITIONS --
30060 !    IN: OLD.STR$ - THE SUBSTRING BEING REPLACED
30070 !        NEW.STR$ - THE SUBSTRING BEING INSERTED
30080 !    OUT: REP.DONE% - INDICATES WHETHER OR NOT
30090 !                       REPLACEMENT WAS PERFORMED
30100 !    IN/OUT: TEXT$ - STRING BEING EDITED
30110 !
30115 !LOCAL VARIABLE
30120 !    REP.POS - FIRST OCCURRENCE OF OLD.STR$
30122 !
30125 !ASSUME REPLACEMENT CANNOT BE PERFORMED
30130      LET REP.DONE% = 0%        !FALSE
30140 !
30150 !REPLACE OLD.STR$ WITH NEW.STR$ IF FOUND
30160      LET REP.POS = INSTR(1, TEXT$, OLD.STR$)
30170      IF REP.POS <> 0 THEN                              &
               !INSERT NEW.STR$ AT POSITION REP.POS          &
               LET TEXT$ = LEFT(TEXT$, REP.POS-1) +          &
                   NEW.STR$ +                                &
                   RIGHT(TEXT$, REP.POS+LEN(OLD.STR$))       &
               \LET REP.DONE% = -1%       !TRUE
30230 !
30240      SUBEND
```

Problem 10C: Room Scheduling

In this program, all three major modules, PRINT.CAP (print room capacity table, see lines 1000-1190), PROCESS (read and process room requests, see lines 2000-4910), and ROOM.ASSIGN (assign a room, see lines 5000-6060), are written as independent VAX-11 BASIC subprograms. Subprograms PRINT.CAP and PROCESS are called by the main program; ROOM.ASSIGN is called by subprogram PROCESS. The two dimensional array ROOM.CAP and its dimensions (NUM.ROWS and NUM.COLS) are passed as arguments to all three subprograms.

For illustrative purposes, a number of subroutines have been left in tact in these subprograms. Thus, for example, the subroutines required to complete the IF-THEN-ELSE at line 2210 are shown nested inside subprogram PROCESS (see lines 3000-4900). In addition, the short fragment of code (see lines 6000-6050) required to actually assign a room to a class has been written as a subroutine (nested inside ROOM.ASSIGN) because it is called in three different places (line 5230) in ROOM.ASSIGN. It is perfectly permissible to nest subroutines inside a subprogram. However, because of the independent nature of the subprogram, a subroutine, and all references to it, must be specified inside the same subprogram. The subroutines should be placed at the end of the subprogram, and the SUBEXIT statement should be used to prevent "falling into" the subroutines.

```
110 !ROOM SCHEDULING PROBLEM
120 !
130 !PROGRAM CONSTANTS
140     LET NUM.ROWS = 3    !FLOORS IN BUILDING
150     LET NUM.COLS = 5    !ROOMS ON FLOOR
160 !
170 !ARRAYS USED
180     DIM ROOM.CAP(3,5)
185 !
190 !ENTER ROOM CAPACITIES TABLE
200     MAT READ ROOM.CAP
210     DATA 30, 30, 15, 30, 40
220     DATA 25, 30, 25, 10, 110
230     DATA 62, 30, 40, 40, 30
240 !
245 !PRINT ROOM CAPACITY TABLE
250     PRINT "INITIAL TABLE OF ROOM CAPACITIES"
255     PRINT
260     CALL PRINT.CAP(ROOM.CAP( , ),                      &
                        NUM.ROWS, NUM.COLS)
270     PRINT
280 !
290 !SET UP HEADING FOR ROOM ASSIGNMENT TABLE
300     PRINT "ROOM ASSIGNMENT TABLE"
310     PRINT "CLASS ID", "CLASS SIZE",                    &
              "ROOM", "CAPACITY"
340 !
350 !PRINT AND PROCESS EACH ROOM REQUEST
360     CALL PROCESS(ROOM.CAP( , ), NUM.ROWS,              &
                      NUM.COLS, NUM.CLASSES)
365     PRINT
370 !
380 !PRINT FINAL ROOM CAPACITY TABLE
385     PRINT
390     PRINT "TABLE OF UNUSED SEATS IN EACH ROOM"
395     PRINT
400     CALL PRINT.CAP(ROOM.CAP( , ),                      &
                        NUM.ROWS, NUM.COLS)
410 !
420 !COMPUTE AND PRINT TOTAL NUMBER OF UNUSED SEATS
430     LET UNUSED.TOTAL = 0
440     FOR I = 1 TO NUM.ROWS
450         LET UNUSED.TOTAL = UNUSED.TOTAL               &
                             + ABS(ROOM.CAP(I,J))         &
                FOR J = 1 TO NUM.COLS
460     NEXT I
470     PRINT
475     PRINT "THE TOTAL NUMBER OF UNUSED SEATS IS";      &
              UNUSED.TOTAL
480 !
490     END    !ROOM SCHEDULING MAIN PROGRAM
```

(continued)

```
1000     SUB PRINT.CAP (ROOM.CAP( , ),                        &
                        NUM.ROWS, NUM.COLS)
1005 !
1010 !PRINTS ROOM CAPACITY TABLE
1015 !
1020 !PARAMETER DEFINITIONS --
1025 !  IN: ROOM.CAP( , ) - ROOM CAPACITY TABLE
1030 !       NUM.ROWS - NUMBER OF FLOORS
1035 !       NUM.COLS - ROOMS PER FLOOR
1040 !
1045 !LOCAL VARIABLE
1050 !  J - LOOP CONTROL VARIABLE
1055 !
1060 !PRINT TABLE HEADINGS
1065     PRINT "                       ROOM NUMBER"
1070     PRINT "FLOOR"; TAB(15); "01"; TAB(25);             &
             "02";"TAB(35);"03"; TAB(45); "04";             &
             TAB(55); "05"
1080     PRINT "-----"; TAB(15); "--"; TAB(25);             &
             "--"; TAB(35); "--"; TAB(45);                  &
             "--"; TAB(55); "--"
1090     PRINT "  1  ";
1100     PRINT TAB(4+10*J); ABS(ROOM.CAP(1,J));             &
           FOR J = 1 TO NUM.COLS
1110     PRINT
1120     PRINT "  2  ";
1130     PRINT TAB(4+10*J); ABS(ROOM.CAP(2,J));             &
           FOR J = 1 TO NUM.COLS
1140     PRINT
1150     PRINT "  3  ";
1160     PRINT TAB(4+10*J); ABS(ROOM.CAP(3,J));             &
           FOR J = 1 TO NUM.COLS
1170     PRINT
1180 !
1190     SUBEND


2000     SUB PROCESS (ROOM.CAP( , ), NUM.ROWS,              &
                     NUM.COLS, NUM.CLASSES)
2005 !
2010 !READ AND PROCESS ROOM REQUESTS
2015 !PRINT ROOM ASSIGNMENT
2020 !
2030 !PARAMETER DEFINITIONS --
2040 !  IN:   NUM.ROWS, NUM.COLS - DIMENSIONS OF
2050 !                            ROOM.CAP
2060 !         NUM.CLASSES - NUMBER OF CLASSES
2070 !  IN/OUT:  ROOM.CAP( , ) - ROOM CAPACITY TABLE
2080 !              SHOWS EMPTY SEATS PER ROOM WHEN DONE
2090 !
2100 !LOCAL VARIABLES - CLASS.ID$, CLASS.SIZE
```

(continued)

```
2110 !                      CLASS.FL.IX, CLASS.I, AS.DONE%
2115 !                      CLASS.RM.IX, CLASS.TEMP
2120 !
2130 !SUBPROGRAM CONSTANT
2140     LET NUM.CLASSES = 15    !CLASSES TO PROCESS
2150 !
2160 !READ AND PROCESS EACH ROOM REQUEST
2170     FOR CLASS.I = 1 TO NUM.CLASSES
2180         READ CLASS.ID$, CLASS.SIZE
2190         !SEARCH FOR A ROOM USING FNASSIGN%
2200         CALL ROOM.ASSIGN(ROOM.CAP( , ),                      &
                    NUM.ROWS, NUM.COLS, CLASS.SIZE,               &
                    CLASS.FL.IX, CLASS.RM.IX, AS.DONE%)
2210         IF AS.DONE% THEN GOSUB 3000                          &
                    ELSE GOSUB 4000
2220     NEXT CLASS.I
2225 !
2230     DATA CIS1, 37, CIS2, 55, CIS3, 100, CIS10, 26
2240     DATA CIS11, 26, CIS25, 39, CIS30, 30,                   &
                    CIS31, 56
2250     DATA CIS101, 20, CIS120, 15, CIS203, 22,                &
                    CIS301, 10
2260     DATA CIS302, 5, CIS324, 28, CIS330, 25
2270 !
2280     SUBEXIT    !RETURN FROM PROCESS
2290 !
2300 !
3000 !SUBROUTINES FOR IF-THEN-ELSE AT LINE 2210
3010 !IF CLASS ASSIGNED THEN COMPUTE ROOM NUMBER
3030     LET CLASS.ROOM = CLASS.FL.IX * 100                      &
                    + CLASS.RM.IX
3040     LET CLASS.TEMP =                                        &
                ROOM.CAP(CLASS.FL.IX, CLASS.RM.IX)
3050     PRINT CLASS.ID$, CLASS.SIZE, CLASS.ROOM,                &
                CLASS.TEMP
3060     LET ROOM.CAP(CLASS.FL.IX, CLASS.RM.IX) =                &
                    -(CLASS.TEMP - CLASS.SIZE)
3070     RETURN
4000 !ELSE NO ROOM AVAILABLE
4010     PRINT "NO ROOM AVAILABLE FOR "; CLASS.ID$
4020     RETURN
4025 !END OF SUBROUTINES FOR IF-THEN-ELSE AT 2210
4030 !
4900     RETURN
4905 !
4910     SUBEND


5000     SUB ROOM.ASSIGN (ROOM.CAP( , ),                         &
                NUM.ROWS, NUM.COLS, CLASS.SIZE,                  &
                CLASS.FL.IX, CLASS.RM.IX, AS.DONE%)
```

(continued)

```
5010 !
5020 !SUBPROGRAM TO ASSIGN A ROOM TO A CLASS
5025 !OF SIZE CLASS.SIZE
5030 !
5040 !PARAMETER DEFINITIONS --
5050 !   IN: ROOM.CAP( , ), NUM.ROWS, NUM.COLS -
5060 !            ROOM CAPACITY TABLE AND DIMENSIONS
5070 !        CLASS.SIZE - SIZE OF CLASS TO ASSIGN
5080 !   OUT: CLASS.FL.IX, CLASS.RM.IX - INDICES OF
5090 !            ASSIGNED ROOM
5100 !       AS.DONE% - INDICATES WHETHER OR NOT FINAL
5105 !                ASSIGNMENT WAS PERFORMED
5110 !
5120 !LOCAL VARIABLES - AS.I, AS.J, AS.SIZE,
5125 !                AS.FOUND%
5130 !
5140 !ASSUME NO ROOM AVAILABLE
5160    LET AS.DONE% = 0%     !FALSE
5170    LET AS.FOUND% = 0%    !FALSE
5175 !
5180 !OUTER LOOP, CHECK EACH FLOOR
5190    FOR AS.I = 1 TO NUM.ROWS
5200       !INNER LOOP, CHECK EACH ROOM ON EACH FLOOR
5210       FOR AS.J = 1 TO NUM.COLS
5220          LET AS.SIZE = ROOM.CAP(AS.I,AS.J)
5230          IF AS.SIZE > CLASS.SIZE AND
                 NOT AS.FOUND% THEN                          &
                 !FIRST FIT -                                &
                 !ASSIGN BUT KEEP LOOKING                    &
                 GOSUB 6000                                  &
              ELSE IF AS.SIZE > CLASS.SIZE AND               &
                 AS.SIZE < ROOM.CAP(CLASS.FL.IX,             &
                          CLASS.RM.IX) THEN                  &
                 !BETTER FIT -                               &
                 !ASSIGN BUT KEEP LOOKING                    &
                 GOSUB 6000                                  &
              ELSE IF AS.SIZE = CLASS.SIZE THEN              &
                 !PERFECT FIT                                &
                 !ASSIGN AND STOP LOOKING                    &
                 GOSUB 6000                                  &
                 \LET AS.DONE% = -1%                         &
                 \SUBEXIT    !EXIT LOOP AND RETURN
5250       NEXT AS.J
5260    NEXT AS.I
5270 !
5280 !ALL FLOORS HAVE BEEN SEARCHED
5290    LET AS.DONE% = AS.FOUND%
5300    SUBEXIT  !RETURN FROM ROOM.ASSIGN
5310 !
5320 !
6000 !SUBROUTINE TO ASSIGN ROOM TO CLASS CLASS.ID
```

(continued)

```
6010    LET CLASS.FL.IX = AS.I
6020    LET CLASS.RM.IX = AS.J
6030    LET AS.FOUND% = -1%     !TRUE
6040    RETURN
6045 !END OF SUBROUTINE TO MAKE ROOM ASSIGNMENTS
6050 !
6060    SUBEND
```

Problem 11B: Updating a Virtual Array

As shown in line 160, the file attribute ORGANIZATION VIRTUAL must be used to specify a virtual array in VAX-11 BASIC. The virtual array is updated by subprogram VIR.UPDATE (starting at line 1000). A virtual array cannot be passed as a subprogram parameter; consequently, the string variable CUR.REC$ is used for temporary storage of the array record being updated and CUR.REC$ is passed to the subprogram (line 230). Upon return from the subprogram, the logical argument UP.DONE% is tested (line 240); the successfully updated record is assigned to the virtual array.

```
100 !UPDATE OF VIRTUAL ARRAY FILE
110 !
120 !PROGRAM CONSTANT
130     LET MAX.STOCK = 1000     !MAX STOCK NUMBER
140 !
150     DIM #1, BOOK$(1000) = 64
160     OPEN "INV.VIR" AS FILE #1,ORGANIZATION VIRTUAL
170 !
175 !PROCESS EACH VALID UPDATE REQUEST
180     INPUT "MORE ORDERS (YES OR NO)"; MORE$
190     WHILE CVT$$(MORE$, 34) = "YES"
200        INPUT "STOCK NUMBER"; STOCK.NUM
210        INPUT "OUT-OF-RANGE, TRY AGAIN"; STOCK.NUM          &
                UNTIL STOCK.NUM > 0 AND                        &
                    STOCK.NUM <= MAX.STOCK
215        INPUT "ORDER"; ORDER
220 !
230        !SAVE BOOK$(STOCK.NUM) AND ATTEMPT UPDATE
225        LET CUR.REC$ = BOOK$(STOCK.NUM)
230        CALL VIR.UPDATE(CUR.REC$, STOCK.NUM,               &
                    ORDER, UP.DONE%)
240        IF UP.DONE% THEN                                   &
                LET BOOK$(STOCK.NUM) = CUR.REC$               &
                \PRINT "UPDATED RECORD:";                     &
                    BOOK$(STOCK.NUM)                          &
            ELSE                                              &
                PRINT "CURRENT RECORD:";                      &
                    BOOK$(STOCK.NUM)                          &
                \PRINT "BAD UPDATE DATA FOR ABOVE RECORD"
```

(continued)

```
250        INPUT "MORE ORDERS (YES OR NO)"; MORE$
260     NEXT    !WHILE
265 !
270     PRINT "FILE UPDATE COMPLETED"
280 !
290 !CLOSE FILE
300     CLOSE #1
310 !
320     END    !VIRTUAL ARRAY UPDATE MAIN PROGRAM


1000    SUB VIR.UPDATE (CUR.REC$, STOCK.NUM,              &
                        ORDER, UP.DONE%)
1010 !
1015 !UPDATES RECORD STOCK.NUM OF VIRTUAL ARRAY BOOK$
1020 !
1025 !PARAMETER DEFINITIONS --
1030 !  IN: STOCK.NUM - STOCK NUMBER OF ITEM PUR-
        CHASED
1035 !      ORDER - PURCHASE AMOUNT
1040 !  OUT: UP.DONE% - INDICATES WHETHER OR NOT
1045 !                  UPDATE WAS PERFORMED
1050 !  IN/OUT: CUR.REC$ - RECORD BEING UPDATED
1055 !
1060 !LOCAL VARIABLES
1065 !  UP.POS1, UP.POS2, UP,STOCK$, UP.QUANT$
1070 !
1080 !FUNCTION CONSTANTS
1095    LET UP.DELIM1$ = ","    !STOCK.NUM DELIMITER
1100    LET UP.DELIM2$ = "\"    !QUANTITY DELIMITER
1105 !
1110 !FIND DELIMITERS FOR STOCK.NUM AND QUANTITY
1120    LET UP.POS1 =                                     &
            INSTR(1, CUR.REC$, UP.DELIM1$)
1130    LET UP.POS2 =                                     &
            INSTR(1, CUR.REC$, UP.DELIM2$)
1135 !
1140 !EXTRACT STOCK NUMBER AND QUANTITY
1145 !SUBSTRINGS OF CUR.REC$
1150    LET UP.STOCK$ =                                   &
            LEFT(CUR.REC$, UP.POS1-1)
1160    LET UP.QUANT$ =                                   &
            RIGHT(CUR.REC$, UP.POS2+1)
1170 !
1180 !UPDATE RECORD DATA IF VALID AND SET UPDONE%
1190    IF UP.POS1 = 0 OR UP.POS2 = 0                     &
            OR UP.POS1 > UP.POS2                          &
            OR VAL(UP.STOCK$) <> STOCK.NUM               &
            OR ORDER > VAL(UP.QUANT$) THEN               &
            GOSUB 2000                                    &
```

(continued)

```
           ELSE                                                    &
               GOSUB 3000
1200 !
1220      SUBEXIT    !RETURN FROM VIR.UPDATE
1230 !
1240 !
2000 !SUBROUTINES FOR IF-THEN-ELSE AT LINE 1190
2010 !IF DATA IS INVALID THEN SET UPDONE% TO FALSE
2020      LET UP.DONE% = 0%    !FALSE
2030      RETURN
3000 !ELSE UPDATE QUANTITY OF CUR.REC$
3010      LET UP.QUANT$ = NUM1$(VAL(UP.QUANT$)-ORDER)
3020      LET CUR.REC$ =                                           &
               LEFT(CUR.REC$,UP.POS2) + UP.QUANT$
3030      LET UP.DONE% = -1%    !TRUE
3040      RETURN
3050 !END OF SUBROUTINES FOR LINE 1190
3060 !
3070      SUBEND
```

Answers to Selected Exercises

Chapter 1

1.1   −27.2, MINE, 0.05

1.3   illegal in EXTEND mode

     12ZIP, P$3, NINE−T, END, DATA$

   illegal in NOEXTEND mode

     all except P$, I1

1.4   Line 110 could be moved anywhere except after line 160
       Line 120 could be moved down but must precede line 160

1.5   35   3.8
       133   108

1.6   40   16.25   650   117   533

1.7
```
100 PRINT "   I   I"
110 PRINT " X I   I"
120 PRINT "---I---I---"
130 PRINT "   I O I X"
140 PRINT "---I---I---"
150 PRINT "   I O I"
160 PRINT "   I   I"
```

1.8   *For Fig. 1.15*

```
100 INPUT "HOURS WORKED"; HOURS
110 INPUT "HOURLY RATE"; RATE
```

Delete 120 and continue with the rest of the program
For Fig. 1.16

```
105 INPUT "DISTANCE IN MILES"; DISTANCE
110 INPUT "AVERAGE SPEED IN MILES PER HOUR"; SPEED
```

Delete 120, 130

```
170 INPUT "ESTIMATED MILEAGE RATE"; MPG
180 INPUT "GASOLINE COST PER GALLON"; GALCOST
```
Delete 190, 200

1.9   Each incorrect line is rewritten below.

```
100 READ HOURS, RATE (extra "," deleted)
105 DATA 5.0, 25.0 (line number and "," inserted)
110 LET RATE = 1.5 * RATE ("*" inserted)
120 LET GROSS = HOURS * RATE (HOUR changed to HOURS)
140 LET NET = NET - 25.0 ("-" moved to right of "=")
145 PRINT HOURS; RATE (line number inserted
                          and ":" changed to ";")
150 PRINT "GROSS =", GROSS (quotation mark
                          transposed with ",")
160 END (END added)
```

Chapter 2

2.1
```
130 INPUT "FIRST NUMBER"; NUMB1
140 INPUT "SECOND NUMBER"; NUMB2
```

Delete 150

2.2   *Input variables*   *Output variables*

NUMB1 ⎫
NUMB2 ⎪ 4 numbers to   SUM: Sum of 4 numbers
NUMB3 ⎬ be summed   AVE: Average of 4
NUMB4 ⎭   numbers

Step 1   Read four data items into NUMB1, NUMB2, NUMB3, and NUMB4
Step 2   Find the sum of the four numbers and store it in SUM
Step 3   Compute the average and store it in AVE
Step 4   Print SUM and AVE

Refinement of Step 2
Step 2.1   LET SUM = NUMB1 + NUMB2 + NUMB3 + NUMB4

Refinement of Step 3
Step 3.1   LET AVE = SUM / 4

2.3   a) true   b) false   c) false   d) true

2.4   a)

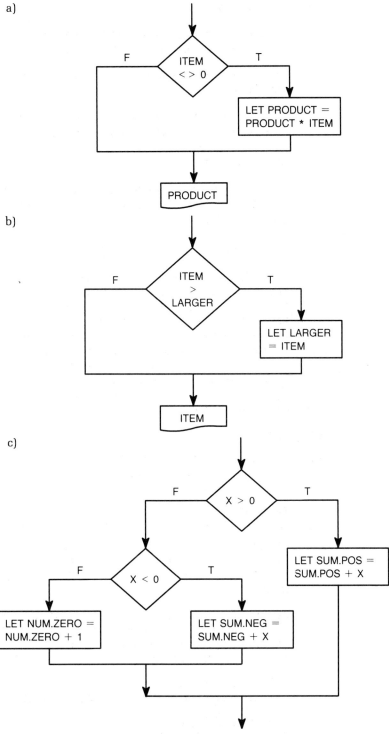

b)

c)

2.5   115.625 (if HOURS = 37.5, RATE = 3.75)
80 (if HOURS = 20, RATE = 4)

2.7   Add the decision step below to the refinement of Step 2

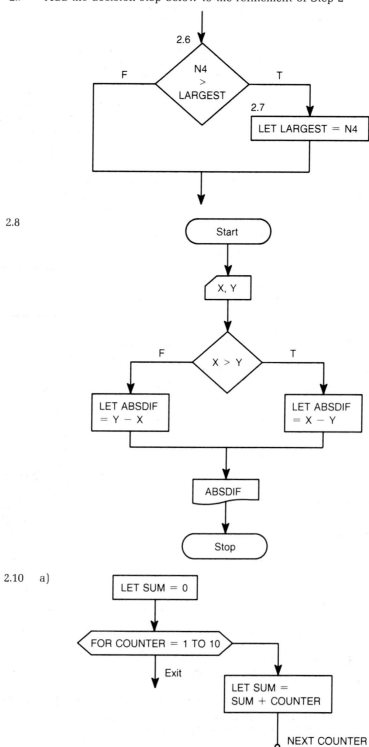

2.6

N4
>
LARGEST

F   T

2.7

LET LARGEST = N4

2.8

Start

X, Y

F   X > Y   T

LET ABSDIF
= Y − X

LET ABSDIF
= X − Y

ABSDIF

Stop

2.10   a)

LET SUM = 0

FOR COUNTER = 1 TO 10

Exit

LET SUM =
SUM + COUNTER

NEXT COUNTER

b)

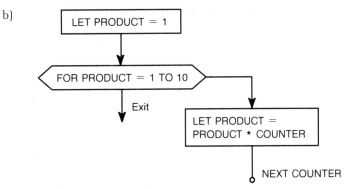

2.13   a) Path 4, Execute 2.3 (LARGEST = 20)
         b) Path 1, N1 = 15, N2 = 5, N3 = 20
                Execute 2.2 (LARGEST = 15)
                Execute 2.5 (LARGEST = 20). Yes
         c) Path 2, Execute 2.2 (LARGEST = 16)
            Yes in the sense that all 4 paths are traced and appear to be correct. It
            would be a good idea to verify that the algorithm still works if two items
            have the same value.

2.15

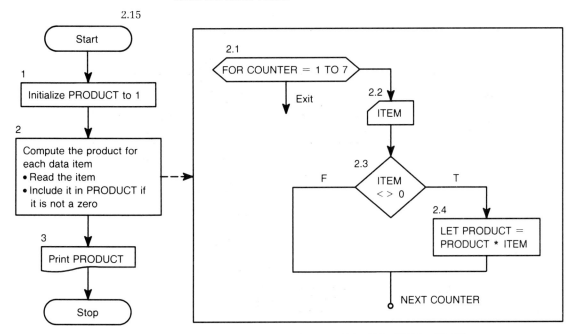

```
100  !PROGRAM TO FIND PRODUCT OF NON-ZERO ITEMS
110  !
120  !INITIALIZE PRODUCT
130       LET PRODUCT = 1
140  !
150  !READ EACH ITEM AND INCLUDE IT IN PRODUCT
155  !IF NOT ZERO
160       FOR COUNTER = 1 TO 7
```

(continued)

```
170        INPUT "NEXT ITEM"; ITEM
180        IF ITEM <> 0 THEN                          &
               LET PRODUCT = PRODUCT * ITEM
190      NEXT COUNTER
200 !
210 !PRINT PRODUCT
220      PRINT "PRODUCT OF ALL NOW-ZERO ITEMS =";      &
               PRODUCT
230 !
240      END
```

2.16   10 and the numbers 10, 20, 30, . . . , 100

Chapter 3

3.1   No. Both X and Y will contain the original value of Y. The statement group
       below will work properly.

```
LET TEMP = Y \ LET Y = X \ LET X = TEMP
```

3.2   a) 200 IF REMAIN = 0 THEN PRINT N

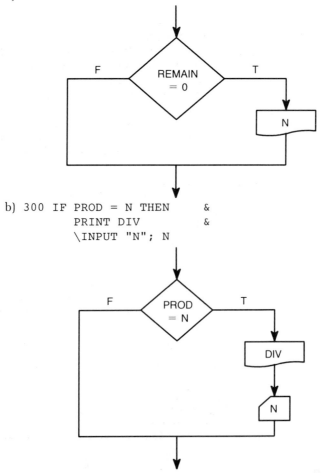

b) 300 IF PROD = N THEN   &
          PRINT DIV   &
          \INPUT "N"; N

```
c) 400 IF NUM.LIGHT > 25 THEN        &
        LET GAL.REQ = MILES / 14     &
        \PRINT "CITY DRIVING"
```

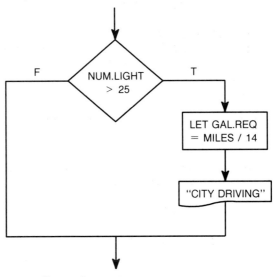

3.3 a) 200 INPUT "ITEM"; ITEM
         210 IF ITEM > 0 THEN LET NPOS = NPOS + 1   &
                 ELSE LET NNEG = NNEG + 1
     b) 300 INPUT "ITEM"; ITEM
         310 IF ITEM = 0 THEN LET NZERO = NZERO + 1
     c) 400 INPUT "ITEM"; ITEM
         410 IF ITEM > 0 THEN LET NPOS = NPOS + 1   &
                 ELSE IF ITEM < 0 THEN LET NNEG = NNEG + 1   &
                 ELSE LET NZERO = NZERO + 1

3.4   200 IF X < 0 THEN   &
           PRINT X; "NEGATIVE" &
       ELSE   &
           PRINT X   &
           \LET SUM = SUM + X

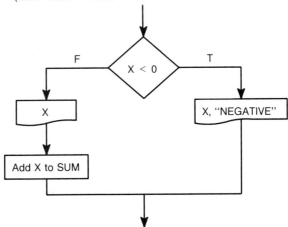

3.5   There should be a STOP before line 220 to prevent the program from "flowing" into the subroutines.

3.9
```
100 IF SALARY > 500 THEN                                  &
        LET TAX.RATE = .30                               &
    ELSE IF SALARY > 300 THEN                            &
        LET TAX.RATE = .20                               &
    ELSE IF SALARY > 150 THEN                            &
        LET TAX.RATE = .15                               &
    ELSE IF SALARY > 50 THEN                             &
        LET TAX.RATE = .10                               &
    ELSE                                                 &
        LET TAX.RATE = .01
```

3.10

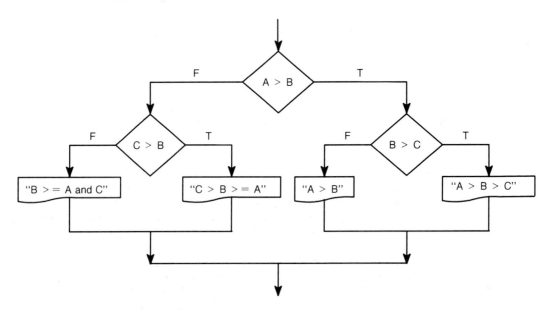

3.11
```
130 LET N = 10
140 LET SUM = 0
150 LET PRODUCT = 1
160 FOR ODD = 1 TO N STEP 2
170     LET EVEN = ODD + 1
180     LET SUM = SUM + ODD
190     IF EVEN <= N THEN LET PRODUCT = PRODUCT * EVEN
200 NEXT ODD
```

3.12 a)
```
160 PRINT "FAHRENHEIT", "CELSIUS"
170 FOR FAHREN = 210 TO -30 STEP -10
180     LET CELSIUS = (FAHREN - 32) / 1.8
190     PRINT FAHREN, CELSIUS
200 NEXT FAHREN
```

b) Change line 170 above

      170 FOR FAHREN = 32 TO 212 STEP 20

3.14
```
100 FOR K = 1 TO 50
110     PRINT K, K ^ .5
120 NEXT K
```

3.15   Insert 165 INPUT "START YEAR"; START.YEAR
        Replace 270 FOR YEAR = START.YEAR TO   &
                             START.YEAR+TERM-1

Chapter 4

4.1   a) $\dfrac{w + x}{y + z}$ e) $(x{\cdot}x - y{\cdot}y)^{.5}$

      b) $g{\cdot}h - f{\cdot}w$ f) $x^2 + \dfrac{r}{365^N}$

      c) $a^{(b^2)}$ g) $p2 - \dfrac{p1}{t2} - t1$

      d) $(b^2 - 4a{\cdot}c)^{.5}$

4.2   a) $\dfrac{5}{7}$ d) $3^{1}/_{3}$

      b) $2^{1}/_{2}$ e) $^{1}/_{4}$ or 2^{-2}
      c) 17   f) 3

4.3   Let X = 6, Y = 3, and Z = 5. Then (X/Y) * Z = (6/3) * 5 = 2 *
     5 = 10. On the other hand, 6/(3 * 5) = 6/15 = 0.4.
     The expression X/Y * Z is equal to (X/Y) * Z. Multiplication and divi-
     sion are on the same level and are performed left-to-right.

4.4   a) LET C = (A ^ 2 + B ^ 2) ^ .5
     b) LET Y = 3 * X ^ 4 + 2 * X ^ 2 - 4
     c) LET W = 3 * K ^ 4 * (7 * K + 4) - K ^ 3
     d) LET X = A ^ 2 * (B ^ 2 - C ^ 2) / (B * C)
     e) LET D = (A ^ 2 + B ^ 2 + C ^ 2) ^ .5
     f) LET Z = 3.14159 * R ^ 2
     g) LET R = 6.27 * 10 ^ (-45) * S
     h) LET P = C0 + C1 * X - C2 * X ^ 2 + C3 * X ^ 3   &
           - C4 * X ^ 4
     i) LET B = A ^ (-5)

4.7
```
100 !AN ILLUSTRATION OF SIN AND COS
120 !
130     PRINT "X(IN DEGREES)", " SIN(X)", " COS(X)"
140 !
145     LET RADIANS = PI / 180
150     FOR X = 0 TO 180 STEP 15
155         Y = X * RADIANS
```

(continued)

```
160          LET SIN.X = SIN(Y)
170          LET COS.X = COS(Y)
180          PRINT X, SIN.X, COS.X
190     NEXT X
200 !
210     END
```

4.8
```
100 !FIND THE ROOTS OF A QUADRATIC EQUATION
110 !
120     INPUT "ENTER A, B AND C"; A, B, C
130 !
140 !COMPUTE THE DISCRIMINANT
150     LET D = B ^ 2 - 4 * A * C
160 !
170     IF D <= 0 THEN                          &
             !NO REAL ROOTS                     &
             PRINT "NO REAL ROOTS"              &
        ELSE                                    &
             !COMPUTE THE ROOTS                 &
             LET R1 = (-B + SQR(D)) / (2 * A)   &
             \LET R2 = (-B - SQR(D)) / (2 * A)  &
             \PRINT "R1 = "; R1, "R2 = "; R2
180 !
190     END
```

4.9
```
100     LET N = 10
110     PRINT "NATURAL LOGARITHM TABLE"
120     PRINT "X", "LOG(X)", "EXP(X)"
130     FOR X = 1 TO N
140         PRINT X, LOG(X), EXP(X)
150     NEXT X
160     END
```

4.10
```
100 !PROGRAM TO COMPUTE .1 TIMES 1000
110 !
120     LET N = 1000
130 !
140 !COMPUTE P
150     LET P = .1 * N
160 !
170 !COMPUTE S
180     LET S = 0
190     FOR I = 1 TO N
200         LET S = S + .1
210     NEXT I
220 !
230 !DETERMINE WHETHER S AND P ARE EQUAL
240     PRINT "P ="; P, "S ="; S
```

(continued)

```
250     IF S = P THEN PRINT "S IS EQUAL TO P"      &
             ELSE PRINT "S IS NOT EQUAL TO P"
260 !
270     END


4.11
100 !INITIALIZE CONSTANTS
110     LET G = 9.81     !GRAVITY IN MTRS/SEC SQUARED
120     LET S = 600      !BUILDING HEIGHT
130 !
140 !COMPUTE THE TIME IT TAKES THE PICKLE
145 !TO HIT THE GROUND
150     LET TGROUND = SQR(2 * S / G)
160 !
170 !PRINT THE VELOCITY OF THE PICKLE
175 !AT FIVE SECOND INTERVALS
180     PRINT "TIME", "VELOCITY"
190     FOR T = 0 TO TGROUND STEP 5
200         LET V = G * T
210         PRINT T, V
220     NEXT T
230 !
240     END
```

4.13   LET X = I - INT(I/J) * J

4.14   LET X = INT(100 * X + 0.5) / 100

4.16   a) Q = A/3 * 2 = 7.5/3 * 2 = 2.5 * 2 = 5
        b) M% = I% + K% * 4 = 3 + 2 * 4 = 11
        c) M% = I%/K% * 5% = 3%/2% * 5% = 5%
        d) Q = I%/K% - 1 = 3%/2% - 1 = 1% - 1 = 0
        e) M% = A/3 + 7 = 7.5/3 + 7 = 2.5 + 7 = 9.5 = 9%
        f) Q = A + B/.5 ^ 2 = 7.5 + 2.5/.5 ^ 2
              = 7.5 + 2.5/.25 = 7.5 + 10 = 17.5

4.18   a) Reads three data items, the string 033-30-0785, and the numbers 40 and
           5.63, into the memory cells SSNO$, HOUR, and RATE, respectively. It then
           prints the string (in SSNO$) to the right of the label SOCIAL SECURITY
           NUMBER.
        b) This sequence is in error because there is no $ in SSNO. String data
           may not be read into a numeric variable.
        c) This sequence is also in error; S should have a $ after it. String data
           may not be assigned to a numeric variable.

Chapter 5

5.1   a) The loop prints the values 5, 3, 1, −1, −3, −5
        b) The loop prints the values

                    1   I
                    2   HIM
                    3   HER
                    4   IT

c) The loop prints 3, 5, 7.

5.3

```
100 !FIND THE LARGEST CUMULATIVE PRODUCT < 10,000
110 !
120     LET PRODUCT = 1
130     FOR I = 1 UNTIL PRODUCT * I >= 10000
140         LET PRODUCT = PRODUCT * I
150         LET LAST.INT = I
160     NEXT I
170 !
180 !PRINT THE HIGHEST INTEGER USED IN COMPUTING THE
190 !PRODUCT AND THE FINAL PRODUCT
200     PRINT "HIGHEST INTEGER "; LAST.INT
210     PRINT "PRODUCT = "; PRODUCT
220 !
230     END
```

5.4   a) The sentinel value would have been printed as the largest score.
       b) COUNTER would have been 1 larger than it should at the end of execu-
          tion.

5.9

```
100 !LOOP TO COMPUTE GALLONS OF WATER REMAINING
105 !AT THE END OF EACH WEEK
110 !
120     LET GAL.LEFT = 10000
130 !
135     PRINT "INITIAL SUPPLY (IN GALLONS) = "; GAL.LEFT
140     PRINT "WEEK", "GALLONS LEFT"
150     FOR WEEK = 1 UNTIL GAL.LEFT < 183
160         LET GAL.LEFT = GAL.LEFT - 183
170         PRINT WEEK, GAL.LEFT
180     NEXT WEEK
190 !
200     END
```

5.11

```
100 !COMPUTE YEAR END SAVINGS WITH COMPOUND INTEREST
110 !
120     LET YEAR = 0
130     LET BALANCE = 10000
135     PRINT "INITIAL BALANCE = "; BALANCE
140     PRINT "YEAR", "BALANCE"
150     UNTIL BALANCE >= 20000
160         LET BALANCE = BALANCE + .125 * BALANCE
170         LET YEAR = YEAR + 1
180         PRINT YEAR, BALANCE
190     NEXT    !UNTIL
200 !
210     END
```

5.13
```
100 !FIRST LOOP IN EXAMPLE 5.5B (LONG FORM)
110     LET N = -1
120     UNTIL N > 0
130         INPUT "ENTER A POSITIVE INTEGER "; N
140     NEXT    !UNTIL
150 !
160 !SECOND LOOP IN EXAMPLE 5.5C (LONG FORM)
170     FOR X = 1 UNTIL X ^ 2 >= 1000
180         PRINT X, X ^ 2
260     NEXT X
270 !
```

5.16   150 FOR COUNTER = 1 WHILE X <> 0   &
                              AND COUNTER < 10

5.17   (only 6 data samples are provided)
```
100 !LOOP TO READ 100 NAME, AGE PAIRS
105 !AND PRINT THE NAMES AND AGES
110 !OF THOSE BETWEEN 25 AND 35
120 !
130     PRINT "NAME", "AGE"
140     FOR I = 1 TO 100
150         READ PER.NAME$, PER.AGE
160         IF PER.AGE >= 25 AND PER.AGE <= 35 THEN            &
                PRINT PER.NAME$, PER.AGE
170     NEXT I
180 !
190 !DATA TO BE PROCESSED
200     DATA "STEVE", 31
210     DATA "MATTHEW", 2
220     DATA "JUDY", 29
230     DATA "PAUL", 27
240     DATA "MEG", 25
250     DATA "CLARE", 35
260 !
270     END
```

5.19   a) false   (false AND true)
       b) false   (true AND false)
       c) false   (true XOR true)
       d) false   (false OR false)
       e) false   (false XOR false)
       f) true   (true OR false)
       g) false   (true AND false)

Chapter 6

6.1   a)

TEAM$(1)	TEAM$(2)	TEAM$(3)	TEAM$(4)	TEAM$(5)	TEAM$(6)
ORIOLES	BREWERS	RANGERS	PHILLIES	PIRATES	CUBS

b)

RUNS(1)	RUNS(2)	RUNS(3)	RUNS(4)	RUNS(5)	RUNS(6)
637	745	526	697	703	512

HITS(1)	HITS(2)	HITS(3)	HITS(4)	HITS(5)	HITS(6)
3075	3483	2927	2718	3231	2620

RBI(1)	RBI(2)	RBI(3)	RBI(4)	RBI(5)	RBI(6)
601	721	500	683	667	493

c)

BA(1)	BA(2)	BA(3)	BA(4)	BA(5)	BA(6)
.272	.242	.266	.233	.281	.297

The legal range of subscripts is 1 to 6.

6.2   If ISUB is equal to 4 —
X(ISUB) refers to the fourth element of X
X(4) refers to the fourth element of X
X(2*ISUB) refers to the eighth element of X
X(5*ISUB-6) is out of range.

6.4   a)

SCORES(1)	SCORES(2)	SCORES(3)	SCORES(4)	SCORES(5)	SCORES(6)
100	42	85	70	58	65

b) and c)

```
100 !PROGRAM SEGMENTS FOR EXERCISE 6.4
110 !
120 !DECLARE SCORES AND READ EACH SCORE INTO ARRAY
130     DIM SCORES(6)
140     READ SCORES(I) FOR I = 1 TO 6
150     DATA 100, 42, 85, 70, 58, 65
160 !
170 !COMPUTE AND PRINT THE SUM AND THE AVERAGE
175 !OF THE ELEMENTS OF SCORES
180     LET SUM = 0
190     FOR I = 1 TO 6
200         LET SUM = SUM + SCORES(I)
205         PRINT I, SCORES(I) SUM
210     NEXT I
220     PRINT "SUM = "; SUM
230     LET AVERAGE = SUM / 6
240     PRINT "AVERAGE = "; AVERAGE
250 !
```

(continued)

```
260  !FIND ABSOLUTE DIFFERENCE BETWEEN EACH SCORE AND
270  !AVERAGE. FIND SUM AND AVERAGE OF DIFFERENCES
290      LET SUM.DIFF = 0
300      PRINT
310      PRINT "I", "SCORE(I)", "ABSOLUTE DIFFERENCE"
320      FOR I = 1 TO 6
330         LET ABS.DIFF = ABS(SCORES(I) - AVERAGE)
340         PRINT I, SCORES(I), ABS.DIFF
350         LET SUM.DIFF = SUM.DIFF + ABS.DIFF
360      NEXT I
370      PRINT
380      PRINT "SUM OF THE ABSOLUTE DIFFERENCES =",        &
               SUM.DIFF
390      LET AVG.DIFF = SUM.DIFF / 6
400      PRINT "AVERAGE ABSOLUTE DIFFERENCE = ";           &
               AVG.DIFF
410  !
420      END
```

6.5   a) G(3) contains −6.1
      b) For I = 3, G(2*I−1) contains 8.2
      c) For I = 3, NO is printed
         For I = 5, YES is printed
      d) FLAG$ will be set to "TRUE" when I is 7, and it will remain that way.
      e)

G(1)	G(2)	G(3)	G(4)	G(5)	G(6)	G(7)	G(8)	G(9)	G(10)
2	4	6	8	10	12	14	16	18	20

      f) The first four elements of G would be changed to 12, 18, 22, and −9.3, respectively. The rest of G would remain unchanged.

6.8   No. Two loops are needed because the average must be computed before the list can be printed.

6.9
```
100  !DECLARE ARRAY PRIME AND READ FIRST 10 PRIMES
110  !
120      DIM PRIME(10)
130      READ PRIME(I) FOR I = 1 TO 10
140      DATA 1, 2, 3, 5, 7, 11, 13, 17, 19, 23
```

6.11 a)
```
160  !PRINT CONTENTS OF FIRST 8 ELEMENTS OF PRIME
170      PRINT "N", "PRIME(N)"
180      FOR N = 1 TO 8
190      PRINT N, PRIME(N)
200      NEXT N
```
      b)
```
250  !PRINT CONTENTS OF MIDDLE 6 ELEMENTS OF PRIME
260      PRINT "N", "PRIME(N)"
270      FOR N = 3 TO 8
280         PRINT N, PRIME(N)
290      NEXT N
```

c)
```
340 !PRINT CONTENTS OF LAST 4 ELEMENTS OF PRIME
350     PRINT "N", "PRIME(N)"
360     FOR N = 7 TO 10
370         PRINT N, PRIME(N)
380     NEXT N
```
d)
```
430 !PRINT CONTENTS OF FIRST K ELEMENTS OF PRIME
440     LET K = 6
450     PRINT "K = "; K
460     PRINT "N", "PRIME(N)"
470     FOR N = 1 TO K
480         PRINT N, PRIME(N)
490     NEXT N
```

6.12   a)
```
100 !PART A
110     DIM LETTER$(26)
120     READ LETTER$(I) FOR I = 1 TO 26
130     DATA "A", "B", "C", "D", "E", "F", "G", "H", &
            "I", "J", "K", "L", "M", "N", "O", "P", &
            "Q", "R", "S", "T", "U", "V", "W", "X", &
            "Y", "Z"
```
   b)
```
150 !PART B
160     DIM S(10)
170     LET S(I) = I FOR I = 1 TO 10
```
   c)
```
190 !PART C
200     DIM T(10)
210     LET T(I) = 11 - I FOR I = 1 TO 10
```
   d)
```
230 !PART D
240     DIM CUBE(10)
250     LET CUBE(I) = I ^ 3 FOR I = 1 TO 10
```

6.13   a) No. Each data item could be processed as it is read. There is no need to
          save the entire collection of data.

6.22
```
1000 !SUBROUTINE TO FIND LETTER GRADE
1005 !USING A SEARCH
1010 !
1080 !SEARCH FOR GRADE CATEGORY
1090     LET FOUND$ = "FALSE"
1100     FOR I = 6 TO 2 STEP -1
1110         IF SCORE >= LOW.GRD(I) AND                              &
                 SCORE < LOW.GRD(I-1) THEN                          &
                 LET FOUND$ = "TRUE"                                &
                 \LET GRD.INX = I - 1
1120     NEXT I
```

```
1130      IF FOUND$ = "TRUE" THEN                                    &
              PRINT "GRADE IS "; LETTER$(GRD.INX)                    &
          ELSE                                                       &
              PRINT "SCORE"; SCORE; "IS OUT OF RANGE"
1140 !
1150      RETURN
1160 !END OF SEARCH SUBROUTINE
1170 !
1180 !
2000 !SUBROUTINE TO COMPUTE LETTER GRADE DIRECTLY
2010 !
2060 !DETERMINE THE GRADE
2070      IF (SCORE < 0) OR (SCORE > 100) THEN                       &
              PRINT "SCORE"; SCORE; "IS OUT OF RANGE"                &
          ELSE IF SCORE = 100 THEN                                   &
              PRINT "GRADE IS A"                                     &
          ELSE IF SCORE <= 49 THEN                                   &
              PRINT "GRADE IS F"                                     &
          ELSE                                                       &
              LET GRD.INX = 10 - INT(SCORE / 10)                     &
              \PRINT "GRADE IS "; LETTER$(GRD.INX)
2080 !
2090      RETURN
2100 !END OF SUBROUTINE TO COMPUTE LETTER GRADE


6.23
 340 !SEARCH TAX TABLE FOR BRACKET INDEX
 345      LET I = 1
 350      LET FOUND$ = "FALSE"
 360      WHILE FOUND$ = "FALSE" AND I <= TABLE.SIZE        &
 370          IF (SALARY >= BASE.SALARY(I)) AND             &
              (SALARY < BASE.SALARY(I+1)) THEN              &
              LET FOUND$ = "TRUE"                           &
              \LET TABLE.INDEX = I
 375          LET I = I + 1
 380      NEXT    !WHILE
```

Chapter 7

```
7.1
IF GPA >= 3.5 THEN PRINT "DEAN'S LIST"                     &
    ELSE IF GPA <= 1 THEN PRINT "ON PROBATION"             &
        ELSE IF GPA <= 1.99 THEN PRINT "WARNING"


7.2
 300 !COMPARE SCORE TO THE MINIMUM FOR EACH GRADE
 310      FOR I = 1 TO 5
 320          IF SCORE >= MINCAT(I) THEN                    &
              LET FREQ(I) = FREQ(I) + 1                     &
              \GOTO 350    !EXIT LOOP
 330      NEXT I
 340 !PRINT A MESSAGE IF SCORE NOT CATEGORIZED
 350      IF SCORE < MINCAT(5) THEN                         &
              PRINT SCORE; "TOO LOW"
```

7.3   first pattern

```
200 IF C1% THEN GOSUB 1000 &
        ELSE GOSUB 2000
               .
               .
               .

1000 !SUBROUTINES FOR IF-THEN-ELSE AT LINE 200
1010 !IF C1% THEN TEST C2%
1020      IF C2% THEN GOSUB 3000   !TASK A &
              ELSE GOSUB 4000          !TASK B
1030      RETURN
2000 !ELSE PERFORM TASK C
2010      GOSUB 5000
2020      RETURN
```

second pattern

```
 300 IF C1% THEN GOSUB 1000          &
        ELSE GOSUB 2000   !TASK D
               .
               .
               .

1000 !SUBROUTINES FOR IF-THEN-ELSE AT LINE 300
1010 !IF C1% THEN TEST C2%
1020      IF C2% THEN GOSUB 3000   !TASK A &
              ELSE GOSUB 4000          !TASK B
1030      GOSUB 5000   !TASK C
1040      RETURN
2000 !ELSE PERFORM TASK D
2010 !TASK D
               .
               .
               .

2090     RETURN
```

7.4   first pattern

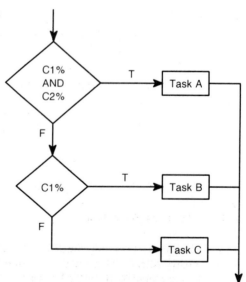

7.6

```
100 !MAIN PROGRAM FOR CAI EXAMPLE
110 !
120 !INITIALIZE CORRECT AND WRONG
130     LET CORRECT = 0
140     LET WRONG = 0
150 !
160 !CONTINUE CAI DRILL UNTIL DONE
165     PRINT "WELCOME TO THE AMERICAN HISTORY "; &
                "CAI REVIEW"
170     LET PERIOD = 0
180     GOSUB 1000 UNTIL PERIOD = 7
190 !
200 !TERMINATE CAI DRILL
210     PRINT "YOU MADE"; CORRECT;                          &
                "CORRECT ANSWERS AND"
220     PRINT WRONG; "INCORRECT ANSWERS"
230     PRINT "END OF CAI SESSION"
240 !
260     STOP
```

Make the following changes to the subroutine at line 1000:

```
1105    PRINT "7 -- STOP THE DRILL"
```

Change number 6 to number 7 at line 1150.

Add a subroutine call (for PERIOD = 7) to line 1160. This subroutine will consist of a RETURN statement only.

7.7   a) line 100, line 60, error

        b) 150, 200, 170, 160, 200

7.8   There is no expression that represents the different cases.

7.9   200 ON INT(X/5) + 1 GOSUB 1000, 2000, 3000, 4000

7.10   240 ON 11 − INT(SCORE/10) GOSUB 1000, 1000,   &
             2000, 3000, 4000, 5000, 5000, 5000, 5000,   &
             5000, 5000

The following subroutines will be executed:

```
1000 for 90 ≤ SCORE ≤ 100 (A)
2000 for 80 ≤ SCORE ≤ 89 (B)
            .
            .
            .
5000 for 0 ≤ SCORE ≤ 59 (F)
```

7.12   1000 times, 50000 times

7.15   Change the FOR loop limit from M.COUNT − 1 to M.COUNT − NUM.PASS where NUM.PASS counts the number of the pass being performed (initially 1). Increment NUM.PASS before repeating the outer loop.

7.16   Change the exchange condition to

```
     M(INDEX) < M(INDEX+1)
```

7.17   Add the lines below to the main program after the sort subroutine call.

```
500 LET MED.INDEX = INT(M.COUNT/2) + 1
510 IF MED.INDEX = M.COUNT/2 + 1 THEN            &
        LET MEDIAN = (M(MED.INDEX) +             &
                      M(MED.INDEX+1))/2          &
ELSE                                             &
        LET MEDIAN = M(MED.INDEX)
```

Chapter 8

8.1
```
120 !PART A
130     DEF* FNAREA.C(R) = PI * R ^ 2
140 !
150 !PART B
160     DEF* FNAREA.R(L, W) = L * W
170 !
180 !PART C
190     DEF* FNVOL.S(R) = 4 / 3 * PI * R ^ 3
200 !
210 !PART D
220     DEF* FNVOL.C(S) = S ^ 3
```

8.2
```
200     DEF* FNMAX(X, Y)
210 !
220 !FIND THE LARGER OF THE TWO NUMBERS X AND Y
230 !
240 !PARAMETER DEFINITIONS --
250 !  X,  Y - THE NUMBERS TO BE COMPARED
260 !
270     IF X > Y THEN LET FNMAX = X            &
            ELSE LET FNMAX = Y
280 !
290     FNEND    !FNMAX

310     DEF* FNMAX$(X$, Y$)
320 !
330 !FIND THE LARGER OF THE TWO STRINGS X$ AND Y$
340 !
350 !PARAMETER DEFINITIONS --
360 !  X$, Y$ - THE STRINGS TO BE COMPARED
370 !
380     IF X$ > Y$ THEN LET FNMAX$ = X$        &
            ELSE LET FNMAX$ = Y$
390 !
400     FNEND    !FNMAX$
```

8.3
```
620     LET LARGEST = FNMAX(FNMAX(A, B), FNMAX(C, D))
```

8.4   a)
```
500     DEF* FNABSOLUTE(X)
510  !
520  !COMPUTE THE ABSOLUTE VALUE OF X
530  !
540  !PARAMETER DEFINITIONS --
550  !   X - NUMBER WHOSE ABSOLUTE VALUE IS COMPUTED
560  !
570     IF X < 0 THEN LET FNABSOLUTE = -1 * X          &
            ELSE LET FNABSOLUTE = X
580  !

590     FNEND !FNABSOLUTE
```
       b)
```
610     DEF* FNSIGN(X)
620  !
630  !DETERMINE THE SIGN OF X
640  !
650  !PARAMETER DEFINITIONS --
660  !X - NUMBER WHOSE SIGN IS TO BE COMPUTED
670  !
680     IF X > 0 THEN LET FNSIGN = 1                   &
            ELSE IF X < 0 THEN LET FNSIGN = -1         &
                ELSE LET FNSIGN = 0
690  !
700     FNEND    !FNSIGN
```
       c)
```
100  !MAIN PROGRAM TO TEST FNABSOLUTE AND FNSIGN
110  !
130     DIM TEST.DATA(3)
140     READ TEST.DATA(I) FOR I = 1 TO 3
150     DATA -50, 0, 50
160  !
170  !TEST FNABSOLUTE
180     PRINT "X", "ABS(X)", "FNABSOLUTE(X)"
190     FOR I = 1 TO 3
200        PRINT TEST.DATA(I), ABS(TEST.DATA(I)),   &
                  FNABSOLUTE(TEST.DATA(I))
210     NEXT I
220  !
230  !TEST FNSIGN
240     PRINT
250     PRINT "X", "SGN(X)", "FNSIGN(X)"
260     FOR I = 1 TO 3
270        PRINT TEST.DATA(I), SGN(TEST.DATA(I)),       &
                  FNSIGN(TEST.DATA(I))
280     NEXT I
290  !
```

(continued)

```
300     STOP
310 !
320 !FUNCTION DEFINITIONS GO HERE
            .
            .
            .
990     END


8.7
300     DEF* FNROUND(X, N)
310 !
320 !FUNCTION TO ROUND X TO N DECIMAL PLACES
330 !
340 !PARAMETER DEFINITIONS --
350 !   X - NUMBER TO BE ROUNDED
360 !   N - NUMBER OF DECIMAL PLACES IN RESULT
370 !
380     LET FNROUND = SGN(X)                                    &
                    * INT(ABS(X) * 10 ^ N + .5) / 10 ^ N
390 !
400     FNEND   !FNROUND
410 !


8.9   a)
340     DEF* FNMOD(I%, J%)
350 !
360 !COMPUTE THE REMAINDER OF I% / J%
370 !
380 !PARAMETER DEFINITIONS --
390 ! I% - POSITIVE INTEGER DIVIDEND
400 ! J% - POSITIVE INTEGER DIVISOR
410 !
420     LET FNMOD = I% - INT(I% / J%) * J%
430 !
440     FNEND !FNMOD
      b)
300     DEF* FNTRUNC(X)
310 !
320 !FUNCTION TO TRUNCATE A REAL NUMBER
330 !
340 !PARAMETER DEFINITIONS --
350 !   X - REAL NUMBER TO BE TRUNCATED
360 !
370     IF X >= 0 THEN LET FNTRUNC = INT(X)                     &
            ELSE LET FNTRUNC = -1 * INT(ABS(X))
380 !
390     FNEND   !FNTRUNC
      c)
410     DEF* FNCEIL(X)
420 !
430 !FUNCTION TO COMPUTE THE SMALLEST INTEGER > X
```

(continued)

```
440 !
450 !PARAMETER DEFINITIONS --
460 !   X - NUMBER WHOSE CEILING IS TO BE COMPUTED
470 !
480     IF X >= 0 THEN                                            &
            LET FNCEIL = INT(X) + 1                               &
        ELSE IF ABS(X) - INT(ABS(X)) = 0 THEN                     &
            LET FNCEIL = -1 * INT(ABS(X)) + 1                     &
        ELSE                                                      &
            LET FNCEIL = -1 * INT(ABS(X))
490 !
500     FNEND    !FNCEIL
```

8.10
```
210     DEF* FNSUMN(N)
220 !
230 !FUNCTION TO SUM ELEMENTS OF AN ARRAY

240 !
250 !PARAMETER DEFINITIONS --
260 !   N - NUMBER OF ELEMENTS IN W
270 !
280 !GLOBAL VARIABLES
290 !   IN: W - ARRAY OF ELEMENTS TO BE SUMMED
300 !
310 !LOCAL VARIABLES - SUM.I, SUM.TEMP
320 !
330     LET SUM.TEMP = 0
340     LET SUM.TEMP = SUM.TEMP + W(SUM.I)                        &
            FOR SUM.I = 1 TO N
350     LET FNSUMN = SUM.TEMP
360 !
370     FNEND    !FNSUMN
```

8.12   Data Table for the Largest Value Function (FNLARGEST)

Parameters
N: The number of items in the array X

Global Variables
X( ): The array containing the data whose largest value is to be determined (input)

Local Variables
LAR.I: Loop control variable for search loop LAR.TEMP: Contains largest value found at any point

The data tables for FNSMALLEST and FNMEAN are similar. (See also the following functions.)

```
290     DEF* FNSMALLEST(N)
300 !
310 !FUNCTION TO FIND SMALLEST ELEMENT OF ARRAY X
320 !
330 !PARAMETER DEFINITIONS --
340 !  N - NUMBER OF ELEMENTS IN X
350 !
360 !GLOBAL VARIABLES
370 !  IN: X - ARRAY TO BE SEARCHED
380 !
390 !LOCAL VARIABLES - SMA.I, SMA.TEMP
400 !
410 !INITIALIZE SMALLEST VALUE (SMA.TEMP)
420    LET SMA.TEMP = X(1)
430 !CHECK FOR VALUES SMALLER THAN SMA.TEMP
440    FOR SMA.I = 2 TO N
450       IF X(SMA.I) < SMA.TEMP THEN                        &
              LET SMA.TEMP = X(SMA.I)
460    NEXT SMA.I
470 !
480    LET FNSMALLEST = SMA.TEMP
490 !
500    FNEND    !FNSMALLEST
510 !
515 !
520    DEF* FNMEAN(N)
530 !
540 !COMPUTE MEAN OF ELEMENTS OF ARRAY X
550 !
560 !PARAMETER DEFINITIONS --
570 !  N - NUMBER OF ELEMENTS IN X
580 !
590 !GLOBAL VARIABLES
600 !  IN:  X ARRAY OF DATA
610 !
620 !LOCAL VARIABLES - MEA.I, MEA.SUM
630 !
640 !COMPUTE THE SUM OF THE ELEMENTS OF X
650    LET MEA.SUM = 0
660    LET MEA.SUM = MEA.SUM + X(MEA.I)                      &
              FOR MEA.I = 1 TO N
670 !
680 !COMPUTE THE MEAN
690    LET FNMEAN = MEA.SUM / N
700 !
710    FNEND    !FNMEAN

8.15
340    DEF* FNBIN(S.KEY, N)
350 !
360 !NONRECURSIVE BINARY SEARCH FUNCTION
370 !
```

(continued)

```
380 !PARAMETER DEFINITIONS --
390 !   S.KEY - ITEM TO BE FOUND
400 !   N - NUMBER OF ELEMENTS IN THE SEARCH ARRAY
410 !
420 !GLOBAL VARIABLES
430 !   IN:  S.LIST - LIST TO BE SEARCHED
440 !
450 !LOCAL VARIABLES - BIN.TEMP
460 !   BIN.FIRST - INDEX TO FIRST ELEMENT IN ARRAY
470 !   BIN.MID - INDEX TO MIDDLE ELEMENT IN ARRAY
480 !   BIN.LAST - INDEX TO LAST ELEMENT IN ARRAY
490 !
500 !INITIALIZE BIN.FIRST AND BIN.LAST
510     LET BIN.FIRST = 1
520     LET BIN.LAST = N
530 !
540     LET BIN.TEMP = 0
550     UNTIL BIN.LAST < BIN.FIRST OR BIN.TEMP <> 0
560         !DEFINE MIDDLE ITEM AND PROBE FOR KEY
570         LET BIN.MID = INT((BIN.FIRST+BIN.LAST) / 2)
580         IF S.LIST(BIN.MID) = S.KEY THEN          &
                !KEY FOUND                           &
                LET BIN.TEMP = BIN.MID               &
            ELSE IF S.LIST(BIN.MID) > S.KEY THEN     &
                !REDEFINE BIN.LAST                   &
                LET BIN.LAST = BIN.MID - 1           &
            ELSE                                     &
                !REDEFINE BIN.FIRST                  &
                LET BIN.FIRST = BIN.MID + 1
590     NEXT    !UNTIL
600 !
610     LET FNBIN = BIN.TEMP
620 !
630     FNEND    !FNBIN


8.16
260     DEF* FNFIB.R(N)
270 !
280 !RECURSIVE FIBONACCI FUNCTION
290 !
300 !PARAMETER DEFINITIONS --
310 !   N - CORRESPONDS TO THE NTH FIBONACCI NUMBER
320 !
330     IF N = 1 OR N = 2 THEN                       &
            !STOP RECURSION                          &
            LET FNFIB.R = 1                          &
        ELSE                                         &
            !DEFINE FNFIB.R RECURSIVELY              &
            LET FNFIB.R = FNFIB.R(N - 1)             &
                        + FNFIB.R(N - 2)
340 !
350     FNEND    !FNFIB.R
```

(continued)

```
370    DEF* FNFIB.NR(N)
380 !
390 !NONRECURSIVE FIBONACCI FUNCTION
400 !
410 !PARAMETER DEFINITIONS --
420 !   N - CORRESPONDS TO THE NTH FIBONACCI NUMBER
430 !
440 !LOCAL VARIABLES - FIB.PREV1, FIB.PREV2,
445 !                  FIB.I, FIB.TEMP
450 !
460    IF N = 1 OR N = 2 THEN                    &
            !TERMINATE                           &
            LET FNFIB.NR = 1                     &
        ELSE                                     &
            !DEFINE FNFIB.NR USING A LOOP        &
            GOSUB 1000
470 !
480    GOTO 1120    !RETURN
490 !
1000 !SUBROUTINE FOR ELSE AT LINE 460
1010    LET FIB.PREV1 = 1
1020    LET FIB.PREV2 = 1
1030    FOR FIB.I = 3 TO N
1040       LET FIB.TEMP = FIB.PREV1 + FIB.PREV2
1050       LET FIB.PREV1 = FIB.PREV2
1060       LET FIB.PREV2 = FIB.TEMP
1070    NEXT FIB.I
1080    LET FNFIB.NR = FIB.TEMP
1090 !
1100    RETURN
1105 !END OF SUBROUTINE FOR ELSE AT LINE 460
1110 !
1120    FNEND    !FNFIB.NR
```

Chapter 9

9.1   Change the PRINT statement in line 240 to

```
PRINT MID(SENT$, START+1, I-START-1); &
      MID(SENT$, START, 1); "AY"
```

add line 280 below

```
280 PRINT RIGHT(SENT$, START+1);                          &
          MID(SENT$, START, 1); "AY"
```

9.2   RON
       , JOHN QUINCY
       LIFORNI
       Y
       QUINCY
       ADAMS, JOHN QUINCY

(continued)

9.3   Extra blank lines would appear in the output.

9.4
```
200 !LOOP TO PRINT NON-BLANK CHARACTERS IN S$
210    FOR I = 1 TO LEN(S$)
220        IF MID(S$, I, 1) <> " " THEN                    &
              PRINT MID(S$, I, 1);
230    NEXT I
```

9.5
```
"JOHN REAGA"
"ADAMS J.Q."
```

9.6
```
100 READ Q$, R$, S$
110 DATA "THE CHAIRMAN SAID"
120 DATA "GENTLEMEN-WOULD EVERYONE"
130 DATA "PLEASE TAKE HIS SEAT"
140 LET Q$ = LEFT(Q$, 9) + "PERSON" +                      &
              RIGHT(Q$, 13)
150 LET R$ = "LADIES AND " + LEFT(R$, 10)
160 LET S$ = LEFT(S$, 7) + "BE" +                          &
              RIGHT(S$, 17) + "ED"
170 END
```

9.7   a,b,c,d,f,g) $<$, $<=$, $<>$
           e) $>$, $>=$, $<>$

9.8
```
180 LET POS.TARG = INSTR(POS.TARG+LEN(REPLAC$),            &
                        SUBJECT$, TARGET$)                 &
        FOR COUNT.TARG = 0 UNTIL POS.TARG = 0
```

9.9
```
300 ON (INSTR(1,"DEREINPRFI",CODE$) + 1) / 2               &
        GOSUB 1000, 2000, 3000, 4000, 5000, 6000
```

9.12   Add ELSE clause to line 180

```
        ELSE IF (NEXT.CODE >= 97) AND                      &
                (NEXT.CODE <= 122) THEN                     &
          LET TEXT$ = LEFT(TEXT$, POS.CHAR - 1) +           &
                      CHR$(NEXT.CODE - 32) +                &
                      RIGHT(TEXT$, POS.CHAR + 1)
```

9.13   Replace 65 with ASCII("A"), 90 with ASCII("Z"), and 32 with ASCII("a") − ASCII("A")

Chapter 10

10.1
```
330    LET CAMPUS = 3
340    LET NUM.STUDENTS = 0
```

(continued)

```
350 !ADD UP ALL STUDENTS AT A SPECIFIED CAMPUS
360    LET NUM.STUDENTS = NUM.STUDENTS +                         &
          ENROLL(COURSE,CAMPUS) FOR COURSE = 1 TO 50
370    PRINT "NUMBER OF STUDENTS AT CAMPUS";                     &
          CAMPUS; "="; NUM.STUDENTS
420    LET NUM.COURSES = 0
430 !COUNT NUMBER OF COURSES WITH NO STUDENTS
440 !PROCESS ONE ROW AT A TIME
450    FOR COURSE = 1 TO 50
460       !PROCESS EACH COLUMN WITHIN ROW
470       FOR CAMPUS = 1 TO 5
480          IF ENROLL(COURSE, CAMPUS) = 0 THEN                  &
                LET NUM.COURSES = NUM.COURSES + 1
490       NEXT CAMPUS
500    NEXT COURSE
510    PRINT "NUMBER OF COURSES WITHOUT ";                       &
          "STUDENTS ="; NUM.COURSES


10.2
2000    DEF* FNSAME%(P1$, P2$, P3$)
2010 !
2020 !IF P1$, P2$, P3$ ARE EQUAL AND NOT BLANK,
2030 !RETURN TRUE (-1%). IF NOT, RETURN FALSE (0%)
2040 !
2050 !PARAMETERS --
2060 !  P1$, P2$, P3$ - ITEMS TO BE COMPARED
2070 !
2080    IF (P1$ = P2$) AND (P2$ = P3$)           &
                      AND (P2$ <> " ") THEN      &
          LET FNSAME% = -1%    !TRUE             &
       ELSE                                      &
          LET FNSAME% = 0%     !FALSE
2090 !
2100    FNEND   !FNSAME%


10.5  b)
290 !ENTER PRICES AND COMPUTE VOLUME FOR EACH STORE
300    MAT READ ITEM.PRICE
310    DATA 15.5, 37.83, 42.55, 95.63, 110.87
320    FOR STORE = 1 TO 3
330       LET STORE.VOLUME(STORE) = 0
340       FOR ITEM = 1 TO 5
350          LET STORE.VOLUME(STORE)            &
                = STORE.VOLUME(STORE) +         &
                + ANNUAL.SALES(STORE, ITEM)     &
                * ITEM.PRICE(ITEM)
360       NEXT ITEM
370    NEXT STORE
380 !
390 !COMPUTE TOTAL GROSS VOLUME, GROSS.VOLUME, AND
400 !DISPLAY ANNUAL VOLUME FOR EACH STORE
```

(continued)

```
410     LET GROSS.VOLUME = 0
420     FOR I = 1 TO 3
430         PRINT "GROSS VOLUME AT STORE "; I;       &
                  "=$"; STORE.VOLUME(I)
440         LET GROSS.VOLUME = GROSS.VOLUME           &
                            + STORE.VOLUME(I)
450     NEXT I
460 !
470     PRINT "TOTAL GROSS = $"; GROSS.VOLUME


10.7
100 !PROGRAM TO SOLVE A SET OF SIMULTANEOUS
110 !EQUATIONS IN 2 UNKNOWNS
120 !
130     DIM A(2,2), X(2), B(2), V(2,2)
140 !
150     MAT READ A
160     DATA 3, 2
170     DATA 1, -1
200     PRINT "COEFFICIENT MATRIX"
220     MAT PRINT A,
230 !
240     MAT READ B
250     DATA 14, 2
260     PRINT "VECTOR OF CONSTANTS"
270     MAT PRINT B
280 !
290 !INVERT MATRIX A
300     MAT V = INV(A)
310     PRINT "INVERSE OF THE COEFFICIENT MATRIX IS"
320     MAT PRINT V,
330 !
340 !SOLVE FOR UNKNOWNS X
350     MAT X = V * B
360     PRINT "SOLUTION VECTOR -- X"
370     MAT PRINT X
380 !
390     END


10.8
1000 !SUBROUTINE TO PRINT THE ROOM CAPACITY TABLE
1010 !
1015     PRINT "                         ROOM NUMBER"
1020     PRINT "FLOOR"; TAB(15);"01"; TAB(25);"02";      &
             TAB(35);"03"; TAB(45);"04"; TAB(55);"05"
1025     PRINT "-----"; TAB(15);"--"; TAB(25);"--";      &
             TAB(35);"--"; TAB(45);"--"; TAB(55);"--"
1030     PRINT "  1  ";
1040     PRINT TAB(4+10*J); ABS(ROOM.CAP(1,J));          &
             FOR J = 1 TO NUM.COLS
1045     PRINT
```

(continued)

```
1050      PRINT "  2  ";
1060      PRINT TAB(4+10*J); ABS(ROOM.CAP(2,J));                    &
              FOR J = 1 TO NUM.COLS
1065      PRINT
1070      PRINT "  3  ";
1080      PRINT TAB(4+10*J); ABS(ROOM.CAP(3,J));                    &
              FOR J = 1 TO NUM.COLS
1085      PRINT
1090 !
1100      RETURN
1110 !END OF PRINT SUBROUTINE
```

Chapter 11

11.1 a) FABIA   62.5 SECONDS
      b) THE D 125.3 SECONDS
      c) HOSS   %1026.2 SECONDS
      d) ACE   -41.0 SECONDS

11.2
```
PRINT USING "SOCIAL SECURITY NUMBER ###-##-####",      &
            S1, S2, S3
PRINT USING "\ \, \ \", L$, F$
PRINT USING "HOURS RATE PAY"
PRINT USING "##.## #.## ###.##", H, R, P
```

11.3 a) -1158
      b) -1,158.45
      c) 1,158.45-
      d) *1,158.5-
      e) $1,158.45-
      f) -1.16E 03

11.4
```
130 PRINT USING "\          \", ANIMAL$(I);             &
        FOR I = 1 TO 4
140 PRINT
150 PRINT USING "#####       ", COUNT(I);              &
        FOR I = 1 TO 4
```

11.5 Extra blank spaces would be inserted in the file and the file would occupy
      more disk space.

11.6
```
240 PRINT #1, STOCK.NUM; ",";                          &
              "'" + AUTHOR$ + "'"; ",";                &
              "'" + TITLE$ + "'"; ",";                 &
              PRICE; ";"; QUANTITY
```

11.7
```
100 !CREATE A GRADE FILE
110 !
120     OPEN "GRADES.DAT" FOR OUTPUT AS FILE #1
130 !
```

(continued)

```
140 !READ ALL STUDENT GRADES
150     INPUT "MORE STUDENTS (YES OR NO)"; MORE$
160     WHILE MORE$ = "YES"
170         INPUT "NAME"; STU.NAME$
180         INPUT "ENTER 3 EXAM SCORES"; EXAM1,          &
                    EXAM2, EXAM3
190         !COPY TO FILE GRADES.DAT
200         PRINT #1, STU.NAME$; ","; EXAM1; ",";        &
                    EXAM2; ","; EXAM3
210         INPUT "MORE STUDENTS (YES OR NO)"; MORE$
220     NEXT    !WHILE
230 !
240 !CLOSE FILE
250     CLOSE #1
260 !
270     END
```

11.10
```
100 !ADD FOURTH EXAM SCORE TO GRADE FILE
110 !
120     ON ERROR GO TO 1000
130     OPEN "GRADES.DAT" FOR INPUT AS FILE #1
140     OPEN "BIGGRD.DAT" FOR OUTPUT AS FILE #2
150 !
160 !READ EACH RECORD AND FOURTH GRADE
170 !WRITE NEW RECORD TO FILE BIGGRD.DAT
180     WHILE -1%        !TRUE
190         INPUT #1, STU.NAME$, EXAM1, EXAM2,           &
                    EXAM3
200         PRINT "ENTER NEW SCORE FOR "; STU.NAME$;
210         INPUT EXAM4
220         PRINT #2, STU.NAME$; ","; EXAM1; ",";        &
                    EXAM2; ","; EXAM3; ","; EXAM4
230     NEXT    !WHILE
240 !
250 !CLOSE ALL FILES AND STOP
260     CLOSE #1, #2
270     STOP
280 !
1000 !ERROR PROCESSING ROUTINE
1010 !CHECK FOR END OF FILE AT LINE 190
1020     IF ERR = 11 AND ERL = 190 THEN RESUME 250       &
            ELSE ON ERROR GOTO 0
1030 !
1040     END
```

11.11 Change line 290

```
290 IF OLD.CLIENT$(1) < UP.CLIENT$(1) THEN               &
        GOSUB 1000                                       &
    ELSE IF OLD.CLIENT$(1) > UP.CLIENT$(1) THEN          &
```

(continued)

```
              GOSUB 2000                                            &
         ELSE
              GOSUB 2040
```

Add the alternative below

```
2040 !ELSE OLD.CLIENT$(1) = UP.CLIENT$(1)
2050     LINE PRINT #3, UP.CLIENT$ (I); FOR I = 1 2 4
2060     INPUT LINE #1, OLD.CLIENT$ (I) FOR I = 1 2 4
2070     INPUT LINE #2, UP.CLIENT$ (I) FOR I = 1 2 4
2080     LET COUNT.UP = COUNT.UP + 1
2090     LET COUNT.OLD = COUNT.OLD + 1
2100     LET COUNT.NEW = COUNT.NEW + 1
2110     RETURN
```

Add the lines below

```
205 LET COUNT.OLD, COUNT.NEW, COUNT.UP = 0
1025 LET COUNT.OLD = COUNT.OLD + 1
1035 LET COUNT.NEW = COUNT.NEW + 1
2015 LET COUNT.UP = COUNT.UP + 1
2025 LET COUNT.NEW = COUNT.NEW + 1
```

11.13

```
100 !COUNT NUMBER OF FILE ITEMS IN EACH DECILE
110 !
120     DIM #1, RAND.INT(500)
130     OPEN "RANDOM.VIR" FOR INPUT AS FILE #1
140     DIM DEC.COUNT(10)
150 !
160 !FIND CORRECT DECILE FOR EACH RANDOM NUMBER
170     MAT DEC.COUNT = ZER
180     FOR I = 1 TO 500
190        LET INDEX = INT(RAND.INT(I)/10) + 1
200        !INCREMENT DECILE COUNT
210        LET DEC.COUNT(INDEX) = DEC.COUNT(INDEX) + 1
220     NEXT I
230 !
240 !PRINT NUMBER IN EACH DECILE
250     PRINT "DECILE", "COUNT"
260     PRINT INDEX, DEC.COUNT(INDEX)                          &
           FOR INDEX = 1 TO 10
270 !
280     CLOSE #1
290 !
300     END
```

11.14

```
100 !CREATE VIRTUAL FILE FROM SEQUENTIAL FILE
110 !
120     ON ERROR GOTO 1000
```

```
130 !
140     OPEN "INVEN.DAT" FOR INPUT AS FILE #1
150     DIM #2, BOOK$(1000) = 64
160     OPEN "INV.VIR" FOR OUTPUT AS FILE #2
165 !
170 !INITIALIZE BOOK$ TO ALL NULL STRINGS
175     LET BOOK$(I) = "" FOR I = 1000 TO 1 STEP -1
180 !
185 !READ EACH RECORD FROM INVEN.DAT AND COPY IT
190 !TO INV.VIR
195     WHILE -1%    !TRUE
200         INPUT #1, STOCK.NUM, AUTHOR$, TITLE$,            &
                      PRICE, QUANTITY
210         LET BOOK$(STOCK.NUM) =                          &
                NUM1$(STOCK.NUM) + "," + AUTHOR$            &
                + "*" + TITLE$ + "$" + NUM1$(PRICE)         &
                + "\" + NUM1$(QUANTITY)
220     NEXT    !WHILE
230 !
240 !CLOSE FILES AND STOP
250     CLOSE #1, #2
260     STOP
270 !
280 !
1000 !ERROR PROCESSING ROUTINE
1010    IF ERR = 11 AND ERL = 200 THEN RESUME 240          &
1020        ELSE ON ERROR GOTO 0
1030 !
1040    END


11.15
100 !CREATE SEQUENTIAL FILE FROM VIRTUAL FILE
110 !
120     DIM #1, BOOK$(1000) = 64
130     OPEN "INV.VIR" FOR INPUT AS FILE #1
140     OPEN "INV.DAT" FOR OUTPUT AS FILE #2
150 !
160 !READ EACH VIRTUAL ARRAY ELEMENT AND EXTRACT
165 !ITS SUBSTRINGS
170     FOR STOCK.NUM = 1 TO 1000
180         !COPY ALL NON-NULL DATA
190         IF BOOK$(STOCK.NUM) <> "" THEN                  &
200             GOSUB 1000 !EXTRACT SUBSTRINGS              &
210             \PRINT #2, STOCK.NUM; ","; AUTHOR$;         &
                       ","; TITLE$; ",";                    &
220                    PRICE; ","; QUANTITY
230     NEXT STOCK.NUM
240 !
250 !CLOSE FILES AND STOP
260     CLOSE #1, #2
270     STOP
```

```
280 !
1000 !SUBROUTINE TO EXTRACT SUBSTRINGS FROM
1005 !BOOK$(STOCK.NUM)
1010    LET POS1 = INSTR(1, BOOK$(STOCK.NUM), ",")
1020    LET POS2 = INSTR(1, BOOK$(STOCK.NUM), "*")
1030    LET POS3 = INSTR(1, BOOK$(STOCK.NUM), "$")
1040    LET POS4 = INSTR(1, BOOK$(STOCK.NUM), "\")
1050    LET STOCK.NUM =                                      &
           VAL(LEFT(BOOK$(STOCK.NUM), POS1-1))
1060    LET AUTHOR$ =                                        &
           MID(BOOK$(STOCK.NUM), POS1+1, POS2-POS1-1)
1070    LET TITLE$ =                                         &
           MID(BOOK$(STOCK.NUM), POS2+1, POS3-POS2-1)
1080    LET QUANTITY =                                       &
           VAL(RIGHT(BOOK$(STOCK.NUM), POS4+1))
1085    LET PRICE = VAL                                      &
           MID(BOOK$(STOCK.NUM), POS3+1, POS4-POS3-1))
1090    RETURN
1100 !END OF SUBROUTINE
1110 !
1102    END
```

Index of Programs

Index of Reference
Tables and Displays

Index of Program
Style Displays

Subject Index

OPEN statement error, 488-489
operator precedence, 129, 200-202
OR, 197-200
out of data, 117
out-of-range subscript, 257, 424
output device, 3, 5
output variable, 44
overlapping FOR loops, 293-294

parallel array, 230, 232, 242, 248-249
passing arrays to functions, 322
payroll program, 12-21
PDP-11 computer, 9
permanent file, 25
PI, 137
precedence of operators, 129, 200-202
prime number, 157, 234
PRINT statement, 11, 19, 29-30, 136
PRINT # statement, 460
PRINT USING statement, 450-455
printing arrays, 233
problem analysis, 42-44
problem solving, 41-77
problem solving principles, 50
processing ASCII files, 458-463
program, 8
program flag, 157-159, 301, 442
program output, 8, 28-30
program system chart, 328-330
program variable, 44
programming, 8
programming language, 9
prompt, 31, 48
protection code, 27

radians, 139
random access, 470
random number, 141-143, 473
RANDOMIZE, 143
READ statement, 18, 31
reading a sequential file, 460-464
reading arrays, 232-234
records, 460
recursion, 340-348
recursion step, 341
redimensioning matrixes, 420-421
registered voters list, 152-157
relational operator, 53
REM statement, 48
remark, 48
RENAME, 25
repetition counter, 66
REPLACE, 25
reserved keyword, 13
RESUME statement, 463

RETURN statement, 93, 206, 298
RETURN without GOSUB, 212
RIGHT, 364, 395-396
RND, 137, 141-142
room assignment problem, 432-442
roots of quadratic equations, 143
rounding numbers, 316
RSTS/E operating system, 22-27
RUBOUT, 24
RUN, 24
RUNNH, 11, 24
run-time error, 117

SAVE, 25
saving a program, 25
scientific notation, 136
searching for a substring, 374-378
secondary memory, 5
secondary storage device, 3, 5
selecting array elements, 248-255
sentinel value, 176, 182-184, 237
sequential file, 456-470
SGN, 137
side effect, 324, 337
simultaneous equations, 430
SIN, 137-140
single-alternative decision, 54, 82-87
single-line function, 314-317
size of an array, 408
social security problem, 58-60
software, 8
sorting an array, 299-302
SQR, 136-137
square matrix, 429
statement group, 82
step-wise programming, 203-205
STOP statement, 96, 112
stopping step, 341
string, 28, 144-156, 362-400
string assignment, 364, 368
string comparison, 149-156, 370-371
string constant, 148, 362
string expression, 368
string field, 453-455
string length, 472
string replacement, 369
string search, 374-378
string variable, 148
structure entry, 297
structure exit, 297-298
structure nesting, 292-296
structured program, 9
stub, 348
subexpression, 128
subroutine, 93-97, 157, 203-210, 272-278
subroutine call, 93, 207